Patterns of Re-use

The transformation of former monastic buildings in post-Dissolution Hertfordshire, 1540-1600

Nicholas Doggett

BAR British Series 331
2002

This title published by

Archaeopress
Publishers of British Archaeological Reports
Gordon House
276 Banbury Road
Oxford
OX2 7ED
England
www.archaeopress.com

BAR 331

Patterns of Re-use: The transformation of former monastic buildings in post-Dissolution Hertfordshire, 1540-1600

ISBN 1 84171 296 5

Printed in England by The Basingstoke Press

All BAR titles are available from:

Hadrian Books Ltd
122 Banbury Road
Oxford
OX2 7BP
England
The current BAR catalogue with details of all titles in print, prices and means of payment is available free from Hadrian Books

"Mergate was a nunnery of late tyme. It standith on a hil in a faire woode hard by Watheling streate on the est side of it; Humfray Boucher, base sunne to the late lorde Berners, did much coste in translating of the priorie into a maner-place."

John Leland, c.1540

Contents

List of figures

I am grateful to Hertfordshire Archives and Local Studies (formerly Hertfordshire Record Office) for permission to photograph the drawings featured in Figs.7, 8, 10, 12, 14, 15, 18, 19 and 20 and similarly to Colin Platt for Fig.17.

Preface and Acknowledgements

The adaptive re-use of monastic buildings in the second half of the 16th century has been relatively little studied. With a few notable exceptions, it has generally been assumed that most former monastic sites were simply plundered for their building materials. Two new approaches suggest that frequently this was not so. First, by examining in detail all the monastic houses of a single county- in this case Hertfordshire- which survived until the Dissolution and secondly, by treating the surviving architectural evidence as a primary source, it can be shown that much medieval fabric is in fact incorporated in later houses on monastic sites, even when this is not readily apparent. Coupled with contemporary documentary records and later antiquarian accounts, this structural analysis allows a reconstruction to be made of the processes of re-use in the half-century after the Dissolution.

Hertfordshire is not a county noted for its monastic remains or well-known examples of conversions to domestic use after the Dissolution. Indeed, as is shown in the detailed architectural descriptions of the thirteen sites which comprise the Appendix to this study, the monastic origins of several of the buildings included here are not immediately obvious and it was therefore necessary to investigate and record these structures thoroughly in order to detect their many phases and the survival or otherwise of medieval fabric. In this way, it has been possible to provide solid evidence from which to draw conclusions.

Too cursory an examination of the buildings could have been misleading and would probably have led to a failure both to recognise monastic fabric and the ways in which individual structures were re-used after the Dissolution. Such lack of observation has unfortunately characterised previous work of this kind in Hertfordshire and accounts for the extraordinary omission of the largely intact 15th-century gatehouse from otherwise detailed architectural descriptions of King's Langley Priory,[1] the absence of any full published description of the 14th-century roofs at Ware Priory or of any description at all of the 15th- and 16th-century roofs at The Biggin, Hitchin and Royston Priory. Similarly, although J.T. Smith's recent comment that "nothing significant is known about the (16th-century) house at Markyate" is happily, if strangely, contradicted by his own very full description of the building elsewhere,[2] his apparently incomplete understanding of Royston could perhaps have benefited from a more rigorous structural analysis of the surviving building.

My purpose, though, is not to be critical of the work of others. Smith in particular casts his net far wider than mine and many of his general conclusions have been invaluable in researching and writing this thesis. Likewise, the considerable limitations of my own work will no doubt be exposed by those who have the opportunity to strip plaster, lift floorboards and carry out measured surveys of the buildings involved.[3]

The essentially building by building approach adopted in Chapters 2 and 3 of this study arises from the detailed site descriptions contained in the Appendix and has, I believe, one significant advantage over the more usual thematic approach, which is itself adopted in Chapters 4 and 5. This is that a thorough examination of the raw data, omitting as far as possible any preconceived notions or ideas obtained from documentary or other sources, enables the conclusions to be drawn primarily from the built evidence itself. That this deductive approach is partially abandoned in Chapters 4 and 5 is not to be regarded as loss of confidence in its validity, but rather as a sign that, as the discussion broadens, it becomes necessary to take a wider and more topic-based view if any significant general observations are to be made. The fundamental point remains, however, that the built evidence is the prime source for a proper understanding of the conversion of former monastic buildings.

Much is made in this study of the importance and limitations of pictorial evidence. Here too, structural analysis of the surviving buildings is vital, acting as an impartial check on the accuracy or otherwise of a particular drawing or plan. The situation can, of course, be reversed, as is well illustrated at Markyate. Here the earliest surviving work is in the short wing of chequered stone and flint at the north-east end of the present house. This appears to have been a service block at right-angles to the main south range, and is shown in what is likely to be basically its original form in Thomas Fisher's 1805 north-east view of the house.[4] This same range was, however, drawn in rather different form by G. Buckler in 1839, which raises some interesting points.[5] The details which Buckler shows of this and the adjoining ranges look like genuine 16th-century

---

[1] See, for example, *R.C.H.M.*, 134-5 and Pevsner, 217.
[2] Smith (1992), 66; Smith (1993), 124-7.
[3] As, for instance, in the recent as yet unpublished investigative work carried out at Ware Priory by the Hertfordshire Archaeological Trust.
[4] B.L., Add. MS. 32,349, fol.2.
[5] H.R.O., Buckler Drawings, IV, 20; Bodl., MS. top. gen. a. 12, fol.90.

work, but a comparison with Fisher's apparently accurate drawing shows that this cannot be the case. Although this might be readily apparent from a site inspection,[6] this would not necessarily be so. Totternhoe clunch stone (of which the house at Markyate is principally constructed) is notorious for its friability and poor weathering qualities and, as at nearby Ashridge, masonry of the 1820s or '30s could quite easily be mistaken for late medieval or Tudor work. The architectural context makes this far less likely at Ashridge, but at Markyate it might have been only too easy without the graphic evidence falsely to identify 19th-century Gothic masonry as medieval fabric.

Documentary evidence can similarly show the dangers of carrying out structural analysis in isolation. Once more Markyate provides the example. Much 13th-century moulded stonework is incorporated in the east wall of the present house, but documentary sources suggest that this re-use took place only in the 19th century.[7] In many cases, of course, such deductions would be possible even without further supporting evidence, but the problem is far more acute with regard to internal fittings and furnishings. Again at Markyate it is known that much late 16th-century panelling was imported from elsewhere only in the 1920s, while at Wymondley Priory the provenance of similar panelling remains unknown. At Beechwood (originally the nunnery of St Giles in the Wood, Flamstead) an early to mid-16th-century fireplace is clearly out of context and not even careful dismantling would establish its origin. In contrast, the recent discovery of *in situ* panelling and blocked windows at Ware Priory has helped to date a particular post-Dissolution remodelling of the south range to c.1600, a conclusion it would otherwise have been considerably more difficult to reach.

Many people have assisted me in carrying out the research for this study, originally undertaken for a Ph.D at the University of Southampton (awarded in December 1997). First, I should mention the many owners and occupiers of the buildings involved, almost all of whom were happy for me to visit their properties and record what I saw. For assistance with the documentary and pictorial evidence I am grateful to the staff of several libraries and museums including the Bodleian Library, Oxford, the British Library and Public Record Office in London, Hitchin and Hertford Museums and particularly the archivists at Hertfordshire Archives and Local Studies (formerly the Hertfordshire Record Office), Hertford, who were unfailingly kind and helpful.

On a more personal note I should record my debt to Malcolm Airs and Jonathan Hunn for their constant encouragement and to Michael Bullen for discussing a number of issues and ideas. My employers, South Oxfordshire District Council, were most generous in providing financial support during much of the time I was working on the thesis. My biggest thanks, however, are to the thesis supervisors, Colin Platt and David Hinton, whose teaching and utilisation of archaeological, architectural and historical sources have been an inspiration since I first went to the University of Southampton as an undergraduate in 1977. Colin Platt in particular was instrumental in the structuring of the thesis and his firm but always friendly cajoling has enabled me at last to complete it. I should also record my gratitude to my external examiners, Maurice Howard and Tom James, for the useful suggestions they made to improve the text. I am grateful too to Colin Platt and Maurice Howard for their continuing encouragement since the thesis was awarded. I should, however, point out that any inaccuracies which remain in the published work are my own.

Finally, I would like to mention my family: my parents for their help and support, my wife, Tace, for her encouragement and forbearance since I began the project in 1989, and most recently of all my sons, Nathaniel and Josiah, for allowing me enough time away from their games to finish its writing.

---

[6] Permission to inspect the house at Markyate was refused by its owner, Mr J. Armstrong. N.M.R., file 77,723.

Chapter One

Introduction: study area, sources and methods

The re-use of monastic buildings in the 16th century is a subject which has been little studied. Despite the vast amount written on medieval monastic buildings, interest generally seems to cease at the Dissolution and few writers have continued the story beyond 1540. This is equally true of archaeologists, documentary and architectural historians. For instance, the splendid series of H.M.S.O. guides to monastic sites prepared by Inspectors of Ancient Monuments for the Office of Works and its successors rarely have much to say about a site after the suppression.

One of the earliest of what could be termed modern, as opposed to antiquarian, accounts of the post-Dissolution history of a monastic site was that of Titchfield (Hants.) by W.H. St John Hope in 1906.[1] St John Hope was attracted to Titchfield by the combination of the extent of the surviving ruins and the unusually detailed documentary sources, which enabled him to reconstruct with great accuracy the sequence of events there. It is perhaps for this reason that St John Hope's account remains a model of its kind, which few later writers have been able to emulate. St John Hope also carried out pioneering studies at many other sites including Fountains and Mount Grace (Yorks.),[2] although at none of these did he examine the adaptive re-use of the buildings in anything approaching the detail he employed at Titchfield.

St John Hope was by no means the first archaeologist or historian to display a serious academic interest in monastic sites. At Fountains he was able to draw on the work of R. Walbran in the 1840s and 1850s,[3] while the stone-by-stone elevation drawings of its buildings by J. Reeve in the 1870s remain, according to Glyn Coppack "the most complete analysis of any abbey ruin."[4] However, most 19th-century archaeologists were content simply to follow the lines of walls in their excavations with the aim of uncovering as much of the original monastic lay-out as possible.[5] Among the exceptions to this rule were A. Lowther and J. Parsons, who at Lewes (Sussex) in the 1840s found clear evidence for the mines used by the Italian engineer, Portinari, to destroy the walls of the Cluniac church.[6] Their interest in the fate of the church at the suppression may, however, have been brought about by the unusual method of its destruction and in general little interest was shown in this phase of monastic sites.

Even among St John Hope's followers, leading exponents of monastic archaeology such as H. Brakspear at Stanley (Wilts.) and Waverley (Surrey), J. Bilson at Kirkstall (Yorks.) and C. Laing at Bardney (Lincs.) displayed little interest in the post-suppression history of the sites they excavated.[7] This attitude was also reflected in the activities of the Office of Works, which after the passing of the Ancient Monuments Act in 1911 took several monastic sites into state care and set about their repair and display to the public. As Coppack has recently commented "The effect that this was to have on monastic sites was dramatic,"[8] and one which remains all too evident even now. Despite radical changes in the management and presentation of such sites in the last few years, the usual image of sites in English Heritage guardianship is still one of ruthlessly mown and manicured lawns with medieval walls heavily repointed in cement-rich mortar and stripped bare of all vegetation.[9]

This approach is not simply one of appearance but in its early days before the First World War and into the 1920s, if not later, also involved the clearing away of later accretions in an attempt to return the surviving ruins to their "original" form. Not only was such an ambition impossible to achieve, since ruins are as much a product of gradual decay and changes through time as the result of a single cataclysmic event, and by today's criteria it would be highly questionable in conservation terms, but it was intensely destructive of archaeological evidence at sites which were among the best preserved in the country.

As Coppack has shown, the work of Sir Charles Peers, Chief Inspector of Ancient Monuments from 1913 until 1933, was instrumental in this process.[10] Peers's own interest in and scholarly approach to the sites in his care is

---

[1] W.H. St John Hope, 'The making of Place House at Titchfield, near Southampton in 1538', *Arch. Jnl.* 63 (1906), 231-43.
[2] W.H. St John Hope, 'Fountains Abbey', *Yorks. Arch. Jnl.*, 15 (1898/9), 269-402 and 'The architectural history of Mount Grace Charterhouse', *Yorks. Arch. Jnl.*, 18 (1905), 270-309.
[3] R. Walbran, *Memorials of the Abbey of St Mary of Fountains, I and II*, Surtees Soc., 42 (1862) and Surtees Soc., 67 (1876).
[4] J.A. Reeve, *A Monograph on the Abbey of St Mary of Fountains* (1892); also printed in St John Hope, op. cit. (1898/9), (note 2), passim; Coppack (1990), 22.
[5] As typified by St John Hope at Alnwick (Northumberland) and Watton (Yorks.). See his 'On the Premonstratensian abbey of St Mary at Alnwick, Northumberland', *Arch. Jnl.*, 44 (1887), 337-46 and 'The Gilbertine priory of Watton in the East Riding of Yorkshire', *Arch. Jnl.*, 58 (1901), 1-34.
[6] M.A. Lowther, 'Reports on the antiquities lately found at Lewes' and 'Further report on discoveries at Lewes', *Jnl. Brit. Arch. Assoc.*, 1 & 2 (1846 & 1847), 346-57 & 104-8; see also W.H. Blaauw, 'On the Cluniac priory of St Pancras at Lewes, its priors and monks', *Sussex Arch. Collns.*, 3 (1850), 185-210.
[7] H. Brakspear, 'Stanley Abbey', *Wilts. Nat. Hist. Mag.*, 35 (1907/8), 541-81 and *Waverley Abbey* (1905); J. Bilson & W.H. St John Hope, *Architectural Description of Kirkstall Abbey*, Publications of the Thoresby Soc., 16 (1907); C.E. Laing, 'Excavations on the site of Bardney Abbey', *Assoc. Soc. Reps.*, 32, pt.i (1913), 21-34. The results of Laing's excavations were fully published by H. Brakspear, 'Bardney Abbey', *Arch. Jnl.*, 79 (1922), 1-92.
[8] Coppack (1990), 25.
[9] See M.W. Thompson, *Ruins: their Preservation and Display* (1981), 29-34 for an attempt to explain the old Ministry of Works policy on the display of ruins and the "advantages" of closely-mown grass in this context. Recently a new, less clinical approach has been evident at sites such as Jervaulx in Yorkshire. For examples of other sites where a more enlightened approach to interpretation has been adopted, see Greene (1992), 215-26.
[10] *D.N.B., 1951-60*, (1971) 800-1.

exemplified by the many site guides he wrote,[11] but his excavations involved the "clearance of all fallen debris, including the evidence for the latest occupation and demolition, (only) stopping at the latest floor levels."[12] Likewise, the concept of bringing a site into guardianship with its emphasis on presenting ruins to the public meant that although the church and claustral buildings were likely to be protected and investigated, the less well-preserved structures and earthworks of the inner and outer courts were often excluded, sometimes as at Buildwas (Shropshire) not even being included within the wider scheduled area.

The attention paid to the church and the least-altered claustral buildings may have been a contributory factor in the general disregard of the post-Dissolution phases of monastic sites. This is typified by the treatment of Rievaulx (Yorks.), a previously largely uninvestigated site, where Peers began major clearance works in 1919. Although Brakspear had earlier shown some interest in the history of the abbey after the suppression,[13] the post-Dissolution archaeological deposits and alterations to the fabric were swept away in the determination to restore the ruins of the church and recover the full plan of the medieval claustral buildings.[14] A similar operation took place at Whitby (Yorks.) in the 1920s and must have occurred at many other places throughout the country.

This cavalier attitude to post-medieval features and deposits extended to buildings erected on monastic sites after the Dissolution. Thus in the 1950s the 17th-century farmhouse at Monk Bretton (Yorks.) was systematically dismantled to expose the medieval fabric of the gatehouse from which it had been fashioned.[15] The disappearance of post-suppression features in this way was the result of a desire to understand and (in the case of sites displayed to the public) to present monastic buildings in a form as close to their original appearance as possible. While such an approach was perhaps considered justifiable in the 1950s, it is even less easy to defend the more recent removal of all traces of the post-medieval domestic use of the former lady chapel at the priory church of St Bartholomew, Smithfield in London.[16] Since then the significance of the re-use of monastic buildings as a social phenomenon has been done a further disservice by the decision to remove the post-Dissolution residential elements from the former church of Blackfriars, Gloucester, although it must be admitted that this could have provided the opportunity to investigate how this transformation had been achieved in the first place.[17]

Nevertheless, it is to be hoped that when restoration programmes take place elsewhere, especially at sites in state guardianship, the post-Dissolution phases of monastic buildings will cease to be regarded as sacrificial.

The 1950s saw the growth of aerial photography of monastic sites by practitioners such as J.K. St Joseph.[18] This drew attention to the outer precinct with its earthworks and outbuildings and was an important factor in the investigation of the monastery as a wider community than that represented simply by church and cloister. This emphasis on the study of the whole monastic complex roughly co-incided with the emergence of post-medieval archaeology as a discipline in its own right in the late 1960s and early 1970s.[19] One of the first of the new generation of scholars to concern itself with events after the Dissolution was David Baker, whose excavation of the small Benedictine nunnery of Elstow (Beds.) included an examination of the mansion erected by Thomas Hillersden in the early 17th century on the site of a house built from the ruins of the nunnery immediately after the Dissolution.[20] Similarly, Edward Johnson's excavations at Sopwell (Herts.) were as much concerned with the post- as the pre-Dissolution phases,[21] while at Norton (Cheshire) Patrick Greene made a detailed study of the way in which the abbot's lodgings were converted to a new house after the suppression.[22] Among other examples of such an approach are Philip Rahtz's work at Bordesley (Worcs.),[23] and at Blackfriars, Gloucester Andrew Saunders has shown how Thomas Bell transformed the Dominican friary into a factory, retaining the church for his own use as a residence.[24]

It is now standard practice for excavators to pay due regard to the post-monastic phases of religious sites, as shown by Tony Musty at Waltham Abbey (Essex), Rick Turner and Robina McNeil at Vale Royal (Cheshire), Barbara Harbottle at the former Carmelite and Dominican friaries in Newcastle-upon-Tyne and P.M. Christie and J.G. Coad at

[11] C.R. Peers, H.M.S.O. guides to *Byland* (1930), *Finchale* (revd., 1973), *Rievaulx* (1933) and *St Botolph's, Colchester* (revd., 1964).

[12] Coppack (1990), 25.

[13] Ibid, 26.

[14] C.R. Peers, H.M.S.O. guide to *Rievaulx* (1933). See also P. Fergusson & S. Harrison, *Rievaulx Abbey* (1999), *passim*.

[15] R. Graham & R. Gilyard-Beer, H.M.S.O. guide to *Monk Bretton* (1966).

[16] M.W. Barley, *Houses and History* (1986), 269-70.

[17] Ibid, 272. No proper account of the post-Dissolution conversion work has been published, Francis Kelly pers. comm. But see Oliver Rackham,

John Blair & Julian Munby, 'The thirteenth-century roofs and floor of the Blackfriars priory at Gloucester', *Med. Arch.*, 22 (1978), 105-22 which, perhaps wisely, offers no comment on the merits of the "restoration" programme.

[18] J.K. St Joseph & David Knowles, *Monastic Sites from the Air* (1952).

[19] The Society for Post-Medieval Archaeology was founded in 1967 and its first journal published in that year.

[20] *Post-Med. Arch.*, 2 (1968), 183.

[21] *Med. Arch.*, 8 (1964), 242; 9 (1965), 179; 10 (1966), 177-80; 11 (1967), 274.

[22] Patrick Greene, *Norton Priory* (1989). See also 'The impact of the dissolution on monasteries in Cheshire: the case of Norton' in A. Thacker (ed.), *Chester: Medieval Archaeology, Art & Architecture*, Brit. Arch. Assoc. Conference Trans. xxii (2000), 152-66.

[23] Philip Rahtz & Susan Hirst, *Bordesley Abbey*, Brit. Arch. Rep., 23 (1976); Susan Hirst, D.A. Walsh & S.M. Wright, *Bordesley Abbey II*, Brit. Arch. Rep., 111 (1983) and G. Astill, 'Monastic research designs: Bordesley Abbey and the Arrow Valley' in Roberta Gilchrist & Harold Mytum (eds.), *The Archaeology of Rural Monasteries*, Brit. Arch. Rep., 203 (1989), 279-93.

[24] Andrew Saunders, 'Blackfriars', *Arch. Jnl.*, 122 (1965), 217-19.

Denny (Cambs.),[25] to name but a few. Nevertheless, the failure in 1989 of even one of the pioneers of post-Dissolution monastic archaeology, Lawrence Butler, to acknowledge the study of the re-use of monastic buildings as one of the research objectives for the "next decades of monastic archaeology" indicates that there may still be some way to go for the topic to be regarded as a priority by archaeologists.[26]

The results of the excavation of post-Dissolution deposits and the archaeological analysis of surviving fabric are slowly beginning to be represented in general surveys of medieval and post-medieval archaeology. As recently as 1984, however, the question of the re-cycling of monastic buildings and materials was completely ignored by Helen Clarke in *The Archaeology of Medieval England* and, although John Steane briefly touches upon the importance of lead to the crown at the time of the Dissolution, he otherwise makes no mention of the topic in *The Archaeology of Medieval England and Wales* (1984), simply contenting himself with the general and rather misleading statement that "Not many complete cloisters survive because after the Dissolution they served no useful purpose and were nearly always destroyed."[27]

Much happier than this is Colin Platt's treatment of the subject in *Medieval England* (1978) and *The Abbeys and Priories of Medieval England* (1984) (see below), while a comprehensive review of recent archaeological work on the re-use of monastic buildings appears in David Crossley's *Post-Medieval Archaeology* (1990). Increasing interest is, however, best illustrated by the devotion of complete chapters to the topic in Coppack's *Abbeys and Priories* (1990) and Patrick Greene's *Medieval Monasteries* (1992). This is in marked contrast to Lionel Butler's and Chris Given-Wilson's earlier *Medieval Monasteries of Great Britain* (1979), which covers much the same ground, albeit from an architectural and historical rather than an archaeological perspective. Apart from these general surveys, there has been rather little in the way of non-site

specific archaeological studies, although David Stocker has tackled the issue of the re-cycling of materials, both within a county context across a wide date range and also with specific reference to the Reformation in Lincoln, while of studies of a particular group of sites before and after the Dissolution, Simon Ward's work on the friaries of Chester is among the most valuable.[28]

If archaeologists were slow to turn to the examination of post-Dissolution deposits and features in their excavation of monastic sites, much the same attitude towards the post-suppression period was evident among architectural and documentary historians. Indeed, it could be argued that the essentially architectural approach of archaeologists like St John Hope, Brakspear and Peers did much to stifle early investigation of the outer precinct buildings, most of which were by then no more than rubble or marked by earthworks. It is true, however, that documentary historians showed no premature enthusiasm to devote themselves to the study of the 16th-century re-use of monastic buildings. Among those concerned with the Dissolution of the Monasteries, early writers like Cardinal Gasquet in his *Henry VIII and the English Monasteries* (1906) and A. Savine in *The English Monasteries on the Eve of the Dissolution* (1909) make no reference to the subject and the topic is only summarily treated by Geoffrey Baskerville in *English Monks and the Suppression of the Monasteries* (1937), although in fairness it should be pointed out that Baskerville's main concern was to trace the post-Dissolution careers of the ex-religious.

The topic was totally ignored by D. Hay in his study of the Dissolution of the Monasteries in the diocese of Durham,[29] but A. Preston, in his transcription of and commentary on a detailed account of the demolition of Reading Abbey in 1549, led the way in showing how documentary sources could be used to illuminate the post-Dissolution history of a particular site.[30] The first documentary historian, however, to give serious consideration to the wider question of the re-use of monastic buildings in general was David Knowles in the third volume (1959) of his magisterial *The Religious Orders in England*. The treatment is necessarily brief in a general survey of this sort and the elegant statement that "In the main, and especially in the numberless small houses in field, forest and dale, the

---

[25] A.E.S. Musty, 'Exploratory excavation within the monastic precinct, Waltham Abbey, 1972', *Essex Arch. & Hist.*, 10 (1978), 127-73 and P.J. Huggins, 'Excavations of the collegiate and Augustinian churches, Waltham Abbey, Essex, 1984-87', *Arch. Jnl.*, 146 (1989), 476-537; *Post-Med. Arch.*, 19 (1985), 159-61 and R. Mc Neil & R.C. Turner, 'An architectural and topographical survey of Vale Royal Abbey', *Jnl. Chester Arch. Soc.*, 70 (1990), 51-79; Barbara Harbottle, 'Excavations at the Carmelite friary, Newcastle-upon-Tyne, 1965, 1967', *Arch. Aeliana*, 4th Ser., 46 (1968), 163-223 and with R. Fraser, 'Black Friars, Newcastle-upon-Tyne, after the Dissolution of the Monasteries', *Arch. Aeliana*, 5th Ser., 15 (1987), 23-150; P.M. Christie & J.G. Croad, 'Excavations at Denny Abbey', *Arch. Jnl.*, 137 (1980), 138-279 and J. Poster & D. Sherlock, 'Denny Abbey: the nuns' refectory', *Proc. Cambridge Antiq. Soc.*, 76 (1987), 67-82.

[26] Lawrence Butler, 'The archaeology of rural monasteries in England and Wales' in Gilchrist & Mytum, op. cit., (note 23), 1-27. The omission of the re-use of monastic buildings as a research objective is even harder to account for in the postscript to Greene (1992), especially given that writer's exemplary treatment of the subject in chapter eight of the same book.

[27] John Steane, *The Archaeology of Medieval England and Wales* (1984), 71.

[28] David Stocker & Paul Everson, 'Rubbish recycled: a study of the re-use of stone in Lincolnshire' in David Parsons (ed.), *Stone Quarrying and Building in England A.D. 43-1525* (1990), 83-101 and 'The archaeology of the Reformation in Lincoln: a case study in the redistribution of building materials in the mid 16th century', *Lincs. Hist. & Arch.*, 25 (1990), 18-32; Simon Ward, 'The friaries in Chester, their impact and legacy', in A. Thacker (ed.), *Chester: Medieval Archaeology, Art & Architecture*, Brit. Arch. Assoc. Conference Trans., xxii (2000), 121-31.

[29] D. Hay, 'The dissolution of the monasteries in the diocese of Durham', *Arch. Aeliana*, 4th Ser., 15 (1938), 69-114.

[30] A.E. Preston, 'The demolition of Reading Abbey', *Berks. Arch. Jnl.*, 39 (1935), 107-44.

work of destruction was swift, and the church and cloister of yesterday were left a stripped and gutted ruin" denies the frequency of re-use,[31] but several residential conversions are cited and Knowles demonstrates a clear understanding of the processes of demolition and re-use.

It is therefore unfortunate that Knowles's example was not followed by other historians of the 16th century. The two volumes covering the period in *The Oxford History of England* make no reference whatsoever to the re-use of monastic buildings,[32] while the topic is conspicuous by its absence from A.G. Dickens's *The English Reformation* (1964). More surprisingly, the situation is no better in two of the most recent general syntheses, Joyce Youings's *Sixteenth-Century England* (1984) and John Guy's *Tudor England* (1988). While it might be argued that extensive treatment of the subject would be out of place in general surveys of the political, social and economic history of the period, its total absence may still reflect a lack of interest among documentary historians.

It is not the case that the wider question of the dispersal of monastic lands has been ignored by historians. This has its own far-ranging literature, including several notable local and regional studies in counties as widespread as Devon, Norfolk and Yorkshire,[33] some of which has been summarised by H. Habbakuk and G.W.O. Woodward as well as in the general surveys referred to above.[34] The general history of the Dissolution of the Monasteries has, of course, been addressed by many writers. Among the more useful recent accounts is Youings's *The Dissolution of the Monasteries* (1971) and the stripping of the Church's wealth is well covered by W.G. Hoskins in *The Age of Plunder* (1976). Platt's *Medieval England* (1978) and *The Abbeys and Priories of Medieval England* (1984) contain references to specific conversion schemes, as does Woodward's *The Dissolution of the Monasteries* (1966), while Felicity Heal's and Clive Holmes's *The Gentry in England and Wales 1500-1700* (1994) provides the most recent summary of the context in which conversions at gentry level took place.

Many of Woodward's examples come from Yorkshire and it is, perhaps, through local and regional studies that the greatest advances have been made in the last 30 years. J. Oxley led the way with *The Reformation in Essex to the Death of Mary* (1965) but, apart from a detailed account of

the destruction of Barking Abbey,[35] his summary of the re-use of monastic buildings in the county is rather superficial and based mainly on the work of the R.C.H.M. and Nikolaus Pevsner.

More disappointing still in view of its recent date is J.H. Bettey's *Suppression of The Monasteries in the West Country* (1989). Despite devoting a complete chapter to the careers of the ex-religious and the fate of the former monastic buildings, his survey (which covers the counties of Dorset, Gloucestershire, Somerset and Wiltshire) is of relatively little value. Admittedly, the area covered is a large one but this perhaps reveals the drawbacks to casting the net so wide, at least until detailed local studies have been undertaken. Bettey cites a number of instances where monastic materials were transported some distance for the building of new houses, but in general he over-emphasises the extent of destruction which took place at the Dissolution. Mention is, of course, made of the region's major conversions, such as Forde and Milton Abbas in Dorset and Lacock and Wilton in Wiltshire, but on the whole the choice of conversions included is unadventurous, the lack of first-hand observation noticeable and the limited amount of space given to the topic seems strangely at odds with the number of photographs of converted monastic buildings found throughout the book. This is particularly frustrating given the number and interest of comparatively obscure sites in the region like Woodspring (Somerset), where part of the church, including the central tower, was converted into a dwelling after the Dissolution, but for which no comprehensive modern account has been published.[36] Bettey's treatment of the subject is probably the result of trying to cover too much ground in one book, but one cannot help feeling that a regional study of this sort would have benefited from a more detailed and analytical account of the re-use of monastic buildings from a smaller number of selected sites.

This criticism cannot be made of Steven Pugsley's recent examination of the country house in Devon,[37] where the role of the monastic conversion in the development of the Tudor and early Stuart country house is more carefully explored and appreciated. It can only be hoped that similar studies will follow elsewhere.

Specific questions have also been examined recently by historians such as J. Horden, who in his study of former monastic churches in Cumbria has advanced the view that while the status of churches as consecrated buildings could prevent the destruction of parish churches at the Dissolution, monastic churches were regarded "first and foremost as monastic buildings, no different from the

---

[31] David Knowles, *The Religious Orders in England*, iii (1959), 387.

[32] J.D. Mackie, *The Earlier Tudors, 1485-1558* (1952); J.B. Black, *The Reign of Elizabeth, 1558-1603* (2nd edn., 1959).

[33] J. Kew, 'The disposal of crown lands and the Devon land market, 1536-58', *Agricultural Hist. Rev.*, 18 (1970), 93-105; T.H. Swales, 'The redistribution of the monastic lands in Norfolk at the Dissolution', *Norfolk Arch.*, 34 (1962-66), 14-44; R.B. Smith, *Land and Politics in the England of Henry VIII: the West Riding of Yorkshire, 1530-46* (1970).

[34] H.J. Habbakuk, 'The market for monastic property, 1539-1603', *Economic Hist. Rev.*, 2nd. Ser., 10 (1957/8), 362-80; G.W.O. Woodward, 'A speculation in monastic lands', *English Hist. Rev.*, 79 (1964), 778-83.

[35] J.E. Oxley, *The Reformation in Essex to the Death of Mary* (1965), 130.

[36] But see Nikolaus Pevsner, *North Somerset and Bristol* (1958), 343.

[37] Steven Pugsley, 'Landed society and the emergence of the country house in Tudor and early Stuart Devon' in T. Gray, M. Rowe & A. Erskine (eds.), *Tudor and Stuart Government, Essays Presented to Joyce Youings* (1992), 96-118.

secular buildings with which they were in physical proximity" and could, therefore, be demolished unless they had also been used for parochial worship.[38] Thus, he argues, it was those churches, such as Lanercost, where the parish had used the nave before the suppression which were most likely to survive wholly or in part after the Dissolution.

It might be expected that architectural historians would have started to examine the question of the re-use of monastic buildings at an earlier date than their documentary colleagues. However, this is not the case. Of the two first reliable modern studies of the period, J. Gotch's *Early Renaissance Architecture in England* (1914) does not address the subject and T. Garner's and A. Stratton's splendid two-volume *The Domestic Architecture of England During the Tudor Period* (1929) makes only passing reference to the conversion of monastic buildings in the introduction, although many examples are included in the gazeteer which forms the main part of the book. The topic is also ignored by D.H.S. Cranage in his otherwise excellent *Home of the Monk* (1934).

In later general works the subject is absent from Sir John Summerson's *tour de force, Architecture in Britain, 1530-1830* (1953) and Eric Mercer's *English Art, 1553-1625* (1962), but Henry VIII's re-use of monastic buildings as royal houses and the re-cycling of materials in the coastal shore forts is considered by Howard Colvin *et al* in *The History of the King's Works, vol.iv, 1485 -1660 (Pt.2)* (1982).

The first general analysis of the re-use of monastic buildings by an architectural historian was by J.C. Dickinson in 1968,[39] although he had earlier touched on the subject in his *Monastic Life in Medieval England* (1961). Dickinson's study was pioneering in that by treating the houses of one order, the Augustinian, he was able to determine the extent and variety of re-use. By this time many individual sites had been thoroughly described by the *R.C.H.M., V.C.H.*, Pevsner and others but Dickinson seems to have been the first to examine the issue within its historical context. His sample is a very large one, "the houses of the English Augustinian canons represent(ing) a quarter of the religious houses in England at the time of the Reformation", and as he rightly points out "only generalities can be offered" until further work has been carried out.[40] Nevertheless, the "generalities" which Dickinson makes are pertinent. For instance, he highlights the difficulties of converting the redundant church to domestic use, emphasises the number of cases where the

former superior's lodging became the basis for a new house on the site, and draws attention to the speed and frequency with which the east claustral range was demolished for the fear that, in the words of one of the new lay owners, "the birds should build therein again."[41] Another innovative aspect of Dickinson's work is that he selected relatively unknown sites among his examples rather than concentrating almost exclusively on the more spectacular conversions as several earlier (and later) commentators have done.

Although not primarily an architectural historian, many useful insights into the process of re-use have been made by Lawrence Stone in a series of books and papers published between 1965 and 1984. Stone's contribution is particularly important for our purposes, because in his study of the aristocracy, Hertfordshire was chosen as a sample area, one paper being entirely devoted to the county's country houses and their owners from 1540 onwards.[42] In his first book, *The Crisis of the Aristocracy 1558-1641* (1965) to consider the topic, albeit in passing, Stone suggests two reasons why it may have been more common for monastic materials to be re-used elsewhere rather than for the buildings themselves to be converted. First, there was the fear that former monastic property could revert to the crown or the Church and, secondly, there was superstition about "wining, dining and sleeping on once holy ground."[43]

Stone goes on to suggest that by the 1570s and 1580s there were overwhelming reasons among the aristocracy for building. At long last new owners felt relatively secure in their possessions, had paid off the purchase price of their properties and had surplus money available. These factors, coupled with the emergence of a new architectural style with its emphasis on symmetry and various technological advances, provided an irresistible urge to build. This stress on the post-1570 period is strangely contradicted in Stone's 1972 paper on Hertfordshire, which notes that "in terms of new construction or substantial rebuilding, the major growth phase...was over by 1580" and that "only in the period 1540-80 does new building or total rebuilding/reconstruction amount to a high proportion of total building activity in this period...the peak of the building boom (being) the 1540s and 1550s when 13 newly built houses entered the sample."[44]

In *An Open Elite? England 1540-1880* (1984) Stone emphasises the role of the Dissolution in the creation of Hertfordshire as "a social and political unit...in its own right" when the break-up of the vast St Albans estate made possible the establishment of new private estates. "Few

---

[38] J. Horden, 'The fate of monastic churches in Cumbria: a consideration of the position at law' in J. Loades (ed.), *Monastic Studies* (1990), 263.

[39] J.C. Dickinson, 'The buildings of the English Austin canons after the Dissolution of the Monasteries', *Jnl. Brit. Arch. Assoc.*, 3rd. Ser., 31 (1968), 60-75.

[40] Ibid, 62.

[41] Thomas Fuller, *The Church History of Great Britain*, iii (ed., J.S. Brewer, 1845), 486.

[42] L. & J.C. Stone, 'Country houses and their owners in Hertfordshire, 1540-1879' in W.O. Aydelotte, A.C. Bogue & R.W. Fogel (eds.), *The Dimensions of Quantitative Research in History* (1972), 56-123.

[43] L. Stone, *The Crisis of the Aristocracy, 1558-1641* (1965), 549-50.

[44] L. & J.C. Stone, op. cit., (note 42), 108, 117, 120.

county elites can have been as heavily dependent upon 16th-century and early 17th-century dispersal of Church and crown properties as was that of Hertfordshire...nearly a half of all seats extant in 1640 (being) built on land which had once been in institutional hands, one third on ex-monastic land."[45]

Several of the issues explored by Stone have been elaborated upon by Malcolm Airs in *The Making of the English Country House, 1500-1640* (1975), which has recently been republished as *The Tudor and Jacobean Country House, A Building History* (1995). Airs makes the point that it was the most powerful men and those who played an active part in the Dissolution who were most likely to be the first to build at ex-monastic property. Others preferred to wait and often it was not until the property had been sold again or passed to later generations that it was exploited. "It is not unreasonable to suggest that this further transaction helped to free it from the inhibitions arising from its religious associations". Airs also notes that many houses occupying former monastic sites "were not begun before the last quarter of the 16th century and some, such as Trentham Hall (Staffs) were not begun until well into the 17th century".[46]

A particularly useful summary of the literature to date from the architectural historian's view-point is contained in chapter seven of Maurice Howard's *The Early Tudor Country House* (1987). In contrast to many writers, Howard emphasises the extent of conversion to other uses which took place at the Dissolution rather than simply concentrating on the amount of destruction which occurred. Howard also plays down the part of superstition or moral scruples in discouraging the conversion process. Rather, he argues, lay involvement in the running of monasteries before the suppression meant "that there was more continuity between the pre-Dissolution situation with regard to monastic buildings and their post-Dissolution history than is sometimes imagined."[47]

Another important point made by Howard is that early lay owners of former monastic property probably went to some length to conceal the ecclesiastical origins of their new houses: it was left to later restorers to reveal monastic features for antiquarian effect. Howard is also the first writer properly to examine the difficulties of converting individual claustral buildings to domestic use, clearly demonstrating that this was often not so easy as might be supposed.

Rosalys Coope has recently discussed the role of monastic conversions in the emergence and development of the long gallery.[48] Citing Lacock and Newstead (Notts.) among others, she suggests that the adaptation of the upper floors

of claustral ranges could create either "corridor-galleries" serving the rooms opening off the galleries or "recreative galleries" of the type well known at houses like Hardwick (Derbys.) or Chastleton (Oxon.). As Howard says "It would be pushing the point too far to suggest that monastic conversions first introduced the idea of a sequence of important rooms on an upper floor, not least because this concept was alien to the monastic lay-out...but (these) conversions undoubtedly accelerated the growing importance of the upper floor."[49]

Equally important is Simon Thurley's *The Royal Palaces of Tudor England* (1993), which not only describes the influential conversions of former monastic property by the crown, but provides new observations on the development of the plan-form of Tudor palaces in the first half of the 16th century, particularly the decline in importance of the great hall. Thurley's book is almost matched in significance by John Schofield's *Medieval London Houses* (1994), which despite its title contains detailed summaries (many based on the writer's own work) of several post-Dissolution domestic conversions in the capital. Some of these were unusual in that they were to lead to multiple occupancy, as at Holy Trinity, Aldgate and St Bartholomew's, Smithfield but as some of the earliest and most comprehensive to be carried out, their significance for an understanding of the subject as a whole should not be under-estimated.

Also useful is Geoffrey Tyack's *Country Houses of Warwickshire* (1994), which includes several monastic conversions in its detailed accounts of individual houses. It is disappointing therefore that the subject receives scant attention in the R.C.H.M.'s *The Country Houses of Northamptonshire* (1996), while its almost complete absence from Nicholas Cooper's *Houses of the Gentry 1480-1680* (1999) is particularly surprising as this authoritative work could have provided the ideal opportunity to investigate on a national basis the context in which conversions at gentry level occurred.

Finally, Roger Stalley's account of the aftermath of the Dissolution in his *The Cistercian Monasteries of Ireland* (1987) provides some valuable insights and sources of comparison for the process of re-cycling of buildings in England,[50] but so far comparable studies have not been produced for Wales and Scotland.

This summary of the available literature has made little reference to books, papers or monographs on individual monastic sites, and in its attempt to survey the contents of what has been written, has probably (at least in some instances) drawn the line too rigidly between the work of archaeologists, documentary and architectural historians.

[45] L. Stone, *An Open Elite? England 1540-1880* (1984), 361.
[46] Airs (1975), 19.
[47] Howard (1987), 143.
[48] Rosalys Coope, 'The "long gallery": its origins, development, use and decoration', *Archit. Hist.*, 29 (1986), 43-84.
[49] Howard (1987), 156.
[50] Roger Stalley, *The Cistercian Monasteries of Ireland* (1987), 227-38.

Some individual studies, like Frederick Hockey's *Beaulieu, King John's Abbey* (1976) contain a limited amount of information on the question of re-use, but others like G. Copeland's work at Buckland (Devon),[51] Paul Drury's study of Walden Abbey (Essex), the precursor of Audley End,[52] or John Hare's excavations at Battle (Sussex) have done much to improve our understanding of the post-Dissolution history of these sites,[53] it undoubtedly being no coincidence that these are all investigations which draw on all forms of evidence. Similarly, the descriptions of individual buildings by the *R.C.H.M.*, *V.C.H.* and Pevsner, particularly those of the *V.C.H.* where they are supplemented by detailed documentary material, are often the best available accounts of particular sites and form a solid basis of information for analysis and comparison.[54]

For the purposes of this study the boundaries of the county of Hertfordshire are taken as those of the post-1974 administrative unit. This means that two former monastic sites which were previously partly or wholly in Buckinghamshire, Ashridge and St Margaret's, Nettleden, are included in this study.

Hertfordshire was chosen as a study area for several reasons. First, it is a relatively small county making a detailed examination of the re-use of its former monastic buildings possible. Its proximity to London means that local conditions and circumstances would be likely to encourage re-use. This is in marked contrast to counties more distant from the capital where lower population densities, the relative lack of sizeable towns and the absence of a courtier class might provide less of an impetus for the adaptation of former monastic buildings to secular use. Also, as recently noted by J.T. Smith,[55] the county is particularly fortunate in the richness of its 18th- and 19th-century histories and pictorial evidence. This is discussed in greater detail below.

The decision to omit the only monastic institution of the first rank, St Albans, from this study was taken at an early stage. St Albans was a major religious community, the fourth wealthiest monastery in terms of net income in the country in 1535,[56] and far outstripped any other Hertfordshire house in size and influence at the time of the Dissolution. The next wealthiest community, Ashridge, had an annual net income over five times smaller than that of St Albans and even this was nearly four times higher than that of the third richest institution, King's Langley.

It was therefore felt that to include St Albans would severely distort the balance of the sample and detract from the significance or otherwise of the remaining religious houses. This is not to deny or underrate the importance of St Albans: clearly its influence was far greater and more profound than that of any Hertfordshire house. Its vast land-holdings, particularly in the south and west of the county, were rivalled only by those of St Paul's in the north and east,[57] while it also held many manors outside the county.[58] The dissolution of St Albans, including the dispersal of its monks and their post-suppression careers,[59] is a subject awaiting its own detailed study.[60]

Even without St Albans, there remains a surprisingly high number of monastic institutions in Hertfordshire. There were at least nine hospitals in the county, of which very little is known,[61] while of the regular houses and friaries several were disbanded long before the 16th century. Of these the earliest casualty was the small Benedictine house of Salburn in Standon, which seems to have become a free chapel by the early 14th century,[62] while the alien priory at Ware was closed in 1414.[63] The collegiate house at Stanstead St Margarets closed in 1431,[64] and the preceptories of Temple Dinsley and Standon, the properties of the Knights Templars and Hospitallers respectively, do not seem to have survived the 15th century as religious institutions.[65]

The Benedictine nunnery of Rowney, Great Munden ceased to function in 1457, although a perpetual chantry was established in its place,[66] but Redbourn Priory, founded as a dependent cell of St Albans in the late 12th century,[67] appears to have survived until the late 15th or early 16th century. A prior, Thomas Albon, is last recorded in 1492,[68] and the house is not referred to again until 1535 when, described as a cell of St Albans, its annual net value was given as £9 2s.[69] It is not at all clear, however, what was meant by the priory at this date and, although the site

---

[51] G.W. Copeland, 'Some problems of Buckland Abbey', *Trans. Devon. Assoc.*, 85 (1953), 41-52.
[52] Paul Drury, 'Walden into Audley End' in S.R. Bassett (ed.), *Saffron Walden: Excavations and Research 1972-80*, C.B.A. Res. Rep., 45 (1982), 94-105 and 'No other palace in the kingdom will compare with it: the evolution of Audley End, 1605-1745', *Archit. Hist.*, 23 (1980), 1-39.
[53] John Hare, *Battle Abbey: the Eastern Range and the Excavations of 1978-80* (1985).
[54] See, for instance, the recent accounts of Buckland and Hexham in the second editions of Nikolaus Pevsner's *Devon* (revd., Bridget Cherry, 1989), 227-9 and *Northumberland* (revd., J. Grundy, G. McCombie, P. Ryder & H. Welfare, 1992), 318-27 respectively, or the R.C.H.M.'s earlier account of Forde in *Dorset*, I (1952), 240-6.
[55] Smith (1992), 9-11.
[56] *Val. Eccl.*, i, 451; Knowles op. cit. (note 31), 473.

[57] Doggett (1991), 47-8.
[58] See P.R.O., SC6/Hen VIII/1619, 1626-31 for its Hertfordshire possessions.
[59] Nicholas Doggett, unpublished paper on the dispersal of the Hertfordshire religious and their post-Dissolution careers.
[60] An introductory study has recently been published. Eileen Roberts, *The Hill of the Martyr, An Architectural History of St Albans Abbey* (1993).
[61] Nicholas Doggett, 'Medieval hospitals in Hertfordshire and their dissolution', *Herts. Past*, 38 (Spring 1995), 8-12.
[62] B.L., Add. MS. 6041, fol.73, nos.20-2.
[63] *Parliamentary Rolls*, v (n.d.), 365. For the background to the closure of the alien houses see Platt (1984), 173-8.
[64] *Cal. Pat. R., 1429-36*, 146.
[65] *V.C.H.*, iv, 444-6.
[66] Dugdale, iv, 343.
[67] H.T. Riley (ed.), *Gesta Abbatum Monasterii Sancti Albani*, ii (1867), 400.
[68] B.L., Add. Chart. 34,350.
[69] *Val. Eccl.*, i, 451.

of the house was granted to John Cokks in April 1540,[70] the royal commissioners in 1537 had described it as uninhabited by religious persons.[71] It therefore seems likely that the land continued to be farmed and presumably some of the buildings were maintained well into the 16th century, but that monastic life had lapsed c.1500.

A similar situation seems to have applied at the Trinitarian friary of Hertford, to which the last certain reference occurs in 1448.[72] Its site is referred to as a messuage called "le Trynytie" when it was granted to Anthony Denny in August 1540,[73] but religious life had apparently come to an end considerably before that date. More certainty attaches to the closure of the Benedictine nunnery of St Mary de Pré near St Albans, which (already deserted by its prioress and nuns) was suppressed by Pope Clement VII in May 1528.[74] In July Henry VIII granted the house to Wolsey, who used its property (with that of several other monasteries) to augment the endowments of his newly-founded Cardinal College, Oxford.[75]

Following the decision to omit St Albans from this project, it was also necessary to consider whether to include hospitals and those houses which did not survive until the Dissolution. The decision to exclude the hospitals can be justified on two counts. First, the hospitals were not truly monastic and, perhaps more importantly in a study primarily concerned with the adaptive re-use of buildings, there are no known surviving buildings in the county which can definitely be associated with the medieval hospitals.

These justifications cannot, however, be made for all those houses which did not survive until the Dissolution. A late 15th-century timber-framed barn remains at Standon Friars, a 19th-century house which stands on the site of the preceptory,[76] and more of this may, of course, be incorporated in the apparently Victorian house. There is good reason to suppose that The Priory in High Street, Redbourn conceals substantial elements of an earlier structure behind its fine early 18th-century facade,[77] while at Ware, No.9 Church Street (the old rectory), a 17th-century and earlier building, has been claimed to be on the site of the alien priory.[78]

The Church of St Margaret, Stanstead St Margarets, has an imposing Decorated chancel, built for the college

established here in c.1316,[79] and Temple Dinsley, a house of 1714 (although extensively remodelled by Lutyens) is said to stand on the site of a house built in 1542, presumably incorporating the remains of the former preceptory.[80] At Rowney, Great Munden the rather unprepossessing Victorian house is believed to have a medieval cellar,[81] and even if this not the case, much undoubtedly survived into the early 19th century, as is shown by Buckler's drawing of the site.[82] Nothing now survives above ground of St Mary de Pré but here too relatively substantial remains were still evident in the early 19th century.[83] There is also an unreliable-looking drawing of the ruins contained in a mid 18th-century manuscript history of St Albans,[84] while more importantly the exact location of the site is known through aerial photographs.[85]

The essential point to make about all these lesser sites (including the hospitals) is that the information about the buildings which survived the Dissolution comes from published material and an examination of the documentary sources. None of these sites has been visited in any detail for this study and it is probable that exhaustive structural analysis of their remaining buildings (of the kind carried out on those sites which have yielded the data for this study) would produce results showing extensive survival of medieval and 16th-century fabric.

Given that seven of the nine religious institutions (excluding hospitals) which failed to survive until the Dissolution appear to have had buildings of pre-Dissolution origin which continued in use well after the Suppression, their omission from this study must be justified. The reason cannot simply be that the remains are too fragmentary to merit inclusion. Such an argument could also be advanced for sites such as Cheshunt and St Margaret's, Nettleden, where nothing now survives above ground, but which survived until the Dissolution and are therefore included in this study. The justification must be that the circumstances of the early closure of these houses was very different from the suppression of the remaining houses at the Dissolution. The conditions surrounding their initial re-use may have been very different from those which prompted the re-use of monastic buildings after c.1540.

It could be argued, of course, that in the case of the Benedictine priories of Redbourn and Rowney and the preceptories of Standon and Temple Dinsley, which as they

[70] *L.P.*, xv, g.611 (46).

[71] *V.C.H.*, iv, 418.

[72] *3rd Rep. of the Royal Commission on Historical Manuscripts* (1872), App., 251.

[73] *L.P.*, xv, g.1027 (25).

[74] Dugdale, iii, 361, no.xi.

[75] *L.P.*, iv (2), no.4472, (3), nos.5714 and 5786. See Knowles, op. cit. (note 31), 161-4.

[76] *V.C.H.*, iii, 350; Pevsner, 273; J.A. Brown, 'The hospice of the Knights Templars at Standon', *Trans. East Herts. Arch. Soc.*, 1 (1899-1901), 289-91 and 'Visit of the East Herts. Arch. Soc., September 1930', Ibid, 8 (1928-33), 265-6.

[77] Pevsner, 277-8; N.M.R., 79,656.

[78] Pevsner, 381; N.M.R., 81,117.

[79] Pevsner, 344.

[80] Pevsner, 359. The pre-18th-century house is illustrated in Chauncy, ii, between pp.176 and 177.

[81] *R.C.H.M.*, 104.

[82] B.L., Add. MS. 36,366, fol.136.

[83] Jonathan Hunn, pers. comm.

[84] Library of Society of Antiquaries, MS. 720, J. Webster, *Gleanings of Antiquity from Verolam and St Albans* (n.d.), 147.

[85] S.M.R., Aerial photographs 3706 and 3906; also many aerial photographs in R.C.H.M. National Library of Air Photographs, Swindon.

are all recorded in the *Valor Ecclesiasticus*,[86] seem to have continued in agricultural if not conventual use until the Dissolution,[87] any modifications which took place after c.1540 can be seen in a similar context to those surrounding the re-use of monastic buildings dissolved between 1536 and 1539. This, however, would be to miss the point of my study, and to allow the inclusion of sites such as Standon and Temple Dinsley would make it impossible not to include the vast numbers of chantries and monastic manors, which would obviously involve research of a very different type and scale.

An argument could also be made for the inclusion of St Mary de Pré in this study as it was a regular house which survived well into the 16th century. Nevertheless, it was undoubtedly suppressed in 1528, its closure being brought about solely to provide further endowments for Cardinal College. Furthermore, it appears that the convent had been deserted since June 1527,[88] so it is unlikely that it would have survived until the Dissolution even without Wolsey's intervention. Although the circumstances surrounding the re-use of the buildings at St Mary de Pré may not be that different from those pertaining some ten years later, Wolsey's suppressions form a separate chapter in the history of the Dissolution of the monasteries and St Mary de Pré is thus excluded from this study.[89]

The sites which are included are all regular houses or friaries which survived until the Dissolution and are as follows: Ashridge (Bonshommes), Beechwood, formerly St Giles in the Wood, Flamstead (Benedictine nuns), Cheshunt (Benedictine nuns), Hertford (Benedictine), Hitchin (Carmelite), The Biggin, Hitchin (Gilbertine), King's Langley (Dominican), Markyate (Benedictine nuns), Royston (Augustinian), St Margaret's, Nettleden (Benedictine nuns), Sopwell (Benedictine nuns), Ware (Franciscan) and Wymondley (Augustinian).

Having defined the area of study and the sources of evidence employed, we must consider the confines and possibilities of the period involved. The survey begins in 1540, chosen as the year in which the last monastery, Waltham Abbey (Essex),surrendered.[90] The selection of 1600 as the finishing point is more problematic, but can be explained in a number of ways. First, it roughly co-incides with the death of Elizabeth in 1603, the last of the Tudor monarchs, and in whose reign the great majority of major monastic conversions were carried out. More important is the perceptible change in plan-form and architectural styles and attitudes at this time. This is a trend which has its roots

in the reign of Henry VIII at the royal palaces of Hampton Court and Nonsuch,[91] develops under the influence of Protector Somerset and his circle in the late 1540s and early 1550s,[92] finds further expression in "prodigy" houses such as Longleat (Wilts.) in the 1570s, Wollaton and Worksop (Notts.) in the 1580s and on a slightly less lavish scale at houses like Condover (Shropshire) and Doddington (Lincs.) in the 1590s.[93] Although great courtyard houses continued to be built in the last part of the 16th century, as at Kirby (Northants.) begun in 1570, Theobalds (Herts.) begun in 1564, and even into the early 17th century as at the remodelled Audley End,[94] the tradition, which stretched back to the 15th century and beyond, was certainly on the wane in late Elizabethan England.

The move towards houses of a compact outward-looking plan, seen in both buildings of the largest scale like Wollaton and Hardwick, built between 1590 and 1597, and at more modest houses like Barlborough Hall, Derbyshire (1583/4), and the now-demolished Heath Old Hall, Yorkshire (c.1585) was reflected in the growing popularity of the E- or H-shaped house,[95] which left the courtyard plan of the monastic conversion increasingly obsolete and isolated. Houses with central courtyards continued to be built in the first decade of the 17th century, but now, as at Chastleton (Oxon.) or Burton Agnes (Yorks.), they usually amounted to no more than light wells.[96] Instead, as Mark Girouard has shown, the emphasis was very much on external show, which at great houses like Hatfield (Herts.) or Blickling (Norfolk) can "supply an almost endless repertory of picturesque groupings."[97] Even at smaller houses like Charlton House, Greenwich (1607) and the contemporary Holland House, Kensington "a strict symmetry, which was perhaps a contribution of the Renaissance, and a feeling for dramatic massing and recession (itself) a discovery of the Elizabethans" are the hall-marks of these early Jacobean buildings.[98]

This emphasis on external display in later Elizabethan and Jacobean architecture had its roots in the medieval period, not least in the great monastic gatehouses of the 14th and 15th centuries.[99] But monasteries were essentially inward-looking communities and their buildings reflected this. The main claustral buildings, which were those most frequently chosen for conversion, were often rather irregularly laid out (perhaps as the result of being of different construction dates) and structures such as the frater could often project at right-angles to the rest of the cloister. Similarly, the buildings of the outer court were often insignificant and

[86] *Val. Eccl.*, i, 451 (Redbourn); iv, 278 (Rowney); i, 403 (Standon and Temple Dinsley).

[87] See W.G. Hoskins, *The Age of Plunder* (1976), 123-5.

[88] P.R.O., E 315/262/79.

[89] But see W. Page, 'The history of the monastery of St Mary de Pre', *Trans. St Albans and Herts. Archit. and Arch. Soc.*, (1895/6), 8-18.

[90] *L.P.*, xv, no.393 (1); *V.C.H., Essex*, ii (1907), 170.

[91] *King's Works*, iv, 126-47 and 179-205.

[92] Colin Platt, *The Architecture of Medieval Britain* (1990), 278.

[93] Girouard (1983), Chs. 1 to 3; M.R. Airs, *The Buildings of Britain, Tudor and Jacobean* (1983), Ch. 1.

[94] See note 52.

[95] Mark Girouard, *Hardwick Hall, National Trust Guide* (1990) and Girouard (1983), 120-5 (Barlborough and Heath Old Hall).

[96] Girouard (1983), 185-91.

[97] Ibid, 36.

[98] Ibid, 32.

[99] Platt, op. cit. (note 92), 148-50.

sprawled over a wide area. Thus, while the courtyard plan of many former monasteries had initially been popular with new lay owners for the ease of conversion, other factors had come to be taken into account by 1600.

The re-use of monastic buildings might have received a fresh impetus around 1600 from the "general predisposition towards nostalgia",[100] typified by Spenser and others, which included in some quarters a melancholy regret for the passing of the monasteries.[101] However, in architecture this took the form of the erection of sham fortresses such as Longford Castle (Wilts.) or Lulworth (Dorset) rather than pseudo-ecclesiastical buildings.[102] Furthermore, the practical difficulties of adapting monastic buildings or conversions to meet the latest architectural styles and fashions meant that, at least at the highest social level, the attempt was largely abandoned by 1600. In some cases, such as Ashridge in 1603/4, it was possible to remodel the already-converted monastic buildings so that from the entrance front they conformed to the fashionable ideal of the H-plan, but even here the details must soon have looked archaic and it is perhaps no coincidence that this was the last full-scale adaptation of a former monastic building in Hertfordshire.

It therefore seems that the increasing dominance of the compact-plan house and to a lesser extent the general collapse of the Gothic architectural tradition by around 1600 provides a logical end-point for this survey. After the beginning of the 17th century, the re-use of monastic buildings can be seen as largely accidental. It might still occur for the first time as a result of local conditions and circumstances, particularly in towns where lack of space could dictate the recycling of otherwise redundant buildings. However, the particular social attitudes and aspirations which had first encouraged the re-use of monastic buildings between 1540 and 1600 were largely extinct after the latter date.

Some former monastic sites experienced another period of activity in the 18th and early 19th centuries, when growing interest in the romantic and the development of antiquarianism led to an appreciation of monastic ruins as objects of the picturesque. This phenomenon was widespread, as evidenced by sites like Bayham in Sussex, Waverley in Surrey and Tintern (Monmouthshire), but was particularly common in Yorkshire, where remote and magnificent ruins like those of Fountains were incorporated in landscaped parks or, as at Jervaulx, became the focal point of a garden.[103] Despite early antiquarian interest in several of Hertfordshire's monastic sites, none seems to

have been used in this way, which is perhaps not surprising in a county not noted for its wild and dramatic landscapes but which instead, in the words of E.M. Forster, is best described as "England at its quietest, with little emphasis of river and hill... England meditative."[104]

Several sources of evidence have been used in this study. The principal is the physical fabric of the buildings themselves. Of the 13 sites included, Cheshunt, Hertford Priory and St Margaret's Nettleden have no remains above ground, while the present houses of Ashridge and Beechwood contain only the scantiest fragments of monastic or immediately post-Dissolution fabric. Sopwell is ruinous and the date of the earliest fabric at The Priory, Royston is contentious. But Hitchin Priory, The Biggin, Hitchin, King's Langley, Markyate, Ware and Wymondley all incorporate substantial elements of their monastic predecessors. The relative survival of early fabric is largely reflected in the published literature. No mention is made by Pevsner of Cheshunt, Hertford Priory or St Margaret's, Nettleden and the *V.C.H.* is exclusively concerned with their documentary history. The early fabric of Ashridge and Beechwood is similarly inadequately treated by both authorities, although the later work in both houses is satisfactorily described, especially by Pevsner.[105] More disappointing though, considering the recent date of the volume, is Pevsner's treatment of the remaining sites. Although basically correct in what little is mentioned, much of significance has apparently gone unnoticed and none of the accounts runs to more than 22 lines, with most much shorter.

The situation is a little better in J.T. Smith's recent book on Hertfordshire houses. Of the three sites where there are no extant remains, only Cheshunt is mentioned and then only in passing.[106] Ashridge is excluded on the grounds that the "plentiful graphic evidence did not sufficiently elucidate (its) plan and development",[107] and although the later phases at Beechwood are well covered,[108] this site's monastic antecedents are totally ignored. Despite its importance and a rather fuller description in the accompanying inventory volume, Sopwell is summarily treated, as are Hitchin Priory, Ware and Wymondley.[109] Although there is a good detailed description with plans in the inventory, the pre-1600 work at Markyate is dismissed in the book with the words "Nothing significant is known about the house at Markyate Cell, begun by one courtier and completed by another before Elizabeth came to the throne."[110] But even this is better than the treatment of The Biggin, Hitchin and King's Langley which are not

[100] Ibid, 293.

[101] See Margaret Aston, 'English ruins and English history: the Dissolution and the sense of the past', *Jnl. Warburg and Courtauld Institutes*, 36 (1973), 231-55.

[102] M.W. Thompson, *The Decline of the Castle* (1987), Ch. 7.

[103] For these and other examples see Greene (1992), 202-4. For Bayham, see also Anthony Streeten, *Bayham Abbey*, Sussex Arch. Soc. Monograph 2 (1983), 50-5.

[104] E.M. Forster, *Howard's End* (1960 Penguin edn.), 185.

[105] Pevsner, 237-40 (Ashridge) and 91-3 (Beechwood).

[106] Smith (1992), 66.

[107] Ibid, xiii.

[108] Ibid, passim and Smith (1993), 55-7.

[109] Smith (1993), 157.

[110] Ibid, 124-7 and Smith (1992), 66.

mentioned at all. The only site to be done anything near justice is Royston,[111] although in the more detailed description contained in the inventory, there is a noticeable failure to record the full extent of the surviving early fabric.[112]

More useful than either Pevsner's or Smith's accounts (and it should be remembered that neither set himself the task of providing exhaustive descriptions of the buildings recorded) are some of the more up-to-date descriptions carried out for the Department of Environment's Resurvey of Listed Buildings.[113] It is therefore unfortunate that only three sites, Beechwood, Markyate and Wymondley, were included in the most recent survey. It is perhaps symptomatic of the Department's earlier surveys that Royston Priory is not even included on the Statutory List of Historic Buildings, while the description of those buildings which are included are singularly inadequate.[114] The *V.C.H.* and *R.C.H.M.* can be excused from this sorry state of affairs on the grounds that the volumes for Hertfordshire were amongst the earliest to be compiled and therefore fall well short of the standards set by later volumes. Individual accounts of particular buildings are dealt with under the site descriptions contained in the Appendix.

Given that the published material on the physical fabric of the sites covered by this study is generally of relatively little use, it remains to be considered how this source of evidence is treated here. The sites of all the former monastic houses covered by this study have been visited. In two cases, Cheshunt and Hertford, nothing now survives above ground, while at St Margaret's, Nettleden only earthworks occupy the site. Elsewhere, the approach adopted was to make a detailed inspection of the exterior and interior of the surviving building or buildings. A comprehensive architectural description was then compiled on site and later written up with the aid of photographs and sketch drawings made on site. In all cases, it was particularly important to carry out a thorough investigation of the roof space, the result of this, as at Royston and Ware, being to provide far more accurate dating than would otherwise have been possible.

Only at Sopwell, Ashridge and Markyate was this approach varied; at Sopwell because the buildings are ruinous, at Ashridge because most of the vast house created by James Wyatt occupies a different part of the site from the old, while at Markyate the owner refused permission to visit the site, as a result of which the description of the house had to be compiled from photographs and published material alone. The decision to compile detailed descriptive accounts of each building may sometimes seem to result in lengthy and apparently irrelevant accounts of the existing structures. This may particularly appear to be the case at Beechwood and Royston and to a lesser extent at Markyate where the present buildings are outwardly 18th and 19th century in appearance. Nevertheless, as will be seen from the Appendix, all contain substantial elements of earlier structures. It is only by fully understanding and describing the evolution of these buildings that it is possible to establish how much pre-Dissolution fabric may have survived and to what extent (if at all) it was incorporated into post-suppression buildings on these sites. Thus it was held necessary to describe fully all elevations and internal features of buildings which may contain elements of pre- or immediately post-Dissolution structures.

That this approach is justified is shown not only by the site descriptions of Beechwood, Royston and Markyate, but by the equally detailed descriptions of those sites which already published material acknowledges contain substantial fragments of monastic fabric. In particular, the full extent of the medieval parts of Hitchin Priory, Ware and Wymondley is only appreciated by a proper understanding of these buildings (notably the roof structures of Ware and Wymondley, no full accounts of which have hitherto been published), while at The Biggin, Hitchin a detailed examination of the roof structure corroborates Smith's footnote in Pevsner that the present almshouses "possibly incorporate medieval timber framed buildings on a cloister plan."[115] Perhaps the most outstanding discovery, however, was the 14th-century gatehouse at King's Langley, converted to domestic use after the Dissolution, which appears to have gone entirely unnoticed by earlier writers.

It is in this detailed examination of the physical fabric of the surviving buildings that this study breaks the most new ground. Seemingly unpromising exteriors and even interiors, as at Royston, have concealed early roof structures, which provide valuable evidence for the buildings' origins and former functions. Nevertheless, it must be acknowledged that while every effort has been made to provide as full an architectural description as possible of each building, there have been unavoidable constraints in compiling these. Royston Priory is divided into three houses; Markyate Cell is a private house and (as noted above) permission was not granted for inspection; Ashridge is a Business Management College; Hitchin Priory is a conference centre and offices; Beechwood is a preparatory school; King's Langley is in mixed residential and institutional use, and The Biggin, Hitchin is divided into almshouses, most of which are currently occupied. At the time of inspection only Wymondley (latterly in use as a private house) was empty, its future uncertain, while the ruins at Sopwell were neglected and partly overgrown.

---

[111] Smith (1992), 62-3.
[112] Smith (1993), 150-1.
[113] For the background to the resurvey of listed buildings see Martin Robertson et al, 'Listed buildings: the national resurvey of England', *Trans. Ancient Monuments Soc.*, 37 (1993), 21-94.
[114] See, for example, the list descriptions of Sopwell, D.O.E. 6th List of Historic Buildings, City of St Albans (1971) and Ware Priory, D.O.E 4th List of Historic Buildings, Ware Urban District (1974).

[115] Pevsner, 201n.

Naturally, these factors all imposed limitations on the extent to which the buildings could be investigated and I am grateful to all owners and occupiers who generously allowed me to tramp through their rooms and crawl through their attics and cellars. (Individual acknowledgments are given in the Appendix). These limitations did mean, however, that while furniture and the like could be and were moved and some disruption to occupants caused, it was not possible to carry out plaster stripping or other invasive recording techniques, which may have answered individual questions. Likewise, all external inspections were carried out from ground level and it should be recognised that examination of some areas of walling at closer quarters may have been rewarding in some instances.

Nevertheless, despite these limitations, the descriptions contained in the Appendix are the most comprehensive and detailed in existence for the buildings covered by this study. It can be confidently stated that (with the exception of Markyate) no significant part of the fabric of any of these buildings was missed during the site inspections.

The documentary evidence used in this study ranges from surveys made by the royal commissioners at the time of the Dissolution and inventories of the former monastic properties made for the new owners, to antiquarian accounts of the 18th century and sales particulars of the 19th century.

Perhaps surprisingly, the later documentary material is often more useful than the contemporary sources. The accounts of the royal visitors and local commissioners are not complete for Hertfordshire, although those that do survive contain useful information on the buildings remaining at the Dissolution and their value.[116] The *Valor Ecclesiasticus* is useful too in recording the incomes of religious houses before the suppression. 16th- and 17th-century grants of sites are usually formalised documents referring to features such as the "gardens, houses, scite and soil" without giving any concrete information on the buildings. Surveys and inventories made for the new owners are sometimes more informative, naming individual buildings and giving their measurements or commenting on their condition,[117] but only in the case of Wymondley is relevant information on the buildings contained in the Ministers' Accounts.[118]

In contrast to official records made for the crown or for the new owners, are descriptive accounts of former monastic properties. Descriptions made by Leland, who appears to have visited Royston in 1540 or 1541 and other Hertfordshire sites in 1544 or 1545,[119] are particularly useful as they offer a first-hand contemporary account of the condition of sites immediately after the Dissolution. Antiquarian interest in the monastic past seems to have developed quickly in the second half of the 16th century,[120] and while the brief descriptions of former monastic buildings by writers such as Camden or Norden are not particularly useful, a manuscript history of St Albans, compiled in c.1610, which includes a brief account of Sopwell, can be viewed in this context.[121]

It is not until the late 17th century, however, with the compilation of Sir Henry Chauncy's *History of Hertfordshire*, published in 1700, that antiquarianism in Hertfordshire can truly be said to come of age. Nevertheless, Chauncy was not merely concerned with items of antiquarian interest; indeed, he seems to have been anxious to record features which contemporaries would have found impressive and worthy of note just as much, if not more so, than relics of the past. It is perhaps significant that of the many 16th- and 17th-century houses shown in the fine Drapentier engravings accompanying Chauncy's text none is of a monastic conversion.

Antiquarianism is more detectable in Nathaniel Salmon's *History of Hertfordshire* (1728), although he was primarily interested in the Roman period and his statements on later buildings are often directly taken from Chauncy. More useful for our purposes are the slightly later, unpublished accounts of Browne Willis and William Cole, which provide much valuable information on Ashridge, St Margaret's, Nettleden and Royston respectively.[122] From the later 18th century, Richard Gough's annotations to his copies of Camden, Chauncy and Salmon provide additional information on several former monastic buildings,[123] while, moving into the early 19th century, works like Brayley's and Britton's *Beauties of England and Wales* (Hertfordshire is covered in volume seven, 1808) refer to several of the sites with which we are concerned. Nevertheless, the relatively poor survival rate of Hertfordshire monastic buildings into this period, especially in the form of romantic ruins so beloved of late 18th- century and early 19th-century topographical writers, means that such works are not so valuable a source as in counties like Yorkshire. However, the antiquarian writers referred to above by no means form an exhaustive list and mention is made of several others in the site descriptions contained in the Appendix.

---

[116] See, for instance, the suppression accounts of Cheshunt, St Giles in the Wood, Flamstead, Sopwell, Royston and Wymondley; P.R.O., E 117/12/30.

[117] See, for example, the surveys of Ashridge (printed in H.J. Todd, *The History of the College of Bonhommes of Ashridge* (1823), 60-4), Hitchin (P.R.O., SC 12/8/29) and King's Langley (P.R.O., E 315/391 (2)).

[118] P.R.O., SC6/Hen. VIII/1606, m.11.

[119] John Chandler, John Leland's Itinerary, Travels in Tudor England (1993), xxx-xxxi.

[120] See note 101.

[121] John Shrimpton, *The Antiquities of Verulam and St Albans* (c.1610), MS. history in H.R.O., 66,296.

[122] Bodl., MS. Willis, passim (Ashridge and St Margaret's, Nettleden) and B.L., Add. MS. 5820, fols.19v-35 (Royston).

[123] Bodl., Gough Gen. Top. 61 (Camden); Gough Herts. 14 (Chauncy); Gough Herts. 11, 16, 17 and 18 (Salmon).

The wide range of documentary sources used is a feature of this study. Even apparently unpromising material like 19th-century sales particulars or newspaper accounts of archaeological discoveries (see below) can contain information not available elsewhere. Although some of the claims of antiquarian writers naturally have to be treated cautiously, one soon obtains a strong feeling for those statements which can be treated as reliable or, alternatively, dismissed.

Documentary records made during the 16th century or at a later period pose problems of a different kind. While not liable to the prejudices or perceptions of writers of "history", whose aim might be to prove an argument or create a literary effect, apparently unbiased records can nevertheless be misleading. Royal commissioners or compilers of surveys and inventories may have been tempted to attribute lower values to former religious houses or exaggerate the dilapidated condition of monastic buildings for their own ends. Similarly, grants of monastic sites are stylised documents containing little information on individual buildings, simply because the new owners were aware of what they were obtaining. That which would seem of interest to us now, may well have been regarded as of no consequence by contemporaries of the actual events and thus have gone unrecorded. Later records, such as inventories, sales particulars or references in deeds, terriers and the like were the product of very different circumstances and their significance for our purposes must therefore be regarded as coincidental to their original purpose.

Finally, the point should be made that, as with all sources of evidence, the wealth of documentary material varies tremendously from one site to another. While to some degree this is likely to be a reflection of a site's relative importance both before and after the Dissolution, it might also be the result of accidental survival. In other words, the absence of documentary material does not necessarily mean that a site was of no significance.

Pictorial evidence for Hertfordshire's former monastic houses is particularly plentiful. The earliest graphic representation of a monastic conversion is the birdseye perspective view of Sopwell on a map of c.1600.[124] There is then a relatively long gap until the next drawing, coincidentally also of Sopwell, in the middle of the 17th century.[125] The likely reason for the absence of early views of former monastic buildings in Hertfordshire has already been touched upon. The lack of spectacular ruins probably played its part. But it is surprising, nevertheless, that for a house as magnificent as Ashridge there are no surviving drawings earlier than the late 18th century. After this date, the number of known views increases dramatically.

The earliest artist regularly to record former monastic buildings was H.G. Oldfield, active between 1790-1803. There is no evidence to suggest that Oldfield had any special interest in former monastic buildings and in fact his main purpose was to provide drawings of country houses and churches which would be attractive to potential patrons.[126] Oldfield's competence as an artist has rightly been called into question,[127] and as Smith has commented he "took pains to accommodate owners' preferences by a careful choice of viewpoint and by the introduction of discreet planting to screen the stables and service ranges."[128] Despite this selectivity, however, Oldfield's views seem to be basically accurate. Comparisons with other evidence, including the work of other artists, suggest that his rather uninspiring and pedestrian drawings can generally be taken as reliable representations of the buildings involved.

Far more accomplished than Oldfield's work is that of the Bucklers. Two generations of the family earned their living as artists, John and his sons, John Chessell and George Buckler. Of the three, the first two carried out the most work in Hertfordshire. Like Oldfield, who seems to have worked exclusively in the medium, the Bucklers painted watercolours but they are more usually represented by their pen and ink drawings and preparatory pencil sketches for these. Buckler drawings are notorious for their accuracy and attention to detail,[129] but even they can be selective in what is shown or omitted and, as Smith has pointed out, there is a suggestion in some cases of an element of archaeological reconstruction rather than literal representation.[130] Nevertheless, comparison between a Buckler drawing and a surviving building is usually a testimony to the precision of the artist. The Hertfordshire drawings with which we are concerned where mostly made between 1830 and 1840, although a few pre-date 1820.

Many other artists made drawings or engravings of former monastic buildings, and are referred to in the site descriptions contained in the Appendix. But two more merit special mention here. These are Thomas Fisher (?1771-1836), noteworthy for his meticulous early 19th-century drawings of Cheshunt, Markyate and Ware,[131] and Thomas Luppino, active between 1790 and 1831, whose work includes a sketch of the now-vanished Hertford Priory.[132]

[124] H.R.O., IV. A. 25.
[125] Ibid, XIII. 30.

[126] H.C. Andrews, 'Henry George Oldfield and the Dimsdale collection of Hertfordshire drawings', *Trans. East Herts. Arch. Soc.*, 11 (1940-44), 212-24.
[127] Stone, op.cit., (note 45), 63.
[128] Smith (1992), 11.
[129] Julian Munby, 'J.C. Buckler, Tackley's Inn and three medieval houses in Oxford', *Oxoniensia*, 43 (1978), 123-69.
[130] Smith (1992), 11.
[131] See J.H. Busby, 'The Hertfordshire drawings of Thomas Fisher (1771?-1836)', *Herts. Arch.*, 1 (1968), 110-16.
[132] The Luppino drawings are kept in the Lewis Evans Collection, St Albans Public Library.

The work of all the artists mentioned here is particularly important, as much of it pre-dates the demolition or extensive alteration of several of the buildings included in this study. The value of pictorial evidence where the building itself has now gone as at Cheshunt, Hertford, St Margaret's, Nettleden or changed beyond recognition as at Ashridge barely needs mention, but it can be almost as critical where the building still survives. In the latter case the building acts as a check to the accuracy of the drawing and the drawing can also provide useful evidence for changes made to the structure.

As Smith has commented, "where drawings show differences of detail in the same building, reliability is hard to judge."[133] This is the case with several of the buildings included in this study, notably in the many views of the north front of the former great hall at Ashridge. Only experience of the competence and limitations of the artist concerned can lead one to a judgment of which representation is to be relied upon in preference to another.

Late 19th- and early 20th-century photographs can be useful in checking the accuracy of drawings and engravings, although in most cases they post-date changes made in the 19th century and are, therefore, less informative than might have been the case. The most useful major collection is the set of photographs taken early in the 20th century by A. Whitford Anderson for the *V.C.H.* (now in Watford Central Library), but there are also collections in the Bodleian Library, Oxford, the Hertfordshire Record Office and the Local Studies Library, Hertford.[134]

Map evidence is dealt with separately in most of the site descriptions contained in the Appendix but its usefulness as a source can be summarised here. Several early estate maps, such as the Sopwell map of c.1600 referred to above, are useful for their pictorial representation of buildings, while later estate, tithe and inclosure maps often show the ground-plans of buildings, sometimes indicating ranges which have now gone and of which little other evidence survives.

More detailed plans of buildings also fall into this category, but it is unfortunate that there are no surviving large-scale plans or even sketch plans of any of the sites included in this study, earlier than the late 17th century. These are the elevation drawings of the pre-1702 house at Beechwood which cast no light on the appearance of the 16th-century house there,[135] but are at least considerably earlier than for any other site, there not being any other plans earlier than the first part of the 19th century.

Archaeological evidence as opposed to antiquarian descriptions of the various sites is relatively slim. Chance discoveries have been made at the majority of the sites and the outlines of the churches at Hertford and King's Langley, along with part of the east end of the church or chapter house at Markyate, were uncovered in the 19th century. Poorly documented excavations took place in the 1950s and 1960s at Cheshunt and The Biggin, Hitchin, the former necessarily amounting to no more than salvage and limited recording in advance of rapid gravel extraction. Only Sopwell has been extensively investigated to anything approaching modern standards, although the excavations carried out in the 1960s have yet to be properly published. Archaeological field evaluations and trial trenching have been carried out recently at Wymondley, Ware, and to a greater extent at Hertford. Full details of all these excavations are contained in the Appendix.

Aerial photography can also play its part, especially in those cases where the post-Dissolution house does not stand directly on the site of the monastic buildings. Thus relatively well-defined parch-marks of possible buildings can be detected at Ashridge and Markyate, although at Beechwood, where the present house stands at a little distance from the site of the monastic buildings, no crop-marks seem to be present in the adjoining arable fields. No geophysical or other non-invasive surveys are known to have been carried out on any Hertfordshire monastic sites.[136]

---

[133] Smith (1992), 9-11.
[134] The photographs in the Bodleian Library are collected together: MS. Top. Eccl. b. 28.
[135] Beechwood Park, Flamstead: a collection of plans and drawings dating from the late 17th to the early 20th centuries. According to Smith (1992), 198 most of the collection was still in the possession of Beechwood Park preparatory school in 1976 but it now appears to have been dispersed.

[136] See, for instance, K. Emerick & K. Wilson, 'Fountains Abbey: some interim results of remote sensing', *Conservation Bulletin*, 18 (October 1992), 7-9.

Chapter Two

Town and Country: Adaptation and Remodelling in the first and second generations

Hertfordshire contains examples of all known types of the adaptive re-use of monastic buildings other than industrial. The process of re-use in the county began immediately after the Dissolution and continued right up to the end of the period with which we are concerned. Instances of re-use range from the minor adaptation of existing buildings at sites like St Margaret's, Nettleden and King's Langley to the transformation of monastic buildings into major country houses as at Ashridge and Sopwell. In this chapter we are concerned with the first category of sites and the re-use of urban monastic buildings, where different circumstances could lead to a wide variety of new uses.

There are many difficulties in establishing the category to which a re-used monastic site should be ascribed. First, the evidence on which categorisations are made is often fragmentary and can vary tremendously in its extent and reliability from one site to another. As shown in Chapter 1, the sources used in this study are extremely diverse and data used for one site, such as that drawn from archaeological excavation, may not exist for another. To take another example, there is historic pictorial evidence for all of the sites included but this ranges from two 19th-century drawings in the case of St Margaret's, Nettleden to sites like Markyate and Sopwell, where there is an abundance of pictorial evidence covering a considerable period of time. It is therefore difficult and perhaps misleading to make direct comparisons between one site and another. Sites like Beechwood and Cheshunt, where the surviving architectural and documentary evidence is slight or non-existent but which seem to have been relatively important conversions, further illustrate the significance of historical accident in the survival rate of relevant evidence and demonstrate that this must always be taken into account when assessing the past status of a particular site. Nevertheless, it would be wrong to deny that the extent of surviving evidence for sites such as Ashridge and Sopwell, compared with that for sites like St Margaret's, Nettleden or Hertford, is not at least indicative of their relative importance in the second half of the 16th century.

Another point to consider in making assumptions about the status of a site in the half century after the Dissolution is that much of the evidence on which these are based comes from material compiled long after the 16th century. To take pictorial evidence as an example, few Hertfordshire sites were reliably recorded in illustrative form before the late 18th century, by which time important sites such as Wymondley had declined in status to little more than farmhouse level, although there is adequate evidence from other sources to show that the original conversion was carried out at a higher social level.

The relative status of a site could change markedly even within the period with which we are concerned. The first grantees or lessees of monastic property often did little to the buildings they acquired and it was frequently left to the second or even third generation of lay owners to implement major conversion works. This is a theme which will be explored in greater depth in Chapter 3, particularly with regard to Ashridge and Sopwell, but the same process can also be found in towns at sites like The Biggin in Hitchin, Hitchin Priory and Ware, where changes in ownership in the decades immediately after the suppression seem to have contributed to the postponement of thorough conversion schemes until later in the century. In this context it is also worth remembering that some sites such as Hertford and Royston, which are now entirely urban, were formerly situated on the fringes of the towns to which they relate, this edge-of-settlement location being a hall-mark of some of the more ambitious conversion schemes like those at Hitchin Priory, Sopwell and Ware, perhaps indicating that the post-Dissolution house at Hertford was of greater importance than some of the other evidence might suggest.

Coupled with changes in the importance of a site, whether in the 16th century or over a longer time span, are the considerable difficulties in accurately dating the various phases of conversion at Hertfordshire's monastic sites. First, the surviving architectural evidence is at best fragmentary or in several cases non-existent, obliging us to rely on incomplete documentary or pictorial evidence, with all the limitations that this can involve. Secondly, even where a building retains fabric or alterations of the period, it is often hard to distinguish work of the late 16th century from that of the mid 16th century, especially in houses below the first rank. It is only rarely, as at The Biggin,[1] that particular fittings or a distinct phase of building work are securely dated or can be directly and without doubt linked to a particular owner.

Developing the issue of the problems of assessing the post-Dissolution status of a site, one has to consider whether much purpose is served by drawing the line too rigidly between a monastic site re-used as a farmstead and one where the buildings were converted into a gentry or courtier house. Even if the evidence allows this distinction to be made, were the sets of circumstances in which re-use occurred so very different in terms of the individual buildings selected for conversion, the time span over which the process took place and the ease with which it was accomplished? In short, should different patterns of re-use be expected at sites of varying status; how will this be detected in the archaeological, architectural and documentary record and, most importantly, how does this reflect the social and economic conditions of the period? It

---

[1] Panelling in the first-floor room in the south-west corner of the building is dated "1585".

is these questions that this and the following chapter will attempt to answer.

Of the sites included in this study, Hertfordshire has five which are urban in character- Hertford, The Biggin and The Priory in Hitchin, Royston and Ware. Although Sopwell was located on the edge of Tudor St Albans, Sir Richard Lee's extensive remodelling of the former Benedictine nunnery resulted in the creation of a country rather than a town house and Sopwell is therefore considered in the next chapter.

The evidence for the re-use of urban monastic sites in Hertfordshire in the four decades after 1540 is patchy and inconclusive. This may be because the documentary evidence does not survive or that the physical manifestation of this in the buildings themselves has been obscured or swept away by later remodelling. However, the fact that this is in stark contrast to the much fuller evidence for re-use after c.1580 suggests that relatively little was done in the way of major conversion works during the period 1540 to 1580. This does not mean to say, of course, that absolutely nothing was done to the buildings during this time. At **Royston**, some work appears to have been carried out by the first lay owner of the property, Robert Chester, who having initially rented the house, bought it from the crown in 1540.[2] Precisely what works Chester undertook it is now impossible to say and it is by no means certain that he retained any of the monastic buildings. Indeed, the sale of the cloister and dorter to Thomas More and John Newport for £24, shortly before the lease of the property to Chester, seems to reflect their value as building materials,[3] suggesting that they were demolished at this time.

It seems that whatever adaptation Chester undertook of any surviving monastic buildings, or any use he made of their materials, was largely complete by 1551 when he entertained Mary of Guise here on her journey from Scotland to France,[4] by which time it appears that Royston was his principal residence.[5] The form that Chester's house took can be seen in a sketch-plan of 1578 when the house was considered as a potential resting-place on a royal progress but was dismissed as "a very unnecessary hows for the receipt of her Majesty; yt stand adjoyning to the Churche on the sowth syde thereof, not haveing any pleasaunt p'spects any way..."[6] The problematic question of whether any of the monastic buildings remained to be incorporated in the house as it was remodelled by Chester's grandson after 1586 is addressed below.

No more certainty attaches to the date or extent of the first conversion scheme at **Hitchin Priory**. On its suppression

in 1538 the site remained in royal hands, Thomas Parrys acting as bailiff for the crown until 1546 when it was granted to Sir Edward Watson and Henry Herdson.[7] From a survey of 1546 made shortly before the site was granted to Watson and Herdson, it appears that demolition and defacing were particularly thorough at the Dissolution. The survey refers to a "mansion house" comprising the "Frater and Dorter with the Cloister whereon the Frater and Dorter is builded with a kitchen...", the priors's lodging and "two little chambers" for the brothers, along with various other service and outbuildings. Apart from the mansion house which was "in good estate being maynteyned and repayred from tyme to tyme since the dyssolucion", all the buildings are described as "sore decayed" and "verrye ruynowce in tymber and tyle for lack of reparacions". The church, which is called "superfluous", had been defaced, the steeple broken down and all the lead, freestone, glass and bells were gone.[8]

The details of the grant of the site to Watson and Herdson suggest that they were primarily interested in the building materials,[9] of which there were many, the presence of Parrys and presumably other servants of the crown apparently having prevented wholesale plundering of the site, although the fact that there was some looting either then or at a later date is shown by the re-use of materials elsewhere in the town.[10] Watson and Herdson do not seem to have engaged in any conversion works and nothing more is known until Watson sold the site to Ralph Radcliffe in 1553.[11] It is far from clear what then remained and which buildings Radcliffe chose to convert, although it does appear that even if it had not already been demolished, the detached prior's lodging played no part in his plans.

The 1546 survey states that "one parte of the said churche is broken and decayed by wether and the other (had) no manner of leade Belles Freestone nor glasse Remanying", implying that substantial sections still survived, a supposition strengthened by the possibility that its west front is depicted in a birdseye perspective map of the town drawn in c.1700.[12] It therefore seems possible that the walls of the church remained standing in the 1550s, even if the roof was gone, and that they were re-used in a range built on its site, some of which may still be incorporated in the core of the present south range, which was comprehensively remodelled in the 1770s.

The cloister lay to the north of the church, with the dormitory in its usual position on the east side and the frater and kitchen on the north and west respectively. There is a well-documented tradition that apart from converting

[2] P.R.O., SC6/Hen. VIII/1607; *L.P.*, xiv (1), p.606; xvi, g.379 (60).
[3] P.R.O., E 315/361, fols.67-9.
[4] *Acts of the Privy Council, 1550-52*, 406.
[5] P.R.O., E 115/86/101.
[6] P.R.O., SP 12/125.

[7] P.R.O., SC6/Hen. VIII/1607-15; E 318/(Box 22)/1190.
[8] P.R.O., SC 12/8/29.
[9] P.R.O., E 318/(Box 22)/1190.
[10] R. Hine, *The History of Hitchin*, i (1927), 147; H.P. Pollard & W.B. Gerish, 'The religious orders in Hitchin', *Trans. East Herts. Arch. Soc.*, 3, pt.i (1905), 7.
[11] *V.C.H.*, iii, 12.
[12] B.L., Add. MS. 32,350, fols.71, 73.

1. Hitchin Priory, north entrance range. Photograph by N.Doggett, April 1989.

its buildings to a residence, Radcliffe established a school in the former friary, the only clue to its precise location being a 17th-century reference to the creation of a stage in a "lower room",[13] whereas the principal domestic apartments were presumably on the first floor. Although there is nothing in the west range which can be securely dated to the 1550s, its brick mullion windows may be of this period, and as in the north range and the service range which projects at an oblique angle to the north-west, there is much medieval fabric within it. The large open space of the refectory could have made it attractive to Radcliffe as the hall of his new house had it not been situated at right-angles to the entrance range, which in the medieval friary would have been in the west range. The hall may, of course, have been in the east range, but the degree of 18th-century and later rebuilding in this range makes this impossible to prove. The only other possibility was that the hall was located to the south where the church had stood, a suggestion made all the more credible by the fact that the north range has been the entrance range since at least the late 17th century.[14] **(Fig. 1)**

This interpretation is largely speculative and all that can really be said with confidence is that Radcliffe appears to have carried out some adaptation of the friary buildings, although it will be noticed that the evidence for this comes primarily from documentary sources rather than the building itself. There is undoubtedly mid- to late 16th-century work in the present building but, as we shall see, this could just as easily have been carried out by Radcliffe's son, another Ralph, who owned the house from his father's death in 1559 until his own demise in 1621.[15]

While the evidence for re-use in the first generation is slight at Royston and Hitchin Priory, it is practically non-existent at Hertford, The Biggin and Ware. The most that can be said is that difficulties in precisely dating the 16th-century work at these three sites mean that it is impossible to be certain that no conversion works took place between 1540 and 1580. Indeed, something must have occurred even if it was only selective demolition and routine maintenance of those parts which were retained. Nevertheless, the surviving architectural and documentary evidence points to the suggestion that major schemes of

---

[13] Anthony Wood, *Athenae Oxonienses*, i (ed., P. Bliss, 1813), 215.

[14] See Appendix, pp.146-7.

[15] *D.N.B.*, xvi, 576-7; *V.C.H.*, iii, 12.

adaptive re-use were not implemented at these sites until the late 16th century. These three properties are therefore treated in this section along with the evidence for further phases of remodelling at Royston and Hitchin Priory.

All traces of **Hertford Priory** and the post-medieval house which succeeded it have now gone. Photographic, map and pictorial evidence show that the latter was an L-shaped building of hall and cross-wing plan. While this structure could well have been of medieval or 16th-century origin, all that can be said with total confidence is that it must be earlier than c.1650. The most likely date for its construction (or remodelling if there had been an earlier structure on its site) would appear to be the 1580s. On its suppression in 1538 the priory had been granted to Anthony Denny and it remained with his family until 1578 when it was sold to Thomas Docwra, Sheriff of Hertfordshire in 1580.[16] Shortly afterwards it seems to have returned to the Denny family but in 1587 it was sold to Henry Colthurst.[17] A terrier of that year refers to the "newe bilt howse, with a dove howse, boornes and stables, the myll newe bilt...the howsinge dove howse and barnes...bilt within thre years coste a thowson markes...the tennants will not be bought out for £300...",[18] which suggests that much of the costs must have been borne by the tenants. Certainly, this documentary evidence is not inconsistent with that for the physical appearance of the building.

Although the possibility that Sir Anthony Denny, who died in 1549, might have converted some of the former monastic buildings here into a town house cannot be ruled out, the lack of any surviving references makes this unlikely and the site is just as likely to have been plundered for its building materials in the years immediately after the Dissolution, its proximity to the town centre probably accelerating this process. The evidence, such as it is, tends to point to a relatively low-key use of the site. The building which was to become known as Priory House may have been retained initially as accommodation for the Denny family on visits to the county town, but by the 1580s it appears to have become a tenanted farmhouse and there is nothing to show that this was not also the case earlier in the century. Further work on the house may have been carried out by Martin Trott, who owned the site between c.1590 and 1617.[19]

If Priory House was a converted monastic building, the prior's lodging emerges as the most likely candidate. The house was situated some 100 yards to the north of the priory church (the site of which is known) and trial trenching in the immediate vicinity in 1988-9 produced no

evidence of any adjoining buildings.[20] The location of the building and its apparent isolation are thus perfectly consistent with the likely position of a late medieval prior's house, the riverside setting providing a pleasant retreat for the prior away from the rest of the monastic community.

There is good surviving architectural evidence for 16th-century re-use at **Ware Priory**, but there are considerable difficulties in pin-pointing the precise date or dates that conversion works took place. Indeed, there is no particular reason why conversion works here or elsewhere should fall into distinct phases, and it is important to remember that in many cases remodelling and adaptation would have been an ongoing process. This said, it is unusually difficult at Ware to hazard anything but the most approximate dating for the comprehensive conversion which undoubtedly took place. There are two main reasons for this. First, the building itself, although undeniably of medieval date and containing much evidence in its fabric for 14th- and 15th-century work, is covered externally with a hard cement render, which makes it impossible to establish whether openings are original or insertions. The situation is further complicated by a thorough restoration which took place in the mid 19th century, the full effects of which are only realised when one looks at the earlier graphic evidence. To some extent, these problems have been mitigated by a scheme of repair and conversion which took place in 1994. This has revealed some features which can be more closely dated, but as the project was quite rightly conservative, involving the minimum of disturbance and plaster stripping or the removal of Georgian and Victorian features, it was not as revealing as might otherwise have been the case.

The other principal difficulty in establishing exactly when conversion works took place at Ware is the long period of ownership by the Byrch family, of whom very little is known. As will be seen in Chapter 3, we should not look solely to changes of ownership as the time when major works are likely to have been carried out. Adaptation and remodelling could have been undertaken at any time, prompted perhaps by a marriage or birth of an heir, or simply because the owner wished to improve his living standards or impress his neighbours. Nevertheless, the long and apparently uneventful ownership by the Byrch family from 1544 to 1628 provides few key moments to which one can attribute a particular phase of work.

On its closure in 1538 the former friary was farmed by Robert Byrch and in 1544 it was sold to Thomas Byrch, who is described in the grant as "yeoman of the crown".[21] Thomas Byrch appears to have been a scrivener and accountant and it has been suggested that he was an agent of Cromwell.[22] It is more likely, however, that as Cromwell

---

[16] P.R.O., C 66/1193/1783; P.R.O., List & Indexes No.9, List of Sheriffs for England & Wales (1898), 64.

[17] P.R.O., C 66/1194/1804; Chauncy, i, 506.

[18] B.L., Lansd. MS. 116, fol.48.

[19] Chauncy, i, 506.

[20] Hester Cooper-Reade, 'Jewson's Yard, Hertford: excavations of St Mary's Priory and St John's Parish Church', *Herts. Past*, 29 (Autumn, 1990), 29-37.

[21] P.R.O., SC6/Hen. VIII/1618; *L.P.*, *xix*, no.610 (68).

[22] R. Walters, 'Ware Priory', *Trans. East Herts. Arch. Soc.*, 1, pt.i (1899), 41.

2. Ware Priory, view of south and west ranges from north-east. Photograph by N. Doggett, April 1989.

had been disgraced and dead since 1540, he received the site in recognition of his services to the crown. For the reasons described above, it is far from clear whether Thomas Byrch (or Robert before him) began the work of conversion. It appears that the friary church was demolished soon after the Dissolution, the proximity to the parish church making its retention unnecessary. Of the claustral buildings, the whole of the south range, along with the southern part of the west range and a hall range projecting at right-angles to the west, were retained, and these form the nucleus of the present house. **(Fig. 2)**

The south and west ranges were originally open to the roof only from first-floor level and, in common with most Franciscan houses, the claustral walks were integral. The upper floor of the south range was probably the refectory and, as in the post-Dissolution house, the kitchen was probably in the south-west corner of the west range on the ground floor. The function of the four-bay hall range is uncertain. Although physically attached to the west range, it is structurally separate from and slightly later than it, there also being evidence that it was possibly open from ground level to its two western bays. It may have served as guest accommodation. All three ranges have fine 15th-century scissor-braced roofs, possibly originally with crown posts throughout, although it is now only in the hall range that these survive.

There is evidence too that the building was much larger in the 16th century. Apart from the obvious truncation of the west claustral range to the north, its present north gable being of 18th-century brick, the presence of rather makeshift roof carpentry towards its southern end and 18th-century brick to the south gable (while they may simply represent rebuilding work) suggests that the range once extended further to the south as well, this projection perhaps having served as the infirmary during the monastic period. It also appears from the 17th-century brickwork in the east gable of the south range and the discovery of foundations to the east of this point in 1892,[23] that the south range was also formerly longer, although it seems that the cloister itself returned to the north where the building now ends. This evidence for the house formerly being larger is neatly confirmed by an inventory of 1715,[24] which clearly relates to a much bigger building than the present structure.

The apparent fact that the house was much more extensive in the 16th century than later does not mean, of course, that all of the former friary was utilised by the Byrch family. Parts of it may have been allowed to become ruinous and in

---

[23] Ibid, 42; H.P. Pollard, 'Franciscan and Benedictine monuments of Ware', in P.C. Standing (ed.), *Memorials of Old Hertfordshire* (1905), 54.
[24] MS. inventory in private ownership. I am grateful to D. Perman for sending me a photocopy of this document.

3. The Biggin, west range. Photograph by N. Doggett, April 1989.

this connection Weever's statement of 1631 that the house was "A Frierie, whose ruines, not altogether beaten downe, are to be seene at this day", while it may simply refer to the church, is particularly interesting.[25] Documentary proof for the involvement of the Byrch family in the conversion of the friary is extremely slight, seemingly being limited to the reference in the verse "The Tale of Two Swannes" (1590) by William Vallans as "Byrches house, that whilom (once) was the Brothers Friers place..."[26]

The date of the poem roughly corresponds with the date of the panelling recently discovered in two first-floor rooms in the south range. This appears to be mainly *in situ* and is of c.1600. A slightly earlier date can be given to the cambered heads of the blocked stone window arches, which have been revealed where plaster has been removed from around the later sash windows inserted in their infill. Both sets of features, while not providing conclusive evidence for a major remodelling at this period certainly show that there was some building activity on the site at about the time of Vallans's poem.

A little more certainty attaches to the date of the 16th-century work at **The Biggin**, Hitchin. (**Fig. 3**) Here it seems that the claustral ranges were retained in a remodelling of the second half of the century. On its suppression in 1538 the former Gilbertine priory remained in royal hands when it was farmed by Robert Marshall and from its apparent decline in value from £13 16s in 1535 to £10 11s 8d in 1544 when it was granted to John Cocks,[27] it can be surmised that little was done to the buildings during this time. That Cocks's interest in the property was speculative, or that he was acting as agent for another party with no intention of converting the buildings himself, seems likely from the large number of similar grants of ex-monastic property he received in Hertfordshire and elsewhere and then sold on to others.[28]

This feeling is strengthened by the fact that there are no further definite documentary references to The Biggin until 1570 when William Croocar bequeathed it in his will to his sons, Thomas and William.[29] That William Croocar the younger undertook some work at The Biggin is made clear

[25] John Weever, *Ancient Funerall Monuments* (1631), 544.

[26] William Vallans, 'A Tale of Two Swannes' (1590), contained in his 'Account of Several Parts of Hartfordshire', which is included as a prefix to Thomas Hearne's 1769 edition of volume five of John Leland's *Itinerary* (Bodl., Douce HH 169).

[27] *Val. Eccl.*, iv, 276; *L.P.*, xix (2), g.166 (25).

[28] For example, *L.P.*, xix (1), g.80 (48), g.1035 (97).

[29] P.R.O., PCC 11 Holney. There are, however, later unsourced references to the property having been conveyed to Thomas Parrys during Edward VI's reign (Salmon, 162), while in Cocks's will of 1553 (P.R.O., PCC 24 Noodes) the manor of The Biggin had been split between his two sons. Croocar's will shows that his wife's mother was named Mary Parrys, raising the possibility that he received the house through his wife.

by the initials "WC" and "IC" (for his wife, Jane) and the date 1585 incised in the contemporary panelling in the first-floor south-west room of the house. **(Fig. 4)** This date is consistent with several other features in the building, including the mullioned and transomed windows and the Tuscan columns of the colonnade to the west range. While this does not, of course, rule out the possibility of earlier domestic use of the site, it shows that there was comprehensive remodelling of the buildings into a comfortable, if comparatively modest, manor house at this time, a use which continued during the ownership of Robert Snagge from c.1587 until his death in 1606.[30]

The presence of the initials and the date 1585 carved in the panelling acutely demonstrates the pitfalls in tying particular fittings or phases of building work to individual owners, the point being that without such evidence one would be just as likely to attribute the panelling to the period of Snagge's ownership as to Croocar's.

As in most cases where claustral ranges were adapted to residential use after the Dissolution, the principal accommodation was on the first floor. There is evidence to suggest that the church was situated on the south side of the cloister, in which case the dormitory would be represented by the present east range and the refectory by the north range. All four ranges have 15th-century roof structures, **(Fig. 5)** the fact that all the ranges are contemporary with each other and thus interconnecting at the same floor and eaves levels making it easier to convert the whole structure to domestic use than would have been the case had the claustral buildings been of different dates and heights.

It is probable that the small size of many claustral garths would have worked against the retention of the cloister's dimensions in the more ambitious remodellings of monastic fabric in the later 16th century. However, this is not likely to have been the case at The Biggin where the relatively modest status of the post-Dissolution house and its position in the centre of Hitchin meant that space would have been at a premium. There is, nevertheless, some suggestion that the late 16th-century house of The Biggin may have been considerably larger than the present structure. First, there was the now-demolished range attached to the south-west corner of the existing building, which cannot have been much later than c.1730 and may well have been considerably earlier.[31] There is also some indication that, just as the west range has a colonnade on its inner face, the east range may have been at least partly open on the ground floor. Excavation in 1968-9 revealed signs of a cobbled driveway running under this range, along with traces of various buildings to the east.[32] The evidence that there was

formerly a gallery in the east range- a feature not commonly found in entrance ranges- further suggests that there may have been an outer court to the east of the present east range. The probability that the former cloister represented the inner courtyard of the new house is indicated, however, by the fine panelled room referred to above, which may have served as a parlour to a first-floor hall in the converted church.

The existing building at **Royston Priory** also contains some evidence for a phase of remodelling in the last quarter of the 16th century. It appears that at this time the house was of two storeys in three unequal bays of close-studded timber framed construction under a steeply pitched plain tile roof. **(Fig. 6)** The house seems to have been open to the roof from the first floor and on this basis and its alignment on a north-south axis, it is tempting to equate those parts of the late 16th-century structure that survive with the west range of the larger double-courtyard house shown in the sketch-plan of 1578, the principal rooms of which were on the first floor. There are, however, several objections to this, not least of which is the fact that the 1578 survey dismissed the house as "a very unnecessary hows for receipt of her Mat.y."[33] As the building was in sufficiently good repair for Robert Chester, who came into possession of the property on attaining his majority in 1586,[34] to entertain James I there in 1603,[35] it is most likely that the late 16th-century work post-dates 1586. Certainly, little would seem to have done during the time of his father, Edward, who held the property only between 1574 and his death in 1577,[36] a suggestion made all the credible by the unfavourable remarks of the queen's surveyors in 1578.

All this is speculative as it must be remembered that houses could often be quickly refurbished for a royal visit and that the house condemned in 1578 could well have been capable of renovation. The work at Royston, though, may have been more than cosmetic as James decided to rent the house for a year during the preparation of his own hunting lodge in the town, a move which seems to have prompted Chester to live at nearby Cockenach, which became his principal residence until his death in 1640.[37]

If there are difficulties in establishing the precise date or the instigator of the late 16th-century work at Royston, it is equally difficult to establish whether any parts of the former monastic buildings remained to be incorporated in the post-Dissolution house. In this regard it is unfortunate that the 1578 sketch-plan does not show the position of the house in relation to the church, although the distance of the present building, which as we have seen contains late 16th-century work, from the site of the monastic nave indicates that it is most unlikely to represent any of the claustral

---

[30] B.L., Lansd. MS. 54, p.65; P.R.O., PCC 31 Stafford. This range is shown in photographs of 1878 and 1897; Bodl., MS. top. eccl. b.27, fol.53.

[31] This range is shown in photographs of 1878 and 1897; Bodl., MS. top. eccl. b.27, fol.53.

[32] C.A. Beresford-Webb, 'The Biggin' (n.d. but c.1969), unpublished manuscript, Hitchin Museum.

[33] P.R.O., SP 12/125.

[34] *V.C.H.*, iii, 260.

[35] J. Nichols, *Progresses of James I*, i (1828), 105.

[36] P.R.O. Lists and Indexes No.26, Index of Inquisitions Post Mortem Preserved in the P.R.O., ii (1908), 74.

[37] *V.C.H.*, iii, 261.

4. The Biggin, panelling dated 1585 in first-floor room at southern end of west range. Photograph by N. Doggett, July 1989.

5. The Biggin, crown-post roof truss in attic of west range. Photograph by N. Doggett, July 1989.

6. Royston Priory, detail of close studding and infilled mullion window to former outside (west) wall of Priory House. Photograph by N. Doggett, February 1992.

buildings. There is absolutely no proof that the house shown on the 1578 sketch-plan has anything to do with the present building, but likewise there is really nothing to suggest that it represents a conversion of the monastic buildings.

Further work also appears to have been carried out at **Hitchin Priory** in the late 16th century. The evidence for this is fairly limited and, as we have seen, it is difficult to distinguish this work from that undertaken in the middle of the century. All that can be attributed with any certainty to this period is the panelling on the north and west walls of the west range and a small closet with plastered decoration of c.1600 in the former service range, both features which can be identified with the long ownership of Ralph Radcliffe the younger. Whether it was he or his father who was responsible for the blocking of the claustral arches it is impossible to say (indeed this could have occurred later), but such an action would have been quite consistent with the concealment of medieval features which was often associated with 16th-century monastic conversions.

At only two of the sites included in this study did the former monastic church remain in ecclesiastical use after the Dissolution. At **Royston**, Leland's description appears to make it clear that the nave was demolished shortly after the suppression of the priory in 1537, and it seems likely that this had already taken place by the time the church was

bought by the townspeople in 1540.[38] That part of the church which survives today is chiefly the chancel, choir and choir aisles of the monastic church, and it seems that relatively little was done to the building in the 60 years after the Dissolution. **(Fig. 7)** Although there may be much exaggeration in the reference of 1600 to the church being "utterly ruinated and fallen downe to the ground",[39] this is probably to some extent a true reflection of the neglect of the church in the second half of the 16th century, while the rebuilding of the tower and north arcade around 1600 was probably a response to this period of inactivity. The statement in the 1578 survey of Priory House that "yt stand(s) adjoyning to the Churche on the sowth syde thereof, not haveing any pleasaunt p'spects any way" suggests, however, that a considerable portion of the nave remained, probably as a ruin, into the last quarter of the 16th century. Whether or not the house shown on the sketch-plan accompanying the survey can be identified with any part of the present house, this suggests that unless it lay considerably to the east, which on the basis of the evidence discussed earlier seems inherently unlikely, it was the ruined nave which spoilt the house's prospects to the north.

---

[38] Alfred Kingston, *A History of Royston* (1906), 71.
[39] Calendar of the Manuscripts of the Marquis of Salisbury Preserved at Hatfield House, pt.x *Hist. MSS. Com. Rep.* (1904), 135.

7. Royston Priory, former priory church viewed from the north-east. Pen and ink drawing by J.C. Buckler, 1832; H.R.O., Buckler Drawings, I, 31.

There can be little doubt that the acquisition of the church in 1540 would have placed a considerable strain on the town's resources and this may have been a factor in the decision to abandon the nave and to retain only the eastern end of the church for parochial worship. Indeed, although it is likely that the population of the town, which until 1540 lay in five parishes,[40] had once worshipped in the nave of the priory church, there is some evidence to suggest that it was already disused and derelict by the time of the Dissolution. Although it was more usual for the nave of a monastic church to be retained after the suppression, if it was already ruinous or dilapidated this would have been sufficient reason to use only the monastic choir and chancel for parochial worship. Certainly, whatever the condition of the nave at Royston, there would have been no incentive to retain the whole building as the parish church of a relatively small town.

At **Hertford** there is less certainty about the sequence of events after the suppression, partly because nothing now survives above ground of the monastic church or its post-Dissolution successor. It seems that before the Dissolution there was only one church in the parish of St John's, in which the priory was situated, and that this was shared by the monks and the townspeople. Archaeological excavation has revealed the lay-out of this church, which comprised a long aisleless nave with transepts and a possible tower to the crossing.[41] Although not fully supported by the archaeological record, documentary sources suggest that the church was neglected during the Later Middle Ages, and one reason why the original post-Dissolution grantee of the site, Sir Anthony Denny, did not appoint a vicar on obtaining the property in 1538 may have been that the church was in need of substantial repair, outweighing any profits he would have derived from the advowson. The church then seems to have fallen into disuse and further deterioration took place in its fabric. The refoundation of the church and its rebuilding to a much smaller scale in the 1620s are difficult to explain, beyond the suggestion that this may have been a belated attempt to breathe new life into an impoverished and neglected area of the town. However, although the new building does not seem to have been particularly poorly constructed by the standards of the time, the project was doomed to failure, as is shown by the church's final demolition before the end of the 17th century.[42]

The majority of the rural sites in the Hertfordshire sample are considered in Chapter 3 but the two sites which never seem to have been converted to anything more than a farming use remain to be dealt with here.

---

[40] Statutes of the Realm, iii (1817), 797.

[41] Cooper-Reade, op. et loc. cit. (note 20); *Hertfordshire Mercury*, 2 December 1893.
[42] Chauncy, i, 506-7.

The post-Dissolution documentary history of **King's Langley** suggests relatively low status use of the site in the second half of the 16th century, an indication which is borne out by the archaeological evidence and the surviving buildings. In 1540 the site was granted to Richard Ingworth, suffragan bishop of Dover and former prior of the friary, and in 1546 it passed to John Lord Russell, first earl of Bedford, whose family still held the property in 1556.[43] Between 1557 and 1558 the surviving buildings housed a small community of Dominican nuns, after which it returned to the crown, being sold in 1574 to Edward Grimston the elder and younger.[44] The Grimstons transferred the site to Robert Cresswell, who in turn conveyed it to Francis, second earl of Bedford.[45] It remained with this family until 1607 when it was sold to Edward Newport, having most recently been tenanted by Thomas Ewer and Peter Edlin.[46]

It is clear that Ingworth actively petitioned Cromwell for the site, and it is likely that he regarded it as his rightful prize for the part he had played as a royal commissioner in the suppression of friaries throughout southern England.[47] It is not possible to say whether Ingworth intended to convert the buildings at Langley for his own use, but the facts that the house was the second wealthiest Dominican friary in the country at the time of its suppression,[48] that Ingworth was not granted any other ex-monastic property, and of his former associations with the house, all mean that this possibility cannot be ruled out. It may be therefore that Ingworth carried out some conversion work to the buildings and that he was prevented from doing more only by his death in 1544.

As little is known about activity at the site during the ownership of John Lord Russell. Towards the end of this period we have a survey of the site carried out in 1555. By then the church was semi-ruinous: "One arche of the sowthe of the seide chaunsell (is) fallen downe", perhaps suggesting that the church had already lost at least part of its south aisle, "the old chapell...on the north seide (?of the nave) is pulled down excepte the walls standing" and there were further dilapidations in the chancel, belfry, lady chapel and "the body of the churche".[49] There are several references to the stonework, glass and ironwork of the church windows being broken down or "utterly defased", a situation attested by archaeological excavation which has shown that the windows may have been smashed from within.[50]

The survey also suggests that many of the other former monastic buildings were by then in a poor state of repair. The frater, dorter and a "doffe" house are described as "sore decayed" and these and several other structures are defective "bothe in tymber work and tylinge", while the "ruffe" of the entrance going out of the cloister is "ready to fall downe". A 1556 survey of the adjoining royal manor with its former palace buildings (little used for their original purpose after the late 15th century),[51] paints a similar picture, stating that "divers edifices within the site of the manor are decayed, pulled down and carried away by the farmers".[52]

It is not known when or by whom the demolition works at Langley were carried out or whether, as seems to have been the case with the palace site, the dilapidation and defacement were largely the result of plunder by local people. It is likely that both occurred and as significant robbing of the site seems to have taken place, this is further suggestion that at least by the 1550s the site was used for farming purposes. Not all removal of building materials from the site, however, was unofficial or unorganised. In 1557 the Dominican nuns were paid £150 by the crown for the stripping of lead from the church roof so that it could be used in the conduit from Windsor Castle to Blakemore Park.[53]

Furthermore, the 1555 survey shows that not all was destruction and dilapidation by this date, as indicated also by the nuns' use of the site. The survey mentions a "fayre" gatehouse and stables, the garner is "littell in decaye" and the great kitchen and the "housse of effyce" (office) are well repaired, all suggesting a well-run and efficient farm complex in accordance with the stipulation in the 1536 First Act of Suppression "to keep or cause to be kept an honest continual house and household in the same site or precinct, and to occupy yearly as much of the said demesnes in ploughing and tillage of husbandry".[54] There is nothing surviving above ground which can be identified with the nuns, and their relatively speedy move to Dartford suggests that their stay may never have been intended to be more than temporary.

Turning now to the surviving buildings, these are entirely consistent with an agricultural use of the site in the second half of the 16th century, both showing signs of low-key remodelling in this period, although as is so often the case it is not possible to give precise dates to the work. The principal building remaining on the site is the long rectangular structure on a north-south axis, traditionally known locally as King John's Bakehouse. (**Fig. 8**) Its function during the monastic period is unknown, but it appears to date to the late 14th century and many

[43] *L.P.*, xv, no.1032 (p.542); P.R.O., E 315/391, fol.40.

[44] Cal. Pat. R., Phil. & Mary, 1555-57, 403 & Cal. Pat. R., 1557-58, 417; P.R.O., C 66/1117/1563.

[45] *V.C.H.*, ii, 238.

[46] Clutterbuck, iii, 433.

[47] *L.P.*, xiii (2), no.1021; David Knowles, *The Religious Orders in England*, iii (1959), 360-5.

[48] Knowles (1953), 185.

[49] P.R.O., E 315/391 (2).

[50] St John O. Gamlen, 'Medieval window glass from the Priory, King's Langley', *Herts. Arch.*, 3 (1973), 73-7.

[51] *King's Works*, ii, 977; David Neal, 'Excavations at the palace of King's Langley, Hertfordshire 1974-6', *Med. Arch.*, 21 (1977), 124-65.

[52] H.R.O., Blackwell papers 20,123.

[53] Bodl., Ashmole MS. 1125, fol.70.

[54] T. Wright (ed.), Three Chapters of Letters Relating to the Suppression of the Monasteries (1843), 110-11.

South East View of the remains of the Palace at Kings Langley, Hertfordshire

8. King's Langley Priory, south-east view of The Priory (mistakenly called The Palace). Pen and ink drawing by J. Buckler, 1830; H.R.O., Buckler Drawings, IV, 107.

adaptations were carried out to it during the second half of the 16th century. These included the insertion of the roughly central stack and the flooring over of the northern part of the building, the southern section apparently always having had a first floor. Various suggestions have been made as to the original use of the range, including an infirmary and "housse of effyce", both of which are referred to in building accounts of the 1360s and '70s, the latter with its "great kychen" also occurring in the survey of 1555.[55] It has also been suggested that it may be the "fayre" stables of the survey, although the fine carpentry of its crown-post roof makes it unlikely that this was its original prime function. There is some evidence to show that the building separated the cloister from the outer court of the friary, in which case it may have served as the refectory or guest house. Whatever its original purpose, there can be little doubt that it was primarily domestic in purpose, a use which would have aided its conversion into a farmhouse in the 16th century, the kitchen on the ground floor of the southern part of the building demonstrating a continuity of use from the monastic into the post-medieval period.

It is difficult to be precise about the relationship of this building to the friary church, save to say that this lay at some considerable distance to the south. As we have seen, the church was already semi-ruinous by the 1550s and in 1591 it is described as completely "ruinated".[56] It therefore seems unlikely that it was used as anything more than a source of building materials during the post-Dissolution re-use of the site.

It is rather easier to reconstruct the original appearance of the gatehouse, which is situated in the range running at right-angles to the east at the northern end of the long rectangular range. The gatehouse is of 15th-century date, comprising a jettied timber-framed superstructure over a gateway, the arch of which was constructed of stone on the external side and of timber to the courtyard side. (Fig. 9) To either side of the gateway there seem to have been chambers. In the 18th century the gatehouse was extended to the south, which means that the inner arch is now embedded in the later structure and concealed from view. This may also have been when the outer arch was infilled. There is nothing to suggest, however, that it did not continue to function as a gatehouse after the suppression, the survival of its late 15th-century crown-post roof suggesting that this occurred with little or no modification to the structure.

[55] P.R.O., E 101/466/3 & 5; *Cal. Pat. R., 1364-7*, 197-8; *Cal. Pat. R., 1370-74*, 431.

[56] H.R.O, Blackwell papers 20,113.

9. King's Langley Priory, gatehouse from the north. Photograph by N. Doggett, May 1989.

Likewise, the relatively sparse evidence for **St Margaret's Nunnery, Nettleden**, where no building traces survive above ground, makes it difficult to reach any positive conclusions about the re-use of the former monastic buildings after the Dissolution. The house was a poor one and it is perhaps no surprise that the re-use was low-key. John Verney, the original lessee of the site from 1536 to 1538, clearly had little time in which to carry out conversion works and these may have been postponed until the house was leased to Sir John Daunce, lessee from 1538 until his death in 1545.[57] Daunce's family had the lease of the site until 1630, but the fact that the crown retained ownership of the site until then may have acted as a disincentive for them to carry out any major conversion scheme, and it seems that throughout this period, as during the long ownership by the Catherall family from the second quarter of the 17th century to c.1800,[58] the buildings served as no more than a farmhouse and associated farmbuildings.

According to the early 18th-century antiquaries, Browne Willis and Edward Steele, the building then surviving (which seems to be the same building drawn by Lysons and B.W. Scott a century later) was constructed during the reign of Henry VII,[59] in which case its relatively recent date would have made it particularly attractive for re-use. The lease to Daunce in 1538 refers to the "church,

campanil(e) and cemetery",[60] while Willis's statement that the church tower stood "ten foot high in the memory of man" suggests that at least parts of the church remained for a considerable time after the Dissolution, even if in ruined form. Whether or not it featured in any conversion scheme at the site is impossible to say.

The building drawn by Lysons and Scott is shown in isolation and it is not known how it related to the other former nunnery buildings. **(Fig. 10)** It appears, however, to have been a domestic building in origin and although a doorway and lancet window shown in the drawing look earlier, there is no real reason to deny Willis's and Steele's assertion that it was late 15th or early 16th century in date. The *V.C.H.* is apparently the earliest authority to identify the building as the monastic refectory, but such a use would be entirely consistent with its character.[61] It is conceivable therefore that the refectory was converted to the parlour and hall of a new house, in which use the surviving structure remained in Willis's time.

The individual buildings selected for re-use at the sites discussed above encompass the full range of buildings commonly chosen for re-use. Perhaps not surprisingly the most frequently re-used structures are the refectory and monastic kitchen. The kitchen was obviously just as

[57] *L.P.*, xiii (1), g.887 (20); Dugdale, iv, 271. Elsewhere, however, it is suggested that Daunce died in 1564, Bodl., MS. Willis 101, p.145.
[58] *V.C.H., Bucks.*, iii (1925), 383.
[59] Bodl, MS. Willis 101, p.143; MS. Top. gen. e. 79, fols.8-11.
[60] *L.P.*, xiii (1), g.887 (20).
[61] *V.C.H.*, ii, 317.

10. St Margaret's Nunnery, north-west view of nunnery ruins. Early 20ᵗʰ-century reproduction of drawing by Benjamin Scott, 1819; H.R.O., Gerish Collection, Box 30.

essential in a post-Dissolution house as in its monastic predecessor and thus the west claustral ranges, which had housed the monastic kitchen and associated offices, continued to serve this purpose at The Biggin, Hitchin Priory, Ware and King's Langley, although it is only at the latter site that clear physical evidence for this survives.

At many former monastic sites the refectory, usually sited on the first floor with an undercroft beneath, was converted into the hall or other domestic apartments of a new house. At none of the sites discussed in this chapter, however, is there unequivocal evidence for the re-use of the refectory as great hall and only at St Margaret's, Nettleden is there any suggestion that this took place. At The Biggin and Hitchin Priory, where the refectory seems to have been situated in the north range, it appears that the hall of the post-monastic house was in the former church, and at Ware it seems that the old guest range was used as the hall in preference to the refectory in the south range. That the former refectory formed an important part of the new house at Ware is suggested, however, by the panelling of c.1600 recently discovered on its first floor, although by this date it appears to have been divided into a series of rooms.

The suggestion that the former church at Hitchin Priory was converted into the hall of the Radcliffes' house is based partly on the fact that it lay directly opposite the north entrance range, which as we have seen had probably housed the refectory on its first floor. At The Biggin the apparent re-use of the church as first-floor hall is harder to explain, as this lay at right-angles to the east range (former dormitory) of what by the second half of the 16th century had become the inner court of a double-courtyard house accessed from the east. It is perhaps the panelled parlour of

1585 at the west end of this range which provides the best evidence for this use.

Similarly, at Ware it is not immediately obvious why the guest range, which projected at right-angles to the west claustral range, was adapted as the hall of the house created for the Byrch family, although here it is far from clear where the entrance range stood, if indeed one existed at all. At King's Langley the suggestion that the principal surviving building was once the guest hall is derived from the fact that it seems to have been the range separating the inner and outer courts of the Dominican friary. It has also been suggested that this range may have been the refectory or "house of office" and stables, while (as discussed above) it retains evidence for a kitchen at its southern end.

At The Biggin it appears that the east claustral range was re-used in the mid- to late 16th-century house, although its use was primarily confined to that of a corridor gallery linking the principal first-floor apartments of the north and south ranges. At Hitchin Priory no early fabric survives in the east wing of the house but the fact that the central courtyard follows the dimensions of the monastic cloister shows that it must have featured in the original conversion. Also at The Priory, medieval fabric in the former service range which runs at an oblique angle to the north-west of the cloister indicates that this must have formed part of the medieval friary. Its use in this period or in the 16th-century house is unclear, but it may originally have been the monastic *cellarium*.

Only at Hertford is there any suggestion that the superior's lodging formed the nucleus of the post-Dissolution house and even here the evidence is at best tenuous, while the possibility at The Biggin of what may have been the prior's house, attached to the south-west corner of the cloister, surviving to be remodelled in the early 18th century is supported on even more fragmentary evidence. Much more certain is the continuing use of the gatehouse at King's Langley, the only example contained in the Hertfordshire sample where the gatehouse is known to have survived the Dissolution. Finally, at Royston it appears that none of the domestic buildings survived to be incorporated in the late 16th-century house built nearby by Robert Chester, although the extremely limited extent to which the 16th-century fabric is visible in the present house makes it impossible to establish whether monastic materials were re-used to a significant extent. If this were the case, as the late 16th-century house was essentially timber framed, re-use would seem to have been confined to the timber work. Indeed, much of the priory stonework was presumably re-used elsewhere following the sale of the cloister as building materials to Thomas More and John Newport in 1537. A similar fate would seem to have befallen the non-claustral buildings at Hitchin Priory when the house was sold to Sir Edward Watson and Henry Herdson in 1546, as their chief interest in the site seems to have been for its value as building materials.

At all the sites discussed above it must be emphasised that the conclusions about which buildings were re-used are based on either the evidence of the surviving buildings themselves or documentary or pictorial evidence often much later than the period with which we are concerned. As a site such as St Margaret's, Nettleden shows, the rate of decay could be very rapid, all above-ground traces of what was a fairly substantial building disappearing within the 19th century, and there is no reason to suppose that a similar pattern of decay cannot have occurred elsewhere between 1540 and 1600. Indeed, we know that several of the houses considered in this chapter were considerably larger in the second half of the 16th century than they were subsequently to become. The late 16th-century houses at The Biggin and Royston were of double-courtyard plan and at Ware the west claustral range not only formerly extended further to the north but to the south of the cloister itself, suggesting that the monastic infirmary may have survived the Dissolution to be incorporated in the house created by the Byrch family.

At all of the sites considered in this chapter none of the buildings selected for re-use seems to have been earlier than the 14th century. The south and west claustral ranges at Ware may date to shortly after the foundation of the priory in 1338, although both seem to have undergone some remodelling in the 15th century when the guest range was added. The long rectangular building at King's Langley is probably late 14th century in origin but the gatehouse seems to be a 15th-century structure. At The Biggin and Hitchin Priory, where all of the claustral ranges and the church appear to have been re-used in the conversions, the buildings seem to be essentially 15th century. At Hertford the building known as The Priory is unlikely to have been earlier than this and the structure

which survived into the early 19th century at St Margaret's, Nettleden was probably remodelled in c.1500. It is only at Royston that there is no evidence for the date of the claustral buildings and here, as we have seen, it is more probable that the post-Dissolution house was built on a new site, rather than that it incorporated any of the conventual buildings.

We have varying degrees of information about the owners and lessees of the ex-monastic property considered in this chapter. As with the buildings themselves, this is so varied in depth and quality that it makes comparisons between sites difficult if not impossible. Nevertheless, it is only by attempting to do this that any general patterns or trends may emerge.

At Royston, Robert Chester having rented the house following its closure in 1537 bought the site in 1540. Born in 1510 of a Hertfordshire family, Chester had first found favour at court as a gentleman usher of the king's chamber.[62] In 1544 he was at Calais with 25 archers, who formed Henry's bodyguard when he departed for the siege of Boulogne.[63] Chester was knighted in 1551 and was made sheriff of Essex and Hertfordshire in 1565.[64] He died in 1574 to be succeeded by his son, Edward. It is likely that the second major phase of 16th-century remodelling at Royston did not occur until after 1586 when Chester's grandson, another Robert, came into possession on reaching the age of 21.[65] A distinguished poet, whose works include *Love's Martyr* (1601), Robert was sheriff of Hertfordshire in 1599,[66] the separate office of sheriff for each county having been created in 1567,[67] and was sufficiently prominent in court circles to have entertained James I at Royston in 1603, shortly after which he was knighted.[68]

Ralph Radcliffe bought Hitchin Priory in 1553. Radcliffe came from a Lancashire family and was born in 1519. He was a scholar of Jesus College, Cambridge and was best known as a scholar and playwright. He died in 1559 after which his son, also Ralph (1543-1621), seems to have taken over at The Priory.[69] Very little is known of this Ralph save that he was a bencher of the Inner Temple.[70] Much more is known of Anthony Denny who bought the site of Hertford Priory on its suppression in 1538 but as it seems unlikely that he carried out much work at Hertford and was more active at Cheshunt, his career is considered in Chapter 3. Denny was succeeded on his death in 1549 by his son, Henry, and it seems that both Hertford and Cheshunt passed to him. Henry died in 1574 but it is not

[62] Kingston, op. cit. (note 38), 61.
[63] *L.P.*, xix (2), nos.424, 524 (8).
[64] W.A. Shaw, *The Knights of England*, ii (1906), 65; *P.R.O., Lists & Indexes No. 9, List of Sheriffs for England & Wales* (1898), 45.
[65] *V.C.H.*, iii, 260.
[66] *D.N.B.*, iv, 203; *P.R.O., List of Sheriffs*, 64.
[67] Smith (1992), 46.
[68] Shaw, op. cit. (note 64), 123.
[69] *V.C.H.*, iii, 12.
[70] *D.N.B.*, xvi, 576-7.

clear whether the Edward Denny who granted Hertford Priory to Thomas Docwra in 1578 was Henry's son, Edward, or Edward, fifth son of Sir Anthony.[71] This, however, is largely irrelevant here as it appears most likely that the remodelling of Priory House before it finally left the ownership of the Denny family in 1587 was carried out chiefly at the expense of tenants whose names are no longer known.

Robert Byrch had the lease of Ware Priory from its suppression in 1538 and in 1544 the site was bought from the crown by Thomas Byrch. In this grant Byrch is described as a "yeoman of the crown" but, apart from the fact that he seems to have been a scrivener and accountant and presumably servant of the crown, nothing more is known of him or his descendants who continued to own the house until 1628.

John Cocks was granted The Biggin in 1544, but although he was to serve as Sheriff of Hertfordshire and Essex in 1548 and was the recipient of many former monastic lands in both counties,[72] he seems to have had little interest in the buildings there. It is not known how or when the property was conveyed to William Croocar beyond the possibility that he acquired it through his wife, Luce, whose mother, Mary, was married to Thomas Parrys, who seems to have had an interest in the former priory lands in the 1550s and to be synonymous with the bailiff to the crown at Hitchin Priory before 1546.[73] Although Croocar left the house to his sons, Thomas and William, in his will of 1570, Mary Parrys, "widow", was paying rent for The Biggin as late as c.1578.[74] Her occupation of the buildings may have been the reason why the second William Croocar waited until the 1580s before carrying out the remodelling works suggested by the date "1585" inscribed in the panelling in one of the rooms. Nothing further is known of the Croocar or Parrys families, while all that is known of Robert Snagge who owned the house between c.1587 and his death in 1606 is that he was a lawyer and second son of Thomas Snagge of Letchworth Hall.[75]

The post-Dissolution career of Richard Ingworth as suffragan bishop of Dover is well known but there is little evidence that he carried out major conversion works at King's Langley. Much is also known of the Russell family, earls of Bedford, who held the property between 1546 and 1556 and again between 1574 and 1607. However, none of the earls seems to have had a direct interest in the house and the low-key conversion scheme there is unlikely to have been due to their personal involvement. A similar situation would have applied at St Margaret's, Nettleden,

dissolved in 1536, at which time John Verney, of the prominent Buckinghamshire family, was granted a 21 year lease of the site. This lease was revoked two years later when the property was leased to Sir John Daunce. Already advanced in years when he acquired the lease, Daunce had been Henry VIII's Treasurer of Wars, through which he was involved in the financing of royal works at Camber, Portsmouth and Portchester.[76] He had also been appointed Commissioner of the Peace for Buckinghamshire in 1536 and for Oxfordshire in 1537.[77] The Daunces remained as lessees of the property until 1630.

Several general points emerge from all this. First, substantial conversion works were more likely to occur during long periods of ownership by one family. Thus at Royston, Hitchin and Ware, owned by the Chesters, Radcliffes and Byrchs from 1540, 1553 and 1544 respectively, major programmes of remodelling took place before 1600. Some explanation is required as to why this did not also happen at Hertford, King's Langley and St Margaret's, Nettleden. At all three sites it may simply be that the properties were too small and unimportant to interest the Denny, Russell or Daunce families on a personal level, while at the latter, although the lease first to the Verneys and then to the Daunces required the remaining buildings to be maintained in reasonable condition, the fact that it remained in royal ownership may also have served as a disincentive to extensive conversion works. An additional factor against major remodelling at St Margaret's may have been its relative proximity to Nether Winchendon (Bucks.), John Daunce's principal residence from 1527 until his death in 1545, and where he carried out much rebuilding during the 1530s.[78] Indeed, that re-use which did occur at St Margaret's may post-date the acquisition of the house at Winchendon by the crown in 1545 or its sale to the Tyringham family in 1574.[79] Similarly, if the Russells had ever intended to carry out more comprehensive works at King's Langley- they did after all take the trouble to recover the site in 1574- it may have been that the break in their ownership dissuaded them from pursuing this further.

The sample is too small to develop the suggestion further, but Robert Chester and Ralph Radcliffe, as well as their later namesakes, were all young men when they embarked on remodelling schemes at Royston and Hitchin. Finally, at The Biggin it seems that individual family circumstances, principally the longevity of Mary Parrys, may have played their part in the postponement of major refurbishment works until the 1580s.

[71] P.R.O., C 66/1193/1783
[72] *P.R.O., List of Sheriffs*, 45; *L.P.*, xix (1), g.80 (48), g.1035 (97).
[73] Pencil transcript by Reginald Hine of a document of 1557, Hitchin Museum. The transcript does not give the location of the original document, but the 18th-century historian, Salmon also refers to the conveyance of The Biggin to Parrys during the reign of Edward VI (Salmon, 162); for Hitchin Priory see P.R.O, SC6/Hen. VIII/1607-15.
[74] P.R.O., PCC 11 Holney; Hine colln., Hitchin Museum.
[75] P.R.O., PCC 31 Stafford; *D.N.B.*, xviii, 610.
[76] *King's Works*, iv, 416, 493, 496; *King's Works*, iii, 291n. An account of Daunce's career is given in given in C.T. Martin, 'Sir John Daunce's accounts of money received from the treasurer of the king's chamber temp. Henry VIII', *Archaeologia*, 47 (1883), 295-336.
[77] *L.P.*, xi, g.1417 (5); *L.P.*, xii, g.1150 (15).
[78] N. Pevsner & Elizabeth Williamson, *Buckinghamshire* (1994), 449-52.
[79] *V.C.H., Bucks.*, iv (1927), 120.

Chapter Three

From Monastery to Country House: high status conversions

This chapter is concerned with those monastic buildings which were converted into gentry, courtier and royal houses. These form a distinct category from those sites examined in the last chapter. Three of the sites- Markyate, Sopwell and Wymondley- retain substantial elements of the immediately post-Dissolution houses and some physical evidence for the monastic buildings which preceded them. Far less now survives at Ashridge, but the post-Dissolution house swept away by Wyatt's early 19th-century mansion is well recorded in documentary and graphic sources. By comparison, Beechwood and Cheshunt are ill recorded, although at both sites there is enough evidence to enable some reconstruction of post-Dissolution events to be made.

As with those sites considered in Chapter 2, it is helpful to deal first with conversions carried out in the period 1540 to 1580 and then to examine separately those conversions made after 1580. By doing this it is possible to establish something of the rate at which conversions were undertaken and also of the processes which enabled them to take place. Again, there is some overlap between those conversions undertaken in the first generation and those of the second and third generations. Indeed, this is even more noticeable as a general trend in the sites considered in this chapter, suggesting that not only did social, economic and political conditions allow higher status conversions to take place earlier, but that the very status of these sites prompted further programmes of extensive remodelling later in the century.

Beechwood and Cheshunt can be described as courtier conversions and at both there is fragmentary evidence for work in the two decades after the suppression. The former Benedictine nunnery of St Giles in the Wood, Flamstead (**Beechwood**) was leased to Sir John Tregonwell soon after its suppression in 1537. It is not clear whether Tregonwell undertook any conversion of the monastic buildings. His complaint in August 1538 when ejected in favour of Sir Richard Page, to whom the crown gave the manor of Molesey in Surrey in exchange for Beechwood, that he had already spent £120 in necessaries for husbandry, hedging, making the ground etc., £40 of which had been paid to the king at the time of the suppression,[1] would seem to refer to general work on the estate rather than to any physical transformation of the buildings themselves, but this does not mean that he was not also involved in conversion works.

Although far from unequivocal proof, the possibility that it may have been Tregonwell's intention to convert at least some of the buildings, including the church, is hinted at by a reference to the "church stepull" in the crown's deed of exchange with Page in September 1538 and then to the "campanile" in the letters patent of the following year.[2] The absence of any reference to the church in Leland's description of the site, which was probably made in 1544,[3] suggests, however, that it did not feature in any conversion which Page may have carried out.

Indeed, there is considerable uncertainty as to whether there was ever a direct conversion of any of the former monastic buildings at Beechwood. In 1548 the house is referred to as the "mansion house Beechwood late callyd the priory of Saint Gyles in the Wood" and in 1564 it is recorded as the "dwelling house now commonly called Beechwood",[4] suggesting that its monastic antecedents were already beginning to be forgotten. This, of course, is anything but conclusive evidence that the new house of Beechwood was not fashioned directly from monastic fabric, and a detailed description of the building in a lease of part of it to John Cheyne in 1564 is equally unrevealing in this respect.[5]

However, what little physical or archaeological evidence there is, either for the nunnery or the 16th-century house which succeeded it, also suggests that the latter does not lie directly on the site of the former. The earliest surviving identifiable fabric in the present building dates to the mid-to late 17th century, and although there is some stonework in the cellar which may be of mid-16th-century or earlier origin, there is nothing which can be linked to the monastic phase of the site. The moulded stone fireplace in what is now the housemaster's study is probably pre-Dissolution- certainly it is not much later- but there is nothing to show that it was monastic and it could have come from elsewhere. **(Fig. 11)**

The early 18th-century front range of the house appears to occupy virgin ground, further suggestion that the nunnery buildings lay elsewhere. The most likely location for these seems to be approximately 110 yards to the east of the present house, where parch marks of a rectangular building, aligned roughly east-west, have been tentatively identified as the site of the monastic church.[6]

It therefore seems that at Beechwood the decision was taken not to convert the monastic buildings but to erect a new house nearby, very probably using materials from the nunnery. The reason for this is not clear, but the small size of the nunnery at the Dissolution may provide some explanation. The buildings recorded in the inventory made

---

[1] *L.P.*, xiii (2), no.74.

[2] *Dugdale*, iv, 301-2; H.R.O., 17,244.
[3] John Chandler, *John Leland's Itinerary, Travels in Tudor England* (1993), xxx.
[4] H.R.O., 17,248; 17,255.
[5] H.R.O., 17,255.
[6] I.V. Bullard, *Flamstead, Its Church and History* (1902), 6.

11. St Giles in the Wood, Flamstead (Beechwood Park), detail of early to mid 16th-century fireplace in housemaster's study. Photograph by N. Doggett, September 1990.

at the house's suppression in 1537- "church (quyre and vestery), parlour, kechyn, high chamber, myddle chamber, buttery and backhowsse"- were not extensive,[7] and although the church is described as in "good repair", with nothing to suggest that the other buildings were in particularly poor condition, it seems likely that both Tregonwell and Page were attracted by the site itself rather than by the buildings. Certainly, neither man would have been deterred from sweeping all away and starting afresh.

The difficulty of distinguishing any work which may have been carried out by Tregonwell from that undertaken by his successor has been referred to above. Indeed, it is only in Page's case that we can be at all certain that building work was carried out, and it may have been that whatever his intentions for the property, Tregonwell's tenure was simply too short-lived for him to have embarked on any major construction activity. Even for Page, we have only Leland's statement that "Master Page the knight hath it now

...(and)...hath translatid the house, and now much lyith there" to rely upon.[8]

The latter part of this remark suggests that Page's work was extensive and that Beechwood was his principal residence. Chauncy recites the "...Tradition that in the Infancy of Edward VI he was removed thither by the Advice of his Physitians for some time, and did reside in the said Religious House..."[9] The date of this stay is unrecorded but it may have provided further incentive, if any were needed, for Page's building work. Page died in 1548 and in March of that year his widow, Elizabeth, leased the house to Sir William Skypwith, whom she was eventually to marry. A lease of 1564 provides some information on the type of house Beechwood had by then become, referring to "the upper end of the house frome the haule porche uppward, the great kytchyn, thre Chambers frome a little entre going to the gardine...(and the) great buttery".[10] This suggests a house of some size, although it is not possible to tell whether this was largely the result of Page's work or whether further additions and alterations were made after 1548. All that can really be stated with certainty is that there was extensive building activity at Beechwood in the two decades after the Dissolution.

Not even this can be established beyond doubt at **Cheshunt**, another small Benedictine nunnery, dissolved in 1536. This is without doubt one of the most poorly documented monastic sites in Hertfordshire. On its suppression it was granted to Anthony Denny, passing on his death in 1549 to his eldest son, Henry, who in 1564 sold the estate to Anthony Throkmerton, Richard Springham and Richard Davys.[11] The inventory made at the house's closure lists a "chauncell, quyre, belfery, dortor, halle, chamber over the halle, maydens chamber, buttery, chamber over the buttery, mylke lofte, chese lofte, bruynge howse, kechyne, my ladys chamber, meanes howsse, priest's chamber and garn(er)".[12]

The recorded annual value of £14 1s and the sale to Anthony Denny of "alle the goods and catalls for £44 7s" suggest that the community was a poor one and the fact that the commissioners valued the church lead at only £2 suggests that the building may have been ruinous before the Dissolution.[13]

Denny is reputed to have been born and to have died at Cheshunt, and as he is not linked with any other house in the immediate vicinity, his death at least is thought to have taken place at the Nunnery, by which name the house continued to be called after the Dissolution.[14] Indeed,

[7] P.R.O., E 117/12/30.

[8] Leland, i, 104.
[9] Chauncy, ii, 514.
[10] H.R.O., 17,255.
[11] *L.P.*, xi, g.519 (12); P.R.O., C 66/1004/584.
[12] P.R.O., E 117/12/30.
[13] P.R.O., SC6/Hen. VIII/1606.
[14] H.L.L. Denny, 'Biography of the right honourable Sir Anthony Denny', *Trans. East Herts. Arch. Soc.*, 3, pt.ii (1906), 210-11.

Denny seems to have had a direct interest in the house before its closure, the indenture of the nunnery's goods, drawn up in May 1536, being made between the commissioners and Denny, rather than with the prioress.[15]

This would all suggest that Denny is likely to have carried out some building work at the nunnery after the Dissolution. Certainly, it would have been a convenient centre from which to administer the considerable estate he put together in Hertfordshire and East Essex from the spoils of monasteries.

Nothing now survives, even below ground, of the nunnery as the whole site was destroyed by gravel extraction in the 1950s, with only the most minimal of archaeological records being made. Even before that few traces of the nunnery or the house which succeeded it remained. During the late 19th and early 20th centuries large glass houses were erected around the buildings of Nunnery Farm, which itself seems to have been built on the site of Cheshunt Nunnery, a mainly 18th-century house, demolished between 1804 and 1811.[16]

This building is known only from brief later 18th-century descriptions and sketch-plans and one late 18th-century and two early 19th-century drawings.[17] These latter drawings are particularly useful and give a good impression of the house's appearance. From the front, the building is entirely 18th century in character but the view of the rear, showing the service areas, depicts a number of earlier ranges. It is not possible to date these accurately, but the more prominent features include a three-storey brick tower which, along with other parts of the building, could belong to the 16th or 17th century. Indeed, there is a possibility that one of the service ranges survived to form Nunnery Farmhouse, when the remainder of the house was demolished.

While this pictorial evidence, along with the discovery of substantial fragments of a mid- to late 16th-century mullion window on the site in the 1950s, are perhaps enough to demonstrate that the house contained 16th-century work, they do not indicate whether this work represented a new house on or near the site of the nunnery or a direct conversion of its former buildings. The extremely fragmentary evidence means that this will never be known. While there may be no particular reason to doubt Richard Gough's assertion that "the principle (sic) staircase (in the house was)...of Denny's time" or his belief, shared by other antiquaries, that the earlier parts of the house were built at or around the time of the Dissolution, this is very little on which to base a reconstruction of the 16th-century house or the nunnery itself.

Writing in 1823, William Caley states that "The refectory (not listed in the 1536 inventory) was the last building to the nunnery which remained entire".[18] This is probably the same structure which William Ellis noted in 1791 "appears to have been built not long before the Dissolution".[19] It is, of course, quite probable that Caley incorrectly identified the surviving building as the refectory and it may well have been one of the other buildings recorded in the inventory. If the structure was indeed "built not long before the Dissolution", it is likely to have been in good enough condition for it to have been re-used in Denny's new house.

During the 1950s' gravel extraction, fragments of Purbeck marble column-shafts, which are most likely to have come from the monastic church, were found on the site. Their exact find-spot is not known but they appear to have come from an area to the south of the main area archaeologically recorded, which seems to have been that occupied by the post-Dissolution house. The column-shafts may not, of course, have been in their original context when recovered in the 1950s, but their location raises the possibility that the church lay to the south of the 16th-century house. If this was a conversion of the monastic buildings- and there is absolutely nothing to show that the church itself was converted to domestic use- this suggests that the cloister lay to the north of the church. It is equally likely, though, that the 16th-century house was not a direct adaptation of the monastic buildings, but was a new building re-using materials from the nunnery, in which case the cloister may have been in the more usual position to the south. Certainly, a man as powerful and ambitious as Denny would not have been deterred from sweeping all away should it have served his purpose.

The evidence for the immediate post-Dissolution phase at Cheshunt is clearly extremely tentative. As we shall see, there is equally inconclusive evidence for further activity at the house later in the 16th century, and all that can be stated with confidence is that Denny is likely to have carried out some work here before his death in 1549, with the strong possibility that further work took place under his son, Henry, before 1564.

The surviving architectural evidence and the archaeological and documentary material for the immediate post-Dissolution phase is much more complete at **Markyate**, another small Benedictine nunnery, which was dissolved by February 1537. Nothing seems to have been done there before 1539 when it was leased for 21 years to Humphrey Bourchier. Having tried unsuccessfully to buy the site, Bourchier died childless in 1540 when the house passed to his widow, Elizabeth. It appears that Bourchier carried out extensive works at Markyate as Leland, who probably saw the house in 1544, writes that "Mergate was a nunnery of late tyme. It standith on a hil in a faire woode hard by Watheling Streate on the est side of it. Humfray Boucher,

---

[15] P.R.O., E 117/12/30.

[16] Ordnance Survey maps, various editions; Dugdale, iv, 328.

[17] H.R.O., Oldfield Drawings, II, 390; B.L., Add. MS. 32,349, fol.45; Bodl., Gough Herts. 16 and 18, MS. notes between pp.10 and 11 of annotated copies of Salmon's *History of Hertfordshire* belonging to Richard Gough.

[18] Dugdale, iv, 328.

[19] William Ellis, *Campagna of London* (1791), 39.

base sunne to the late lorde Berners, did much coste in translating of the priorie into a maner-place: but he left it nothing endid."[20]

The house created by Bourchier has been much altered since, with additions of c.1600, the mid-17th century and the 18th century, and it owes its present neo-Elizabethan appearance to a major remodelling by Robert Lugar in 1825/26. Despite this, it is still possible to reconstruct the form of the mid-16th-century house, which seems to have consisted of a long hall range on the south aligned roughly east-west, with cross-wings projecting to the north. The eastern of these may have acted as a service range, the massive projection to the base of the external lateral stack possibly housing a garderobe, while the staircase may have been at the northern end of the west cross-wing. The hall range was almost certainly of two storeys from the start and may have been heated by a large stack on the north wall. The principal rooms appear to have been on the upper level above an undercroft or semi-basement and it seems that the main entrance was on the south side, probably approached by a flight of steps, giving direct access to the hall range.

The earliest surviving fabric in the present house is in the short wing of chequered stone and flint to the north east and in the lower range on the south side, both of which date to this period. While it is possible that this work could immediately precede the Dissolution, it is quite clear that neither the church nor any of the claustral buildings were converted to domestic use. The east end of the church or possibly chapter house was uncovered in 1805 some 40ft to the west of the terrace to the north of the present house, indicating that the cloister must also have lain at some distance to the west. If the present building is monastic in origin, the only possible candidate which emerges is a detached superior's lodging, although the distance from the remainder of the nunnery buildings and the community's relative poverty and small size at the time of its suppression make this inherently unlikely.

It therefore seems that Bourchier made the decision to start afresh on a new site higher up the hill side, no doubt using the old buildings as a convenient quarry. The east wall of the existing house does in fact incorporate much 13th-century moulded stonework, although it seems likely that a lot of this was only re-used during the remodelling of the east range in the 19th century, very possibly following the discovery of the east end of the church or chapter house in 1805. Elsewhere in the house, material which is almost certainly monastic in origin, was probably recycled at a much earlier period. This includes a beam in the old kitchen, on the end of which was a carved shield, surviving to be illustrated by Thomas Fisher in 1805.[21] The flint and stone chequerwork pattern on the north wall of the east range may also be re-used material, although as noted above, its continuation on to the east wall of the same range is more likely to be the result of 19th-century remodelling. **(Fig. 12)**

12. Markyate Priory, north-east view of house. Pen and ink drawing by G. Buckler, 1839; H.R.O., Buckler Drawings, IV, 20.

---

[20] Leland, i, 104.

[21] B.L., Add. MS. 32,349, fol.6.

Bourchier's widow married George Ferrers in 1541 but it was not until 1548 that the site was granted to him. During this time, the property presumably remained with the crown and, despite Leland's reference to Bourchier having left it "nothing endid", there is no documentary evidence to suggest that anything further was done. The house remained with the Ferrers family until the mid-17th century, but as the next phase of remodelling does not seem to have occurred until c.1600 this is discussed below.

The Augustinian priory of **Wymondley** was dissolved in 1537 and passed to James Nedeham, in whose family the property was to remain until 1733. For much of this period the site was little more than a large farm, the converted west end of the former monastic church serving as the farmhouse, but there is some evidence to suggest that in its immediate post-Dissolution phase the site was of higher status.

The principal surviving monastic buildings are the west part of the nave of the Augustinian church, converted with various additions and alterations to domestic use in the 16th century, and the late 15th-century aisled barn, both of which stand within a well-preserved moated enclosure. Outside the moated area are a conduit house to the north east and a dovecote to the north west, both probably of 16th-century date.

Although it has been suggested that the building converted to domestic use is not in fact the church but the western part of a conventual building, possibly the refectory,[22] this is not generally accepted and what remains of the monastic fabric of this structure is perfectly consistent with use as a church. The conversion to domestic use was effected by inserting first and second floors and fireplaces and refenestrating the building with mullioned and transomed windows.

Although a case has been argued for the cloister being in the usual position to the south,[23] it seems more likely that it lay to the north. Evidence for this can be seen in the existing building in the form of a blocked processional door in the north wall and the height of the two 13th-century lancets in the south wall, which do not allow for a cloister walk beneath them. The suppression inventory of 1537 lists a hall, servants' chamber, kitchen, bakehouse, brewhouse, buttery and pantry but it is not possible from this to identify their locations.[24] Unless it should be identified as the hall, no mention is made of the refectory but as it is referred to in a bishop's visitation of 1530 as being newly rebuilt, it is unlikely that it failed to survive the Dissolution. This visitation is particularly useful for the light it sheds on the condition of the buildings so shortly before the house's closure.[25] It shows that although 100 marks had been spent on repairs to the church since 1520 and two windows at the east end had recently been renewed, the nave and chancel were still in need of further work. The bell tower was being rebuilt after a collapse, and it can be surmised that this was a free-standing structure, presumably at the west end of the church, as there is no record of its collapse having caused damage to the rest of the structure.

Repairs did not stop there. In 1537 Nedeham paid £15 4s 8d to the former prior, John Atow, "for repairs this year made on the house and church buildings of the former priory where they were greatly ruined and defective." Indeed, £5 more than this was set aside for maintenance, which indicates that repairs were still ongoing after the Dissolution.[26] This suggests that Nedeham, who had been managing the priory's financial affairs since April 1537, planned from the start to convert some of its buildings to domestic use. In December 1537 he obtained the lease of the property, but it may not have been until after he bought the site in April 1538 that building works began.

It is not easy to reconstruct the appearance of the house created by Nedeham. It is probable that it was much larger than the remaining structure would indicate. Writing in c.1700, Chauncy states that "this Priory has been a fair old building with cloysters",[27] which perhaps suggests that although the cloister had disappeared by then, some vestiges had remained well after the Dissolution. An estate map of 1731 shows the buildings to have been far more extensive than now, especially to the east. It is tempting to equate the formerly greater extent of the house with a survival of the eastern part of the church and it is possible to interpret the roughly cruciform shape of the larger building as following the plan of the church. Certain irregularities suggest, however, that these ranges represent structures added after the Dissolution, albeit on the site of the eastern end of the church. Similarly, if the formerly greater extent of the building does represent the crossing, transepts and quire of the monastic church, they may not have survived as habitable structures but may have been shown on the map simply because their walls remained above ground.

It is unlikely, though, that in such an early conversion Nedeham would have been prepared to tolerate the survival of ruins directly abutting his house- certainly, it is unlikely that he would have displayed any antiquarian interest in such features- and if they did survive, it is more likely that they would have been put to domestic use. This is all the more likely when one recalls the recent repairs to the church, even though it is not specified to which areas the repairs were carried out. Finally, the current eastern wall of the house is somewhat thinner than those on the north and

[22] Smith (1993), 218.
[23] Gil Burleigh *et al*, *Wymondley Priory, Hertfordshire: An Archaeological Evaluation* (North Herts. District Council Museums, 1989), 4.
[24] P.R.O., E 117/12/30.

[25] Noel Farris, *The Wymondleys* (1989), 157.
[26] P.R.O., SC6/Hen. VIII/1606, m.11.
[27] Chauncy, ii, 110.

south, suggesting that originally it may have been internal, although like that on the west it may simply have been rebuilt.

It is, of course, quite possible that the eastern part of the house had become ruinous by 1731, particularly as the status of the site appears to have declined during the 17th century. If Nedeham was prompted to convert the church to domestic use partly on account of its apparently good condition, it is unlikely that he would have ignored the recently rebuilt refectory, especially as its most likely position -directly opposite the church- would have led to the adoption of a convenient and fashionable courtyard plan. If there was a prior's lodging, and it is possible that the reference to a hall in the 1537 inventory is to the refectory, this may have been in the west claustral range. It is likely that, along with the dormitory in the east range, this would have been converted to lodgings as the church appears to have served as the hall and parlour of Nedeham's new house.

Nedeham died in 1544 and it is not possible to tell how much had been accomplished by his death. This is partly because, as is so frequently the case, it is extremely difficult to distinguish between work carried out in the mid-16th century and that undertaken later in the century, a problem exacerbated at Wymondley by an insensitive "restoration" in the 1970s, which destroyed all the 16th-century windows and many other potentially datable features. It is therefore not possible to say whether it was Nedeham or one of his successors who added the short brick range on the south west of the main range. Other elements of the 16th-century house, such as the triple gables on the north front, are more likely to have been added later and are therefore discussed with other work of the later 16th century, but we can be certain that, with the title to the property assured, Nedeham's successors would have continued to work on the house. Indeed, even if the physical evidence had survived, it is very doubtful that it would be possible to differentiate work carried out for Nedeham before 1544 from that undertaken for his son, John, after that date, and since the work would seem to have been an ongoing process, it is debatable as to whether this would in any case be particularly informative.

It is difficult to visualise the appearance of the mid-16th-century house, but it is worth commenting that Nedeham would probably have gone to some pains to disguise the most obvious ecclesiastical features. Thus, although the lancet windows in the south wall of the former nave are at the right level to serve as first-floor doorways to the south-west range, the ground-floor ceiling cuts across them, and it must be questioned whether they served as such in the 16th-century house. If they did, it is likely that their 13th-century nook-shafts would have been concealed from view. **(Fig. 13)**

13. Wymondley Priory, 13th-century lancet window in south wall of former church truncated by inserted 16th-century floor. Photograph by N. Doggett, November 1989.

Of the other former monastic buildings, the barn would have continued in much the same use as before, while it is impossible to tell whether the dovecote, which must date to between the 1520s and 1550s, was built before or after the suppression, although the absence of any reference to it in the 1537 inventory perhaps tips the balance in favour of the latter. The evidence for the date of the conduit house is far from conclusive but points marginally to later in the 16th century, which means that it is discussed below. It is not known when the land to the north of the moated platform was first called "the Park", the name which it is given on the 1731 map, but this probably happened in the mid-16th century. This area of land contains the earthworks of house platforms and enclosures, demarcated on the west by ponds and a hollow-way on the east. It has been suggested that these are the remains of a tenant settlement linked to the priory,[28] which may have been deliberately depopulated by the Nedehams after the Dissolution. Certainly, a fine parkland landscape is just the sort of setting the family would have desired for their new house.

---

[28] D.O.E. List of Scheduled Ancient Monuments, National Monument Number 11,518.

A large park was one of the key components created by Sir Richard Lee at **Sopwell**, a small Benedictine nunnery just outside St Albans. The house was dissolved in 1537 and was granted to Lee in December 1538, with confirmation in 1540. The suppression inventory records a "hall, kychen, churche and quyre", the confirmation grant also referring to the tower and cemetery of the church.[29]

Archaeological excavation has provided evidence for lead melting at the site and it is likely that this was carried out as part of the crown's stripping of the site rather than by Lee. Lead was the most valuable building material from the nunnery, being valued at £40 in the Ministers' Accounts for 1537.[30] Much of this lead was re-used for the king's manor of The More at nearby Rickmansworth. This was still taking place as late as 1542,[31] which suggests either that the lead was being stored before removal to The More or, as was usually the case, the sale to a lay owner of the former monastic property excluded the lead. Other building materials were sold in 1538 to John Shreve and Thomas Maydewell, presumably local men, whose purchases included the "Tymber worke in the Quyre" for 40s. Maydewell also bought the "stones in the churche wt the vestery Stuff" for 40s.[32]

Lee had been bailiff and farmer of the nunnery since 1534 and as he does not appear to have participated in the purchase of materials before he received the grant of the site, it must be assumed that he was content to see the buildings left as little more than shells. Lee does not seem to have been in any hurry to begin work on converting the buildings. Leland is thought to have passed through St Albans on his return to London from his north-eastern itinerary in 1539 and makes no mention of Sopwell. However, as he also gives no description of St Albans itself, it would be unwise too read to much into this. In 1550 Lee was granted the greater part of the abbey buildings and there is a persistent tradition that he used materials from there at Sopwell.[33] While this cannot be disproved, it is likely that the remains of the buildings at Sopwell would have provided all that was necessary, at least for the first house which Lee built on the site.

The most likely date for the commencement of Lee's building activity at Sopwell would seem to have been after 1548 when he withdrew from public life and spent almost a decade of retirement in Hertfordshire. The reasons for this delay are not clear. Lee's title to the property was secure, he was prominent in royal service and he had been knighted in 1544, at about which time he became surveyor of the king's works in succession to James Nedeham.

Furthermore, as early as 1538 he had acted as advisor to Thomas Wriothesley at Titchfield, one of the earliest and most daring of the first phase of monastic conversions. It may simply have been that he was too busy to attend to Sopwell and wished to wait until he had enough time to devote his energies solely to that project. He also had other houses, including the former alien priory of Newent in Gloucestershire.[34]

Lee came from a Hertfordshire family and it may have been partly for this reason that he was particularly keen to make Sopwell a house of the first rank. Although it was not until the second phase of remodelling, which probably took place in the late 1560s and 1570s and which is discussed later, that the old monastic plan was discarded completely, Lee never appears to have felt constrained by re-using the fabric of the existing buildings in the construction of his new house, which, with his experience of building, we can be confident that he was closely involved in and very probably provided the design for himself. This perhaps explains why Lee does not appear to have been overly concerned by the demolitions and dilapidations at Sopwell after 1537 and why, although the buildings seem to have been in reasonable repair at the time of the Dissolution, only their ground-plan and perhaps some of the structural fabric were re-used in the domestic conversion.

The existing ruins on the site relate to the later 16th-century house and this makes it difficult to determine the extent to which any surviving monastic buildings may have been re-used in the first phase of domestic conversion. However, as the site has been archaeologically excavated, albeit that the results have not been properly published, it is possible to say a little more about this first conversion than would otherwise be the case. Nothing is known from documentary sources about the lay-out of the medieval nunnery, but the cloister seems to have been situated in the usual position to the south of the church. This seems to have been rebuilt no earlier than the 14th century, as the remains of an unrelated smaller 12th-century church, which continued in use throughout the 13th century, were also uncovered in the excavations. The nave of the later medieval church and perhaps part of the central tower seem to have provided the floor-plan for the hall of Lee's first house, although the archaeological evidence suggests that the walls themselves were not retained but were rebuilt on the old foundations. A wide fireplace was built in the north wall of the hall, but the excavator does not suggest whether this was of one or two storeys, although in a house of this status by the mid-16th century one would expect the latter.

The dimensions of the medieval cloister seem to have been followed exactly by the courtyard of the Tudor house, but the walks appear to have been demolished. The east range, which seems to have had an undercroft on the lower level, was also rebuilt on the old foundations and, although the

[29] *L.P.*, xii (1), no.571 (1); H.R.O., IV. A. 1; *L.P.*, xv, no.282 (123); P.R.O., E 117/12/30.

[30] P.R.O., SC6/Hen. VIII/1606, m.8.

[31] Bodl., MS. Rawl. D. 809.

[32] P.R.O., E 315/361, fols.63-63b.

[33] *Cal. Pat. R., Ed. VI*, iv, 5; John Shrimpton, *The Antiquities of Verulam and St Albans* (c.1610), 78: MS. volume in H.R.O., 66,296; *D.N.B.*, xi, 811.

[34] John Harvey, *English Mediaeval Architects* (revd. edn., 1984), 175-7; *King's Works*, iii, 13-14, iv, 410-11.

archaeological work was less extensive to the south and west, this also seems to have applied to the south and west ranges. The puzzle remains, however, as to why, given that Lee apparently chose to follow the ground-plan of the medieval nunnery so slavishly, he did not re-use more of its fabric. Even allowing for ten years or so of demolition, decay and perhaps plunder by local people, it is hard to believe that some walls did not remain standing. The sweeping away of the first house by the later building makes it impossible to prove, but one wonders whether the first phase of rebuilding was as total as the excavator of the site would have us believe.

A series of plaster and stone medallions now at Salisbury Hall in the neighbouring parish of Shenley are said to have been purchased by Sir Jeremiah Snow from Sir Harbottle Grimston, who bought Sopwell in 1669 and who is believed to have demolished at least some of its buildings.[35] The medallions are of very fine quality and depict the busts of Roman emperors and other figures from classical antiquity. They are almost certainly of English workmanship and would seem to have been expressly commissioned for Lee's Sopwell, but even their general context within the house is unknown. Their exact date is also uncertain. Although their fine quality would seem in some ways to be more in keeping with the more lavish second phase of Sopwell, they are precisely the kind of work associated with the mid-Tudor Renaissance of Protector Somerset and his circle and were perhaps ultimately inspired by the very similar terracotta roundels of the 1520s at Hampton Court.[36] As such, they are useful confirmation that even in its first, comparatively modest phase, Sopwell is likely to have been a house of more than local significance. This is further reflected by the choice of the house as a stopping-place for Elizabeth on a royal progress in 1564.[37] The queen's reaction to the house is not known, but as her stay was some years before Lee's second phase of remodelling it can be assumed that the house was of a sufficiently high standard to meet the requirements of even this most demanding of visitors.

Although it is not known when Lee began work on the formal gardens at Sopwell, it is likely that at least some of these were laid out as part of the first phase of operations. It seems, however, that the boundaries of the large park with which Lee surrounded the house and gardens were not defined before the first house was complete and it was not until 1562 that the London Road was diverted around the park.[38] Large sections of the wall surrounding the park were made up of moulded stonework and other materials, which probably came from the former nunnery. Further brick and stone in the wall may have come from St Albans Abbey, this also being precisely the time when Nicholas Bacon was removing building materials from the abbey for

his new house of Gorhambury a few miles to the west of the town.[39]

It is not entirely clear what happened in the first phase of domestic re-use at **Ashridge**. The college of Bonshommes was dissolved in January 1540 and the site was leased to John Norrys for 21 years.[40] Nothing is known of Norrys and it seems that he simply farmed the land and was responsible for keeping the buildings in good repair, as is shown in a dispute between him and Robert Emys, the last tenant of the former college, in 1540.[41] In 1550 the lease was revoked and the site was granted to Princess Elizabeth, who in 1555 leased the site to Richard Combes for another 21 years.[42] One reason why the property was leased rather than sold to either Norrys or Combes may have been that the crown wished to retain ownership of the house but preferred to make others responsible for its day-to-day maintenance.

Henry VIII had visited Ashridge on at least two occasions before the Dissolution, once in 1523 when its pleasures were described in verse by the court poet, John Skelton,[43] and again in 1530 when the king gave 7s 6d to the shrine of the "Holy Blood there" and 4s 8d "To Edmonde the footman for so moche by him given in rewards at Ashridge to one that made the dogges to draw water",[44] which is probably a reference to the use of dogs to lift up water buckets from the deep monastic well.

In August 1543 a meeting of the privy council was held at the house,[45] and at various times all three of the royal children lived there. In 1544 a letter from Prince Edward's tutor, Dr Richard Cox, complains about living conditions and in the 1540s and first half of the 1550s Princess Elizabeth spent long periods at the house,[46] its grant to her in 1550 presumably enabling her to make any further changes she saw fit.

Much of the documentary evidence for the buildings at Ashridge comes from later 16th-century sources and, as all of the conventual buildings except a late medieval barn and an early 14th-century undercroft have been swept away by the Gothic fantasy of Wyatt's early 19th-century mansion, it is difficult to reconstruct the appearance of the house during the 1540s and '50s.

---

[35] Mark Girouard, 'Salisbury Hall, Hertfordshire- II', *Country Life*, 126 (29 October, 1959), 711; Pevsner, 322-3; Smith (1993), 157.

[36] Simon Thurley, *The Royal Palaces of Tudor England* (1993), 106-9.

[37] P.R.O., E 351/3202.

[38] *V.C.H.*, ii, 15, 470.

[39] J.S. Rogers, 'The manor and houses at Gorhambury', *Trans. St Albans and Herts. Archit. and Arch. Soc.*, n.s., 4 (1933-5), 41.

[40] Knowles (1953), 176; H.J. Todd, *The History of the College of Bonhommes of Ashridge* (1823), 83.

[41] Todd, op. cit., 84-6.

[42] *Cal. Pat. R., Ed. VI*, iii, 238; Todd, op. cit, 31-2; an original copy of the lease is kept in the present house.

[43] John Skelton, *The Garden of Laurell* (1523): see A. Dyce (ed.), *The Poetical Works of John Skelton*, i (1843), 361-424 and L.J. Lloyd, *John Skelton* (1938), 123-30.

[44] *L.P.*, v, 321, 751.

[45] Cal. S.P. Dom., ix, 489.

[46] B.L., Harl. MS. 6986, fol.15, Lansd. MS. 1236, fol. 39; Portland MS. II, *Historical Manuscripts Comm.*, 13th Rep. App., pt.2 (1893), 7; Cussans, iii, pt.1, 138.

It is probable that the relatively recent date of much of the claustral ranges, a large part of which seems to have been reconstructed in the mid-15th century, meant that the principal buildings were still in good condition at the Dissolution, when Ashridge was the second wealthiest monastic community in Hertfordshire.[47] It therefore seems unlikely that there would have been a pressing need to carry out major alterations to the buildings, which appear already to have offered a relatively high standard of domestic comfort.

A great deal of work was carried out to the house by Thomas Egerton after 1604 and probably also by the Cheyney family, who owned the house from 1575 to 1602. It is essentially this house which is described by Thomas Baskerville, Browne Willis and other late 17th-century and early 18th-century antiquaries and which also survived to be recorded by Henry Oldfield and other artists before its demolition in the early 19th century. **(Fig. 14)**

There is good reason to suppose, however, that whatever the work carried out later, Ashridge was- in Norden's words- "a more stately house" when Elizabeth "lodged (there) as in her owne",[48] and that this statement was not entirely the result of sycophancy to the monarch. Much of the monastic lay-out is recognisable in Egerton's house and

this must therefore also to a large extent reflect its character and appearance during Elizabeth's occupation.

The cloister appears to have lain to the north of the church with the early 14th-century refectory in its northern range. The undercroft of this survives beneath the dining room and drawing room on the south (garden) front of the existing mansion. The refectory certainly served as the great hall of Egerton's house and there is no good reason to suppose that this was not also the case in Elizabeth's time. Indeed, it may have been because the refectory was selected for re-use as the great hall in the first post-Dissolution house that it continued to be used for this purpose in the house's later phases.

A long gallery seems to have occupied the upper level of the north and east cloister walks and, although this is a feature more often associated with late 16th-century and early 17th-century architecture, there are parallels with other converted monastic buildings of the 1540s to suggest that this formed part of the first phase of post-Dissolution re-use.[49]

Working back from later documentary evidence like a survey of 1575, an inventory of 1701 and a sale catalogue of 1800, it appears that there was an entrance hall in the

14. Ashridge, view of cloister walk and detail of angel bosses with armorial shields. Pen and coloured ink drawing by H.G. Oldfield, c.1800; H.R.O., Oldfield Drawings, III, 189.

---

[47] *Val. Eccl.*, iv, 227.
[48] John Norden, *Speculi Britanniae Pars, The Description of Hartfordshire* (1598), 11-12.

[49] As at Lacock and Newstead. See Chapter 4.

west claustral range- perhaps the "Maynes Hall of the 1575 survey- which also had a gallery apparently linking with the gallery over the north cloister walk. By the late 18th century the south and west ranges were "divided into suites of rooms", with the upper floor of the south range containing "a suite of four bedrooms", including the apartment traditionally said to have been used by Elizabeth.[50] This range was presumably on the site of the monastic church, which appears to have survived and perhaps to have remained in at least partial use for some time after the Dissolution. The evidence for this comes from the former presence in the church of the tomb of Sir Ralph Verney, who did not die until 1546, and the reference to its repaired lead roofs in the survey of 1575.[51] There is also a reference in the survey to "Mr Chamberlen's lodging called the Tower", the 30ft-square dimensions of which accord exactly with those of "le steple", recorded in the same survey, making it likely that they were one and the same structure. This then was probably the central tower of the cruciform church, which along with the monastic nave or possibly the north aisle and transept- depending on the lay-out of the medieval church- was converted into the south range of the post-Dissolution house.

If there had been continuing ecclesiastical use of the monastic church after the suppression- as suggested by the Verney tomb- it was probably confined to the choir and this use may have declined or ceased altogether after the departure of Elizabeth in 1554, although it was probably to be another 20 years before the choir was demolished. Indeed, there seems to have been a general deterioration at the house after Elizabeth left and by 1560 many of the buildings were in poor condition. Despite £55 3s 8d having been spent on repairs since the first year of her reign, a good part was falling down "namely the lodging that Master Treasurer laye in, which accoumpted the fayrest lodging of the howse next where the Quene's highness laye" and £200 would not make "a house meete for her highness to lye in yt three dayes".[52]

During the 1560s it must be assumed that maintenance was the responsibility of the lessees of the estate and this may have been one of the reasons why it was necessary to spend £67 10s 7d on repairs to the house in preparation for a royal progress through Hertfordshire in 1564.[53] It may have been the result of these repairs which attracted the attention of Sir Nicholas Throckmorton, Ambassador to France, towards the house. In 1566 he was advised in a letter from Peter Osborne that "Ashridge is worth the having...The situation and walls about it will save you money, and the translating of it will be done with small charge in comparison of building a new house".[54] It is not known whether Throckmorton displayed any further

interest in Ashridge but Osborne's comments are enough to suggest that although it had many attractions, there was felt to be a need for another phase of "translating" to take place.

Meanwhile, the farmbuildings of the former monastery would have continued in agricultural use, including the surviving late 15th-century five-bay timber-framed barn, while, whether or not it was of monastic origin, the dovecote referred to in the 1575 survey, may be identified as the large circular structure shown on an estate map of 1762.[55] The continuing use of the house between 1575 and the early 17th century is discussed below.

It has already been suggested that the former monastic buildings at Beechwood, Cheshunt and Markyate were effectively demolished during the 1540s and that, although some of their materials were almost certainly re-used, they played no direct part in shaping the new houses erected at these sites. A brief account should, however, be given of the later 16th-century phases of these houses, not only because monastic materials were re-used once more but, more importantly, because this helps to provide a context for Ashridge, Sopwell and Wymondley where the former monastic plan and building fabric continued to influence the evolution of these houses into the 17th century and beyond.

Very little evidence survives at **Beechwood** for any building activity carried out by the Smith family, who owned the property between c.1575 and 1628.[56] There is no identifiable fabric in the present building from before the mid-17th century and the original H-plan is also likely to date to this period. All that is contemporary with the Smiths' ownership of the house is some panelling and an early Jacobean overmantel over the early to mid-16th-century fireplace in the present housemaster's study, but even these could be later imports to the building.

Cheshunt Nunnery remained in the hands of the Denny family until 1564 when Henry Denny sold it to Anthony Throkmerton, Richard Springham and Richard Davys. Nothing is known of these men and this, along with their group purchase of the property, suggests that they were agents acting for another party. How long the house remained in their hands or with their client is also unknown but in 1590 Edward Denny, younger brother of Henry, bought back the estate. Denny did not retain it long, however, selling it to Sir William Cecil in 1592, the property remaining with the Cecils until 1608.[57] Owing to the extremely fragmentary nature of the data discussed earlier, it is not possible to attribute precise dating to the 16th-century work carried out at Cheshunt or to determine

[50] *The Topographer*, ii, no.3 (March 1790), 150.
[51] Todd, op. cit. (note 40), 60-4.
[52] P.R.O., SP 12/12/38.
[53] P.R.O., E 351/3202.
[54] *Cal. S.P. Dom., Addenda 1566-79*, 16.
[55] H.R.O., AH. 2770.
[56] Smith (1993), 55.
[57] Clutterbuck, ii, 108; *V.C.H.*, iii, 448, 454.

15. Markyate Priory, house (south and west fronts) viewed across park with parish church in foreground. Watercolour by unknown artist, c.1800; H.R.O., Knowsley Clutterbuck, iii, 346d.

whether it took place in distinct phases. The only evidence we have for work carried out later rather than earlier in the second half of the century are the tantalising references in William Vallans's *A Tale of Two Swannes* (1590), which run "From thence to Broxbourne, and to Wormley wood/ And so salute the holy house of Nunnes,/ That late belong'd to captaine Edward Dennie,/ A knight in Ireland of the best accompt/...There now Lord Talbot keepes a noble house". Both the reference to "late belong'd to...Dennie" and to Lord Talbot (presumably the sixth earl of Shrewsbury, who died in 1590) are puzzling, especially the latter as the earl is not known to have had any connection with Cheshunt, and perhaps they should not be relied upon. Nevertheless, there is no reason to doubt the main thrust of Vallans's lines, namely that in around 1590 Cheshunt Nunnery remained a house of the first rank.

The evidence is rather fuller at **Markyate** for a second phase of remodelling in the later 16th century. As we have seen, it is likely that the first post-Dissolution house on the site was started by Humphrey Bourchier before his death in 1540, but it is also likely that much remained to be carried out by his successor, George Ferrers, between 1548 and his death in 1579. Much of the work undertaken by Ferrers could relate to this first phase, although as the extent of Bourchier's work remains unknown, this is impossible to prove. This first phase of building is, however, quite distinct from the second in which a west range was added to the original house. This is now so much altered by later

remodellings that the possibility that it belongs to another burst of activity in the mid-17th century cannot be ruled out, but it is more probable that it was added before c.1600.[58] The main reason for believing that the west range was an addition to the original building is that it was at a different level to the south range. **(Fig. 15)** In the early 17th century a short one-storey and attic range with a timber-framed east gable was added to the north-east corner of the west range.

Several candidates emerge as the possible builder of the west range. It may have been George Ferrers, his son, Julius, between 1579 and his death in 1596 or George's grandson, John, after the latter date. John did not die until 1640 and he is therefore also likely to have added the range to the north-east corner of the west range. Lack of surviving architectural detail means that the answer will never be known.

The absence of specific documentary evidence at **Wymondley** and the problems of precisely dating the 16th-century work make it difficult to distinguish between the work of James Nedeham before 1544 and that carried out by his son, John, or grandson, George, who owned the property between 1544 and 1591 and from 1591 to 1626 respectively. These are long periods of ownership and it is likely that both men carried out work at the house. Various

---

[58] Smith (1993), 124-5.

41

16. Wymondley Priory, north front with triple gables. Photograph by N. Doggett, April 1989.

features can be dated to between c.1590 and c.1600. The most prominent of these are the three gabled ranges, which from their queen-strut roof structures appear to have been added to the north front of the former nave at this time, suggesting that if this was not already the case, the north front had become the main entrance front of the house by this date. **(Fig. 16)**

Also dating to c.1600 are the various panelled rooms in the house, the panelling on the north wall of what was formerly a ground-floor passage-way concealing the internal face of the west processional doorway in the north wall of the monastic nave. While the panelling may not be *in situ*, this raises the possibility that although the post-Dissolution house may have originated with a courtyard plan based on the monastic cloister, it had been reduced in size by c.1600, with the removal of the claustral ranges and the addition of the three smaller gabled projections on the north front.

The suggestion that the house had declined in importance as early as 1600 is not entirely consistent with some of the features of this period which still remain or formerly existed in the building. For instance, the panelling appears to have been considerably more extensive before the remodelling of the 1970s when much of it was destroyed or replaced by "replica" panelling. It is therefore not possible to date the panelling exactly or even to be sure that it was not brought in from elsewhere at a later date, but the panelling does at least suggest a house of some status.

More revealing of the relative importance of the house at the end of the 16th century was the discovery in 1973-4 of a wall painting in a late medieval traceried recess in the

north-east corner of the house. The function of the recess is unclear but the late 16th-century painting of running soldiers in classical armour is work of the highest quality.[59] It has been suggested that the recess is where the south walk of the cloister should have been,[60] but as it is situated in what is clearly a late 16th-century addition (the eastern of the three gabled projections), it is much more likely to have been reset. In this case it may have served as the piscina of the chapel which Chauncy says was "consecrated since the Dissolution" and the location of which is not known.[61] As only part of the painting is now visible, it is not possible to say whether the subject depicted was of a secular or religious nature and this suggestion must remain tentative. All that can really be concluded is that although the house seems to have been reduced in scale by the end of the 16th century, it remained an important building, a status that it was to retain throughout the following century during which further improvements were made.[62]

Before leaving Wymondley mention should be made of the conduit house, which stands some 500 yards to the north-east of the house. Only fragmentary ruins remain and even these are mainly the result of a reconstruction of the structure by the East Hertfordshire Archaeological Society

[59] Clive Rouse, 'Domestic wall and panel paintings in Hertfordshire', *Arch. Jnl.*, 146 (1989), 448.
[60] D.O.E. 54th List of Historic Buildings, District of North Hertfordshire (28 May 1987), 87; Stuart Rigold, 'Wymondley Priory', *Med. Arch.*, 18 (1974), 191.
[61] Chauncy, i, 110.
[62] George Nedeham was assessed for 16 hearths here in 1662; P.R.O., E 179/375/30.

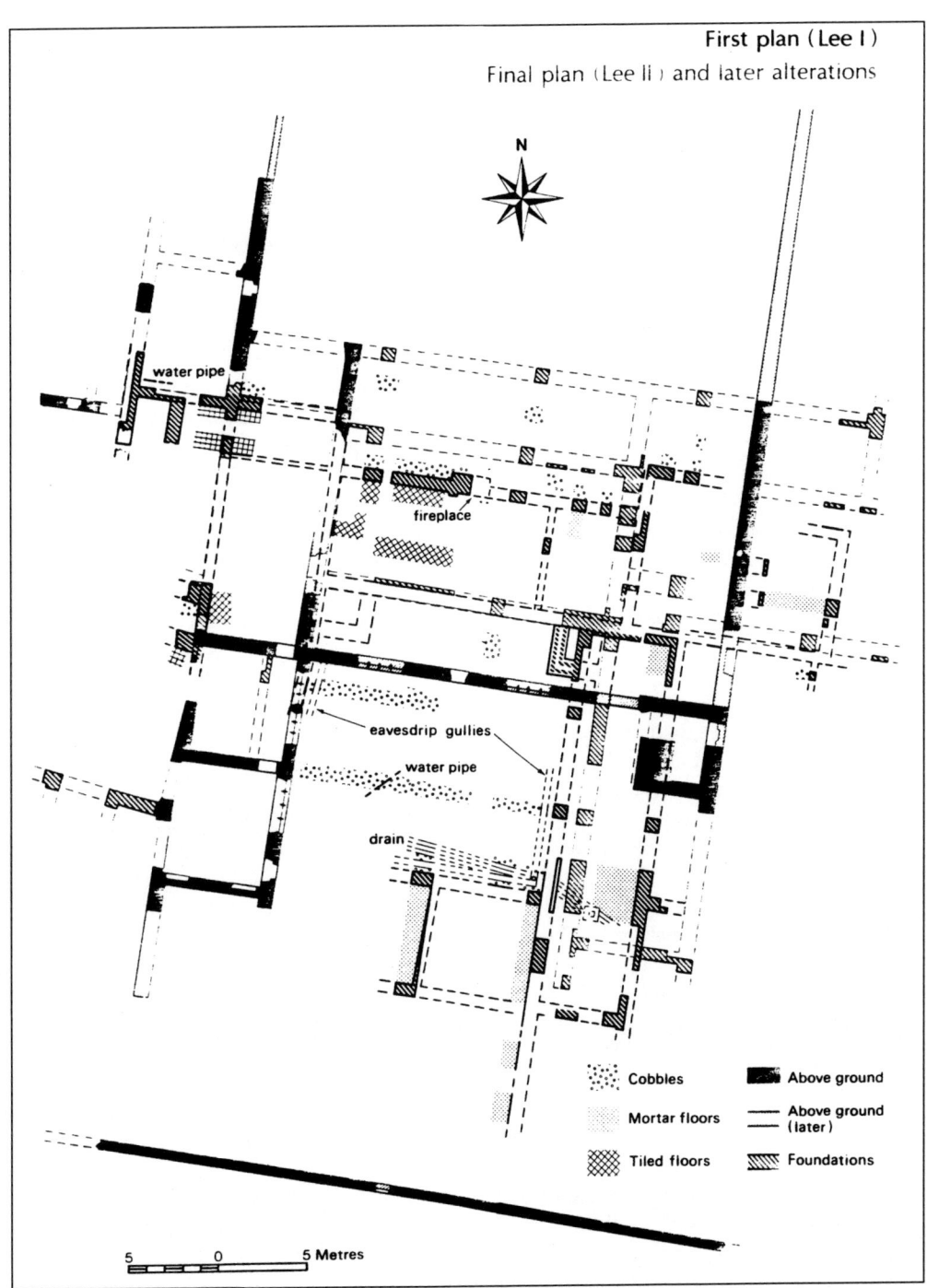

17. Sopwell Nunnery, superimposed plan of Lee's Sopwell, phases one and two. Reproduced from C. Platt, *Medieval England* (1978), 216.

in c.1905.[63] Chauncy records that the conduit provided "sufficient water to turn the spit in the kitchen (of the house) upon all occasions", a purpose it still served in the mid-19th century,[64] the supply of piped water to the house being the reason for building the conduit in the first place. Although the conduit may be of monastic origin, the

conduit house itself seems more likely to have been erected after the Dissolution, what is known of its former roof structure suggesting that it was built towards the end of the 16th century.

The second phase of post-Dissolution remodelling at **Sopwell** seems to have taken place in the late 1560s or early 1570s, only some 10 to 15 years after work on the first house was complete. In the second phase, although the

---

[63] 'Twenty Fourth Excursion', *Trans. East Herts. Arch. Soc.*, 3 (1906), 230-1.
[64] Chauncy, i, 110; *V.C.H.*, iii, 189.

hall still occupied the site of the church it was considerably widened and the monastic plan was effectively abandoned, giving way to a fashionable double-courtyard plan. **(Fig. 17)** It is the remains of this house which is the principal survival on the site today, the ruined walls of the west range, which is of double width at its northern end, and the south wall of the hall standing to a considerable height.

The circumstances which prompted Lee to embark on such a comprehensive remodelling of his comparatively recently finished first house are not known. Whether, as slightly later at Gorhambury,[65] it could have been at least partly the result of unfavourable remarks during the royal progress of 1564 is purely speculative, while unlike the period during which Lee constructed the first house, its building does not seem to have coincided with any withdrawal by Lee from public life. Lee remained active in royal service virtually until his death in 1575 and similarly it seems from the archaeological evidence that he continued to work on the house, which was still incomplete when he died.

That many of his intentions for the house were by then fulfilled, however, is suggested by the terms of his will (made in 1570) which states that "if any of the persons mentioned in this entail do altar, change, transforme digge cutt dowen or deface the said howses, edifices, buyldynges or walles of the mansion house...and shall not within the space of three years next folowinge the said alterynges etc...in like or better form and fashion ereckt buylde upp or make the same againe...from henceforth the sd persons so doing shall forfeit their interest in the premises".[66] This is a clear reflection of Lee's pride in his house and also perhaps of his anxiety at not having a male heir. This lack of a son may well have been a long-standing concern of Lee's and may have been the reason why in 1557 he had conveyed the estate to trustees for the use of his younger daughter Anne.[67] It was, however, his elder daughter, Mary, wife of Humphrey Coningsby, who inherited the property, although whether she continued to live there until her death in 1610 is not known.

That the house remained, even in its apparently incomplete state, an important building is suggested by the imposing appearance it presents in a birdseye perspective view on an undated estate map of c.1600,[68] **(Fig. 18)** which ties in quite neatly with the archaeological and surviving architectural evidence. Similarly, in his manuscript *History of St Albans* (c.1610) John Shrimpton describes Sopwell as "a fair house."[69] Shrimpton also states that the "stones and cheife stuffe (were)...taken out of the abbey" and makes no mention of the former nunnery buildings.[70] Although it is quite certain that building materials from the nunnery must have been re-used and it is possible that in its first phase

some of the buildings may have been a direct conversion of the monastic structures, Shrimpton is writing so soon after the completion of Lee's second house, that his claim must be treated with some seriousness.

It is conceivable that the supply of building materials from the already extensively-robbed small nunnery may largely have been exhausted by the erection of Lee's first house, forcing him to resort to using materials from the abbey for his much more extensive second stage of remodelling. There are other reasons too for thinking that Lee may have been more likely to re-use material from the abbey in his second house rather than in the first. Lee was granted the greater part of the abbey buildings only in 1550,[71] by which time work was already under way at Sopwell. It might be argued that Lee's sale of the abbey's domestic buildings in 1551 to its last abbot, Richard Boreman, who it seems entertained hopes of refounding the monastic community,[72] means that he would not have been able to re-use materials from there at Sopwell, but he may, of course, have stockpiled sufficient for his needs. Furthermore, it is likely that after the death of Mary in 1558 and the final abandonment of any plans to re-found the abbey, there were fewer inhibitions to taking stones from the abbey for recycling elsewhere.

At **Ashridge** it is more difficult to distinguish the later 16th- and early 17th-century work from that carried out for Elizabeth in the 1540s and 1550s, not least because nothing of either period now survives above ground. The transfer of ownership to the Cheyney family in 1575 when, after a series of leases, the property finally left royal hands can probably be regarded as a watershed. As noted above, the tower and possibly the nave of the monastic church appear to have been converted to residential use after the Dissolution, with only the choir remaining as the chapel of the new house. In 1576 the tomb of Sir Ralph Verney and the 15th-century monument of Sir Richard Whittingham were transferred to the nearby church of Aldbury,[73] suggesting that the choir was demolished at about this time.

A house of Ashridge's size, however, must have continued to have had a chapel and it is possible that it was moved to the ground floor of the former monastic nave below the domestic apartments on its first floor, which would explain the otherwise puzzling reference to the church in James I's grant of the site to Sir Thomas Egerton in 1604.[74] As part of his remodelling of the house, Egerton built a new chapel, which from Gough's late 18th-century account of the house appears to have adjoined the great hall.[75] A

---

[65] Eric Mercer, *English Art, 1553-1625* (1962), 14.

[66] P.R.O., C 142/189/86.

[67] *Cal. Pat. R., Philip & Mary, 1557-8*, 243.

[68] H.R.O., IV. A. 25.

[69] Shrimpton, op. et loc. cit. (note 33).

[70] Ibid.

[71] *Cal. Pat. R., Ed. VI*, iv, 5.

[72] Doggett (1991), 50.

[73] See Appendix (Ashridge).

[74] Bodl., MS. Willis 102, fol.15v; 40, fols.139-40.

[75] Bodl., Gough Herts. 18; MS. account in annotated copy of Salmon's *History of Hertfordshire*, belonging to Richard Gough, between pp.134-8 of published volume.

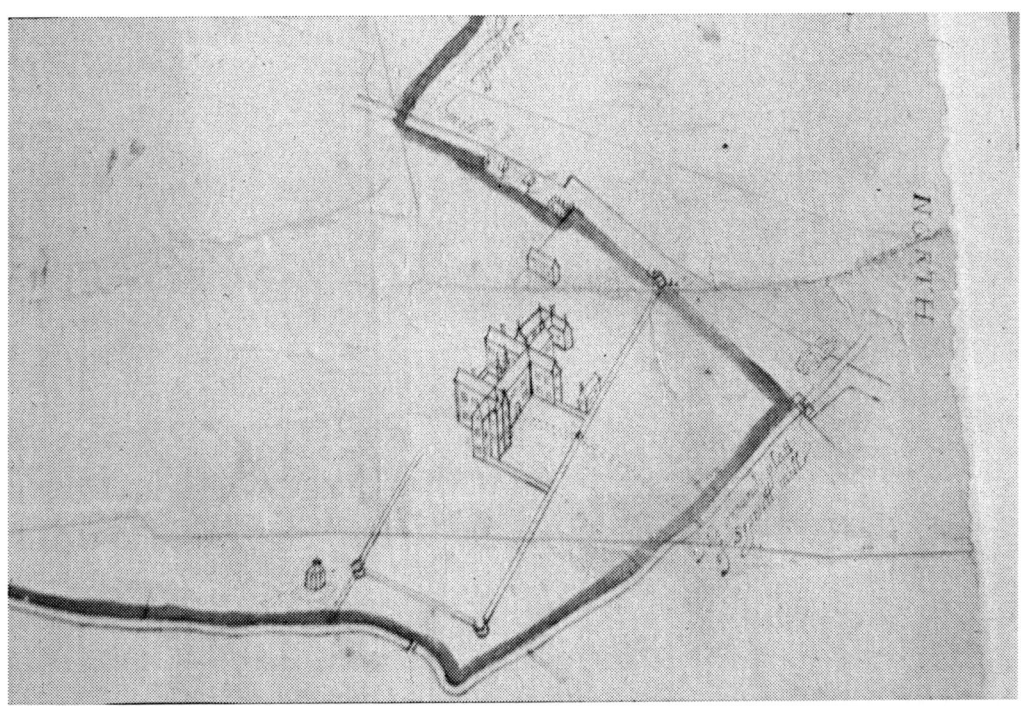

18. Sopwell Nunnery, estate map with birdseye perspective view of house. Map by M. Pierce, c.1600; H.R.O., IV. A. 25.

further chapel was built on the south side of the cloister in 1699, thus returning the wheel full circle.[76]

Egerton's rebuilding of Ashridge was so comprehensive that it tends to overshadow the work carried out by the Cheyney family between 1575 and 1602. It is therefore worth remembering Norden's statement that "this place is lately beautified by the Lord Cheyney", although to precisely what this refers is unknown. Egerton's building activity was largely concentrated between 1604 and 1607, the relative speed with which it was carried out suggesting that it was essentially a remodelling and refurbishment of existing fabric. Some additions were made, however, including the lower Dutch-gabled ranges flanking the great hall and the many two-storey canted bay projections on the south side of the house. While it is conceivable that the so-called White Lodge was a rebuilding of the former monastic gatehouse, both it and its companion Red Lodge are more likely to have been built at this time, along with the large outer court to which the White Lodge formed the entrance. **(Fig. 19)**

As with those sites examined in Chapter 2, structures from the full range of former monastic buildings were selected for re-use at the sites considered above. It is perhaps significant, however, that less attention appears to have been paid to the monastic plan at these higher status sites. Indeed, at Beechwood, Cheshunt and Markyate it seems likely that, even in the first period of post-Dissolution

activity, the monastic buildings were abandoned and used as no more than a convenient building quarry for the new houses erected nearby. In the first phase at Wymondley, the claustral ranges appear to have been retained with the western part of the nave of the monastic church converted into the hall of the new house. At Sopwell too the claustral plan was followed, with the nave and tower of the nunnery church being transformed into the hall of Lee's first house, although here the archaeological evidence suggests that the walls were rebuilt on their old foundations rather than that the monastic buildings themselves were converted. At both sites, however, the cloister was abandoned in the second phase, at Sopwell being replaced with a larger and fashionable double-courtyard plan and at Wymondley apparently being demolished as the house declined in importance.

At Ashridge the cloister was re-used in both the first and the second post-Dissolution mansions. Here the refectory was converted into the great hall, with the nave and tower of the church, along with the east and west claustral ranges, being transformed into domestic apartments. The external elevation of the refectory overlooked a large outer court, which is more likely to have been created after the Dissolution rather than to have served as the outer precinct of the monastery. Various alterations to the refectory, which was now entered through a porch leading to a screens-passage at the lower end, included the addition of projecting ranges with prominent bay windows at each end. These enabled the building to present the outward appearance of a hall with symmetrical cross-wings in the fashionable H-plan. Internally, the refectory/hall overlooked the former monastic cloister, which now

---

[76] Todd, op. cit. (note 40), 67.

19. Ashridge, north front of house (top) and north front of gatehouse- 'The White Lodge' (bottom). Pen and coloured ink drawings by H.G. Oldfield, 1802; H.R.O., Oldfield Drawings, III, 186.

The earliest re-used building among the higher status sites was the church at Wymondley, which from its trussed rafter roof, lancet windows and west processional doorway can be dated to no later than c.1250. Documentary sources suggest that the claustral ranges retained by Nedeham in his conversion of the 1540s had been extensively remodelled in the 15th century with further repairs in the 1520s and '30s. The church and much of the claustral ranges at Sopwell appear from archaeological evidence to have been built in the 14th century with further remodelling in the 15th century. At Ashridge the lancet windows and the surviving vaulted undercroft of the refectory suggest that it was built in the late 13th or early 14th century, while it appears that the majority of the other claustral buildings were reconstructed during the 15th century.

Far less certainty attaches to the date of the buildings at Beechwood, Cheshunt and Markyate, but as none of them appears to have been converted to secular use after the Dissolution, this is perhaps not directly relevant. Nevertheless, the stray finds of stonework fragments at Cheshunt suggest the former presence of a major 13th-century ecclesiastical building, while at Markyate the discovery in 1805 of what was probably the east end of the church or chapter house, along with various pieces of stonework, shows that considerable work was carried out on the church in the 13th century. Part of a late 12th-century capital was also found at Markyate in 1805 and although its precise context is unknown, it too may have come from the church. The discovery of these stray finds does not, of course, mean that further work was not undertaken on the church in the Later Middle Ages and the age of the claustral buildings remains unknown.

It now remains to examine what is known of the lives and careers of those who adapted to new uses the former monastic buildings considered in this chapter. Unlike some of those discussed in the previous chapter, all the new lay owners referred to here had the authority and resources to do what they wished with their new properties. This is reflected in two principal ways. First, these men (for with the exception of Elizabeth they were all men) do not appear to have felt constrained by the fabric or the lay-out of the buildings which they acquired. This is expressed in the most obvious way at Beechwood, Cheshunt and Markyate where the old monastic buildings were unceremoniously swept away and replaced by new houses on or near the sites. At Sopwell, Lee retained the claustral plan only while it suited him and even in the first building phase it appears that the monastic buildings were effectively demolished and their walls rebuilt on the old foundations. Lee also displayed his disregard for the medieval buildings and also his status and ambition by transforming the church itself into the hall of his new house.

Such motives may also have inspired Nedeham to make the western part of the church at Wymondley the hall of his

became the inner courtyard of the new house. As shown above, these conversion works probably took place as early as the 1540s or '50s, the former claustral walks, which may always have been integral in the east and west ranges, being raised in height to form corridor galleries around the courtyard, in what must be regarded for its date as a remarkably innovative design, **(Fig. 20)** paralleled in other major monastic conversions such as Newstead and Lacock. That the cloister remained to be incorporated in the successive remodellings which took place until all was destroyed by Wyatt in the early 19th century was probably due to its substantial proportions, its description by Thomas Baskerville in 1682 as "a fine cloister remarkable...for having in paint upon the walls some scripture and monkish stories" paying tribute to its qualities.[77]

---

[77] Portland MS. II, *Historical Manuscripts Commission*, 13th Rep. App., pt.2 (1893), 306.

20. Ashridge, the cloister looking north with great hall beyond. Watercolour by unknown artist, 1788; H.R.O., D/ECl/Z8/181b.

new home and here it is likely that the good condition and recent date of the claustral ranges ensured their survival. At Ashridge Elizabeth and her successors, the Cheyneys and the Egertons, clearly had the means to demolish the monastic buildings should they have wished to do so and the fact that they did not is adequate testimony to the high quality of the medieval buildings, which is further brought out by the relatively few structural changes made after the initial conversion in the 1540s and early '50s.

The early date of the conversions discussed in this chapter is in marked contrast to the urban and lower status sites considered earlier. The evidence at Beechwood, Cheshunt and Markyate is not particularly good, but at all three places we can be reasonably confident that the new houses built from the materials of these former nunneries were erected within a decade of the Dissolution. At Beechwood, although it seems likely that the principal conversion was carried out by Sir Richard Page after 1538, it is quite possible that some work had been carried out by Sir John Tregonwell before him. This is suggested partly by the pains that Tregonwell took before the Dissolution to secure the property and also his extreme reluctance to relinquish the house to Page.[78] It is said that Tregonwell, who had been made a privy councillor by 1532 and who took an

active role in the suppression of many monasteries, especially in the south and west, sometimes complained about the lack of reward he received for his services. Nevertheless, his acquisition of Milton Abbey (Dorset) in 1540 must have proved more than adequate compensation for the loss of Beechwood and there, of course, he was able to embark on a major conversion project.[79]

Page's career was less distinguished than Tregonwell's and at the time of Anne Boleyn's execution he was imprisoned in the Tower. Later, however, he was made a privy councillor and lieutenant of the band of gentlemen pensioners. He attended the christening of Prince Edward in October 1537 and the reception for Anne of Cleves at Greenwich in January 1540 and, if Chauncy is to be believed, he was sufficiently favoured by the crown for the prince to stay at Beechwood "for some time" during his bouts of childhood sickness.[80]

Anthony Denny was one of the most prominent men of his generation and his career is well-enough known for no more than a brief outline to be given here. Denny came from a long-established Hertfordshire family and was born at Cheshunt in 1500. After early service as a diplomat

---

[78] *L.P.*, xi, nos.1390, 1391; xiii (2), no.74.

[79] *L.P.*, xv, g.282 (90); Howard, 203.
[80] Chauncy, ii, 514.

under Sir Francis Bryan, he attracted the attention of the king and his early appointments at court included those of groom of the privy chamber and yeoman of the royal wardrobe. Knighted after the Boulogne campaign of 1544, he succeeded in building up a vast landed estate on the spoils of the monasteries, including St Albans and Waltham. An ardent convert to Protestantism, Denny was instrumental in furthering the Reformation and the story of how he had the courage to warn Henry on his death-bed of his imminent end and the need to repent of his sins is proof of the high esteem in which the king held him. Appointed as an executor to Henry's will, he served as a privy councillor and before his death in 1549 as member for Hertfordshire in Edward VI's first parliament.[81]

Relatively little is known of Denny's first son and heir, Henry, who sold Cheshunt Nunnery ten years before his death at the age of 34 in 1574, but his younger brother, Edward (1547-99), who bought back the property in 1590, held a number of important offices, including those of gentleman of the privy chamber to Elizabeth and governor of Kerry and Desmond in Ireland. He was also member of parliament for Liskeard and later for Tregony in Cornwall.[82]

Little is known of Humphrey Bourchier who began the conversion works at Markyate but who died, childless, in 1540 with his work on the house "nothing endid". He was a member of the king's household, although what position he held is unknown. Otherwise, we simply have Leland's description of him as the "base" (illegitimate) son of the second Lord Berners, who had translated Froissart's *Chronicles* and was deputy of Calais until his death in 1533.[83] Bourchier's widow, Elizabeth, married George Ferrers in 1541, although it was not until 1548 that he obtained the grant of the site. Ferrers was from a Hertfordshire family and as a lawyer renowned for his oratory came to prominence in 1534 for his publication of an English translation of Magna Carta. In 1542 he was returned as M.P. for Plymouth and although he is said to have taken part in the war against France, his most likely role was as a legal advisor to the king, for which he was rewarded with a bequest of 100 marks in Henry's will. Ferrers, who received the grant of several other ex-monastic properties, continued to serve the crown after Henry's death, helping to suppress Wyatt's rebellion in 1554. In 1567 he became escheator for Hertfordshire and Essex and died in 1579, Markyate remaining with his family until the mid-17th century.[84]

The life and career of James Nedeham, granted Wymondley Priory in 1537, are well documented and only a brief outline is necessary here. The son of a London carpenter, Nedeham was an apprentice and then warden of the London Carpenters' Company, serving with the king's army in France in the 1520s. He later worked for Wolsey and then for the king at York Place, Westminster and following his appointment as chief master carpenter in 1531 and then surveyor of the king's works in 1532, at the Tower of London, Hampton Court, St Augustine's, Canterbury and various coastal forts, among other places. He was also involved in the demolition and conversion of Dartford Priory and Chertsey Abbey and the recycling of materials from the religious houses of Barking and Merton for the royal palaces at Greenwich and Nonsuch, all projects which would have provided useful experience for his work at Wymondley. Nedeham died in September 1544 while on Henry VIII's Boulogne campaign and was buried there.

Although considered a gentleman, Nedeham had a practical knowledge of the building trade, particularly of carpentry, and it may have been partly this, as well as his rapid rise to prominence, which made him enemies among the long-established clerics of the civil service. On several occasions he was accused of financial mismanagement, but nothing was ever proved against him and the charges failed to dent his reputation as a pushing and able administrator.[85]

Virtually nothing is known of Nedeham's son, John, who inherited Wymondley on his father's death and apparently continued to live there until his own death at the age of 70 in 1591, and we have no way of telling whether it was he or his son, George (1557-1626), who made the late 16th-century additions and alterations to the priory.

Nedeham's successor as surveyor of the king's works, Richard Lee, was born in c.1513 of a Hertfordshire family and it is likely that both his father and grandfather were masons. He first came to prominence in the king's army at Calais and from 1536 to 1542 he was surveyor and paymaster of the fortifications there. In 1538 he advised Thomas Wriothesley on the conversion of Titchfield and in 1544 he was inspecting and advising on royal fortifications in the north, being present at the attack on Edinburgh in the spring of that year. This led to his knighthood in October 1544, at about which time he became surveyor of the king's works.

Lee's passage into the ranks of the elite was certainly aided by his marriage to Margaret, daughter of Sir Richard Grenville who had been with him at Calais, and his own ambitious and forceful personality. In early 1545 he was responsible for the restoration of the defences at Calais and Boulogne, but after 1547 when he accompanied Protector Somerset in his campaign against the Scots, he resigned the post and withdrew from public life for nearly a decade, during which time he built the first house at Sopwell. In 1557, however, Lee returned to royal service and was heavily involved for the next few years in the refortification

[81] Denny, op. cit. (note 14), 197-216.
[82] H.L.L. Denny, 'Biography of Sir Edward Denny', *Trans. East Herts. Arch. Soc.*, 2 (1904), 247-60.
[83] *D.N.B.*, ii, 920-2.
[84] S.T. Bindoff (ed.), *The History of Parliament: the House of Commons, 1509-1558*, ii (1982), 129-31.
[85] Harvey, op. cit. (note 34), 210-13; *King's Works*, iii, 10-14.

of Berwick and the Scottish border. In 1560 he prepared plans for Upnor Castle (Kent) and was again involved in works at Berwick. In 1562 Cecil sent Lee to Dieppe and Le Havre and he remained in demand for his work as a military engineer almost until the end of his life, the earl of Essex requesting that he should build a fort near Belfast as late as 1573. Lee died in 1575.[86]

Relatively little is known of Henry, Lord Cheyney who was in his mid-thirties when he acquired Ashridge after it finally left royal ownership in 1575. He had been commissioner of the peace in Kent, where he was a prominent landowner, in 1564 and 1569, a commissioner for enforcing the Act of Uniformity in the dioceses of Lincoln and Peterborough in 1571 and in 1573 he was made Sheriff of Kent.[87] Although Cheyney died in 1587 his family continued to own Ashridge until 1602 when it passed, through various agents, to Sir Thomas Egerton. Already in his sixties when he bought Ashridge, Egerton was one of the most distinguished political figures of his day, having served as M.P. for his native Cheshire between 1584 and 1587 and being made Attorney-General in 1592. Two years later he was knighted and appointed Master of the Rolls, becoming in 1596 Lord Keeper of the Seal. Shortly after his accession in 1603 James I made Egerton Lord Chancellor, a post he was to hold until his death in 1617.[88]

A number of shared characteristics appear to link the men who acquired the higher status former monastic properties in the first generation after the Dissolution. Of those whose ages are known, all were relatively young, with Tregonwell at the age of 39 being the second oldest recorded recipient of a former monastic property in Hertfordshire at this period, Sir John Daunce referred to in the last chapter being in his fifties when he acquired St Margaret's, Nettleden in 1538. Anthony Denny, Ferrers and Lee were from local families, Denny and Lee having close connections before the Dissolution with the houses which they were to be granted. James Nedeham too was involved with Wymondley before its suppression and it is not surprising that with the added advantage of their prominent positions in the king's service, such men were able to secure the properties they most desired. That an important office at court, a foreknowledge or even an active role in the Dissolution did not always bring a man what he sought is, however, demonstrated by the failure of Bourchier to buy Markyate or of Tregonwell to retain the lease of Beechwood and serve as a reminder that all was ultimately in the gift of the king.

The crown's usual method of disposing of former monastic property in the years immediately after the Dissolution was by lease. Leases were usually for a period of 21 years, although later, especially after 1550, the number of years'

purchase was often increased to 30 or more.[89] Very few outright gifts of monastic sites were made and none is recorded in Hertfordshire. Unlike some of the leases of the lower status sites considered in the previous chapter, the lease rather than a sale of a site does not seem to have acted as a disincentive to conversion or other building work. At Beechwood and Markyate, the fact that the properties were initially leased rather than sold to their grantees did not prevent an apparently immediate start on building work, while at Wymondley there is nothing to show that it was the transfer from a lease to ownership of the property in 1538 that prompted Nedeham to begin conversion works, although the possibility cannot, of course, be ruled out.

Indeed, whether the grantees were lessees or owners of the property, the real key to major conversion works, as at the lower status sites, was a long period of occupation by an individual or family and the degree of security the grantee felt in his new home. Thus, while work could begin immediately a site was granted to a new lay occupant, as at Beechwood and Markyate, it could be a number of years in a case like Sopwell before conversion works began in earnest. At Ashridge, circumstances were different again, its retention in royal ownership leading to the creation of a house of the first rank in the 1540s and early '50s, followed by a period of abandonment and partial neglect from the mid-'50s to 1575, during which time it was let to a series of tenants, followed by a period of renewed investment and rebuilding, first under the Cheyneys and then from 1604 under the Egertons.

---

[86] See note 34.
[87] *Cal. Pat. R., 1560-3*, 149; P.R.O., C 66/998/125; C 66/1073/1894; C 66/1077/2161; *Cal. S.P. Dom., 1547-80*, 471.
[88] *D.N.B.*, vi, 579-81.

---

[89] Joyce Youings, *Sixteenth-Century England* (1984), 161-2. See also Helen Miller, *Henry VIII and the English Nobility* (1986), ch.7.

Chapter Four

The conversion of monastic buildings: blind alley or wasted opportunity?

It has frequently been stated that the claustral buildings of a former monastery would most easily lend themselves to re-use.[1] Structures such as the dormitory, refectory, kitchen, lay brothers' quarters or guest range were all of domestic character and function and could be adapted with the minimum of difficulty to secular residential use after the Dissolution. This could involve little structural alteration to the fabric and in the case of some buildings, such as the kitchen, the transition from monastic to lay ownership could in theory involve no changes to the building at all. Similarly, the large open space and internal volume of the refectory, whether open to the roof from ground or first floor, was well suited to a new use as the great hall of a secular mansion, as at Ashridge, Cleeve (Somerset) or Horsham St Faith in Norfolk.[2]

In cases where more than one of these buildings was situated in the claustral ranges and the physical condition of the buildings was good enough to encourage re-use, this could lead to the retention of the claustral lay-out in a new courtyard-plan house. The recycling of these buildings would be even more likely to occur where they had been constructed or rebuilt in the century preceding the Dissolution. While refectories or kitchens erected in the 13th or 14th centuries would usually be obsolete or their fabric in desperate need of repair by the 1530s, buildings post-dating 1400 could often be expected to meet many of the stylistic fashions and functional requirements still evident in such buildings in the first part of the 16th century and, because of their more recent date, they would be likely to be in better condition than their earlier counterparts.

Although the Hertfordshire sample contains no certain examples, superiors' lodgings were frequently situated in the cloister and were often prime candidates for re-use. Not only were they entirely domestic in character but, as a result of the status of their former occupants, they could be expected to provide more lavish accommodation and a higher standard of privacy and comfort than other claustral buildings. Furthermore, many superiors' lodgings were of very recent date. "As the life-style of an abbot had become increasingly secularized",[3] so monastic communities had spent an ever growing proportion of their income on the

domestic quarters of their heads. The Benedictines of Milton Abbas (Dorset) and Muchelney (Somerset) built new abbots' lodgings in the years around 1500,[4] while among the other orders the Augustinian houses of Notley (Bucks.) and St Osyth (Essex) and the Cistercian abbeys of Cleeve, Forde and Fountains provide some of the best examples of this practice.[5] Equally sumptuous was Abbot King's remodelling of the superior's lodgings at Thame (Oxon.) in the 1530s, further evidence (if any were needed) that Bernard of Clairvaux's directives had been largely forgotten by Cistercian abbots of the 16th century. King's work included a new three-storey tower containing chambers with linenfold-panelled walls and fashionable Renaissance plasterwork. **(Fig. 21)** It is no surprise then to find that with very little modification these lodgings formed the nucleus of the post-Dissolution house of Thame Park.[6]

21. Thame Park (Oxfordshire), Renaissance panelling and plasterwork in abbot's parlour. Photograph by N. Doggett, August 1997.

---

[1] See, for example, the statement made by Coppack (1990), 137 that "Cloister ranges might easily be converted into a house for the new owner with little effort".
[2] Appendix (Ashridge); R. Gilyard-Beer, H.M.S.O. guide to *Cleeve Abbey* (1959); Nikolaus Pevsner, *North-East Norfolk and Norwich* (1962), 172; David Sherlock, 'Discoveries at Horsham St Faith Priory, 1970-73', *Norfolk Arch.*, 36 (1976), 202-23.
[3] Platt (1984), 210.

[4] Ibid, 210-11.
[5] The relatively little-known site of Notley is described in W.A. Pantin's 'Notley Abbey', *Oxoniensia*, 6 (1941), 36-41.
[6] Walter Godfrey, 'The abbot's parlour, Thame Park', *Arch. Jnl.*, 86 (1929), 59-68; Jennifer Sherwood & Nikolaus Pevsner, *Oxfordshire* (1974), 809-11; *V.C.H., Oxon.*, vii (1962), 168-70, 177; a recent study of the building by the R.C.H.M. has yet to be published.

Whether the superior's lodgings formed an integral part of the cloister as at Norton (Cheshire), were totally divorced from it as at Much Wenlock (Shropshire) or as possibly appears to have been the case at Hertford,[7] or only tenuously linked in cases like The Biggin in Hitchin, Battle, Castle Acre (Norfolk) or Canterbury Cathedral Priory,[8] they could provide an enormous incentive for re-use and it is certainly no coincidence that at all these sites extensive remodelling had taken place shortly before the Dissolution.

Although it was usually one or more of the claustral buildings which were most likely to be converted to domestic use after the Dissolution, other buildings could be adapted in this way. Thus it was the gatehouses at King's Langley, Beaulieu (Hants.), Bolton Priory (Yorks.), Bromfield (Shropshire), Montacute and Hinton in Somerset and Maxstoke (Warwicks.) which formed the basis for the post-suppression conversion schemes at these sites, while the gatehouse from Ramsey in Huntingdonshire was dismantled and re-erected at nearby Hinchingbroke (itself a former monastic site) in c.1600.[9] In towns, however, while the Hertfordshire sample provides no examples, the gatehouse, which so often had provided a very real defence for the monastic community against its secular neighbours, was more likely to find a civic use. For instance, the gatehouse at St Albans became the sessions house and those at Bury St Edmunds (Suffolk) were put to a variety of uses, only the Norman gate tower remaining in ecclesiastical use after the Dissolution as the bell tower of the adjoining Church of St James.[10]

In other instances where great courtyard houses emerged from monastic fabric, it may appear surprising that the monastic gatehouse did not survive more often as the gatehouse to the new house. There are, of course, cases like Battle, Michelham (Sussex) and St Osyth's where this did occur,[11] but these usually belong to the 1540s and 1550s and by the later Elizabethan period there was a tendency for gatehouses to be broader and lower in keeping with the classical form, as at Burton Agnes in Yorkshire and Charlecote (Warwicks.).[12] This meant that the tall and ostentatious, if sometimes forbidding, medieval gatehouse with its emphasis on display but which so often concealed the buildings behind from view, was not considered appropriate in a context such as Ashridge where views through to the house beyond were positively encouraged.

While the frequency with which individual claustral buildings were converted to residential use cannot be doubted, it should not be assumed that the process was always straightforward. Although as long ago as 1968 Dickinson estimated that well over half of the houses of Augustinian canons were converted wholly or in part to domestic use and that in the majority of cases this involved the claustral buildings,[13] the Augustinian order as yet remains the only one to be studied at all systematically, and even in this case, as Dickinson himself admitted, the treatment was far from exhaustive.

What is clear, however, is that it was unusual for complete claustral ranges to be retained in residential conversions. This can be explained in a number of ways. First, in the majority of cases the various ranges of the cloister were of different dates and were not usually directly linked to each other, having different floor and eaves levels. Second, as Howard has pointed out "in the conventional courtyard house, such as Compton Wynyates (Warwicks.), the entrance range faced the largest ground-floor space, the hall, across the court, but in the monastery the western, entrance range faced the subdivided chapter-house range".[14] This meant that the claustral range which most readily lent itself for conversion to the hall of a secular house, the raised frater, would lose some of its potential attraction by its usual position at right-angles to the monastic entrance range, making it unlikely that both ranges would be retained in a conversion to a courtyard house of the first order. In the case of the earlier Cistercian houses where the refectory had characteristically been built on a north-south axis to the south of the south range, the relationship to the western entrance range would be equally inconvenient, as is shown at Netley where it was demolished as part of the post-Dissolution conversion.[15]

In practice, of course, where there were overwhelming reasons to convert the frater into the hall of a new mansion this might simply lead to the abandonment of the old monastic entrance range and the creation of a new entrance range on the site of the church to face the hall. This is well illustrated at Titchfield where it seems that Wriothesley may well have had in mind the contemporary advice of

---

[7] Patrick Greene, *Norton Priory* (1989), 144-5; *V.C.H., Shropshire*, ii (1973), 46; the prior's lodging at Much Wenlock has recently been redated through dendrochronology to c. 1420, Paul Stamper, pers. comm. Appendix (Hertford).

[8] Appendix (The Biggin); Platt (1984), 158-64.

[9] Appendix (King's Langley); *V.C.H., Hants.*, iv (1911), 652; Nikolaus Pevsner & David Lloyd, *Hampshire and the Isle of Wight* (1967), 96-7 (Beaulieu); A. Hamilton Thompson, *History and Architectural Description of the Priory of St Mary, Bolton-in-Wharfedale*, Publications of the Thoresby Soc., 30 (1928), 174-8 (Bolton); *V.C.H., Shropshire*, ii (1973), 29 (Bromfield); N. Pevsner, *North Somerset and Bristol* (1958), 204-6 (Montacute); Philip C. Fletcher, 'Recent excavations at Hinton Priory', *Proc. Somerset Arch. and Nat. Hist. Soc.*, 96 (1951), 160-5 (Hinton); *V.C.H., Warwicks.*, iv (1947), 136-7 (Maxstoke); N. Pevsner, *Bedfordshire and the County of Huntingdon and Peterborough* (1968), 264, 332 (Hinchingbroke).

[10] Doggett (1991), 57; P.L. Drewett & I.W. Stuart, 'Excavations in the Norman gate tower, Bury St Edmunds Abbey', *Proc. Suffolk. Inst. Arch.*, 33 (1973-5), 241-52.

[11] Ian Nairn & Nikolaus Pevsner, *Sussex* (1965), 404 (Battle) and 568-9 (Michelham); Howard (1987), 205 (St Osyth's).

[12] Nikolaus Pevsner, *Yorkshire: York and the East Riding* (1972), 207 (Burton Agnes); N. Pevsner & Alexandra Wedgwood, *Warwickshire* (1966), 227; Geoffrey Tyack, *Warwickshire Country Houses* (1994), 42-7.

[13] J.C. Dickinson, 'The buildings of the English Austin canons after the Dissolution of the Monasteries', *Jnl. Brit. Arch. Assoc.*, 3rd. Ser., 31 (1968), 64.

[14] Howard (1987), 145.

[15] John Hare, 'Netley Abbey: monastery, mansion and ruin', *Proc. Hants. Field Club*, 49 (1993), 218.

Andrew Boorde, who in his *A Compendyous Regyment or a Dyetary of Health* (1542) wrote "Then devyde the lodgynges by the cyrcuyte of the quadryuyall courte, and let the gate-howse be opposyt or against the hall-dore (not dyrectly) but the hall-dore standynge a base, and the gate-howse in the mydle of the front entrynge in to the place."[16] A plan of precisely this sort also appears to have been created at Ashridge, although here a new courtyard and gatehouse were laid out to the north of the former frater.

In terms of its position with regard to the entrance range, the dormitory might emerge as a strong contender for re-use as the hall of a new house, but although there are instances of this happening as at the Premonstratensian monastery of Egglestone in Yorkshire, the Augustinian house of Launde (Leics.) or in rather different contexts at St Helen's, Bishopsgate in London where Thomas Kendall bought the east claustral range on behalf of the Leathersellers' Company in 1544, or at Whitefriars, Coventry,[17] the dormitory's chances of retention in this way were often blighted by its being placed "inconveniently upstairs and off-centre, stretching beyond the square of the cloister itself",[18] and there are no examples of the east range being re-used as a great hall in the Hertfordshire sample.

Where the east range was retained in the post-Dissolution house it was usually as part of the conversion of the whole cloister as at Ashridge, Sopwell and Wymondley or, outside the county, at places like Lacock and Newstead, in all of which cases it appears to have been used as domestic apartments. At the urban Hertfordshire sites of The Biggin and Hitchin Priory, the function of the retained east range is unclear, but at the former its narrow width suggests that it served chiefly as a corridor gallery linking the first-floor apartments of the north and south ranges.

Another factor which worked against the retention of the east range was the likelihood that, as it contained two of the buildings most essential to monastic life- the dormitory and the chapter house, it would have been partially demolished at the suppression or at least "defaced" by the king's commissioners to prevent the possibility of the monks returning.[19] This may well account for the disappearance of the east range at many sites, including Ware, where the east range was demolished, although the

south and part of the west ranges were retained in the 16th-century house.

It is therefore the case that while "it might seem that adapting the four basic ranges of a cloister into a house would be relatively straightforward",[20] there were often considerable difficulties in retaining the whole of the claustral ranges in conversions to courtyard houses. In this respect the Hertfordshire sample appears to be far from typical, with examples of such conversions from the highest rank at Ashridge, Sopwell and Wymondley to those of a slightly lower social level at The Biggin and Hitchin Priory. It is almost certain that in the relatively rare cases where this did occur elsewhere, as at Lacock or the first post-Dissolution phase of Walden Abbey (Audley End), and apparently at Mottisfont,[21] this was due to the unusually good condition of the claustral ranges, and this also seems to be the case with the Hertfordshire examples.

In the Hertfordshire sample, the cloisters of Ashridge, Wymondley, The Biggin and Hitchin Priory were all rebuilt in the 15th century, while at Mottisfont and Walden the satisfactory state of the cloisters probably owed much to the fact that they too had been rebuilt in the 15th century, which is almost certainly the reason why they were left intact at the suppression. At Lacock there was already a passage at upper level on the south side of the cloister connecting the former abbess's chapel in the west range with the dorter in the east range. This somewhat unusual feature probably encouraged the new lay owner, Sir William Sharington, to retain all of the cloister and to build new connecting corridors on the upper floors of the east and north ranges.[22]

Similar situations may have existed at Ashridge and Hitchin Priory where the claustral walks were retained in the mid-16th century conversions. The evidence is less clear at Wymondley, while at The Biggin the west claustral walk appears to have been replaced by a timber Tuscan colonnade. At Sopwell, where most of the cloister seems to have been no later than 14th century in date and was therefore perhaps somewhat old-fashioned if not dilapidated by the time of the Dissolution, its age may have been a contributory factor in the decision to demolish and rebuild it on the old foundations. This can be contrasted with Newstead where, although much of the cloister dated to the early 13th century with the west range possibly having been remodelled c.1300,[23] Sir John Byron was not

[16] Andrew Boorde, *A Compendyous Regyment or a Dyetary of Health* (1542), ed. by F.J. Furnivall and printed in *Early English Text Ser., Extra Ser.*, x (1870), 238.
[17] J.F. Hodgson, 'Eggleston Abbey', *Yorks. Arch. Jnl.*, 18 (1904-5), 154-7 (Egglestone); Dickinson, op. cit. (note 13), 68-9; Nikolaus Pevsner, *Leicestershire and Rutland* (2nd edn., revd. Elizabeth Williamson, 1984), 197-8 (Launde); John Schofield, 'Building in religious precincts in London at the Dissolution and after', in Roberta Gilchrist & Harold Mytum (eds.), *Recent Advances in Monastic Archaeology*, Brit. Arch. Reps., 227 (1993), 38 (St Helen's, Bishopsgate); Charmian Woodfield, 'Finds from the free grammar school at the Whitefriars, Coventry, c.1545-c.1557/8', *Post-Med. Arch.*, 15 (1981), 81-3.
[18] Howard (1987), 149.
[19] Dickinson, op. cit. (note 13), 72.

[20] Howard (1987), 149.
[21] See Howard (1987), 225-6 (footnotes 34 and 36) for references to Mottisfont and Lacock. The retention of the medieval cloister of Walden Abbey as the inner (and later only) courtyard of Audley End is graphically shown in plan form in Paul Drury's 'No other palace in the kingdom will compare with it: the evolution of Audley End, 1605-1745', *Archit. Hist.*, 23 (1980), 26.
[22] Nikolaus Pevsner, *Wiltshire* (2nd. edn., revd. Bridget Cherry, 1975), 284-9.
[23] Rosalys Coope, Eric Fernie & Maurice Howard, *Newstead Abbey. Papers and Discussion From a Day Symposium organised by the Society of Architectural Historians in association with the Thoroton Society*

deterred from retaining the whole of it as the nucleus of his new house. As at Lacock, access corridors were formed at first-floor level by building above the old claustral walks although, unlike Lacock, here they were rebuilt, possibly because of structural weakness. "It may well be that Newstead is the only example among converted monasteries where a double-storey cloister/corridor runs around the entire internal court, uninterrupted by a gatehouse, a hall bay window or some other feature."[24]

These examples of complete cloister conversions are not, of course, the only cases where this occurred, but although the relatively small Hertfordshire sample contains three high status examples- Ashridge, Sopwell and Wymondley- such conversions were perhaps more common at a slightly lower social level, as at The Biggin and Hitchin Priory in Hertfordshire and elsewhere at Hinchingbroke and Ivychurch (Wilts.), where all of the claustral ranges were initially retained in the post-Dissolution houses.[25]

Nevertheless, Ashridge, Lacock, Mottisfont and Newstead are particularly interesting. Unlike other places where the whole of the cloister was initially retained, such as Titchfield where Sir Thomas Wriothesley drove his celebrated gatehouse through the nave of the former church, Battle Abbey or Leez Priory (Essex), the retention of the claustral walks themselves is significant. All are early conversions, Leland's description of the house at Mottisfont as "onperfecte" suggesting that work had already stopped on the death of William, Lord Sandys in 1540,[26] while although Leland makes no mention of the work at Lacock in the description of his journey to the west country in 1542,[27] it is unlikely that Sharington would have waited much longer than this before starting the work of conversion there. Similarly, although Leland's reference to the ruins at Newstead in 1544 can be taken as an indication that conversion work had yet to begin in earnest,[28] the delay was probably only temporary and may have been attributable simply to uncertainty over the stability of the claustral walks. As we have seen in Chapter 3, Ashridge and probably Wymondley too were early conversions. Whatever the exact starting date on all these houses there can be no doubt that they were conversions of the first generation and were carried out by men of far more than local importance, several of whom had been involved in the suppression of the monasteries.

Like Wriothesley at Titchfield and Paulet at Netley, Sandys, Sharington and Byron knew exactly what they wanted from their new properties and their extensive

lobbying of the crown for their acquisition immediately before the Dissolution suggests that they already had a good idea how their architectural ambition could be achieved,[29] while the speed with which Nedeham set about the remodelling at Wymondley suggests that he too was similarly motivated. It is indeed unfortunate that the extensive correspondence relating to the transformation of Titchfield is the exception rather than the rule.

If instances of the total re-use of the claustral buildings are relatively rare, a number of explanations can be offered for this. Despite the Hertfordshire and other examples mentioned above, the small size of many cloisters was often a disincentive in conversions of the first rank and it is perhaps no surprise that even in some cases where the new house followed a courtyard plan as at Battle, the monastic cloister was relegated to being little more than a service court, while at Wilton it now appears that the courtyard plan of the mid 16th-century house may not have been based on the dimensions of the monastic cloister at all.[30]

In the case of friaries where cloisters were already particularly compact owing to the small size of the communities involved, the lack of claustral walks could prove a further disadvantage as the fact that the connecting walks were internal restricted the amount of space available on the ground floor. Nevertheless, as the Hertfordshire conversions of Ware and Hitchin Priory show, this was not an insurmountable difficulty as the principal accommodation of both friaries and their post-Dissolution successors was on the first floor.

The comparative infrequency with which claustral walks at houses of the regular orders were re-used intact or, as at Lacock or Newstead and possibly Ashridge and The Biggin, raised in height to form "corridor-galleries" may result from their commonly being roofed in lead which would usually have been removed by the royal commissioners before the transfer to lay ownership. Another explanation may be that, while connecting corridors or "cloisters" as they were contemporaneously known are by no means unknown in early Tudor houses like Cadhay (Devon) and Hengrave (Suffolk), they are heavily outnumbered by houses of courtyard plan where there are no corridors connecting the various ranges, examples including Compton Wynyates, Cotehele in

---

(April 1992). I am grateful to Maurice Howard for providing me with a copy of this unpublished document.

[24] Ibid.

[25] Nikolaus Pevsner, *Bedfordshire and the County of Huntingdon and Peterborough* (1968), 264; R.C.H.M., *Churches of South-East Wiltshire* (1987), 145-53.

[26] Howard (1987), 151.

[27] John Chandler, *John Leland's Itinerary, Travels in Tudor England* (1993), 490.

[28] Ibid., 354. See also note 23.

[29] For instance, in 1536 Sandys was writing to Cromwell from his "new house of Mottisfont which by your help I have of the king's late gift", *L.P.*, xi, no.241.

[30] John Hare, *Battle Abbey, The Eastern Range and the Excavations of 1978-80* (1985), 38-42. The view that the courtyard plan at Wilton may not follow the dimensions of the medieval cloister was advanced by Paul Drury in his paper 'The origins and development of some country houses converted from monastic buildings', delivered at the 1985 Oxford conference 'Dissolution and Resurrection, the Re-use of Monastic Buildings'. John Bold in *Wilton House and the Story of English Palladianism* (1988), 31 appears, however, to accept that the courtyard is based on the form of the monastic cloister. For Walden/Audley End, again see Paul Drury, 'Walden into Audley End' in S.R. Bassett (ed.), *Saffron Walden: Excavations and Research 1972-80*, C.B.A. Res. Rep., 45 (1982), 104.

22. Cotehele (Cornwall), courtyard showing chapel and hall range. Photograph by N. Doggett, August 1993.

Cornwall, **(Fig. 22)** Cowdray (Sussex), Ingatestone in Essex, Sutton Place (Surrey) and Temple Newsam (Yorks.).[31] As Howard has commented "It seems that no early Tudor courtyard house quite took the step of unifying an inner court by means of a continuous cloister until the conversions of the monasteries themselves sometimes dictated the preservation of the monastic arrangement".[32] For the reasons explained above, the circumstances in which this could take place were relatively uncommon and may have contributed to the failure of the connecting corridor or gallery to realise its full potential in Elizabethan architecture.

The extent to which claustral or indeed other buildings were re-used may be blurred by the accident of survival and the many rebuildings which have taken place since the Dissolution. This may seem an obvious point but it is worth remembering that many monastic conversions, such as Ashridge or Bermondsey Abbey, south of the Thames in London, are now recorded only through 19th-century or earlier drawings.[33] As explained in Chapter 1, this difficulty is even more acute with regard to monastic conversions than to other classes of medieval or 16th-century building, as post-Dissolution accretions have so often been removed in the desire to see a building returned to its "original" form.

The Hertfordshire sample is further evidence that the instances in which the monastic church was converted to residential use are far more frequent than has been commonly supposed. Earlier studies such as Copeland's work on Buckland tended to exaggerate the rarity of such conversions but more recently a number of examinations of individual buildings and Howard's general survey have shown that the re-use of the church was in fact relatively widespread. It has sometimes been suggested that the internal volume of the church with the whole structure open to the roof might deter domestic conversion but this would not necessarily be so where the nave or other part of the church was re-used as the great hall of a secular mansion as at Leez Priory or Netley.[34] In other cases like Buckland, **(Fig. 23)** Hinchingbroke and Mottisfont as well as Sopwell and Wymondley and possibly The Biggin and Hitchin Priory in Hertfordshire, where the nave was converted into a two-storey hall, it was relatively simple to insert a first floor and fireplaces to transform the building in this way. Similarly, at Ashridge where it appears that the former church was transformed into domestic apartments, the conversion was affected in much the same way. Certainly, the tendency to insert first floors and fireplaces into the open halls of secular buildings from the early 16th century onwards would have provided a precedent for similar work

---

[31] Howard (1987), 73-83.
[32] Ibid, 95.
[33] B.L., Add. MS. 24,432-3 (Bermondsey). For Ashridge see Appendix.

[34] *R.C.H.M., Essex*, ii (1921), 158-61 and David Crossley, *Post-Medieval Archaeology* (1990), 54-5 (Leez); Platt (1984), 240 and Hare, op. cit. (note 15), 217 (Netley). The process of converting the church into a house was also relatively common in Ireland: Roger Stalley, *The Cistercian Monasteries of Ireland* (1987), 228-34.

23. Buckland (Devon), general view from south-west showing converted nave. Photograph by N. Doggett, August 1993.

to churches and the technical problems posed by such an operation would have been easily overcome by the Tudor builder.

In many cases, however, the church, along with the dorter, chapter house, frater and other claustral buildings would have been "defaced" by the king's commissioners at the suppression. It is important to remember that the reason this was done was simply to render the buildings uninhabitable in order to prevent the monastic community from re-establishing itself. Although in some counties like Lincolnshire the destruction could be very thorough,[35] it was more usual for it to amount to no more than breaking the windows and removing the roof covering, especially if, as at King's Langley or Sopwell, it was of lead. The buildings would then be left to the vagaries of the weather and plunder by local people, who are likely to have viewed the abandoned structures as a convenient source of building materials.

In the event some were soon to mourn the passing of the monasteries- "it was never merie world since",[36] a trend which was to grow more noticeable by the end of the century, especially among antiquaries and other members of the intelligentsia, and certainly not one confined to those with Catholic sympathies. It was, of course, not only the

dispersal of monastic libraries and other treasures and the despoliation of the buildings themselves which were to be seen as a cause for regret, but also the disappearance from English life of the monastery as charitable and social institution. It seems to have been this that was uppermost in the mind of John Shrimpton of St Albans when he wrote in c.1610: "Howsoever these things were applyed and used by the papists, yet were they the gifts and religious offerings of devout men, and therefore ought to have been bestowed to the mentainance of learninge and releife of the poore, and not to mentaine the pride and prodigallity of those to whom both religion lerning and charity was wanting."[37] The interest of Shrimpton's contemporary, Sir John Oglander, in the monastic past was more overtly antiquarian in character, leading him to embark on an excavation of the once great Cistercian abbey of Quarr on the Isle of Wight when he inherited the property in 1607.[38] Weever and Fuller were by no means the first to criticise the destruction of former church property, and even actual contemporaries of the Dissolution such as Leland and John Bale seem not to have been unaware of the importance of what was being destroyed or looted.[39]

[35] David Knowles, *The Religious Orders in England*, iii (1959), 385.

[36] These are the words of Francis Trigge, a Lincolnshire cleric in 1589, quoted in A.G. Dickens (ed.), *Tudor Treatises*, Yorks. Arch. Soc. Rec. Ser., 125 (1959), 38.

[37] H.R.O., 66,296, John Shrimpton, *The Antiquities of Verulam and St Albans* (n.d.), 77.

[38] Stuart Piggott, *Ruins in a Landscape, Essays in Antiquarianism* (1976), 113.

[39] Margaret Aston, 'English ruins and English history: the Dissolution and the sense of the past', *Jnl. Warburg and Courtauld Institutes*, 36 (1973), 245-6.

Melancholic regret for what had gone or antiquarian interest in what remained would not, of course, have had such strong a grip on the less high-minded. Thus the remains of Repton Priory in Derbyshire were apparently speedily removed one Sunday in Mary's reign by one Gilbert Thacker, determined to "destroy the nest, for fear the birds should build therein again".[40] Equally typical of the unscrupulous or opportunistic man is the oft-quoted remark of Michael Sherbrook's father when questioned by his son as to why he had removed timber from the bell-frame of Roche Abbey in Yorkshire when he had held the monks in high esteem- "What should I do...might I not as well as others have some Profit of the Spoil of the Abbey? For I did see all would away; and therefore I did as others did".[41]

Despite the instructions to the king's commissioners that they were to "pull down to the ground all the walls of the churches, stepulls, cloysters, fraterys, dorters, chapter howsys" and the like,[42] the degree to which the "defacing" of the church and claustral buildings was official government policy is unclear and "as happened so often in Tudor affairs, there were certainly gaps of varying dimensions between central precept and local practice".[43] It is particularly likely that buildings would have been spared from major demolition works in cases like Beechwood, Markyate and Wymondley in Hertfordshire or Mottisfont and Titchfield in Hampshire where the site passed quickly from the crown to other hands, although even here the most valuable materials such as lead or the copper from the church's bells were excluded from the conditions of sale or lease and reserved to the king.

Although it is no longer fashionable to ascribe any reluctance to convert the monastic church itself into a house to any moral or religious objections and there is no evidence for this concern in Hertfordshire, such scruples did in fact exist. An example of this is provided by John Crayford's and Ronald Lathom's letter of January 1538 to Thomas Wriothesley's wife concerning the conversion of Titchfield, suggesting that no harm could come from the sale of "marble stones, aulters, ymages, tables etc." with the words- "Mres (Mistress) Wriothesley nor yo neither be not meticulous ne scrupulous to make sale of such holly (holy) thinge having ensample of a goode devoute bisshop of Rome called Alexander whos epitaphie ys writ after this sorte: *vendit Alexander cruces altaria Christi vendere jure potest/ emerat illius prius*".[44] Superstition of this sort is even more likely to have been prevalent among the workmen engaged in the physical process of demolition

and conversion. Again Titchfield provides the example, Wriothesley being advised in another letter that one of the carpenters "stayeth from his labour taking down the Churche of the Abbey because we wold be loth to adventure wyt hym before the change of the moon".[45] Nevertheless, instances such as this are likely to have been little more than an irritation to men like Wriothesley or Lee and Nedeham in Hertfordshire and certainly insufficient to thwart ambitious conversion plans.

The scale and type of work undertaken at an individual site was to a large extent conditioned by the ideas and aspirations of the new owner. At the Dissolution all former monastic sites passed into royal hands but the great majority were soon leased, sold or granted away. The precise details of this process are not directly relevant to this study, but in general the transfer from royal to lay ownership was remarkably quick and it has been estimated that by 1547 almost two-thirds of former monastic property had been alienated in this way. By 1558 this figure had risen to over 75% and the remaining lands were sold by Elizabeth and the early Stuarts.[46]

In the relatively few cases where the crown held on to former monastic property for any significant time, the resulting conversion works could be spectacular as at Ashridge, St Augustine's Abbey, Canterbury or Dartford Priory but they could also be low-key as at St Albans where only the Great Court and the stables remained with the crown after 1550, earlier plans for the conversion of the domestic buildings apparently having come to little or nothing.[47] From the Hertfordshire sample only Ashridge remained in royal hands for some time after the Dissolution, but in general the comparative lack of interest that the crown showed in converting monastic buildings which remained in its ownership may have stemmed from the fact that it had sufficient resources to build afresh rather than needing to adapt outmoded and inconvenient buildings to domestic use.

The same could equally have applied, however, to the first rank of royal favourites and other members of the nobility. Men such as Lee, Wriothesley, Paulet, Nedeham, Sandys, Sir Anthony Denny and Sir Richard Rich in the first generation, and Sir Nicholas Bacon, Sir Francis Willoughby, Sir Thomas Egerton and Sir John Thynne in the second, all had the means to build on virgin sites and indeed did so, but they all also converted monastic buildings or at least re-used materials from former monasteries to construct new houses. Furthermore, Sandys even abandoned his great house of The Vyne, finished only

---

[40] Thomas Fuller, *The Church History of England*, iii (ed., J.S. Brewer, 1845), 486.

[41] Quoted in Dickens, op. cit. (note 36), 125.

[42] Knowles, op. cit. (note 35), 384.

[43] Dickinson, op. cit. (note 13), 62.

[44] W.H. St John Hope, 'The making of Place House at Titchfield, near Southampton in 1538', *Arch. Jnl.*, 63 (1906), 235. One can only assume that Patrick Greene has not read St John Hope, when he writes of Titchfield "No feelings of sacrilege seem to have troubled Wriothesley" (Greene, 1992, 188). Certainly, they troubled his wife.

[45] St John Hope, op. cit., 236.

[46] John Guy, *Tudor England* (1988), 145.

[47] For the conversion works at these sites see Appendix (Ashridge); Simon Thurley, 'English Royal Palaces, 1450-1550', unpublished Ph.D. thesis (London, 1991), 247-57 (Dartford) and *King's Works*, iv, 59-63 and 240 (St Augustine's, Canterbury & St Albans respectively).

in the 1520s, in favour of Mottisfont as his principal residence.[48]

A potential trap when considering the residential conversion of former monastic buildings is to assume too readily that if a man was granted a site he would automatically wish to use at least some of the buildings for domestic purposes. As at St Margaret's, Nettleden, however, this may not always have been the case and frequently the grantee may simply have farmed the land and allowed the buildings to fall into decay or leased them to a local tenant who is likely to have done little or nothing to them. Thus two of the country's best-known monasteries, Rievaulx and Fountains, were effectively ignored by their new owners at the Dissolution, although many of the materials of the latter were re-used in the construction of nearby Fountains Hall by Sir Richard Proctor in the early 17th century.[49] Likewise, of the many sites acquired by men such as Sir Anthony Denny or Sir Richard Rich, at only a few were houses of the first rank created from their monastic predecessors. For every Buckland, Sopwell or Titchfield there are scores of monastic sites the buildings of which were abandoned or partially demolished and adapted to farming or, in fewer cases, industrial use, while in other instances like Beechwood or Markyate, new country houses were constructed close by, re-using materials from the former monastic buildings.

Another contributory factor to the late conversion of many monastic buildings below the highest social level was the time needed for the families involved to acquire sufficient resources to carry out major works of adaptive re-use. In many cases it was not financially possible to undertake major schemes until the often crippling mortgages with which the property had been purchased in the first place were paid off.[50] As is now commonly acknowledged, very few former monastic sites were given away by the crown and the great majority were sold or leased.[51] In the years immediately following the Dissolution leases were particularly common and although the Hertfordshire evidence at higher status sites like Beechwood and Markyate does not seem to support this idea, the insecurity of tenure that this provided, plus the fact that the ownership of the property concerned remained with the crown, may have proved a further disincentive to conversion. This certainly appears to have been so at St Margaret's, Nettleden, and it is unlikely to be coincidental that even at the highest social level there are many cases where conversion was postponed until leases had been superseded by purchase, Wymondley and Newstead being but two examples of this probably widespread practice.[52]

In other cases, conversion works were not carried out by the families of the original grantees but by succeeding owners, whose families were to own the site for many generations thereafter. Examples of this sort include Thame Park, where after a relatively brief time during which the property formed part of the endowments of the new diocese of Oxford, the original secular grantee, Lord Williams of Thame, seems to have done little to the buildings and it was left to the Wenmans, who bought the site in 1559, to carry out the first major phase of post-monastic work, the family continuing to own the property until early this century.[53] Similar patterns can be detected in the Hertfordshire sample at Hitchin Priory and elsewhere at Forde, St Osyth's Priory and Wroxton (Oxon.).[54] At Ashridge a change of ownership in the early 17th century led to a remodelling of the earlier conversion, while at Audley End this prompted a total reworking of the previous relatively modest conversion.[55] That it was not always a change in family which prompted major rebuilding work is shown, however, from the Hertfordshire evidence by examples like Markyate and Royston and from further afield by Elstow in Bedfordshire and Wilton. In some cases the original instigator of conversion works could remodel his own work, as did Lee at Sopwell and Sir John Thynne at Longleat.[56] More rarely a house could be reduced in size towards the end of the century, as seems to have happened at Wymondley.

It is not easy to explain why there are so many instances where ownership by the families of the original post-Dissolution grantees was short-lived. By the middle of the 17th century writers such as Fuller and Sir Henry Spelman were anxious to ascribe this to what they considered to be the sacrilegious treatment of monastic sites by new lay owners, attributing the misfortunes of various families to their involvement in the demolition and conversion of monastic buildings, while as early as c.1610 John Shrimpton was referring to "the impious sacraledg comitted at that time (the Dissolution) heaven lift not long unpunished, as by many examples I would declare were it not for giving offence to these these envious times".[57] Spelman, in particular, sought to prove a direct link between the secular use of former monasteries and the downfall of the families concerned,[58] a connection which C.F.S. Warren still felt obliged to make as late as 1898.[59]

---

[48] Howard (1987), 151.
[49] Airs (1975), 125; B.L., Harl. MS. 6853, fol.450.
[50] Airs (1975), 18.
[51] Guy, op. et loc. cit. (note 46).
[52] Appendix (Wymondley); Coope, Fernie & Howard, op. cit. (note 23) (Newstead).

[53] *V.C.H.*, op. et loc. cit. (note 6).
[54] Appendix (Hitchin Priory); *R.C.H.M., Dorset*, i (1952), 240-6 (Forde); Howard (1987), 205 (St Osyth's); Sherwood & Pevsner, op. cit. (note 9), 862 and *V.C.H., Oxon.*, ix (1969), 172-3 (Wroxton). Other examples of this pattern are given by Airs (1975), 19.
[55] For Ashridge see Appendix; Drury, op. cit. (note 30), 97 (Audley End).
[56] Appendix (Markyate and Royston); David Baker, 'Excavations at Elstow Abbey, 1965-66', *Beds. Arch. Jnl.*, 3 (1966), 29; Bold, op.cit. (note 30), 33 (Wilton); Appendix (Sopwell); Girouard (1983), Ch.1 (Longleat).
[57] Shrimpton, op. et loc. cit. (note 37).
[58] Sir Henry Spelman, *The History and Fate of Sacrilege*, 1632 (published posthumously in 1698), Ch.6.
[59] C.F.S. Warren (ed.), *An Appendix Bringing the Work The History and Fate of Sacrilege up to the Present Date* (1898), 347-8 where he relates

Such conclusions are clearly difficult to sympathise with today and there were, of course, many families which profited from the fall of the monasteries and whose fortunes continued to prosper for many years to follow. Nevertheless, as at The Biggin and King's Langley, there are many instances where former monastic property changed hands with sometimes bewildering frequency during the course of the 16th century.

It was once usual to ascribe rapid changes in ownership of former monastic property to speculation on the part of the new owners,[60] and the number of instances where exchanges took place between the crown and new owners and among the grantees themselves, particularly during the 1540s,[61] indicates that it would still be unwise to deny that this was a factor. It has now long been recognised, however, that brief periods of apparent ownership by otherwise unknown or relatively lowly men, as at Ashridge, The Biggin or Hitchin Priory, are more often a reflection of the activities of agents who were appointed by their clients to acquire and dispose of properties in an attempt to secure the most desirable sites or to build up compact landholdings.[62] Thus a number of individuals frequently appear in the records of the Court of Augmentations who, when also referred to in subsequent deeds of sale or exchange, are revealed to be agents acting for others. The search for the required property may therefore have contributed to a slight delay in the conversion process but it is unlikely to have been a major factor. Its effects would not have been felt much beyond the 1540s and would certainly have been over by the next boom in monastic conversions during the 1570s.

If the rapid turnover of owners after the Dissolution was a factor, however small, in delaying conversion works, the age of the owner at the time he obtained a site may also have played its part. Indeed, it may not be coincidental that, with the exception of Sir Thomas Egerton at Ashridge in the early 17th century, all those men from the Hertfordshire sample whose ages are known when they acquired and converted former monastic property were in fact relatively young. It is also conceivable that those who had been contemporaries of the religious or who had been encouraged by their elders to respect the monks may have been more reluctant than those of a later generation to transform monasteries into secular residences. Thus it might be left to the sons or grandsons of the original grantees to carry out the first major conversion works. That any lingering respect for the religious life was not shared by many of the original grantees is, however, made abundantly clear by the number of men, like Tregonwell at

Beechwood or Ingworth at King's Langley, who actively petitioned the crown for the grant of sites at the suppression, while others, such as Denny at Cheshunt and Hertford or Lee at Sopwell, used their pre-Dissolution involvement with particular monasteries to obtain possession at their closure.[63] This is a situation which is found outside Hertfordshire, especially at the top of the social scale in the cases of men like Charles Brandon, Thomas Howard and Edward Seymour, who all quickly used their positions to secure what they wanted.[64]

A frequently overlooked reason for the fact that often little was done to the buildings immediately after the Dissolution may simply be that the buildings themselves were in good condition at the time of suppression and needed little in the way of adaptation to make them suitable for secular residential use. This was, of course, particularly likely to be so where the new use was relatively low-key and did not call for radical modification of the buildings. This was probably the case at King's Langley and St Margaret's, Nettleden and possibly also at Hertford. A similar example can be found in the neighbouring county of Bedfordshire where John Cheney, granted the lease of Harrold Priory in 1537, did little beyond carrying out minor adaptation of the existing buildings. Despite the construction of a new house in the early 17th century, the monastic buildings were still standing in 1614 when the reference to "the auncient mancion house of the said Priory or Mannor of Harrold with the outhouses thereunto belonging" suggests that, although they were abandoned, the buildings still remained in reasonable condition.[65] A further parallel can be found at Whalley (Lancs.), where the immediately pre-Dissolution abbot's house formed the nucleus of a new country house.[66]

Elsewhere, owners of former monastic property may have delayed or refrained altogether from conversion because they wished to use the building materials to erect a new house on, near, or at some distance from the site. While there can be little doubt that the extent to which monastic stone was re-used away from its original context has been somewhat over-emphasised to the detriment of a proper appreciation of the process of conversion itself,[67] it should still be recognised that this was an important factor throughout the 16th century and later. Thus just as stone from the Hertfordshire nunneries of Cheshunt, St Giles in the Wood, Flamstead and Markyate was used to build houses nearby, a similar process can be seen at Chertsey in

the misfortunes of the Egerton family directly to their ownership of former monastic property.
[60] S.B. Liljegren, *The Fall of the Monasteries and the Social Changes in England* (1924), 118-24.
[61] W.G. Hoskins, *The Age of Plunder* (1976), 132-4.
[62] H.J. Habbakuk, 'The market for monastic property, 1539-1603', *Economic Hist. Rev.*, 2nd. Ser., 10 (1957/8), 378-80; Knowles, op. cit. (note 35), Ch.32.

[63] Appendix (Beechwood, Cheshunt, Hertford, King's Langley, Sopwell).
[64] Howard (1987), 138-42; Knowles, op. cit. (note 35), Ch.32.
[65] Airs (1975), 18; Beds R.O., TW 11/110.
[66] Owen Ashmore, H.M.S.O. guide to *Whalley* (1962), 18-19.
[67] For a recent example of this see J.H. Bettey, *The Suppression of the Monasteries in the West Country* (1989), Ch.7. A similar lack of understanding of the complexity of the conversion process is displayed by Mick Aston in his otherwise exemplary *Monasteries* (1993), 144 where he makes the rather curious assertion that the evidence for conversion to residential use "comes not so much from the buildings themselves, although there are numerous good examples...but from the new interest in the history and archaeology of gardens".

Surrey and Waltham in Essex.[68] Meanwhile, John Hynde, grantee of Anglesey Abbey (Cambs.) chose to use stone from there to build the kitchen range at nearby Madingley Hall in the 1540s rather than undertake conversion works at Anglesey itself.[69] Others, like Thomas Kytson who bought materials from Bromehill Abbey and Thetford Priory in Norfolk and Ixworth Priory in Suffolk for his massive building project at Hengrave, preferred to buy materials from a number of sites,[70] while to the number of later examples cited by Airs and others, can now be added the recent discovery of 12th-century stonework re-used in the basement of Wollaton House (Notts.), completed only in 1588, which is most likely to have come from nearby Lenton Priory.[71]

In 1575 Edward Paston of Binham Priory (Norfolk) refused to sell Nathaniel Bacon stone from there for use in the construction of nearby Stiffkey Hall on the grounds that he was possibly going to use it for a new house himself, this act providing yet further evidence that uncertainty over a site's use could lead to the effective sterilisation of its buildings for many years after the Dissolution, while in the same county as late as 1621 stone from Coxford Abbey was used for the foundations of Raynham Hall.[72]

Brief consideration was given in Chapter 1 to the fact that the circumstances of re-use changed markedly after c.1600 and that after this date it is probably correct to attribute most cases of re-use to convenience and coincidence rather than to anything more significant. One reason for selecting 1600 as the end-point for this study is the major change in floor-plan and to a lesser extent architectural style which occurs at the beginning of the 17th century. We have seen that by this time the courtyard plan was largely obsolete, even for relatively minor houses, and the trend towards taller houses of compact plan had become firmly established. Although the Gothic style was undergoing a brief revival at this period, classicism was still in the ascendancy and with the appointment of Inigo Jones, who was active in the production of royal masques as early as

1603, to the post of surveyor of the king's works in 1615, its triumph was almost complete.[73]

As Summerson has written "Three generations participated in the Elizabethan age. First there were the men...of the Burghley generation who, if they had an eye for architecture, would look back to the time when Henry VII's Chapel was still a recent marvel, who remembered the building of Nonsuch and the way that Somerset House had seemed to open up a new and charming future for English building. Second, there was the generation born within a decade, either way, of 1540. They were the real makers of the age...the builders of the prodigy palaces, of Kirby, Holdenby, and Wollaton. Third, there was the generation born around 1570...To them, the Reformation was already history (and) architecture...a living art rather than a 'new fashion'. They were the builders of Audley End, Bramshill, Hatfield, and Blickling: houses in which the discoveries of the previous generation were exploited with supreme confidence and lavish elaboration".[74]

To members of this third generation the houses which their fathers and grandfathers had created from former monasteries must have seemed unfashionable and inconvenient. Reasons which had earlier prompted re-use were of little or no significance by the close of the 16th century. To men born after 1570 the events of the Dissolution and the following 30 years were remote and irrelevant and converted monastic buildings must have been seen in this light. One has only to compare the irregular and rambling plan of Buckland with the compact plan and symmetrical elevations of the rebuilt Longleat, itself originally fashioned from monastic fabric, to appreciate that even by the 1570s, just as the number of monastic conversions was peaking, the converted monastery was becoming largely irrelevant to architectural innovation and development.

While this is difficult to illustrate from the Hertfordshire evidence, it is better demonstrated at Montacute where, excepting the church, the whole site of the Cluniac monastery was granted to Dr. William Petre in 1539.[75] The buildings were then leased to John Birt, who appears to have converted the gatehouse into a farmhouse and whose family continued to farm the land until c.1600.[76] Between c.1590 and 1601 Sir Edward Phelips, Speaker of the House of Commons, was less than a mile away building Montacute House. **(Fig. 24)** The significance here is that Phelips, whose family had been in the parish since the late 15th century, and who was to acquire the manor in 1608,[77] made no attempt to buy the site of the former monastery before starting work on his new house. As a result Abbey House (as the gatehouse was known) became virtually redundant and by 1633 it is described as "almost desolate"

---

[68] Greene (1992), 183 and *King's Works*, iv, 207-9 (Chertsey); P.J. Huggins, 'Excavations of the collegiate and Augustinian churches, Waltham Abbey, Essex, 1984-87', *Arch. Jnl.*, 146 (1989), 481.

[69] S.D.T. Spittle, 'Madingley Hall', *Arch. Jnl.*, 124 (1967), 225.

[70] Cambridge University Library: Hengrave Hall Deposit 80.

[71] Airs (1975), 125; Simon Thurley, *The Royal Palaces of Tudor England* (1993), 56; Steven Pugsley, 'Landed society and the emergence of the country house in Tudor and early Stuart Devon' in T. Gray, M. Rowe & A. Erskine (eds.), *Tudor and Stuart Government, The Common Estate and Government, Essays Presented to Joyce Youings* (1992), 109; Pamela Marshall, 'The archaeological survey at Wollaton Hall: some revelations' in Malcolm Airs (ed.), *The Tudor and Jacobean Great House* (Oxford University Dept. Continuing Education, Conference Proceedings, 1994), 80 (Lenton).

[72] E.R. Sandeen, 'The Building Activities of Sir Nicholas Bacon', unpublished Ph.D. thesis (Chicago, 1959), 188. A microfilm copy is deposited in the Bodleian Library (1959 Chicago 9); H.L. Bradfer-Lawrence, 'The building of Raynham Hall', *Norfolk Arch.*, 23 (1927), 101; Linda Campbell, 'Documentary evidence for the building of Raynham Hall', *Archit. Hist.*, 32 (1989), 52-63.

[73] Summerson (1977), Chs.7 and 8.

[74] Ibid, 111.

[75] P.R.O., SC6/Hen VIII/3137, m.24.

[76] *V.C.H., Somerset*, iii (1974), 214.

[77] Ibid.

24. Montacute (Somerset), general view from south-east. Photograph by N. Doggett, August 1993.

25. Abbey House, Montacute, converted monastic gatehouse. Photograph by N.Doggett, August 1993.

because Phelips's son, Sir Robert "seldom makes use of it".[78] The apparent fact that Sir Edward Phelips did not consider utilising the former abbey gatehouse or conventual buildings as the basis for his new mansion is all the more surprising when one looks at the surviving gatehouse. It is an imposing embattled structure with two-storey ranges to either side of a fan-vaulted gateway with an oriel window above. **(Fig. 25)** This carries the carved coat-of-arms of Thomas Chard, prior from 1514-32, showing that the gatehouse had been remodelled shortly before the Dissolution, elegant testimony indeed that even the most fashionable work of the earlier 16th century (Montacute was the third wealthiest Cluniac house in England in 1535)[79] was no longer suited to the aspirations or needs of an ambitious builder of the 1590s.

To cite Montacute and other examples is not to deny that the conversion of monastic buildings produced some interesting and occasionally spectacular routes along the by-ways of 16th-century architectural history. But ultimately it was to end in a blind alley. The decline in popularity of the courtyard plan towards the end of the century was partly responsible, but it would be far too simplistic to attribute the failure of the converted monastery to achieve a more significant place in the history of English architecture to this factor alone. There were, after all, a substantial number of courtyard houses of the first rank built after 1570 including the second phases of Cecil's Burghley and Theobalds and the even more extravagant Audley End, rebuilt between 1603 and 1616, which suggest that at the highest social level the courtyard plan was not completely obsolete. Why then did converted monastic buildings not feature more prominently in this final flowering of the courtyard plan? The explanation for this would seem to lie mainly in the comparatively small size of many medieval cloisters. Although monastic cloisters had proved large enough to form the basis for new houses at places like Ashridge, Lacock, Newstead and Wymondley and the earliest phases of Sopwell, Longleat and Audley End, the great majority were quite simply insufficient in scale to be incorporated in the larger double-courtyard houses of the late Elizabethan period. Thus, while as late as 1612 Francis Bacon could write in his influential essay 'Of Building' (which was to be revised many times before taking its final published form in 1625),[80] that in an ideal "palace" the "inward court...(should be) in the inside, cloistered on all sides, upon decent and beautiful arches, as high as the first story",[81] it is doubtful whether many former monastic cloisters would have been large or grand enough to meet this requirement.

The post-Dissolution history of the cloister at Longleat provides a good example of this situation. Although it appears to have formed an integral part of Thynne's initial adaptations of the monastic buildings, it was "too small to be used as an internal courtyard of the traditional kind". This seems to have encouraged Thynne to realise the potential of an outward-looking plan, which he "exploited...as the house developed", the monastic cloister becoming no more than a small internal court.[82] At Longleat, therefore, the presence of a small medieval cloister seems to have had a positive effect on the development of the house's plan, but it must have been far more common for it to have been disregarded completely in the pursuit of a larger double courtyard house, as occurred at Sopwell.[83]

The smallest monastic cloisters were little bigger than the small courtyards or large light wells found at some early 17th-century houses like Burton Agnes or Chastleton, but such plans were the exception rather than the rule after 1600. From the 1580s onwards the U-plan and the characteristic H-plan became the dominant plan-form in houses as different in scale and ambition as medium-sized manor houses like Pyrton Manor in Oxfordshire, larger houses such as Condover (Shropshire) and Mapledurham (Oxon.), and virtual palaces like Wimbledon House and the colossal Hatfield. In houses of this plan, irrespective of their scale, the straight monastic conversion clearly had no role to play.

Changes in emphasis in the internal planning of great houses also made it difficult for the monastic conversion to suit the needs and aspirations of the most fashionable and ambitious men by 1600. The provision of separate sets of lodgings, those which Summerson has termed "a suite of two or three rooms suitable for the (temporary) residence of a person of quality",[84] initially ensured the continuation of the old courtyard plan. In houses of this type the two long sides of the courtyard were dedicated to lodging accommodation, while the side opposite the entrance formed the hall and kitchen ranges. Those ancillary rooms which had now become essential to any substantial house-the summer and winter parlours and perhaps, too, a withdrawing room were also located in this part of the building.

The adaptation of monastic buildings could clearly provide accommodation of this sort, although it is interesting to note that even in the early royal conversions of Rochester and St Augustine's, Canterbury, where all the claustral buildings were initially retained, only one of the claustral ranges was re-used as lodgings.[85] The reason may simply have been that, as often seems to have occurred elsewhere,

---

[78] J.H. Bates (ed.), *The Particular Description of the County of Somerset, Drawn up by Thomas Gerard of Trent, 1633*, Someset Rec. Soc., 15 (1900), 99.

[79] Knowles (1953), 98.

[80] Francis Bacon, *Essays* (1955 Everyman edn.), xviii.

[81] Ibid, 135-6.

[82] Girouard (1983), 56-9.

[83] See Appendix (Sopwell).

[84] Summerson (1977), 62.

[85] Thurley, op. cit. (note 71), 57 (St Augustine's, Canterbury), 115-19 (Rochester); *King's Works*, iv, 59-63 (St Augustine's) and 234-7 (Rochester).

the monastic cloister was considered to be too small for this purpose. Certainly such cloisters would have been insufficient for the type of building erected in response to the royal Progresses of Elizabeth's reign so that, at least in the greatest houses, the monastic cloister's route to survival was blocked by its own inadequate dimensions, this surely being the reason for the sweeping away of the cloister in the second phase at Sopwell.

Assuming that it was of sufficient length, the re-use of the upper level of a claustral range could conveniently provide a long gallery and the lower level could be adapted to create an open loggia for summer exercise, while in many cases the great chamber of an Elizabethan house could be accommodated by placing it in the former superior's lodgings. Far greater difficulties were, however, encountered in adapting monastic buildings to the late Elizabethan and Jacobean innovation of placing the hall on a central axis, as at Hardwick and Charlton House, Greenwich, rather than in its traditional position to left or right of the main entrance. The problems that this caused were not insurmountable when the hall was entered on its long axis but it would have been much more difficult to create a hall from a narrow claustral range if it was desired that the entrance to it should be on its short axis. The only claustral buildings from which a hall entered on its short axis could be devised would be the chapter house or the fraters built at right-angles to the south or north ranges of some early Cistercian houses,[86] of which there are no examples in the Hertfordshire sample. In any case, few of the latter would have survived by the late 16th century, while those of the former which remained from the demolitions of the Dissolution would have been disadvantaged by their overtly ecclesiastical appearance and their location at the end of the east range.

Thus even at houses as grand as Ashridge, halls which had been created from claustral ranges were beginning to look distinctly archaic by the end of the 16th century, although the way in which the traditional positioning of the hall at Chastleton was concealed externally could in theory just as easily have been achieved in a monastic conversion, as indeed was to some extent the case at Ashridge. Similarly, it would be mistaken to think that the asymmetrically-entered hall disappeared quickly after 1600. As late as 1638 Sir Edmund Wright, a Cheshire merchant who was soon to become Lord Mayor of London, was building Swakeleys (Middx.) in which the hall was still entered in the old asymmetrical way, although as at Chastleton and countless other houses this arrangement was completely concealed by the building's outward symmetry.[87] Although

Summerson is, of course, correct to draw attention to the gulf in taste between court and city that Swakeleys represents, it should also be recognised that by his own standards Wright was an influential and in some ways sophisticated man. Indeed, it would not be until well after 1650 that the traditional position of the hall would be abandoned in new-built houses.[88] Furthermore, it perhaps persisted longer in the homes of the gentry and wealthy merchants than in the houses of prosperous yeoman farmers, where the central lobby-entry plan was superseding the old hall and cross-wing plan from the late 16th century onwards.

If changes in the positioning of the hall, which ultimately resulted from its decline in importance,[89] were difficult to accommodate in monastic conversions, the growing significance of the staircase presented an even greater problem. A grand or ceremonial staircase was becoming an essential ingredient of a house of any pretension from the mid-16th century onwards. Unlike medieval or early Tudor spiral staircases which took up very little space and were well suited to claustral ranges and courtyard houses in general, even an enclosed stair within a square or rectangular tower was greedy by comparison. The only way such stairs could be incorporated in interconnecting ranges without eating into the ranges themselves was by means of extruded corner towers which, if they were not to appear on the outward elevations, then had the effect of impinging on the courtyard instead. Clearly, this was far from desirable, especially where the courtyard was based on the restricted dimensions of the old cloister garth, while if a grand open staircase of the lavish proportions recommended by architectural treatise writers like Francis Bacon and Sir Henry Wotton and found at houses such as Hatfield and Knole was required, this would be impossible to achieve without total remodelling.[90] It is undoubtedly for such reasons that no grand staircases are found in any of the Hertfordshire monastic conversions.

It is therefore apparent that by 1600 the type of house created by a typical monastic conversion was largely obsolete. This does not mean to say, of course, that all houses created from former monasteries would have been completely rebuilt after this date or that they would automatically have descended the social scale. As J.T. Smith has written on a slightly later period for Hertfordshire "Many...houses were now sufficiently well built and sufficiently large to outlive the social and economic conditions which produced them; and although...(it might) be unsuitable for the needs of an heir or a new owner, its complete replacement by a house of comparable size represented a waste of resources for all but

---

[86] See Peter Fergusson's 'The twelfth-century refectories at Rievaulx and Byland Abbeys' in E.C. Norton & W.D. Park (eds.), *Cistercian Art and Architecture in the British Isles* (1986), 160-80 where, interestingly, it is pointed out that in the very first Cistercian houses refectories were often located in the north or south claustral range rather than at right-angles to the cloister, as was to become standard practice by the second half of the 12th century.

[87] Summerson (1977), 158.

[88] Smith (1992), 83.

[89] See Thurley, op. cit. (note 71), 113-20 for the earliest manifestations of this.

[90] John Newman, 'The development of the staircase in Elizabethan and Jacobean England' in A. Chastel & J. Guillaume (eds.), *L'Escalier dans l'architecture de la Renaissance* (1985), 175-8.

the very richest".[91] This meant that in most cases there would have to be compromises in terms of the very latest ideas on planning or architectural style and that houses would be modified or rebuilt piecemeal, but it would nevertheless be true to say that the social, political, religious and economic factors which had prompted monastic conversions in the first place were all but extinct by 1600.

It is probably the case that the architectural significance of monastic conversions would have been more far-reaching had circumstances allowed a greater number to take place in the 1540s and early 1550s when the courtyard house was still very much in vogue. Instead, with the exception of a relatively small number of important conversions like Ashridge, Sopwell and Wymondley, the majority of substantial conversions rather than comparatively simple adaptation of existing buildings to secular purposes took place only in the 1570s and '80s by which time the courtyard house was already approaching terminal decline. Although it was possible for a double-courtyard house such as the post-1568 Longleat to be essentially outward looking in exactly the same way as houses of compact plan like Hardwick and Wollaton, this was considerably more difficult where the size of a house was dictated by the retention of a small monastic cloister with its inward-looking ranges.

Another possible explanation of why the conversion of monastic buildings ended in an architectural *cul-de-sac* is that there were few religious houses of the first rank where major conversion works were carried out. Of the 30 or so wealthiest communities at the time of the Dissolution only four- Ramsey, Reading, St Augustine's, Canterbury and Syon- were the subject of a thorough conversion to domestic use. This can be explained partly by the fact that several of the greatest monasteries, including those which had been monastic cathedrals before the suppression- Christ Church, Canterbury, Durham, Ely, Norwich, Winchester and Worcester- became secular cathedrals as did the former abbeys of Chester, Gloucester, Oxford, Peterborough and Westminster.[92] Even in those cases where the now redundant cloister was not demolished or vandalised at the Dissolution, the new circumstances did not permit single residential use of the former conventual buildings, although many were of course adapted to form accommodation for the new dean and chapter or other associated uses.[93]

In the cases of Croyland, St Albans and Tewkesbury where the abbey church became parochial after the Dissolution, similar factors applied. But these examples are heavily outnumbered by major monastic churches which were completely abandoned after the Dissolution. This occurred in both town and country and included those at Abingdon, Bury St Edmunds, Cirencester, Evesham, Fountains, Leicester, Lewes, Merton, Reading, Shaftesbury and St Mary's, York, all of which had become ruinous by 1600.[94]

Even at those major monastic houses like Abingdon, Glastonbury and St Albans where there was some domestic re-use not directly connected with a continued religious function of the site in the 16th century, this tended to be piecemeal and unimpressive in scale and vision.[95] The only real exceptions to this were at St Augustine's, Canterbury, Ramsey, Reading and Syon. At the former, the buildings were converted to a royal palace in time for the arrival of Anne of Cleves in December 1539; at Syon, Protector Somerset spent some £5000 in transforming the Bridgettine nunnery into a brick quadrangular house; at Reading, a "mansion" was made for the king from the abbot's lodging in the west range; and at Ramsey in the late 16th century, after a period during which the site was used as little more than a source for building materials, the Cromwell family converted the former lady chapel of the Benedictine monastery into a house.[96]

By the second half of the 16th century few, if any, of these houses would have provided accommodation fit for the queen. Elizabeth built no palaces for herself, preferring to rely on her great magnates and courtiers to provide the most sumptuous accommodation during her summer Progresses. Some of the remarks notoriously attributed to the queen and the responses supposedly made by those addressed may be little more than apocryphal, but there can be little doubt that, if uttered, the comment she is reported to have made to Sir Nicholas Bacon on the occasion of her

---

[91] Smith (1992), 83.

[92] Taken from the list of religious houses with annual incomes exceeding £1000 at the time of the *Valor Ecclesiasticus*, printed in Knowles, op. cit. (note 35), 473. See also ibid, Ch.31.

[93] This is a subject which has received relatively little attention, as typified by Francis Woodman in his otherwise authoritative *The Architectural History of Canterbury Cathedral* (1981), 226-30. One of the best general treatments of the topic remains Gerald Cobb's *English Cathedrals, The Forgotten Centuries: Restoration and Change from 1530 to the Present Day* (1980), while John Crook has explored in some detail the post-Dissolution history of the close at Winchester- 'The Cathedral Priory and Deanery, Winchester', paper read at the 1996

Hampshire Field Club Conference 'Hampshire Monasteries: the Aftermath of the Dissolution'. Earlier studies, such as R.V.H. Burne's *Chester Cathedral from its Founding by Henry VIII to the Accession of Queen Victoria* (1958) tended to concentrate on spiritual and administrative matters rather than on physical changes to the buildings themselves.

[94] A detailed account of the demolition of the church of Reading Abbey, based on a survey of 1549, is given by A.E. Preston in his 'The demolition of Reading Abbey', *Berks. Arch. Jnl.*, 39 (1935), 107-44. The churches at Bury St Edmunds and Cirencester are among a number of great monastic churches demolished in the years immediately after the Dissolution, the sites of which have been at least partially excavated. See R. Gilyard-Beer, 'The eastern arm of the abbey church at Bury St Edmunds', *Proc. Suffolk Inst. Arch.*, 31 (1967/9), 256-62 and John Wacher, 'Cirencester 1964', *Antiquaries Jnl.*, 45 (1965), 105-10.

[95] Thurley, op. cit. (note 71), 56-7. Abingdon was considered but rejected as a house for the king on account of its dilapidated buildings and because there was no land which could "be conveniently imparked for the king's disport and pleasure"; G.H. Cook (ed.), *Letters to Cromwell and Others on the Suppression of the Monasteries* (1965), 145-6.

[96] *King's Works*, iv, 59-63 (St Augustine's, Canterbury); ibid, 272-3 and Bridget Cherry & Nikolaus Pevsner, *London 3: North West* (1991), 442-6 (Syon); *King's Works*, iv, 220-22 (Reading); *V.C.H., Hunts.*, ii (1932), 192-3, N. Pevsner, *Bedfordshire and the County of Huntingdon and Peterborough* (1968), 330-2 and *Med. Arch.*, 13 (1969), 246 (Ramsey).

visit to Gorhambury in 1572- "My Lord Keeper, what a little house you have gotten"- prompted him to add the long two-storey west 'cloister' before her second visit in 1577.[97] Similar circumstances may have prompted Lee's remodelling of his first conversion at Sopwell, while at Theobalds Cecil "came to enterteyne the quene so often there, he was inforced to enlarge it, rather for the quene and her great traine, and to sett (the) poore on worke, than for pompe or glory".[98]

In such circumstances, where both Cecil and Sir Christopher Hatton "confessed to having spent more than even they could afford on houses which they did not need",[99] it is perhaps not surprising that the buildings of the largest and wealthiest monasteries, many of them already old fashioned at the time of the Dissolution or hemmed in by other buildings in crowded urban locations, proved unattractive to those who could have afforded to convert them to domestic use.

It was thus more often monastic houses of the second rank which were selected for re-use. This is amply illustrated from the Hertfordshire sample, in which no houses except Ashridge and Hertford (and then only as a dependent cell of St Albans) were large enough to survive the First Act of Suppression. Elsewhere the same phenomenon can be seen at sites like Hinchingbroke, Horsham St Faith, Mottisfont and Netley, all of which were either poor or not particularly wealthy at the time of the Dissolution and closed before the Second Act of Suppression.[100] All, however, offered considerable advantages to their new lay owners in terms of location, buildings suitable for adaptation, and good wholesome country air. Furthermore, it was not the case that houses of this sort appealed only to the less influential courtiers or to nobility of the second rank, as the activities of Nedeham at Wymondley, Lee at Sopwell, Rich at Leez Priory, Sharington at Lacock and Wriothesley at Titchfield, among others of the first generation, clearly show.

During the 1540s and early 1550s it was still possible for a fashionable house to be created from a direct conversion of monastic buildings but at this time it was only the most powerful and ambitious men in the kingdom who had the resources or the opportunity to carry out such work, thereby limiting the extent to which conversions were undertaken. By the 1560s and '70s a greater number of men were in a position to carry out the adaptation of monastic buildings to domestic use but by then fashions were changing and it was necessary for monastic buildings to be altered far more radically, as the remodelling of sites like Hinchingbroke, Longleat and Sopwell shows, to enable them to meet the latest ideas in planning or architectural style. After c.1580 it is doubtful whether the effort was still worth making even below the highest social level, as is shown by Sir Stephen Proctor's decision simply to use

Fountains Abbey, the buildings and estates of which he had bought in 1597, as a stone quarry for his Fountains Hall which was completed by c.1611 nearby.[101] Although Ashridge and Wymondley show that remodelling schemes were still being carried out at the more important monastic conversions as late as c.1600, it is more usual to find examples of late conversions or substantial reworkings of earlier conversions at the homes of the less wealthy members of the gentry or prosperous yeoman farmers. For such men convenience and comfort would have been more pressing concerns than the latest architectural theory, and thus we find evidence for building activity at The Biggin, Hitchin Priory, King's Langley, Royston and Ware in the last two decades of the 16th century.

---

[97] D. Lloyd, *State Worthies* (1779), 355; Smith (1993), 158.
[98] F. Peck, *Desiderata Curiosa* (1779), 25.
[99] Summerson (1977), 62-3.
[100] Knowles (1953), passim.
[101] Girouard (1983), 192-7; B.L., Harl. MS. 6853, fol.450.

Chapter Five

Conclusions: the theory of adaptive re-use and suggestions for further work

As shown in Chapter 4, the Hertfordshire evidence largely confirms what is known from elsewhere about the re-use of monastic buildings in the second half of the 16th century. While there may be no major surprises from the Hertfordshire sample, the concentration on the data from a single county is in itself a useful discipline and helps to cast additional light on the complexities and shifts of emphasis in this undoubtedly important, but as yet imperfectly understood, process.

The purpose of this chapter is to draw the various strands together: to examine in more detail what might be termed the theory of adaptive re-use and to offer speculations and suggestions for further work.

The Hertfordshire material helps to dispel some of the myths and unfounded generalisations surrounding the question of the re-use of monastic buildings. At all of the sites contained in the sample there is at least some evidence to show re-use after the Dissolution. In all cases save Beechwood, Cheshunt, Markyate and Royston, where new houses appear to have been built nearby from monastic materials, this seems to have taken the form of direct adaptation and conversion of the monastic structures. At Ashridge, Hitchin Priory, King's Langley, Sopwell, Ware and Wymondley this is fairly readily apparent, but at The Biggin, Hitchin, Hertford and St Margaret's, Nettleden the deduction needs to be teased out from a detailed examination of the surviving or now-demolished buildings or from other sources.

This high level of re-use in a county not noted for the quality of its monastic remains is remarkable. Indeed, it may well be that the high incidence of re-use is a direct result of the comparatively unimposing character of Hertfordshire's religious houses. This is in direct contrast to counties like Yorkshire, where the remote locations and magnificent ecclesiastical architecture of sites like Byland, Fountains and Rievaulx do not seem to have encouraged adaptive re-use. It therefore seems possible to argue that re-use was more likely to occur in areas where monastic buildings were smaller in scale and more conveniently situated. A similar pattern might be expected in counties like Buckinghamshire, Hampshire and Oxfordshire, but even here circumstances may have been very different from those in Hertfordshire.

Hertfordshire was a particularly attractive county in which to build a country house in the second half of the 16th century. This is amply demonstrated throughout the period

by houses as varied in scale as Berkhamsted Place (c.1580), Little Gaddesden Manor (1576) and Standon Lordship (1546), to the palaces of Gorhambury (1563 ff.), Hatfield (1607-12) and Theobalds (1564 ff.). Indeed, from c.1550 onwards, developing a trend already observable in the 15th century,[1] Hertfordshire experienced a considerable influx of new families, whether of courtiers or merchants, drawn from London by the combined attractions of pleasant countryside and good, wholesome air. By the 17th century this phenomenon was so widespread that Sir Thomas Fuller could comment wittily that "such who buy a house in Hertfordshire pay two years' purchase for the air".[2] The proximity to the capital, where the court was becoming increasingly permanently based, and the relatively good road system were no doubt also influential in this process.

Two themes emerge from this background. First, the evidence that direct adaptive re-use of monastic buildings was widespread casts doubt on the generally-held assumption that it was more usual simply to re-cycle materials elsewhere. The importance of the latter practice has been amply demonstrated by David Stocker,[3] but others have viewed the evidence less critically and have perhaps concluded too quickly that re-cycling of materials rather than adaptation of monastic buildings was the norm after the Dissolution.[4] The re-use of materials away from their original context is, of course, not unknown in Hertfordshire, and there are clear signs of this process at most, if not all, of the sites included in the sample. It should also be pointed out that the extent of the process is very difficult to quantify, as without a detailed examination of every historic structure in the vicinity of a former monastery it is impossible to ascertain even the surviving evidence for the recycling of building materials. In addition, some buildings containing re-used stonework will have been demolished and in other cases materials will have been transported considerable distances from their original sites.

Nevertheless, it can be argued that while the evidence for the plunder and re-cycling of materials is unsurprising, the evidence for the adaptive re-use of buildings is more striking. Such re-use appears to have occurred equally at all site types contained in the sample, from urban friaries like Hitchin and Ware, to conversions to farmhouse use at King's Langley, to those of the first rank at Ashridge, Sopwell and Wymondley.

The comparative unimportance of the re-cycling of monastic materials in Hertfordshire is perhaps also reflected in the relatively slight evidence for demolition at the county's religious sites. There can be little doubt that

---

[1] Lionel Munby, *The Hertfordshire Landscape* (1977), 139.
[2] Thomas Fuller, *The Worthies of England* (ed., John Freeman, 1952), 229.
[3] See Chapter 1, note 28.
[4] See, for example, J.H. Bettey, *The Suppression of the Monasteries in the West Country* (1989), Ch.7.

deliberate programmes of demolition took place at many sites in the second half of the 16th century, and these are clearly hinted at through documentary sources at Ashridge, Hitchin Priory, King's Langley and Sopwell. However, it is notable that it is only at the latter two sites that the process has been detected archaeologically, although this may simply reflect the relative lack of archaeological investigation at monastic sites in the county rather than anything more significant.

The second theme to emerge from the Hertfordshire sample is the idea that adaptive re-use might be more likely to occur at the less important sites, where the prospects of conversion were financially and physically less daunting. It has already been shown in Chapter 4 that very few of England's wealthiest monastic houses were converted to full residential use and the practical difficulties of converting large churches into domestic accommodation must have been a factor in this. Several churches were, of course, converted in just this way in Hertfordshire. But it is probably significant that, with the possible exception of Ashridge, they were not ecclesiastical buildings of the first order. Indeed, it may be equally significant that where important churches did exist- at King's Langley and Royston- the former was effectively ignored by the post-Dissolution owners and at the other the nave was demolished and the east end remained in religious use.

Certainly, it would have been far easier to convert an aisleless church to two-storey domestic use, whether to form a hall and parlour as at Wymondley, or a lodging range as at Titchfield (Hants.), than would have been the case with an aisled building. Thus, at Netley (Hants.) the hall created from the aisled church was open to the roof, while at Mottisfont, also in Hampshire, and Sopwell the two-storey conversions resulted in the removal of the aisles.

The location of sites was also a major influence on the likelihood that they would be re-used. The position of the priories of Hertford, The Biggin, Hitchin and Royston and the friary at Ware on the edges of their respective towns was ideal for the apparently relatively modest manor houses that they became. The Carmelite friary at Hitchin was situated at the southern extremity of the medieval town, no doubt as a result of its late foundation, and its extensive precinct was readily transformed into the park, gardens and orchards of the post-Dissolution house. Indeed, it is tempting to attribute the seemingly slightly higher status of Hitchin Priory over the other urban sites in the 16th century- a pre-eminence it had certainly achieved by the 17th century- to the particular attractions and advantages of its edge-of-town location.

This certainly seems to have been the case at Sopwell, where Sir Richard Lee's house, built from the materials and on the site of the former Benedictine nunnery, was located conveniently close to St Albans but sufficiently far from the town to be surrounded by its own extensive parkland.

The siting of Ashridge, Beechwood, Markyate and Wymondley are clearly different again and proved suitable for the country houses that they became, while it might be argued that the comparative inaccessibility of St Margaret's, Nettleden was a factor in its becoming no more than a farmhouse.

Thus the positions of the religious houses of The Biggin, Hitchin Priory, Hertford, Royston and Ware in or on the edges of their respective towns may have played their part in the relatively low-key transformations of these sites, while the more attractive locations of Ashridge, Beechwood, Markyate, Sopwell and Wymondley may have been equally instrumental in their conversion into houses of the first rank.

If the location and physical setting of sites was an important influence on the type and extent of conversions undertaken, the resources and aspirations of the new lay owners were equally significant. These naturally varied enormously, although there is a surprising degree of correlation between the practical problems of converting individual buildings and the dates at which this occurred, at whatever social level they took place.

A shared factor between many of the less intensive conversion schemes was the relatively late date in the 16th century that they were carried out. Indeed, it could be argued that a prosperous yeoman farmer or one of the less wealthy members of the gentry would have been more reluctant to indulge in the conversion of monastic buildings in the years immediately after the Dissolution than a favoured courtier or member of the aristocracy, particularly as the former were more likely to be motivated by purely practical concerns such as the condition and suitability of individual buildings for re-use. In short, those lower down the social scale had less to invest and therefore arguably more to lose from premature involvement in conversion schemes than their wealthier and more influential counterparts. Thus, while there is some evidence for conversion works in the first generation at Hitchin Priory and Royston, it is singularly lacking at The Biggin, Hertford, Royston and Ware where no major works of adaptive re-use seem to have taken place until after c.1580. At King's Langley and St Margaret's, Nettleden, lack of precise dating evidence makes it difficult to state exactly when the buildings were adapted to domestic use.

It is surely no coincidence, however, that the conversion of Ashridge, Sopwell and Wymondley into houses of the first rank took place in the two decades after the Dissolution, albeit with further remodelling later in the century, and there is similar evidence for building activity at Beechwood, Cheshunt and Markyate in the same period. This is mirrored nationally by other early and innovative conversions like Lacock (Wilts.), Newstead (Notts.) and the Hampshire trio of Mottisfont, Netley and Titchfield, all the work of some of the most powerful and influential men in the kingdom.

The first-generation conversions of Sopwell and Wymondley and, to a slightly lesser degree the building of new houses at Beechwood, Cheshunt and Markyate, are a reflection of the atypically high number of grants of former monasteries in Hertfordshire to courtiers and other royal favourites. This can be contrasted with the situation in counties such as Devon and Norfolk, remote from London's influence, where the former monastic lands were just as, if not more, likely to be acquired eventually by members of the gentry or of the aspiring yeoman farmer class.[5]

The crown's grants of former monastic properties to courtiers were no doubt partly caused by the requirement to ensure their continuing support, but the far greater need to gain revenue was probably even more important and it was, of course, courtiers who were able and willing to pay the highest prices. Thus it was in Hertfordshire that the earliest grants were predominantly to courtiers.

As shown in Chapter 4, it has been estimated on a national basis that over 75% of former monastic property had been transferred from royal to lay ownership by 1558.[6] Hertfordshire was certainly no exception to this pattern, only Ashridge- held until 1575- remaining with the crown for any significant time after the Dissolution. Indeed, it has been noted for the county as a whole that "of 395 manors or similar estates, whose successive owners can be traced through the county histories, 168 (42.5%) were in the hands of the crown in 1540. By 1550 only twelve (7%) of these 168 properties remained in the hands of the crown",[7] although it should be pointed out that the number of manors owned by the crown in 1540 had been artificially inflated by the temporary appropriation of monastic manors between 1536 and 1540. However, it is probably significant that by 1700 only 42 of the 395 properties were owned by the same family or institution as in 1540.

This remarkable transfer of ownership was due partly to the widespread sale of privately owned manors, beginning in the 1540s, but the dispersal of former monastic lands through the king was even more significant. During the second half of the 16th century in Hertfordshire, as in many counties, the most likely purchasers of manors, including former monastic ones, were members of the gentry.[8] Whether from old or new families, men with sufficient means were anxious to build up country estates and the fluid land market provided them with the perfect opportunity to do so. It should be emphasised, however, that the Hertfordshire gentry, while able to buy former monastic manors, were generally excluded from purchasing the buildings and sites of the monasteries themselves, not least because the majority had been bought already by courtiers and other royal favourites.

Many members of the gentry were, of course, royal officials and it is not always easy to distinguish between a man who would be regarded as a courtier and one who would not.[9] Nevertheless, there is probably a useful distinction to be made between men like Robert Byrch and Sir Robert Chester, both apparently minor figures in the royal household, and the holders of the major offices of state like Denny, Egerton, Lee and Nedeham. Not surprisingly, the status of the man is often reflected in the quality of the house he created from his former monastic property, although as we have already seen there is often not a direct relationship between the pre- and post-Dissolution importance of individual sites. However, while the relatively modest nature of the post-suppression houses of Hitchin Priory and The Biggin can be seen as an indication of the comparatively limited means of their successful lawyer owners, considerably more influential men like Denny and Sir John Daunce, Henry VIII's Treasurer of Wars, could acquire minor sites such as Hertford Priory and St Margaret's, Nettleden, with which they did little or nothing as they also had other houses elsewhere.

In this context it is probably significant that work on Sopwell was never completed after Lee's death in 1575 and that Wymondley appears to have been reduced in size in c.1600. One explanation for the rebuilding work carried out at Beechwood, Cheshunt and Markyate in the late 16th century may be that they were in any case relatively newly-built houses rather than conversions made obsolete by changing architectural fashions. Another is that, as their then owners were of slightly lesser status than elsewhere, expectations and aspirations were fewer and the houses were still thought worthy of remodelling. Only at Ashridge did an owner of the first rank consider the buildings suitable for further extension and remodelling after 1600.

The contraction or stabilisation at houses of the first order in the late 16th century contrasts markedly with the situation at the urban sites, where the picture is one of rebuilding and expansion in the two decades after 1580. While it is only at Hitchin and Royston that there is evidence for adaptive re-use between 1540 and 1560, there is clear evidence for major schemes of work at Hertford Priory, The Biggin and Ware Priory after c.1580, with further phases of remodelling at Hitchin and Royston before 1600. The sample is perhaps too small to draw definitive conclusions but may suggest that, while men of the highest rank were less prepared to tolerate the somewhat old-fashioned standards that many monastic conversions were seen to represent by the late 16th century,

---

[5] Felicity Heal & Clive Holmes, *The Gentry in England and Wales 1500-1700* (1994), 326; W.G. Hoskins, *The Age of Plunder* (1976), 137.

[6] John Guy, *Tudor England* (1988), 145.

[7] Munby, op. cit. (note 1), 139-40.

[8] Heal & Holmes, op. et loc. cit.

[9] Ibid.

such buildings could still provide very acceptable houses for those slightly lower down the social ladder.

Passing reference was made in Chapter 1 to the probability that when a former monastic building was adapted to secular residential use, the new owner would have gone to some pains to disguise the building's ecclesiastical origins. It is certainly true that the trend for exposing features of historical or archaeological interest in buildings established itself only in the 18th and 19th centuries. Before then fashion usually dictated that every effort should be made to conceal obsolete features and to make a remodelled building appear as up-to-date as possible, thereby accounting for the vast number of timber-framed houses refronted in brick or stone from the 17th century onwards.

The situation may not have been quite so simple, however, in the case of monastic buildings converted to domestic use in the second half of the 16th century. As Malcolm Airs has written, "The cultured mind of the 16th century delighted in anything that could be called 'curious' or 'ingenious'...(for example) in allegory and metaphor which characterise much of the literature and painting of the period (and in)...emblems and devices, in which a philosophical truth or a line of conduct was reduced to an allegorical picture supported by a cryptic motto or some lines of verse".[10]

One of the ways that this phenomenon could be developed was through architecture and perhaps its clearest expression can be found in the so-called allegorical buildings of the late 16th and early 17th centuries, among the best-known examples being Longford Castle (Wilts.) and Sir Thomas Tresham's Triangular Lodge and Lyveden New Build in Northamptonshire.[11] It may not therefore be too fanciful to suggest that some monastic conversions should be seen in this light, although in the absence of literary or other documentary material this is impossible to prove. It is conceivable, moreover, that an intellectually sophisticated owner of particular religious persuasions could have taken "delight" in the allegory or symbolism of converting a former monastery to domestic use. Certainly, it is easy to imagine that the physical challenge of conversion, if not the difficulty of concealing the monastic origins of the building, would have appealed both to practical men like Nedeham and Lee in the first generation and to skilled political operators like Egerton towards the end of our period. It is pure speculation, however, whether devotees of the old or new religion would have found greater intellectual and moral fulfilment in making use of former monastic buildings in this way.

Various factors could act as a bar to the early re-use of monastic buildings whatever the social level of their new owners. The principal of these was perhaps the religious uncertainty of the period. The accession of Mary in 1553 must have worried many who had acquired former monastic property during the reigns of her father and younger brother. Several religious houses were re-established under her, including Westminster, and a house of Dominican nuns, formerly of Dartford in Kent, was refounded at King's Langley in 1557 before moving back to Dartford in the following year.[12] There were also plans to re-endow several more (including St Albans) which remained unrealised at the time of Mary's death in 1558.[13] These refoundations were viewed by many at the time as the tip of the iceberg and there can be little doubt that Mary herself would have liked to have gone much further in the restoration of confiscated Church property, being prevented from so doing only by political expedience and the practical difficulties of unravelling nearly 20 years' secular ownership of former ecclesiastical lands and buildings. How much more she might have achieved in this regard is now only a matter for speculation but the circumstances of her reign were clearly not propitious for the conversion of monastic buildings into country or town houses.

The succession of Elizabeth and the 1559 Act of Uniformity are often viewed as a turning point in the religious climate of the times,[14] but this certitude is only possible with the benefit of hindsight. To contemporaries who had experienced the brief reigns of Edward and Mary and the very different attitudes of the two monarchs and their governments, the early years of Elizabeth's reign can have offered little in the way of security, and it is perhaps no coincidence that nationally the conversion of the great majority of former monastic buildings did not peak until the 1570s and '80s, decades in which much new building work was also undertaken.[15]

The significance of converted monastic buildings in the development of architectural styles and ideas in the 16th century, both within a county and a national framework, is difficult to assess. Hertfordshire has many examples of town and country houses of this period, several of which have been usefully brought together and compared by J.T. Smith in his recent publications.[16] A particularly relevant comparison can be made between monastic conversions and other houses of courtyard plan, in the anticipation that the success or ultimate failure of the latter may tell us something about the importance or otherwise of the former.

[10] Airs (1975), 3.
[11] Summerson (1977), 77-80.

[12] See Appendix (King's Langley).
[13] David Knowles, *The Religious Orders in England*, iii (1959), Ch.34.
[14] See G.R. Elton, *England Under the Tudors* (2nd. edn., 1974), 273-4 for an expression of this traditional view.
[15] Airs (1975), 18-19.
[16] J.T. Smith, *English Houses 1200-1800: the Hertfordshire Evidence* (1992) and *Hertfordshire Houses: Selective Inventory* (1993).

As Smith has shown, the medieval tradition of the courtyard house lasted well into the 17th century in Hertfordshire, the remodelling of Beechwood, completed only in 1702, representing one of the last examples of this building type. While the medieval relationship of gatehouse to main hall range was retained in this planform, there were severe limitations to linear extensions, and it was more convenient to extend the hall range at right-angles to each end, creating an enclosed inner courtyard, with only the outer courts completely or partly open. The converted buildings of a monastic cloister could in theory lend themselves quite easily to such an arrangement, although as pointed out in Chapter 4 there were in fact often practical difficulties in doing this, owing to the frequently different ages and varying heights of the individual buildings in the cloister. Nevertheless, these difficulties could be overcome as the courtyard houses of The Biggin, Hitchin Priory and on a larger scale Ashridge, Sopwell and Wymondley clearly show.

These sites can be seen in the wider context of other 16th-century courtyard houses in the county such as Broxbourne Bury, Hatfield Palace, Standon Lordship, Theobalds and Watton Woodhall, all of which developed in several stages, or the smaller number of houses like Berkhamsted Place and Gorhambury, which were planned and built to a courtyard lay-out from the start.[17]

The halls of several of these houses were open to the roof, as at Gorhambury and Knebworth, and this certainly seems to have been the case at Ashridge, while at The Biggin, Sopwell and Wymondley the hall range was probably divided into two storeys. Likewise, it should not be assumed that the hall range would always lie directly opposite the gatehouse range in courtyard-plan houses. At Standon Lordship, for example, the hall is situated at right-angles to the entrance range and this suggests that at monastic conversions like Hitchin Priory, where the position of the hall is unclear, it would be unwise automatically to deduce that it lay opposite the entrance range. Indeed, at The Biggin it appears that the hall was in the south range of the old priory cloister, the east range having become the entrance range to the inner court of the 16th-century house.

The principal reasons why the conversion of former monastic buildings ended in an architectural blind alley towards the end of the 16th century have been outlined in Chapter 4, and it now remains only to offer some speculations and ideas for further work. First, to adopt a similar approach to that taken to the Hertfordshire sample in an investigation of the 16th-century re-use of monastic buildings in another part of the country might produce a very different picture. For example, Hertfordshire's proximity to London and its growing prosperity at this period mean that it is far from being a typical county and in other parts of the country, remote from the capital's influence, where many former monastic buildings were acquired by members of the gentry or yeoman farmer class, rather than by royal favourites or officials, another pattern of re-use is likely to have emerged.

Second, the question of whether Catholics or Protestants were the more likely to convert monastic buildings to domestic use remains open. In theory either group would have found the proposition attractive, Catholics possibly seeing in the re-use of the buildings themselves some continuity with the monastic past, Protestants regarding the secularisation of the buildings as the triumph of reason and reform over the perceived ignorance and superstition of medieval religion. England had, of course, not become an exclusively Protestant country by the late 16th century and, as various recent studies have shown, adherence to the old religion remained strong in some regions.[18] But the fact that, officially at least, Protestantism was predominant by this time may have been a contributory factor in the peaking of monastic conversions in the 1570s and '80s.

There are, of course, frequently difficulties in establishing whether an individual subscribed to the Protestant or Catholic faith. Some men, such as Sir Richard Rich or Sir William Paulet could switch their adherence to suit the mood of the time, a change in monarch often signalling a shift in allegiance, while others like Wriothesley could disguise their private belief in one creed by a show of public devotion to the other.[19] One barrier to further investigation is the almost total lack of supporting documentary material, followers of the old religion being particularly reluctant to commit to writing anything that might jeopardise their careers or the welfare of their families.[20]

Another possible area for further work might lie in the marked changes in architectural development and landscape appreciation evident towards the end of the 16th century, several of which are likely to have had implications for the adaptive re-use of monastic buildings, at least at the highest social level. This was precisely the period when the importance of views and vistas was beginning to be valued for the first time, being reflected in the building of look-out towers which, although they seem

---

[17] Smith (1992 & 1993), passim.

[18] Two of the most recent studies to show the continuing strength of Catholicism in various regions of the country in the Tudor and Elizabethan period are Eamon Duffy's *The Stripping of the Altars, Traditional Religion in England 1400-1580* (1992) and Christopher Haigh's *English Reformations, Religion, Politics and Society Under the Tudors* (1993).

[19] See *D.N.B.*, xvi, 1009-12; xv, 535-9 & xxi, 1063-7 for the religious leanings of Rich, Paulet and Wriothesley. The topic can be explored further through the publications of the Catholic Record Society (Records Series) and its journal, *Recusant History*. I am grateful to Edward Chaney for drawing my attention to these publications.

[20] The difficulty of identifying the true religious persuasions of individuals is comprehensively covered by J.A. Williams in his 'Sources for recusant history (1559-1791) in English official archives', *Recusant Hist.*, 16 (1983), 331-451.

to have had their origins earlier in the century, were becoming more popular by c.1550 as typified at Bisham Abbey (Berks.), Lacock in Wiltshire and St Osyth's (Essex).[21] By the time Sir Francis Bacon wrote 'Of Building', the recreational use of the lead flats of parapeted or balustraded roofs was likewise well established- "As for the tower, I would have it two stories, of eighteen foot high a-piece, above the two wings; and a goodly leads upon the top, railed with statuas interposed...[22] In the same spirit, prospect mounds, like that constructed for Bacon's father, Sir Nicholas, at Gorhambury,[23] were raised not only to give views over surrounding formal gardens but over the wider countryside beyond.

Similarly, an elevated position was often considered to be the best location for a new house. As early as 1542 Andrew Boorde was writing in his *Compendyous Regyment* that "Then he that wyll buylde, let hym make his fundacyon upon a gravaly grownde myxt with clay, or els let hym buylde upon an hyll or a hylles syde".[24] While this advice was not necessarily intended to advocate building on a hill-top, such a practice was certainly adopted by Sir Francis Willoughby at Wollaton (Notts.) in the 1580s when he abandoned the valley site of his ancestral home and built anew on the nearby hill.[25]

The value of a hilly position was increasingly appreciated by architectural treatise writers. Although Sir Henry Wotton warned against the perils of hill-top building in the inclement North, he also wrote in his *The Elements of Architecture* (1624) that a house should not "be subject to any foggy noysomnesse, from Fenns or Marshes neere adjoyning; nor too Mineral exhalations, from the soile it selfe. Not undigested, for Want of Winde..." Instead, he extolled "the properties of a well chosen Prospect...there is a Lordship likewise of the Eye which being a raunging and Imperious and (I might say) an usurping Sence, can indure no narrow circumscription; but must be fedde with extent and varietie".[26]

The impracticalities of building on top of a hill were later recognised by Roger North- he considered that the best place to build was at the "medium" between "mountanous country" and the "plain"..."on the side of an hill, a little rising, and not farr from the bottom"- but he acknowledges that this opinion was not shared by all of his contemporaries: "It was the usage in ancient times, to build low, and neer water, but that is found or thought unwholesome, and the next course is to take the other

extream and build, as our age doth, upon the summit of hills, where they are intollerably exposed to weather".[27]

As North was clearly aware, this predisposition towards building on a hill-top contrasted markedly with the medieval and early Tudor tendency to select a low-lying and sheltered spot, close to abundant and convenient supplies of water and firewood, in which to build a house: features equally sought and exploited by the builders of medieval monasteries. In many cases, of course, the English climate ensured that houses continued to be erected in these sheltered valley locations, and as on many other topics, the advice of architectural treatise writers on siting was not entirely practical. But that the advice went not completely unheeded is demonstrated by a group of hill-top houses built in the North Midlands from the 1580s into the early 17th century. Apart from Wollaton in Nottinghamshire, these included the Derbyshire houses of Chatsworth and Hardwick, as well as a number of rather smaller buildings like Barlborough and The Little Castle at Bolsover, also in Derbyshire, Heath Old Hall in Yorkshire and Wootton Lodge in Staffordshire, all, of course, influenced by, if not directly built to, the designs of Robert Smythson.[28]

Elsewhere, great magnates were building lodges where they could retreat with their friends and a few essential servants to hunt or to relax from the pressures of public life. Some of these lodges, like Manor Lodge at Worksop (Notts.) or Wothorpe in Cambridgeshire, which Thomas Cecil, Lord Exeter built on a Greek-cross plan in the early 17th century "to retire to out of the dust when his house of Burleigh was sweeping",[29] were close to the main residences of their owners but large enough to provide temporary accommodation when required. Others, like the rather earlier Hunting Tower at Chatsworth, were built as 'stands', points from which to shoot at deer or from which to watch their hunting.[30]

Several of these buildings, like Robert Cecil's Cranborne in Dorset (1608-11),[31] were on the sites of medieval hunting lodges, while others, including the earliest of its kind, Mount Edgcumbe in Cornwall (1546),[32] Sir Walter Raleigh's Sherborne (Dorset) and Wootton (Staffs.) would soon prove so attractive to their owners that they were enlarged to form their principal residences.[33] Indeed, in both the smaller and the great country house of the late 16th and early 17th centuries, the ever increasing emphasis on the compact plan, an innovation that was to become the

---

[21] Girouard (1983), 106-7.

[22] Francis Bacon, *Essays* (1955 Everyman edn.), 134. See also Paula Henderson, 'Life at the top: sixteenth- and seventeenth-century roofscapes', *Country Life*, 177 (3 January, 1985), 6-9.

[23] Jonathan Hunn, pers. comm.

[24] Andrew Boorde, *A Compendyous Regyment or a Dyetary of Health* (1542), ed. by F.J. Furnivall and printed in Early English Text Ser., Extra Ser., x (1870), 238.

[25] Airs (1975), 17.

[26] Sir Henry Wotton, *The Elements of Architecture* (1624), 3-4.

[27] Roger North, *Of Building* (eds., Howard Colvin & John Newman, 1981), 89-90.

[28] Girouard (1983), passim.

[29] Richard Gough, *Camden's Britannia*, ii (1806 edn.), 292.

[30] Girouard (1983), 119.

[31] R.C.H.M., *Dorset*, v (1975), 7-12.

[32] Girouard (1983), 97-101.

[33] R.C.H.M., *Dorset*, i (1952), 66-9; Girouard, 199-204.

norm by time of the Restoration,[34] meant that there was little or no role for the converted former monastic building.

Many new houses would, of course, yet be built in styles, plan-forms and locations not favoured by the architectural treatise writers or their readers, and many more existing buildings remained to be adapted and remodelled by their owners: certainly, it is true that in all periods (except our own) most construction work has consisted of "alterations, additions or repairs to an older structure".[35] Nevertheless, by c.1600 a combination of factors, not least the marked changes in architectural ideas and direction, had created a set of circumstances where, at the highest social level, it was no longer worth the effort to continue to convert former monastic buildings to domestic use.

---

[34] Colin Platt, *The Great Rebuildings of Tudor and Stuart England* (1994), passim.
[35] L. Stone, *An Open Elite? England 1540-1880* (1984), 352.

ABBREVIATIONS

Add. Chart.	British Library, Additional Charters
Add. MS.	British Library, Additional Manuscripts
Airs (1975)	Malcolm Airs, *The Making of The English Country House 1500-1640* (1975)
Arch. Jnl.	*Archaeological Journal*
Archit. Hist.	*Architectural History*
Assoc. Soc. Rep.	*Associated Societies Reports*
B.L.	British Library, London
Bodl.	Bodleian Library, Oxford
Brayley & Britton, vii	E.W. Brayley & J.Britton, *The Beauties of England and Wales, Vol.7, Hertfordshire* (1808)
Brit. Arch. Rep.	British Archaeological Report
Cal. Pat. R.	*Calendar of Patent Rolls Preserved in the Public Record Office* (1903- (in progress)
Cal. S.P. Dom.	*Calendar of State Papers, Domestic Series, of the Reigns of Edward VI, Mary, Elizabeth & James I*, 12 vols. (1856-72)
C.B.A. Res. Rep.	Council for British Archaeology Research Report
Chauncy	Henry Chauncy, *The Historical Antiquities of Hertfordshire*, 2 vols. (1700, reprinted 1975)
Clutterbuck	Robert Clutterbuck, *The History and Antiquities of Hertfordshire*, 3 vols. (1815-27)
Coppack (1990)	Glyn Coppack, *Abbeys and Priories* (1990)
Cussans	J.E. Cussans, *The History of Hertfordshire*, 3 vols. (1870-81)
D.N.B.	*Dictionary of National Biography*, 22 vols. (revd. edn. 1921/2)
Doggett (1991)	Nicholas Doggett, 'The demolition and conversion of former monastic buildings in Hertfordshire at the Dissolution' in D. Jones-Baker (ed.), *Hertfordshire in History: Papers Presented to Lionel Munby* (1991), 46-64.
Dugdale	William Dugdale (ed.), *Monasticon Anglicanum*, (re-ed. J. Caley, H. Ellis & B. Bandinel, 6 vols. in 8, 1817-30)
Girouard (1983)	Mark Girouard, *Robert Smythson and the Elizabethan Country House* (1983)
Greene (1992)	Patrick Greene, *Medieval Monasteries* (1992)
Harl. MS.	British Library, Harleian Manuscripts
Herts. Arch.	*Hertfordshire Archaeology*
Herts. Past	*Hertfordshire's Past*
Howard (1987)	Maurice Howard, *The Early Tudor Country House* (1987)
H.M.S.O.	Her Majesty's Stationery Office
H.R.O.	Hertfordshire Record Office, Hertford
Jnl. Brit. Arch. Assoc.	*Journal of the British Archaeological Association*
King's Works	Howard Colvin *et al*, *The History of the King's Works, the Middle Ages & 1485-1660*, 4 vols. (1963-82)
Knowles (1953)	David Knowles & R. Neville Hadcock, *Medieval Religious Houses* (1953)
Lansd. MS.	British Library, Lansdowne Manuscripts
Leland	Lucy Toulmin Smith (ed.), *The Itinerary of John Leland in or about the Years 1535-43*, 5 vols. (1906-10)
L.P.	*Calendar of Letters and Papers, Foreign and Domestic, of the Reign of Henry VIII*, eds. J.S. Brewer, J. Gairdner & R.H. Brodie, 21 vols. (1862-1932)
Med. Arch.	*Medieval Archaeology*
misc.	miscellaneous
n.d.	no date
N.M.R.	National Monuments Record, Swindon
Parliamentary Rolls	*Rotuli Parliamentorum ut et Petitiones et Placita in Parliamento*, 6 vols. with index (1832)

Pevsner   Sir   Nikolaus   Pevsner, *Hertfordshire* (2nd edn., revd. Bridget Cherry, 1977)

Platt (1984)   Colin Platt, *The Abbeys and Priories of Medieval England* (1984)

Post-Med. Arch.   *Post-Medieval Archaeology*

P.R.O.   Public Record Office, London

R.C.H.M.   Royal Commission on Historical Monuments, *An Inventory of the Historical Monuments in Hertfordshire* (1910). Other counties are indicated by the addition of county name, volume number and publication date.

Salmon   Nathaniel Salmon, *The History of Hertfordshire* (1728)

Smith (1992)   J.T. Smith, *English Houses 1200-1800: the Hertfordshire Evidence* (1992)

Smith (1993)   J.T. Smith, *Hertfordshire Houses: Selective Inventory* (1993)

S.M.R.   County Sites and Monuments Record, Hertford

Statutes of the Realm   *The Statutes of the Realm, from Original Records and Authentic Manuscripts*, 11 vols. in 12 (1810-28)

Summerson (1977)   John Summerson, *Architecture in Britain, 1530-1830* (6th edn., 1977)

Trans. East Herts. Arch. Soc   *Transactions of the East Hertfordshire Archaeological Society*

Val. Eccl.   *Valor Ecclesiasticus*, eds. J. Caley & J. Hunter, 6 vols. (1810-34)

V.C.H.   *The Victoria History of the Counties of England: Hertfordshire*, 4 vols. (1902-14). Other counties are indicated by the addition of the county name with volume number and publication date.

BIBLIOGRAPHY

A. MANUSCRIPT SOURCES

(NB- only the principal record classes and collections are cited here).

1. *British Library, London*
   Additional Manuscripts: topographical drawings by the Buckler family and other artists, mainly at Add. MS. 32,349-50 and 36,365-6; description of Royston Priory (1747) by William Cole, Add. MS. 5820, fols.19v-35
   Harleian Manuscripts: various
   Lansdowne Manuscripts: various, including a 1587 terrier of Hertford Priory, Lansd. MS. 116, fol.48
2. *Public Record Office, Chancery Lane, London*
   SC6/Hen. VIII/1606-32: ministers' accounts
   SC 12/8/29: survey of Hitchin Priory (1546)
   SP/12/125: survey of Royston Priory (1578)
   E 117/12/30: suppression inventories of Cheshunt, Royston, St Giles in the Wood, Flamstead, Sopwell and Wymondley
   E 315/361: commissioners' returns for Cheshunt, Royston, St Giles in the Wood, Flamstead, Sopwell and Wymondley
   E 315/391 (2): survey of King's Langley Friary (1555)
3. *Library of Society of Antiquaries, London*
   MS. 720: Webster, J., *Gleanings of Antiquity from Verolam and St Albans* (n.d.)
4. *Bodleian Library, Oxford*
   Gough Herts.: annotated books formerly belonging to Richard Gough
   Gough MS.: topographical collections and notes by Richard Gough and others
   MS. Top. Eccl. b. 28
   MS. Willis: topographical collections and notes by Browne Willis
5. *Hertfordshire Record Office, Hertford*
   Buckler Drawings: reference by volume and folio number
   Oldfield Drawings: reference by volume and folio number
   Gerish Collection: collection of late 19th- and early 20th-century newspaper cuttings and other miscellaneous material compiled by W.B. Gerish
   Shrimpton, J., *The Antiquities of Verulam and St Albans* (c.1610): MS. volume, 66,296
6. *County Sites and Monuments Record, Hertford*
   Aerial photograph collection and files and record cards on individual sites and buildings
7. *Hertford Museum*
   Miscellaneous unpublished material on Hertford Priory
8. *Hitchin Museum*
   Miscellaneous unpublished material on The Biggin and Hitchin Priory, mainly collected by Reginald Hine
9. *Museum of St Albans*
   Topographical drawings in the Lewis Evans Collection
10. *St Albans Public Library*
    Luppino drawings in the Lewis Evans Collection
11. *Watford Central Library*
    Photographic collection
12. *National Library of Air Photographs, the Royal Commission on Historical Monuments, Swindon*
    Aerial photographs of individual sites and buildings
13. *National Monuments Record, The Royal Commission on Historical Monuments, Swindon*
    Files and photographs of individual sites and buildings, accessed by computer catalogue in the public search room

B. PRINTED SOURCES

Place of publication is London unless otherwise stated.

1. Primary Sources

Acts of the Privy Council, ed. J.R. Dasent, 32 vols. (1890-1970).

Bates, J.H. (ed.), *The Particular Description of the County of Somerset, Drawn up by Thomas Gerard of Trent, 1633*, Somerset Rec. Soc., 15 (1900).

Boorde, A., *A Compendyous Regyment or a Dyetary of Health* (1542), ed. F.J. Furnivall and printed in Early English Text Ser., Extra Ser., x (1870).

Calendar of the Manuscripts of the Marquis of Salisbury Preserved at Hatfield House, pt.x *Historical Manuscripts Commission Report* (1904).

Calendar of Patent Rolls Preserved in the Public Record Office (1903- (in progress).

Calendar of State Papers, Domestic Series, of the Reigns of Edward VI, Mary, Elizabeth and James I, 12 vols. (1856-72).

Calendar of State Papers, Domestic Series, Addenda, 1547-65, 1566-79, 1580-1625, 3 vols. (1870-2).

Department of the Environment, Lists of Historic Buildings.

Department of the Environment, Lists of Scheduled Ancient Monuments.

Dickens, A.G. (ed.), *Tudor Treatises*, Yorks. Arch. Soc. Rec. Ser., 125 (1959).

Dugdale, W. (ed.), *Monasticon Anglicanum*, (re-ed. Caley, J., Ellis, H. & Bandinel, B., 6 vols. in 8, 1817-30).

Letters and Papers, Foreign and Domestic, of the Reign of Henry VIII, eds. Brewer, J.S., Gairdner, J. & Brodie, R.H., 21 vols. (1862-1932).

Norden, J., *Speculi Britanniae Pars, The Description of Hartfordshire* (1598).

Portland MS. II, *Historical Manuscripts Commission*, 13th Rep., App., pt.2 (1893).

Public Record Office, Lists and Indexes No.9, List of Sheriffs for England and Wales (1898).

Public Record Office, Lists and Indexes No.26, Index of Inquisitions Post Mortem Preserved in the P.R.O., vol. ii (1908).

Riley, H.T. (ed.), *Gesta Abbatum Monasterii Sancti Albani*, 3 vols. (1867).

Rotuli Parliamentorum ut et Petitiones et Placita in Parliamento, 6 vols. with index (1832).

Skelton, J., *The Garden of Laurell* (1523).

The Statutes of the Realm, from Original Records and Authentic Manuscripts, 11 vols. in 12, (1810-28).

Third Report of the Royal Commission on Historical Manuscripts (1872).

Toulmin Smith, L. (ed.), *The Itinerary of John Leland in or about the Years 1535-43*, 5 vols. (1906-10).

Vallans, W., 'A Tale of Two Swannes' (1590), contained in the same writer's 'Account of Several Parts of Hartfordshire', which appears as a prefix to Thomas Hearne's 1769 edition of vol. 5 of John Leland's *Itinerary* (Bodl., Douce HH 169).

Valor Ecclesiasticus, (eds. Caley, J. & Hunter, J.), 6 vols. (1810-34).

Wright, T. (ed.), *Three Chapters of Letters Relating to the Suppression of the Monasteries*, Camden Series, 26 (1843).

2. *Secondary Sources*

Airs, M.R., *The Making of the English Country House 1500-1640* (1975).
　　The Buildings of Britain, Tudor and Jacobean (1983).
　　The Tudor and Jacobean Country House, A Building History (Stroud, 1995).

Andrews, H.C, 'Henry George Oldfield and the Dimsdale collection of Hertfordshire Drawings', *Trans. East Herts. Arch. Soc.*, 11 (1940-44), 212-24.

Ashmore, O., H.M.S.O. guide to *Whalley* (1962).

Astill, G., 'Monastic research designs: Bordesley Abbey and the Arrow Valley' in Gilchrist, R. & Mytum, H. (eds.), *The Archaeology of Rural Monasteries*, Brit. Arch. Rep., 203 (Oxford, 1989), 279-93.

Aston, Margaret, 'English ruins and English history: the Dissolution and the sense of the past', *Jnl. Warburg and Courtauld Institutes*, 36 (1973), 231-55.

Aston, Mick, *Monasteries* (1993).

Bacon, F., *Essays* (1955 Everyman edn.).

Baker, D., 'Excavations at Elstow Abbey, 1965-66', *Beds. Arch. Jnl.*, 3 (1966), 22-30.

Barley, M.W., *Houses and History* (1986).

Baskerville, G., *English Monks and the Suppression of the Monasteries* (1937).

Beresford-Webb, C.A., 'The Biggin' (n.d. but c.1969), unpublished manuscript, Hitchin Museum.

Bettey, J.H., *The Suppression of the Monasteries in the West Country* (Gloucester, 1989).

Bilson, J. & St John Hope, W.H., *Architectural Description of Kirkstall Abbey*, Publications of the Thoresby Soc., 16 (1907).

Bindoff, S.T. (ed.), *The History of Parliament: the House of Commons, 1509-1558*, 3 vols. (1982).

Blaauw, W.H., 'On the Cluniac priory of St Pancras at Lewes, its priors and monks', *Sussex Arch. Collns.*, 3 (1850), 185-210.

Black, J.B., *The Reign of Elizabeth, 1558-1603* (2nd. edn., Oxford, 1959).

Bold, J., *Wilton House and the Story of English Palladianism* (1988).

Bradfer-Lawrence, H.L., 'The building of Raynham Hall', *Norfolk Arch.*, 23 (1927), 93-146.

Brakspear, H., *Waverley Abbey* (1905).
　　'Stanley Abbey', *Wilts. Nat. Hist. Mag.*, 35 (1907/8), 541-81.
　　'Bardney Abbey', *Arch. Jnl.*, 79 (1922), 1-92.

Brayley, E.W. & Britton, J., *The Beauties of England and Wales, Vol. 7, Hertfordshire* (1808).

Brown, J.A., 'The hospice of The Knights Templars at Standon', *Trans. East Herts. Arch. Soc.*, 1 (1899-1901), 289-91.

Bullard, I.V., *Flamstead, its Church and History* (Rochester, 1902).

Burleigh, G. *et al*, *Wymondley Priory, Hertfordshire: An Archaeological Evaluation* (North Herts. District Council Museums, Hitchin, 1989).

Burne, R.V.H., *Chester Cathedral from its Founding by Henry VIII to the Accession of Queen Victoria* (1958).

Busby, J.H., 'The Hertfordshire drawings of Thomas Fisher (1771?-1836)', *Herts. Arch.*, 1 (1968), 110-16.

Butler, Lawrence, 'The archaeology of rural monasteries in England and Wales' in Gilchrist, R. & Mytum H., (eds.), *The Archaeology of Rural Monasteries*, Brit. Arch. Rep., 203 (Oxford, 1989), 1-27.

Butler, Lionel & Given-Wilson, C., *Medieval Monasteries of Great Britain* (1979).

Campbell, L., 'Documentary evidence for the building of Raynham Hall', *Archit. Hist.*, 32 (1989), 52-63.

Chandler, J., *John Leland's Itinerary, Travels in Tudor England* (Stroud, 1993).

Chauncy, H., *The Historical Antiquities of Hertfordshire*, 2 vols. (1700, reprinted Dorking, 1975).

Christie, P.M. & Croad, J.G., 'Excavations at Denny Abbey', *Arch. Jnl.*, 137 (1980), 138-279.

Clarke, H., *The Archaeology of Medieval England* (Oxford, 1984).

Clutterbuck, R., *The History and Antiquities of Hertfordshire*, 3 vols. (1815-27).

Colvin, H.M. *et al*, *The History of the King's Works, the Middle Ages & 1485-1660*, 4 vols. (1963-82).

Cobb, G., *English Cathedrals, The Forgotten Centuries: Restoration and Change from 1530 to the Present Day* (1980).

Cook, G.H. (ed.), *Letters to Cromwell and Others on the Suppression of the Monasteries* (1965).

Coope, R., 'The "long gallery": its origins, development, use and decoration', *Archit. Hist.*, 29 (1986), 43-84.

With Fernie, E. & Howard, M., *Newstead Abbey. Papers and Discussion From a Day Symposium organised by the Society of Architectural Historians in Association with the Thoroton Society* (April 1992).

Cooper, N., *Houses of the Gentry 1480-1680* (New Haven: London, 1999).

Cooper-Reade, H., 'Jewson's Yard, Hertford: excavations of St Mary's Priory and St John's Parish Church', *Herts. Past*, 29 (Autumn 1990), 29-37.

Copeland, G.W., 'Some problems of Buckland Abbey', *Trans. Devon. Assoc.*, 85 (1953), 41-52.

Coppack, G., *Abbeys and Priories* (1990).

Cranage, D.H.S., *Home of the Monk* (Cambridge, 1934).

Crossley, D.W., *Post-Medieval Archaeology* (Leicester, 1990).

Cussans, J.E., *The History of Hertfordshire*, 3 vols. (1870-81, reprinted Wakefield, 1972).

Denny, H.L.L., 'Biography of Sir Edward Denny', *Trans. East Herts. Arch. Soc.*, 2 (1904), 247-60.
    'Biography of the right honourable Sir Anthony Denny' *Trans. East Herts. Arch. Soc.*, 3, pt.ii (1906), 197-216.

Dickens, A.G., *The English Reformation* (1964).

Dickinson, J.C., *Monastic Life in Medieval England* (1961).
    'The buildings of the English Austin canons after the Dissolution of the Monasteries', *Jnl. Brit. Arch. Assoc.*, 3rd. Ser., 31 (1968), 60-75.
    Dictionary of National Biography, 22 vols. (revd. edn., Oxford, 1921/2).
    Dictionary of National Biography, 1951-60 (Oxford, 1971).

Doggett, N.D.B., 'The demolition and conversion of former monastic buildings in Hertfordshire at the Dissolution' in Jones-Baker, D. (ed.), *Hertfordshire in History: Papers Presented to Lionel Munby* (Hertford, 1991), 46-64.
    'Medieval hospitals in Hertfordshire and their dissolution', *Herts. Past*, 38 (Spring 1995), 8-12.
    Unpublished paper on the dispersal of the Hertfordshire religious and their post-Dissolution careers.

Drewett, P.L. & Stuart, I.W., 'Excavations in the Norman gate tower, Bury St Edmunds Abbey', *Proc. Suffolk Inst. Arch.*, 33 (1973-5), 241-52.

Drury, P.J., 'No other palace in the kingdom will compare with it: the evolution of Audley End, 1605-1745', *Archit. Hist.*, 23 (1980), 1-39.
    'Walden into Audley End' in Bassett, S.R. (ed.), *Saffron Walden: Excavations and Research 1972-80*, C.B.A. Res. Rep., 45 (1982), 94-105.

Duffy, E., *The Stripping of the Altars, Traditional Religion in England 1400-1580* (New Haven: London, 1992).

Dyce, A. (ed.), *The Poetical Works of John Skelton*, 2 vols. (1843).

East Hertfordshire Archaeological Society, 'Twenty fourth excursion (to Wymondley)', *Trans. East Herts. Arch. Soc.*, 3 (1906), 230-1.

'Visit of the East. Herts. Arch. Soc. (to Standon), September 1930', *Trans. East Herts. Arch. Soc.*, 8 (1928-33), 265-6.

Ellis, W., *Campagna of London* (1791).

Elton, G.R., *England Under the Tudors* (2nd. edn., 1974).

Emerick, K. & Wilson, K., 'Fountains Abbey: some interim results of remote sensing', *Conservation Bulletin*, 18 (October 1992), 7-9.

Farris, N., *The Wymondleys* (Hertford, 1989).

Fergusson, P.,'The twelfth-century refectories at Rievaulx and Byland Abbeys' in Norton, E.C. & Park, W.D. (eds.), *Cistercian Art and Architecture in the British Isles* (Cambridge, 1986), 160-80.

with Harrison, S., *Rievaulx Abbey* (New Haven: London, 1999).

Fletcher, P.C., 'Recent excavations at Hinton Priory', *Proc. Somerset Arch. & Nat. Hist. Soc.*, 96 (1951), 160-5.

Forster, E.M., *Howard's End* (Harmondsworth, 1960 Penguin edn.).

Fuller, T., *The Church History of Great Britain*, 6 vols. (ed. Brewer, J.S., Oxford, 1845).
    The Worthies of England (ed. Freeman, J., 1952).

Garner, T. & Stratton, A., *The Domestic Architecture of England During the Tudor Period*, 2 vols. (1929).

Gamlen, St John O., 'Medieval window glass from the Priory, King's Langley', *Herts. Arch.*, 3 (1973), 73-7.

Gasquet, F.A., *Henry VIII and the English Monasteries* (1906).

Gilchrist, R. & Mytum, H., *The Archaeology of Rural Monasteries*, Brit. Arch. Rep., 203 (Oxford, 1989).
    Recent Advances in Monastic Archaeology, Brit. Arch. Rep., 227 (Oxford, 1993).

Gilyard-Beer, R., H.M.S.O. guide to *Cleeve Abbey* (1959).
    'The eastern arm of the abbey church at Bury St Edmunds', *Proc. Suffolk Inst. Arch.*, 31 (1967/69), 256-62.

Girouard, M., 'Salisbury Hall, Hertfordshire- II', *Country Life*, 126 (29 October, 1959), 708-11.
    Robert Smythson and the Elizabethan Country House (New Haven: London, 1983).
    Hardwick Hall, National Trust Guide (1990).

Godfrey, W., 'The abbot's parlour, Thame Park', *Arch. Jnl.*, 86 (1929), 59-68.

Gotch, J.A., *Early Renaissance Architecture in England* (1914).

Gough, R., *Camden's Britannia*, 4 vols. (1806).

Graham, R. & Gilyard-Beer, R., H.M.S.O. guide to *Monk Bretton* (1966).

Greene, J.P., *Norton Priory* (Cambridge, 1989).
    Medieval Monasteries (Leicester, 1992).
    'The impact of the dissolution on monasteries in Cheshire: the case of Norton' in Thacker, A. (ed.), *Chester: Medieval Archaeology, Art & Architecture*, Brit. Arch. Assoc. Conference Trans., xxii (2000), 152-66.

Guy, J., *Tudor England* (Oxford, 1988).

Habbakuk, H.J., 'The market for monastic property, 1539-1603', *Economic Hist. Rev.*, 2nd. Ser., 10 (1957/8), 362-80.

Haigh, C., *English Reformations, Religion, Politics and Society Under the Tudors* (Oxford, 1993).

Hamilton Thompson, A., *History and Architectural Description of the Priory of St Mary, Bolton-in-Wharfedale*, Publications of the Thoresby Soc., 30 (1928).

Harbottle, B., 'Excavations at the Carmelite friary, Newcastle-upon-Tyne, 1965, 1967', *Arch. Aeliana*, 4th Ser., 46 (1968), 163-223.

with Fraser, R., 'Black Friars, Newcastle-upon-Tyne, after the Dissolution of the Monasteries', *Arch. Aeliana*, 5th Ser., 15 (1987), 23-150.

Hare, J., *Battle Abbey, The Eastern Range and the Excavations of 1978-80* (1985).

'Netley Abbey: monastery, mansion and ruin', *Proc. Hants. Field Club*, 49 (1993), 207-27.

Harvey, J., *English Mediaeval Architects* (revd. edn., Gloucester, 1984).

Hay. D., 'The dissolution of the monasteries in the diocese of Durham', *Arch. Aeliana*, 4th Ser., 15 (1938), 69-114.

Heal, F. & Holmes, C., *The Gentry in England and Wales 1500-1700* (Basingstoke: London, 1994).

Henderson, P., 'Life at the top: sixteenth- and seventeenth-century roofscapes', *Country Life*, 177 (3 January, 1985), 6-9.

Hine, R., *The History of Hitchin*, 2 vols. (1927-9).

Hirst, S., Walsh, D.A. & Wright, S.M., *Bordesley Abbey II*, Brit. Arch. Rep., 111 (Oxford, 1983).

Hockey, F., *Beaulieu, King John's Abbey* (Old Woking, 1976).

Hodgson, J.F., 'Eggleston Abbey', *Yorks. Arch. Jnl.*, 18 (1904/5), 129-82.

Horden, J., 'The fate of monastic churches in Cumbria: a consideration of the position at law' in Loades, J. (ed.), *Monastic Studies* (Bangor, 1990), 255-66.

Hoskins, W.G., *The Age of Plunder* (1976).

Howard, M., *The Early Tudor Country House* (1987).

Huggins, P.J., 'Excavations of the collegiate and Augustinian churches, Waltham Abbey, Essex, 1984-87', *Arch. Jnl.*, 146 (1989), 476-537.

Kew, J.,'The disposal of crown lands and the Devon land market, 1536-58', *Agricultural Hist. Rev.*, 18 (1970), 93-105.

Kingston, A., *A History of Royston* (1906).

Knowles, M.D., *The Religious Orders in England*, iii (Cambridge, 1959).

with Hadcock, R.N., *Medieval Religious Houses* (1953).

with St Joseph, J.K.S., *Monastic Sites from the Air* (Cambridge, 1952).

Laing, C.E., 'Excavations on the site of Bardney Abbey', *Assoc. Soc. Reps.*, 32, pt.i (1913), 21-34.

Liljegren, S.B., *The Fall of the Monasteries and the Social Changes in England* (Lund, 1924).

Lloyd, D., *State Worthies* (1779).

Lloyd, L.J., *John Skelton* (Oxford, 1938).

Lowther, M.A., 'Reports on the antiquities lately found at Lewes' and 'Further report on discoveries at Lewes', *Jnl. Brit. Arch. Assoc.*, 1 & 2 (1846 & 1847), 346-57 & 104-8.

Mackie, J.D., *The Earlier Tudors, 1485-1558* (Oxford, 1952).

Marshall, P., 'The archaeological survey at Wollaton Hall: some revelations' in Airs, M.R. (ed.), *The Tudor and Jacobean Great House* (Oxford University Dept. Continuing Education, Conference Proceedings, 1994), 73-90.

Martin, C.T., 'Sir John Daunce's accounts of money received from the treasurer of the king's chamber temp. Henry VIII', *Archaeologia*, 47 (1883), 295-336.

McNeil R. & Turner, R.C., 'An architectural and topographical survey of Vale Royal Abbey', *Jnl. Chester Arch. Soc.*, 70 (1990), 51-79.

Mercer, E., *English Art 1553-1625* (Oxford, 1962).

Miller, H., *Henry VIII and the English Nobility* (Oxford, 1986).

Munby, J., 'J.C. Buckler, Tackley's Inn and three medieval houses in Oxford', *Oxoniensia*, 43 (1978), 123-69.

Munby, L., *The Hertfordshire Landscape* (1977).

Musty, A.E.S., 'Exploratory excavation within the monastic precinct, Waltham Abbey, 1972', *Essex Arch. & Hist.*, 10 (1978), 127-73.

Neal, D.S., 'Excavations at the palace of King's Langley, Hertfordshire 1974-6', *Med. Arch.*, 21 (1977), 124-65.

Newman, J., 'The development of the staircase in Elizabethan and Jacobean England' in Chastel, A. & Guillaume, J. (eds.), *L'Escalier dans l'architecture de la Renaissance* (Paris, 1985), 175-8.

Nichols, J. (ed.), *Progresses of James I*, 4 vols. (1828).

North, R., *Of Building* (eds., Colvin, H.M. & Newman, J., Oxford, 1981).

Oxley, J.E., *The Reformation in Essex to the Death of Mary* (Manchester, 1965).

Page, W., 'The history of the monastery of St Mary de Pre', *Trans. St Albans and Herts. Archit. and Arch. Soc.*, (1895/6), 8-18.

Pantin, W.A., 'Notley Abbey', *Oxoniensia*, 6 (1941), 36-41.

Peck, F., *Desiderata Curiosa* (1779).

Peers, C.R., H.M.S.O. guides to *Byland* (1930), *Finchale* (revd., 1973), *Rievaulx* (1933) and *St Botolph's, Colchester* (revd., 1964).

Pevsner, N., *North Somerset and Bristol* (Harmondsworth, 1958).

North-East Norfolk and Norwich (Harmondsworth, 1962).

Bedfordshire and the County of Huntingdon and Peterborough (Harmondsworth, 1968).

Yorkshire: York and the East Riding (Harmondsworth, 1972).

Wiltshire (2nd edn., revd. Cherry, B., (Harmondsworth, 1975)

Hertfordshire (2nd edn., revd. Cherry, B., Harmondsworth, 1977).

Leicestershire and Rutland (2nd. edn., revd. Williamson, E., Harmondsworth, 1984).

Devon (2nd edn., revd. Cherry, B., Harmondsworth, 1989).

Northumberland (2nd edn., revd. Grundy, J. *et al*, Harmondsworth, 1992).

Buckinghamshire (2nd edn., revd. Williamson, E., Harmondsworth, 1994).

with Lloyd, D., *Hampshire and the Isle of Wight* (Harmondsworth, 1967).

with Nairn, I., *Sussex* (Harmondsworth, 1965).

with Sherwood, J., *Oxfordshire* (Harmondsworth, 1974).

with Wedgwood, A., *Warwickshire* (Harmondsworth, 1966).

with Cherry, B., *London 3: North West* (Harmondsworth, 1991).

Piggott, S., *Ruins in a Landscape, Essays in Antiquarianism* (Edinburgh, 1976).

Platt, C.P.S., *Medieval England* (1978).

Abbeys and Priories of Medieval England (1984).

The Architecture of Medieval Britain (New Haven: London, 1990).

The Great Rebuildings of Tudor and Stuart England (1994).

Pollard, H.P., 'Franciscan and Benedictine monuments of Ware' in Standing, P.C. (ed.), *Memorials of Old Hertfordshire* (1905), 53-7.

with Gerish, W.B., 'The religious orders in Hitchin', *Trans. East Herts. Arch. Soc.*, 3, pt.i (1905), 1-10.

Poster, J. & Sherlock, D., 'Denny Abbey: the nuns' refectory', *Proc. Cambridge Antiq. Soc.*, 76 (1987), 67-82.

Preston, A.E., 'The demolition of Reading Abbey', *Berks. Arch. Jnl.*, 39 (1935), 107-44.

Pugsley, S., 'Landed society and the emergence of the country house in Tudor and early Stuart Devon' in Gray, T., Rowe, M. & Erskine, A. (eds.), *Tudor and Stuart Government, Essays Presented to Joyce Youings* (Exeter, 1992), 96-118.

Rackham, O., Blair, W.J. & Munby, J., 'The thirteenth-century roofs and floor of the Blackfriars priory at Gloucester', *Med. Arch.*, 22 (1978), 105-22.

Rahtz, P. & Hirst, S., *Bordesley Abbey*, Brit. Arch. Rep., 23 (Oxford, 1976).

Reeve, J.A., *A Monograph on the Abbey of St Mary of Fountains* (1892).

Rigold, S., 'Wymondley Priory', *Med. Arch.*, 18 (1974), 191.

Roberts, E., *The Hill of the Martyr, An Architectural History of St Albans Abbey* (Dunstable, 1993).

Robertson, M. *et al*, 'Listed buildings: the national resurvey of England', *Trans. Ancient Monuments Soc.*, 37 (1993), 21-94.

Rogers, J.S., 'The manor and houses at Gorhambury', *Trans. St Albans and Herts. Archit. and Arch. Soc.*, n.s., 4 (1935), 35-112.

Rouse, C., 'Domestic wall and panel paintings in Hertfordshire', *Arch. Jnl.*, 146 (1989), 423-50.

Royal Commission on Historical Monuments, *An Inventory of the Historical Monuments in Hertfordshire* (1910).

Essex, ii (1921).

Dorset, i (1952, reprinted with amendments 1974) & v (1975).

Churches of South-East Wiltshire (1987).

The Country Houses of Northamptonshire (1996).

St John Hope, W.H., 'On the Premonstratensian abbey of St Mary at Alnwick, Northumberland', *Arch. Jnl.*, 44 (1887), 337-46.

'Fountains Abbey', *Yorks. Arch. Jnl.*, 15 (1898/9), 269-402.

'The Gilbertine priory of Watton in the East Riding of Yorkshire', *Arch. Jnl.*, 58 (1901), 1-34.

'The architectural history of Mount Grace Charterhouse', *Yorks. Arch. Jnl.*, 18 (1905), 270-309.

'The making of Place House at Titchfield, near Southampton in 1538', *Arch. Jnl.*, 63 (1906), 231-43.

St Joseph, J.K.S. & Knowles, M.D., *Monastic Sites from the Air* (Cambridge, 1952).

Salmon, N., *The History of Hertfordshire* (1728).

Sandeen, E.R., 'The Building Activities of Sir Nicholas Bacon', unpublished Ph.D thesis (Chicago, 1959). A microfilm copy is deposited in the Bodleian Library, Oxford (1959 Chicago 9).

Saunders, A., 'Blackfriars', *Arch. Jnl.*, 122 (1965), 217-19.

Savine, A., *The English Monasteries on the Eve of the Dissolution* (Oxford, 1909).

Schofield, J., 'Building in religious precincts in London at the Dissolution and after' in Gilchrist, R. & Mytum, H. (eds.), *Recent Advances in Monastic Archaeology*, Brit. Arch. Rep., 227 (Oxford, 1993), 29-41.

Medieval London Houses (New Haven: London, 1994).

Shaw, S., 'Account of Ashridge', *The Topographer*, ii, no.3 (March 1790), 131-54.

Shaw, W.A., *The Knights of England*, 2 vols. (1906).

Sherlock, D., 'Discoveries at Horsham St Faith Priory, 1970-73', *Norfolk Arch.*, 36 (1976), 202-23.

Smith, J.T., *English Houses 1200-1800: The Hertfordshire Evidence* (1992).

Hertfordshire Houses: Selective Inventory (1993).

Smith, R.B., *Land and Politics in the England of Henry VIII: the West Riding of Yorkshire, 1530-46* (Oxford, 1970).

Spelman, H., *The History and Fate of Sacrilege*, 1632 (published posthumously in 1698).

Spittle, S.D.T., 'Madingley Hall', *Arch. Jnl.*, 124 (1967), 225-6.

Stalley, R.A., *The Cistercian Monasteries of Ireland* (New Haven: London, 1987).

Steane, J.M., *The Archaeology of Medieval England and Wales* (1984).

Stocker, D. & Everson, P., 'Rubbish recycled: a study of the re-use of stone in Lincolnshire' in Parsons, D. (ed.), *Stone Quarrying and Building in England A.D. 43-1525* (1990), 83-101.

'The archaeology of the Reformation in Lincoln: a case study in the redistribution of building materials in the mid 16th century', *Lincs. Hist. & Arch.*, 25 (1990), 18-32.

Stone, L., *The Crisis of the Aristocracy, 1558-1641* (Oxford, 1965).

> *An Open Elite? England 1540-1880* (Oxford, 1984).

With Stone, J.C., 'Country houses and their owners in Hertfordshire, 1540-1879' in Aydelotte, W.O., Bogue, A.C. & Fogel, R.W. (eds.), *The Dimensions of Quantitative Research in History* (1972), 56-123.

Streeten, A.D.F., *Bayham Abbey*, Sussex Arch. Soc. Monograph 2 (Lewes, 1983).

Summerson, J., *Architecture in Britain, 1530-1830* (revd. edn., Harmondsworth, 1977).

Swales, T.H., 'The redistribution of the monastic lands in Norfolk at the Dissolution', *Norfolk Arch.*, 34 (1962-66), 14-44.

Thacker, A. (ed.), *Chester: Medieval Archaeology, Art & Architecture*, Brit. Arch. Assoc. Conference Trans., xxii (2000).

Thompson, M.W., *Ruins: their Preservation and Display* (1981).

The Decline of the Castle (Cambridge, 1987).

Thurley, S., 'English Royal Palaces, 1450-1550', unpublished Ph.D. thesis (London, 1991).

> *The Royal Palaces of Tudor England* (New Haven: London, 1993).

Todd, H.J., *The History of the College of Bonhommes at Ashridge* (1823).

The Topographer, ii, no.3 (March 1790), 131-54.

Tyack, G., *Warwickshire Country Houses* (Chichester, 1994).

The Victoria History of the Counties of England,

> *Buckinghamshire*, iii (1925), iv (1927).
> *Essex*, ii (1907).
> *Hampshire*, iv (1911).
> *Hertfordshire*, 4 vols. (1902-14).
> *Huntingdonshire*, ii (1932).
> *Oxfordshire*, vii (1962), ix (1969).
> *Shropshire*, ii (1973).
> *Somerset*, iii (1974).
> *Warwickshire*, iv (1947).

Wacher, J., 'Cirencester 1964', *Antiquaries Jnl.*, 45 (1965), 105-10.

Walbran, R., *Memorials of the Abbey of St Mary of Fountains, I and II*, Surtees Soc., 42 (1862) and 67 (1876).

Walters, R., 'Ware Priory', *Trans. East Herts. Arch. Soc.*, 1, pt.i (1899), 39-43.

Ward, S., 'The friaries in Chester, their impact and legacy', in Thacker, A. (ed.), *Chester: Medieval Archaeology, Art & Architecture*, Brit. Arch. Assoc. Conference Trans., xxii (2000), 121-31.

Warren, C.F.S. (ed.), *An Appendix Bringing the Work the History and Fate of Sacrilege up to the Present Date* (1898).

Weever, J., *Ancient Funerall Monuments* (1631).

Williams, J.A., 'Sources for recusant history (1559-1791) in English official archives', *Recusant Hist.*, 16 (1983), 331-451.

Wood, A., *Athenae Oxonienses*, 5 vols. (ed., Bliss, P., 1813-20).

Woodfield, C., 'Finds from the free grammar school at the Whitefriars, Coventry, c.1545-c.1557/8', *Post-Med. Arch.*, 15 (1981), 81-159.

Woodman, F., *The Architectural History of Canterbury Cathedral* (1981).

Woodward, G.W.O., 'A speculation in monastic lands', *English Hist. Rev.*, 79 (1964), 778-83.

> *The Dissolution of the Monasteries* (1966).

Wotton, H., *The Elements of Architecture* (1624).

Youings, J.A., *The Dissolution of the Monasteries* (1971).

> *Sixteenth-Century England* (Harmondsworth, 1984).

Appendix

The purpose of the appendix is primarily to provide a detailed architectural description of each site included in Chapters 2 and 3 (the Hertfordshire sample), together with an inventory of all known visual evidence and a list of all primary and secondary sources consulted in drawing up these descriptions.

The bulk of the fieldwork from which the site reports in the Appendix are compiled was carried out between 1989 and 1992 with an additional visit to Ware Priory in February 1994 when extensive repairs were being carried out to the building as part of a conversion project. The criteria and methodology applied in examining the fabric of each site are described in Chapter 1 (pp.10-11). It is intended in due course to deposit the notes and files which make up the archive at the Hertfordshire Record Office.

In the lists of sources for each site, place of publication for all printed works, both primary and secondary, is London unless otherwise stated.

ASHRIDGE

History

College of Bonshommes founded by Edmund, Earl of Cornwall in 1283; dissolved January 1540.[1] The property was then leased in November 1540 for 21 years to John Norrys,[2] but in 1550 the lease was revoked and the site granted to Princess Elizabeth.[3] In 1557 she leased the house to Richard Combes for 21 years,[4] and in 1572 to William Gorge for 31 years after the expiry of the lease to Combes.[5]

In 1575 the property passed to John Dudley and John Ayscough,[6] agents to Henry, Lord Cheyney and his wife, Jane.[7] It remained with this family until 1601 when it was conveyed to Ralph Marshall and then in 1603 to Randolph Crew and Thomas Chamberlain.[8] In 1604 Ashridge was bought by Thomas, Lord Ellesmere,[9] remaining with the Egerton/Brownlow family until 1925.[10] The estate was then sold, the buildings serving first as a political training college and then, from 1959, as a business management college.[11]

INTRODUCTION: THE BUILDINGS

The site of the monastic college and the 16th-/17th-century house which succeeded it is now largely covered by James Wyatt's vast Gothic fantasy of 1808-13, completed by his nephew, Sir Jeffry Wyatville between 1813 and 1821.[12] The only monastic buildings to survive are the 14th-century undercroft and the late medieval barn, both of which are described below. No attempt is made here to describe the early 19th-century house, as this bears no direct relation to the monastic buildings or to the immediately post-Dissolution house, and the reader's attention is drawn to published accounts of this elsewhere.[13] Until 1895 the majority of the house was in Buckinghamshire, although most of the service buildings of both the old and new houses have always been in Hertfordshire.[14]

INTRODUCTION: DOCUMENTARY EVIDENCE

The documentary evidence for Ashridge is particularly abundant and, by way of introduction, it is worth considering the detailed survey of the site made in October 1575 by the supervisors of the queen's lands in Buckinghamshire and Hertfordshire, Sir Richard Asshefyld and Richard Young, after its acquisition by Henry, Lord Cheyney.[15] The survey is especially useful for the measurements and values it gives for the buildings then surviving:-

---

[1] Knowles (1953), 176; *V.C.H., Bucks.*, i (1905), 386-7.I

[2] H.J.Todd, *The History of the College of Bonhommes at Ashridge* (1823), 83. Hereafter described as Todd. Todd's *History* is a particularly valuable source as it refers to several important documents which are now lost.

[3] *Cal. Pat. R. Edw. VI.*, iii, 238.

[4] Todd, 31-2; an original copy of this lease is kept in the present house.

[5] P.R.O., C 66/1087/2679.

[6] H.R.O., AH 943B; P.R.O., C 66/1127/2823.

[7] Bodl., MS Willis 102, fol.15v.

[8] Ibid.

[9] Ibid.

[10] H. Senar, *Little Gaddesden and Ashridge* (1983), 9. Hereafter described as Senar.

[11] Ibid; ex. inf. Ashridge archivist, Kay Sanecki.

[12] Pevsner, 237-40. Although Jeffry Wyatt did not adopt the name Wyatville until 1824, this name is used throughout here to avoid confusion with his uncle, James Wyatt.

[13] Ibid; *V.C.H.*, ii, 210-11; Todd, 70-7; G. Lipscomb, *The History and Antiquities of Buckinghamshire*, iii (1847), 444-7; *Saturday Magazine*, no. 774 (July 27, 1844), 29-30; A.J. Bolton, 'Ashridge Park', *Country Life* (Aug. 6 and 13, 1921), 160-6 and 192-8.

[14] D. Coult, *A Prospect of Ashridge* (1980), 230-1. Hereafter described as Coult.

[15] Printed in Todd, 60-4. The survey is mainly written in Latin and is here translated and much abbreviated: the original spelling has been retained where English words are used in the survey.

"It is stated on oath that the building and structure of the mansion house as to lead, iron, timber, tiles, stone, glass, le paning tyle (?pantiles) and all other materials of the same is valued, as if it were to be sold, as follows:-

The church

The body of the church, 51ft long by 32ft wide; St. Jones Chapell 51ft by 21ft; Our Lady Chappell 51ft by 21ft; le South Ile 26ft by 32ft; le North Ile 26ft by 32ft; Chancel 81ft by 32ft; le steple 30ft by 30ft. The church with all its limbs is covered with lead, of which a large part is entirely clear and in many places is late repaired with le soder and in various other places there has been work of alteration.

The cloisters are covered with lead and its dimensions are: west side 90ft by 10ft; south side 42ft by 9ft; north side 42ft by 9ft.

There are various other places covered with lead as follows: the Sextrye (sacristy) 33ft by 22ft; the plate howse 18ft 8in by 11ft; the dorter howse 108ft by 34ft; the Librarye 33ft by 23½ft; the howse of Evidence 10ft by 8ft; the Maynes Hall with certain places annexed to the same 64ft by 24ft; the greate Chamber 64ft by 24ft; the pryve Chamber 28ft by 18ft; the Lordes Chappell 20ft by 10ft; the greate Hall 66ft by 28ft; Mr Chamberlens lodging called the Tower 30ft by 30ft; le 200 stayers to the said tower 10ft; the gromes Chamber 15ft by 9ft; the Bed Chamber 48ft by 24ft; chapel adjoining the said chamber 18ft by 14½ft; the Taylery 14ft by 12ft; the Chapman's parlour 15ft. That all places, cloisters, rooms, halls and various edifices above mentioned are covered in lead, although in many parts damaged (value not recorded).

It is stated on oath that the stone, iron, le seeling, timber, glass, le pavingtyle, doors and windows of the church with their tracery are worth £151 if sold. The cloisters from the Gromes Chamber up to le Sextre is worth £4; le Sextre on the south cloister £4; le Dortery and the howse of Evidence £50; the Maynes hall £7; the greate hall £30; le Librarye with the Chapter-howse beneath £8 10s; the gromes Chamber above the cloister 33s 4d; the greate Chamber with the Chamber of presens above £20; the Bed chamber above which is le Fermery with two chapels adjoining £10; the pryve Chamber with chapel below £6; the Taylery gate 40s.

It is further stated that there are various houses and edifices called the owtehowses which, if sold, are worth as follows: le Deyrey with an old house adjoining called a cartehowse 100s; the chapel outside the gate and the hunters Lodge 40s; the porters Lodge £10; stables £8 6s 8d; the plommery howse and le chaundery howse £3; a barn £20; the Bayliffs chamber £7; a dovecote £3 6s 8d; the well howse with appendages £7; le Boyling-howse and Fyshhowse with a room adjoining £6 8s 4d; the drye Larder with two rooms adjoining 50s; a little room adjoining le dry larder 30s; the kechin 66s 8d; a house called Callys 106s 7d; a house called Copthall with various rooms adjoining £7 10s; a small house on the wall on the south side of the church 26s 7d an old house called the Tower 66s 8d; the stone wall with tiles on top surrounding the house of Assheridge £13; two chambers within le Meynes hall 40s. The value of all the houses and edifices (except the lead, much damaged) is £363 13s 4d."

It is clear that the values assigned to the buildings represent the amount which could be obtained on the sale of their materials and we will look later at the evidence the survey gives for the survival of individual structures in 1575. For the moment, it is sufficient briefly to record the information that it gives on the lay-out of the monastic buildings. The surviving undercroft lies under the drawing and dining rooms of the 19th-century house. Its actual dimensions and the measurements of the great hall in the 1575 survey are virtually identical. This makes it clear that the undercroft lay under the great hall, which is likely originally to have been the refectory on the north side of the monastic cloister. The large cruciform church with its long choir, transepts and short nave with north and south aisles would have lain to the south, with the dorter on the east, presumably with the chapter house and sacristy beneath (although there is a reference to the sacristy being on the south cloister), and "Maynes Hall" (possibly the guest range) would have occupied the west side. To the north would have been an outer court, with a gatehouse on its north side, apparently with a chapel outside. The service and farmbuildings lay to the west, as is confirmed by the surviving 15th-century barn, and the whole complex seems to have been enclosed by a precinct wall.

THE SURVIVING BUILDINGS

The undercroft, well and barn are the only structures from the monastic college surviving *in situ* in the present house and grounds.

The undercroft. This is situated under the drawing room, ante-room and dining room of the Wyatt house, extending in length from the middle of the bay windows in both of the principal rooms, and measures 68ft by 26ft. There are eight octagonal pillars with chamfered plinths to the centre, including the responds at the east and west ends, dividing the space into 14 equal-sized compartments. There are corresponding pillars to both the north and south walls, flanked by deep recesses with later stone shelves, the bays immediately to the east of the entrance, which is in the centre on the north wall, being less deeply recessed on both the north and south sides. Each section of the roof is vaulted with intersecting chamfered ribs springing directly from the pillars, which do not have capitals. There are no bosses. The pillars are built of Totternhoe ashlar, which is also the material used for the roof and the upper parts of the walls on all four sides, with brick used beneath the shelves and to the lower parts of the end walls. The floor is stone-flagged except under the shelves, where it is of brick.

Various dates have been speculated for the undercroft,[16] but it is most likely to have been built in the early 14th century.

No other medieval or 16th-century work can be identified in the extensive cellars, which are mostly constructed of brick and relate directly to the Wyatt house. There is a band of stonework in the passage-way to the north of the undercroft, which turns at right-angles to run under the early 19th-century house. Although the stone itself may be of monastic origin, it was probably simply re-used after the demolitions of 1800-02 and there is nothing to suggest that it relates to the pre- or immediately post-Dissolution buildings.

A pair of substantial oak doors near the entrance to the present chapel is said to have come from the monastic college.[17] They have blind tracery patterns including window designs of two trefoil-headed lights with quatrefoils above. They are probably late 14th century and were re-used when the new house was built; unfortunately, their location in the previous building is unknown.

The Well. This is situated in a well house under the present chapel. Traditionally believed to be 275ft deep,[18] it was in fact found to be 224ft deep when explored by the Watford Underwater Club in 1970-71.[19] Cut through the solid chalk, it is flint lined for the top 28ft. The cast-iron donkey wheel was installed in the early 19th century and it seems that the well house was remodelled at the same time.

"Monks' Barn". This is situated to the south-west of the house on the south side of the stable yard. It is a structure which has undergone much modification, most notably by Wyatville in 1816-17 and then in a conversion to bedroom accommodation by Andrew Carden Associates in the early 1970s.[20] The monastic barn forms the eastern part of the existing structure, which was extended by Wyatville to its present length to create additional stabling. Before the residential conversion, which occupies the whole of the building, the old part of the barn was used as a cart shed and storeroom,[21] although on the plan of the early 19th-century house in Todd's *History* it is marked as a coach house.[22]

The original form of the barn is most clearly visible on the north side. This shows it to have been a timber-framed structure with heavy close studding and wall posts; mainly red brick infill with some vitrified brick on a brick plinth with chamfered stone capping. This plinth stops at the point where Wyatville's brick addition begins. Before the residential conversion there were seven gabled dormers in the bottom of the tiled roof slope,[23] four (including the large central dormer) in the original barn and three in the 19th-century extension, but there are now only four, three being destroyed by the late 20th-century additions at right-angles to the north at each end. All the dormers were inserted by Wyatville, along with the Gothic lantern to the ridge (the current lantern is a late 20th-century reconstruction) and have characteristic cusped bargeboards and decorative iron finials (now missing). The largest dormer to the centre also has intersecting tracery in four lights and timber colonettes. The former panelled double doors directly below the central dormer have now been replaced by a late 20th-century glazed screen and there is another one to the left. The paired Tudor-arched timber windows between the middle rail and the wall-plate are also by Wyatville.

Wyatville's work is even more evident on the south and east sides of the barn. On the south side he set back the original outside wall to form a covered walk-way of 18 timber segmental-pointed arches with hollow spandrels. It is possible that at least some of the posts which form these arches are the original wall timbers of the barn, although their octagonal shape and straight-cut stops to top and bottom clearly show that they have been recut. The recessed wall is of early 19th-century red brick in Flemish bond, a change in the brickwork being detectable at the point where the original barn abuts the westward extension.

There were formerly six single-light Wyatville dormers in the bottom of the roof slope flanking a larger one to the centre with intersecting tracery in four lights.[24] This is the only one to survive, although it now has plain Y-tracery in two lights, and there are five late 20th-century hipped dormers to either side. The walk-way continues around the east end of the building, although here it seems to represent an extension, the recessed brick wall (although rebuilt in Wyatville's remodelling) marking the original extent of the barn. The timber frame with its herringbone brick infill and elaborately cusped bargeboards above the walk-way are all Wyatville's work. There is also some red brick in English bond in the west gable end, which may have been re-used when this part of the barn was built.

The original character of the medieval barn is more clearly visible internally, although much has now been obscured or destroyed by the insertion of a full-length first floor as part of the residential conversion. The ground-floor corridor on the south side, however, has five massive wall-posts exposed with huge curving braces supporting the tie beams. There is also evidence for another wall-post at the east end on the line of the recessed wall, making the original barn a five-bay structure. There are also intermediate wall timbers exposed in the south wall and the remains of further close studding below the tie beam of the original west gable end.

[16] *R.C.H.M.*, 143; D.O.E. 30th List of Buildings of Special Architectural or Historic Interest, The Borough of Dacorum, 95.
[17] Todd, 74.
[18] Ibid, 70; J. Lucas (tr.), *Kalm's Account of his Visit to England on his way to America in 1748* (1892), 228.
[19] Coult, 230.
[20] Pevsner, 238, R.I.B.A. Drawings colln., Wy Je [1] 354-70.
[21] Ex. inf. Kay Sanecki; Bodl., MS. Top. eccl. b.27, fol.50v.
[22] Todd, no page no.

[23] Photograph in Bodl., see note 21.
[24] Drawings by F. MacKenzie in Todd, between pp.68-9.

As a result of the formation of bedrooms on the upper level and the boxing in of the trusses, it is difficult to establish the exact form of the original roof structure. This is visible only in the area of the lantern, although here much has obviously been cut away to form this feature. Nevertheless, it seems that the roof trusses were of collar and tie beam type (presumably with supporting queen struts, although these are not visible) with double butt-purlins and two tiers of substantial curved windbraces, one of which survives to the westernmost roof truss. To the west of this point the sawn roof trusses of the Wyatville extension are visible. On the evidence of the wall framing and roof structure, it seems most likely that the barn was constructed in the mid- to late 15th century.

Although no other features of the former monastic buildings are visible as physical remains, it is worth noting the marked drop in ground level to the east of a line of yew trees, which lies directly to the south of the south-east corner of the terrace outside the drawing room and dining room of the present house. This is in the area most likely to have been occupied by the conventual buildings (see below), and the break in slope may possibly indicate the eastern extent of the cloister buildings. In this connection, it is worth noting a reference by Humphry Repton to "large yew trees still growing in rows near the site of the monastery."[25]

PICTORIAL EVIDENCE

Having briefly examined the 1575 survey and the information it provides for the probable lay-out of the pre-Dissolution buildings, we now turn to the abundant pictorial evidence for the site. From this a relatively clear impression can be obtained of the appearance of the house before the third Duke of Bridgewater's demolitions and Wyatt's rebuilding. Used in connection with the documentary material (examined in detail below), it is possible to draw some conclusions about which monastic buildings were re-used in the 16th-century royal conversion and the early 17th-century mansion of the Egertons which succeeded it.

The principal drawings of the pre-Wyatt Ashridge are in the Hertfordshire Record Office and the British Library, with one important view in the Bodleian Library and two original drawings dated 1761 kept in the present house. The most frequently depicted building is the great hall (probably the monastic refectory), which is shown in a number of important views,[26] used here to compile the following description:-

North side. A long hall range with seven tall pointed windows set high in the wall. At the east and west ends are projecting matching gabled ranges. In the angle with the west projecting range is a porch with a four-centred archway and a crenellated parapet, which leads to the screens-passage. The hall range has a cupola to the centre with a clock on the north face, surmounted by a weathervane. In some views this cupola is shown, probably inaccurately, as a taller and more elaborate structure. Each gabled range has a tall bay window to the front divided into four sections, apparently with leaded lights, and a crenellated parapet. Above are large three-light mullion windows and the gables have pointed finials. The inner returns of the gabled ranges have prominent lateral stacks with tall shafts. The outer slope of the west projecting range has gabled dormers. From coloured views it appears that the whole range is constructed of stone under a plain tile roof.[27]

Some useful details are added from a view in the British Library.[28] The hall windows are shown as two-light lancets. To the projecting ranges, the three-light mullion windows are smaller, the four-light bay windows are shown to have king mullions with narrower mullions dividing the sections to either side and the crenellations above are much more closely spaced. There is a sundial attached to the left corner of the porch and the cupola is shown as having two pointed open arches to the top under a lead cap with weathervane.

This view and others show lower two-storey gable-fronted ranges to the east and west of the great hall. To the east the twin Dutch-gabled range has large three-light mullioned and transomed windows on the first floor and elongated oculi to the gables. Apparently in front of the ridge is a massive stack with a brick shaft, shown as two shafts in some views. To the west of the great hall a very similar twin Dutch-gabled range is repeated, with twin Dutch gables to the right return, which then gives way to a long range of outbuildings with a wide variety of gabled and hipped roof forms. Many tall stacks cluster behind. The date of all the twin-gabled ranges and the outbuildings is apparently early 17th century, although the possibility that they are remodellings of earlier buildings cannot be ruled out. Again the materials appear to be stone under a plain tile roof.

Views of the **south side** of the great hall are less plentiful but a view of the cloisters from the south, dated 1788, shows that the south wall has a high parapet rising to a gable at the east end. This has a mullioned and transomed window at first-floor level. Roughly to the centre of the range, slightly to the right of the cupola, is an integral lateral stack with three tall detached shafts.[29]

[25] H. and J.A. Repton, *Fragments on the Theory and Practice of Landscape Gardening* (1816), 139.

[26] H.R.O., Oldfield Drawings, III, 181, 186; D/EC1/Z8/181a; B.L., K. Top. VIII. 10. 1. b.; Add. MS. 32,349, fols.95, 96, 110a, 110b; Add. MS. 9063, fols.304, 304v,a; 1761 view kept in present house; *The Topographer*, ii, no.3 (March, 1790), opp. 131.

[27] H.R.O., Oldfield Drawings, III, 181; B.L., K. Top. VIII. 10. 1. b.

[28] B.L., Add. MS. 9063, fol.304v,a.

[29] H.R.O., D/EC1/Z8/181b.

To the north of the great hall was a large courtyard in the centre of which on the north side stood the gatehouse, known as "The White Lodge", which was probably erected by Lord Ellesmere in the early 17th century. The north front of this is shown in several drawings.[30] It bears a marked resemblance to the wings on either side of the hall range, consisting of a three-storey stone structure with three symmetrical Dutch gables to the front, the outer two higher than that to the centre, under a plain tile roof. The end walls are also crowned by Dutch gables, all of the gables having oval-shaped windows to the apexes. One:one:one bays, the outer bays having three-light mullion windows with leaded latticed lights on each floor. The centre bay has a four-light mullion window to its upper level flanked by small square windows. The central archway is round headed with plain pilasters to either side of a tall open-panelled double gate. The front roof slope has four tall stacks with moulded capping and there are two similar stacks visible behind the ridge to the rear.

The view from which the above description of the gatehouse is compiled,[31] is largely confirmed by a drawing made by H.G. Oldfield in 1802.[32] This, however, is different in several important respects. First, it shows pronounced alternating quoins and tall integral end stacks with moulded capping. The outer gables are largely as in the other drawing but are surmounted by obelisks. The centre gable is quite different, taking the form of a blind traceried curved gable, crowned by a large cross. Below this is a four-light mullion window sitting on a string course with small windows in the angle between the string course and the mullion window. At first-floor level is a four-light mullion window directly above the central archway, which here is represented as semi-circular but infilled, with three windows divided by buttresses to the blocking and a triangular light above the centre window. The windows on either side of the archway are shown as triple lancets.

Comparison with a drawing of 1814 by J.C. Buckler,[33] probably the most reliable of early 19th-century topographical artists, confirms the basic accuracy of Oldfield's view, the major differences between the two apparently being attributable to alterations carried out to the lodge between 1802 and 1814, rather than to different artistic representations of the building. In both views it is clear that the two outer gables conceal roofs behind, the inner returns of which have plain stepped gables. Buckler's drawing shows the traceried arrangement to the centre of the building more clearly. The tracery is Gothic in style and may have been the work of Wyatt, who is known to have drawn up plans for the remodelling of the lodge as part of his early proposals for the building of the new mansion.[34]

The Buckler drawing does not show the cross to the centre but does show a tall stack to the rear of the building. The archway is shown as completely blocked with triple lancet windows to the infill. The caption to one of the copies of the drawing states that the lodge was demolished in 1816.[35]

Various views show the boundary wall to the east and west of the lodge. Relatively little of the boundary wall to the east is visible in the 1790 drawing but what can be seen is punctuated by a gate flanked by plain gate piers with finials.[36] A little to the left of this is the end of a hip-roofed range straddling the boundary wall. More of this building is visible in a drawing of 1796 by Thomas Baskerfield and its position is confirmed by Grey's map of 1762;[37] the building may have served as stables. In Oldfield's 1802 drawing of the lodge, the boundary wall is shown in a chequerwork pattern, perhaps consisting of alternating panels of flint and clunch.

To the west the boundary wall runs some distance before being intersected by a gate flanked by plain gate piers with finials. To the right of this is another outbuilding with a gabled range to the left, which is bisected by the end of the drawing in several views. More of this gatehouse is shown in Baskerfield's drawing of 1796 and in a roughly contemporary drawing, probably by Richard Gough, in the Bodleian Library.[38] These indicate the gatehouse to be at the far end of the boundary wall and to be a three-storey structure with triple gables to the front, the right largely obscured by trees in the drawing. The gables run back to a ridge, which has a prominent central stack (shown as two ridge stacks in the Bodleian view). The drawing is at too small a scale clearly to detect the window details but there are symmetrically spaced three-light mullion windows to the first floor directly above two-light mullion windows on the ground floor; the attic storey has lozenge-shaped windows or reliefs to the gables. There is a large square-headed carriage arch, through which the main drive to the house runs, an arrangement confirmed in Grey's map of 1762 and clearly identifying the gatehouse as the so-called "Red Lodge", which name perhaps suggests that it was primarily constructed of brick (see below).

There is only one known drawing of the south front of the White Lodge and there are no views of the south side of the boundary wall, although the 1762 estate map shows the area to the east of the square courtyard directly in front of the great hall to have been occupied by formal gardens at this date. This drawing, made by Baskerfield in 1796,[39] shows the rear of the lodge as follows, usefully confirming the accuracy of Oldfield's and Buckler's illustrations of the front: the lodge is of three storeys in three sections with Dutch gables surmounted by obelisks to the outer sections and a lower gabled centre section, crowned by a tall stack.

[30] H.R.O., Oldfield Drawings, III, 181, 186; Buckler Drawings, I, 138; B.L., K. Top. VIII. 10. 1. b.; Add. MS. 9063, fol.304.

[31] B.L., K. Top. VIII. 10. 1. b.

[32] H.R.O., Oldfield Drawings, III, 186.

[33] H.R.O., Buckler Drawings, I, 138.

[34] D. Linstrum, *Catalogue of the Drawings Collections of the R.I.B.A., The Wyatt Family* (1973), 33.

[35] H.R.O., Knowsley Clutterbuck, iii, 386d.

[36] H.R.O., Oldfield Drawings, III, 181; B.L., K. Top. VIII. 10. 1. b.

[37] B.L., Add. MS. 9063, fol.304; H.R.O., AH 2770.

[38] B.L., Add. MS. 9063, fol.304; Bodl., Gough Maps 11, fol.62.

[39] B.L., Add. MS. 9063, fol.304v,b.

The gables have oval-shaped windows to their apexes and there are symmetrically spaced three-light mullion windows on both the first and second floors. The centre section has three symmetrically spaced windows on the first and second floors with a pointed doorway to the left and a window to the centre on the ground floor. All the windows have intersecting tracery which, along with the Y-tracery to the overlight of the door, may be another result of Wyatt's gothicization of the lodge.

Returning to the north front, the Buckler drawing of 1814 gives useful information on the appearance of the site between 1762 and Wyatt's building of the new mansion. To the east of the lodge, roughly in the position of the hip-roofed stable range, is a two-storey hip-roofed building with seven evenly spaced glazing bar sashes under segmental heads on the first floor with five sash windows on the ground floor, the third and fourth bays from the left being occupied by a large flat-roofed open porch with balustraded parapet. There are ridge stacks at each end of the building and more are visible to the returns. To the south of the west return a full-height block with sash windows and two ridge stacks (with clustered chimney pots as on the main range) runs at right-angles to the west to link with a tall projecting hip-roofed range, which has a tall integral stack to its west face, with a cupola behind to the ridge. Although apparently of two-storey height, this range has only one window visible- a tall segmental-headed three-light window on the north side. Slightly recessed from this range a single-storey range runs at right-angles to the west to meet the lodge, from which it is slightly set back and behind which part of the new mansion can be seen. This range has a wide segmental-headed doorway flanked by large segmental-headed windows.

Buckler also drew the other side of this range of buildings in 1814.[40] The seven-bay range is shown to have five glazing bar sashes on the first floor with a blank section of wall to the third bay from the east, marked by a straight joint, above which is an integral stack. The east return has two glazing bar sashes on the first floor and a wide segmental-headed four-light French window to the lower left and another window to the right, the latter partly obscured by bushes. The west return, visible in the front view of the range, ends in a gable to the south with coped verges and kneelers and an integral end stack. There are two glazing bar sashes on the first floor. To the west is the link block with three glazing bar sashes on the first floor, running into a recessed two-storey range. The whole of this elevation is dominated on the ground floor by two polygonal conservatories with elaborate trellis work flanking French windows linked by two lean-to verandahs to an ornate tent-like structure to the centre gable.

A small sketch, dated 1809, also shows this side of the range. The central gable is pedimented and the range ends in another gable three bays to the east, at the position of the

straight joint shown in the Buckler view, clearly indicating that everything to the east of this point is an addition to the original structure.[41] It has been suggested that Wyatville was responsible for adding the trellis work and generally upgrading the standard of accommodation for the seventh earl.[42]

None of this range of buildings is depicted on the 1762 map and, like the early 17th-century lodge, it appears to have been demolished in 1816. These dates provide a *terminus post quem* and a *terminus ante quem* for the range and it is worth noting that the 1809 sketch referred to above is captioned "Part of (the) New House". Despite the date, it is clearly not part of Wyatt's new mansion, nor is it part of the 17th-century and earlier house. The range therefore seems most likely to have been constructed in the late 18th or early 19th century, before the decision to embark on the building of the new house. This would seem to tie in well with the architectural details shown in the two Buckler drawings. The range is last seen in this form in a plan drawn by J. Taylor in February 1816 (by which time the lodge had already gone),[43] although it later seems to have been incorporated in the orangery on the same site.[44]

To the south of the great hall was the cloister, of which a number of illustrations survive.[45] It appears to have been square in plan and may represent the site of the monastic cloister (see below). The south side of the hall range has been described above. Directly in front is the north cloister walk consisting of a two-storey flat-roofed range with a coped parapet and a large projecting oriel to the centre. This has a three-light mullioned and transomed window in the centre with narrow transomed windows to the angled returns. To either side of the oriel are two three-light mullioned and transomed windows with a prominent lead downpipe between those to the left. On the ground floor are eight pointed moulded archways with hoodmoulds, separated by slender stepped buttresses, the fifth arch from the left carried down to form a doorway.

The east and west walks are also visible in the same view, which is dated 1788.[46] The east walk is the same height as the north and has similar archways on the ground floor. There is a three-light mullioned and transomed window on the first floor towards the north end and a gabled dormer breaking the eaves line with two ridge stacks to the left. The west range has the same eaves line as the others but has a pitched tile roof. It has a large gabled dormer with a six-light mullion window on the right and a similar dormer, only partly in the drawing, to the left. There is a large five-light mullioned and transomed window on the first floor and a three-light mullioned and transomed window to its

---

[40] H.R.O., Buckler Drawings, I, 137.

[41] B.L., Add. MS. 9063, fol.305v.
[42] D. Linstrum, *Jeffry Wyatville, Architect to the King* (1972), 98.
[43] Repton, op. cit. (note 25), plan between pp.140-1.
[44] Ex. inf. Kay Sanecki.
[45] H.R.O., D/ECl/Z8/181b, 182b, 183; Oldfield Drawings III, 189; B.L. Add. MS. 9063, fols.119v, 120.
[46] H.R.O., D/ECl/Z8/181b.

left. The ground floor has similar archways and buttresses as the other ranges.

In the centre of the cloister is a statue, probably for a fountain, of Jonah and the Whale. This is also shown in a sepia drawing,[47] where Jonah is depicted as a bearded figure, naked, except for a loincloth, standing in front of a whale: the whole sculpture sits on a panelled plinth and the centre of the cloister is shown surrounded by a balustrade.

There are several views of the cloister walks themselves. The most accurate appears to be that by Oldfield of c.1800.[48] This shows a long cloister alley (which range it represents is not specified) with slender clustered shafts supporting a fine sexpartite vault with carved bosses to the ridge. Two of these bosses are shown as details and are of angels bearing armorial shields. A nail-studded oak panelled door is visible at the end of the alley. The arches themselves are not shown full on in this view so it is not possible to tell whether they were filled with tracery. However, another more romanticized view, dated 1796, does not show tracery to the arches.[49]

A full-page pencil sketch by Lysons in the British Library of "part of the cloister" shows a corner of the cloister with pointed doorways in both walls.[50] The doorways have deeply recessed, richly moulded segmental-pointed arches, that fully visible in the sketch having heavy timber doors. Over this is a painting, details of which are shown in another sketch.[51] The painting is of Christ appearing to two of his disciples, with what are probably donor figures below to either side of the doorhead. The left is a cardinal, holding a scroll and pointing upwards, the right is a female figure holding a book: the costume of both is 15th century. Accompanying this sketch is one of an armorial shield and a beast head corbel holding a shield; the wording "in a vaulted room adjoining the cloister called the Scotchman's Hall" may refer to these sketches.

There are no known views of the south cloister range from within the cloister but an important drawing of 1790 shows the south front of the house at that date.[52] It depicts a long stone-built range with a clay tile roof, which may actually conceal the south cloister range from view. As in the associated drawing of the north front, the buildings shown appear to be early 17th century in date. In front is a high stone boundary wall with coped parapet, pierced by a gateway to the left with plain piers and finials. These flank wrought-iron gates with a small ornamental overthrow. Behind is a long two-storey range, to the approximate centre of which, behind a coped parapet, are four gables forming attics. The left gable has a small three-light mullion window, the centre gables have two-light mullion

windows and the right is blind. The basic accuracy of this view is confirmed by the original 1761 drawing of the south-east front, kept in the present house.

This range also has four full-height canted bays with five-light mullioned and transomed windows on the first floor. There are also two cross windows to the left of the left bay window on the first floor and another between the third bay window from the left and the right bay window. The perspective of this drawing is poor, probably even worse than that of the associated drawing of the north front. It appears in fact that the right bay window is probably at the front of a long range which runs at right-angles to the north or at an oblique angle to the north-east. This has three full-height bay windows with three-light mullioned and transomed windows to the front of each bay and cross windows to the returns, alternating with mullioned and transomed windows to the main front wall. Behind this range is a much taller gable-fronted building with a blind front wall and three ridge stacks. To the right is a two-storey range, which ends to the right in three Dutch gables with mullioned and transomed windows on the first floor. The flank wall has two cross windows on the first floor.

To the left of the long range described above is a projecting range, which also seems to extend considerably to the rear. At the front this has a gabled attic with a small three-light mullion window above a large two-storey canted bay with a six-light mullioned and transomed window. To the right of this a massive integral lateral stack with two tall diagonal shafts forms the front of the side wall which has two gables with mullion windows near the top to the right. Below and to the left of this range is a two-storey structure with gables to front and side. There is a tall stack to the left, one of the many visible in this view. Behind the roof of the long range, another ridge is visible, which may be that of the south claustral range. Unfortunately, none of the buildings shown in this drawing can be clearly identified with the buildings marked on Grey's 1762 map.

Views of the interior of the old house are rare. An undated sepia drawing gives a good impression of the appearance of the interior of the hall shortly before its demolition. Six bays of the hall are shown, the view apparently being towards the east as the windows in the front wall are shown. The open-trussed roof is supported by tall slender wall shafts and has timber spandrels pierced by open trefoils in the angle between the capitals of the shafts and the principal rafters. There is a panelled dado running around the entire room with a doorway in the presumed south-east corner.[53]

A few more details are added in the apparently more accurate view by Lysons showing the hall in the process of demolition. The dado panelling is seen to have an embattled cornice with carved quatrefoils to the frieze.

[47] Ibid, 183.
[48] H.R.O., Oldfield Drawings, III, 189.
[49] B.L., Add. MS. 9063, fol.305.
[50] B.L., Add. MS. 9460, fol.119v.
[51] Ibid, fol.120.
[52] H.R.O., Oldfield Drawings, III, 183; B.L., K. Top. VIII. 10. 1. b.

[53] H.R.O., D/ECl/Z8/182a.

Windows are shown in both the long walls and have moulded nook-shafts.[54]

There is a fine drawing of 1813 by J. Buckler of the undercroft but this adds no further information to that which can be obtained from an inspection of the existing structure,[55] while the earliest known surviving drawings of the barn show it after its gothicization by Wyatville.[56] The caption to a reconstruction drawing by Oldfield of "a room on one side (of) the cloister at Ashridge supposed to have been a study" states that the roof, walls, chimney and windows "remained as represented".[57] The roof is a shallow-pitched timber roof and there are two trefoil-headed two-light windows, one in each wall; the fireplace is Tudor-arched with hollow spandrels. Despite Oldfield's claim to the authenticity of the features shown, the drawing, complete with religious occupant, was clearly intended as a reconstruction of a monk's cell and it is perhaps unsafe to place too much reliance on its accuracy.

CARTOGRAPHIC EVIDENCE

There is abundant map and plan evidence for the pre-Wyatt house but nearly all of it dates to the years immediately preceding the destruction of the old house or was compiled during the actual process of demolition. The earliest known surviving map showing the house is Grey's estate map of 1762, the relevant features of which have been referred to above. The basic features of this map are repeated in Dury and Andrews' map of c.1766,[58] but as this is primarily a road map, the details of the buildings are less clearly shown and it is not so reliable for our purposes.

A plan drawn by the Earl of Essex in October 1805, the original of which is in the Bridgewater papers at Belton House (Lincs.),[59] shows what was then still left of the old house in relation to what was being proposed. The plan is rather confusing and mainly seems to show the intended remodelling of the surviving buildings after the substantial demolitions of 1800-02. Only the White Lodge, here called "The Old Lodge", and the courtyard to the south can be clearly equated with the pre-19th-century house.

The situation is slightly clearer in a series of plans which survive in the R.I.B.A. Drawings Collection. These relate to the building of the new house by Wyatt and Wyatville. Although it was James who was to gain the commission to build the new mansion, the earliest drawings are those of his nephew, who was employed in 1803-04 (and perhaps

earlier) to improve the accommodation in the relatively small 18th-century house, left after the demolition of most of the old buildings on the site. Two elevation drawings show the 18th-century house,[60] later drawn by Buckler,[61] and it seems that Wyatville not only added the trellis and verandah on the south side,[62] but he or Wyatt added the porch on the north, extended the building slightly to the east and linked it to the White Lodge to the west.

In 1807 a plan was drawn showing all the buildings then surviving on the site.[63] The White Lodge and the 18th-century block are both marked. Also shown are the boundary wall running from the White Lodge to the approximate position of the Red Lodge and the coach house and stables in the stable yard. More significant, though, is the plotting of a block measuring 72ft 6" by 29ft some 168ft to the south of the White Lodge.

A proposal plan drawn in the same year by Wyatt for a new mansion slightly to the north of the final site shows the retention of the White Lodge.[64] The eastern section is marked as "Porter's Lodge" and the western as "House Steward's Room" with the central section vaulted, indicating that it was intended to reopen the blocked archway. Parts of the 18th-century block are also marked as retained. To the south is a building referred to as the "Present Laundry and Washhouse". The dotted lines in which it is drawn presumably indicate that it was scheduled for demolition, and it seems very likely to be the south range shown in the 1807 site plan mentioned above.

The significance of this increases still further when these drawings are compared with an undated plan and elevation drawing by Wyatville of a range referred to as laundry, wash house and chapel.[65] These drawings certainly relate to the first period of the architect's involvement with Ashridge. The plan indicates that the chapel occupied the eastern section of the range, the laundry the centre and the wash house the west. The south wall is shaded in grey, perhaps indicating that it is old work retained. At right-angles to the south at the west end is a building marked as bakehouse and scullery. The elevation drawing, which shows a two-storey hip-roofed range with two ridge stacks, four windows on the first floor and a Tudor-arched doorway with hollow spandrels and dripstone to the left is therefore of the north wall of the range. The site plan of 1807 and Wyatville's plan drawing both show a porch at the west end of the building.

---

[54] D. & S. Lysons, *Magna Britannia*, i (1806), 492; the original pencil sketch of this is in B.L., Add. MS. 9460, fol.121.

[55] H.R.O., Buckler Drawings, III, 136.

[56] R.I.B.A. Drawings colln., see note 20.

[57] H.R.O., Oldfield Drawings, III, 191.

[58] A. Dury & J. Andrews, *A Topographical Map of Hartfordshire* (London 1766; facsimile edn., Stevenage 1980).

[59] Egerton Papers, unindexed collection at Belton House (Lincs.); photocopy in H.R.O., D/EC o F44. At the time of writing (1993) the collection was in the process of transfer to the Lincolnshire Record Office.

[60] R.I.B.A. Drawings colln., Wy Je [1] 1, 2.

[61] H.R.O., Buckler Drawings, I, 137, 138.

[62] Linstrum, op. et loc. cit. (note 42).

[63] R.I.B.A. Drawings colln., Wy Jas [1] 1.

[64] Ibid, Wy Jas [1] 2. Although this drawing bears the later pencilled date "1804" and this is the date ascribed to it in the catalogue by Linstrum, op. et loc. cit. (note 34), it is more likely to date to 1807, the first year of Wyatt's involvement at Ashridge. See Linstrum (note 34), explanatory text.

[65] Ibid, Wy Je [1] 11, 12. The elevation drawing (12) has the later pencilled date "1801".

From this it can be deduced that the building represented in these drawings is a rebuilding on the site of the great hall, which was demolished in 1800-02. It certainly bears no resemblance to the appearance of the great hall before 1800 and is probably best interpreted as Wyatville's rebuilding of this range on a much smaller scale, work which was in turn soon to be swept away by Wyatt. Significantly, the 1800 sale catalogue of building materials from the old house (see below) specifically refers to taking down the cloisters without damaging the north wall, which would also have formed the south wall of the great hall. Confirmation that this laundry, wash house and chapel range occupied the site of the old great hall comes from another Wyatt proposal plan of 1808, which shows the "Present brewhouse, wash house and laundry" occupying the position of what was to be the present dining room and drawing room, which as we have seen, lie directly above the medieval undercroft.[66] The Wyatville plan of the range also has a caption to the window in the east wall of the bakehouse stating that it is "in the middle of the old doorway opening into the cloisters", which again ties in with the laundry, wash house and chapel range lying on the north side of the old cloisters.

Two sketch plans and a series of measurements by Lysons, relating to the pre-Wyatt house, are now in the British Library. The measurements are not particularly informative as it is very difficult to establish precisely to what they relate. One of the sketch plans is more useful as it clearly indicates the great hall 68ft in length and 22ft across, which it states is now a barn. To the east of the hall/barn, on the same building line, is a stable and in the south wall, near the dividing wall with the stable, a "pointed arch stopped up" and a "cusped rib with foliage" are indicated. At the west end of the hall/barn is what appears to be a through-passage, which is said to be "vaulted with common stone". Part of the cloister to the south of the hall is also clearly marked.[67] The other sketch plan of the hall helpfully confirms the arrangement of the hall seen in the drawings referred to earlier, showing a doorway at the west end of the north wall and a fireplace roughly to the centre of the south wall.[68]

WRITTEN EVIDENCE

This is covered in two sections, firstly records compiled in connection with the house's ownership from the Dissolution to the early 19th century and secondly the accounts of visitors during the same period.

Documentary Sources. These are fuller than for most former monastic properties in Hertfordshire. As is frequently the case, no information on the buildings can be obtained from the Ministers' Accounts and no detailed records seem to have been made by the royal

commissioners at the time of the house's surrender.[69] The lease to John Norrys similarly contains nothing on the buildings,[70] but the details of a dispute between Norrys and Robert Eme,[71] who had had the lease of a messuage called the Dairy House situated outside the monastic precinct since 1537,[72] offer a useful insight into the situation at Ashridge immediately after the Dissolution. In a bill of complaint in 1542 Norrys states that he had been granted the "...governance and keeping... of Ashridge" by the king. He had committed to his servant, Oliver Lowthe, all the "...lede, ireons, glasse, locks, bolts and hengys, with divers other necessaries therein remaining..." Since then, in the absence of Lowthe, Robert Eme, "late fermer ther", has "...broken up the dores where the premises did remayne..." and has "...imbessilled thens so well diverse evidence and wrytynges as led, iron, glass, loks, bolts and henges with the divers other things therein remaynynge to no small value in substance, to the no littell detrement of your highnes".

On his return, finding the doors etc open, and suspecting Eme, Lowthe organised a search of Eme's house, where the missing articles were found. In reply, Eme stated that he had bought "...iii old dores with the locks upon them, paying 5s for the same..." from Lowthe and that he had not at any time broken into the monastery in an "unlawful manner". He further complained that Lowthe had entered his house without reason and arrested his wife, various servants and himself for felony, imprisoning them within the former monastery. Among the allegations of cruelty against Lowthe was the charge that he "did hang uppe by the hands" a twelve-year old boy called Arthur Dagnall. He also said that, as a tenant of the former monastery, he had "good authoryte" to enter it and that the convent seal was wrongfully withheld from him by Norrys.[73] The outcome of the case is unknown but some settlement must have been reached as Eme was still tenant of the Dairy House in 1550.[74]

It is known that both Edward VI and Elizabeth spent considerable parts of their childhoods at Ashridge and both were living at the house in 1543 when Mary was also brought there for her health.[75] In 1550 the former college buildings were granted to Elizabeth;[76] several letters written by Elizabeth from Ashridge survive.[77]

Elizabeth's position at court was in danger after Mary's accession to the throne and in December 1553 she once

[66] Ibid, Wy Jas [1] 12.
[67] B.L., Add. MS. 9460, fol.122.
[68] Ibid, fol.120.

[69] P.R.O., SC6/Hen. VIII/238, m.18.
[70] Todd, 83.
[71] Ibid, 84-6.
[72] Ibid, 82.
[73] Ibid, 84-6.
[74] See note 3.
[75] Cussans, iii, pt.1, 138.
[76] See note 3.
[77] E.g.,Bodl., MS. Cherry 36, fols.1-2; B.L., Harl. MS. 6986, fol.15; Lansd. MS. 1236, fol.39; Portland MS., II, *Historical Manuscripts Commission*, 13th Rep. App., pt.2 (1893), 7.

more retired to Ashridge.[78] In the new year Elizabeth was implicated in Wyatt's rebellion and in February 1554 she was virtually forcibly removed from Ashridge.[79] Elizabeth did not return to Ashridge to live and in March 1557 the house was leased for 21 years to Richard Combes of Hemel Hempstead.[80]

By 1560 it seems that many of the buildings were in poor condition. Although £55 3s 8d had been spent on repairs since the first year of Elizabeth's reign, a good part was falling down "namely the lodging that Master Treasurer laye in, which accoumpted the fayrest lodging of the howse next where the Quene's highness laye" and £200 would still not make it "a house meete for her highness to lye in yt three dayes".[81]

Throughout Henry's, Edward's and Mary's reigns there is no reference to the surveyor of the royal works being concerned with Ashridge,[82] and presumably maintenance there was the responsibility of the lessees of the estate. Money spent on the buildings may therefore have been minimal and perhaps was one of the reasons why it was necessary to spend £67 10s 7d on repairs in connection with a royal progress in Hertfordshire in 1564.[83]

These repairs were presumably sufficiently extensive for the house to have attracted the attention of Sir Nicholas Throckmorton, Ambassador to France, who in February 1566 was advised in a letter from Peter Osborne that "Ashridge is worth the having...The situation and walls about it will save you money and the translating of it will be done with small charge in comparison of building a new house".[84] It is not known, however, whether Throckmorton pursued any interest in the house.

In January 1575 a survey was made of the property prior to the grant to Henry, Lord Cheyney, which "valued all and singuler the brick, stone, iron, leade, glasse, tymber, and tyle thereof, in such sorte as if all the severall things shud presently be pulled asunder, taken downe, and then solde". It found as follows: "In brick £10 15s, stone £53 15s 8d, iron £29 10s 3d, glasse £13 8d, timbre £212 14s 4d, wainscot £30 13s 4d, paving tyle £7 22d, tyle £50 20d and lead £163 3s 4d", amounting to a total of £614 17s.[85]

This was followed in October 1575 by the survey, which has already been referred to above. It is worth noting that, in addition to the parts quoted earlier, the commissioners presented that "there has not been devastation or unroofing in or around the mansion house of Ashridge aforesaid except to certain ruinous houses, for they had fallen down

by reason of age, of which the timber still exists in the same place, useful for nothing but burning. And another part of the ruined houses in the same place was destroyed by a certain _____ Stockwood, supervisor of work of the Queen, and with them he repaired and mended other houses in the same place. They present further that a house called the outhouses, other necessary buildings called houses of office, which at present are to some extent decayed, are not able sufficiently to be repaired and mended for the sum of 100 marks." This clearly shows that, although they were in poor condition, the principal buildings at least still remained and some work of maintenance was continuing.

It is usually assumed that the church was demolished at some date between 1575 and 1604,[86] but the wording of the grant of the site to Thomas Egerton in the latter year suggests that this may not have been the case. It refers to "... the scite, circuit and precinct of the said late dissolved College and all that church voc. Ashrudge Church als. Asheridge Colledge Church and all those Messuages Cottages Lands Tenements Houses Edifices Buildings barnes Stables Sollars, Cellars Gatehouses the Courts Orchards..."[87] Although this is obviously not conclusive, it does pose the possibility that parts at least of the church survived at this date.

It appears that the change of ownership to the Egerton family was accompanied by a comprehensive programme of remodelling, which took place between 1604 and 1607,[88] although it seems that Sir Thomas may have been in occupation a year before the house was formally conveyed to him.[89] Todd, drawing on sources now lost, refers to "the names of such as did gratefie my Lorde Chancelor with carriage" of timber and stone in 1604, among whom was Sir Edmund Ashfield, one of the October 1575 commissioners. He also refers to a document, again now lost, in the Lord Chancellor's own hand, which was entitled "A remembrance for more buylding and reparacons at Ashridge" and to "estimates of all the charges for the newe byldinge, bothe for all manner of stuffe and workmanshippe, as also for carriages". These clearly indicate that considerable work was being carried on at the house at this time.[90] Particularly long lists of fittings and furnishings for 1607 suggest that the work was largely completed in this year.[91] It is not necessary to quote at length from these and a few extracts are enough to show something of the splendour of the new house:

"For two suytes of tapistrye hanginges for the purple bedchamber and the withdrawinge chamber to yt; the one

[78] *S.P. Dom. 1547–80*, 29; F. Mumby, *The Girlhood of Queen Elizabeth* (1909), 102-3; Maria Perry, *Elizabeth I* (1990), 87-8.
[79] *S.P. Dom., 1547–80*, 60.
[80] See note 4.
[81] P.R.O., SP/12/12/38; *S.P. Dom., 1547–80*, 154.
[82] *King's Works*, iv, 48.
[83] P.R.O., E 351/3202.
[84] *S.P. Dom., Addenda 1566–79*, 16.
[85] Todd, 32-3.

[86] *V.C.H.*, ii, 210.
[87] Bodl., MS. Willis, fols.139-40.

[88] Coult, 110.
[89] Huntingdon Library, San Marino, California, Ellesmere MS. EL 1179 & 1180; M. Girouard, *Life in the English Country House* (1978), App. 1.
[90] Todd, 64.
[91] Ibid, 64-5.

of 7 peeces, (storye of Alexander) and the other (storye of Elyas) 5 peeces; both 5 sticks deepe a peece; at severall rates, the bill...£132 15s"

"For Sir Tho. Egerton his daughters, 15 May, 1607. For two bedds of blew and whyte carroll, furnished with feather bedds, and boulsters, pillowes, mattresses, matts, 4 kersey stooles, and a bed furnished for the chambermayd, the bill...£25 16s"

"For the la: Frauncis's Nurcerie, 22 May, 1607. For three bedds of myngle colerd caroll, furnished with feather bedds and boulsters, pillowes, matts, mattresses, and 7 kersey stooles, the bill...£33 6s".
A reference to 8s "For a handbell for the Chapel" is useful evidence for the existence of such a building at this date.

It is not possible from these sources to say with certainty which parts of the house were rebuilt at this date but the pictorial evidence referred to above is a clear indication that much was done at this time. Certainly, the architectural details of the lower ranges flanking the great hall suggest that they were at least remodelled, if not added at this date, while the two-storey canted bay windows on the south side are also likely to be of the late 16th or early 17th century. The likelihood is strong too that the main lodge or gatehouse, and probably the subsidiary gatehouse to the west, were built at this time.

After this date, we are concerned here with documentary sources only for the information that they give on the early 17th-century and earlier buildings. In 1641 one John Williams wrote to John, first Earl of Bridgewater, concerning "worke aboute the Cloysters pond", which may be a reference to the erection of the fountain and statue of Jonah and the whale, informing him that "the courte is gravelled and made very neat".[92]

The household book of John, second Earl of Bridgewater, gives instructions to the "Huisher (usher) of My Hall" in 1652, which show that the great hall was by then the room where the less important servants took their meals. That the hall remained of some importance, at least as a space to process through, is made clear, however, by the order to "Permit none, after meales are done, to sitt drinkinge in the hall; but speedily make it cleane againe, that it may be fitt for Company to passe through...."[93]

An inventory drawn up in 1663 has recently been studied by Paul Hunneyball and enables a full reconstruction to be made of the house's appearance at this time, which is likely to have been very similar to the form in which it was left by Thomas Egerton some 60 years earlier. From the upper end of the hall a passage led eastwards to the principal staircase, which in turn led to the great chamber and other adjacent reception rooms on the first floor. From the main stairs, the west range of the house, which contained a selection of private suites, was approached by a gallery built over the north cloister running alongside the upper level of the hall. This gallery, which appears to have been used for the display of pictures, also gave access to a library to the east of the hall. A second picture gallery, broader and apparently with windows to either side, ran above the east cloister and ended in what was still known in 1663 as the king's (James I's) chamber. Beyond this lay a set of first-floor suites spread along the south side of the house.[94]

In April 1701 a full inventory of the household goods at Ashridge was taken after the death of John, third Earl of Bridgewater. This is useful for the information it reveals on the rooms of the house at this time, of which there are no contemporary drawings and which is otherwise known only from the writings of Browne Willis and other antiquaries. The following rooms are mentioned: "My Lady's Chamber, My Lord's Dressing Room, My Lord Mary's Chamber, Mrs Granjon's room, Mr Savage's chamber, Library Passage, Lobby, The Gentlemen's Parlour, The Supping Room, The Wainscot Drawing Room, The Drawing Room Adjacent, The Virginal Passage, My Lord Chancellor's chamber, The Little Room adjoining, Room over the Chapel, The little room adjacent, The Room called Mars and Venus, The little room adjacent, The King's Bedchamber, The King's Dressing Room, The Great Hall, The Cedar Gallery, The Great Stairhead, Room over the Best bedchamber, The Best Drawing Room, The Great Dining Room, The Wainscot Gallery, Passage leading to the Guilt Parlours, The stone room leading to the parlours, The Guilt Parlour, The Guilt Drawing Room, The Guilt Closet, The old Nursery that was, The little room adjoining, The Wardrobe, The room formerly My Lady Mary's, The room next, The maid's room adjoining, The Dark green chamber, The little room joining, The footboys chamber overhead, Passage leading to the Paper room, The Gilt leather Bed Chamber, The Closet, The Dressing Room, The Room overhead, The next room (James the footman), The next room (over the Gilt Leather room) Mr Wood's room, The passage, The room that was Mr Dale's, The store room, The room over the Still house, Mr Peircy's room, The preserving room, Mr Foulkes chamber, The next room, The room over the King's Bedchamber, The long hole in the Cloysters, The Chappell, The room over the King's Dressing Room, The White Lodge (the main gatehouse), The porter's room, Middle chamber at the west end of the lodge, The room over the last, Room over the gateway, The room called Tho: Thomas's chamber, The next room even with the former, The middle room at the east end of the lodge, Upper room at the east end of the lodge, The Kitching, The Larder, The porter's room, The Still house, The rear hall, The bakehouse, The brewhouse, The little brewhouse, The first of the uppermost rooms in

[92] H.R.O., AH 996.
[93] Todd, 53.

[94] Huntingdon Library, San Marino, California, Ellesmere MS. 8094, fols. 9r, 10v, quoted in Paul Hunneyball, *Status, display and dissemination: social expression and stylistic change in the architecture of 17th-century Hertfordshire*, Oxford D.Phil. thesis, 1994, 309.

the wellhouse at the west end, The uppermost room, The Brewer's chamber, The Cook's chamber, The next room, Mr Slater's chamber that was, The maid's chamber next adjoining, The next maid's chamber, The Laundry, The Wash house, The Cheese room below stairs, The sinkman's chamber, The sinkmaid's Chamber, The store, The coachman's chamber, The next room, The rooms over the pad stable, The rooms over the Hunting Stable, The dogkennel room, The smith's room, The Gardener's chamber, In the Red (west) Lodge Mr Morasted's chamber, Mr Morasted's closet, The footboy chamber."[95] The inventory shows that the principal rooms were lavishly furnished but, other than indicating the considerable extent of the house and its many outbuildings, is of only minor help in reconstructing the actual plan of the buildings at this time.

The next important sources for the appearance of Ashridge before Wyatt's rebuilding date from a century later, being the sales catalogues of 1800 and 1802, compiled at the time of the old house's demolition. The former, which deals with both building materials and furnishings, is particularly comprehensive and lists the following rooms: "South side garrets; West side garrets; North-west garrets; North-west End garrets; North Roof between the Breaks over the Hall including the turret, clock and its two bells; North Roof East Return, over Assembly Room; North-east Wing Roof; Roof adjoining Southward; East Roof; Bath; One Pair Floor, South side; Room adjoining Westward; Room adjoining Westward and Landing; One pair South-west Room, over Chapel; Room adjoining and Passage Eastward; Long Gallery over the North cloister; North-east Return, Ball Room; North-east Wing; Closet adjoining; Best Staircase and Landing; Billiard Room; Two Pair, South-west Room, over Entrance; Small Rooms and Landing; North-west Room, two pair; North-west Return; Library; Passage; Landing and Passage; Ground Floor, South-west Room; Basement; Stone Passage; Ground Floor; Passage, Foot of best Staircase; Basement, Stone Parlour including an oval marble fount, two feet by one foot six, pedestal, and slab behind; Cloisters; Chapel; West Entrance Hall including all the Purbeck paving, about 350 feet and nine steps; West Entrance (again with Purbeck paving); the North and East garden wall; South Side; old garden house; west wall next the lodge from north-west corner."[96]

Many building materials are listed in the catalogue, including wainscotting, floor boards, doors, roof timbers, tiles, staircases, fireplaces and windows (both sashes and leaded casements), all with their values given, the great majority being sold. The section relating to the cloisters is particularly interesting: "All the Purbeck paving, about 700 feet, to the north side and also to the east, south and west sides; All the brick and stone work to the north cloister

from the one pair floor to the ground- to be taken down without damaging the north wall; All the brick and stone work from the one pair floor to the ground to the east and west sides of the east cloister; also to the south and west sides; Jonah on a pedestal in the centre of a quadrangle, the ballustrades, and all the brick work to ditto; two large garden seats, a pedestal, and a pair of lattice gates; the stairs and linings from No. 23 (Room adjoining Westward and Landing) to ground." It is worth noting that only these last two lots were sold. The fact that the Purbeck paving was not sold may be significant. Todd refers to "carved table-frames of oak; some covered with oriental alabaster, and some with polished Purbeck marble slabs, which were formerly used on the gravestones of Brethren of the College" in the present staircase hall.[97] It may be therefore that some of the paving slabs were re-used in the new mansion. More importantly, the reference to not damaging the north wall of the cloister implies that it was to remain standing. If this was the case, it is possible that some of it still remains in the south wall of the Wyatt dining room and drawing room, which occupy the site of the monastic refectory and later great hall.

Apart from this, however, the conditions of sale make it quite clear that demolition was to be carried out quickly but carefully after the auction. The total amount brought in from the five-day long sale was £1481 11s 5d, from which £154 15s was deducted for expenses.[98] The balance of £1326 16s 5d was to be paid to James Lewis for his work for the Bridgewater family at Cleveland Court House, London.[99]

The 1802 catalogue is rather less useful as it is principally concerned with the sale of fittings, furnishings and brewing utensils. Nevertheless, it is informative for the lists of outbuildings and offices it contains. These are the "Kitchen, Still Room; Larder; Pantry; Laundry; Coachman's Room; Glazier's Shop; Carter's Room; Brewhouse; Passage Yard; All the Brick Wall South side of Pleasure Garden; Court Garden; Large wrought iron gate, North side of garden and another of the same size at the south side; lower Granary; Blacksmith's Shop; Carpenter's Shop; Cooper's Shop; Wheelwright's Shop; Riding House; Ox Yard; Bake-house; Wellhouse: Venison House; Dairy; Plumber's House; Brick and panel tiled wood barn and Kiln".[100]

Virtually all the building materials from these structures were sold, bringing in a gross amount of £1439 4s, which after the expenses of the auction left a net profit of £1212 6s 1d.

[95] Egerton papers (see note 59); photocopy and partial transcript in H.R.O., D/EC o F43.

[96] H.R.O., 49,211. Another copy at Belton has the values of the building materials recorded; photocopy in H.R.O., D/EC o F43.

[97] Todd, 72.

[98] See note 95.

[99] H.R.O., AH 1835.

[100] Original copy at Belton; photocopy in H.R.O., D/EC o F43.

ANTIQUARIAN ACCOUNTS

Leland's sole reference to Ashridge is "there the king lodgid",[101] and this may relate to Henry VIII's visit before the Dissolution.[102] Norden in 1598 writes "...Queene Elizabeth lodged [there] as in her owne, (being then a more stately house) at the time of Wyatt's attempt in Queene Maryes dayes...This place is lately beautified by the Lord Cheyney."[103]

Fuller, writing in the mid-17th century, says that he was informed that "more of a Monastery is visible this day (at Ashridge) than in any other House in England."[104] Thomas Baskerville visited the house in 1682 and left the following account "...As to the fabric or form of the house within the gatehouses, for it hath one fair gatehouse which gives entrance through a large court on the northern side of the house to the hall to which they ascend by steps on a terrace walk which leads to the hall, and another gatehouse which leads to the stables, where Mr Blower had his lodgings. It is a square containing in it a small quadrangle, and in that a little pond of water, walled about with freestone, fed with the water which first comes from a deep well drawn up by a horse in a great wheel in two barrels or large buckets, a man always standing by as soon as the bucket comes above the collar of the well to empty it into a leaden cistern and here the ingenuity of the horse must not be forgotten, for as soon as the man lays hold on the bucket to empty it, the horse turns himself in the wheel without bidding or forcing and travels the other way to draw up the next bucket, and so this water after it hath served all the offices of the house runs into the pond as aforesaid, where do live some few hungry carp, and this is all the fish pools that I saw about the house. Here doth also enclose this pool and quadrangle a fine cloister, remarkable for this, because my lord will not have it blurred out, for having in paint upon the walls some scripture and monkish stories.

The hall is a noble room in which some good horses which my lord hath been owner of are drawn in full proportion. From hence at the lower end you descend into the buttery or pantry, being a fair room vaulted over and adorned with many heads and horns of stags or red deer which have been killed out of my lord's own park, and out of this room the friendly gentleman of the house led us into the cellars of wine, ale and beer; in that for beer was a range of vessels bound with iron hoops, each vessel containing the quantity of two pipes; and in some peculiar rooms made on purpose for them, for here was but one great vessel in a room, where some might vie with the Prince of Heidelberg's tun, they look so big upon you..."[105]

In 1699 the house and gardens were the subject of "The Vision, or a Poeticall View of Ashridge...written by one of the female sex...and dedicated to Mary, Lady Egerton." This describes the lodge as follows: "The very anti-palace seem'd to be/ Sufficient subject for my muse and me:/ 'Tis fairly wrought throughout, and so compact/ And every frosted stone laid so exact/ With such a symmetry, it may be sworn/ All the whole mass is but made up of one."[106] This would appear to confirm that the lodge was faced with fine-quality ashlar, as the drawings referred to earlier suggest.

Much more detailed information is added by Browne Willis, the eccentric Buckinghamshire historian, who visited the former monastery on at least one occasion in the early 18th century. His most detailed account is as follows: "In this parish is Ashridge Monastery or College which is converted into the Earl of Bridgewater's seat. The college church which stood in the garden there is entirely demolished and has been so ever since Q. Elizabeth's time if not soon after the surrender: in so much as no tradition is to be pickt up about it, save that several of the materials were converted into the building a large Farm house or two, it stood ranging with the Cloysters. There have been several stone Coffins dugg up in the garden and by the length of the Foundations which were sometime since discovered it was a large pile. Good part of all the rest of the Monastery has been in some measure rebuilt and metamorphosed except the Great Hall and Cloysters, both which entirely remain and are Noble Buildings. The former of which is very large being 44ft in length x 22ft in Bredth and shews 7 or 8 windows in front. Tis an very high lightsom Building curiously roofd at Top the Side Pillars which range with the Windows are very neat and in the Windows there remain these Arms viz [he then lists the armorial bearings, which include those of France and England in the third and fourth windows and those of the Beauchamps in the sixth window].

In the aforesaid Cloysters which are Entirely arched over with Tattenhall [Totternhoe] Stone neatly wrought are cut in the Centers of the Arches in diverse places the Arms of the said Monastery or College, viz an Holy Lamb standing on the Sepulchre displaying a Banner and round the sides of the Cloyster was beautifully painted the History of Our Saviour taken out of the New Testament which of late has been much impared by the Weather it being done in Water Colours tho' with very great Art and Life. In the long Gallery are diverse Coats of Arms of the Lord Bridgewater's Family but nothing else as I could see relating to the Convent."

Later in the same account he gives the dimensions of the cloister walks as 41ft in length by 10ft in width and describes the paintings on their walls: "1. Defaced two If not Herod's Cruelty. 2. Our Saviour disputing in the Temple. 3. The Baptism. 4. The Temptation. 5. The

---

[101] Leland, i, 104-5.
[102] *L.P.*, v, pp.321, 751.
[103] J. Norden, *Speculi Britaniae Pars, The Description of Hartfordshire* (1598), 11-12.
[104] T. Fuller, *Church History of Britain*, ii (1868 edn., revd. by J. Nichols), 177.
[105] Portland MS., II, *Historical Manuscripts Commission*, 13th Rep. App., pt.2 (1893), 306.

---

[106] Todd, 57.

Healing of the Infirm at the Lake. 6. Ezechiel I. The Vision of Ezechiel. 7. Lazarus raised from the Dead. 8. Our Saviour's riding to Jerusalem. 9. The Turning the Mony Changers out of the Temple. 10. Psalm 2. 11. Mark II. Jesus's Appearance to 2 of his disciples. 12. The Passover. 13. Our Saviour Betrayed by Judas. 14. He is apprehended and the Healing of the Solders Ear. 15. Our Saviours Tryal. 16. His Crowning with a Crown of Thorns and the robes put upon him. 17. Pilate washing his hands. 18 and 19. Defaced. 20. The Bearing of the Cross. 21. The Putting up of the Cross. 22. The Crucifixion between 2 Thieves. 23. Our Saviour taken down from the Cross. 24. The Placing Him in the tomb. 25. His descent into Hell. 26. His appearance to one of his disciples. 27. His Ascension. 28. His appearance to all of his disciples. 29. *Tres Videt* and *unum adoravit*. 30. *His Tres unum sunt*-Holy Trinity. 30 to 40. Defaced."[107]

Elsewhere Willis writes "The monastery church of Ashridge stood at some distance from the conventual house. Twas pulled down in Queen Elizabeth's time and several of the material employed towards building a Farmhouse abt half a mile off where there is yet some Coats of arms etc which see there was great Buildings..."[108] It appears from another manuscript, where Willis states that the coats-of-arms in the farmhouse came from the "Abby church", that he visited Ashridge in 1709.[109]

In a letter of September 1723 to the Duke of Bridgewater, Willis writes of the church: "What sort of fabrick it was...is not easy to guess, tho' I presume it was two thirds longer than the Cloysters, which, in religious Houses, generally made a third part of the church...By a legacy of £100 of Cardinal Beaufort, Bishop of Winchester, Anno 1447, I judge the Cloysters and good part of the House now standing was built temp. Hen. VI within less than 100 years before the Reformation, and being a good building occasioned its being preserved."[110]

In 1730 the antiquary, Thomas Hearne, was informed by Mr Frewin, vicar of Ivinghoe, that "the Abbey of Ashridge is still a vast noble thing",[111] but the next major account of the former college is that by Richard Gough, dated September 3rd 1767.[112] He writes "...in front of the house stands a large lodge with circular gabels, and a round gate, now disused. The house was probably rebuilt after it came into lay hands, only the hall, cloisters and a kind of back porch leading to the hall with a groined roof and two clustered pillars remaining of the antient Structure. The hall is wainscotted and over the pannels an embatled moulding of quatrefoils. In the windows on one side (being all plain

and of two bays) are these shields, two in each window...[described]...This room is hung round with bad pictures of horses, one a grey starved to death by order of the late Duke for having killed his rider. The ceiling oak. Adjoining to it a neglected parlour said to have been the original chapel now wainscotted and decaying with damp as are most of the ground rooms from the low situation. In the window of a small passage, the Egerton arms...[described]...In the window of the picture gallery a great number of quarterings in garters and in plain shields ducally crowned, some supported by a goat and a bear or ram dated 1578 (The same arms and date are in an outhouse)...Pictures in the Gallery...[long list described] Other pictures here as well are almost spoilt by damp. In a small passage closet a head of Sir Christopher Hatton on board in a circle with the signs of the Zodiac...[other pictures described]...In another room these family pictures...[gives list]...In another gallery whole lengths of 8 daughters of the first Earl of Bridgewater...[list given]...Another large room in good repair has the portraits of William and Mary and fresco histories...In another gallery heads of the 12 Caesars and smaller ½ lengths of Turkish emperors with their names. On the great staircase a whole length of Isaac wedding Rebecca in grotesque habits on board large as life. Peeping Tom a man in the dress of the 16th century looking through a casement- board. Many of the best pictures are carried to London.

The cloisters are pointed arches with buttresses but no tracery round a square court in whose center a square reservoir of rainwater supplying the house, and divided into two by a brick wall: in the middle a statue of Jonah and the whale. The inner opposite arches are walled up and have been beautifully painted with New Testament histories in lively colours, only the upper parts of some remain: the late Duke offered £5000 to have them repaired but nobody would undertake them. I distinguisht Christ disputing with the Elders, raising Lazarus, crucifixion, burial, one with devils at top, a devil [two sketch drawings are shown of this] another flying like a serpent to one sitting in a niche like bacchus. Each history is inclosed in a kind of arched frame on whose pillars are painted Saints holding labels with black small letters and Latin sentences expressing the subject and the Gospel whence taken: the figures of the chapters singular Arabic numerals...One arch seems to contain a wedding, above is the altar and candlestics...The south cloister leads into the later ground floor chapel now disused, all the books but two are old print 1578."

There then follows a largely duplicate account,[113] only the significant differences in which are noted here. The picture gallery is "wainscotted with cedar painted", "in two rooms [in the picture gallery] they say Q. Eliz was prisoner", "the roof [of the cloisters is] groined springing from round clustered columns with square capitals", the New Testament "histories" are said to have "more expression

---

[107] Bodl., MS. Willis 102, fols.10b-14b.
[108] Bodl., MS. Willis 34, fol.120b.
[109] Bodl., MS. Willis 68, fols.148-148b.
[110] Todd, 59.
[111] Bodl., Hearne's Diaries 127, fol.37.
[112] MS. account in annotated copy of N. Salmon's *History of Hertfordshire* (1728) in Bodl., Gough Herts. 18, between pp.134-5 of published volume.

[113] Ibid.

than such old paintings usually have" and the "one with devils at top" has a devil "farting".

A letter from William Cole to Gough of May 1773 simply repeats the account given by Willis but Gough has altered the description of cloister painting number six from The Vision of Ezechiel to The Transfiguration.[114] Gough used his manuscript account of the house to compile a much shorter description of Ashridge for his 1789 edition of Camden's *Britannia*,[115] which contains no additional information.

A very full description was made of the house by the Revd. Stebbing Shaw in 1790,[116] the important additions to and differences from the accounts made by Willis and Gough being noted as follows: "[The hall] is a noble sized room, very lofty, with a wooden covered fret-work roof. It is crowded with stag's horns, and a large gallery over the screens." In a footnote Shaw writes that the dimensions given by Gough "appeared to us much larger" and this would accord well with the measurements of the great hall given in the 1575 survey and the actual size of the surviving undercroft. "Returning into the Hall, we passed thro' a door at the upper end, into a passage, on the left of which are several rooms, now much injured by the damp, and uninhabitable...This passage led us to the staircase, which is hung with old portraits etc, too much neglected...From hence we passed into the gallery. This has two sides, over two sides, of the Cloyster. The other two sides are divided into suites of rooms...At the end of the gallery we pass thro' a suite of rooms, over the next side of the Cloysters...In a small passage room is a splendid genealogical tree of the family, framed in the wainscot, with portraits, arms etc and the paternal coat at the bottom with 84 quarterings. Over the third side of the cloyster we passed thro' a suite of four bedrooms, principally hung with old tapestry, one of which is still called Q. Eliz.'s apartment, and has an ancient bed, said not only to have belonged to her, but to have been most of it her work. Over the fourth side of the cloyster is another picture gallery; whose farthest end joins the first gallery before described. The windows are full of arms...[six described] Carey, Gray of Wilton, Cecil, Egerton and Bassett of Blore, Dudley and Powlett," making it appear that there were six windows over this range of the cloisters.

"One of the bay windows [of the hall] mentioned in front is occupied by a very large room, which is entered out of the gallery. The library takes up the other, but this we could not see. The lodge was fitted up as a temporary habitation for the Duke, at the time the house was intended to be rebuilt, which was so near being put into execution, that many of the materials were prepared, and are still lying at the back of the house. It consists of a vestibule, a neat dining and drawing room, and some comfortable bedchambers...At the back door of the mansion is a porch, and some arches, of the old structure. The chapel is entered from the Cloysters, and is small but neat."

Not surprisingly perhaps Todd's account of old Ashridge draws heavily on that contained in *The Topographer*.[117] He does, however, add a little information on the galleries and rooms over the cloister: "One was called the Billiard Gallery and contained the following arms in the windows; most of which are preserved, and form part of the ornaments in the Ashridge of our time." The glass in the sixth and seventh windows is said to date to 1575 and 1578 respectively and this armorial glass may be that now contained in the windows in the porch added by Wyatville over the main entrance of the present house. Todd goes on to say that this gallery linked with the "Cedar Gallery". In the so-called Queen Elizabeth's apartment "a kind of toilet remain[ed]", while the chapel is described as "a neat but not ancient structure...entered from the cloisters... It appears to have been built in 1699; for there is, among the Ashridge manuscripts now belonging to Lord Stafford, 'A Sermon preached at the opening of the new Chapell at Ashridge, August 27, 1699 by Geo. Burghope.'" This chapel may have been new built in 1699, or it may have been a comprehensive remodelling of an earlier chapel provided as part of the domestic conversion of the former monastic buildings. However, it could just conceivably have been of monastic origin. The church is known to have been on the south side of the cloister and to have had two chapels, one of which- St John's Chapel- may have been on the north side of the nave. If so, it is, of course, likely to have undergone very considerable remodelling at a later date. On balance, however, the survival of anything but the most vestigial fragments of the monastic church beyond the early 17th century seems unlikely, although elsewhere in his *History* Todd states in a footnote "I remember an old drawing, in watercolours, of Ashridge, in which the Church made the most conspicuous part of it; which has been lost since the College was pulled down in 1800."[118] Whatever the precise origins of the chapel, it seems clear that part of the south claustral range was occupied by a chapel, which survived into the early 19th century.

In the garden "Plans of the strangest invention, the meander, and the maze, were visible, tho' in ruins." The library "consisted of three rooms, known by the distinctions of the Great Library, the lesser library, and the little closet. The two latter were small rooms. But the first was a large and well-proportioned apartment, yet injudiciously contrived, by doors resembling a panelled wainscot thro'out, to conceal the library treasures within it. The case was much the same in one of the other apartments."

Some insight into the process of the demolition of the old house is given by Lysons, who writes that "the cloisters by

---

[114] Ibid, between pp.132-3 of published volume.
[115] R. Gough (ed.), *Camden's Britannia* (1789), 319.
[116] *The Topographer* (note 26), 131-54.
[117] Todd, 66-8.
[118] Ibid, 62n.

accident were not lotted when the materials were sold, and therefore were not pulled down at the same time with the other parts of the building; but they are considerably damaged by the fall of the adjoining walls."[119] Otherwise, nothing is added by Lysons or by Lipscomb,[120] whose account is based on those by Willis and later visitors. This also applies to the short description by Sheahan, who repeats the tradition, apparently first referred to by Todd, that "An oblong square, with high box hedges, called the Monks' Garden, is supposed to have been the entrance to the west end of the old conventual church."[121] This garden lay immediately to the south-west of the chapel of the present house, but there is no reason to connect it with the site of the former monastic church.

THE BUILDING OF THE NEW HOUSE

As stated earlier, it is not the purpose here to give an architectural description of the house built by Wyatt and completed by his nephew, Wyatville. Nevertheless, some of the sources for the building of the new house cast light on the appearance of the old one. Demolition of the old buildings seems to have begun in 1800 during the time of the third duke. Apart from his reference to the cloisters (see above), Lysons writes that the great hall was "entire in 1800."[122]

Although it was the third duke who began the work of demolition and much had been carried out by his death in 1803, it seems unlikely that he intended to destroy completely the existing buildings. The plans of the third duke's successor, John, the seventh earl (the dukedom having expired on the death of the third duke), were more ambitious but even he initially intended to spare the unpretentious 18th-century house and the gatehouse,[123] in the latter of which he (like the duke before him) continued to live during the building of the new house.[124] In fact, it was not demolished until 1816, three years after the completion of Wyatt's original mansion. By 1817 the old monastic barn had been enlarged and remodelled and further offices added to the west, behind a screening wall, which linked the new house to the surviving Red (West) Lodge, which was itself comprehensively rebuilt at this time.

Wyatt and Wyatville were not the only architects to draw up plans for Ashridge, although in the event they were the only two architects whose proposals were implemented. Unsigned plans of 1760 survive for a Palladian house and there are also unattributed drawings of neo-classical facades in the manner of Sir Robert Taylor. In 1800 James Lewis, who worked for the Bridgewaters at Cleveland House, London, produced plans for a classical house, which would appear to have retained none of the old buildings.[125] In 1805 the Earl of Essex drew a sketch plan (referred to earlier) and elevations for a Gothic-style mansion. The plan shows the White Lodge retained and a passage to the "present (i.e. the 18th-century) buildings". However, as the elevation drawings do not include the north elevation, we cannot be sure if it was intended to retain the gatehouse and the 18th-century range or whether the earl was simply showing the relationship of old to new buildings in his sketch plan.

Ground plans of what was probably intended to be a classical-style house were prepared by Thomas Cundy in 1806 but for the purpose of reconstructing the lay-out of the pre-Wyatt house, the most useful scheme is that formed by plan and elevation drawings of a Gothic-style mansion by William Wilkins in 1807.[126] Used in conjunction with the Earl of Essex's sketch plan and a plan made by Repton of the new house and his own proposals for the gardens,[127] they confirm that the White Lodge lay to the north of the former monastic cloister with the surviving undercroft under the north range of the cloister.

FITTINGS AND FURNISHINGS

Various fittings and furnishings from Ashridge have found their way elsewhere. Beginning at the Dissolution, six bells were sold for £82 to John a Marlowe,[128] it is suggested before November 1540.[129] What became of them, however, is not known. Some 15th-century panelling at Little Gaddesden Manor House is reputed to have come from Ashridge.[130] As the manor house was extensively rebuilt in 1576,[131] it seems quite conceivable that this occurred after the sale of materials from Ashridge in the previous year.

1575/6 is also the date when the tombs of Sir Robert Whittingham (d.1452) and wife and Sir Ralph Verney (d.1546) and wife were taken by Edmund Verney from Ashridge to the parish church at Aldbury. This removal is documented on a brass of 1588 in the Pendley chapel at the east end of the south aisle where the Whittingham monument now stands. This magnificent monument, which consists of two life-size effigies on a tomb-chest with weepers and armorial shields, has variously been thought primarily to commemorate Sir John Verney (d.1505) and wife or the second Sir Robert Whittingham (d.1471) and wife, but is now thought most likely to have first been erected by the second Sir Robert in memory of his father,

[119] Lysons, op. cit. (note 54), 492n.
[120] Lipscomb, op. cit. (note 13), 443-4.
[121] J.S. Sheahan, *The History and Topography of Buckinghamshire* (1862), 734.
[122] Lysons, op. cit., 620.
[123] R.I.B.A. Drawings colln. (see note 64).
[124] Todd, 57.

[125] Egerton papers, Belton (see note 59).
[126] Ibid.
[127] Repton, op. cit. (note 25), between pp.140-1.
[128] Mentioned in the "Declaracon of Joise Carleton, wydowe, 8 March 1555", which is quoted in A.H. Cocks, *The Church Bells of Buckinghamshire* (1897), 550-1.
[129] Cocks, op. cit., 467.
[130] Pevsner, 237; Senar, 100.
[131] D.O.E. 30th List of Historic Buildings (note 16), 112.

the first Sir Robert Whittingham (d.1452) and wife,[132] although the 1588 brass makes it clear that the remains of other members of both families were later interred in the tomb. The tomb slab has a gadrooned edge in Elizabethan style, presumably added after its removal to Aldbury. The fine 15th-century stone parclose screen, which surrounds the Pendley Chapel, is clearly an insertion and, along with the medieval floor tiles in the chapel, was probably also brought from Ashridge.

The circumstances surrounding the removal of Sir Ralph Verney's tomb are equally interesting. Sir Ralph was Edmund's father and his will stipulated that he was to be buried at Ashridge.[133] The 1588 brass, however, shows that by this date he was buried in "the Chauncell of Aldeburie." Although the brass does not state when this occurred, it seems most likely that the change of ownership at Ashridge in 1575 would have occasioned the removal of this and perhaps other monuments to Aldbury.

It has been suggested that Verney's tomb was not put together again after it was taken to Aldbury. Writing in the mid- 19th century, J. Bruce describes it thus: "The flat stone which formed the top of it was placed over his grave, one of the sides inserted in the paving of the chancel floor on each side of the top stone, and one of the ends in the pavement of the south aisle. The sides and end are despoiled of the heraldry which at one time adorned them, but the fourth or top stone retains handsome brasses, which represent Ralph and the heiress of Lord Bray with their nine children."[134] By the time of the *V.C.H.* account in the early 20th century, the monument had been reassembled in its present position in the north chancel chapel, almost certainly during the restoration of 1866.[135] In fact, it seems unlikely that the tomb would not have been properly re-erected following its removal from Ashridge. It seems improbable that Edmund Verney would have allowed the constituent parts of his father's monument to be scattered throughout the church, particularly considering the dignified treatment given to his more distant ancestors in the Pendley chapel. Indeed, the reference on the 1588 brass to Sir Ralph Verney being buried in the chancel suggests that his tomb chest was given pride of place in that part of the church, its prominent position later resulting in its dismantling. A further intriguing aspect about the date of the Sir Ralph Verney memorial- if it truly did come from Ashridge- is that it post-dates the Dissolution, suggesting that the church remained in use after the closure of the monastic college, a possibility already hinted at by the reference to repairs to the church in the 1575 survey.

Aldbury was not the only church to acquire new fittings as a result of the suppression of Ashridge. Writing a description of Nettleden Chapel in 1711, Willis refers to "an antient Brown Velvet Hearse cloath which is adorned in divers places with fleur de lys, on it wrought in gold is the Holy Lamb sitting on an altar displaying a Banner, which Lamb being the Arms of Ashridge monastery at a mile distant from hence confirms it to have come from hence."[136] This is almost certainly the same "ancient Communion Table Cloth", described by Willis's contemporary, Edward Steele, who also made two drawings of the cloth.[137] What the original function of the cloth was- it may have been a vestment of some kind- or the circumstances in which it reached Nettleden are not known. Another description of the chapel by Willis shows it to have been unusually well furnished for a small parochial chapel,[138] raising the possibility that other fittings too came from Ashridge.

One other feature from Ashridge found its way elsewhere. This is the statue of Jonah and the Whale, which formerly stood in the fountain at the centre of the monastic cloister. In 1844 it was placed in the grounds of Turvey Abbey (Beds.), probably by its then owner, John Higgins.[139]

INTERPRETATION AND CONCLUSIONS

It is clear that much survived the Dissolution at Ashridge, most of the monastic buildings still remaining in 1575, even if by then in poor condition and ready for demolition. The relatively late survival of the buildings and the lack of destruction which took place after the suppression may have been largely due to the property remaining in crown hands, continuing in active royal use until the mid-1550s and then being retained as a leased property until 1575. A letter from Prince Edward's tutor, Doctor Richard Cox, to Sir William Paget in 1544 complains about the living conditions at Ashridge,[140] but this is not evidence for the neglect of the buildings and it is perhaps more significant that deterioration seems to have set in after the end of royal residence in the 1550s.

It might, of course, be argued that the relatively late survival of pre-Dissolution buildings at Ashridge is a sign, not of royal interest in the house, but rather the reverse. There are indeed many instances where the crown or another new owner of former monastic property, finding the buildings obsolete or particularly unsuited to an ambitious conversion scheme, simply swept them away and started again. That this was not the case at Ashridge, however, is more likely to be a reflection of the good condition of the buildings at the suppression. In August 1530 Henry VIII himself seems to have stayed at the

---

[132] J. Bruce (ed.), *Letters and Papers of the Verney Family...to 1639*, Camden Soc., 56 (1853), 84; *V.C.H.*, ii, 147; H.F. Chettle, 'The Boni Homines of Ashridge and Edington', *Downside Review*, 42 (1944), 53; Pevsner, 65.

[133] Bruce, op. cit., 53.

[134] Ibid, 84-5.

[135] N. Doggett, 'Church building patterns in Dacorum, 1000-1550', *Hertfordshire Archaeology* (forthcoming).

[136] Bodl., MS. Willis 34, p.124b.

[137] Bodl., MS. Top. gen. e.79, fols.3-3b; Gough Bucks. 5, fol.15.

[138] Bodl., MS. Willis 102, fols.19-23.

[139] H.R.O., Gerish colln., Box 30; Senar, 43.

[140] *L.P.*, xix (2), no.726.

college when he offered 7s 6d to the "Holy Blood there",[141] and payments of 7s 6d and 4s 8d respectively were made to a servant of Sir Edward Donne "for bringing a bucke to the King at Ashridge" and "To Edmonde the footman for so moche by him given in rewards at Ashridge to one that made the dogges to draw water",[142] the latter probably referring to the use of dogs to lift up water buckets from the deep monastic well. Only seven years earlier the court poet, John Skelton, had written the following lines on the pleasures of Ashridge: "...Of the Bonhoms of Ashridge beside Bercamsted/ That goodly place to Skelton most kind/ Where the sang royal is, Christes blood so red/ Whereupon he metrified his mind/ A pleasanter place than Ashridge is, hard were to find..."[143]

Even after the Dissolution, Ashridge continued to be visited by Henry. A meeting of the privy council was held here in August 1543,[144] and the house was lived in for varying periods by all three of his children, Elizabeth in particular spending much of her adolescence and young womanhood here.

The extent to which the relative modernity of the buildings played a major part in their continuing use after the surrender is difficult to assess owing to their almost total disappearance and to the lack of accurate dating evidence for those destroyed in the early 19th century. In the early 15th century Richard Petworth, a clerk to Henry Beaufort, Bishop of Winchester, gave £100 towards the rebuilding of the cloister, dorter and quire.[145] In 1413 the bishop himself granted the Bonshommes the rectory of the church of nearby Ivinghoe (Bucks.) and this was later followed, probably shortly before his death in April 1447, by his gift of £50 for further work to the cloister, dorter, infirmary and sacristy.[146] Certainly, what is known of the cloister ranges through the accounts of various antiquaries and late 18th-century drawings would not contradict a 15th-century date for their construction.

Further evidence for the prosperity of the house in the later 15th century comes from the building of the five-bay monastic barn, while the *Valor Ecclesiasticus* net income of £416 16s 4d and the value of £467 3s 7½d recorded at the Dissolution make Ashridge the second wealthiest monastic community in Hertfordshire.[147] This would all tend to suggest that the buildings remained in good condition and suitable for re-use at the Dissolution.

The 1575 survey forms the basis for our knowledge of the lay-out of the monastic buildings, the reference to repairs to the church and the tomb of Sir Ralph Verney (d.1546),

now at Aldbury, making it appear that at least part of the church continued in use after the Dissolution, perhaps until the building of a chapel by Sir Thomas Egerton, Lord Ellesmere in the early 17th century.[148] Some of the church, however, may have been converted to domestic use. The reference in the survey to "Mr Chamberlens lodging called the Tower" being 30ft square accords exactly with the dimensions given for "le steple", making it likely that they were one and the same.[149]

When used in conjunction with the roughly contemporary accounts by Baskerville and Browne Willis, the 1701 survey is useful in determining which parts of the monastic buildings were converted to domestic use, although not the dates at which this occurred. Taking the great hall (probably the former monastic refectory) in the north range of the cloister as a starting point, the inventory reveals something of the lay-out of the claustral ranges at this time. As no major work is known to have been carried out to the house at this period, this plan could very possibly reflect the work undertaken by Lord Ellesmere and his predecessors. The great hall seems to have led into a passage leading to the principal staircase, which from the account in *The Topographer* seems to have been at the east end of the great hall.

The sale catalogue of 1800 confirms that the great hall with its cupola and clock tower was on the north side of the cloister and the chapel on the south. A long gallery seems to have occupied the upper level of the north cloister walk and there was an entrance hall (perhaps the successor of the "Maynes Hall" referred to in the 1575 survey) in the west range.

The west end of the great hall, behind the porch, was the lower end giving access to the buttery and pantry, which like the screens passage itself, appears to have been stone vaulted. Todd remarks that "the western end of the Dining Room is the precise spot of the Old Buttery."[150] Gough states that the "south cloister leads into the later ground-floor chapel now disused," but intriguingly he also refers to a "neglected parlour said to have been the original chapel" adjoining the great hall.[151] Clearly the position of this room shows that it cannot have been the original monastic church but it could perhaps have been the chapel built by Sir Thomas Egerton.

Both the accounts in *The Topographer* and Todd's *History* make it clear that the gallery, which at least as early as 1663 was used for the display of pictures and certainly by the late 18th century was hung with many paintings, occupied the upper level of the north cloister walk and the east claustral range. The south and west ranges were "divided into suites of rooms", the south range containing a "suite of four bedrooms", including the apartment

[141] *L.P.*, v, p.321.
[142] *L.P.*, v, p.751.
[143] J. Skelton, *The Garden of Laurell* (1523); see A. Dyce (ed.), *The Poetical Works of John Skelton*, i (1843), 361-424 and L.J. Lloyd, *John Skelton* (1938), 123-30.
[144] *S.P. Dom.*, ix, 489.
[145] Todd, 21.
[146] *Cal. Pat. R., 1413-16*, 174; *V.C.H.*, ii, 210.
[147] *Val. Eccl.*, iv, 227; Dugdale, vi, pt.1, 517.

[148] Todd, 65.
[149] *King's Works*, iv, 48.
[150] Todd, 74.
[151] Gough, op. et loc. cit. (note 112).

reputedly used by Elizabeth I. The west range also seems to have contained a passage, which apparently linked with the gallery over the north cloister.

The acquisition of Ashridge by the Egertons in 1604 and the comprehensive remodelling which they undertook so tends to overshadow the ownership of the property by the Cheyneys for a period of nearly 27 years that it is worth repeating Norden's statement that "this place is lately beautified by the Lord Cheyney." Norden qualifies this statement by saying that Ashridge was a more "stately house" when Elizabeth "lodged (there) as in her owne," although this may simply be political deference to the monarch rather than truly objective judgement of the work carried out by Cheyney. Relatively little is known of Cheyney. He was in his mid-thirties when he acquired Ashridge,[152] and had been Commissioner of the Peace in Kent, where he was a prominent landowner, in 1564 and 1569.[153] In 1571 he was appointed as a commissioner for enforcing the Act of Uniformity in the dioceses of Lincoln and Peterborough,[154] and in 1573 he was Sheriff of Kent.[155] Although Cheyney himself died in 1587, the long period for which his family continued to hold the property would seem to suggest that considerable effort and financial resources were put into its embellishment.

There can be no doubt, however, that much building work was carried out by his successor, Sir Thomas Egerton. Egerton was already in his sixties when he acquired Ashridge and was one of the most distinguished political figures of his day. He had served as M.P. for his native Cheshire from 1584 to 1587, was appointed Attorney-General in 1592 and two years later was knighted and made Master of the Rolls. In 1596 he became Lord Keeper of the Seal and, shortly after the accession of James I in 1603, Lord Chancellor, an office he was to hold until the year before his death in 1617.[156] The shaped gables of the wings flanking the great hall and the architectural details of both the White Lodge and Red Lodge are clearly indicative of an early 17th-century date and the abundant documentary evidence for a comprehensive remodelling at this time has been referred to above.

It seems then that at Ashridge we have a cloister to the north of a cruciform collegiate church, the large size of the choir relative to the nave probably being attributable to the fact that, although Ashridge was a popular place of pilgrimage and its relic of the holy blood attracted many important burials,[157] its church was not commonly used for public worship. The refectory was on the north side of the cloister and it was this that became the great hall of the

post-Dissolution house. The east and west claustral ranges were also converted to domestic use, their comparatively recent date, in common with those of other Hertfordshire religious houses, making them particularly suitable for residential accommodation. It is perhaps not entirely irrelevant that the only other English house of Bonshommes, Edington (Wilts.), also had its claustral buildings to the north of the church.[158]

The post-Dissolution history of the church at Ashridge is especially interesting. The burial of Sir Ralph Verney in 1546 and the reference to repairs lately carried out in 1575 both suggest that parts at least remained in religious use after the suppression. On the other hand, the reference to Mr Chamberlen's lodging in the tower and the reputed location of Elizabeth's apartments in the south claustral range, the probable location of the monastic nave or north aisle (St John's Chapel), seem to indicate that parts were converted to domestic use. It therefore appears possible that the choir only remained in religious use after the Dissolution. The transfer of the Verney and Whittingham memorials to Aldbury in 1576 probably marked the end of this function and possibly also the choir's physical destruction, active religious use perhaps having ceased with the departure of Elizabeth in the 1550s. That part of the church which remained after 1575 was possibly incorporated in the chapel built on the south side of the cloister in 1699. It thus seems conceivable that the nave or north aisle had a first floor inserted after the Dissolution, the upper floor being used for residential accommodation, perhaps Elizabeth's apartments, the ground floor possibly having been used as a chapel after the likely demolition of the monastic choir in c.1575. All this, however, must remain conjectural and is further complicated by Gough's mention of a chapel adjoining the great hall, although it is quite likely that a house of Ashridge's size would have had more than one chapel.

The outer or north court of the college formed a natural entrance courtyard to the new house, with a new gatehouse or the old monastic gatehouse remodelled on its north side. Another significant aspect of the 19th-century house lying to the north of its predecessor is that it is likely that the foundations of the east and west cloister ranges and the church itself, which along with the north range, formed the basis of the 16th- and early 17th-century domestic conversion, remain under the lawns to the south of the present house.[159] Indeed, it is conceivable that some of the south wall of the hall range, albeit much altered and disturbed by the insertion of large windows, remains in the south wall of the dining room/drawing room range.

Of the ancillary and service buildings, the barn and well house obviously remained in use after the Dissolution and a

[152] Cheyney was granted a licence to enter his lands on reaching the age of 21 by the Court of Wards in 1561. *Cal. Pat. R., 1560-63*, 149.

[153] P.R.O., C 66/998/125, C 66/1073/1894.

[154] Ibid, C 66/1077/2161.

[155] *S.P. Dom., 1547-80*, 471.

[156] *D.N.B.*, vi, 579-81.

[157] White Kennett, *Parochial Antiquities of Ambrosden and Burcester*, i (1695), 440.

[158] N. Pevsner & B. Cherry, *The Buildings of England: Wiltshire*, (2nd. edn., 1975), 238-9; K.J. Rogers, 'The Priory Church of St Mary, St. Katharine and All Saints Edington, Wiltshire', (1980), 11-13.

[159] As well as there being marked changes in ground slope on the lawns, a series of parch marks are clearly visible from the air.

large circular structure shown on Grey's 1762 map may be the dovecote referred to in the 1575 survey, although whether or not it was built before or after the Dissolution it is now impossible to tell.

Bibliography

PICTORIAL SOURCES

(NB- this includes references to plans, which in the site report are treated under cartographic evidence. Maps are, however, listed below under Cartographic Sources).

Hertfordshire Record Office

Buckler Drawings, I, 136-8.

Knowsley Clutterbuck, iii, 386d.

Oldfield Drawings, III, 181, 186, 189, 191.

D/ECl/Z8/181a, 181b, 182a & b, 183.

D/EC o F44.

British Library, London

Add. MS. 9063, fols.304, 304v, a & b, 305, r & v.

Add. MS. 9460, fols. 119v, 120, 121, 122.

Add. MS. 32,349, fols. 95, 96, 110a, 110b.

K. Top. VIII. 10. 1. a. & b.

Bodleian Library, Oxford

Gough Maps 11, fol.62.

R.I.B.A. Drawings Collection, London

Wy Jas [1] 1, 2, 12, 354-70.

Wy Je [1] 1, 2, 11, 12.

Miscellaneous

1761 view kept in present house.

Printed

Lysons, D. & S., *Magna Britannia*, i (1806), 492.
Repton, H. & J.A., *Fragments on the Theory and Practice of Landscape Gardening* (1816), plan between pp. 140-1.
Drawings by F. MacKenzie in Todd, H.J., *The History of Ashridge* (1823), between pp.68-9.

The Topographer, ii, no.3 (March, 1790), opp. p.131.

PHOTOGRAPHIC SOURCES

Bodleian Library, Oxford

MS. Top. eccl. b.27, fol.50v.

CARTOGRAPHIC SOURCES

Hertfordshire Record Office

AH 2770.

Printed

Dury, A. & Andrews, J., *A Topographical Map of Hartfordshire* (London 1766; facsimile edn., Stevenage 1980).

OTHER PRIMARY SOURCES

Manuscript:-

Public Record Office, London

SC6/Hen. VIII/238, m.18.

SP/12/12/38.

E 351/3202.

C 66/998/125; C 66/1073/1894; C 66/1077/2161; C 66/1087/2679; C 66/1127/2823.

Hertfordshire Record Office

AH 943B; 996; 1835.

D/EC o F43.

49,211.

Gerish Collection, Box 30.

British Library, London

Harl. MS. 6986.

Lansd. MS. 1236.

Bodleian Library, Oxford

Gough Bucks. 5.

Gough Herts. 18.

Hearne's Diaries 127.

MS. Cherry 36.

MS. Top. gen. e.79.

MS. Willis 34, 40, 68, 102.

Huntingdon Library, San Marino, California

Ellesmere MS. 8094; 1179; 1180.

Printed:-

Bruce, J. (ed.), *Letters and Papers of the Verney Family...to 1639*, Camden Soc., 56 (1853).

Calendar of Patent Rolls Preserved in the Public Record Office (1903- (in progress).

Calendar of State Papers, Domestic Series, of the Reigns of Edward VI, Mary, Elizabeth and James I, 12 vols. (1856-72).

Calendar of State Papers, Domestic Series, Addenda, 1547- 65, 1566-79, 1580-1625, 3 vols. (1870-2).

Dugdale, W., (ed.), *Monasticon Anglicanum*, (re-ed. Caley, J., Ellis, H. & Bandinel, B., 6 vols. in 8, 1817-30).

Letters and Papers, Foreign and Domestic, of the Reign of Henry VIII, eds. Brewer, J.S., Gairdner, J. & Brodie, R.H., 21 vols. (1862-1932).

Portland MS., II, *Historical Manuscripts Commission*, 13th Rep. App., pt.2 (1893).

Toulmin Smith, L. (ed.), The Itinerary of John Leland in or about the Years 1535-43, 5 vols. (1906-10).

Valor Ecclesiasticus, (eds. Caley, J. & Hunter, J.) 6 vols. (1810-34).

SECONDARY SOURCES

Bolton, A.J., 'Ashridge Park', *Country Life* (Aug. 6 and 13, 1921), 160-6 and 192-8.

Chettle, H.F., 'The Boni Homines of Ashridge and Edington', *Downside Review*, 42 (1944), 40-55.

Coult, D., *A Prospect of Ashridge* (Chichester, 1980).

Cocks, A.H., *The Church Bells of Buckinghamshire* (1897).

Colvin, H.M., *et al*, *The History of the King's Works*, iv (1982).

Cussans, J.E., *The History of Hertfordshire*, iii, pt.1 (1879, reprinted Wakefield 1972).

Department of the Environment 30th List of Buildings of Special Architectural or Historic Interest, the Borough of Dacorum.

Dictionary of National Biography, 22 vols., (revd. edn., Oxford 1921/22).

Doggett, N., 'Church building patterns in Dacorum, 1000-1550', *Hertfordshire Archaeology* (forthcoming).

Dury, A. & Andrews, J., *A Topographical Map of Hartfordshire* (London 1766; facsimile edn., Stevenage 1980).

Dyce, A., (ed.), *The Poetical Works of John Skelton*, i (1843).

Fuller, T., *Church History of Britain*, ii (1868 edn., revd. by Nichols, J.).

Girouard, M., *Life in the English Country House* (New Haven: London, 1978).

Gough, R. (ed.), *Camden's Britannia* (1789).

Hunneyball, P., *Status, display and dissemination: social expression and stylistic change in the architecture of 17th-century Hertfordshire* (Oxford D. Phil. thesis, 1994).

Kennett, W., *Parochial Antiquities of Ambrosden and Burcester*, i (Oxford, 1695).

Knowles, M.D. & Hadcock, R.N., *Medieval Religious Houses* (1953).

Linstrum, D., *Jeffry Wyatville, Architect to the King* (Oxford, 1972).

-*Catalogue of the Drawings Collections of the R.I.B.A., The Wyatt Family* (Farnborough, 1973).

Lipscomb, G., *The History and Antiquities of Buckinghamshire*, iii (1847).

Lloyd, L.J., *John Skelton* (1938).

Lucas, J. (tr.), *Kalm's Account of his Visit to England on his way to America in 1748* (1892).

Lysons, D. & S., *Magna Britannia*, i (1806).

Mumby, F., *The Girlhood of Queen Elizabeth* (1909).

Norden, J., *Speculi Britaniae Pars, The Description of Hartfordshire* (1598).

Perry, M., *Elizabeth I* (1990).

Pevsner, N. & Cherry, B., *Wiltshire*, (2nd. edn., Harmondsworth 1975).

-*Hertfordshire*, (2nd. edn., revd. Cherry, B., Harmondsworth 1977).

Repton, H. & J.A., *Fragments on the Theory and Practice of Landscape Gardening* (1816).

Rogers, K.J., *The Priory Church of St Mary, St. Katharine and All Saints Edington, Wiltshire* (Edington, 1980).

Royal Commission on Historical Monuments, *An Inventory of the Historical Monuments in Hertfordshire* (1910).

Salmon, N., *History of Hertfordshire* (1728).

Saturday Magazine, no. 774 (July 27, 1844).

Senar, H., *Little Gaddesden and Ashridge* (Chichester, 1983).

Sheahan, J.S., *The History and Topography of Buckinghamshire* (1862).

Skelton, J., *The Garden of Laurell* (1523).

Todd, H.J., *The History of the College of Bonhommes at Ashridge* (1823).

The Topographer, ii, no.3 (March, 1790), 131-54.

The Victoria History of the Counties of England, *Buckinghamshire*, ii (1905).

-*Hertfordshire*, ii (1908).

THE BIGGIN, HITCHIN

History

Gilbertine house founded in 1361/2 by Edward de Kendale; dissolved in September 1538.[1] Ralph Morice had unsuccessfully petitioned Cromwell for the site in 1536,[2] but it was not until 1544 that it was sold to John Cocks of Broxbourne,[3] Robert Marshall having resided there as bailiff of the crown since 1539.[4]

Cocks subsequently subdivided the property, which included other buildings and land in Hitchin,[5] with the result that The Biggin itself was acquired by William Croocar, whose will (1570) bequeathed "the house called the Biggin to Thomas and William my sonnes".[6]

Shortly after 1585 it seems to have bought by Robert Snagge of Letchworth, who in 1587 described it as my "poore house called the Biggin".[7] Snagge died in 1606, leaving the property to his sister, Anne Dallison.[8] By 1635 the house was in the ownership of Joseph Kempe, who founded a school here.[9] In 1723 it became a poorhouse, being converted into almshouses c.1812,[10] in which use it remains today under the administration of the Hitchin United Charities.[11]

THE BUILDINGS

Introduction

Situated on the southern side of St Mary's Square near the parish church and immediately to the east of the River Hiz, the surviving buildings consist of four brick and timber-framed ranges around a small central courtyard. From external evidence these appear to date mainly to the late 16th century and some authorities have claimed that nothing survives above ground of their medieval predecessors.[12] This, however, is not the case and a detailed investigation of the site suggests that much of the fabric of the monastic claustral ranges remains in the present buildings. The courtyard plan of the 16th-century domestic conversion and of the religious house which preceded it was easily adapted to use as a school in the 17th century and subsequently as a poorhouse/almshouses in the 18th and 19th centuries.

---

[1] Knowles (1953), 173.
[2] *L.P.*, xi, no.1479.
[3] Ibid, xix (2), g.166 (25).
[4] P.R.O., SC6/Hen. VIII/1617, m.1.
[5] L.P., xix (2), g.166 (25).
[6] P.R.O., PCC 11 Holney.
[7] B.L., Lansd. MS. 54, p.65.
[8] P.R.O., PCC 31 Stafford.
[9] R.L. Hine, *The History of Hitchin*, i (1927), Museum. 165; *V C.H.*, ii, 12.
[10] Hine, op. cit., 170.
[11] Information from clerk to trustees, Mr C.W. Hawkins, Messrs John Shilcock, Chartered Surveyors, Hitchin.
[12] *V C.H.*, ii, 6; *R. C.H.M*, 124.

The property was thoroughly repaired at the beginning of the 20th century and again in 1958 and, although several of the rooms were unoccupied at the time of inspection in July 1989, is still in use as almshouses today.

Description

Each elevation is first described from the exterior and then from the courtyard side. The materials are timber frame with rendered infill on a high red brick plinth, parts of the walls having been rebuilt in red brick (mixed bond). The whole building is of two storeys under a modern plain tile roof, which is hipped on all sides except the east where there are two gables at each end of the range.

West elevation. Timber-framed first floor with red brick to the ground floor. The frame consists of closely-spaced verticals with several sawn-off tenons, especially on the members immediately to the right of the prominent external lateral stack to the left and right of the first-floor two-light window. The width between these members and the presence of the sawn-off projecting timbers to the tops of the respective members suggests that there was formerly a two-storey range projecting at right-angles to the west. There is a curved tension brace to the wall-post at the right corner. This post has several sawn-off mortice and tenon joints on its two visible faces and there is a sawn-off beam at the top on the west face, which again suggests there may have been a projecting range at this point. Similar sawn-off mortice and tenon joints to the corner post at the north-west angle, however, probably indicate nothing more than a re-used timber. The timber frame on the first floor probably originally extended to the ground floor.

Irregular fenestration on both floors; six windows to the ground floor and three on the first floor, all 20thcentury replacement leaded casements except a two-light window immediately to the left of the lateral stack on the ground floor and a large eight-light mullioned and transomed window (probably of the late 16th century) directly below the eaves to the right. Prominent external lateral red brick stack to left and a large red brick ridge stack to right of centre; gabled dormer in roof slope directly in line with lateral stack.

South elevation. The materials are the same as on the west elevation, except that the whole of the right part has been rebuilt in brick. The brick is 18th century but the pointing and the soldier courses to the windows indicate a 20th-century rebuilding. The timber frame to the left part extends to the ground floor on the left of the entrance but has been underbuilt in brick to the right. There is a reset projecting bracket to the member to the right of the left corner post with the remains of a tension brace below. There are also several sawn-off tenons, which may be associated with the 18th-century brick range which formerly abutted this elevation (see below). The curved brace in the red brick infill panel to the left of the modern door may represent the spandrel of an original entrance arch in line with the west cloister walk. The right part of this elevation has two windows directly below the eaves and two on the ground floor, all 20th-century casements except the two-light leaded window to the left on the first floor. External lateral stack to right.

East elevation. This is timber framed with rendered infill on the first floor; red brick on the ground floor except the left gable which is mostly timber framed. There are flush gables to the left and right but the original four bays can be detected, one to each gable and with a thick wall-post to the centre dividing the inner bays, all the wall-posts extending into the brick ground floor. The gables themselves are 16th century but the close-studded frame (including that to the ground and first floors of the gabled sections) is substantially medieval, although it contains a straight tension brace to the centre.

The gables have bargeboards, moulded bressumers and louvred openings to the attic and renewed twelve-light mullioned and transomed leaded windows on the first floor with infilled two-light mullion windows directly to either side. The centre section has two eight-light mullioned and transomed windows directly below the eaves divided by the central wall-post. The ground floor has a twelve-light mullioned and transomed window to the left gable and one of six larger lights to the right gable, both renewed, the former with an infilled two-light mullion window to the left. There are also three 20th- century leaded windows to the centre range.

North elevation. This has been substantially rebuilt in red brick (mixed bond) to the eastern two-thirds, although this may simply be cladding as it projects from the right section, which has close-studded timber framing with rendered infill on the first floor and brick to the ground floor. Integral lateral stack in the roof slope to far left. Irregular fenestration; six-light mullioned and transomed window directly below the eaves to the right corner. Entrance on left of timber-framed part has 16th- or 17th-century plank door with strap hinges; blocked window to right. The brick section has two leaded windows directly below the eaves with another at lower level to the right. The ground floor has a leaded cross window to the centre in the position of an infilled doorway with a two-light leaded window on the right and a six-light mullioned and transomed window to the left; blocked window to left of the latter.

Courtyard side

West elevation. This is timber framed with rendered and brick infill to the first floor; colonnade to ground floor. The first floor has four posts, the third from the right being the thickest and supporting a principal truss with a curved brace to the right. There is a similar but straight tension brace to the left corner. Three leaded windows directly below the eaves, two to the left rectangular and the right in two lights: these look relatively modern. The colonnade

has five wooden Tuscan columns with plain impost blocks and wooden pads, dividing the west range into four bays. Mortices to the underside of the beam supported by the colonnade show that there were previously close-studded posts in this position. At the northern end are the remains of a doorway to a possible north walk; cambered head with the door jambs cut away. There are three similarly shaped arches beneath the first floor of the west range itself, the supporting beams of which run on a north-south axis. Also behind the colonnade is the set-back ground-floor east wall of the west range, which has 20th-century doors and windows.

South elevation. Any evidence for a south walk has been obliterated by later work. There are two late 16th-century mullioned and transomed windows directly below the eaves, the left of six lights and the right of eight lights to either side of a massive wall-post.

East elevation. Again any evidence for a claustral walk is not readily detectable in the fabric. There are prominent stacks in the angles with the north and south ranges, the latter especially massive with two small windows in it. Between the two stacks are two small windows above a modern lean-to porch.

North elevation. The western part is open on the ground floor with the slight suggestion of an arch cut into the girding beam of the first floor; the eastern part is brick with a small leaded window. Late 16th-century ten-light leaded latticed mullioned and transomed window to the left on the first floor with six vertical posts beneath. From the right corner of its window cill a curving tension brace links with a massive timber wall-post in the angle with the east range.

Interior.
Much altered in 1958 when it was divided into 12 self-contained flats with shared staircases. There are late 20th-century doors and fireplaces throughout except where stated. The ground floor of each range is described in the same sequence as the exterior, then the first floor.

Ground Floor

West Range. There are no features of particular note.

South range. The north-south running wall in Flat No.5 has square and rectangular oak panelling like that in Flats No.11 and 12, but possibly reset, with fluting to the cornice. To the west of this wall the wall-posts of the external walls have curved braces supporting the massive beam of the inserted first floor. More timber framing is visible in the kitchen and the bathroom of this flat.

East range. Flat No.4 in the southern part of this range has reset rectangular panelling like that in Flats No.5, 11 and 12 in the lavatory to the right of the entrance. A curved brace to a beam supporting the first floor may indicate the former presence of a claustral walk, but if one did exist, its inner (i.e. western) wall has subsequently been pushed out to west. Running east-west across this flat is a timber-framed wall which appears to be of medieval construction and has sawn-off joist ends showing that the ceiling has been raised. Flat No.3 in the northern part of this range has an elaborate moulded beam with run-out stops running north-south across the main room. The curved brace supporting a beam in the kitchen of Flat No.3 is the corresponding brace to that in the lavatory of Flat No.4.

North range. Flat No.2 in the eastern part of this range has a moulded spine beam with run-out stops running north-south across its main room.

First Floor

West range. Flat No.7 in the northern part of this range has several exposed timbers which appear to be of medieval date. The main room of Flat No. 12 in the southern part of the range is completely panelled to e south and east walls and to the southern part of the west wall: rectangular panels, some apparently reset but most *in situ.* Fluted frieze and guilloche pattering to cornice. The panelling on the south wall has three round-headed arches with carved leaves to the spandrels and wide fluted Ionic pilasters with moulded imposts rising from a dentilled plinth. Carved initials and date "WC 1585 IC" from left to right in centre of each arch-way. Immediately to the left of these arches is a massive jowled wall-post (now boxed in by late 16th-century panelling with guilloche pattering), which supports the southern end of the massive tie beam of the west truss of the south range. The corresponding wall-post to the north has had most of its 16th-century 'boxing' removed and its original medieval form is visible. This shows a sawn-off tenon below the jowling, which indicates the former presence of a brace to the plastered tie beam, the reconstructed size of the brace suggesting that the first floor is an insertion. The east and west faces of this wall-post also have sawn-off tenons, indicating the presence of bracing to the wall-plate, although a mortice is now visible only to the west of the wall-post. On this side of the wall-post is an inserted fireplace (now infilled). There is also a section of late 16th-century panelling fixed to the wall at this point: it consists of six panels with diamond shapes having rosettes to the centre and carved leaves to the spandrels; guilloche patterns to the rails and muntins. There is a large cupboard to the left of the fireplace.

In the room to the north is the principal truss of the west range: massive wall-posts with the lower parts of crudely chamfered braces supporting the tie beam visible. The tie beam of an additional truss to the north is also visible.

South range. Flat No.11 in the south range is separated from Flat No.12 by a landing with a straight-flight staircase down to the courtyard. This staircase is probably of early 18th-century date with turned newels and a handrail on three sides at the top. The triangular stick balusters are later replacements. Immediately above the entrance to Flat No.11 is a cambered tie beam with moulded arch braces from the wall-posts. There are substantial wall-plates visible to the north and south walls.

The main room of Flat No.11 has late 16th- or early 17th-century rectangular oak panelling with a fluted cornice (probably not *in situ*) and traces of contemporary painted strapwork decoration. The east and west walls have the vestiges of painted mottoes. These are thought to date to the period when Robert Snagge was owner of The Biggin and one, accompanied by a painting of a woman watching a man (presumably her husband) as he walks away and with the legend "In things abroad be ye a wary man, At home I'll be as thrifty as I can" issuing from her mouth, may represent Snagge and his wife. Other rhyming couplets, such as "Two lawyers thus their clients doe uphold/ Till they consume and their estates be sold", appear to be satires on the legal profession, of which Snagge was a member.[13]

East range. The southern half of this range forms Flat No.10 but this was not accessible at the time of inspection. Flat No.9 in the northern half of this range is separated from No.10 by a landing with a modern straight-flight staircase leading down to the courtyard; there is a piece of reset Purbeck marble carving in a quatrefoil pattern towards the foot of this staircase. The carving is probably of late 14th-century date.

Flat No.9 has a close-studded wall (some of the framing removed) separating it from Flat No.8 in the north range. There is a massive chimney breast visible in the cupboard immediately to the left of the entrance and the small kitchen has a plastered-over brace from the wall-post to the tie beam on the east side.

North range. Flat No.8 has an exposed tie beam with a plastered-over brace on the south side. There is a blocked doorway on the landing leading to Flat No.7 in the west range. A semi-winder staircase leads down to the courtyard and there is a straight-flight staircase behind a plank door up to the attic.

The attic. This is the part of the building where the original construction is most clearly visible. The roof structure is of crown-post type, although only two actual crown-posts now survive in the west range. Each range is of four bays.

West range. The first truss from the south has a tall crown-post with curved braces to the east and west in a wattle and daub partition. The collar purlin has now gone at this point. The next truss to the north is the best preserved in the building: a tall crown-post, square in section with straight braces to the north-south aligned

---

[13] Hine, op. cit., 162-3.

collar purlin, which is cut by the inserted stack to the south. The crown-post rests on a slightly cambered tie beam, which is chamfered to the underside and has the chamfered braces to the wall posts below visible. The collar purlin, which retains its collar bracing to the common rafters, is spliced, has empty mortices and is apparently reused.

The next truss to the north, which consists simply of a tie beam, is not original and was probably inserted in the 16th or 17th century to give the roof extra strength. The next truss is medieval and consists of a tall thin crown-post with a downward-curving brace to the east in a wattle and daub partition; there is no mortice or groove for a similar brace or partition to the west. The collar purlin, which does not extend to the north, stops at this point.

South range. This has a coupled rafter roof throughout. The eastern bay has complete floor boards (probably of 16th- or 17th- century date), its truss being a modern partition. The second truss from the east has a tie beam, chamfered to the underside and with an empty mortice for a crown-post; the tie beam of the third truss is concealed by a modern piece of timber. Several of the rafters and collars appear to be smoke blackened.

East range. Like the south range, this has a coupled rafter roof. The collar purlin is present for a short length at the northern end and a mortice to this, rather than the absent or concealed tie beam, indicates the position of the first truss from the north. The next tie beam is probably of the 16th century as it is not chamfered to the underside, while the appearance of the third tie beam is concealed by plaster.

North range. The west bay retains its collar purlin with a crown-post to its truss, also acting as a door jamb; chamfered collar to this truss concealed by plaster. The second tie beam has an empty mortice for a crown-post but any mortice to the third tie beam is concealed by a modern partition.

General comments on roof structure. The roof structure is 15th century in date with some 16th- and 17th-century remodelling. Only the roof structure of the west range remains in anything like its original condition, but the inconsistent chamfering and poor detailing of the central tie beam and crown-post suggest that, while the truss would have been exposed to view from the first floor, or possibly the ground floor, the room in which it was situated is likely to have been comparatively unimportant. The partitions to the trusses to the north and south also appear to be original. It is not possible to reconstruct the precise details of the roof to the other ranges but enough remains to suggest that it was originally of crown-post construction throughout.

Other features

On the east wall of the west range to the left of the entrance to Flat No.6 are fixed the remains of the top section of a late 14th-century timber window. This is square headed and has four pointed lights with cusped quatrefoils to the spandrels. It was discovered in 1907 just below the eaves of the south wall of the south range,[14] leading to the suggestion (see below) that the south range represents the former monastic church.

Until its demolition in 1958 a red brick range abutted the south-west corner of the building. It was gable fronted to the west with leaded windows and dentilled floor bands to the first floor and attic. On the south side there was a corbelled oriel window directly below the eaves with a tall external lateral stack immediately to the right. The appearance of this range in late 19th- and early 20th-century photographs raises the possibility that, although it was extensively remodelled in c.1730,[15] the range was in origin a very much earlier structure. At the time the photographs were taken the gable was weatherboarded with render to the first floor on the south side, both finishes suggesting the existence of timber framing beneath. That this frame was substantial is further suggested in the photographs by the presence of a large wall-post to the south-east corner.

PICTORIAL EVIDENCE

This is probably slimmer for The Biggin than for any other monastic site in Hertfordshire with surviving buildings, and even at sites like Cheshunt and St Margaret's, Nettleden, where all above-ground traces of the former monastic structures have long gone, the graphic evidence is rather more useful than it is for The Biggin. Apart from the photographs referred to above, there are a number of late 19th-century drawings, including several of the central courtyard,[16] but few add much information that cannot be obtained from an examination of the existing buildings. There is also an undated but apparently late 18th- or early 19th-century coloured drawing in the Museum of St Albans of a painted panel on a door at The Biggin, but even this is of little use as the precise location of the door is not stated on the drawing's caption.[17] The panel is painted with Jacobean strapwork decoration and the door can presumably be identified with remodelling work of that period.

DOCUMENTARY EVIDENCE

Nothing is known of the condition of the buildings at the time of the Dissolution beyond Ralph Morice's claim that they were in "ruinous state" when he made his petition to Cromwell for the property in 1536.[18] This should not necessarily be taken at face value, however, for Morice may have been deliberately distorting the situation to improve his chances of obtaining the site.

[14] Ibid, 161; letter (1927) from Walter Millard to Hine, Hine colln., Hitchin Museum.

[15] H.R.O., Gerish colln., Box 47; Bodl., MS. Top. eccl. b.27, fol.53.

[16] For example in The Museum of St Albans, 82.2451.

[17] Ibid, Lewis Evans colln., Scrapbooks.

[18] *L.P.*, xi, no.1479.

As is frequently the case in Hertfordshire, there is no information from the Ministers' Accounts on the buildings. There is also no commissioners' record made at the suppression, the prior, John Mounton, having been sent, as was the prior of Hertford, direct to the Chancellor of the Court of Augmentations.[19] Nevertheless, we can surmise that between 1538 and 1544, during which time the property remained in royal hands, Robert Marshall residing there as bailiff of the crown from 1539, little was done to the house, its value apparently declining from £13 16s in 1535 to £10 11s 8d in 1544.[20]

It was in 1544 that the house was sold to John Cocks of Broxbourne for £254 12s 9d, "with which" the crown stated "we are fully contented and satisfied."[21] Cocks was an important and influential man. Apart from being appointed Sheriff of Essex and Hertfordshire in 1548 and being returned along with Sir Robert Sadleir as Member for the latter county in 1553, he served as Master of Requests to both Edward VI and Mary.[22] However, it seems that he did not plan to retain the property, but acquired it simply with the intention of splitting it up and selling it on. This suggestion is given further weight by the fact that Cocks obtained many other such grants, not only in Hertfordshire but elsewhere,[23] which he then transferred to other owners. Whether Cocks was acting purely on his own account or as an agent for others is not known, but the status and position of the man suggest that in his case personal ambition and speculation are likely to have been the primary motivators. Be this as it may, beyond the splitting of the manor between his two sons in his will of 1553, there is no further reference to The Biggin until 1570, when William Croocar bequeathed it in his will to his sons, Thomas and William.[24] How Croocar obtained the property is not known but he may have acquired it through his wife, Luce, whose mother, Mary, was married to Thomas Parrys, who seems to have had an interest in the former priory lands in the 1550s and who is almost certainly the same Thomas Parrys, who was bailiff to the crown at Hitchin Priory between 1538 and 1546.[25]

Nothing more is known of the Croocar or Parrys families beyond the fact that, despite William Croocar the elder's will of 1570, Mary Parrys, "widow", was still paying rent for The Biggin in c.1578.[26] There is little more information on Robert Snagge, who owned the house between c.1587 and his death in 1606, other than that he was a lawyer and

second son of Robert Snagge of Letchworth Hall, who served as Speaker of the House of Commons from 1588 to 1592.[27]

ARCHAEOLOGICAL EVIDENCE

In 1968 a survey of the building was undertaken by C.A. Beresford-Webb and in this and the following year some archaeological excavation was carried out under his direction. Neither the results of the survey nor the excavation have been published but there is a manuscript report in Hitchin Museum.[28] Although some of Beresford-Webb's conclusions (especially from the excavation) are dubious, he recognised that the present building retains much of its medieval fabric. In this he follows the views of the architect, Walter Millard, who after the discovery in 1907 of the 14th-century window in the south wall of the south range (see above), argued that this range represents part of the medieval church. The exact location of this window when discovered is not known as no proper record seems to have been made or survives, but it appears to have been "set high up in the wall close beneath the eaves".[29] The tracery of the surviving fragment and such a position would not be inconsistent with the use of the range as a church/chapel, although this is by no means proven.

On the evidence of his excavations, Beresford-Webb suggested that the church lay on the south side of the cloister, postulating a nave beginning immediately to the east of the staircase in the south range and terminating just to the east of the east range of the present building, where the floor stepped up to continue, according to Beresford-Webb, as the canons' choir and presbytery. His assertion that the church ended in a semi-circular apse is less reliable and the suggestion that the west range formed the lay brothers' quarters, kitchen and lavatorium, while credible, does not appear to be based on solid evidence.[30]

Likewise, his suggestion that the west end of the church may have had a gallery leading to the prior's lodging in the south-west corner of the site appears to be based entirely on the situation at the far larger Gilbertine house of Watton (Yorks.), rather than on the evidence from The Biggin.[31] Indeed, the range at the south-west corner of The Biggin (demolished in 1958) seems to have dated chiefly to c.1730, although as noted earlier it may have been remodelled from an earlier structure, perhaps even the prior's lodging. In this connection, it is also worth recalling the early 20th-century antiquary, W.B. Gerish's claim that this range may have served as a chapel in the

[19] V.C. H., iv, 443 n.

[20] *Val. Eccl.*, iv, 276; L. P., xix (2), g.166 (25).

[21] L.P., xix (2), g.166 (25).

[22] Hine, op. cit. (note 9), 161; a full biography of Cocks's life and career is given in S.T. Bindoff (ed.), *The History of Parliament. The House of Commons 1509-58*, i (1982), 662-4. Cocks had earlier been returned as M.P. for Hertfordshire in 1545 and 1552.

[23] For example, *L.P.*, xix (1) g.80 (48); xix (1) g.1035 (97).

[24] P.R.O., PCC 24 Noodes; Cocks did not die until 1557 and his will was proved in the following year (P.R.O., C 142/111/82). P.R.O., PCC 11 Holney (Croocar).

[25] P.R.O.1 SC6/Hen. VIII/1607-15; miscellaneous documents and papers in Hine colln., Hitchin Museum; Salmon, 162.

[26] Hine colln., Hitchin Museum.

[27] D.N.B., xviii, 610.

[28] C.A. Beresford-Webb, *The Biggin* (no date but c.1968), unpublished manuscript in Hitchin Museum.

[29] Hine, op.cit. (note 9), 161; letter (1927) from Walter Millard to Hine, Hine colln., Hitchin Museum.

[30] Beresford-Webb, op. cit., 22.

[31] W.H. St. John Hope, 'The Gilbertine Priory of Watton in the East Riding of Yorkshire', *Arch. JnL*, 58 (1901), 1-34, esp. plan opp. p.34.

post-Dissolution house.[32]

Beresford-Webb suggests that the north range would have housed the canons' frater on the first floor over an undercroft and that the warming house with dorter above lay at right-angles to this range, but further east than the present east range, the night stair entering the church "at a position below the sanctuary and just above the quire".[33]

INTERPRETATION AND CONCLUSIONS

The foundation date of 1361/2 provides a *terminus post quem* for The Biggin, with the details of its construction suggesting a 15th-century date for the basic fabric. The most reliable evidence for this primary phase comes from the least disturbed part of the building, the crown-post roof structure. Crown posts in Hertfordshire tend to be taller in the 15th century than in the 14th century,[34] those at The Biggin falling into the former category. It is difficult, however, to give a more precise date than this for the monastic phase because of the comprehensive nature of the 16th-century and later remodellings.

The first date positively associated with post-Dissolution re-use at The Biggin is 1585, the date inscribed in the panelling in the first-floor south-west room of the building, with the accompanying initials "WC" and "IC", which are probably those of William Croocar (the second) and his wife. The panelling itself, along with that in other rooms, and other features such as the mullioned and transomed windows, is also consistent with this date and while this does not, of course, show that there was not also earlier residential use of the building, it clearly indicates that there was extensive remodelling of the structure at this time.

The work undertaken by Croocar seems to have had the effect of converting the building into a comfortable, if comparatively modest, manor house. The next owner, Robert Snagge, who was probably responsible for the rhyming couplets on the walls of the first-floor room in the south range, appears to have made similar use of the building.

There remains the question of which parts of the former monastic buildings are represented by the existing structure and to what extent they were altered by the 16th-century conversion. In answering this, especially in view of the comparative lack of documentary and pictorial evidence for The Biggin, comparisons with other Gilbertine houses may be useful.

Relatively little is known of the plans or architecture of Gilbertine houses. They are few in number and even fewer survive in anything like their original condition or have been archaeologically investigated. It should also be emphasised that even by the standards of Gilbertine houses, which were usually comparatively small, The Biggin was a very small establishment, never seeming to have accommodated more than two canons and the prior,[35] although the number at the Dissolution is not known. This perhaps means that we should not automatically expect there to have been a conventional claustral lay-out, although the surviving courtyard plan suggests that it is probably correct to assume there to have been one. These difficulties are exacerbated by the substantial changes to the building in the 17th-century and later. Similarly, the demolition in 1958 of the supposedly 18th-century wing attached to the south-west corner of the building and the conversion of the then 18 rooms into 12 self-contained flats was not archaeologically recorded.

Of excavated Gilbertine houses, St Andrew's, York and Watton have produced evidence for north cloisters,[36] while others like Mattersey (Notts.) and the mother house of the order, Sempringharn (Lincs.), had the cloister in the more usual position to the south.[37] Old Malton (Yorks.) and Chicksands (Beds.) have cloisters to the south, both converted to domestic use in the 16th century, although at the latter site there is a tradition that there was also a cloister to the north, Chicksands being a 'double' use.[38]

Comparisons between The Biggin and the large 'double' houses of Chicksands, Sempringham and Watton may not, however, be particularly rewarding and even Mattersey and St Andrew's, York were originally intended for six and twelve canons respectively,[39] although by the time of the Dissolution there were only the prior and four canons at Mattersey and a prior and three canons at St Andrew's.[40] Indeed, it seems that, like The Biggin, both communities had been very small for a considerable time before the suppression: only the prior and three canons are recorded at St Andrew's in 1380/1 and at Mattersey excavations have produced clear signs of retrenchment in the late medieval period.[41]

All the evidence at The Biggin points to the cloister having been on the north side, a practice remarkably common in Hertfordshire, as at Ashridge, King's Langley, Wymondley and nearby Hitchin Priory. The explanation for this at The Biggin may lie partly in its central urban location with the River Hiz running only yards to the west. The late

[32] H.P. Pollard and W.B. Gerish, 'The religious orders in Hitchin', *Trans. East Herts. Arch. Soc.*, 3, pt.i (1905), 4; H.R.O., Gerish colln., Box 46.
[33] Beresford-Webb, op. cit., 23.
[34] But see Smith (1992), 177 and more particularly Graham Bailey and Barbara Hutton, *Crown-Post Roofs in Hertfordshire* (1966), 5-6 for the dangers of dating crown-posts according to their length or other typological features.

[35] Knowles (1953), 173.
[36] *Med. Arch.*, 31 (1987), 170; St. John Hope, op. et loc. cit. (note 31).
[37] C.R. Peers, 'Mattersey Priory, Notts.', *Arch. Jnl.*, 87 (1930), 16-20; Rose Graham, 'Excavations on the site of Sempringham Priory', *Jnl. Brit. Arch. Assoc.*, 3rd Ser., 5 (1940), 73-101.
[38] N. Pevsner, *The Buildings of England. Yorkshire, The North Riding* (1966), 232-3; *VC.H., Beds.*, ii, 274.
[39] Knowles (1953), 174-5.
[40] Ibid.
[41] Ibid, 175; Peers, op.cit., 19.

foundation date may also have been a factor; certainly, the lay-out of The Biggin would have been influenced by the existence of other buildings in the immediate vicinity.

If it can be agreed that the present south range of the building represents the nave of the Gilbertine church, it is nevertheless still difficult to accept the rest of Beresford-Webb's reconstruction of the monastic layout. The strange elongated plan of his cloister is most unusual and it seems far more likely that the footings of the buildings which he discovered running at right-angles to the north at the supposed east end of the church are those of buildings in some kind of outer court, rather than those of the east claustral range. A more probable position for the latter structure would seem to be on the site of the present east range, especially as it appears to contain a substantial amount of 15th-century work in its fabric. If this was case, the reconstructed plan of the cloister would be more conventional, the east claustral range joining the church between nave and choir. This would then allow the refectory to have occupied the present north range. The east end of the church would also have terminated further to the west, a more likely arrangement than the very long choir and presbytery postulated by Beresford-Webb. Finally, it would mean that the semi-circular 'apse' detected in the footings to the east would have belonged to a building other than the church. These suggestions undoubtedly contribute to a more credible reconstruction of the church's plan, as an apse would be a most unusual feature in a monastic church of the 14th or 15th century.

Further credence to this alternative reconstruction is given by the 1986 excavation at St Andrew's, York. At this house, the east range lay at right-angles to the junction between nave and chancel, the chapter house being immediately to the north with dorter and possibly scriptorium also in the east range. The refectory occupied the north range but the footings of the west range have been destroyed by post-medieval activity.[42]

The main objection to this reconstruction of the cloister lay-out at The Biggin might be that the claustral garth would be extremely small, as is indeed the present courtyard, but it will be recalled that this was a very small house, never seeming to have accommodated more than three canons, including the prior. By these standards, and even allowing for the presence of several lay brothers, the accommodation would in fact have been quite adequate.

To return to Beresford-Webb's report, he asserts that the west range is late 16th century in date, although it contains the two surviving crown-posts, and that the Tuscan columns to its ground-floor arcade come from a dividing screen wall in the former church, a most unlikely proposition given the overtly classical form of the columns

and the fact that The Biggin was never a 'double' house.

Beresford-Webb goes on to state that the present east range is also of late 16th-century construction and was built to link the medieval north and south ranges, whereas the evidence from the surviving building shows that it is essentially of the same date as the other ranges, only the gables at the north and south ends on the eastern side being post-Dissolution additions. More attention can, however, be given to Beresford-Webb's claim that this range was formerly open to the ground floor, his excavations having revealed the foundations of a driveway consisting of "a loosely-packed chalk surface with traces of cobblestones on top" directly beneath the present building.[43] While this range was almost certainly not originally open on the ground floor, part of it may have been opened up in the 16th century to provide an entrance into the courtyard of the post-suppression house.

There is strong suggestion of just such an arrangement in an undated engraving in Cussans's *History of Hertfordshire* and the first floor of this range seems formerly to have had a 'long gallery' running the full length of the range on the east side.[44] This was later subdivided, perhaps when the building was converted into a school in the 17th century, and all traces of it were effectively removed during the 'restoration' of 1958, only the two large 16th-century mullioned and transomed windows in the centre of the range remaining as evidence for its former existence. The exact date of this 'gallery' is not known but it must have been created as part as part of the 16th-century conversion.

It seems likely that the principal domestic apartments of the post-Dissolution house were at first-floor level, this floor, at least to the south and possibly the west ranges, being an insertion of this period. From the evidence of the surviving panelling it appears that the most important parts of the building were the south range and the southern half of the west range, especially the room in the south-west corner, which may have been some kind of parlour to a first-floor hall in the south range. It should be remembered, however, that there have been many alterations which have changed the original arrangement of the 16th- century conversion and even much of the contemporary panelling seems to have been reset. Furthermore, the presence of the 'long gallery' in the east range suggests that there was probably another courtyard to the east, as a gallery is not usually a feature found directly over the main entrance to an Elizabethan house.

Owing to the many structural alterations, it is difficult to be precise about the date when the conversion took place, although the evidence, such as it is, seems to point to the main phase having taken place in the 1570s and '80s. Likewise, we cannot be sure which parts of the priory the surviving building represents. Despite the apparent traces

[42] *Med. Arch.*, 31 (1987), 170; *Interim Bulletin of the York Archaeological Trust*, Vol.11, no.2 (Summer 1986), 19-27 and Ibid, Vol. 1 1, no.4 (Winter 1986/7), 12-19; Richard Kemp 'Anglian York- the missing link', *Current Arch.*, No.104, Vol.ix, no.9 (April 1987), 259-63.

[43] Beresford-Webb, op. cit. (note 28), 31.
[44] Cussans, ii, pt.1, 54; H.R.O., Gerish colln., Box 47.

of smoke blackening in its roof structure, the idea that the south range may be the nave of the former church seems credible, and if this was the case, its conversion to domestic use may have been inspired by the rather earlier transformation of the nave at nearby Wymondley Priory to residential accommodation.

Finally, it will be noted that if the south range does represent the nave of the Gilbertine church, it, like the other claustral buildings, would have been of timber-framed construction. This, while unusual among monastic churches of this date, is not implausible considering the small size and relative poverty of the community at the Biggin.[45]

Bibliography

PICTORIAL SOURCES

Museum of St Albans

82.2451.

Lewis Evans Collection, Scrapbooks.

PHOTOGRAPHIC SOURCES

Hertfordshire Record Office

Gerish Collection, Box 47.

Bodleian Library, Oxford

MS. Top. eccl. b.27, fol.53.

OTHER PRIMARY SOURCES

Manuscript:-

Public Record Office, London

SC6/Hen. VIII/1607-15, 1617, m.1.

PCC 11 Holney.

PCC 24 Noodes.

PCC 31 Stafford.

C 142/111/82.

Hertfordshire Record Office

Gerish Collection, Box 46.

British Library, London

Lansd. MS. 54, p.65.

Hitchin Museum

C.A. Beresford-Webb, *The Biggin* (no date but c.1969), unpublished manuscript.

Miscellaneous documents and papers in Hine collection.

Printed:-

Letters and Papers, Foreign and Domestic, of the Reign of Henry VIII, eds. Brewer, J.S., Gairdner, J. & Brodie, R.H., 21 vols. (1862-1932).
Valor Ecclesiasticus, (eds. Caley, J. & Hunter, J.), 6 vols. (1810-34).

SECONDARY SOURCES

Bailey, G. & Hutton, B., *Crown-Post Roofs in Hertfordshire* (Hitchin, 1966).
Bindoff, S.T. (ed.), *The History of Parliament: The House of Commons 1509-58*, i (1982).
Cussans, J.E., *The History of Hertfordshire*, ii, pt.1 (1874, reprinted Wakefield 1972).
Dictionary of National Biography, 22 vols. (revd. edn., Oxford 1921/2).
Graham, R., 'Excavations on the site of Sempringham Priory', *Jnl. Brit. Arch. Assoc.*, 3rd Ser., 5 (1940), 73-101.
Hine, R.L., *The History of Hitchin*, i (1927).
Interim Bulletin of the York Archaeological Trust, Vol.11, no.2 (Summer 1986), 19-27 and ibid, Vol.11, no.4 (Winter 1986/7), 12-19.
Kemp, R., 'Anglian York- the missing link', *Current Arch.*, No.104, Vol.ix, no.9 (April 1987), 259-63.
Knowles, M.D. & Hadcock, R.N., *Medieval Religious Houses* (1953).
Medieval Archaeology, 31 (1987), 170.
Peers, C.R., 'Mattersey Priory, Notts.', *Arch. Jnl.*, 87 (1930), 16-20.
Pevsner, N., *Yorkshire, The North Riding* (1966).
Pollard, H.P. & Gerish, W.B., 'The religious orders in Hitchin', *Trans. East Herts. Arch. Soc.*, 3, pt.i (1905), 1-9.
Royal Commission on Historical Monuments, *An Inventory of the Historical Monuments of Hertfordshire* (1910).
St. John Hope, W.H., 'The Gilbertine Priory of Watton in the East Riding of Yorkshire', *Arch. Jnl.*, 58 (1901), 1-34.
Smith, J.T., *English Houses 1200-1800: the Hertfordshire Evidence* (1992).
The Victoria History of the Counties of England, *Bedfordshire*, ii (1908).
-*Hertfordshire*, ii (1912); iv (1914).

---

[45] Parish churches of timber-framed construction are not, of course, uncommon at this date, especially in counties like Herefordshire, Shropshire and Cheshire.

CHESHUNT NUNNERY

History

Benedictine nunnery established before 1183, founder unknown.[1] Dissolved September 1536 when the site was granted to Anthony Denny.[2] On his death in 1549 the property passed to his eldest son, Henry, who in 1564 sold the estate to Anthony Throkmerton, Richard Springham and Richard Davys for 44s 6d.[3] In 1590 Edward Denny, younger brother of Henry, bought back the estate but sold it to Sir William Cecil in 1592.[4]

Introduction

Nothing now remains of the nunnery or the house which succeeded it. It was situated in the north-eastern part of Cheshunt parish immediately to the west of the Small River Lea but the last vestiges were removed by gravel extraction between 1954 and 1958.[5] It seems, however, that little survived by this date, the last monastic buildings and the main parts of the mainly 18th-century house which succeeded it, having been demolished c.1811.[6] Maps of 1785 and 1802 show the location of the nunnery but, although the 18th-century house is clearly shown, do not help in the identification of other individual buildings.[7] Further maps of 1896 and 1898 show "Nunnery Farm on (the) site of (the) Nunnery" and confirm that only a farmhouse and farmbuildings remained by this date. An arm of a moat immediately to the north possibly suggests that the whole site was moated but it may represent the remains of a monastic fishpond.[8]

THE BUILDINGS

Documentary Evidence

A number of documents relating to the closure of the nunnery survive but as is usually the case they do not allow a full reconstruction to be made of the monastic plan or that of the immediately post-Dissolution house which succeeded it. For instance, no information on the lay-out of the buildings is included in an undated survey made during the reign of Henry VIII or in the surviving sets of Ministers' Accounts.[9] The inventory of the nunnery taken at the suppression is, however, rather more informative and records the following buildings: the "chauncell, quyre, belfery, dortor, halle, chamber over the halle, maydens chamber, buttery, chamber over the buttery, mylke lofte,

chese lofte, bruynge house, kechyne, my ladys chamber, meanes howsse, priest's chamber and garn(er)".[10]

These structures are no more than would be expected at a small monastic house like Cheshunt and the annual value of £14 1s recorded at the suppression and the sale to Anthony Denny of "alle the goods and catalls for £44 7s" suggest that the community was a poor one.[11] Nothing is known of the actual process of demolition at the site but the fact that the Commissioners valued the lead from the church at only £2 suggests that it may already have been in ruins before the Dissolution.[12]

It is not known what became of the buildings after the suppression but the speedy grant of the site to Denny at the annual rent of 40s suggests that he coveted the house even before its closure.[13] In fact, he may already have had a direct stake in the house, perhaps as steward or corrodian, as the indenture of the nunnery's goods, drawn up in May 1536, was made between the Commissioners and Denny, rather than with the prioress.[14]

Denny succeeded in building up a considerable estate in Hertfordshire and East Essex on the spoils of the monasteries. He was a favourite of Henry VIII and a privy councillor and in 1541 obtained large tracts of land which had belonged to the wealthy abbeys of St Albans and Waltham (Essex). He was knighted in 1544 and on Henry's death in 1547 was appointed as executor to his will and as counsellor to Edward VI, appearing as member for Hertfordshire in the young king's first parliament.[15]

Denny is reputed to have been born and to have died at Cheshunt. This and the fact that the former nunnery remained in the family after his death suggest that he may have converted the buildings there into a house for himself: certainly it would have been a useful centre from which to have administered the vast landed estate he had created.

There is, however, nothing in the surviving 18th- and early 19th-century views of the house built on the site which show this to have been the case (see below). Some of the fabric at the rear of the house may have been of 16th-century date but in the absence of any supporting evidence it is not possible to be certain about this.

Pictorial Evidence

The following description is compiled from two early 19th-century drawings by Thomas Fisher in the British Library, supplemented by two very similar drawings by the same

[1] Knowles (1953), 211.
[2] *L.P.*, xi, g.519 (12).
[3] P.R.O., C 66/1004/584.
[4] Clutterbuck, ii, 108.
[5] H.R.O., D/EHw Z 13; J. Edwards, *Cheshunt in Herts* (1974), 20.
[6] Dugdale, iv, 328.
[7] H.R.O., D/ECr 125/2-3.
[8] Bodl., c 17: 70a 452; Ordnance Survey 2nd edn. 25" map.
[9] P.R.O., SC 12/22/71; SC6/Hen. VIII/1606, 1632.

[10] P.R.O., E 117/12/30.
[11] P.R.O., E 315/361, fol.71; Dugdale, iv, 329.
[12] P.R.O., SC6/Hen. VIII/1606.
[13] Clutterbuck, ii, 106.
[14] P.R.O., E 117/12/30.
[15] *D.N.B.*, v, 823-4; H.L.L. Denny, 'Biography of the Right Honourable Sir Anthony Denny', *Trans. East Herts. Arch. Soc.*, 2, pt.iii (1906), 197-216.

artist dated 18th June 1804 in the Museum of St Albans,[16] with additional information from a slightly earlier view by H.G. Oldfield.[17] The first early 19th-century drawing entitled "South-East View of Nunnery" shows a substantial early to mid-18th-century house of red brick (described as "good red brick" on the St Albans drawing) under a hipped plain tile roof with modillioned eaves cornice. The house is of two storeys and attic with three stacks directly behind the ridge and another smaller stack to the right end. It is of two: five: two bays, the outer bays projecting and defined by plain pilasters. There is a continuous string course and the windows are glazing bar sashes, those to the ground floor in tall round-headed recesses. There are four flat-roofed multi-paned dormers in the roof slope.

This view is largely corroborated by the Oldfield drawing, which was made from a position completely parallel with the elevation and also shows to the right an equal-height but slightly set-back range with hipped roof and string course continued round from the main range. Although the Oldfield drawing is less detailed than Fisher's, there is no reason to doubt the existence of this secondary range, which is hidden from view in the Fisher drawing. The Oldfield view otherwise differs from Fisher's only in that it depicts the openings at each end of the centre section on the ground floor as doorways rather than as windows and in the greater number of stacks it shows.

The left return (shown only on the Fisher drawing) has three blind windows on the first floor and a pedimented portico with coupled Ionic columns flanking a round-headed fixed-light window with glazing bars to the ground floor. Attached at right-angles to the left of the left return, and apparently slightly set back from it, is a low single-storey red brick range with slate roof and modillioned eaves cornice. It has five shuttered windows in slight square-headed recesses. To the left is a slight projection which has a projecting portico (very similar to the one attached to the left return of the main house) with a round-arched window. The top of another pediment is visible behind to the left and attached to the left of the range is a lean-to orangery or greenhouse.

The second early 19th-century view entitled "North-west view of Nunnery" shows the rear of the house and what appears to be earlier work than that on the main front, as is suggested by the reference on the St Albans version of this drawing to the brickwork on this side of the house being "old, dirty and patched". To the left is a square three-storey brick tower on a stone plinth with a steeply gabled or pyramidal roof surmounted by a weatherboarded cupola with a pyramidal tile cap and weathervane. (This cupola and weathervane are also visible in the Oldfield drawing). The top floor of the tower is separated from the two lower

stages by a corbelled string course and has a three-light leaded latticed mullion window, apparently of stone but probably plastered as the reveals are brick. There are infilled windows on the ground and first floors. There seems to be an angled buttress to the left corner, behind which is a shallow two-storey lean-to, with behind again the gabled projection of a large and tall external stack. To the rear of this can be glimpsed the tiled roof of an apparently lower range.

To the right of the tower is a single-storey brick lean-to, to the right of which is a rendered stone-coped shaped gable end with a tall external lateral stack attached by iron ties to the tower and the roof behind the gable end. Behind the gable-ended range a two-storey range is visible, which has a gable to the right with a two-light leaded latticed window. To the right of this can be seen a short section of roof with a ridge stack and to the right again a projecting gabled range with an integral end stack, two small latticed windows to the attic, two segmental-headed glazing bar sashes to the first floor with a floor band below and two doorways or windows on the ground floor, the heads only of which are visible, the rest being concealed by a brick wall which runs to the left into the gable-ended range. This wall is pierced by two doorways, the left in the angle with the gable-ended range and the right with a circular leaded window to the right.

Behind the wall are low slate-roofed outbuildings, the tallest and rear of which is probably that seen in the south-east view, a tall chimney with a curved flue being visible in both views. To the left of the outbuildings is what is almost certainly the rear wall of the left return of the main range; the modillioned eaves cornice visible to the right corner is not carried round to the back wall.

It is difficult from the evidence of this drawing alone to give accurate dates to the parts of the building shown: some parts are concealed by others but the two-storey projecting range with floor band is probably of the early to mid-18th century and the outbuildings to its right are probably slightly later. To the left of the two-storey projecting range are what appear to be earlier ranges but precise dating is not possible. The tower, however, is unlikely to be later than the 17th century and could be of 16th-century date. Its character suggests a primarily domestic function, although the cupola may be associated with partial use as a dovecote.

The evidence of the two early 19th-century views and the Oldfield drawing is usefully confirmed by a near contemporary note-written account (see below) and rough sketches of the building by Richard Gough,[18] although the orientation he gives to the various elevations of the building do not accord with the captions on the early 19th-century Fisher drawings. A pencil sketch of the rear of the

---

[16] B.L., Add. MS. 32,349, fol.45; Museum of St Albans, Lewis Evans colln., Scrapbooks, Hertfordshire Vol.2, p.118.

[17] H.R.O., Oldfield Drawings, II, 390; Bodl., Gough Herts. 11, opp. p.10 of extra-illustrated copy of Nathaniel Salmon's *History of Hertfordshire* (1728).

[18] Bodl., Gough Herts. 16, Ms. notes between pp.10 and 11 of annotated copy of Salmon's *History of Hertfordshire* (1728).

building, made from the other side to that made by Fisher, confirms what is shown in Fisher's view. A sketch-plan is also informative. It shows the main range of the house with bedchamber and library separated from a breakfast room and parlour by a central passage. Off this passage to the right is a broad staircase and at the back "kitchen and offices". The long, low range attached at right-angles to the left return of the main front is marked as a gallery. This is presumably where the then owner, Mrs Blackwood, kept her renowned collection of pictures,[19] the shutters shown in Fisher's drawing no doubt being to protect the paintings from the effects of sunlight. The structure to the left of the gallery is marked as a greenhouse.

Antiquarian and other Accounts

In his written account of the building Gough states that the "house at Cheshunt...appears to have been rebuilt about the beginning of the last ____ of the preceding (ie 17th) century of brick." The east front "consists of a small paved hall with 2 porphyry and 2 bronze busts opening s(outh) to a greenhouse and leading n(orth) into a drawing room furnished with capital made by pictures - B out of the old Greenhouse and opening into a dining parlour in wch are about 16/14 more this into a breakfast room and library and beyond that a bedchamber. The rest of the house being a century or more older is appropriated to rooms and offices for servants. A kitchen part may by the fascia be of ____ time. The principle staircase supposed of ____ or Dennys time goes out of the 2d passage. The s(outh) front may be of the beginning ____ of last or end of preceding century by Ld. Bingley."

The details of this account, along with the accompanying sketches, make it likely that Gough actually visited the house himself. It is possible that his interest may have been sparked by his ownership of a copy of Nathaniel Salmon's *History of Hertfordshire* (1728) containing an unattributed manuscript note, dated 1762, which gives the following description of the former nunnery. "Mr Benson rebuilt or cased the principal part: so that only the north end or offices are of the original brick, or perhaps not older than the Dissolution. In the gardens which contain eleven acres is a large canal in the form of a cross east and west but inverted, also a large elm, both perhaps coeval with the Nunnery. The greenhouse is fitted up as a modern saloon to which adjoins a room of the house..."[20] The Benson family were owners of the property in the early 18th century and this statement implies that the 18th-century work is simply a remodelling of an earlier structure, parts of which dated from the time of the Dissolution if not before.[21]

This account and Gough's own can be tied in with other descriptions of the building compiled in the late 18th and early 19th centuries. William Ellis in his *Campagna of London* (1791) writes that "A very small part of the Nunnery remains, and that appears to have been built not long before the Dissolution. The inside of it has been modernised and it is now used as a kitchen".[22] This probably refers to one of the ranges at the rear of the house but there is no means of telling which one. William Caley in his 1823 edition of Dugdale's *Monasticon* states that the nunnery's "last remains were taken down about twelve years ago by the then possessor, William Butt...who in 1811 sold the nunnery lands, about a 100 acres, to John Early Cook, the present possessor. The refectory was the last building to the nunnery which remained entire".[23] This is probably the same building to which Ellis referred in 1791.

Little is added by the account in *The Beauties of England and Wales* (1808) which reads "...for some years the seat of the late Mrs Blackwood, who had a very valuable collection of paintings, by the first masters. The remains of the Nunnery forms the domestic parts of a large mansion, that has been erected at different periods and contains some elegant apartments. The grounds are disposed with taste and the River Lea has been formed into a canal before the east end of the house".[24] Bickerton Bayley in his manuscript history of Cheshunt (1859) merely adds that "the house was pulled down soon after the death of Mrs Blackwood".[25]

By the late 19th century little seems to have remained. It is possible that some destruction was caused by the building of the railway but this lay immediately to the west of the site and no record of any damage occasioned by this has been found. Cussans (1876) simply states that "nothing of the old buildings, beyond the foundations now remains".[26] A report of 1888 in *The Hertfordshire Mercury* is more informative and probably more accurate. It records that all that then survived of both nunnery and "mansion" was a large walled garden and dovecote and an "unpretentious farmhouse and homestead, probably built with the old materials of the mansion, which appears to have stood close by on the east side". The buildings were surrounded on three sides by a broad moat, "nearly filled up in places".[27] The statement that the mansion (by which presumably the main part of the early 18th-century house is meant) was demolished c.1820 is, however, probably less reliable. No supporting evidence is given for this assertion and it seems more likely that both the mansion and the majority of the service buildings were demolished between

[19] Brayley and Britton, vii, 236; details of the paintings are recorded by Richard Gough, see note 18.

[20] Bodl., Gough Herts. 18, Ms. note between pp.10 and 11 of annotated copy of Salmon's *History of Hertfordshire* (1728). The Catalogue of Western Manuscripts in the Bodleian Library suggests that Gough may have annotated the volume himself, but the clear hand in which it is done is most certainly not his.

[21] The site was sold to Samuel Benson in 1713. He conveyed it in the following year to Robert Benson, Lord Bingley, who left it by will in

1729 to Robert, son of Samuel Benson, who released it to William Jansen. *V.C.H.*, iii, 454. See also note 18.

[22] W. Ellis, *Campagna of London* (1791), 39.

[23] Dugdale, iv, 328.

[24] Brayley and Britton, vii, 236.

[25] B. Bayley, *Cheshunt, Herts* (1859), 27: MS. history awaiting H.R.O. catalogue number, November 1990.

[26] Cussans, ii, pt.2, 207.

[27] *Hertfordshire Mercury* (28 April 1888).

1804 and 1811 when William Butt was owner of the property.

Nothing is added by the *V.C.H.* account of 1912,[28] but a paper written by W.B. Gerish for the visit of the East Hertfordshire Archaeological Society to the site in 1914 is more useful. Gerish writes that "All that we can show is an extensive range of outbuildings, whose sphere of usefulness has long since departed, a small homestead, probably of 18th-century date and an extensive walled-in-garden, much of the brickwork apparently being of 17th-century construction. Its shape is curious, leading one to assume that the mansion specified (by Ellis) as standing here in 1791 was located in the portion to the east. Whether this was also the exact site of the nunnery cannot be definitely stated, but the balance of probability is in favour of this conjecture".[29] The "curious" shape of the walled garden can be clearly seen on the 1898 25" Ordnance Survey map covering the site.

Gerish repeats Caley's statement that the refectory was the last conventual building to have remained on the site and also adds as a footnote to his paper a short account of some wall footings discovered in 1914. These were of brick, some two or three feet deep, and a sketch-plan of them was made by F.W. Martin.[30] This shows the walls running under an "existing building" to the north and under the "stack yard ground" to the south. From their nature Gerish concluded that the walls "represent(ed) the later mansion erected upon or near the site (of the nunnery)".[31]

The "homestead" and the "existing building" respectively referred to in Gerish's account and Martin's plan is probably the structure shown in an apparently contemporary photograph of the site.[32] This building is a low brick structure of two storeys with a gable-lit attic. The roof is pantiled with coped verges and continues as a catslide outshut on the side nearest the camera. The outshut has a central entrance with three-light segmental-headed shuttered casements to either side. There is a tall brick stack to the left at the junction between the outshut and the main range and the latter has a central ridge stack.

Despite the comment in *The Hertfordshire Mercury* article of 1888 that the farmhouse then existing, was "probably built with the old materials of the mansion", the building appears to pre-date the demolition of the mansion and looks more likely to have been built in the mid-to late 18th century. Furthermore, although there is nothing in the photograph which can definitely be said to be earlier than this, the possibility remains that it incorporates part of an older structure which is not visible in the photograph.

Indeed, while the building cannot be positively identified with any of the structures shown in Fisher's rear view of the the Nunnery, it is very similar in character to these buildings and there is a strong likelihood that the building was one of the service ranges of the former mansion. Unfortunately, however, the building shown in the photograph cannot be positively equated with the buildings shown on the 1898 25" Ordnance Survey map of the site.

In the 1880s the site became the property of Joseph Rochford,[33] and during the late 19th and early 20th centuries large glass houses were constructed in the immediate vicinity as the land was used for nursery gardens.[34]

Archaeological Evidence

By the late 1940s the farmbuildings of the Nunnery Farm seem to have been derelict and the site was ear-marked for gravel quarrying. In granting permission for the quarrying, the District Council stipulated that "any remains of archaeological interest should be notified to the Council".[35] Despite this condition, no official recording work seems to have been undertaken during the site's destruction.

Although some Purbeck marble columns, thought to have come from the nunnery, were discovered in 1954,[36] gravel extraction on the site of the Nunnery Farm did not begin in earnest until the summer of 1957. It was then that a local amateur archaeologist, Thomas Howlett, began to show an interest in the site and it is his notes, photographs and drawings (now in the Hertfordshire Record Office) which form what little record there is of the site's archaeology.[37]

Without much help from the then Ministry of Works or other official bodies, Howlett made a valiant attempt to record what was left of the site in the face of considerable difficulties. As the gravel was extracted, the excavated areas were immediately flooded and Howlett was not able to be present on site for most of the time work was in progress. He therefore had to rely a great deal on the finds and verbal reports of the two men operating the mechanical excavators.

For these reasons, it is probably not safe to place too much reliance on Howlett's records but they do at least give some information on the site, which would otherwise have been lost. Howlett's notes begin in September 1957 recording the discovery of "huge chunks of brick foundations, possibly from old farmbuildings still being dug out, about 60 yards south of (the) remaining small surface structure of the old farmbuilding ruins, which are about 10 yards south of the moat or fishpond".

[28] *V.C.H.*, iii, 444-5.
[29] W.B. Gerish, 'Cheshunt Nunnery', *Trans. East Herts. Arch. Soc.*, 5, pt.iii (1914), 288.
[30] Ibid, 289; there is a copy of this sketch in H.R.O., Gerish colln., Box 25.
[31] Ibid.
[32] H.R.O., Gerish colln., Box 24.

[33] Gerish, op. cit. (note 29), 289.
[34] Ordnance Survey Maps, various editions.
[35] *East Herts. Arch. Soc. Newsletter*, 1 (1949).
[36] H.R.O., D/EHw Z 13.
[37] Ibid.

Many human bones were discovered at the same time, some of which were dated by Cambridge University to the 16th century. According to an entry in Howlett's notes for 30th September 1957, one of the excavator operators said that several months previously he had found "a whole row of long shafts of Purbeck marble and that because nobody seemed to want them he threw them back into the water!" Some of those column shafts were reputed to have been several feet long.

On another visit to the site in October 1957 Howlett recorded another area of brick foundations, about 20 ft to the east of the first area and two wells, estimated to have been between 12 and 16 ft deep. Later in 1957 he "noticed several pieces of masonry and bricks lying on the bed of the moat, which appeared to be material of old standing", while on its southern edge, along with more human bones, substantial sections of mid-to late 16th-century chamfered stone mullion window were discovered. The reveals of the mullion and its cill or head had double grooves, one probably being for glazing and the other possibly for an iron grille in front.[38]

A letter from Stuart Rigold of the Ministry of Works in January 1958 states that the ministry was unable to carry out any recording work and goes on to say that "most of the masses of brickwork remaining on the site belonged to post-Dissolution structures". By September 1958 the site had been totally flooded and all traces removed, including the surviving section of moat which had formed its northern boundary.

It is difficult to be certain about the date of the structures recorded by Howlett but his notes suggest that most of the foundations uncovered did indeed relate to post-Dissolution buildings. The recorded dimensions of the bricks in the foundations discovered in September and October 1957 would seem to be consistent with a 16th-century date and the foundations may represent the service ranges of the house demolished in the early 19th century. Howlett thought that some of the foundations related to a cellar but whether the foundations were associated with the farmbuildings which remained on the site until the 1950s or the footings discovered in 1914, it is not possible to say. Areas of clunch masonry were also discovered to the east and west of the brick foundations but Howlett ascribed no date to these.

Even less certainty attaches to buildings which can be positively identified with the nunnery. The Purbeck marble column-shaft fragments came from the area to the south of the brick foundations and were discovered before Howlett started his recording work so it is not possible to be more precise about their exact location. Apart from a 13th-century crocketed capital found near the mullion window fragment, the only other features definitely connected with the nunnery were a series of encaustic floor tiles. Again

these were found out of context on one of the spoil heaps. They were dated to the mid-14th century by the British Museum and their provenance is almost certain to have been the tile factory at Penn (Bucks.).[39] They are most likely to have come from the nunnery church and, if so, suggest that this building was in its prime a higher status building than is suggested by the evidence for its condition at the time of the Dissolution. Alternatively, the tiles may have come from a chapter house although none is listed in the suppression inventory.

With the exception of one tile depicting three swans and oak leaf motifs, which was donated to the British Museum, the other tiles were given by Howlett to Cheshunt Public Library, along with the mullion window fragment, some sections of Purbeck marble column-shaft and the crocketed capital. Other fragments from the nunnery found their way elsewhere. Photographs taken by Howlett at nearby Nunsbury House in 1957 show an arch and summerhouse in the garden. Both are clearly modern and incorporate moulded stonework, which was probably taken from the site of the nunnery.[40]

Hurried and incomplete as it was, the recording work carried out by Howlett appears to have been the only documented archaeological work carried out on the site, which is particularly unfortunate as all the evidence has now been destroyed. For instance, there are apparently no references to any discoveries having been made when the railway was built in the 19th century immediately to the west of the site, nor when the River Lea Navigation was dug in the 18th century, although as this lies some distance to the east this is perhaps not surprising.

While Howlett's work does not add a great deal of information to what is known about the site, it usefully confirms what can be learnt from other sources. The discovery of the Purbeck marble shafts to the south of the other material recovered perhaps suggests that the church and cloister lay to the south of the farmbuildings which survived on the site until the 1950s. Which part of the nunnery site or of the house that succeeded it these latter buildings represent is, however, unknown.

One other feature destroyed during the gravel working and which may have been connected with the nunnery was a moat some distance to the south. This moat surrounded a square platform with traces of a building on it. An aerial photograph of 1955 clearly shows it in complete condition,[41] but Howlett makes no reference to it in his notes and nothing further is known of its function.

---

[38] I am grateful to Tace Parminter for this observation.

[39] H.R.O., D/EHw Z 13; C. Hohler 'Medieval paving tiles in Buckinghamshire', *Records of Bucks.*, 14 (1942), 1-49.

[40] H.R.O., D/EHw Z 5.

[41] Ibid, D/EHw Z 13.

INTERPRETATION AND CONCLUSIONS

Cheshunt is without doubt one of the least well-recorded monastic sites in Hertfordshire. It appears to have been in poor condition at the Dissolution and the low values assigned to its buildings in the Commissioners' inventory make it likely that several of them were already derelict. We do not know the full extent of the buildings or their lay-out and, as mentioned earlier, it is not clear whether the section of the moat which survived until 1958 was a fishpond or should be seen as an indication that the whole complex, like the Augustinian priory at Wymondley, was moated. The latter is, however, a possibility as the maps of 1785 and 1802 show a stretch of water to the south of the buildings flowing at right-angles to the west of the Small River Lea. This stretch of water may represent another section of moat and the river presumably formed the eastern boundary of the site. This would give three arms to the moat, as stated in *The Hertfordshire Mercury* report of 1888.

Equally little is known about the immediately post-Dissolution re-use of the site. All that can be asserted with any confidence is that Anthony Denny's apparently close connections with the locality make it likely that he converted the former buildings or possibly re-used materials from them to build a new house on or near the site for his own use. Little weight can be attached to Gough's statement that "the principle staircase (in the house is) supposed of ____ or Denny's time", especially as the actual reference to Denny is struck out in this manuscript account.[42]

The discovery of the mullion window fragments is, however, indicative of some 16th-century domestic re-use of the site, the details of the window moulding suggesting a relatively high-status building. We also have the unsubstantiated statement of 1762 that the offices of the 18th-century house "are of the original brick, or perhaps not older than the Dissolution", an assertion which is not inconsistent with the early 19th-century drawing of the rear of the house.

Caley also states that the refectory was the last building of the nunnery "which remained entire" and if this is the same building which Ellis says "has been modernised and is now used as a kitchen", the fact that it "appears not to have been built long before the Dissolution" (and was therefore presumably in relatively good condition at the time of the suppression) may have been instrumental in its re-use.

Although it is not possible to be certain whether it was Anthony Denny before 1549 or his son, Henry, before 1564 who first adapted the monastic buildings to domestic use, it is much more likely that the earliest phase of post-Dissolution work was carried out by one of these two men than by Anthony Throkmerton, Richard Springham and Richard Davys, of whom nothing is known and whose group purchase of the property suggests that they were agents acting for another party. That a second phase of building activity took place later in the century is hinted at by the reference to the former nunnery in a verse by William Vallans entitled "A Tale of Two Swannes" (1590).[43] This verse, which also refers to Ware Priory and Sir Richard Lee's Sopwell, is apparently the earliest literary (as opposed to documentary) allusion to a former monastic house in Hertfordshire:

> "...From thence to Broxbourne, and to Wormley wood
>   And so salute the holy house of Nunnes,
>   That late belong'd to captaine Edward Dennie,
>   A knight in Ireland of the best accompt
>   Who late made execution on our foes,
>   I meane of Spanyardes, that with open armes
>   Attempted both against our Queene and us:
>   There now Lord Talbot keepes a noble house"

Although these lines give no concrete information on the site, they appear to suggest that a dwelling of some significance had been created here. The references to "late belong'd to Dennie" and to Lord Talbot (presumably the sixth earl of Shrewsbury, who died in 1590 and who had no known connection with Cheshunt) are puzzling, however, and perhaps warn us not to place too much reliance on Vallans's verse.

If a house of the first rank had been fashioned from the former nunnery, it is surprising that so little record survives of this building. Certainly, however, extensive remodelling of the house known as "Cheshunt Nunnery" took place in the 17th and 18th centuries and its almost total demolition in the early 19th century means that it was not the subject of Victorian antiquarian study. Similarly, the existence of other large houses in the parish, most notably Cheshunt Great House and Sir William Cecil's great mansion of Theobalds, may have led to any house erected on the site of the former nunnery being overlooked by earlier commentators or antiquaries, as indeed largely seems to have been the case.[44]

Bibliography

PICTORIAL SOURCES

Hertfordshire Record Office

Oldfield Drawings, II, 390.

---

[42] See note 18.

[43] 'A Tale of Two Swannes' is contained in William Vallans's 'Account of Several Parts of Hartfordshire', which appears as a prefix to Thomas Hearne's 1769 edition of volume 5 of John Leland's *Itinerary* (Bodl., Douce HH 169).

[44] The house is similarly ignored in J.T. Smith's recent study of Hertfordshire houses (1992), 66.

Gerish Collection, Box 25.

British Library, London

Add. MS. 32,349, fol.45.

Bodleian Library, Oxford

Gough Herts. 11.

Museum of St Albans

Lewis Evans Collection, Scrapbooks, Hertfordshire Vol.2, p.118.

CARTOGRAPHIC SOURCES

Hertfordshire Record Office

D/ECr 125/2-3.

Bodleian Library, Oxford

c 17: 70a 452 (map room).

PHOTOGRAPHIC SOURCES

Hertfordshire Record Office

Gerish Collection, Box 24.

OTHER PRIMARY SOURCES

Manuscript:-

Public Record Office, London

SC 12/22/71; SC6/Hen. VIII/1606, 1632.

E 117/12/30.

E 315/361.

C 66/1004/584.

Hertfordshire Record Office

B. Bayley, *Cheshunt, Herts* (1859), 27: MS. history awaiting H.R.O. catalogue number, November 1990.

D/EHw Z 5; D/EHw Z 13.

Bodleian Library, Oxford

Douce HH 169.
Gough Herts. 16, 18.

Printed:-

Dugdale, W., *Monasticon Anglicanum*, (re-ed. Caley, J., Ellis, H. & Bandinel, B., 6 vols. in 8, 1817-30).
Letters and Papers, Foreign and Domestic, of the Reign of Henry VIII, eds. Brewer, J.S., Gairdner, J. & Brodie, R.H., 21 vols. (1862-1932).

SECONDARY SOURCES

Brayley, E.W. & Britton, J., *The Beauties of England and Wales, Vol. 7, Hertfordshire* (1808).
Clutterbuck, R., *The History and Antiquities of Hertfordshire*, ii (1815).
Cussans, J.E., *The History of Hertfordshire*, ii, pt.2 (1876, reprinted Wakefield, 1972).
Denny, H.L.L., 'Biography of the Right Honourable Sir Anthony Denny', *Trans. East Herts. Arch. Soc.*, 2, pt.iii (1906), 197-216.
Dictionary of National Biography, 22 vols. (revd. edn., Oxford 1921/2).
East Herts. Arch. Soc. Newsletter, 1 (1949).
Edwards, J., *Cheshunt in Herts* (Cheshunt, 1974).
Ellis, W., *The Campagna of London* (1791).
Gerish, W.B., 'Cheshunt Nunnery', *Trans. East Herts. Arch. Soc.*, 5, pt.iii (1914), 288-9.
Hertfordshire Mercury (28 April 1888).
Hohler, C., 'Medieval paving tiles in Buckinghamshire', *Records of Bucks.*, 14 (1942), 1-49.
Knowles, M.D. & Hadcock, R.N., *Medieval Religious Houses* (1953).
Salmon, N., *The History of Hertfordshire* (1728).
Smith, J.T., *English Houses 1200-1800: The Hertfordshire Evidence* (1992).
The Victoria History of the Counties of England, Hertfordshire, iii (1912).

HERTFORD PRIORY

History

Benedictine priory founded by Ralph de Limesi as a dependent cell of St Albans between 1086 and 1093.[1] Dissolved in 1538 and granted to Anthony Denny, the property remained in the Denny family until 1578 when it was granted to Thomas Dockwra.[2] Shortly afterwards it seems to have returned to the Denny family but in 1587 it was sold to Henry Colthurst, passing to Martin Trott in c.1590.[3] In 1617 Trott sold the site to Richard Willis, whose son conveyed it to John Harrison in 1637 whereupon it became part of the Balls Park estate.[4]

THE SITE

Introduction

The site of the priory lies on the south-east bank of the River Lea, bounded by Railway Street to the south, St John's Street to the east and Priory Street to the west. No buildings earlier than the 19th century remain above ground, although parts of the church have been excavated on two separate occasions.

Description

The present buildings are a mixture of 19th-century terraced housing and industrial structures. The late 19th-century "Priory House", which bears no relation to the former Priory House which stood by the bank of the River Lea, is situated at the junction of Priory Street and Railway Street. Most of the area to the north-west of Priory Street running towards the river is occupied by an extensive late 20th-century housing development, while to the south-west are the school, presbytery and church of the Roman Catholic Church of The Immaculate Conception and St Joseph (1858).

THE FORMER BUILDINGS

Documentary Evidence

Hertford Priory is among the most poorly documented of those Hertfordshire monastic houses which survived until the Dissolution. There are no commissioners' returns and the ministers' accounts for 1537-8, as is frequently the case, give no information on the buildings.[5] The grant of the site to Anthony Denny in February 1538 makes the standard reference to the "howse, edifice, dove howses, gardens" etc. of the "scite" but contains no specific details.[6] The earliest useful reference is a terrier of the

manor made at the time of its sale by Edward Denny to Henry Colthurst. This mentions a "watter myle, a newe bilt howse, with a dove howse, boornes and stables, the myll newe bilt, orchards and gardens..." Edmund Gravener of Hertford is described as "farmer in the manner house" valued at £86. The total value of the property is given as £262 1s 8d. "The howsinge dove howse and barnes were bilt within thre years coste a thowson markes the hole being lesed for 17 years to come for wch the tennants will not be bought out for £300..."[7]

There is some confusion as to whether before the Dissolution there were one or two churches connected with the priory site. The priory church itself was dedicated to St Mary the Virgin but it was in St John's parish.[8] In the endowment of a vicarage for the parish in 1209, the words "Vicaria in ecclesia Sancti Johannis, Hertford, qua est monachorum ibidem..." suggest that the Church of St John was the parochial part of the monks' church, while a slightly later institution refers simply to "perpetuam vicarium ecclesie beate Marie Monachorum."[9] Whether or not the two churches were one and the same, the last pre-Dissolution reference to St John's Church is in 1535,[10] and after the grant to Denny in 1538 it does not appear to be recorded again until 1622 when John Hume was appointed vicar.[11]

In 1621 a survey of Hertford mentions the borough boundary as being near the "stile and gate of St John's churchyard", which lay outside the borough,[12] but by 1624 the churchyard seems to have closed as it is described as forming part of the mill close of Lykermill.[13] In 1629 it is said that Thomas Willis rebuilt the church and dedicated it to St John the Baptist.[14] In 1638, however, the parish was combined with the larger parish of All Saints,[15] and by the end of the century (according to Chauncy) the church had been "lately demolisht by Order of the Bishop of Lincolne."[16]

The documentary evidence is not conclusive in establishing whether there were separate parish and priory churches and, if so, which was the first to be built. It appears, however, from the archaeological evidence discussed below that the nave of the excavated church dates to the 13th century. This ties in with the endowment of the vicarage in 1209 and seems to imply that the excavated

---

[1] *V.C.H.*, iv, 419; Knowles (1953), 68.
[2] *L.P.*, xiii (1), g.384 (47); P.R.O., C 66/1193/1783.
[3] P.R.O., C 66/1194/1804; Chauncy, i, 506.
[4] B.L., Harl. MS. 756, fol.182; *V.C.H.*, iii, 506.
[5] P.R.O., SC6/Hen. VIII/1596.
[6] B.L., Add. MS. 32,579, fols.11-20.
[7] B.L., Lansd. MS. 116, fol.48.
[8] Dugdale, iii, 299; A. Gibbons (ed.), *Liber Antiquus Hugonis de Welles* (1888), 29.
[9] Gibbons, op. et loc. cit; W.P.W. Phillimore (ed.), *Rotuli Hugonis de Welles*, Lincs. Rec. Soc., 3 (1912), 138.
[10] *Valor Eccl.*, i, 451.
[11] *Hertfordshire Mercury*, Dec. 2 1893.
[12] J.Norden, *MS. Survey of the Borough of Hertford in 1621*: 19th-century transcript by H.G. Andrews in Hertford Museum. Also printed in Cussans, ii, pt.2, 261-66.
[13] *V.C.H.*, iii, 509.
[14] Chauncy, i, 506.
[15] L. Turner, *History of the Ancient Town and Borough of Hertford* (1830), App. iv, 472-3.
[16] See note 14.

nave was the parochial church of St John, a suggestion which is perhaps strengthened by the apparent absence of any claustral buildings found adjoining it.

The foundation charter, early charters of confirmation and gifts of land to the priory make it clear, however, that there was a priory church here long before the early 13th century and that this church was dedicated to St Mary,[17] the foundation charter, for instance, referring to "ecclesia sancta Maria". There is some confusion over whether the church was also called St Mary the Less to distinguish it from the parish church of St Mary the Great elsewhere in the town or whether in fact it was the other way round. Chauncy claims that it was the other church, which stood between the Old Cross and Cowbridge, which bore the suffix "The Great" but there appears to be no documentary evidence to support this and the *V.C.H.* takes the opposite view.[18] Although the evidence for this assertion is similarly missing, it is perhaps the more likely, as presumably the priory church was the greater church. As we have seen, the parish in which the priory church was situated was dedicated to St John the Evangelist, although the names "parochia de monachorum", St Mary Monachorum and Monkenchurch were also used in the Middle Ages.[19]

Furthermore, the words of the 1209 endowment quoted above seem to show that there was still only one church at this date. It therefore appears that before this time the parishioners of St John's and the monks shared one church, the former probably worshipping in the nave and the latter in the chancel. It is possible that this church is not the building which has been archaeologically excavated (it may even have been a timber structure) but it is more likely to have been the same building. It is particularly unfortunate then that neither the excavation of 1893 nor 1988-89 included an exploration of the east end of the church and it should be pointed out that neither excavation produced positive evidence of a date earlier than the 13th century. It is most likely, however, that it would be the east end of the church which would retain vestiges of the building's late 11th-century origins if these existed.

The supposition that there was only one church, the nave of which was rebuilt or extended in the early 13th century following the establishment of the vicarage, therefore seems quite credible. It is possible that the crossing and chancel were re-dedicated to St Mary and reserved to the use of the monks at this time, while the nave was dedicated to St John the Evangelist and used by the parishioners. This may simply have been the formalisation of an existing arrangement but it may be significant that there is no reference to a dedication to St John before this date.

The apparently close link between St Mary's and St John's is also shown by the fact that the prior and convent were patrons of the living of St John's. It appears that from 1209 until 1349, the vicarage was served by the monks themselves but in the latter year the death of one Philip led to the appointment of Robert West, the first vicar who was not also a member of the priory.[20] Ordinations continued without a break until 1423 when the last known medieval vicar, Walter Barbur, was appointed.[21] After this date there are no further recorded appointments until that of John Hume in 1622. There are several possible explanations for this. One is that the parochial part of the church became ruinous and was no longer used, while another is that it was once again served directly by the monks. That the latter was the case is suggested by the payment in 1525-26 of an additional mark's stipend to the monk who was in charge of St John's Church,[22] and the inclusion of the advowson of the vicarage in the grant of the priory manor to Denny in 1538. Nevertheless, the fact that it was no longer considered necessary to appoint a vicar after William Barbur had resigned or died suggests that the church had declined in importance or that the population of the parish had fallen by this time.

This suggestion is backed up by the general economic decline of Hertford during the 15th century.[23] Very little is known, however, of the later medieval history of the church itself. In his will of 1525 John Purfote requested to be buried in the priory church,[24] but this does not make it clear whether the burial was to take place in the parochial or monastic part of the church or whether such a distinction could still be made.

The precise date of the suppression of the priory is not known. Its net value in 1535 was £72 14s 8d,[25] and the grant to Denny in February 1538 suggests that by then it had been dissolved, although it should be noted that in March 1537 the royal commissioners had not taken the surrender of the house but instead sent the prior, Thomas Hampton, to the Court of Augmentations.[26] A dispute over the tithes of Amwell in July 1539 is not conclusive proof of the priory's continued existence at this date,[27] but it is likely that its formal closure was postponed until the surrender of the mother house of St Albans in December 1539.[28]

After the reference to St John's churchyard in the borough survey of 1621 and the union of the parish with All Saints in 1638, documentary sources seem to suggest that the church fell into disuse, and after the 1587 terrier there are no relevant references to Priory House until the mid 18th century.[29] It is unfortunate that Chauncy's statement

[17] Dugdale, iii, 299-301.
[18] Chauncy, i, 512; *V.C.H.*, iii, 509n.
[19] *Taxatio Ecclesiastica*, iv, 37; *Cal. Pat. R., 1381-85*, 207; *Feudal Aids*, ii, 461.
[20] See note 11.
[21] Ibid.
[22] P.R.O., E 315/272/77.
[23] *V.C.H.*, iv, 207; *Feudal Aids*, ii, 461.
[24] P.R.O., PCC 1 Porch.
[25] See note 10.
[26] *V.C.H.*, iv, 420n.
[27] B.L., Add. Chart. 35,315.
[28] Dugdale, ii, 249-50; *L.P.*, xiv (2), no.635.
[29] H.R.O., D/Z3. T3.

regarding Willis's rebuilding of the church in 1629 is unsubstantiated and it would be unwise to set too much store by his recording of the dedication to St John the Baptist rather than the Evangelist. It is possible, of course, that the dedication was changed following the rebuilding but it is just as likely that Chauncy simply got the dedication wrong- there are several other instances of Chauncy incorrectly recording church dedications in his *History*.[30]

It is indeed conceivable that Chauncy is mistaken in saying that the church was rebuilt in 1629. The date is rather surprising given the evidence that the churchyard had closed by 1624 and the union of the parish with All Saints shortly afterwards, especially as it was All Saints' Church rather than St John's which continued to be used for parochial worship after 1638. Equally puzzling, though, is the appointment of a new vicar in 1622, particularly after a break of almost 200 years in the institution of vicars to St John's, and it is possible that the reputed rebuilding of 1629 represented a desperate, last attempt to instill new life into an ailing parish. It is significant that the archaeological evidence discussed below for a smaller church built within the ruins of the larger medieval church is perfectly consistent with a date in the 1620s.

Mention should be made here of an important piece of "negative" evidence. No reference is made to either St John's or St Mary's Church in the return of church goods drawn up in 1553.[31] This suggests that the church fell into disuse after the Dissolution and is perhaps further evidence that the appointment of Hume in 1622 and the subsequent rebuilding of the church within the apparently ruinous shell of the medieval church was a deliberate attempt to revive the parish.

Antiquarian accounts of the priory site are few and brief in content, probably because little of interest survived into the 17th century. Weever refers to several burials in the Church of St Mary but does not make it clear whether there were any significant remains of the building to be seen in his day.[32] Although the Church of St John had apparently only just been rebuilt, he makes no reference to this. Chauncy adds nothing further about the site than that which is referred to above, while Nutt's edition of Camden's *Britannia* simply repeats the information given by Chauncy.[33] Salmon gives a rather fuller account: "A good House is built upon the Scite of the Priory, near Dicker Mill [probably the Lykermill of 1624], which belongs to it. This is upon a Cut out of the Lea, near the Place where water is raised to serve the Town, and this Water falls again into the Lea before it receives the Beane. This Priory stood in the East Part of the Town. If the Church of St

Mary Monk was rebuilt in 1629 by Mr Willis, and anew dedicated to St John Baptist, 'tis much it should be so ruinous in Sir John Harrison's Time. For Sir John, who procured the Parish to be added to that of All Saints, himself died in the year 1669. And 40 Years being too short a space for such Decay, we must imagine Mr Willis only bestowed some repairs. There were two monuments in it when pulled down..."[34]

When Browne Willis visited the town in March 1740 he simply commented that there were no remains of the "priory church which was called St John's and lay near the new Hospital [Christ's Hospital in Fore Street]. They shewed me the scite of the church which was very small consisting of one little Isle."[35] From this description it seems that Willis was shown the site of the 17th-century church, which was by then in ruins. An annotated copy of Gough's 1789 edition of *Britannia* states that "a modern brick house occupies the site of the priory,"[36] while Brayley and Britton refer to "a good modern house" having been erected on the site, a statement which is repeated almost *verbatim* in Caley's and Ellis's edition of Dugdale's *Monasticon*.[37]

The post-medieval lay-out of the site is more fully discussed under cartographic evidence but, following the sale of the priory manor to John Harrison in 1637, the property became part of the Balls Park estate and so remained until the sale of the estate in 1830.[38] For most of this time the site appears to have been largely open with only Priory House and its barn next to the river.[39] By 1802 part of the land was in use as a timber yard and in 1877 a large, cellared sawmill was built to the north of the site of the church.[40] In 1853 the priory estate itself was split up and sold in lots, Priory Street and St John's Street being laid out in 1857 and 1858 respectively.[41] A variety of buildings, including those of the Roman Catholic Church of The Immaculate Conception and St Joseph, were then erected on the site.[42] The portion of the land known as Priory Wharf was acquired by S. Andrews,[43] father of R.T. Andrews who uncovered the remains of the church in 1893. By the early 20th century the extent of the timber yard had increased and in 1912 it was occupied by Messrs. Ewen and Tomlinson.[44] This later became Jewson's timber yard and the site remained in this use until the late 1980s when

---

[30] See N. Doggett, 'Medieval church dedications in Hertfordshire: two early eighteenth-century lists', *Hertfordshire's Past*, 35 (Autumn 1993), 14-15.

[31] P.R.O., E 315/497/82.

[32] J. Weever, *Antient Funerall Monuments* (1631), 543.

[33] M. Nutt (ed.), *Camden's Britiannia et Hibernia*, ii (1720), 986.

[34] Nathaniel Salmon, *The History of Hertfordshire*, 40.

[35] Bodl., MS. Willis 51, fol.40.

[36] Bodl., MS. Gough Gen. Top. 61, p.344 of printed text.

[37] Brayley and Britton, vii, 265; Dugdale, iii, 299.

[38] H.R.O., D/EL 4371 A.

[39] H.R.O., Gerish colln., Box 39.

[40] R.T. Andrews' Book of Plans, Hertford Museum.

[41] H.R.O., D/EL 4363, 4363 A; R.T. Andrews' Gazeteer and Notebook, Hertford Museum.

[42] A. Baker and W.D. Fenning, *MS. History of the Ancient Borough and Honour of Hertford* (c.1929), copy in Hertford Museum (loose notes contained therein).

[43] *Hertfordshire Mercury*, Dec. 2 1893.

[44] *V.C.H.*, iii, 509.

the majority of the land was developed for housing by McLean Homes Ltd.[45]

CARTOGRAPHIC EVIDENCE

The earliest cartographic representation of the site is on Speed's map of 1611.[46] This is highly stylised but seems to indicate that the site was already largely open. Five gabled buildings are shown grouped around an irregularly shaped enclosure to the south-west of which there appears to be a battlemented wall, which may have formed the precinct wall to the site. An apparently more reliable map is an estate map of c.1733, the whereabouts of which is now unknown but which survives in a 19th-century copy by R.T. Andrews.[47] Priory House is marked as a large rectangular structure on the south-east bank of the River Lea. To the south-west is an area marked as "Yard" which has a large, irregularly shaped outbuilding directly bordering the river on its north-west side. Immediately to the south of the yard is a narrow piece of land, widening towards its south end, marked as "Old Churchyard" and on which there are no buildings. Directly to the west of the "Old Churchyard" is a plot named as "Garden of Mr Maylin", while to the east is the larger "Priory Close" which continues right up to the river to the east of the "Priory House" plot. Towards the north-east corner of "Priory Close", which is bounded on its east side by a road, are the buildings of "Priory Farm".

The open nature of the site in the 18th century is largely confirmed by J. Andrews's and M. Wren's 1766 plan of Hertford,[48] although in this case the whole area of the site is simply termed "The Priory". On this map Priory House is shown as an L-shaped building with a large L-shaped outbuilding directly to the south-west. The road defining the eastern boundary of the site is called "Sow Lane" and the buildings of what must be "Priory Farm" are again shown in the site's north-east corner. To the west of the farm is an orchard extending towards "Priory House" and a smaller orchard is marked directly to the west of the L-shaped outbuilding. From the south-west corner of this orchard a straight hedge boundary forms the western side of the property. The most significant feature of the map is that, although the "Old Churchyard" of the c.1733 map is no longer defined as such, the map marks the feature "Church in Ruins" some distance to the south of Priory House, a location which ties in neatly with the archaeological evidence discussed below.

An undated late 18th-century map covering nearly all of Hertford's parishes is at too small a scale to be much use but appears largely to depict the same situation as on the 1766 map.[49] An estate map by J. Charlton of 1802, which also only survives in a copy by R.T. Andrews,[50] shows Priory House in rather more detail, the rectangular building of 1733 apparently having been extended towards the river, which it now directly borders as on the 1766 map. The outbuilding to the south-west, marked on earlier maps, appears again, this time with a smaller L-shaped outbuilding between it and Priory House. The area to the south-west of the outbuilding is now shown as a "Timber Yard" but no use is given for the land directly to the south of Priory House. The buildings of Priory Farm are again marked.

The 1808 Inclosure map, which covers the relevant part of Hertford, is most uninformative, the priory site and Priory Farm being represented by a highly stylised drawing of a house.[51] A map by E. Johnson for Turnor's *History* and a slightly later unattributed map show much the same lay-out as the 1802 map,[52] although neither map can agree on the precise shape of Priory House or the exact position or number of outbuildings shown at both Priory House and Priory Farm. Johnson's map shows the site of St John's Church to the south of Priory House.

Two maps made in the 1840s are particularly useful for our purposes in that they were drawn before the extensive changes to the site in the 1850s. The tithe map of 1847 is another map at too small a scale to be truly useful in this context, but at least it seems to confirm the lay-out of the priory premises shown in a plan drawn before 1847, which again survives in a later copy made by R.T. Andrews.[53] On this map Priory House is shown in a form which can be closely equated with the plan of the house on the 1802 map and, even more importantly, clearly identified with the pictorial evidence discussed below. The irregularly shaped outbuilding, here marked as "Barn and Shops", is recognisable from the c.1733 estate map, the smaller outbuildings between it and Priory House are marked and the area to the south-west is still shown to be a timber yard as in 1802. The buildings of Priory Farm are again shown adjoining the road, by then called Priory Lane, which defines the eastern boundary of the site. Later cartographic material is discussed under archaeological evidence.

PICTORIAL AND PHOTOGRAPHIC EVIDENCE

The earliest known surviving drawing of Priory House is one by H.G. Oldfield made in the 1790s.[54] This shows what the pre-1847 map of the priory premises referred to above proves to be the north-west elevation of the house. The building is of two storeys, rendered and with a steeply pitched tiled roof. The hall range is on the left with a

[45] H. Cooper-Reade, 'Jewson's Yard, Hertford: excavations of St Mary's Priory and St John's Parish Church', *Hertfordshire's Past*, 29 (Autumn 1990), 29.

[46] Bodl., Gough Maps 92; reproduced in *V.C.H.*, iii, opp. p.500.

[47] See note 40.

[48] B.L., K. Top. XV. 52; extract printed in Cooper-Reade (note 45), 32.

[49] H.R.O., D/EX 367. P1.

[50] See note 40.

[51] H.R.O., QS/E 30.

[52] H.R.O., Map No. 3 of Hertford Borough Records, Vol. 43.

[53] H.R.O., D/P 48/27/IC; see note 40.

[54] H.R.O., Oldfield Drawings, III, 387.

doorway to the right where it meets a flush range projecting to the rear under a steeply pitched hipped roof, the eaves of which are slightly higher than that of the hall range. The hall range has four windows directly beneath the eaves, two-light leaded casements to the left and centre with a narrow rectangular window to the right of the latter and a small twelve-paned sash window to the right where the hall range meets the hip-roofed range.

On the ground floor of the hall range there is a prominent canted bay projection with sash windows, sixteen-paned to the centre and twelve-paned to the splays, the whole under an ogee-capped lead roof. Immediately to the left of the canted bay is another small twelve-paned sash window. To the right where the two ranges meet is an elaborate late 17th-century or early 18th-century doorcase with barleysugar columns supporting a decorated, segmental shell pediment; decorative panelled door. The hip-roofed range has two symmetrically spaced twelve-paned sashes on each floor. Two chimney stacks are visible in the view: a prominent square brick ridge stack with an ornamental panel to the front in the centre of the hall range and what is probably an external lateral stack on the left of the rear projection of the hip-roofed range, of which only the triple diagonal shafts can be seen in this drawing.

The basic accuracy of Oldfield's view is confirmed by what appears to be a slightly later watercolour by an unknown artist.[55] This drawing shows the house in its setting on a bend in the river, the main difference between this and Oldfield's drawing being that, as the perspective is not flat on, the gable end of the hall range is also visible. The eaves of Oldfield's hip-roofed range are shown to be parapeted and the apex appears to be gableted. Behind the prominent ridge stack of the hall range, which also has a small integral stack to the left gable end, the ridge of a rear range (confirmed on the pre-1847 map) is just visible. Attached to the left gable end of the hall range, and continuing behind it is a single-storey service range which projects outwards into the river. This also has a stack to its left gable end and where the range attaches to the main house it takes the form of a lean-to. The only other significant difference between this view and Oldfield's drawing is in some of the fenestration details. The hall range has three leaded windows to the right at the junction with the hip-roofed/gableted range. The ground floor has an additional sash window directly below this latter window and the canted bay projection is shown with two sashes to the front instead of one large sash. The triple chimney shafts of Oldfield's view are here shown as a prominent single stack.

The appearance of the building in this view is very nearly completely corroborated in all important respects by another later watercolour, which is known to have been painted before 1860.[56] It adds the detail of alternating quoins to the left corner of the hall range and seems to

indicate that only the two left windows directly below the eaves are leaded casements. All other windows, the positions of which accord exactly with those shown in the earlier watercolour, plus the addition of windows to left and right of the canted bay are evidently timber and are presumably sashes, although the meeting rails are not evident. There are lead downpipes and it appears that by this date there was a fanlight over the door, in front of which is a porch. The outer windows to the bay projection seem to have timber shutters and the hipped/gableted range is shown in the former form. The outbuildings to the left of the hall range are shown as separate weatherboarded structures with plain tile roofs. The rear outbuilding has a leaded window and a boarded door. The most striking features are two carved stone eagles with outstretched wings on moulded square pedestals in front of the house, the front garden of which is enclosed by a picket fence. A later note on the back of the watercolour says that the eagles were taken to the stable yard, Porthill (Hertford) but removed and sold c.1925. Their present whereabouts is unknown.

There is only one known drawing of Priory House from another perspective and this was executed by Luppino c.1817.[57] It is rather a faint sketch drawing and shows Priory House from the river. The form and positioning of the outbuildings can be equated with those shown on the pre-1847 map. The single-storey outbuilding in the foreground of the picture appears as a weatherboarded structure over a high brick plinth disappearing into the river. The range running at right-angles to the rear of the house on its north-west side is also shown. There are two full-height gables on its north-west side towards the river, to the northern one of which is a very large ridge stack, part of which can be seen in the drawings of the front of the house.

There is only one known view of the interior of the house. This is an undated watercolour, captioned on the reverse "A room in _____ once lived", almost certainly painted by Charlotte Bosanquet in the early 1840s.[58] It shows a room with two sash windows to the front, confirming that it is the ground-floor front room of the hipped/gableted range, completely panelled with large, tall rectangular panels above the dado rail; moulded cornice. There is a boxed-in cross-beam ceiling and a stone-flag floor with black tiles at the interstices with the paviors. A six-panel door is situated in the long side wall, which presumably gave access to a passage-way behind the front door seen in external views of the house.

[55] B.L., Add. MS. 32,350, fol.42.
[56] Hertford Museum, Cat. no. 2983.1.
[57] Lewis Evans colln., St Albans Public Library.
[58] H.R.O., Hertf./163. The watercolour is unattributed but it is identical in style to several others by Charlotte Bosanquet, now contained in an album in the Ashmolean Museum, Oxford, Dept. of Western Art (Print Room). See also J. Cornforth, 'Some early Victorians at home' *Country Life*, (Dec. 4 1975), 1530-4.

A series of photographs was taken of Priory House shortly before its demolition in 1906.[59] It is not immediately easy to equate these with the earlier drawings and paintings of the house, although the basic accuracy of the latter is confirmed by the map evidence. It certainly seems that the house's appearance changed dramatically between the mid-19th century and the time the photographs were taken. The photographs seem to show that the greater part of the hall range had disappeared by 1906, leaving a short three-window range as the only remnant of the former entrance front. This truncated range has three symmetrically spaced glazing bar sashes on the first floor with two windows below to left and centre and a recessed doorway to the right. The roof is now hipped with a prominent brick stack to its apex. The range running at right-angles to the rear of the hall range and facing the river appears largely to survive, although the south of its two projecting gables has gone. Its place has been taken by two hip-roofed dormers in the roof slope. The north gable survives and has a prominent brick stack to the apex, corresponding with the position of the same stack in the Luppino view. Towards the bottom of the roof slope of the gable, near where it meets the main part of the range, is a subsidiary stack. The wall of the gable, which is flush with the remainder of the range, is completely blind but the main section has three irregularly spaced 19th-century sash windows on the first floor (the left narrow) and three sashes on the ground floor plus a doorway; all appear to be Victorian. The attached outbuildings shown in the earlier drawings have been demolished.

To the rear of the house, the north gable of the range facing the river runs back at right-angles to it. There are two symmetrically spaced flush-framed twelve-paned glazing bar sashes on each floor with a central hip-roofed dormer in the roof slope. A lean-to porch stands to the right. The left return of this range is not so clearly shown in the photographs and (if the interpretation that the old hall range had been truncated by this date is correct) it would originally have been an internal wall, but it appears to have few openings. Areas of roughcast render have come away from this wall and from the range with the flush-framed sashes revealing lath and plaster to the former and timber framing with brick infill panels to the latter.

The plain tile roofs to the whole building are irregular and partially sagging, suggesting that much of the old roof structure still survived in 1906. All around the building are the stacked materials and outbuildings of the timber yard, including a large open-fronted structure where the remainder of the hall range once stood.

Apparently photographed at the same time as Priory House was a large barn, which an Ordnance Survey map of 1881 shows lay on the western side of the former farmyard of

Priory Farm,[60] the farmhouse and several other buildings of which were presumably destroyed by the construction of the Great Northern Railway before 1850.[61] The barn was a large weatherboarded structure on a brick plinth with a plain tiled roof, half-hipped at the southern end and gabled to the north. There were full-height double doors on the eastern side, but if opposing doors once existed on the west they had been removed and the opening boarded over by the time the photographs were taken. A photograph of the interior shows that the barn was of close-studded construction with a mid-rail. The roof structure appears to have been of collar and tie beam type, originally with raking struts from the tie beams to the principal rafters which have very slightly curved windbraces to the single purlins; jowled wall posts with long curving braces to the tie beams. Intermediary collars shown in the photographs may well be later insertions and much of the thin-scantling wall framing visible (particularly in the end wall) also appears to be a replacement of the original heavy close studding. The most likely date for the barn on the slender evidence of this one photograph of the interior, which only shows part of the building, seems to be the late 16th or early 17th century, but it had clearly been much altered by the time the photograph was taken and an earlier origin cannot be entirely ruled out. Photographs of the exterior show that there were further weatherboarded barns and outbuildings in the immediate vicinity but their relatively shallow roof pitches and general appearance suggest that none was of any great antiquity.

ARCHAEOLOGICAL EVIDENCE

The site of Hertford Priory has been archaeologically investigated on two occasions- in 1893 and 1988-89- and chance finds have also been made. The earliest recorded discovery was in 1877 when a well constructed of clunch was found to the east of Priory Street. Further finds of human bone, stone coffin lids and the "loose remains of an old rubble wall about 12ft long" were made in the 1870s and 1880s in the area bounded by Priory Street, St John's Street and Railway Street.[62] The location and high density of human remains found suggest that they represent the site of the monastic cemetery.

In October 1893 the foundations of the monastic/parochial church and the smaller church built within its shell in the early 17th century were discovered. The earlier building was a large cruciform structure with a long aisleless nave measuring 87ft by 29ft internally, transepts of 30ft 4" by 20ft and a chancel of 24ft in width, the eastern extent of which lay outside the area investigated. The west end of this building, which R.T. Andrews claims first came to light as "the loose...rubble wall..." located in 1877, lay about 200ft to the west of St John's Street and was laid out

[59] Hertford Museum, cat. nos. 6036. 191-8.

[60] Hertford Museum, uncatalogued; 1:500 scale map, Bodl., Map Room C 17:70 a 189.

[61] L. Munby, *The Hertfordshire Landscape* (1977), 212.

[62] See note 41; *The Antiquary*, v (1882), 34, 134.

on an approximate east-west axis.[63] It should be emphasised that, although the dimensions of the church appear to have been carefully measured and recorded, the discovery was initially a chance one made during the laying of a water supply in the timber yard and was simply a matter of tracing the extent of the walls. Consequently important evidence may have been lost.

The north-west angle of the nave is reported to have been "very much broken down, because originally the ground at the west end was a very steep slope."[64] The position of the church in relation to the human remains found, and further graves found on the same alignment immediately to the north-west of Railway Street in 1906,[65] suggest that the monastic cemetery lay to the south-west of the church.

The published account of the 1893 excavation provides no date for the medieval church, stating that "No moulded stones of any kind were met with to show the style of architecture which was adopted in the church, but from a small block of moulded clunch-stone, which was found some 15 years ago in a disused well on the premises, it is judged to have been Early English."[66] The *V.C.H.*, however, later asserts that, as the walls of the church were approximately four foot thick, it must have been "at least as early as the 12th century."[67] This statement is difficult to substantiate, but the basic accuracy of the 1893 investigation was confirmed by the work which took place in 1988-89, although these excavations were smaller in area and only uncovered some of the walls located in 1893. Again the east end of the church lay outside the area investigated.

The most significant new evidence from the 1988-89 excavations was that the medieval church was of at least two principal phases. The earliest structural phase of the excavated nave can be dated no earlier than the 13th century, although there was equivocal evidence for a building (not certainly a church) preceding this period. This evidence comes chiefly from two large post holes discovered towards the east end of the excavated area, but their symmetry in relation to the outer walls of the 13th-century church makes the excavator believe that they are more likely to represent a structural division within this church. Also associated with the first certain phase of the church was a wall of uncertain function running at right-angles to the south wall of the church and immediately pre-dating it or associated with its construction was an oval-shaped furnace, probably used for the casting of a bell.[68]

It seems that the church was remodelled in the late 15th or early 16th century, principally taking the form of an extension of the nave to the west, where it appears there

was a doorway in the north-west corner. As in the 1893 excavation the full plan of the early 17th-century church was revealed in the 1988-89 excavation. This church utilised the south wall of the medieval church, had an octagonal apse with brick corners, measured approximately 20 by 53ft with walls approximately 20" thick and was poorly constructed on shallow footings.[69]

Neither excavation located positive evidence for any other monastic buildings, but there can be no doubt that the 19th- and 20th-century warehouses and the large cellared Victorian sawmill to the north of the site of the church would have destroyed large areas of any surviving medieval stratigraphy, while the considerable slope in ground level in the north-west corner of the excavated area would probably have limited monastic activity in this part of the site.

With the exception of a north-south wall 59ft north of the church and part of a building with a cobbled yard or path on its northern edge 95ft to the north of the church, to neither of which does the excavator attribute a date, the only feature which could possibly be associated with the domestic buildings of the priory was a wall running at right-angles to the south wall of the church in its first phase.[70]

Finally, mention should be made of a boundary ditch, marked on the c.1733 map, which formerly ran from the River Lea in a southerly direction on a roughly parallel line some 89ft to the west of the west wall of the phase two medieval church, but which was infilled in the first half of the 19th century.[71] The ditch is thought to have dated to the 14th century and may have represented the western boundary of the monastic precinct,[72] but the circumstances of its backfilling and any evidence this may have concealed are unknown. Another boundary ditch of uncertain date and infilled at some time in the 18th or 19th century was picked up in one of the evaluation trenches of the 1988-89 excavation. The ditch ran on a north-south axis, on a line roughly parallel with and to the west of St John's Street.[73] Although it should be emphasised that only a very small section of this ditch was examined and it may actually turn off and continue on a totally different alignment, it appears that it may have enclosed the site of the priory, and it could conceivably have been the eastern boundary of the precinct.

INTERPRETATION AND CONCLUSIONS

Relatively little is known of the late medieval documentary history of the site and although the 18th-century and 19th-century cartographic and pictorial evidence can be tied

---

[63] See note 43.
[64] Ibid.
[65] See note 41.
[66] See note 43.
[67] *V.C.H.*, iii, 509.
[68] Cooper-Reade, op. cit. (note 45), 33-4.

[69] Ibid, 34-6.
[70] Ibid, 36.
[71] See note 40.
[72] Cooper-Reade, op. cit., 30.
[73] Ibid.

together in a particularly satisfying way, much remains unknown about Hertford Priory.

The likelihood seems to be that there was only one church before the Dissolution and that this was shared by the monks and the parishioners of St John's. This is by no means certain, however, and it should be emphasised that the site appears to have been of considerable extent and that only a very small proportion of it has been archaeologically investigated. It is therefore quite conceivable that there were two churches, at least for part of the priory's history, but that only one has so far been located.

The almost total lack of documentary material contemporary with the suppression of the house is frustrating but its absence may itself be a reflection of the house's abandonment for all practical purposes by this date, although its formal closure was postponed until the fall of St Albans. Certainly, the fact that there is apparently no reference to any monks other than the prior at the time of the Dissolution suggests that the priory had by then effectively closed.[74] If further evidence is needed to support this argument, it should be remembered that the site was granted to Denny well before the suppression of St Albans.

The degree of Denny's involvement at Hertford is problematic. The outline of his political career has already been given in the section on Cheshunt and the particular reasons why he or his son, Edward, are likely to have established a residence there explained. The suggestion that Denny may have had a house at Cheshunt is in itself no reason why he should not also have maintained a house at Hertford, particularly as one is in a rural location and the other in an urban (or more precisely at this period a suburban) context but Denny cannot have had a house at every former monastic property, including the many monastic manors he was granted, on his vast estate. Perhaps, though, Hertford would have been a more likely place for a house than some of his other properties. Certainly, its status as county town, along with its relative proximity to Cheshunt and its central position in relation to the estate as a whole would have made Hertford attractive to Denny.

The evidence for the appearance of the now demolished Priory House tends to suggest that at least parts of it were of 16th-century date. Despite many of the fenestration details, including the sash windows and the canted bay projection and the segmental-pedimented doorcase which are all likely to be of the 18th century, the essential character of the house derived from its steeply pitched roofs, the prominent chimney stacks and the evidence for timber framing, which all suggest a much earlier origin. Although it would be unwise to place too much reliance on the details of the map evidence, the house seems to have

grown considerably between its appearance on the c.1733 estate map and its form on late 19th-century maps. What the cartographic evidence and that of various drawings does show, however, is that its basic plan-form was that of an L-shaped hall and cross-wing house. It seems likely that the front door gave access onto a through-passage which separated the hall from the cross-wing. This is a plan type which has long medieval antecedents but continued well into the 17th century. The paucity of evidence obviously means that it is impossible to determine even an approximate date for the building, but at least it can be stated with confidence that it cannot post-date c.1650. On the evidence available it is indeed just as likely to be a remodelling of a medieval open-hall structure with inserted stack and first floor, as a house built with a first floor from the start.

If it is a remodelling of a medieval structure, the most likely candidate for such a remodelling is the prior's lodging. Perhaps significantly the house was situated some 300ft to the north of the excavated church and the trial trenches dug in 1988-89 in the immediate vicinity of the house's site produced no evidence of any adjoining buildings. The location of the building and its apparent isolation are thus perfectly consistent with the likely position for the prior's house. Even its setting by the river may be important, providing a pleasant retreat for the prior away from the rest of the monastic community. If Priory House is a remodelling of the prior's lodging- and even its name may be a clue to this - it is likely to have been a late medieval building, as detached lodgings for the head of a monastery are rare before the 15th century.[75]

A relatively recent construction date for the building, of course, means that it is likely to have been in better condition at the time of the Dissolution than an earlier structure and this, along with its domestic function and presumably reasonably up-to-date lay-out and standards of comfort, may have encouraged its re-use in preference to other buildings on the site. Virtually nothing is known about the other conventual buildings. As pointed out earlier, the site has been much disturbed by later building activity. The 1893 excavation did, however, uncover the plan of the monastic/parochial church. This had a long aisleless nave, north and south transepts and a possible tower to the crossing. Only the west end of the north and south walls of the chancel were located and a recent reconstruction by A.G. Davies, showing it as apsidal-ended and flanked by shorter semi-circular, apsidal transeptal chapels, seems purely speculative.[76] Certainly, the extent of the footings uncovered in 1893 does not rule out a square-ended chancel and there does not seem to have been any indication of transeptal chapels found at this time. Neither the 1893 nor the 1988-89 excavations produced evidence for the position of the claustral ranges, although traces of

---

[74] See note 26.

[75] C. Platt, *Medieval England* (1978) 169-70.

[76] A.G. Davies, personal communication. I am grateful to Mr Davies, the former curator of Hertford Museum, for drawing several references to my attention.

walls were found to both north and south of the church on the latter occasion.

The documentary evidence referred to above suggests that the priory as a whole had experienced some financial difficulties before the Dissolution, although it was by no means the poorest religious house in Hertfordshire at the time of the suppression. The apparent lack of a vicar after the appointment of Walter Barbur in 1423 may reflect deterioration and neglect of the church, if not poverty and population decrease in the parish as a whole. This picture is not, however, borne out by the archaeological evidence which suggests some remodelling of the church in the 15th or 16th century. Nevertheless, the excavator of the 1988-89 programme herself points to the inconclusive nature of the archaeological data and, although believing it to be inherently unlikely, she does not altogether rule out a post-Dissolution date for the second phase of the church.[77]

In this context it should be pointed out that the phase two work was not that extensive (it was not deduced at all by Andrews in 1893) and on its own is not enough to contradict the documentary evidence for the neglect of the church in the Later Middle Ages. One reason why Denny did not appoint a vicar on obtaining the property may have been that the church was in need of substantial repair, outweighing any profits he would have derived from the advowson. It is important to remember that there is no reference to the church in the 1553 list of church goods.

The circumstances of the refounding of the church and its rebuilding in the 1620s fall outside the period with which we are primarily concerned and it is difficult to offer a plausible explanation for this work, beyond the suggestion that it may have been an attempt to inject new life into an impoverished and neglected area of the town. The new building itself does not seem to have been particularly poorly constructed by the standards of the time, but the project was doomed to failure, as is shown by the church's demolition before the end of the 17th century.

It is likely that many of the building materials on the site were plundered by local people after the Dissolution, although rather surprisingly the archaeological evidence for this or for the deliberate destruction of the church at this time is only touched upon by the site's recent excavator. Speed's 1611 map suggests that the site was already fairly open by this date and its proximity to the town perhaps accelerated the clearance process. The absence of any early antiquarian accounts of the property may in itself be significant and tends to suggest that the re-use may have amounted to no more than a conversion of the prior's lodging into a relatively small house for the accommodation of Denny and his family during visits to the county town. Alternatively, the house may simply have acted as a farmhouse to serve the former priory lands, although the proximity of Priory Farm perhaps makes this less likely. Virtually nothing is known of the history of this farm. Some buildings are shown in this location on Speed's map but whether it was on the site of a monastic farm or was established after the Dissolution it is now impossible to say.

It is indeed speculative to suggest that Denny or succeeding members of the family were responsible for the conversion or erection of Priory House. There seems to have been considerable indecision as to what to do with the property in the late 1570s and early 1580s. In June 1578 it was granted by Edward Denny to Thomas Dockwra but in December of the following year Denny was issued a licence to alienate "the late priory of St Mary" to William Crooke.[78] Nevertheless, the terrier of 1587 referring to the "newe bilt howse, with a dove howse, boornes and stables, the myll newe bilt...the howsinge dove howse and barnes...bilt within thre years coste a thowson markes" attests to considerable remodelling, if not rebuilding, at the former priory shortly afterwards. The reference to the fact that "the tennants will not be bought out for £300..." perhaps suggests that some of the substantial costs may have been borne by the tenants rather than by the Denny family, who were by then prepared to relinquish the property. Further building work may have occurred after 1587 when the house finally left the ownership of the Denny family, in which case Martin Trott, who held the property between c.1590 and 1617, would seem the most likely candidate, but as elsewhere in Hertfordshire, short periods of ownership do not necessarily preclude building work on former monastic sites. It is therefore really only safe to say that the former Priory House was a building of pre-1650 date.

Bibliography

PICTORIAL SOURCES

Hertfordshire Record Office

Oldfield Drawings, III, 387.

Hertf./163.

British Library, London

Add. MS. 32,350, fol.42.

Hertford Museum

Cat. no. 2983.1.

St Albans Public Library

Lewis Evans Collection.

[77] Cooper-Reade, op. cit. (note 45), 37 footnote 15.

[78] P.R.O., C 66/1194/1804.

CARTOGRAPHIC SOURCES

Hertfordshire Record Office

D/EX 367. P1.

QS/E 30.

Map No. 3 of Hertford Borough Records, Vol. 43.

D/P 48/27/lC.

British Library, London

K. Top. XV. 52.

Bodleian Library, Oxford

Bodl., Map Room C 17:70 a 189; Gough Maps 92.

Hertford Museum

Uncatalogued 1:500 scale map.

R.T. Andrews' book of plans.

PHOTOGRAPHIC SOURCES

Hertford Museum

Cat. nos. 6036. 191-8.

OTHER PRIMARY SOURCES

Manuscript:-

Public Record Office, London

SC6/Hen. VIII/1596.

E 315/272/77.

E 315/497/82.

PCC 1 Porch.

C 66/1193/1783.

C 66/1194/1804.

Hertfordshire Record Office

D/EL 4363, 4363 A; 4371 A.

D/Z3. T3.

Gerish Collection, Box 39.

British Library, London

Add. Chart. 35,315.

Add. MS. 32,579, fols.11-20.

Harl. MS. 756, fol.182.

Lansd. MS. 116, fol.48.

Bodleian Library, Oxford

MS. Willis 51, fol.40.

MS. Gough Gen. Top. 61, p.344.

Hertford Museum

Norden, J., *MS. Survey of the Borough of Hertford in 1621*: 19th-century transcript by H.G. Andrews.

R.T. Andrews' Gazeteer and Notebook.

Printed:-

Inquisitions and Assessments Relating to Feudal Aids, 5 vols. (1899-1920).
Calendar of Patent Rolls Preserved in the Public Record Office (1903- (in progress).
Dugdale, W., *Monasticon Anglicanum*, (re-ed. Caley, J., Ellis, H. & Bandinel, B., 6 vols. in 8, 1817-30).
Gibbons, A. (ed.), *Liber Antiquus Hugonis de Welles* (Lincoln, 1888).
Letters and Papers, Foreign and Domestic, of the Reign of Henry VIII, eds. Brewer, J.S., Gairdner, J. & Brodie, R.H., 21 vols. (1862-1932).
Phillimore, W. (ed.), *Rotuli Hugonis de Welles*, Lincs. Rec. Soc., 3 (1912).
Taxatio Ecclesiastica (Record Commission, 1802).
Valor Ecclesiasticus, (eds. Caley, J. & Hunter, J., 6 vols., 1810-34).

SECONDARY SOURCES

The Antiquary, v (1882), 34, 134.
Baker, A. & Fenning, W.D., *MS. History of the Ancient Borough and Honour of Hertford* (c.1929), copy in Hertford Museum.
Brayley, E.W. & Britton, J., *The Beauties of England and Wales, Vol. 7, Hertfordshire* (1808).
Chauncy, H., *The Historical Antiquities of Hertfordshire*, i (1700, reprinted Dorking 1975).
Cooper-Reade, H., 'Jewson's Yard, Hertford: excavations of St Mary's Priory and St John's Parish Church', *Hertfordshire's Past*, 29 (Autumn 1990), 29-37.
Cornforth, J. 'Some early Victorians at home', *Country Life*, (Dec. 4 1975), 1530-4.

Cussans, J.E., *The History of Hertfordshire*, ii, pt.2 (1876, reprinted Wakefield 1972).

Doggett, N. 'Medieval church dedications in Hertfordshire: two early eighteenth-century lists', *Hertfordshire's Past*, 35 (Autumn 1993), 14-16.

Hertfordshire Mercury, Dec. 2 1893.

Knowles, M.D. & Hadcock, R.N., *Medieval Religious Houses* (1953).

Munby, L., *The Hertfordshire Landscape* (1977).

Nutt, M. (ed.), *Camden's Britiannia et Hibernia*, ii (1720).

Platt, C., *Medieval England* (1978).

Salmon, N., *The History of Hertfordshire*.

Turnor, L., *History of the Ancient Town and Borough of Hertford* (Hertford, 1830).

The Victoria History of the Counties of England, *Hertfordshire*, iii (1912); iv (1914).

Weever, J., *Antient Funerall Monuments* (1631).

HITCHIN PRIORY

History

Carmelite friary founded in 1317 following grants of lands and buildings by John de Blomville, Adam le Rous and John de Cobham.[1] Dissolved in October 1538, Thomas Parrys acting as bailiff for the crown until 1546.[2] In that year the house and lands were granted to Sir Edward Watson and Henry Herdson and in 1553 Watson sold the property to Ralph Radcliffe.[3] The house remained with the Radcliffe family (latterly the Delme-Radcliffes) until 1965.[4]

THE BUILDINGS

Introduction

Located by the River Hiz on the edge of the medieval town to the south of the junction between Sun Street, Bridge Street and Tilehouse Street, the buildings are principally situated around a central courtyard, which represents the friary cloister. The church probably lay to the south but all traces of it were destroyed by the wing built to the designs of Robert Adam for John Radcliffe between 1770 and 1777.[5]

Substantial parts of the claustral ranges remain, however, in the north and west wings, the north front being remodelled for Ralph and Sara Radcliffe in 1679. Running at a slight angle to the west of the north front is a two-storey flint range which probably comprised the service buildings of the friary.

The buildings were extensively restored in the mid-1920s by Ralph Delme-Radcliffe and were transferred to Hertfordshire County Council in 1965. In 1984-5 the buildings were the subject of another drastic restoration programme, which involved the refacing of the whole of the Adam wing, the erection of a large conservatory in the courtyard and many internal alterations. The Priory (as the building has generally been known since at least the 18th century) was in 1990 in use as a residential conference centre administered by Hitchin Priory Limited.

Description

Each range is described from the exterior side and then in the same sequence from within the courtyard.

South range.

Entirely rebuilt in Palladian style to the designs of Robert Adam in 1770-7. It was originally intended to build a new house at Highdown approximately four miles to the west of Hitchin and plans for this survive in the Sir John Soane Museum, London.[6] In the event the proposals were abandoned and it seems that the decision was taken to remodel The Priory instead. It has been suggested that Adam's plans were modified and the work itself carried out by a local architect builder.[7] Certainly, the proportions of the south front are less satisfactory than Adam's original plans for Highdown but there is no positive evidence that he was not directly involved at The Priory.

The south range is in two high storeys with projecting wings forming a rough U-plan. The whole is faced in Totternhoe stone ashlar (recently entirely renewed) with a moulded cornice under a parapeted hipped slate roof. The south elevation is of one: five: one bays, the windows all glazing bar sashes including the Venetian windows to the ground floor of the projecting wings. Central entrance; semi-circular porch with moulded entablature and Doric columns over glazed door. Rainwater heads to the lead downpipes in the angles with the projecting wings were formerly dated "1777" but are now dated "1984".

The inner returns of the projecting wings have two blind semi-circular headed niches, now filled by modern statuary, on the ground floor and also to the first floor of the wing on the east side. The first floor of the wing on the west has two sash windows in the corresponding position. Internal lateral stack to the wing on the east side.

The outer return of the wing on the east side has three sash windows to each floor but the wing on the west is of greater depth in five bays with sash windows and blind openings symmetrically placed on three floors. There are two prominent integral lateral stacks to this wing.

East range.

To the north of the east return of the south range is the lower east range. This is also faced in Totternhoe stone and has sash windows high in its wall; like the south range there is no visible sign of any medieval fabric.

North range.

This was remodelled in 1679 but contains a substantial amount of earlier fabric. Of red brick construction under a flat lead roof with a raised and somewhat recessed stone centre section, which has a wooden modillion eaves cornice. This apart, the range is of two storeys with a moulded stone cornice and stone-coped brick parapet. Three: one: three bays, the centre bay forming a slightly

---

[1] Knowles (1953), 197.

[2] P.R.O., SC6/Hen. VIII/1607-15.

[3] P.R.O., E 318/(Box 22)/1190; *V.C.H.*, iii, 12.

[4] G.Savage, *A Brief History of Hitchin Priory, 1371-1967* (1970), 5.

[5] Pevsner, 204-5.

[6] Sir John Soane Museum, London, Adam Drawings Vol. 46, no.90.

[7] David King, *The Complete Works of Robert and James Adam* (1991), 386; Alastair Rowan, *Designs for Castles and Country Houses by Robert and James Adam* (1985), 44. Drawings by Adam of proposed battlemented additions to Hitchin Priory can be seen in the Soane Museum, Adam Drawings Vol. 29, nos.49-53. The proposals were never implemented.

projecting full-height open porch and the two inner bays to either side with round-headed arches. Multi-paned cross windows (probably late 17th century but much renewed) across the first floor and to the outer bays on the ground floor. In 1924, however, a photograph shows the whole of the north front rendered with blind windows over the outer arches of the five central bays.[8]

The five central bays, including the porch, form a ground-floor loggia, which has semi-circular arches with keystones and stone imposts supported by octagonal brick piers on stone bases. Each arch has a plaster tympanum with rosette and cable-moulded decoration (not shown in a photograph of c.1910 in the Hertfordshire Local Studies Library and much renewed in the recent restoration). The central arch below a moulded brick cornice also has carved stone spandrels with strapwork, a shield bearing the Radcliffe and Potts family coats-of-arms and the date and initials "R R S 1679" (for Ralph and Sara, nee Potts, Radcliffe) to the right spandrel. There are lead downpipes in the angles to the left and right of the porch, the left with its rainwater head dated "1761". The outer bays project slightly and represent the north terminations of the east and west ranges.

Under the arcade or loggia in line with the two-storey porch is the main entrance to the courtyard behind; a nail-studded double door in a moulded surround with ogee stops. To the left of this doorway is a three-light stone mullion window and a small two-light one to the left of that, both probably late 16th century in date. In the east wall of the arcade is another nail-studded plank door with decorated strap hinges and a moulded surround with ogee stops; this too is probably of the late 16th century.

West range.

The west elevation is much altered and is almost completely obscured by later outbuildings, which do not contain any monastic or 16th-century fabric.

Running at an oblique angle to the west of the north range is a **two-storey range**, which may represent the domestic offices of the Carmelite friary. It is constructed of flint with the eaves raised in brick under a slate roof. Its east wall projects slightly from the north range and is also of red brick with a leaded latticed window on the ground floor. The north elevation has a multi-paned cross window to the left on the first floor and two glazing bar sashes with segmental heads below the brick eaves to the right. The ground floor has a two-light casement window with glazing bars in a brick surround with segmental head to the left and a rectangular projection immediately to the right of centre. This may be the remains of a buttress but is more likely to be the base of a truncated external lateral stack. The narrow rectangular chamfered windows to either side, now both infilled, are of the 15th century. To the right again is a

flush-panelled door with a rebuilt brick head. The north wall has several pieces of worked medieval stone and some tile patching. Also visible on the first floor are the west jambs of two blocked openings and a line of infilled putlog holes. Until the recent restoration there was a tall red brick ridge stack to the left of centre. At the north-west angle of the range is a massive ramped buttress with a round-headed arch and tile relieving arch over the River Hiz. This also has a putlog hole in its north face.

The **courtyard** is now infilled by a large conservatory erected in the recent restoration. There had previously been a late 19th-century conservatory in much the same position, which was removed in the 1920s.[9] The structure of the four claustral ranges is fully visible behind the present conservatory.

South range

Like the south front, the courtyard elevation of this range appears to be entirely the work of the 1770s. The ground floor or *piano nobile* is at a higher level than that of the other ranges and the central entrance is approached by a straight flight of external steps. The six-panel door sits under a bracketed flat hood which is surmounted by a semi-circular fanlight with projecting keystone. The entrance is flanked by round-headed sash windows and there are further sash windows to both the ground and first floors. There are four flat-roofed dormers directly above the eaves parapet.

East range.

This is of red brick construction and has irregularly spaced sash windows on both floors.

North range.

The first floor is of 17th-century red brick but the ground floor is of the original flint rubble construction and contains four broad 15th-century arches. These are of clunch, are two-centred and continuously moulded with double ogee chamfers and have wide piers between. All the tracery is now cut away and the third arch from the east is in line with the main north entrance: the other arches were blocked until the 1920s restoration as is shown in a photograph of 1924.[10] The first floor has four cross windows with glazing bars, one to the left of the west arch, two over the next arch and one over the east arch. Wooden modillion eaves cornice.

West range.

This is almost entirely of flint rubble with red brick to the parapet, which has been raised and has stone coping. There is also red brick at the southern end, marking the position

[8] H. Avray Tipping, 'Hitchin Priory-I', *Country Life* (Oct.17, 1925), 596.

[9] Ibid.
[10] Ibid.

of the staircase. Running from north to south the following windows are on the first floor: one 15th-century trefoil-headed lancet, a late 16th-century three-light brick mullion window, a 15th-century trefoil-headed lancet, another two-light brick mullion window, a trefoil-headed lancet and finally a two-light stone mullion window lighting the staircase between the west and south ranges. The windows have leaded latticed lights and ornamental metal catches which look to be of the late 16th century. There are several putlog holes visible.

The ground floor has two broad 15th-century arches (like those in the north range) with a later ramped brick buttress between; the northern arch has a flight of semi-circular stone steps behind. The blocking of a third arch is detectable in the north-west corner but is more clearly visible internally, where the details of its moulding show it to be of the same date as the others; a blocked fourth arch can be seen in the south-west corner. All the arches in this range and the three cusped windows on the first floor were all blocked before the 1920s restoration.[11]

INTERIOR

This was much altered in the 18th century and again in the restorations of the 1920s, 1960s, and 1980s. It is particularly unfortunate that it was not possible to investigate the building before the most recent renovations as these involved considerable stripping out and much is now concealed or replaced by modern fittings.

South range.

This range, which contains the principal rooms of the late 18th-century house, is not described here as it appears to have been entirely rebuilt between 1770 and 1777 and contains no visible earlier fabric. Descriptions of its fittings and former contents are, however, made in articles by H. Avray Tipping and George Whiteman and there is also a typescript description in the National Buildings Record compiled by J.T. Smith during the recent restoration.[12]

It should be noted that many of the 18th-century cornices, skirtings, door surrounds and other details were renewed or replaced in the recent work. No features of an earlier date are reported to have been found during these operations.

East range.

This also is not described here as the only visible features it contains are of 18th-century or later date.

North range.

This preserves the width of the original north claustral walk

between the arches in its south wall and the wall to the north. To the north of this the fabric probably dates to 1679 and after. Photographs taken after the 1920s restoration show chamfered beams running north-south across the plastered ceiling of the cloister walk but these are now concealed. The eastern end of the cloister walk is currently occupied by a reception area for the conference centre. There is reputed to be cellarage under this range,[13] but it was not possible to inspect this at the time of inspection in November 1989.

West range.

This is the most archaeologically complex part of the building and contains the greatest amount of medieval and 16th-century fabric. On the ground floor there is a thick cross-wall which has a nail-studded plank door with strap hinges. This is approached by a short semi-circular flight of steps to the north. The first floor is reached by a short staircase with square newels and turned balusters at the southern end of the range. The first floor has renewed late 16th-century or early 17th-century panelling to the north and west walls, wide floor boards and a much restored trussed rafter roof (formerly plastered over). Photographs taken in 1985 show that the roof is probably contemporary with the remainder of the monastic fabric in this range as the majority of the ashlar pieces are embedded in the top of the flintwork of the walls. No sole pieces are visible in the photographs and the original masonry has been carried upwards to keep the ashlar pieces vertical (otherwise there is no longitudinal stiffening), but some make use of the timber lintel of the inserted three-light mullion window towards the northern end of the range. The photographs also show high-level collars.[14] Towards the southern end of the range an 18th-century straight-flight staircase, which is linked by a handrail with turned balusters to the contemporary staircase leading down to the ground floor, leads up to the later service buildings to the west. At the southern end of the range is a gallery with balusters similar to those on both staircases.

The **range at an oblique angle to the north range** is now largely converted to bedrooms with many modern partition walls. The original outside wall construction is, however, visible on the first floor; flint rubble with exposed wall-plate and ashlar pieces. The original back (south) wall, which is now internal owing to the additions behind, also has its flint rubble construction exposed on the first floor and contains the following features from west to east: a single-light window with cusped head, a broad lancet, an original opening (now with a modern fire door inserted) and a two-light trefoil-headed window. A Totternhoe stone chimney breast is visible in one of the bedrooms.

Projecting at right-angles to the east end of this range is a small closet entered by a late 16th-century or early 17th-

---

[11] Ibid; *V.C.H.*, iii, 13; *R.C.H.M.*, 120.
[12] H. Avray Tipping, 'Hitchin Priory-II', *Country Life*, (Oct.24, 1925), 632-9; G. Whiteman, 'Hitchin Priory', *The Antique Collector* (July/Aug. 1944), 108-17.

[13] *V.C.H.*, iii, 13; *R.C.H.M.*, 119.
[14] N.M.R., file 39,620.

century plank door in a pilastered wood surround with imposts, carved spandrels bearing the date "1679" and a key block (now removed). Inside, the closet is fully plastered. Each wall has blind semi-circular arches with plastered keystones and simple rosettes; stars and fleur de lys to the spandrels. Above is a frieze with guilloche, cable moulding and medallions below the cornice. A deep semi-circular arch leads to the doorway, which has cornucopia to the spandrels and is surmounted by a shell between scrolls and leafage. In the centre of the coved ceiling is a trailing branch from which sprout leaves and acorns. There is a window in the south wall. Despite the date "1679" on the internal arch and the plaster motifs over the internal arch, which "do not appear widely until c.1640," the most likely date for the plaster decoration appears to be c.1600.[15]

The roof structure of the whole building was inspected but appears to contain nothing earlier than the 18th century with much later renewal.

DOCUMENTARY EVIDENCE

The present building is not particularly revealing about the plan of the Carmelite friary or the 16th-century house which succeeded it, beyond showing that the post-Dissolution conversion incorporated the cloister as its nucleus. The documentary evidence is, however, reasonably complete and can be used to trace the course of events after the suppression.

Before the site was sold to Sir Edward Watson and Henry Herdson in 1546, there seems to have been systematic slighting of the friary. The king's commissioners, William Coffyn and Henry Crwche, who supervised the surrender in October 1538, were instructed to "proceed to the dissolution and defacing of the said house",[16] and it appears that they were unusually thorough in this task.

A survey of 1546, made shortly before the site was sold to Watson and Herdson for £1,541, is particularly useful in establishing the extent of the destruction after 1538 and also what remained eight years later.[17] The buildings then comprised a "mansion house" with a frater and dorter over the cloister, the prior's lodging and "two little chambers" for the brothers, a kitchen, barn and other offices. Except for the mansion house which was "in goode estate beinge maynteyned and repayred from tyme to tyme since the dyssolucion", all the buildings were "sore decayed" and "verrye ruynowce both in tymber and tyle for lack of reparacions". The church, which is described as "superfluous", had been defaced, the steeple broken down and all the lead, freestone, glass and bells were gone. It was valued at 66s 8d plus "certain old settes of wentscotte remaining in the quire" at an additional 6s 8d.

The grant of the site to Watson and Herdson goes into some detail about the building materials which they acquired as part of the purchase.[18] They obtained all the "macrium" (possibly limestone or clunch), tiles, lime and stone and four large stones "vulgarly called gravestones" from the church and seven other stones "called gravestones" and "all the stones, vulgarly called the paving tiles in the cloister and all the old seats of waynescott in the quire of the church". They also received the materials from the majority of the other buildings referred to in the survey.

The survey enables some reconstruction to be made of the friary's plan. The gatehouse was in Bridge Street but there is no evidence to show that it was on the site of No.17 (now No.32) as suggested by Hine.[19] In fact, this timber-framed building, while of medieval date, shows no sign of having been a gatehouse and it is too far to the west of the priory complex to make this likely in any case. Indeed, it needs to be pointed out that the rest of Hine's reconstruction of the friary plan, as published in *The History of Hitchin* is equally unreliable. Likewise, the conjectural plan of the friary as drawn in G. Savage's *A Brief History of Hitchin Priory* (1970) closely follows Hine's interpretation and is best ignored.[20] For the record, Hine believed that the chapter house (such a structure is not even mentioned in the survey) was a free-standing structure some distance to the west of the cloister and also invented a scriptorium and 'solarium', which he placed to the south-east.

From the information actually contained in the survey and the evidence from the standing building it appears that the church probably lay on the south side of the cloister, the dormitory occupied the east range, the refectory was on the north and the kitchen was probably in the west range.[21] Further domestic offices were probably contained in the range at an oblique angle to the west of the north range: the survey refers to "two other old houses whereof the one is called Friar Butler's Colehouse (John Butler was the last head of the community) and the other is called a hen house being both ruinous and in a manner clean untiled". Adjoining the "cole house" was "another house being like to fall down and takine away by Thomas Parrys towards the repairing of the said tenantries".

The survey also mentions "four several houses lying under one roof whereof the one is called the owlde halle (valued at 40s) the other called the prior's lodging (53s 4d) with two little chambers (46s 8d) reserved for two friars".[22] It is not possible to locate the position of this building.

The process of demolition at Hitchin seems to have been more than usually complete. The earliest reference to the condition of the buildings at the time of the suppression

---

[15] Monika Puloy, 'Decorative plasterwork in Hertfordshire', *Herts. Arch.* 8 (1980-2), 179.

[16] Clutterbuck, iii, 20.

[17] P.R.O., SC 12/8/29.

[18] P.R.O., E 318/(Box 22)/1190.

[19] R. Hine, *The History of Hitchin*, i (1927), 128.

[20] Savage, op.cit. (note 4), 11.

[21] P.R.O., SC 12/8/29.

[22] Ibid.

appears to be in a list of friaries made in September 1538, which "have no substance of lead, save only some of them have small gutters".[23] It seems, however, that extensive work had only recently been carried out on the church. For instance, in 1523 James Chetham left 2000 tiles in his will for its repair,[24] while as late as 1530 Thomas Wynch bequeathed several sums of money for the "giltinge" of altars, the provision of vestments, the "mending of the organs of said Friers" and a further gift of £3 6s 8d "to the repair of the church in tyle and lathe and nayle".[25] It was also in 1530 that the king himself gave 40s to the friary, although it is not recorded how this comparatively small gift was used.[26]

The fact that the buildings were not granted to new owners until 1546 means that, after the commissioners had departed, the local townspeople had the opportunity to plunder the site for building materials. Materials which may have come from the former friary are found in several buildings in the town, such as The Cock Hotel and The Old Red Lion.[27] Likewise, when No. 29 Market Place was demolished in 1899 it was found to contain many re-used materials ranging in date from the 13th to the 16th century. One massive chimney breast was constructed entirely of moulded clunch blocks, among which were arch mouldings, portions of roll- and ogee-moulded mullions and part of a chimney piece.[28] It should be emphasised, however, that the circumstances in which these materials came to these buildings are not known and there is no direct evidence that the friary was their ultimate provenance.

Nevertheless, it is almost certainly the case that many building materials were removed from the friary between 1538 and 1546. Further damage was caused by the weather as the buildings lay largely unattended. In 1546 the church is described as "broken and decayed by wether" and "four little graven stones remayning in the said church (had been) brused and broken by the taking down of the said steeple",[29] while the ruinous condition of the other buildings has been noted above.

Further despoliation probably ceased with the grant of the site to Watson and Herdson in 1546, who as they appear to have been agents are unlikely to have done much to alter the buildings, but nothing more is known until Watson sold the property to Ralph Radcliffe in 1553.[30] Radcliffe came from a Lancashire family and was a scholar of Jesus College, Cambridge: he is also known as a schoolmaster and playwright.[31] It seems that in addition to converting the

former friary buildings into a residence, he also founded a school here.

Thomas Fuller drawing on a statement by Radcliffe's contemporary, John Bale, records that Radcliffe converted part of the priory into a stage for his pupils to perform plays from,[32] many of which no doubt were written by Radcliffe himself. This tradition is also refered to by the 17th-century Oxford antiquary, Anthony Wood, who writes that Radcliffe "framed out a lower room into a stage for his scholars to act Latin and English comedies, to the end that they might be emboldened for speaking and pronunciation which practice being used by them several years, his school was in great renown, he grew rich and was held in much veneration in the neighbourhood".[33] It is not known precisely where in the friary this stage was situated. With characteristic confidence Hine asserts that it was in the refectory but provides no evidence to support this view.[34] In any case, Wood states that the stage was in one of the lower rooms, whereas the refectory was presumably at first-floor level.

It is not known which other parts of the friary Radcliffe converted to domestic use but it seems likely that both the east and west ranges, as well as the north entrance range, formed part of his new house. What appears to have been the almost total destruction of the church implies that it did not feature in Radcliffe's plans. However, it is not certain whether or not another range of buildings was constructed on its site or whether parts of it may be incorporated in the present late 18th-century south range (see below), while its position directly opposite the 17th-century entrance range raises the possibility that it may have been converted into the hall range of the post-Dissolution house.

PICTORIAL EVIDENCE

Although there are many views of The Priory after its remodelling in the 1770s, these are invariably of the south front, the part reconstructed at this time.[35] This is perhaps not surprising as it was (and is) the most architecturally distinguished part of the building but this is not helpful in establishing the extent of the domestic conversion in the second half of the 16th century.

Only two views of the pre-Adam phase are known to exist and neither corresponds with the other. The first is on the birdseye perspective map of the town engraved by John Drapentier in c.1700 for inclusion in Chauncy's *History of*

[23] *L.& P.*, xiii (2), no.489.
[24] P.R.O., Arch. Hunts. 2/262.
[25] P.R.O., Arch. Hunts. 4/32.
[26] *L.P.*, v, p.751.
[27] Hine, op.cit. (note 19), 147.
[28] H.P. Pollard and W.B. Gerish, 'The religious orders in Hitchin', *Trans. East Herts. Arch. Soc.*, 3, pt.i (1905), 7.
[29] P.R.O., SC 12/8/29.
[30] *V.C.H.*, iii, 12.
[31] *D.N.B.*, xvi, 576-7.

[32] T. Fuller, *Worthies of England*, i (ed. J. Nichols, 1811), 190.
[33] A. Wood, *Athenae Oxonienses*, i (ed. P. Bliss, 1813), 215.
[34] Hine, op. cit. (note 19), 131.
[35] H.R.O., sepia drawing of south front by J. Crane (1783), D/EC1, no.405; 18th-century print of exterior from garden, County Views, HIT/18; view of south front by Oldfield, Oldfield Drawings, IV, 149; pen and ink drawing of south front from south-east by G. Buckler (1840), Vol.8 of Knowsley edn. of Clutterbuck, fol.20b. B.L., K. Top. 15. 56. c.; Add. MS. 9063, fol.92b. Brit. Mus. Dept. of Prints and Drawings, 1790s watercolour of south front by T. Hearne, 1859. 5. 28. 210. Bodl., pencil drawing of south front by G. Buckler, MS. top. gen. a.12, fol.73.

Hertfordshire.[36] A larger version of this map is in the British Library and shows what appears to be the loggia on the north front, which had then only recently been constructed, surmounted by a tall cupola or bell tower, a design which it has been suggested was ultimately inspired by the entrance facade of Hatfield House.[37] There is a small building to the east but nothing on the south. At the south-west angle is a long narrow building aligned east-west with a similar but lower structure on its north side.[38] To the west of the latter is what the early 20th-century antiquary, W.B. Gerish, interpreted as the west front of the church comprising a nave with north and south aisles.[39] To the north, the house was enclosed by a forecourt with a high wall or railings along the north side. This forecourt survived well into the 20th century, when the house was approached from the north between two 18th-century rusticated stone gate piers.[40]

Although the small 'scale' of the map and its draughtsman's undoubted artistic licence make it far from reliable evidence, it poses the interesting possibility that part of the church survived at this date and had been incorporated in the post-Dissolution house. The 1546 survey states that "one parte of the said churche is broken and decayed by wether and the other (had) no manner of leade Belles Freestone nor glasse Remanyng" but it does not specifically state that the whole of the church, which as noted above was extensively refurbished in the 1530s, had been demolished.[41] Similarly, the grant of "all the church of the late priory" to Watson and Herdson implies that something remained,[42] even if by then the church's main value lay in its building materials. It therefore seems possible that the walls of the church remained standing after the suppression, even if the roof was gone, and were then re-used in a range built on its site, some of which may still be incorporated in the present south range.

The second view of the house before the late 18th-century alterations is in an engraving showing "The Garden View of the Priory".[43] This appears in William Dunnage's *History of Hitchin* (1815), where it is dated to 1762, and a copy was sent by Robert Hinde of Preston Castle near Hitchin to the author of *The London Magazine* in November 1770 as a record of the old building.[44] A painting of the same view, attributed to Paul Braddon and dated c.1765, is reproduced in Hine's *History of Hitchin*.[45] The view shows a long structure of two storeys and an attic

divided into four bays by narrow stepped buttresses with larger angle buttresses at the gable end. This has a wide doorway on the ground floor with Venetian windows to the first floor and attic, the latter window narrower and with the mullions missing. The long side has a window on each floor to each bay and there are seven gabled dormers, five to the left and two to the right of a tall internal lateral stack. There is an integral stack to the far gable end and a ridge stack to the left of centre. Lower projecting ranges are shown to the left and right at the far end of the building, the former with the gable end of another range visible behind. Both ranges have what appear to be mullion windows on both floors.

It is difficult to reconcile the building shown in this view with that shown in the Drapentier map or with the present building. As far as the latter point is concerned, the assumption must be that the drawing shows a structure destroyed during the remodelling of the 1770s but the failure to equate this building with any of those depicted in Drapentier's map is more worrying. If, as the caption to the engraving suggests, the view is from the south-east, and this is the view favoured by later artists, the principal range shown must be the south range. In this case it must represent the converted church or at least a building on its site. No date can be positively attributed to the range shown in the view. The stepped buttresses possibly indicate a medieval origin but the Venetian windows suggest a date no earlier than the late 17th century, possibly contemporary with the 1679 remodelling of the north front. It may be, of course, that the building is medieval but reworked at a later date. If the identification of the range shown in the engraving with the south range is correct, the range to the right must be the east range, although unlike the present east range, it seems to be set back from rather than flush with the south range. This in itself is not a problem if the main range does represent the converted church as the east part of the church would presumably have extended beyond the east claustral range. The range to the left cannot be identified and must be assumed to be a structure destroyed during the 1770s' remodelling as it is not shown in later views.

INTERPRETATION AND CONCLUSIONS

None of the pictorial evidence really helps to reconstruct the plan of the post-Dissolution conversion. The reference in the 1546 survey to "the frater and dorter with the Cloyster whereupon the said frater and dorter ys buylded" suggests a conventional claustral arrangement of first-floor refectory and dormitory.[46] The ground floor of the north range was presumably occupied by an undercroft and the east range, as paralleled at the Carmelite friaries of Coventry, Newcastle-upon-Tyne and Norwich,[47] would

---

[36] Chauncy, ii, opp. p.161.

[37] Paul Hunneyball, *Status, Display and Dissemination: Social Expression and Stylistic Change in the Architecture of 17th-Century Hertfordshire*, unpublished University of Oxford D. Phil. thesis (1994), 135.

[38] B.L., Add. MS. 32,350, fols.71, 73.

[39] Pollard and Gerish, op.cit. (note 28), 6; H.R.O., Gerish colln., Box 46.

[40] Avray Tipping, op. et loc. cit. (note 8).

[41] P.R.O., SC 12/8/29.

[42] P.R.O., E 318/(Box 22)/1190.

[43] B.L., K. Top. 15. 56. b.

[44] *London Magazine*, 40 (1771), 104.

[45] Hine, op. cit. (note 19), 125.

[46] P.R.O., SC 12/8/29.

[47] *Med. Arch.*, 11 (1967), 278-9; Barbara Harbottle, 'Excavations at the Carmelite friary, Newcastle-upon-Tyne', *Arch. Aeliana*, 4th Ser., 46 (1968), 163-223; *Med. Arch.*, 3 (1959), 305.

have contained the chapter house, slype and warming house. It should be emphasised, however, that there is nothing surviving at Hitchin to confirm this interpretation, and all that is known of the later use of the east range is that by 1815 it had for "several years" been in use as a picture gallery.[48]

On the evidence from the surviving building it seems most likely that the principal apartments of Radcliffe's house were in the west range. This was often the range chosen for conversion and examples can be found at sites as diverse as Lanercost (Cumbria), Elstow (Beds.), Hailes (Glos.) and Monk Bretton (Yorks.).[49] There is, however, nothing remaining in this part of the building, which can be positively associated with immediate post-Dissolution re-use. The brick mullion windows may be of mid-16th-century date but the panelling on the north and west walls is probably of the late 16th or early 17th century. Similarly, the small closet with plastered decoration in the former service range is unlikely to be earlier than c.1600.

This may suggest that the hall and parlour of Radcliffe's house were situated elsewhere, possibly in the south range on the site of the church or even incorporating its remains. While there is nothing in the surviving building to indicate this, the location of the south range directly opposite the entrance range makes it a strong candidate for having been the hall of the 16th-century house, although it should, of course, be remembered that it is not known whether the north range was in fact the entrance range before the remodelling of 1679.

Further tenuous support for the south range having been an important part of the building prior to its late 18th-century refronting comes from a series of aerial photographs showing possible garden earthworks to the south of the house.[50] In this connection it may be significant that the earthworks are not directly aligned on the present garden entrance to the south range but lie off-centre to the east.

Whether the south or the west range formed the main part of the post-Dissolution conversion, several of the later 16th-century features of the west range suggest a period of activity associated with the second Ralph Radcliffe, son of the first Ralph Radcliffe and bencher of The Inner Temple, who owned The Priory between his father's death in 1559 and his own death in 1621.[51] The difficulties of dating exactly the remains of the 16th-century work mean that it is not possible to be certain at which time the buildings were first converted to domestic use but it may have been the second Ralph Radcliffe who carried out the major

conversion works. This would accord well with the sequence at other urban sites locally like The Biggin, Hitchin and Royston Priory, where the main work of conversion seems to have taken place in the late 16th century. At both these houses it seems that the former monastic buildings were first adapted to domestic use soon after the Dissolution, but it was left to the second generation of lay owners to carry out the full work of conversion. Similar sequences can be seen elsewhere in Hertfordshire, as at Hertford and possibly Ware, and further afield at sites like Buckland (Devon) and Hinchingbrooke (Cambs.).[52]

Another feature that The Priory has in common with other sites like Buckland and St Bartholomew's Priory, Smithfield in London,[53] is that the 16th-century conversion work probably attempted to conceal as much of the house's monastic origins as possible, only for much of this work subsequently to be unpicked or removed by later restorers, keen to expose the medieval monastic fabric. A similar situation seems to have occurred nearby at Wymondley, where several of the medieval features, concealed for many years, perhaps since the first post-Dissolution conversion, have only recently been brought to light.[54]

At Hitchin the three 15th-century windows and all four cloister arches in the west range are known to have been infilled before the windows and two of the arches were unblocked in the 1920s' restoration, while in the north range all the arches, except that in the line with the entrance arch in the 17th-century loggia, were also blocked before being reopened in 1924/5.[55] It is not known when the arches were originally infilled, partly because no adequate archaeological record seems to have been made when they were unblocked, but it is unlikely that the blocking had recently been made. The most probable dates for building up the arches would appear either to be the time of the post-Dissolution conversion or during the remodelling of 1679, although due to the lack of positive evidence, other dates cannot be ruled out.

Bibliography

PICTORIAL SOURCES

Hertfordshire Record Office

Oldfield Drawings, IV, 149.

Vol.8 of Knowsley edn. of Clutterbuck, fol.20b.

D/EC1, no.405.

[48] W. Dunnage, *The History of Hitchin* (1815), 246. MS. volume in Hitchin Museum.
[49] N. Pevsner, *Cumberland and Westmorland* (1967), 156-7; D. Baker, 'Excavations at Elstow Abbey, 1965-66', *Beds. Arch. Jnl.*, 3 (1966), 29; M. Aston, *Monasteries* (1993), 146; L. Butler and C. Given-Wilson, *Medieval Monasteries of Great Britain* (1979), 297.
[50] R.C.H.M., National Library of Air Photographs, Swindon: Accession no. CAP 8211, frame 55, 56.
[51] *D.N.B.*, xvi, 576; *V.C.H.*, iii, 12.

[52] Howard (1987), 144, 149-50.
[53] Ibid, 144; M. Barley, *Houses and History* (1986), 269-71.
[54] See report on Wymondley Priory.
[55] Avray Tipping, op. et loc. cit. (note 8).

HIT/18.

British Library, London

K. Top. 15. 56. b. & c.

Add. MS. 9063, fol.92b.

Add. MS. 32,350, fols.71, 73.

British Museum Department of Prints and Drawings

1859. 5. 28. 210.

Bodleian Library, Oxford

MS. top. gen. a.12, fol.73.

Sir John Soane Museum, London

Adam Drawings Vol. 29, nos.49-53; Vol. 46, no.90.

PHOTOGRAPHIC EVIDENCE

National Library of Air Photographs, The Royal Commission on Historical Monuments, Swindon

Accession no. CAP 8211, frames 55-6.

National Monuments Record, The Royal Commission on Historical Monuments, Swindon

File 39,620.

OTHER PRIMARY SOURCES

Manuscript:-

Public Record Office, London

SC6/Hen. VIII/1607-15.

SC 12/8/29.

E 318/(Box 22)/1190.

Arch. Hunts. 2/262.

Arch. Hunts. 4/32.

Hertfordshire Record Office

H.R.O., Gerish Collection, Box 46.

Printed:-

Letters and Papers, Foreign and Domestic, of the Reign of Henry VIII, eds., Brewer, J.S., Gairdner, J. & Brodie, R.H., 21 vols. (1862-1932).

SECONDARY SOURCES

Aston, M., *Monasteries* (1993).
Avray Tipping, H. 'Hitchin Priory-I & II', *Country Life* (Oct. 17, 1925, 592-8; Oct. 24, 1925, 632-9).
Baker, D., 'Excavations at Elstow Abbey, 1965-66', *Beds. Arch. Jnl.*, 3 (1966), 22-30.
Barley, M., *Houses and History* (1986).
Butler, L. & Given-Wilson, C., *Medieval Monasteries of Great Britain* (1979).
Chauncy, H., *The Historical Antiquities of Hertfordshire*, ii (1700, reprinted Dorking 1975).
Clutterbuck, R., *The History and Antiquities of Hertfordshire*, iii (1827).
Dictionary of National Biography, 22 vols. (revd. edn., Oxford, 1921/2).
Dunnage, W., *The History of Hitchin* (1815). MS. volume in Hitchin Museum.
Fuller, T., *Worthies of England*, i (ed. Nichols, J., 1811).
Harbottle, B., 'Excavations at the Carmelite friary, Newcastle-upon-Tyne', *Arch. Aeliana*, 4th Ser., 46 (1968), 163-223.
Hine, R., *The History of Hitchin*, i (1927).
Howard, M., *The Early Tudor Country House* (1987).
Hunneyball, P., *Status, Display and Dissemination: Social Expression and Stylistic Change in the Architecture of 17th-Century Hertfordshire*, unpublished University of Oxford D. Phil. thesis (1994).
King, D., *The Complete Works of Robert and James Adam* (Oxford, 1991).
Knowles, M.D. & Hadcock, R.N., *Medieval Religious Houses* (1953).
London Magazine, 40 (1771), 104.
Medieval Archaeology, 3 (1959), 305; 11 (1967), 278-9.
Pevsner, N., *Cumberland and Westmorland* (Harmondsworth, 1967).
-*Hertfordshire* (2nd. edn., revd. Cherry, B., Harmondsworth, 1977).
Pollard, H.P. & Gerish, W.B., 'The religious orders in Hitchin', *Trans. East Herts. Arch. Soc.*, 3, pt.i (1905), 1-9.
Puloy, M., 'Decorative plasterwork in Hertfordshire', *Herts. Arch.*, 8 (1980-2), 144-99.
Rowan, A., *Designs for Castles and Country Houses by Robert and James Adam* (Oxford, 1985).
Royal Commission on Historical Monuments, *An Inventory of the Historical Monuments in Hertfordshire* (1910).
Savage, G., *A Brief History of Hitchin Priory, 1371-1967* (Hitchin, 1970).
The Victoria History of the Counties of England, Hertfordshire, iii (1912).
Whiteman, G., 'Hitchin Priory', *The Antique Collector* (July/Aug. 1944), 108-17.
Wood, A., *Athenae Oxonienses*, i (ed. Bliss, P., 1813).

KING'S LANGLEY PRIORY

History

Dominican friary founded in 1308 by Edward II; dissolved in late 1538.[1] In June 1557 Mary founded here a small house of Dominican nuns, who had formerly been at Dartford (Kent),[2] but in September 1558 it appears that the nuns returned to Dartford.[3] Before this, the house and site had in February 1540 been granted to Richard Ingworth, suffragan bishop of Dover and the last prior of King's Langley.[4] In 1546 the property had passed to John, Lord Russell whose family still held it in 1556.[5]

In April 1574 the house was granted to Edward Grimston the younger and elder, who transferred it to Robert Creswell, who in turn conveyed it to Francis, earl of Bedford.[6] It remained in this family until 1607, when it was sold to Edward Newport and John Compton, having most recently been tenanted by Thomas Ewer and Peter Edlin.[7]

THE BUILDINGS

Introduction

The main structures now on the site are a long rectangular building, aligned north-south, with another range (now attached to the rectangular range by later outbuildings) extending at right-angles to the east on the north. To the south of the rectangular building is a section of boundary wall running north-south and another section formerly ran eastwards from its south-eastern corner. A further wall on an east-west axis to the south may represent part of the former friary church.

Little is known from documentary sources about the immediate post-Dissolution history of the buildings but they appear to have been used as part of a farm by both Ingworth and Russell, a use to which the site seems to have returned after the departure of the Dominican nuns in 1558. A survey undertaken in 1555 is not particularly helpful in identifying individual buildings, although it does show that considerable demolition had already taken place by that date.[8] In 1591 the church is described as completely "ruinated" and further destruction occurred in the late 17th century under the ownership of William Houlker.[9] In 1831 the foundations of the church are said to have been exposed and cleared away by a Farmer Betts, an event witnessed by the young George Gilbert Scott, who later described the

remains as those of "a conventual church of the first class".[10]

Considerable additions and alterations were made to the surviving monastic structures by Barry Parker after 1911, although some of these were demolished in c.1975,[11] and the buildings are now used by a school and a small Christian community. Limited trial excavations took place in 1970 in conjunction with David Neal's more thorough investigation of the nearby royal palace but the results have not been fully published.[12] Some of the site and in particular the boundary walls were overgrown with ivy and other vegetation at the time of inspection in July 1989.

DESCRIPTION

West range

This is the main surviving building on the site and was formerly known locally as King John's Bakehouse.[13] It is mainly of 14th-century date with mid- to late 16th-century adaptations and alterations, many unfortunately removed since the *V.C.H.* account of 1908.[14] Rectangular in plan, the building is constructed of flint rubble with clunch dressings; it is of two storeys under a clay tile roof. There are prominent additions of 1911 and later to both the south-east and north-east corners, but for clarity these are omitted from the description.

Owing to the many alterations, the original appearance of the building is difficult to establish. The Gothic tracery to the arches on the west side is entirely the result of early 20th-century speculative restoration and the majority of the stone mullion windows are also of this date. The best evidence for the pre-20th-century appearance of the building therefore comes from drawings, especially those of the 1830s by J. and J.C. Buckler, and old photographs,[15] combined with a detailed investigation of the surviving fabric, which was carried out in July 1989.

Lying on the west side of a large enclosure, the building originally seems to have been free standing, abutted by a wall at the south-east corner only, all the other corners having angle or diagonal buttresses.

[1] *Cal. Pat. R., 1307-13*, 453; *L.P.*, xiii (2), nos.1021, 1022.

[2] *Cal. Pat. R., Phil. & Mary, 1555-57*, 403.

[3] *Cal. Pat. R., Phil. & Mary, 1557-58*, 417; C.F.R. Palmer, 'Prelates of the black friars of England', *The Antiquary*, 27 (1906), 114.

[4] *L.P.*, xv, no.1032 (p.542).

[5] P.R.O., E 315/391, fol.40.

[6] P.R.O., C 66/1117/1563; *V.C.H.*, ii, 238.

[7] Clutterbuck, iii, 433.

[8] P.R.O., E 315/391 (2).

[9] H.R.O., Blackwell papers 20,113; Nathaniel Salmon, *The History of Hertfordshire* (1728), 113.

[10] G.G. Scott (ed.), *Personal and Professional Recollections by the Late Sir George Gilbert Scott* (1879, repr. 1995), 68-9; R.I.B.A. Drawings colln., Scott sketchbook no.2 (1830-31).

[11] J.P. Haythornthwaite, *The Parish of King's Langley* (1924), 51; Scott Hastie & David Spain, *King's Langley, A Hertfordshire Village* (1991), 92.

[12] D.S. Neal, 'Excavations at the palace and priory at King's Langley, 1970', *Herts. Arch.*, 3 (1973), 31-72. See also the same writer's 'Excavations at the palace of King's Langley, Hertfordshire, 1974-1976', *Med. Arch.*, 21 (1977), 124-65.

[13] *V.C.H.*, ii, 238.

[14] Ibid, 238-40.

[15] H.R.O., Buckler Drawings, IV, 107, 108; Bodl., MS. top. eccl. b. 28, fol.14; Watford Central Library, photographic colln.

East elevation

Before the 20th-century restoration the main section of the east elevation had on the ground floor five small rectangular windows, probably 14th century in date, plus two 19th-century windows replacing late 16th-century mullioned and transomed windows.[16] The larger of these two windows is to the left and has now been superseded by a four-light mullioned window of c.1911; the other window to the right is now blocked. Towards the southern end of the range is a narrow pointed 14th-century doorway with chamfered head, which is now incorporated within what remains of this part of Parker's addition. A photograph of 1899 shows a brick-infilled doorway between the two northern windows, which by the time of another photograph, taken in c.1911, had been unblocked.[17] On the first floor were four small rectangular windows, similar to those on the ground floor, and the wall was divided by three roughly evenly-spaced stepped buttresses (probably original to the building),[18] that to the north corner still surviving internally behind the 20th-century addition. There is a prominent rendered ridge stack roughly to the centre of the range.

Immediately to the left of the pointed doorway the wall projects about a foot (this is now obscured by the truncated 20th-century addition at this point) to form a steeply pitched gable. A low wall ran at right-angles to the east from the north-east corner of this slight projection.

West elevation

The most prominent features on this side of the building are the three wide arches on the ground floor at the northern end, separated by largely rebuilt buttresses, which were formerly stepped and, like those on the east elevation, are probably original to the structure. The arches now have inserted 20th-century Gothic tracery but previously were probably open or contained doors. Drawings, although perhaps significantly not an apparently accurate watercolour of 1809 and a view by J.C. Buckler, that most reliable of topographical artists,[19] certainly imply the former existence of a fourth arch to the south.[20] This feature is very clearly shown in one drawing, which is probably not that accurate, and more conclusively in a photograph taken at the turn of the century, in which the first, second and fourth arches from the north are shown blocked and the third arch is open.[21]

There is no certain indication of this arch in the present fabric, but all traces may, of course, have been obliterated by the extensive 20th-century restoration of the building. In this connection, it is therefore worth noting that the left of three rectangular windows to the right on the first floor appears to be reset as it has what seems to be the remains of a buttress directly below and a large blocked door opening immediately to the right. Below is an area of disturbed masonry which is precisely where the fourth arch would have been located. The third arch from the north formerly had a doorway directly above,[22] now cut and replaced by a three-light mullion window of c.1911. There is also one other buttress, traces of which remain, towards the southern end of the building, making with the corner buttresses a total of six buttresses to this elevation. The other openings to this elevation are, on the ground floor, a narrow rectangular window immediately to the right of the fourth buttress from the north, to the right again a Tudor-arched doorway, now filled with a leaded window of c.1911, and a roughly square-shaped chamfered window. On the first floor are a three-light mullioned window and a narrow rectangular window to the first and second bays from the north respectively, both of c.1911.

North gable wall

This has a 14th-century pointed chamfered doorway behind a 20th-century timber lean-to with a former doorway,[23] now converted to a two-light mullion window, directly above on the first floor. To the apex of the gable is a narrow louvred rectangular opening.

South end wall

The ground floor has a small narrow rectangular window to the left and a narrow 14th-century doorway with a chamfered pointed head, formerly infilled but now open again and converted into a leaded window, to the right. There is a 20th-century two-light mullion window, which replaced a 19th-century casement, itself the replacement of a small rectangular window, to the centre on the first floor.[24]

Interior

Apparently much altered in the mid- to late 16th century and again after c.1911, it is divided into two roughly equal parts by a thick cross wall, possibly original on the ground floor but inserted on the first floor, to the south of which there are fireplaces on both floors. The ground-floor fireplace formerly had a low four-centred stone arch but now has a wooden lintel of c.1911.[25] The room to the north of the cross wall was used as a store until the 20th-century alterations and has a late 16th-century beamed ceiling, consisting of two chamfered cross beams with straight-cut and ogee stops and ten joists running north-south. The room on the south was probably a kitchen from the 16th

[16] H.R.O., Buckler Drawings, IV, 107.

[17] Watford Central Library, photographic colln.

[18] H.R.O., Buckler Drawings, IV, 107; plan in *V.C.H.*, ii, 239 and more detailed original plan (1907) by A. Whitford Anderson for *V.C.H.* in Hertford Museum store. Both plans seem to suggest that the buttresses are additions to the building.

[19] B.L., Add. MS. 32,350, fol.122; H.R.O., Buckler Drawings, IV, 108.

[20] *The Builder*, 2 (1844), 66.

[21] H.R.O., Gerish colln., Box 52; Hastie & Spain, op. cit. (note 11), 82.

[22] H.R.O., Oldfield Drawings, IV, 384.

[23] B.L., Add. MS. 32,350, fols.121, 124.

[24] Ibid, fol.123.

[25] *V.C.H.*, ii, 239.

century onwards, if not before, and had a newel staircase leading to the first floor, immediately to the south of which there was formerly a built-up late 15th-century doorway with splayed jambs and a flat four-centred arch.[26] This room is now one large space but was formerly subdivided into three, one room serving as a pantry, the divisions marked by changes in direction to the flat medieval ceiling joists. In the west wall is a plain recess with a pointed arch which appears never to have been a doorway.

The main feature of the first floor is the magnificent 14th-century crown-post roof running in five bays up to the point where the east wall slightly projects to form the steep gable. The area between this break and the south end wall is divided into two further bays and there was formerly a crown-post to the gable.[27] The crown-posts are short and plain with curved braces to the collar purlin but the undersides of all the tie beams are moulded and have straight-cut chamfer stops. The large brick chimney breast on the first floor is definitely an insertion, which suggests that the ground-floor fireplace was also of the 16th or 17th century rather than of 14th-century date as implied by the *R.C.H.M.*[28] There was formerly an early 17th-century corner fireplace with three-centred head and splayed edges in the north-west angle of the room to the south of the stack on the first floor.[29] There is an oak-framed doorway with a flat four-centred arch connecting the rooms to either side of the chimney breast on the first floor. There is also a timber doorway (c.1600) with chamfered semi-circular head, presumably re-used from elsewhere in the building, leading from the projecting gable to the c.1911 addition. All the original narrow rectangular windows on the first floor are deeply splayed with rectangular insets for the window-frames and concave-shaped rere-arches.

North (gatehouse) range

This now consists of a weatherboarded outbuilding connected to the c.1911 addition at the north-east angle of the west range, a former barn converted to residential use and the gatehouse itself, which is partially embedded in an early 18th-century red brick cottage extended in c.1911.

By again using drawings and old photographs, it is possible to reconstruct the appearance of this range before the extensive early 20th-century alterations and additions. The outbuilding is of this period and links on the east to a barn of c.1700, now converted to domestic use. The barn is weatherboarded and has a clasped purlin queen-post roof covered with plain tiles. It is now partially incorporated in the 20th-century additions to the 18th-century cottage to the east, and its formerly hip-roofed cart entrance on the

south side is now gabled.[30] The cottage is constructed of red brick (mixed bond) with some stonework to the original north-east corner. It has a hipped plain tile roof and 19th-century casements; the most noticeable feature on the south side is the prominent external stack. There are extensive early 20th-century additions to the south and west. A series of photographs taken at this time are useful for showing further details of the cottage's construction.[31] The west elevation has vertical timber studding with two diagonal braces running across above a brick and flint ground-floor lean-to. The southern gable end is weatherboarded to the apex with brickwork below.

The original form of the gatehouse is still visible on the north elevation. The gateway itself, now blocked and with two 19th-century casements inserted in the infill below a blind recessed centre panel, has a double-chamfered three-centred arch beneath a jettied timber-framed first floor with long curving braces and three early 20th-century leaded windows directly below the eaves. A watercolour of 1809 shows that the upper floor was formerly weatherboarded with the left and centre windows infilled and the right window leaded. The windows in the blocking of the arch were then cross-windows, the left infilled and the right leaded. A square infilled opening can be seen to the right of the arch.[32] This is now occupied by a 19th-century casement. The style of the now-exposed timber framing is repeated in the 20th-century extension of the gatehouse to the west and the roof is now hipped at this end, whereas before the extension it was gabled.[33] The photographs referred to above show the first-floor construction of the south elevation to be of brick to the left and timber framed to the right. The timber framing is rather indistinct in the photograph but a substantial mid-rail is clearly discernible.

Interior

Details of the arch-way are visible in the cramped space between the present ground-floor ceiling and the first floor. The arch is triple-stepped internally and constructed of clunch. There is a corresponding three-centred chamfered arch to the south- the inner arch of the gate-way-constructed of timber. This has square corner posts (now cut away below the ground-floor ceiling) from which curved braces support the probably formerly jettied first floor and the originally open side walls. It seems that there were chambers to either side of the gate-way.

It should be noted that the southern face of the south arch is not visible even internally as the gate-way has been infilled by a thick wall marking the junction between the original gatehouse and the 18th-century addition at this point. This division is also marked externally by a straight joint visible in the east elevation of the cottage. There is good early

---

[26] Ibid.

[27] The former presence of a crown-post to the gable can be inferred from an east-west running collar purlin at the southern end of the surviving roof structure.

[28] *R.C.H.M.*, 134.

[29] Ibid.

[30] B.L., Add. MS. 32,350, fol.123.

[31] Watford Central Library, photographic colln.

[32] B.L., Add. MS. 32,350, fol.124.

[33] Ibid.

18th-century wall panelling to the ground floor of both the original part of the building and the 18th-century addition.

The gatehouse has a very roughly constructed crown-post roof with arched braces to the tie beams and struts to the collar purlin. The poor construction suggests a mid- to late 15th-century date and that the structure was never intended to be visible. Such a date would be consistent with the exposed framing on the north elevation and the construction of the two arch-ways. Stone quoins can be seen at the north-east corner of the original building within the roofspace.

Other Structures

Running southwards from the south-west angle of the c.1911 addition at the south-east corner of "King John's Bakehouse" is a thick flint and clunch rubble wall. This formerly began as a thinner and much later wall running southwards from the south-east corner of the gabled projection, but this section was destroyed by the c.1911 addition. Further south, the surviving wall is again thinner but unlike the now-destroyed section is probably not on the medieval line. In the west face of the thick section is a small, presumably post-medieval, brick-arched oven. The existence of the 14th-century doorway and window in the south wall of "King John's Bakehouse" suggests that the wall was either a boundary wall or part of a covered walk-way or pentice, although it should be said that no scars of such a structure can be seen on the south wall of the building. A watercolour of 1809 appears to show a series of blocked arches in the east face of the wall.[34]

The wall continues south to a point where it meets a wall running east-west, which can be interpreted as either the south wall of the chancel or the south aisle/lady chapel of the friary church, which marked the boundary between the friary and the adjacent royal palace. As the moulded plinth uncovered in the 1970 excavation clearly shows the wall to have been external,[35] the latter alternative is the more likely. Only the small fragment of wall in the angle between the east-west running wall and the wall running north-south is actually medieval but the continuation of the wall to the east is probably on the medieval line and is also likely to represent the south wall of the church.

At the time of inspection in July 1989 owing to dry weather conditions, the outline of a wall running east-west was visible in the field to the east of "King John's Bakehouse" bordering Langley Hill. How this might relate to the rest of the priory site is not clear but it may have been part of a precinct or other boundary wall. The site of a supposedly medieval oven was discovered a little to the east of the gatehouse range in 1912,[36] a position which could correspond with the reference to the "brewe housse and back house" in 1555,[37] although this is far from conclusive.

Running west from the west wall of "King John's Bakehouse" near its southern end is a low wall, apparently fairly recently constructed, comprising salvaged medieval materials, mostly 14th-and 15th-century window mouldings. This probably dates to c.1911 or later.

DOCUMENTARY EVIDENCE

Little is known about the plan of the church apart from the rough sketch-plan made by Farmer Betts when he exposed its foundations in 1831.[38] From documentary sources it is known that the church was consecrated in 1312 and that it was an aisled building, largely completed by 1368.[39] The survey of 1555 helps a little in identifying its constituent parts: the building, which by then was already partly ruinous, consisted at this date of chancel, belfry, nave, north chapel and lady chapel and possibly also a south chapel.[40]

In 1557 mention is made of the removal of six fothers of lead from the south aisle, and seven from the revestry and lady chapel.[41] Although at this date the word "aisle" may sometimes imply a chapel rather than what is now understood by the term, the dimensions of the church as recorded by Betts would seem to confirm that the building was aisled. Furthermore, Gilbert Scott, who as a young man witnessed Betts's clearing of the site, later described the remains as those of "a conventual church of the first class with pillar bases of Purbeck marble and columns composed of eight shafts around a central pier".[42] Although it is possible that what Scott was describing was not the church at all- his account in *The Recollections* post-dates his actual witnessing of Betts's clearing operation by nearly 50 years- but a building associated with the royal palace, there is no particular reason to suppose this, particularly as a sketch of one of the column bases appears in his own contemporary notebook.[43] Indeed, a column base exactly fitting Scott's description stands *ex situ* a little to the south-east of the building known as Priory House and would certainly seem to have come from a major ecclesiastical building like the friary church. Another column base formerly stood in the grounds of nearby Langley Hill House.[44]

Little more is likely to be established about the plan or precise position of the church without detailed

---

[34] B.L., Add. MS. 32,350, fol.123.

[35] Neal (1973), op. cit. (note 12), plate 6 D. at end of volume.

[36] Notes & drawings by R. Fisher (c.1957) in H.R.O., D/EX 76 P1.

[37] Ibid.

[38] H.R.O., Gerish colln., Box 52.

[39] Lincs. Record Office, Episcopal Registers, Dalderby Mem. fol.227d; P.R.O., E 315/391 (2) and E 101/544/22.

[40] See note 8.

[41] Bodl., Ashmole MS. 1125, fol.70.

[42] Scott, op. et loc. cit. (note 10).

[43] Scott notebook (note 10).

[44] H.R.O., Gerish colln., Box 52; '49th excursion of the East Hertfordshire Archaeological Society, Sep. 23, 1914', *Trans. East Herts. Arch. Soc.*, 5, pt.iii (1914), 306.

archaeological investigation of the site. In fact, on present evidence it is difficult to determine clearly which buildings belonged to the priory and which were part of the palace. That church and palace buildings were very closely situated is, however, suggested by a reference in 1388/9 to the fixing of a lock on the door of the church "to exclude and keep the said friars from the king's household".[45] Could this have been a door in the south wall of the south aisle, which it seems may have formed the boundary between the two sites? As suggested above, the east-west wall, which now separates the properties of the Old and New Schools, is probably on the line of this wall.

It is difficult too to establish the original function of the building known as King John's Bakehouse. All the surviving architectural details such as the arches on the west elevation, the crown-post roof and the deep internal splays to the original windows tend to suggest a late 14th-century date. This accords well with the many documentary references to the construction of the conventual ranges in the late 1360s and early 1370s.[46] These include the mention in building accounts of an infirmary, which does not seem to have formed part of the cloister itself, a refectory, dormitory, chapter house and "a house of office".[47] Both the infirmary and "house of office" would seem to be possible candidates for "King John's Bakehouse", although the latter would perhaps seem more likely as "a house of office" is also mentioned in the survey of 1555.[48]

While it has also been suggested that "King John's Bakehouse" was in fact a bakehouse,[49] a more plausible possibility is that it was the "fayre stables" mentioned in the 1555 survey.[50] The dimensions of 72ft by 18ft given for this building in the survey certainly accord closely with the actual dimensions of 76ft 8" by 18ft 1" of the surviving building. Clearly, however, a structure of this quality- the crown-post roof represents work of the highest standard- was not originally constructed simply as stables, although it is, of course, quite conceivable that this is what it had become by the mid-16th century. It is also possible that this was part of its original function in a multi-purpose building.

The structural evidence, however, seems instead to point to the present form of "King John's Bakehouse" being the result of a conversion of a domestic range into a farmhouse in the mid- to late 16th century. This would not be inconsistent with the documentary information on the use of the site at this period. It should also be noted that even if the building was in use as stables in 1555, there is no reason why (under different ownership) it could not have become a farmhouse later in the century.

There is nothing surviving at the site which can clearly be equated with the community of Dominican nuns housed here from 1557 to 1558.[51] Indeed, it seems that their stay here may never have been intended to be more than temporary. The church was already in poor condition when they arrived, while the payment to the nuns of £150 in 1557 for the stripping of lead from the church roof, to be used in the conduit from Windsor to Blakemore Park,[52] suggests that they never planned to use the building for worship.

The seven nuns established at Langley were all pensioners and former inmates of the house at Dartford.[53] It would not be surprising therefore if they actively sought a return to their previous home: certainly, the poor condition of the buildings at Langley would have done little to dissuade them from this.

Whatever the thoughts or motives of the nuns, the 1555 survey clearly indicates that the church was by then semi-ruinous. "One arche of the sowthe of the seide chaunsell (is) fallen downe", which perhaps suggests that the church had already lost at least part of its south aisle, "the old chapell... on the north seide (of the nave?) is pulled downe excepte the walls standing" and there were further dilapidations in the chancel, belfry, lady chapel and the "body of the churche".[54]

The removal of the remaining lead in 1557 undoubtedly hastened the process of decay and by 1591 the church is described as "ruinated", a reference to "the hills of the said wall (of the church)" perhaps implying that by this date this part of the site was already marked by little more than earthworks.[55]

There are several references in the 1555 survey to the stonework, glass and ironwork of the windows being broken down or "utterly defased" and this has been archaeologically attested. In the excavation of 1970, 14th-century window glass was found immediately to the south of the probable lady chapel and south chancel aisle.[56] Presumably, this glass became dislodged from the windows as the church fell into disrepair- that this happened relatively quickly is suggested by the lack of the pitting to the back of the glass which is so common in medieval glass remaining in church windows today- and it is possible that the windows were deliberately smashed from within.

The survey of 1555 suggests that many of the other buildings were by then in a poor state of repair, which may be the result of their having been plundered by local people for their materials. The frater, dorter and a "doffe" (dove)

---

[45] P.R.O., E 101/473/5.

[46] P.R.O., E 101/466/3 & 5; *Cal. Pat. R., 1364-7*, 197-8; *Cal. Pat. R., 1370-74*, 431.

[47] P.R.O., E 101/544/22; E 101/544/20; E 101/466/6 & 9; E 101/544/20.

[48] See note 8.

[49] R. Gee, *The Two Langleys* (1853), 10.

[50] See note 8.

[51] *Cal. Pat. R., Phil. & Mary, 1555-57*, 403; C.F.R. Palmer, 'The history of the priory of Dartford, in Kent', *Arch. Jnl.*, 36 (1879), 270.

[52] See note 41.

[53] C.F.R. Palmer, 'The Friar Preachers or Blackfriars of King's Langley', *Reliquary*, 19 (1878-9), 218.

[54] See note 8.

[55] H.R.O., Blackwell papers 20,113.

[56] St John O. Gamlen, 'Medieval window glass from the priory, King's Langley', *Herts. Arch.*, 3 (1973), 73.

house were "sore decayed" and these and several other buildings were defective "bothe in timber work and tylinge", while the "ruffe" of the entrance going out of the cloister was "ready to fall downe". Although it is difficult to determine the precise degree of dilapidation from these statements, it therefore seems that a significant amount of destruction had taken place by the mid-1550s. Indeed, a survey of 1556 of the adjoining royal manor with its former palace buildings states that "divers edifices within the site of the manor are decayed, pulled down and carried away by the farmers",[57] a fate no doubt shared by the priory buildings.

Not all the buildings, however, were in quite such poor condition. The 1555 survey mentions a "fayre" gatehouse and stables, the garner is "littell in decaye" and the great kitchen and the "house of effyce (office)" were well repaired. As suggested earlier, the "fayre" gatehouse and stables (or perhaps the house of office) are the most likely candidates for the surviving building known as King John's Bakehouse and possibly they were originally selected for re-use on account of their relatively good condition. At a site of this sort (relatively low-status farm use) the main criterion for re-use would have been the condition and adaptability of surviving buildings. Even if the church had remained in good condition, and all the evidence suggests that it had not, as a large aisled structure it would have been less easy than other buildings to convert to domestic use and this is probably the reason why all trace of it has long since disappeared. In this connection, it is significant that the grant of the site to Edward Newport and John Compton in 1607 refers to the "conventual church, now destroyed".[58]

There is no documentary record of what became of the fittings and furnishings of the church at the Dissolution, but the fine chest tomb of Edmund of Langley (d.1402) and the memorial to Sir Ralph Verney (d.1528),[59] both formerly in the friary church are now in the parish church in the village, where it appears they have occupied various positions.[60] Although it has been suggested that the tombs were removed to the parish church in 1557,[61] when much of the lead was stripped from the friary church roof, it is generally held that they were not transferred until 1574.[62]

Likewise, there is nothing in written sources to suggest that either in the 16th century or later the surviving buildings served as anything other than as part of a farm. Indeed, in the mid-19th century it is known that "King John's Bakehouse" was divided into labourers' cottages.[63]

Materials from the church and other buildings were probably plundered by local people, not only immediately after the Dissolution but in later years, and much may be incorporated in the cottages on Langley Hill and very possibly further afield.

INTERPRETATION AND CONCLUSIONS

It has been suggested above that the building now known as King John's Bakehouse, and which despite its ground-floor arches does not seem to have formed part of the claustral ranges, may have originated as the stables, "house of office" or infirmary of the friary, or as a combination of all three uses. Another plausible suggestion is that it may have served as a guest house, possibly with stables at the north end. This idea is strengthened by its position on what appears to have been the western side of an outer court, although it should be pointed out that it would be more usual to find arches, such as those present on the ground floor of the west elevation, on the enclosed rather than what seems to have been the external face of the building. Indeed, the position and purpose of the arches remain an enigma, whatever the original function of the building.

One possible explanation for the arches is that they gave access to an undercroft, but this is difficult to prove as there is no indication in the surviving structure of springing for a vaulted ceiling or any form of ground-floor ceiling earlier than the present one. Instead, there is some evidence to suggest that the building was originally open to the roof to its northern part. As referred to earlier, the ground-floor ceiling is of late 16th-century date and the apparently contemporary stack is clearly an insertion. The southern section of the building, however, seems always to have had a first floor, supported at its northern end by the thick cross wall. This raises the possibility that there was some kind of timber partition at first-floor level between the northern and southern parts of the building, but any traces of this have been obliterated by the inserted stack.

Another possibility, that the gabled projection at the southern end of the building on the east elevation formerly continued eastwards to form another range corresponding with the gatehouse range to the north and closing what seems to have been an outer court, appears unlikely. While the steep gable might suggest such a truncated range, John Buckler's drawing of 1830 clearly shows what look like original angle quoins to both the north and south corners of the projection,[64] which can be seen as further evidence against this theory. This drawing and a number of old photographs also show a stepped wall running eastwards from the north-east corner of the projection,[65] the outline of which was visible in the dry grass during July 1989. This appears to have been quite a substantial wall and may have separated the inner and outer courts of both the friary and its post-Dissolution successor.

[57] H.R.O., Blackwell papers 20,123.

[58] See note 7.

[59] Verney's will is printed in L. Munby (ed.), *Life and Death in King's Langley, Wills and Inventories 1498-1659* (1981), 8-9.

[60] Chauncy, ii, 470-1; Clutterbuck, i, 436-7; Cussans, iii, pt.1, 200-2; *V.C.H.*, ii, 242-3; Pevsner, 218.

[61] L. Munby (ed.), *The History of King's Langley* (1963), vii.

[62] J. Evans, 'Edmund of Langley and his tomb', *Archaeologia*, 46 (1881), 309-10, 317; Haythornthwaite, op. cit. (note 11), 64.

[63] Gee, op. et loc. cit. (note 49).

[64] H.R.O., Buckler Drawings, IV, 107.

[65] Ibid; Watford Central Library, photographic colln.

The position of the church in relation to the surviving buildings is unclear, but it has been suggested by R. Fisher that the cloister lay to the north rather than to the south.[66] Indeed, it is possible that the 14th-century doorway in the south wall of "King John's Bakehouse" led into a covered walk-way and on Betts's sketch-plan of the foundations uncovered in 1831, it appears that the cloister lay to the south of this building. Given the situation of the palace buildings immediately to the south of the church, this would certainly seem the most likely location for the cloister, to the north of the nave. Nevertheless, the doorway is unlikely to have given direct access to the cloister, as the angle buttress to the south-west corner of "King John's Bakehouse" means that the north claustral walk must have lain further to the south. A short passage-way may have linked "King John's Bakehouse" to the cloister itself.

Interestingly, the cloister itself probably did not abut directly onto the nave as the 14th-century building accounts refer to the four **outer** walls of the enclosure.[67] This was a fairly standard feature of Dominican houses, an open space being left between the nave and the north or south wall of the cloister as applicable, thus affording better lighting to the nave.[68] Further evidence for this arrangement is found in the survey of 1555, which refers to "an entrance going oute of the cloyster into the churche conteyning 15 yardes in length and 3 in breadth".[69]

Another feature of Dominican architecture adopted at Langley was the building over of the claustral walks rather than treating them as separate structural units, as at houses of most other monastic orders. This was done on at least two sides of the Langley cloister, certainly with the dormitory and probably also the refectory, which formed the east and north ranges respectively.[70]

This still leaves the problem of the cloister lying to the west of "King John's Bakehouse" and seemingly being unprotected on this side. Reference has already been made to the apparent peculiarity of the entrances to the presumed stables in "King John's Bakehouse" lying on the west rather on the east side of the building, that is on the side facing away from the courtyard. This anomaly can be overcome, however, if another courtyard or precinct is postulated to the west of "King John's Bakehouse". This seems quite plausible as the western boundary of the site as a whole appears to lie along a field boundary some distance to the west.[71] In such a plan, horses would have been led through the gatehouse into the stables from around the northern side of "King John's Bakehouse"- the presence of original buttresses to the north wall suggests that it was not abutted by other buildings- and there may also have been access directly from the west.

Bibliography

PICTORIAL SOURCES

Hertfordshire Record Office

Buckler Drawings, IV, 107, 108.

Oldfield Drawings, IV, 384.

Gerish Collection, Box 52.

DSA 4/64/1.

British Library, London

Add. MS. 32,350, fols.121-4.

R.I.B.A. Drawings Collection, London

Scott sketchbook no.2 (1830-31).

Hertford Museum Store

Original plan (1907) by A. Whitford Anderson for *V.C.H.*

Printed

The Builder, 2 (1844), 66.

PHOTOGRAPHIC SOURCES

Bodleian Library, Oxford

MS. top. eccl. b. 28, fol.14.

Watford Central Library

Photographic Collection.

OTHER PRIMARY SOURCES

Manuscript:-

Public Record Office, London

E 101/466/3, 5, 6 & 9.

E 101/473/5.

---

[66] H.R.O., D/EX 48 P2-3; D/EX 76 P1.
[67] P.R.O., E 101/544/20, m.2; E 101/544/22, m.3.
[68] *King's Works*, i, 261.
[69] See note 8.
[70] *King's Works*, i, 260-1, where it is incorrectly stated that the refectory probably lay on the south side of the cloister.
[71] Plan in Neal, op. cit. (note 12), 33; H.R.O., tithe map, DSA 4/64/1.

E 101/544/20; 22.

E 315/391.

C 66/1117/1563.

Hertfordshire Record Office

Blackwell papers 20,113; 20,123.

D/EX 48 P2-3.

D/EX 76 P1.

Bodleian Library, Oxford

Ashmole MS. 1125, fol.70.

Lincolnshire Record Office

Episcopal Registers, Dalderby Mem. fol.227d.

Printed:-

Calendar of Patent Rolls Preserved in the Public Record Office (1903- (in progress).
Letters and Papers, Foreign and Domestic, of the Reign of Henry VIII, eds. Brewer, J.S., Gairdner, J. & Brodie, R.H., 21 vols. (1862-1932).

SECONDARY SOURCES

Chauncy, H., *The Historical Antiquities of Hertfordshire*, ii (1700, reprinted Dorking 1975).
Clutterbuck, R., *The History and Antiquities of Hertfordshire*, iii (1827).
Colvin, H.M. *et al.*, *The History of the King's Works*, i (1963).
Cussans, J.E., *The History of Hertfordshire*, iii, pt.1 (1879, reprinted Wakefield 1972).
'49th excursion of the East Hertfordshire Archaeological Society, Sep. 23, 1914', *Trans. East Herts. Arch. Soc.*, 5, pt.iii (1914), 306.
Evans, J., 'Edmund of Langley and his tomb', *Archaeologia*, 46 (1881), 297-328.
Gamlen, St John O.,'Medieval window glass from the priory, King's Langley', *Herts. Arch.*, 3 (1973), 73-7.
Gee, R., *The Two Langleys* (St Albans, 1853).
Hastie, S. & Spain, D., *King's Langley, A Hertfordshire Village* (King's Langley, 1991).
Haythornthwaite, J.P., *The Parish of King's Langley* (1924).
Munby, L. (ed.), *The History of King's Langley* (King's Langley, 1963).
　　-Life and Death in King's Langley, Wills and Inventories 1498-1659 (King's Langley, 1981).

Neal, D.S., 'Excavations at the palace and priory at King's Langley, 1970', *Herts. Arch.*, 3 (1973), 31-72.
-'Excavations at the palace of King's Langley, Hertfordshire, 1974-1976', *Med. Arch.*, 21 (1977), 124-65.
Palmer, C.F.R., 'The Friar Preachers or Blackfriars of King's Langley', *Reliquary*, 19 (1878-9), 209-18.
-'The history of the priory of Dartford, in Kent', *Arch. Jnl.*, 36 (1879), 241-71.
-'Prelates of the black friars of England', *The Antiquary*, 27 (1893), 111-14.
Pevsner, N., *Hertfordshire* (2nd edn., revd. Cherry, B., Harmondsworth 1977).
Royal Commission on Historical Monuments, *An Inventory of the Historical Monuments in Hertfordshire* (1910).
Salmon, N., *The History of Hertfordshire* (1728).
Scott, G.G. (ed.), *Personal and Professional Recollections by the Late Sir George Gilbert Scott* (1879, re-ed. Stamp, G., Stamford, 1995).
The Victoria History of the Counties of England, *Hertfordshire*, ii (1908).

MARKYATE PRIORY

History

Benedictine nunnery founded before 1145 by Abbot Geoffrey of St Albans with Christina of Markyate as the first prioress;[1] dissolved before February 1537.[2] It remained in royal hands until March 1539 when it was leased to Humphrey Bourchier for 21 years.[3] In July 1548 the property was granted to George Ferrers, remaining in the Ferrers family until the mid 17th century.[4]

THE BUILDINGS

Introduction

The house is in the parish of Markyate, formed in 1897, but was formerly in the Hertfordshire part of the parish of Caddington, some of which was in Bedfordshire.[5] It is situated on rising ground in landscaped parkland above the River Ver and Watling Street. Approximately 100 yards east of the house is an old bowling green, bounded on the west by a yew hedge. Other features associated with the house are described below.

The earliest part of the present house is the short mid 16th-century service wing in chequered stone and flint on the east side of the building. The south range was added c.1600 but was remodelled in the mid 17th century with two large rear stair towers. A long mid 17th-century west range was fronted by a two-storey classical range in the 1730s, to which a single-storey library was added at the north end in the late 18th century. This range was demolished and the remains of the building remodelled in 1825-26 as a compact rectangular house with corner turrets in neo-Elizabethan style. Further alterations were carried out in the early 20th century, including moving the main entrance to the north side in the redesigned courtyard.

There is no direct evidence that the existing house contains any fabric of pre-Dissolution date and what appears to have been either the east end of the monastic church or the chapter house was uncovered in 1805 some 40ft to the west of the present terrace on the north side of the house.[6]

Description

It was not possible to gain permission from the present owner, Mr J. Armstrong, to visit the property and consequently this description has had to be compiled from various published accounts and photographs.[7] It may not therefore be entirely accurate in all respects, owing to a lack of photographs of some parts of the house and the inevitable errors which arise from working from photographs alone.

South elevation. Two storeys and attics to main range with lower range to right. The main range is of narrow red brick in English bond, refaced in 19th-century Flemish bond brickwork on the ground floor and above the sills of the attic windows; moulded stone string courses, red brick window dressings (partly obscured by later stucco surrounds) and steeply pitched plain tiled roofs, which are present throughout the building. The octagonal corner turrets are of blueish brick with lead caps and weathervanes. The lower range is of roughly coursed clunch rubble and knapped flint to the ground floor with red brick to the upper storey, which has a roughly central stone pilaster carried up from the ground floor with traces of a similar pilaster to the right corner.

The main range is of three bays with coped parapets to shaped outer gables and a steeply pointed centre gable; boldly projecting string courses. The centre gable has a two-storey bay projection with strapwork decoration and corner obelisks to its parapet. Three-light mullion windows to the gables, and three-light mullioned and transomed windows elsewhere, except to the ground floor right where the mullioned and transomed window is of four lights, all lights above the transoms being segmental pointed. All casements are leaded; diagonal latticed cames to the attic, decorative to the first floor and plain rectangular cames on the ground floor. The returns of the bay projections have narrow rectangular transomed windows and there are similar but still narrower false windows to the ground- and first-floor stages of the slightly projecting corner turrets, which have slit windows to their cardinal faces at their top level. Symmetrically spaced ridge stacks to either side of the centre gable, the left with four decorated octagonal shafts, moulded capping and bases, the right with three such shafts. There is a prominent external end stack to the right gable end of the main range with four octagonal shafts similar to those of the ridge stacks.

The lower range has a three-light and a four-light wooden mullion window to left and right on the first floor respectively and a two-light and a five-light stone mullioned window in corresponding positions on the ground floor. All the windows have diagonal latticed cames, segmental-pointed heads and hoodmoulds. The tracery of the ground-floor windows looks older than that on the first floor and has hollow spandrels. The right gable end of this range forms part of the **east elevation**, which is

---

[1] Dugdale, iii, 368; H.T. Riley (ed.), *Gesta Abbatum Monasterii Sancti Albani, i, 793-1290* (1867), 95-103; M. Gibbs (ed.), *Early Charters of the Cathedral Church of St Paul, London*, Camden Soc., 3rd series, 58 (1939), 119-20.

[2] *L.P.*, xiii (1), no.1520.

[3] *L.P.*, xiv (1), p.610.

[4] *Cal. Pat. R., Edw.VI, 1547-8*, 314-15; B.L., Harl. MS. 7389, p.34.

[5] *V.C.H.*, ii, 187; S. Coleman, *Caddington and Kensworth*, Bedfordshire Parish Surveys, 4 (1985), 9.

[6] B.L., Add. MS. 32,349, fols.5-6; *Gentleman's Magazine*, n.s., 26 (1846), 469-70.

[7] The principal of these are the accounts in *V.C.H.*, ii, 190; *R.C.H.M.*, 150 and D.O.E. 34th List of Buildings of Special Architectural or Historic Interest, The Borough of Dacorum, 90-1. There is also a useful set of photographs taken by the R.C.H.M. in 1981 in the N.M.R. (red boxes) and typescript notes by J.T. Smith and others, file 77,723.

of clunch rubble construction (partly rendered over) with Totternhoe stone quoins at its south end, giving way to a regular knapped flint and stone chequerwork pattern incorporating much 13th-century moulded stonework at its north end. The most prominent feature of this elevation is the large external gable end stack to the left, the upper section of which has been rebuilt in brick with three attached diagonal shafts, which have corbelled capping. To the left of this on the first floor is a small two-light leaded mullion window and in the angle to the right is a two-storey lean-to. To the right of this is a tall rectangular two-light mullion window and to the right again a similar but less elongated window. Both are on the first floor and between is a blind pedimented brick gable rising from the parapet.

The **west elevation** of the house, the whole of which is refaced in 19th-century Flemish bond brickwork, is similar to the south elevation but shorter. It too has slightly projecting corner turrets, that to the south also being the west turret of the south elevation. Two slightly projecting steeply pitched gables break the eaves, the heads of their three-light mullion windows being at parapet level. Below these windows are a two-storey rectangular bay projection to the left and a canted bay projection to the right, string courses continuing round from the south elevation to form dripstones to the windows, which are again mullioned and transomed. Both projections have three-light windows, of reduced proportions to the first floor, following the same glazing and tracery details as on the south elevation. The canted bay has transomed windows to the returns. Between the projections there are cross windows on each floor. Roughly central ridge stack with three ornamental shafts as on the south elevation and another to the far left with four ornamental shafts.

The **north elevation** of the building is more difficult to describe owing to the relative lack of photographs and the complex plan of this part of the house, but there is a roughly rectangular courtyard to the north. Beginning at the north-west corner turret described under the west elevation, to the left is a tall two-light mullion window on the first floor directly above a doorway. To the left again is a shaped gable with a two-light mullion window to the attic and a larger two-light mullioned and transomed window on the first floor; string courses continued round from the west elevation. Within the courtyard, the north elevation exhibits some of the earliest remaining fabric in the building, although again the photographic coverage is poor. There is a chequered stone and flint projecting gabled wing at the east end (the north gable end of the east range) with two 17th-century style red brick gabled projections to the west, the right taller and projecting further forwards, and having between them a tall brick stack with decorated octagonal shaft and moulded capping. The stone and flint gable has a two-light moulded mullion window with four-centred heads on the ground floor. All these gables are set back from the remainder of the north elevation. Attached to the central of the three gabled ranges facing into the courtyard is a two-storey gabled entrance porch with a carved stone plaque

over a round-headed arch-way with pendant keystone and moulded imposts. On the first floor of the porch is a three-light mullioned and transomed window and immediately to the right of the porch, the front wall of the centre gable has a tall three-light mullioned and transomed window.

The courtyard is bounded by single-storey brick service ranges on its north, east and west sides. The north range has a roughly central arched carriage-way, which externally takes the form of a round-headed Bath stone arch-way with lion-head and pendant keystone and moulded entablature (at eaves level of the remainder of the range), flanked by three-quarter length Doric columns. Above the arch-way is an old stone plaque with carved strapwork in a shaped gable. It is suggested that the old stonework and the columns in the arch-way came from the former south entrance (see below).[8] On its inner (courtyard) face the arch is also round-headed and has a five-light mullioned window like those in the house to its right. Above the windows is a brick ridge stack with two decorative octagonal shafts. Adjoining the north end of the east range is a wide four-centred arch-way in brick with a bell in the triangular gable above. This was formerly the carriage entrance to the courtyard when it was a stable court but was blocked in the early 20th century by a corridor which links the service ranges to the north-east corner of the house.

Returning to the external face of the north range of the courtyard, there is a break in the north-west corner where there is a distinct section (the former gun room) defined by ridge stacks with paired decorative shafts to coped verges, the right (on the gable end) crow-stepped. This gable end has a cross-window to the apex and below are evenly-spaced rectangular windows with leaded latticed lights. To the north and south sides of this section are steeply-pitched brick dormers, the former overlooking the walled garden (see below) and the latter giving access on to the flat, parapeted roof of the west range of the courtyard. This has four four-centred arches with three-light leaded mullion windows in its west wall.

The **walled garden** is very extensive and the stretch of wall which directly adjoins the north-west corner of the former gun room incorporates medieval stonework and flint to its lower courses. Elsewhere, it is of red brick, in 16th-century English bond on the west side and to the south, where it runs to the east of the south side of the courtyard, and in Flemish bond to the sections heightened in the 18th century, which are chiefly on the north and east. The wall is stepped on its north side. There are terraces to the south and west of the house, defined by low 19th-century brick walls with decorative pierced balustrades forming alternating diamond and quatrefoil patterns. There is a projecting bastion to the south-west corner of the terrace.

---

[8] D.O.E. List, 91.

The **interior** of the house is even less easy than the exterior to describe accurately, as there is apparently only one set of photographs available for public inspection.[9] These photographs were taken in c.1899 and, along with the various published accounts of the house, from the basis for the following description. Where possible the rooms photographed have been matched to a ground-plan made for proposed alterations by E.A. Sursham in 1926.[10]

The house is now entered through the two-storey porch on the north elevation facing the courtyard described above. Although some earlier features remain, the interior seems to have been comprehensively remodelled in 1825-26 and again in the early 20th century. The principal staircase towards the north-west corner of the house belongs to this earlier period. It is of oak, Jacobean in style and rises around three sides of an open well with moulded string, rusticated square newels and tall pierced finials. Panelled oak double doors at the foot of the stairs in a vigorous Jacobean-style doorcase with double pilasters, fluted entablature and brackets with acorn drops. This doorcase previously took the form of an open screen and is on the axis of the former south entrance hall, now thrown together with the large adjoining room to the east to create the billiard room shown on the 1926 plan.

The billiard room has a rich plaster ceiling of moulded ribs in geometric patterns with charges in the spaces; deep arcaded frieze with Ionic pilasters and oak scratch-moulded panelling. There is a four-centred Tudor-arched stone fireplace with a carved strapwork band at the top, similar to the fireplaces in most of the principal rooms of the house, in the wall dividing the billiard room from the room to the east. This room is shown on the 1926 plan as the dining room but was previously the kitchen and represents the earliest part of the present building. The rather less heavy plaster ceiling in this room dates to after 1910, when the room was still in use as a kitchen, and this is the date of the other accomplished Arts and Crafts-style moulded plaster ceilings elsewhere in the house. Particularly noteworthy is the segmental vault with bands of vine scroll decoration in the west link block to the north courtyard. There is an early 19th-century classical white marble fire surround with carved urns on the corner blocks and centre panel and a decorated cast-iron basket grate in the northern room on the west elevation (school room on the 1926 plan but earlier the library).

Apparently the only readily detectable early feature in the present fabric is what is now an arch-way in the west wall of the former scullery, which after 1926 became incorporated in the present entrance hall. The wall itself at this point is over three foot thick and contains a depressed pointed stone arch, partly exposed over a corridor with three moulded orders consisting of a chamfer, a hollow chamfer and a chamfer on each face. This arch-way seems originally to have been a fireplace.

PICTORIAL AND PHOTOGRAPHIC EVIDENCE

This is particularly abundant and is used here to highlight the many significant differences between the building's former appearance and its appearance today. The earliest view of the house seems to be a late 18th-century drawing by Oldfield.[11] This shows the house from some distance away with the former two-storey brick range of c.1734 on the west side. This is of brick in a classical style with a hipped roof partly concealed by a parapet; 2:3:3:2 bays with sash windows and a string course. There is a shallow porch approached by a short flight of steps to the centre of the third group of windows from the left and to the left of the range is a single-storey hip-roofed structure (the late 18th-century library) with a Venetian window to the front. There is another single-storey hip-roofed outbuilding in a corresponding position to the south of the range. The south range is also shown in this drawing, consisting of five flat-topped gables with oval-shaped medallions to the centre and outer gables.

The south range is shown in more detail in an undated but probably slightly later watercolour attributed to C.D. Clarke (d.1840).[12] This shows the south elevation full on. The five flat-topped gables project from a long range behind, only the ridge of which and a stack between the second and third gables are visible. Symmetrical four-light mullioned and transomed windows throughout on the first and second floors, their heads protected by continuous string courses, which are bisected by pilasters carried up as verges to the gables, the outer of which have oval-shaped medallions as in the Oldfield drawing with two-light mullion windows to the three centre gables. There is also a string course above the partly submerged ground floor, which apparently has an infilled doorway to the left bay, two infilled doorways to the second bay from the left, that to the right Tudor-arched, and wide infilled mullion windows to the centre and right bays. There is a row of single-storey outbuildings attached to the left corner of this range running at right-angles to the south.

The south and west ranges are again shown in an attractive watercolour of the house viewed from across the park,[13] but this adds little further information beyond showing a boundary wall continuing to the north on a line level with the west front, behind which are outbuildings to the east. Much more detail of the south front is shown, however, in an 1805 watercolour by Thomas Fisher,[14] one of a series of views made by this artist. This view of the south front confirms the basic impression given by Clarke but adds many useful details and appears to be the more accurate of

[9] H.R.O., D/Z 59 Z1.
[10] N.M.R., file 77,723.

[11] H.R.O., Oldfield Drawings, IV, 502
[12] Victoria and Albert Museum, Dept. of Prints and Drawings, Pressmark 93 A9.
[13] H.R.O., Knowsley Clutterbuck, iii, 346d.
[14] B.L., Add. MS. 32,349, fol.1.

the two drawings. The differences on the upper floors are the presence of a clock in a square plaque dated "1789" to the centre gable, the presence of two mullions to the oval-shaped medallions, showing that these are likely to have been windows, and the mullion windows to the other gables are shown as having three lights. In addition to the ridge stack there is a tall end stack with two octagonal shafts and one twisted shaft (to the centre), surmounted by ornamental moulded capping to the right end wall.

Red brick is confirmed as the predominant building material, including to the coping of the gables, and the stone pilasters of the Clarke drawing are shown terminating at eaves level. Alternating quoins are shown to the right corner at first-floor level and the mullioned and transomed windows, all of which have latticed leaded lights, are shown as considerably less deep than in the Clarke view. The main difference between the two views, however, is on the ground floor, which is shown in far greater detail and apparently accuracy by Fisher, who was perhaps aided by the fact that the ground appears to have been at a lower level when he drew the house.

The ground floor is of coursed rubblestone. Below the string course and aligned with the left jamb of the left first-floor window is a twelve-paned sash window. Aligned between the right jamb of the second window from the left on the first floor and the second pilaster from the left (none of which it should be noted continues below the first-floor string course as in Clarke's drawing) is a Tudor-arched doorway with plank door and hollow spandrels plus a two-light arched window directly above under the string course. To the right of this and continuing to the right of the third pilaster from the left is a wide, eight-light Tudor-arched mullion window with hollow spandrels divided to the centre by a king mullion. Approximately aligned with the centre of the fourth pilaster from the left is a two-light square-headed window and to the right again is a three-light Tudor-arched mullion window with hollow spandrels, its jamb adjoining the end pilaster (neither end pilaster is shown in Clarke's view). Fisher shows all windows with leaded latticed lights.

Directly attached to the right end pilaster and running at right-angles to the south is a high stone wall with tile or brick coping, forming the eastern boundary of a courtyard. The top of the wall is level with the first-floor string course and towards its southern end a straight joint can be detected. Also shown in Fisher's drawing is the south end wall of the 18th-century west range, in which two blind windows and alternating quoins can be seen, along with a tall stack at the junction with the south range. Below this range a series of single-storey outbuildings is visible as in Clarke's view.

It seems probable that Fisher's view pre-dates Clarke's, although as stated above the latter is undated. The reasons for supposing this are that Fisher's drawing shows a boundary wall to the east side of the courtyard, whereas Clarke's shows a fence in this position and in the relatively short time span between 1805 and the major remodelling of 1825-6, which must provide a *terminus ante quem* for Clarke's watercolour, it is more likely that the ground level to the south of the house rose in height, rather than that it was reduced and infilled openings unblocked. It therefore seems likely that Clarke drew the house relatively shortly before the remodelling of 1825-6, by which time the wall to the courtyard had been replaced by a fence.

Returning to Fisher, he also drew the house from the north-east in 1805. This drawing survives in several forms, including an engraving published in *The Gentleman's Magazine*.[15] The most useful version is the watercolour in The British Library, incorrectly captioned as the north-west view, the details of which are confirmed by a pencil drawing in the Hertfordshire Record Office.[16] The short east range is shown as being in two sections. To the left are the brick triple octagonal shafts of the massive chimney to the right gable end of the south range, which is shown to be considerably broader to its projecting stone base, which has alternating quoins and a small fire window underneath tile capping. To the right of the stack are windows placed directly above the one below on each floor, a three-light mullion window on the ground floor, and two-light mullion windows of decreasing size on the first and second floors, all with Tudor-arched heads and with hoodmoulds on the ground and first floors. The ground- and first-floor windows are set within an area of roughly coursed stonework, which continues to the left of the stack and terminates in a former steeply-pitched roof line which shows that the south range has been raised in height, further evidence of which is given by the transition to brickwork above the former roof line. A stone-coped brick parapet screens a steeply-pitched gable running to the rear of the south range, the render to the face of which suggests the possibility of timber frame. The gable also has an infilled window. Below the gable and continuing flush with the east wall of the higher section is a two-storey range, particularly notable for its chequered stone and flintwork, and having a tall three-light mullion window with Tudor-arched heads to the first floor on the east side and a small four-light mullion window on the ground floor to the north.

Directly adjoining this range to the west, and apparently slightly set back from it, is a full-height brick range which runs at right-angles to the rear of the south range. It is fronted by a steeply-pitched flat-pedimented stone-coped gable, which has a moulded stone cornice at eaves level and a three-light mullion window, the outer lights of which are blind, in a moulded surround, surmounted by a small round-headed window. Directly below the string course to the left is a three-light mullioned and transomed window, to the right of the cill of which is another three-light mullioned and transomed window. Immediately below the left window is another three-light mullioned and transomed

[15] *Gents. Mag.*, op. cit. (note 6), opp. p.467.
[16] B.L., Add. MS. 32,349, fol.2; H.R.O., D/EX 55 Z 2/84.

window, the head of which is at the same level as the transom of the right window and directly below the right window is a two-light mullioned and transomed window. Immediately underneath the left windows is a two-light mullion window which acts as an overlight to a boarded door in moulded surround. To the right of this range is a continuous catslide outshut down to the ground floor, with a nine-paned sash window breaking the eaves, to the left of which a pump is attached to the wall. This lean-to links to another full-height gabled brick range, which differs from the other principally in that the coped parapet terminates in a small pedimented gable to the right and the moulded cornice continues round to the left return. The gable has a three-light mullion window to the centre and directly below the cornice to the right is a three-light mullioned and transomed window, below which is another three-light mullion and transomed window and finally a boarded door under a simple bracketed canopy. To the left corner there are also three-light mullioned and transomed windows, one directly above the other, the head of the upper one at cill level of the right upper window and the head of the lower one mid-way between the transom and cill of the right lower window. To the left of the doorway there is a section of chamfered stone plinth. It should be noted that all the windows to both rear ranges have moulded surrounds and dripmoulds without labels and like those to the east range leaded lights. A variety of lead rainwater goods is shown throughout.

The Fisher view also shows the rear of the classical range of c.1734 which runs at right-angles to the north-west of the ranges described above. This range with its hipped roof to the right, partly concealed by a parapet to the brick facade with two sash windows on the first floor, actually appears to be much earlier than c.1734. There are two prominent external stone stacks to the back wall, which itself is of coursed rubble, the left with a rectangular brick shaft and the right with triple brick shafts. Between the windows is a tall probably original three-light mullion window with a hoodmould, the outer parts infilled and with a twelve-paned sash window inserted to the centre. Directly below is an infilled three-light mullion window again with a hoodmould. It therefore appears that the work of c.1734 simply represents the refronting of an earlier range. A short section of brick wall can be seen running to the north of the range.

Running at right-angles to the east of the north end of the c.1734 range is a lower service range, which was perhaps a stable. It has a steeply-pitched roof, gable ended to the east which is timber framed above tie beam level with vertical studs and has a small two-light window above the collar. There is a gabled eaves hatch on the north side towards the gable end.

Fisher also drew in 1805 some foundations which were discovered in that year "under the lawn in front of the house."[17] These are usually interpreted as part of the east and north walls of the east end of the monastic church and were situated immediately below top soil level, but they could just as easily be the corresponding walls of the chapter house. The drawing is made from within the structure and shows two buttresses against the east wall framing the remains of a single-light window opening, consisting of the bases of elaborately moulded triple nook-shafts. At cill level there is a continuous moulded string course which links with ring-shafts in the east wall and the north-east angle and continues along the north wall where there is an identical window towards the east end. The details of the mouldings suggest work of the early 13th century and the windows were almost certainly lancets.

Also included on the drawing are "miscellaneous fragments found in removing the Blockading Terrace before the House." These comprise a fragment of an inscription "n EDE" found with bones etc," part of a coffin lid with a raised foliated cross, "a fragment seemingly part of a Norman capital", two fragments of 13th-century foliated capitals and a "section of bases found among the rubbish". Fisher also drew at this time the "form of a shield on the end of a beam in the kitchen" and part of the Tudor-arched brick fireplace in the kitchen which he measured as nine foot six inches wide, along with the "section of a groin" and the "section of the arch of a doorway", which were presumably also in the house.

Fisher also made a ground-plan of the house, which confirms the lay-out shown on other drawings. The courtyard wall is shown running to the south of the south-east angle of the south front and the west side of the courtyard is bounded by outbuildings, while to the east in the courtyard itself is a rectangular structure marked as a "Dove House". The plan also marks the position of the excavated remains of the church or chapter house in relation to the house.[18]

An important drawing was made of the house from the south west by Robert Lugar in c.1825. This shows the building as transformed by his remodelling of 1825-26 and is usefully accompanied by plans of the ground and first floors.[19] As the outward appearance of the house today is substantially the same as it was left by Lugar, only the significant differences are noted here, although it is important to emphasise that the drawing may represent the house as Lugar intended to leave it rather than being a totally accurate record of the work actually carried out. The most noticeable differences are the plain rectangular and rebated shafts to the chimney stacks and the fact that the centre bay to the south range projects slightly from the others. The two-storey porch below this has a shaped pedimented parapet with a blank armorial shield and a round-headed doorway with imposts and projecting

[17] B.L., Add. MS. 32,349, fol.6.
[18] Ibid, fol.5.
[19] R. Lugar, *Villa Architecture* (1828), pl.40.

keystone flanked by plain Doric pilasters with moulded entablature supporting strapwork decoration. Several of the fenestration details are different from those on the house today. All of the windows on the south and west elevations of the main house are shown deeper in Lugar's drawing than on the building today, while those on the lower range on the south are shown as less deep than in fact they are. Those window openings which are shown by Lugar that can be compared with the windows in the present building show no sign of having been altered since the early 19th century and, together with a discrepancy in the number of lights to two of the windows shown, add to the impression that the Lugar drawing shows the ideal rather than the execution of the architect's remodelling.

Equal caution should be applied to Lugar's representation of the low range on the north-west side of the house connecting it with the stable range, especially as it does not correspond with the appearance shown by the usually reliable Buckler (see below), although the form in which it is shown by Lugar with its three Tudor arches (in reality there are four) infilled by three-light mullion windows (albeit with transoms in Lugar's drawing) is closer to Lugar's original concept than the open form in which they are shown by Buckler. Lugar also shows shallow stepped buttresses with pinnacles between the arches and the precise details of the gable end of what was to become the gun room should probably be attributed to the architect's imagination rather than taken as evidence for what was finally built. The Lugar engraving, along with an unattributed sketch drawing of much the same date,[20] is useful, however, in showing that the enclosed courtyard to the south had by then been swept away. Lugar also shows that a terrace bounded by a low retaining wall with urns had been created or was proposed on the south and west sides of the house.

Much the same view as shown by Lugar is depicted in a pen and ink drawing of 1832 by J. Buckler.[21] This shows the house in almost exactly the same form as today, the only significant differences being the presence of the doorway (almost identical to the appearance of the one drawn by Lugar with the exception of the absence of strapwork carving above the entablature) in the two-storey entrance porch, some of the details of the leaded lights to the windows and the size of the lower right window to the lower section of the south range, which looks very similar to the form in which it is drawn by Lugar. To the north of what was to become the gun room, which is shown in all important respects as it stands today, a high boundary wall can be seen running to the north.

Another pen and ink drawing of 1838 by J.C. Buckler made from a position to the north west of the house is also remarkably similar to the appearance of the building

today,[22] the only major difference being that the four arches of the 19th-century single-storey link range on the west elevation are shown in their former open form. More information, however can be obtained from another pen and ink drawing of 1839 by G. Buckler,[23] the preparatory pencil sketch for which (dated July 1838) also survives.[24] This shows the house from the north east from almost exactly the viewpoint adopted by Fisher in 1805. There are, however, several important differences, which seem to show that even at the rear of the house much remodelling had been undertaken during the intervening period. First, the low range attached to the north end of the east range has been raised in height, the chequerwork of the old part giving way to plain ashlar blocks to the upper part of this gable. An internal lateral stack (the truncated remains of which still survive) with diamond shafts and moulded capping has been added at the former junction between the two sections and the three-light mullion window in the east wall of the lower range from the 1805 drawing has been supplanted by the large two-light window with hoodmould which survives today, along with the other two-light mullion window to the right of the left stack.

Moving to the north side, the four-light mullion window to the ground floor of the lower range has been replaced by the extant two-light mullion window. The doorway and two-light overlight to the left corner of the range to the right are recognisable from the 1805 drawing but, apart from the three-light mullioned and transomed window at eaves level to the left corner, the rest of this range is considerably altered, the two windows to the right having been replaced by a tall three-light mullioned and transomed window with dripmould. The shaped gable of the 1805 drawing has given way to an asymmetrically-pitched plain gable on the right side of which, in the angle with a narrow gabled range projecting to the north, the tall surviving stack (described above) is clearly visible, although at this date it had octagonal corbelled capping.

The rest of what is visible in this Buckler drawing has already been described above under the description of the present building, the only significant difference being that, in contrast to their earlier depiction by J.C. Buckler, the four attached shafts to the north end stack of the west range are shown as three tall octagonal shafts with corbelled capping. The drawing is also useful in that it depicts the west side of the low link range, which is shown as having a plain tile roof and screened by a stone-coped boundary wall with a boarded doorway, small window and a canted bay projection (identifiable on the 1926 plan) adjoining the tall three-light mullioned and transomed window referred to above. It should also be noted that the Buckler drawing shows that the apparent projection of the chequerwork-patterned range shown in the 1805 Fisher drawing is false,

[20] B.L., Add. MS. 32,349, fol.4
[21] H.R.O., Buckler Drawings, IV, 18.

[22] Ibid, 19.
[23] Ibid, 20.
[24] Bodl., MS. top. gen a. 12, fol.90.

as this range is shown by Buckler as flush with the range to the right.

Of later drawings, reference should be made to A. Whitford Anderson's unpublished measured drawings of 1906 for the *V.C.H.*[25] These show an elevation and section of the fireplace archway in the west wall of the former scullery and the "jamb and mullion of the scullery window," which are shown to be cavetto moulded. Undated early 20th-century drawings showing the interior of the drawing room must be earlier than 1926 as they relate to the south-west room of the house,[26] referred to as the drawing room on Lugar's 1828 plan (see below), but which by 1926 had become the library. The drawings show the room before and after proposed alterations. Pre-alterations, the fireplace has a classical surround and there is dado panelling to the walls but after the alterations the whole room is panelled, including the fireplace surround.

We now turn to photographs for evidence of further alterations to the house in the later 19th and early 20th centuries, although in the absence of a site inspection, some of these have already been used in compiling the description of the existing building. A photograph taken at the turn of the century and another of 1905 show the two-storey entrance porch in almost the same form as depicted by J. Buckler in 1832, except that it now has the strapwork decoration to the parapet.[27] By c.1920, however, the present three-light mullioned and transomed window has appeared in place of the doorway.[28]

The earlier photographs and others of c.1910 also show that the east elevation had timber sash windows on the first floor and timber casements on the ground floor at this time.[29] A photograph of 1915 is useful for the information it gives on the courtyard to the rear of the house before the alterations of the 1920s,[30] showing that there had formerly been an entrance through the north range of outbuildings before this was reopened by Sir John Pennefather. Only one other photograph not referred to earlier gives any additional information. This is a photograph of 1905 which shows the kitchen (now dining room) fireplace: Tudor-arched and chamfered, springing (like the fireplace arch in the former scullery) directly from the jambs.[31]

MAP AND PLAN EVIDENCE

Considering the abundance of pictorial evidence for the house, this is surprisingly slim. The earliest detailed plan of the building appears to be that made by Fisher in 1805,[32] which usefully confirms the information given in his

drawings of the house. The plan shows the main block of the pre-1825-26 house with the south, east and the east end of the north walls heavily delineated, presumably indicating old work. This shading also applies to the east side of the west range, while the partly timber-framed stable range running at right-angles to the west range and closing the north side of the courtyard to the rear of the house is also marked in this way. To the south of the main range of the house the large courtyard is shown with a range of outbuildings on its west side and the boundary wall to the east. Within the courtyard towards its west side a rectangular structure named as a "Dove House" is marked. The plan also shows the location, approximately 55ft to the west of the north-west corner of the late 18th-century library attached to the north end of the west range, of the excavated remains of the east end of the church or chapter house discovered in 1805.

Owing to the late date of the creation of the parish of Markyate, there are no tithe or inclosure maps of the parish and there appear to be no surviving estate maps. The house is, however, shown on the Caddington Inclosure map of 1798-1800,[33] which is really at too small a scale to be useful but confirms the basic lay-out depicted by Fisher.

Much more informative for our purposes are the ground- and first-floor plans of the remodelled house prepared by Robert Lugar for publication in his *Villa Architecture* (1828).[34] To a large extent these correspond with the internal arrangement of the house shown in the plan of 1926 referred to above, but there are several important differences. On the ground floor, the billiard room of 1926 is divided into two rooms, the west an entrance hall, measuring ten by fifteen foot aligned on the porch to the south front. The dining room of 1926 is also divided into two rooms, the west the servants' hall, the east the kitchen. In the north-east corner is the scullery with a large inglenook fireplace to its east wall, having a large bread oven and a copper to its south-east and north-east corners respectively. On the east side of the principal staircase, which occupies the same position as in 1926, a service corridor leads eastwards towards the Butler's pantry, which by 1926 along with the scullery had been transformed into a hall following the transfer of the entrance from the south to the north side of the house. On the first floor there are fewer differences between the two plans, the principal one being that the large bedroom No. Three on the south side of the house in 1926 consists of a bedroom and a dressing room to the west extending into the two-storey porch on Lugar's plan. Neither of the back stairs on the 1926 plan is shown by Lugar, although as discussed below, it is likely that the one at the eastern end of the long axial corridor existed by this date, albeit in a different form.

[25] Hertford Museum store, uncatalogued.
[26] H.R.O., D/Ecd F13.
[27] H.R.O., Gerish colln., Box 55; Bodl., MS. top. eccl. b. 28, fol.14.
[28] N.M.R., file 77,723.
[29] Hertfordshire Local Studies Library, Hertford, photographic colln.
[30] H.R.O., MARK/13.
[31] Bodl., MS. top. eccl. b.28, fol.14.
[32] B.L. Add. MS. 32,349, fol.5.
[33] Beds. R.O., A and MA 46.
[34] Lugar, op. et loc. cit. (note 19).

By the time of an undated map made in c.1877 the plan of the house had largely taken its present form,[35] which is also that shown (in relation to the now-demolished ranges) by A. Whitford Anderson in an unpublished plan of 1906 prepared for the *V.C.H.*[36]

DOCUMENTARY EVIDENCE

Apart from the Ministers' Accounts of 1536/37 and a valor of the demesne made shortly before the house left royal ownership,[37] neither of which gives any information on the buildings, the earliest post-Dissolution reference to Markyate is in March 1539 when it was leased to Humphrey Bourchier for 21 years.[38] Bourchier subsequently tried to buy the estate, but owing to his own onerous liabilities and the fraudulent activities of his kinsman, Sir Francis Bryan, to whom the purchase money was entrusted,[39] the transaction was not completed when Bourchier died heirless in 1540.[40] That he had already carried out some work to the house, however, is shown by Leland's contemporary description of the site: "Mergate was a nunnery of late tyme, it standith on an hil in a faire woode hard by Watheling (Watling) Streate on the est side of it. Humfray Boucher, base sunne to the late lorde Berners, did much coste in translating of the priorie into a maner-place: but he left it nothing endid."[41] In 1541 Bourchier's widow, Elizabeth, married George Ferrers, who was granted the manor in July 1548.[42] This grant contains no information on the buildings beyond the usual references to the "gardens, howses, scite and soil".

Ferrers died in 1579,[43] the estate passing to his son, Julius, and then in 1596 to his grandson, Sir John.[44] By 1630, at which time the house was still in possession of the Ferrers family, a deed refers to it as "known by the name or names of Markeyate Cell, or the house and scite of the late monastery or Priory of Markeyate...And all houses, dovehouses, edifices, buildings, barnes, stables, yardes, gardens, orchards, backsydes, and other the appurtenances to the same Capitall Messuage or mansion place..."[45]

The house seems to have been ignored by all antiquaries after Leland until the early 19th century when it was noticed by Clutterbuck, who wrote "The mansion-house, disencumbered from large gloomy yews and a blockading terrace, now forms an interesting object from the public road. Under the terrace were discovered some remains of the original Cell, which have been preserved by the

drawings of Mr Fisher,"[46] while to the information discussed above a later account in *The Gentleman's Magazine* adds only that "the three upper stories (of the house) were...probably of the age of Charles I."[47]

Later surveys, including those by the *V.C.H.* and the *R.C.H.M.* have been used in compiling the description of the existing building, but it is worth correcting here some of the erroneous information given in other sources and adding those details which have not already been mentioned. For instance, Cussans, writing in the late 1870s, states that "The priory appears to have been rebuilt at the time of Henry VIII and some substantial remains of the pre-Reformation edifice exist in the scullery and kitchen of the present mansion. About 40 years ago an iron door was found some 10 or 12 feet up the kitchen chimney. On opening the door a stone staircase was discovered, leading to a small chamber on the ground level. The doorway was built up, but the hiding place and stairs still remain". In a footnote he adds that "The late Mr Adey, who pulled down a large portion of the old building after the fire of 1840, determined to re-open the doorway...On opening the doorway, a narrow stone staircase was found. At the top was a stout oak door, which was broken down, but it afterwards appeared that it might have been opened by pressing a concealed spring. Nothing was found in the room but innumerable bats, which had gained an entrance through a small opening in the wall".

Cussans also seems to have been the originator of the apparently unsubstantiated story, repeated by the *V.C.H.* and the *R.C.H.M.*, that "Three times during as many centuries the mansion has been destroyed by fire. The last time was in 1840. It was then rebuilt on a smaller scale and the present house contains 36 fewer rooms than its predecessor, though it still retains the fair proportions of a country gentleman's residence. The cemetery was on the north side of the present mansion as appears by the number of stone coffins and human bones which have been found there".[48] Although Cussans is correct in saying that the rebuilt house was much smaller than the previous one, he is probably confusing the supposed rebuilding of 1840 (to which there is no earlier reference) with Lugar's remodelling of the house for Daniel Goodison Adey in 1825-26.

INTERPRETATION AND CONCLUSIONS

The building history of Markyate Cell is particularly long and complex, stretching from the 1540s to the 1920s. The complicated nature of this evolution and the fact that it is not possible to ascribe distinct elements of the building to any one period means that it is necessary to understand fully how the various periods interact before attempting to

[35] H.R.O., D/P 38A 3/4.
[36] See note 25.
[37] P.R.O., SC6 Hen. VIII/8 m.9; E 315/402, fols.1-12.
[38] See note 3.
[39] W. Brigg (ed.), *Herts. Genealogist & Antiquary*, iii (1899), 108-9.
[40] Ibid; P.R.O., PCC Alenger 16.
[41] Toulmin Smith, i, 104.
[42] See note 4.
[43] P.R.O., C 142/186/2.
[44] *V.C.H.*, ii, 190.
[45] H.R.O., D/E Ay T.2, bdle.1, no.1.

[46] Clutterbuck, i, 348.
[47] *Gents. Mag.*, op. cit. (note 6), 469.
[48] Cussans, iii, pt.1, 115.

reconstruct the appearance of the house in the second half of the 16th century.

The earliest surviving work is the short wing in chequered stone and flint at the north-east end of the house. This appears to have been a service block at right-angles to the main south range, and is shown in what is likely to be basically its original form in Fisher's 1805 north-east view of the house. As discussed above, this range is shown in rather different form by G. Buckler in 1839 which raises some interesting points. The details which Buckler shows of this and adjoining ranges look like genuine 16th-century work, but a comparison with Fisher's apparently accurate drawing shows that this cannot be the case. Although this might be readily apparent from a site inspection, this would not necessarily be the case. Totternhoe clunch stone is notorious for its friability and poor weathering qualities and, as at Ashridge, masonry of the 1820s or '30s could easily be mistaken for late medieval or Tudor work. The architectural context makes this far less of a problem at Ashridge, but at Markyate it might be quite easy falsely to identify 19th-century Gothic masonry as medieval.

This certainly seems to have been the case with the *V.C.H.*'s description of the two-light scullery window, shown as a four-light window in the Fisher drawing, although the *V.C.H.* does acknowledge that the eastern wall of this range had been rebuilt and a chimney added c.1840 (*sic*).[49] Of this chimney only a fragment now survives as the blind pedimented gable on the east front of the house. Comparison between the Fisher and Buckler drawings also shows that the majority of the other windows on the north and east elevations of the house, while 16th century in style, are in fact work of the first half of the 19th century. On the north side of the house the massive chimney between the second and third gabled ranges from the east, which themselves have changed dramatically in shape since Fisher's drawing, also dates to this period. It appears that only the massive end stack to the east gable of the south range with its reputed secret chamber (more likely a garderobe) is genuine old work, although even here the brick triple shafts appear to be 19th century.

Moving round to the south elevation, it appears that the lower range contains some 16th-century fabric, although here too there have been many alterations. Fisher's 1805 drawing of the south front shows it as a five-bay three-storey range with gabled attics, the ground-floor stage being of rubblestone and the upper floors of brick. At this time there was no lower range but it is interesting to note that Fisher's north-east view of the house shows a former steep-pitched roof line to the end wall of the south range. It therefore seems that the east end of the south range had been raised in height before the time of Fisher's drawing, probably as early as the mid 17th century (which seems the most likely date for the five gabled bays), and then reduced to something like its original height and appearance as part

of Lugar's 19th-century remodelling. In this connection it is worth remarking that, although the *V.C.H.* and the *R.C.H.M.* appear to treat the five-light former kitchen window as 16th-century work, the present windows in the lower range are much more similar to those in Lugar's and Buckler's drawings than Fisher's. This tends to suggest that the original work in the lower range is confined to the rubblestone fabric on the ground floor and perhaps the brickwork on the first, with sections of two pilasters surviving. Nevertheless, as explained above, the basic form of the lower range may well be similar to the 16th-century original.

If the lower range represents the lower part of the two eastern bays of the mid 17th-century five-bay south range and its 16th-century predecessor, it seems quite conceivable that the three western bays are represented by the three-bay south range of Lugar's compact house. In the absence of a site inspection, however, this must remain conjectural. Certainly any early fabric has been completely concealed externally but the length of the south front, including the lower range, makes the suggestion entirely feasible.

J.T. Smith has suggested that the former west range was added before c.1600,[50] although his evidence for doing so is not altogether clear. Fisher's north-east view of the house strongly suggests that the long west range shown by Oldfield and others was merely an 18th-century refronting, not least from his depiction of the two large external stacks to its back wall and the hoodmoulds to its windows, but other than the likelihood that the Ferrers family who held the property from 1548 until the 1640s are likely to have carried out some work to the house, there seems no conclusive architectural reason why this range, like the remodelled south range, cannot belong to the mid 17th century rather than any earlier.

Citing Aston Bury as his model, Smith also believes that the mid 17th-century remodelling, which was probably carried out for Thomas Coppin after 1657,[51] also involved the provision of two staircase towers to the rear of the house. It is these which appear as the centre and west gables in Fisher's north-east view of the house, the apparently irregular fenestration pattern being the result of windows lighting the staircases. Both staircase projections can clearly be identified in Lugar's plan and the 1926 plan and the western staircase, although remade by Lugar, still occupies its original position. The most likely candidate for refronting the west range is John Coppin, who built the chapel in the park in 1734,[52] while the addition of the single-storey library to the north end of the west range, probably for Revd. John Pittman Coppin before 1794,[53] completes the pre-19th-century building history.

[49] *V.C.H.*, ii, 190.

[50] N.M.R., file 77,723.
[51] Ibid; Beds. R.O., GA 727.
[52] *Beds. Notes and Queries*, iii, 198.
[53] Clutterbuck, i, 347; D.O.E. List (note 7), 90.

Lugar's remodelling of the house has been adequately described above and it is evident that the house owes much of its present appearance to his hand. Of later work, it only needs to be said that the west link on the north side of the house was remade in its present form as a drawing room by the then owner, a Mr McLeod, between 1910 and 1916, and that further extensive alterations were carried out for Sir John Pennefather in the early 1920s.[54] Pennefather imported panelling and other features, blocked the doorway to the two-storey porch on the south elevation and, as part of his reordering of the rear courtyard, moved the entrance to the north side. C.1925 he moved to Eastwell Park (Kent), which he rebuilt in imitation of Markyate Cell, re-using several fittings including panelling and a carved overmantel (which may have been late 16th century or early 17th century and original to the house) from Markyate at Eastwell.[55] Relatively little work seems to have been undertaken by the next owner, E.A. Sursham, who took possession in 1928 (although the plan showing alterations for him is dated 1926) and who lived at the house until the mid 1980s. It is not known what alterations may have been carried out by the present owner, Mr J. Armstrong.

It is very difficult to reconstruct the form of the 16th-century house, but it is clear that it bore no relation to the former conventual buildings. The discovery in 1805 of what was almost certainly the east end of the church or chapter house some 40ft to the west of the terrace to the north of the present house indicates that the claustral buildings must also have lain at some distance to the west. The alterations to the windows of the surviving 16th-century work make it impossible to attribute a more precise date to this part of the house and it is just conceivable that it could pre-date the Dissolution. If this were the case, the only likely candidate for such a building would be a detached superior's lodging, although the considerable distance from the rest of the monastic buildings and the community's relative poverty and small size immediately before the suppression (what is known of the building's architectural details would not allow an earlier date) make this inherently unlikely.[56]

It seems then that Bourchier made the decision to start afresh on a new site higher up the hill side, although he would doubtless have made use of materials from the former monastic buildings. The east wall of the present building does in fact incorporate much 13th-century moulded stonework in its fabric, although it seems likely that much of this was only re-used during the remodelling of the east range in the 19th century, quite possibly as Sursham suggests,[57] following the discovery of the east end of the church or chapter house in 1805.

This still leaves the problem of reconstructing the appearance of Bourchier's house, but it can be assumed to have comprised a long hall range aligned roughly east-west with cross-wings projecting to the north. The eastern of these may have formed a service range, the massive projection to the base of the external lateral stack possibly housing a garderobe,[58] while the staircase may have been at the northern end of the west cross-wing. The hall range may have been heated by a large stack on the north wall, of which there is still some suggestion on Lugar's plan. Some material from the former nunnery was almost certainly re-used in the house, including a beam in the old kitchen on the end of which a shield was carved, surviving to be illustrated by Fisher in 1805.[59] The flint and stone chequerwork pattern on the north wall of the east range may also be re-used material, although as noted above its continuation on to the east wall of the same range is more likely to be the result of 19th-century remodelling. The *V.C.H.* remarks that, although chequerwork-patterned walling is found in 14th- and 15th-century buildings such as the churches of Abbots Langley, Puttenham and Redbourn, it was also used in later buildings as at Berkhamsted Place (c.1580) or Oxhey Chapel, erected as late as 1612.[60]

As the 1805 Fisher drawing of the south front appears to show that the principal rooms were at an upper level above an undercroft or semi-basement, Smith suggests that the main entrance to the mid 16th-century house was on this side, probably approached by a flight of steps. Just such an arrangement seems to have been followed at the slightly earlier Wyddial Hall, although there the hall range was initially open to the roof,[61] whereas at Markyate it was almost certainly of two storeys from the start.

The apparent difference of levels between the south and west ranges seems to be the main reason why Smith suggests that the latter was an addition, probably of the late 16th or early 17th century. Fisher's north-east view of the house shows a first-floor window to the rear of this wing as rather taller than the one below it, suggesting that the principal rooms were on the same level as those of the building to which it was added. If this were so, the entrance may have remained on the south side at this time. The one storey and attic range with the timber framed east gable was probably added to the north-east corner of the west range shortly afterwards.

The next major transformation of the house occurred in the mid 17th century when Thomas Coppin recased in brick all of the south front except the semi-basement or undercroft and probably added the five gables. The provision of staircase towers to either side of the stack to the rear of the hall range was also carried out as part of this work and Smith suggests that, as the Fisher drawing of the south

[54] N.M.R., file 77,723.
[55] Ibid, inf. P.M. Reid.
[56] For an illustration of the house's poverty shortly before the Dissolution, see A. Hamilton Thompson (ed.), *Visitations in the Diocese of Lincoln, 1517-31*, Lincs. Rec. Soc., 37 (1947), 15.
[57] N.M.R., file 77,723.
[58] Ibid.
[59] H.R.O., Knowsley Clutterbuck, iii, 348d.
[60] *V.C.H.*, ii, 190.
[61] Smith (1992), 1-4.

front shows no sign of a 17th-century doorway to this elevation (any previous doorway presumably being removed as part of the recasing), Coppin probably added a two-storey porch to the north-west corner of the west wing. The porch itself was later incorporated in the west wing of c.1734 but the entrance remained on the same axis, as is shown by the position of the porch in Oldfield's south-west view of the house. The suggestion that the porch was incorporated into the 18th-century wing would account for its being more than one room deep, the late 16th- or 17th-century range being doubled in width to the west at this time.

It remains only to examine the lives and careers of the men who carried out the immediate post-Dissolution phases of work at Markyate and, so far as it is possible, to examine their motives for doing so. Little is known of Humphrey Bourchier. Leland describes him as the base (illegitimate) son of the second Lord Berners,[62] who had translated Froissart's *Chronicles* and was Deputy of Calais until his death in 1533.[63] Bourchier was a member of the king's household,[64] but it is not known what position he held when he died childless in 1540, with his work on the house "nothing endid".

His widow, Elizabeth married George Ferrers in the following year but it was not until 1548 that the site was granted to him.[65] During the intervening period, although Elizabeth may have continued to live here, the property presumably remained in crown hands (Bourchier's attempts to buy it having failed), but the absence of any reference to it in the accounts of the surveyor of the king's works suggests little or nothing was done to the house during this period. Ferrers was from a Hertfordshire family and came to prominence in 1534 when he published an English translation of Magna Carta.[66] As a lawyer he was renowned for his oratory and in 1542 became M.P. for Plymouth. Although he is said to have taken part in the war against France, he most probably advised the king on legal matters, for which he was rewarded with a bequest of 100 marks in Henry's will.[67] Ferrers continued to serve the crown during the reigns of Edward VI and Mary, assisting in the suppression of Wyatt's rebellion in 1554,[68] and in 1567 he held the office of escheator for Hertfordshire and Essex.[69] Ferrers died in 1579,[70] the property passing to his son, Julius and then in 1596 to his grandson, Sir John, who died as late as 1640.[71]

There is no reason to disbelieve Leland's statement concerning Bourchier's work at Markyate, while the building evidence is equally consistent with the second phase being carried out by any of the three members of the Ferrers family referred to above. Why Bourchier chose to build on a new site rather than utilise the remains of the conventual buildings is not clear. There is no evidence relating to the condition of the buildings at the time of the Dissolution and it may simply be that Bourchier and his successors thought a site further up the hillside away from the river to be more imposing and, therefore, fitting for the status of the new mansion.

Bibliography

PICTORIAL SOURCES

Hertfordshire Record Office

Buckler Drawings, IV, 18-20.

Oldfield Drawings, IV, 502.

Knowsley Clutterbuck, iii, 346d, 348d.

D/EX 55 Z 2/84.

D/Ecd F13.

British Library, London

Add. MS. 32,349, fols.1-2, 4-6.

Victoria and Albert Museum, London

Dept. of Prints and Drawings, Pressmark 93 A9.

Bodleian Library, Oxford

MS. top. gen a. 12, fol.90.

Hertford Museum Store

Original Drawings by A. Whitford Anderson (1906) for *V.C.H.*

Printed

Gentleman's Magazine, n.s., 26 (1846), opp. p.467.

Lugar, R., *Villa Architecture* (1828), pl.40.

PHOTOGRAPHIC SOURCES

Hertfordshire Record Office

D/Z 59 Z1.

[62] Toulmin Smith, i, 104.
[63] *D.N.B.*, ii, 920-22.
[64] *L.P.*, xiv (1), p.610.
[65] *Cal. Pat. R., Edw. VI, 1547-48*, 314-15.
[66] J. Bale, *Index Britanniae Scriptorum*, (ed., R.L. Poole, 1902), 83.
[67] S.T. Bindoff (ed.), *The History of Parliament: The House of Commons 1509-1558*, ii (1982), 130.
[68] B.L., Harl. MS. 425, p.94.
[69] P.W. Hasler (ed.), *The History of Parliament: The House of Commons 1558-1603*, ii (1981), 113.
[70] P.R.O., C 142/186/2.
[71] *V.C.H.*, ii, 190.

MARK/13.

Gerish Collection, Box 55.

Hertfordshire Local Studies Library, Hertford

Photographic Collection.

Bodleian Library, Oxford

MS. top. eccl. b. 28, fol.14.

National Monuments Record, The Royal Commission on Historical Monuments, Swindon

Red Boxes.

File 77,723.

CARTOGRAPHIC SOURCES

Bedfordshire Record Office

A & MA 46.

Hertfordshire Record Office

D/P 38A 3/4.

OTHER PRIMARY SOURCES

Manuscript:-

Public Record Office, London

SC6 Hen. VIII/8 m.9.

E 315/402, fols.1-12.

PCC Alenger 16.

C 142/186/2.

Bedfordshire Record Office

GA 727.

Hertfordshire Record Office

D/E Ay T.2, bdle.1, no.1.

British Library, London

Harl. MS. 425, p.94; 7389, p.34.

Printed:-

Calendar of Patent Rolls Preserved in the Public Record Office (1903- (in progress).

Dugdale, W., *Monasticon Anglicanum*, (re-ed. Caley, J., Ellis, H. & Bandinel, B., 6 vols. in 8, 1817-30).

Gibbs, M. (ed.), *Early Charters of the Cathedral Church of St Paul, London*, Camden Soc., 3rd series, 58 (1939).

Hamilton Thompson, A. (ed.), *Visitations in the Diocese of Lincoln, 1517-31*, Lincs. Rec. Soc., 37 (1947).

Letters and Papers, Foreign and Domestic of the Reign of Henry VIII, eds. Brewer, J.S., Gairdner, J. & Brodie, R.H., 21 vols. (1862-1932).

Riley, H.T. (ed.), *Gesta Abbatum Monasterii Sancti Albani, i, 793-1290* (1867).

Toulmin Smith, L. (ed.), *The Itinerary of John Leland in or about the Years 1535-43*, i (1906).

SECONDARY SOURCES

Bale, J., *Index Britanniae Scriptorum*, (ed. Poole, R.L., Oxford, 1902).

Beds. Notes and Queries, iii, 198.

Bindoff, S.T. (ed.), *The History of Parliament: The House of Commons 1509-1558*, ii (1982).

Brigg, W. (ed.), *Herts. Genealogist & Antiquary*, iii (1899), 108-9.

Clutterbuck, R., *The History and Antiquities of Hertfordshire*, i (1815).

Coleman, S., *Caddington and Kensworth*, Bedfordshire Parish Surveys, 4 (Bedford, 1985).

Cussans, J.E., *The History of Hertfordshire*, iii, pt.1 (1870, reprinted Wakefield 1972).

Department of the Environment 34th List of Buildings of Special Architectural or Historic Interest, the Borough of Dacorum.

Dictionary of National Biography, 22 vols. (revd. edn., Oxford 1921/2).

Gentleman's Magazine, n.s., 26 (1846), 469-70.

Hasler, P.W. (ed.), *The History of Parliament: The House of Commons 1558-1603*, ii (1981).

Royal Commission on Historical Monuments, *An Inventory of the Historical Monuments of Hertfordshire* (1910).

Smith, J.T., *English Houses 1200-1800: the Hertfordshire Evidence* (1992).

The Victoria History of the Counties of England, Hertfordshire, ii (1908).

ROYSTON PRIORY

History

Augustinian house founded before 1179 by Ralph de Rochester.[1] Dissolved in 1537,[2] it was then leased to Robert Chester.[3] Chester obtained a new lease in May 1539 and in 1540 was granted the site.[4] The property remained in the Chester family until 1759 when it was sold to Thomas Plumer Byde of Ware Park.[5]

THE BUILDINGS

Introduction

The priory church, which since the Dissolution has served as Royston's parish church, stands near the middle of the town on the south side of Melbourn Street, the principal east-west thoroughfare. Immediately to the south-west is Priory House, a large red brick house, possibly occupying the site of the west range of the former claustral buildings, facing Fish Hill on its west side. The site is most conveniently described under two headings- the church and Priory House.

Description

The nave and aisles of the present **church** are the choir, choir aisles and chancel of the 13th-century monastic church. The west tower was once central and the wall which runs westwards from this on the same line as the south wall of the present nave aisle is probably the south wall of the former south aisle to the monastic nave. The existing chancel is a late Victorian addition. The church was substantially restored in the 19th century and refaced in flint with ashlar dressings and parapets, except for the two centre bays to the north aisle which are entirely of (restored) ashlar. There is a copper roof to the nave and lead roofs to the chancel, aisles and north vestry.

The much restored **tower** is rectangular in shape and of three stages with chamfered string courses and stepped angle buttresses; 19th-century embattled parapet with crocketed corner pinnacles. The belfry stage has three Victorian lancets to the east and west faces and two on the north and south, all with continuous hoodmoulding. The second stage has a clock on the north face and a quatrefoil window in a square surround to the west but is blank on its less restored south side. The three-light Victorian west window breaks through the string course to the first stage and below is a triple-gabled entrance porch (erected in 1891), now with late 20th-century glass doors to the centre. There is a late 19th-century window to the first stage on the north side and the flat-roofed vestry to the south was added

c.1927.[6]

Of the **nave** only the clerestory is visible externally, indicated by a two-light Victorian window to the east on the north side and a probably late 16th-century three-light window to the west on the south. The coped east gable with foliated cross is Victorian. **North aisle**. This is in four bays with stepped buttresses, including a diagonal buttress to the north-east corner, the buttress between the two eastern bays carried up to form an ashlar-faced chimney. The west wall is much restored and has a pointed Victorian doorway with a square-headed window above. To the north wall the east and west bays have 19th-century two-light Decorated-style windows. Of the two centre bays, the eastern has a two-light Decorated-style window with an ornate ogee-arched canopy and is flanked by similar traceried slate slabs with inscriptions to members of the Beldam family. The bay to the west has a similar window directly adjoining the buttress to its left, while immediately to the west of this window is a large, elaborately carved 18th-century wall monument with broken scrolled pediment, again commemorating members of the Beldam family. Late 19th-century east window in three lights.

South aisle. The medieval aisle was the same length as the north aisle but was increased by two bays to the east in 1891.[7] The medieval section is now divided into four unequal bays by later or rebuilt buttresses. At the south-west corner there is no buttress on the south side, although there is a slender buttress (rebuilt in the late 19th century) to the west wall, which also has a two-light Victorian window. On the south wall the first buttress from the west may be of medieval origin, although it has been widened to form the present massive, stepped buttress in 18th-century red brick. There is an infilled, narrow, pointed brick arch-way in the east face of this buttress. The next buttress to the east is much narrower and appears to have been rebuilt in the late 19th century. To the east again is a wide, stepped red brick buttress and the junction between the medieval aisle and the Victorian extension is marked by a 19th-century narrow, stepped buttress. All the windows in the original aisle are Victorian, those to the east and west bays with Decorated tracery in two lights. The two windows to the centre bays, separated only by the slender, rebuilt buttress, are broad lancets remodelled in 1859-61.[8] Immediately to the east of these is a blocked, small, pointed doorway. The eastern extension of the aisle is in two bays with two-light Decorated-style windows flanking a narrow, pointed doorway. The east wall has a diagonal, stepped buttress and a three-light Decorated-style window.

Returning to the north side of the church, the north wall of the medieval chancel, the eastern part of which formed the short post-Dissolution chancel, is visible to the west of the

[1] Knowles (1953), 151; *V.C.H.*, iv, 436.
[2] P.R.O., SC6/Hen. VIII/1606, m.1d; *L.P.*, xiii (1), no.571.
[3] P.R.O., SC6/Hen. VIII/1607.
[4] *L.P.*, xiv (1), p.606; *L.P.*, xvi, g.379 (60).
[5] Clutterbuck, iii, 561.

[6] H.R.O., D/P 87 6/15.
[7] H.R.O., D/P 87 6/13; DSA 2/1/282.
[8] H.R.O., Gerish colln., Box 64; A. Kingston, *A History of Royston* (1906), 186.

1891 chancel. The wall contains a tall 13th-century lancet, the only medieval window (albeit restored) still visible externally. There are also traces of a blocked opening immediately to the east of this, a section of cill at a lower level than the cill of the lancet just being apparent. The flintwork in this section of wall has a less restored appearance than elsewhere in the church. To the east are the gabled **vestry** and **organ chamber** of 1891 and the east wall of the contemporary **chancel** has angle buttresses, triple lancets and a Celtic cross to the gable. There are two identical lancets in the north wall.

Adjoining the south-west corner of the present south aisle is a high wall which forms the boundary between the churchyard and The Priory (see below). The easternmost part of this wall is concealed on its northern face by the c.1927 vestry. To the west, however, the fabric is visible, principally being of roughly coursed clunch with some flint and brick, the upper part of the wall having been rebuilt in the latter material. The wall contains several fragments of carved and moulded stonework, including a carved cross-bones which is probably from a post-medieval funerary monument, suggesting that, although the wall is on the line of the south aisle wall of the monastic nave, it has been at least partly rebuilt. The eastern section of wall contains the right jamb of a large opening which ran at right-angles to the wall with to the right at ground level the remains of a tomb recess. Both these features appear to be *in situ*. The south side of the wall was much obscured by vegetation at the time of site inspection (February 1992) but, although it contains some flint, it is mainly of red brick construction in a combination of mixed and header bonds. A small section has been rebuilt in 20th-century brick, probably where a modern structure formerly abutted.

Interior. The architectural development of the church is more readily apparent internally. The present four-bay nave is principally the choir of the monastic church, the rood screen or pulpitum having stood one bay to the east of the tower arch, and the monastic chancel beginning to the east of the third column from the west. Judging from the details of the remains of the lancets in the north and south walls and the original moulded capitals of the arcades, the choir and chancel seem to date to between c.1250 and 1260. The north and south choir aisles were probably originally of only three bays, the easternmost bay on each side having been added in the 14th century. That the westernmost bays of the aisles were possibly earlier than the remainder is shown by the mouldings (c.1220-50) of the western arch on the south side, although there is some evidence to suggest that this has been rebuilt (see below). This arch abuts the tower indicating that this face of the tower is also likely to be of primary construction, although the rest was probably rebuilt in the late 16th or early 17th century.

Virtually every capital to the arcades is different. Beginning on the north side, the west respond of the west arch has a capital (A) with egg and dart moulding to the impost (cut away on the south side, probably for a screen)

above a half-octagonal pillar. The single-chamfered pointed arch which springs from this respond is post-medieval. This must also be the date of the west half of the capital (B) into which the arch dies. Again this has egg and dart moulding but the eastern half is deeply moulded in a style consistent with a date of c.1250. The pillar on which the capital rests is octagonal and the arch, like all those in the north arcade, is steeply pointed and single chamfered. The central column of the north arcade is clustered with four half-round shafts and smaller intermediate rolls. The capital (C) is richly moulded and appears to be of c.1250. The capital (D) to the next octagonal pillar has the same moulding as the east half of capital B. The same moulding appears on the capital (E) of the half-octagonal east respond of the arcade, but here the carving looks crisper and is probably Victorian. There is foliage carving to its south-east corner.

The capital (F) of the west respond of the south arcade has very similar moulding to capital C, except that it is not quite so elaborate and the moulding does not run around the top of the clustered respond beneath. The capital supports a low, almost semi-circular arch which has undercut pointed rolls and a moulded label. The base of the respond is also moulded. The arch dies into a very similar capital (G) on its eastern side, the respond below being almost identical to that to the west except that it has no moulded base. There is then a short section of walling in which the position of the entrance to the rood loft, discovered in 1859,[9] is just visible under the plaster. The east respond to this section of wall is very close in style to that beneath capital C, except that the moulding to the capital (H) is heavier and probably the result of Victorian restoration, while the clustered respond itself has pointed rolls. From the respond springs a richly moulded, pointed arch of two orders, the outer of a hollow in a chamfer and the inner of two hollow chamfers. The east end of the arch rests on a clustered column with capital (I), identical to H, except that the column has a moulded plinth and the whole is 19th-century work. The next arch, respond and capital (J) to the east are identical to I (again recut). A short section of wall to the east denotes the former presence of a screen to north and south. On the east side of this section of wall is a half-octagonal respond with capital (K) like I and J. This marks the position of the north-east corner of the south aisle before it was extended to the east in the 14th century. The two-bay arcade to the east of this respond must post-date the remains of the 13th-century lancets above as it cuts these, but the stonework of only the western arch is old. This is pointed with a plain label and is of two orders, the outer of one hollow in a chamfer and the inner of two. The central octagonal column with its capital and the eastern respond, like the eastern arch itself, are Victorian.

[9] H.R.O., Gerish colln., Box 64; T. Milbourn, 'Notes on the history of Royston', *Proceedings of the Evening Meetings of the London & Middx. & Surrey Arch. Socs.* (n.d. but paper read in 1874), 224, 278; H. Fowler, 'Church of St. John the Baptist, Royston', *Trans. St. Albans Archit. & Arch. Soc.*, no vol. no. (1884), 16.

As the arches of the two-bay arcade are lower than those of the 13th-century aisle, enough remains of the three lancets above to reconstruct the original form of these windows. There are clustered shafts with rolls and finely moulded capitals in the splayed jambs and the richly moulded arches have dogtooth ornament. The two easternmost windows are blocked but the western one is open above the intrusive 14th-century arch. There were originally three corresponding lancets on the north wall but only the eastern of these now survives, the other two having been destroyed by the 18th-century east bay of the north arcade except for a tiny fragment of the centre window. The surviving window has been restored to its presumed original appearance and has shaft-rings to its clustered shafts with rolls between. The present chancel arch is just to the east of the lancets. It is steeply pointed with moulded responds and, like everything to the east of this point, dates to 1891.

In the third bay from the west in the north aisle is an infilled 14th-century arch-way which cuts across an eaves cornice. This arch was probably one of two leading into a two-bay north chapel, the jambs of the arch-way having clustered shafts, rolls and moulded capitals, although the foliage carving to the bases of the jambs looks Victorian. The capital of the west jamb seems to belong to a detached pier rather than to a respond, seeming to indicate the former presence of another arch to the west. The surviving arch is in two orders, the inner hollow chamfered and the outer with undercut rolls, surmounted by a plain hoodmould terminating in a label-stop carved as a king's head to the east. The wide tower arch with its pointed segmental head was probably rebuilt in the late 16th century. The jambs have crudely moulded capitals of this date but the arch incorporates re-used stonework, similar in section to that of the 14th-century arch-way which cuts the lancets in the south wall of the present nave. The shallow-pitched nave roof with moulded principals and carved bosses is probably late 15th or early 16th century. The south aisle has a plain trussed lean-to roof with short principals supported on carved stone face corbels. There are three wingless angels holding shields to the wall-plate and carved bosses at the intersections between the moulded main rafters and the longitudinal member. There has been some resetting of the timberwork to both the east and west ends of the aisle. The north aisle roof is probably also of 15th-century origin but is plainer, without corbels or bosses, and has been much reconstructed.

Fittings and Furnishings. Various fittings and furnishings survive from the pre-Dissolution church, although not many in their original form or location. The 13th-century piscina has been reset in the south wall of the present chancel and sections of the elaborately traceried 15th-century former rood screen have been used in the making of two prayer desks. Fragments of the screen have also been incorporated in the pulpit, the stone base of which is made up from a panelled tomb chest. All of these fittings were assembled in the 19th century.

The font at the west end of the nave was in the garden of a house to the north-east of Royston Palace in the early 20th century.[10] It consists of an octagonal basin (probably 13th century) on a 15th-century panelled pedestal with blank shields to the base. The 15th-century stained glass traceried canopies in the second window from the west in the north aisle may be *in situ* but the 14th-century oval panels of angels below are reset. The *R.C.H.M.* states that the traceried and panelled former west door of the tower (now propped against the west wall of the north aisle) is made up from screens,[11] although there is no direct evidence to show this.

There is a Jacobean altar table in the present chancel and reset early 17th-century panelling, elaborately carved with fluted, foliage and geometrical patterns on the ground-floor stage of the tower, above which is a Victorian gallery. Two headless medieval alabaster statues, now on the cills of the north and south windows of the present sanctuary, represent respectively the Virgin and Child, the latter holding a bird in his left hand, and a bishop with his pastoral staff broken away. They are 15th century in date and were found, along "with a large quantity of human bones regularly piled up", during repairs to "the middle of the south wall" of the church in 1823.[12] There is no positive evidence to support the idea that the statue of the bishop is Thomas Becket,[13] one of the former patron saints of the church.

Monuments. Only those dating to before 1600 are listed here. In a recess in the south wall of the chancel is the reset alabaster effigy (c.1415) of a knight in plate armour and surcoat with two angels by his head. A stone slab underneath the communion table has a long brass cross on a stepped base, incised with a bleeding heart and the other four wounds of the passion. This is probably 15th century. In the nave are brasses to an unidentified man and woman (c.1500) with an indent for another woman, and the half-figure of a priest in hood and tippet under a crocketed and cusped canopy representing William Tabram, rector of Therfield, d.1462. The east wall of the north aisle has three brass inscriptions commemorating William Chamber (d.1546), Robert White, prior of Royston (d.1534) and a plate of c.1500 with a verse in English but neither name nor date.

Priory House

This stands to the south of the former south nave aisle of the monastic church. It is aligned roughly north-south and is now divided into three separate dwellings. The principal building materials are red brick with plain tile and slate roofs. The basic plan consists of a long main block with projecting wings at right-angles to the east at each end.

---

[10] *R.C.H.M.*, 174.

[11] Ibid.

[12] J. Warren, Appendix to *Origines Roystonianae* (1825), 33-4.

[13] Kingston, op. cit (note 8), 87.

Behind the main block is a two-storey lean-to fronting Fish Hill.

East elevation. This is the entrance front and is of two storeys and attic with a late 19th-century machine tile roof. The south section of the main range is roughcast and has a two-light casement with glazing bars and overlight on the first floor to the left. There is a similar window to the right but this has paired eight-paned sashes. Below the left first-floor window is a window opening which has been cut down and narrowed to form a 20th-century glazed door. To the right of this is a 19th-century two-light casement with transom and two top-opening vents, below which the brick plinth has a straight joint in line with the left jamb, while to the right again is a narrow larder window. Immediately to the right of the larder window is a line of alternating chamfered quoins, presumably marking a break in building.

The centre section of this range is rendered including the plinth. There are prominent late 19th-century two-storey canted brick bays with stone coping to each side of the 20th-century pedimented centre section, which has a wide stone Doric portico. The walling of the left bay projection is thicker, although the external brickwork and the plate-glass sash windows (like those to the right bay) are Victorian. To the left of the left bay is a plain sash window directly beneath the eaves and the render has incised lines to resemble ashlar. Underneath the portico is a 20th-century six-panel door flanked by contemporary side-hung casements. Above is a 16-paned sash window with plain pilasters supporting the pediment. To the right of the right bay are narrow 20th-century windows on each floor and the range terminates in alternating chamfered quoins. There is a tall red brick ridge stack to the far left of the range, immediately to the right of the hipped junction with the left projecting range.

This is entirely Victorian in character, the part projecting from the main range being a late 19th-century addition. It is built in Flemish bond with vitrified headers (some of which are paired) and has cross casements with gauged heads and stone cills on each floor to the front. Timber bargeboards to the gable with a vertical strut from the apex to the collar carried down as a pendant below the collar. The right return has a similar window in the angle with the main range to those on the front.

The north projecting range is also entirely late 19th century, constructed in Flemish bond with vitrified headers. The south wall has a half-glazed door to the left with an overlight under a gauged segmental head. The window above, with gauged segmental head, directly under the eaves is similar to those in the south projecting range. To the right is a 20th-century fictive timber-framed panel with four-light mullioned and transomed windows on each floor, the upper under a gable breaking the eaves. The east gable has similar fictive framing to a two-storey canted bay projection under a small, steep-pitched hipped roof. Six-light mullioned and transomed windows on each floor and

a small two-light casement lighting the attic above the bay projection. Projecting purlin ends and plain bargeboards with pendant. The north wall has a small external lateral stack to the west, on the right of which is a narrow 19th-century window on each floor. To the left of the stack are two four-paned sashes directly below the eaves and another sash window and a half-glazed door with margin lights and overlight in corresponding positions on the ground floor. All of the openings have gauged segmental heads. There is a prominent red brick ridge stack to this range, to the right of which is a rooflight. Weathervane at the junction with the roof of the main range.

South elevation. This comprises the south end of the main north-south range and the south wall of the south projecting range. The south-west corner has some apparently 17th-century red brickwork in mixed bond, which is separated by a straight joint in line with the left corner of the porch from the 19th-century brickwork to the right. This is a mixture of mixed and Flemish bonds, including some paired headers, suggesting that a substantial section of the south wall of the main range was rebuilt when the south projecting range was added in the 19th century. This elevation is of two storeys and attic, lit by a steeply pitched gabled dormer in the roof slope; old clay tile roof. The area of 17th-century brickwork has a wide eight-paned sash window on the first floor and a 16-paned sash directly below, both with segmental heads. Small narrow 20th-century window directly to the right of the first-floor window. The rebuilt section has a 20th-century lean-to porch to the left over an inner boarded door and two 20th-century segmental-headed casements on the first floor, the left carried down to form a door opening. On the ground floor is a segmental-headed 16-paned sash window. The 19th-century extension has an internal lateral stack to the left and to the right a 12-paned sash window with gauged segmental head above a 20th-century flat-roofed addition.

West (rear) elevation. This basically comprises a full-height catslide outshut with slate roof. There are three tall stacks in the roof slope, the left much more substantial than the other two, and a tall integral stack to the far right. The south section of the lean-to projects further than the remainder and has 17th-century brickwork similar to that on the south elevation, except where it has been replaced in 20th-century brick to the lower left. Two eight-paned sashes with timber lintels directly under the eaves to the left and a segmental-headed three-light casement to the lower left.

Immediately to the left of the lean-to projection, which has a narrow sash window in its north end wall is an eight-paned glazing bar sash with segmental head on the first floor of the main lean-to. This is directly above a 20th-century glazed metal door with overlight and gauged head. To the left of the door is a red brick boundary wall which runs at an oblique angle to the lean-to. It has a straight joint approximately to the centre, the section to the west consisting of 18th-century brick below and 19th-century brick above, the east section being 17th-century brick, predominantly in header bond.

The 17th-century brickwork continues to the ground floor of the lean-to to the north of the wall but the first floor is in 18th-century Flemish bond. There are eight-paned glazing bar sashes with segmental heads to left and right on the first floor and a round-headed sash window (lighting a staircase) to the centre with plain timber spandrels directly below the eaves. The ground floor has a twelve-paned sash window below the staircase window and eight-paned sashes beneath the other first-floor windows, all with segmental heads and set high in the wall.

There are two virtually flat-roofed dormers in the roof slope directly above the lean-to projection and three 19th-century rooflights immediately to the north of the left stack. To the left of the main two-storey lean-to, which has 17th-century brickwork to its north return on the ground floor, 17th-century brickwork is also present to the west wall of the north projecting range. This brickwork continues in a boundary wall which runs a short distance to the north, then returns to the west, before continuing once more to the north. This wall has a weatherboarded outbuilding with a plain tile roof abutting its south side.

Other features. Bordering Fish Hill immediately to the south-west of the house is an apparently 19th-century flint boundary wall with red brick coping and dressings, behind which are a series of 19th- and 20th-century outbuildings. Further to the south is another substantial section of brick and flint wall which runs at right-angles to the east of Fish Hill and then returns at right-angles to the south. A section of clustered column shaft lying by the main doorway to the north projecting range of the house may come from the church.

Interior. The house is now divided into three separate units and, apart from the roof space, is most conveniently described in three sections- South Priory (the south range), No.2 (the centre range) and No.3 (the north range). **No.3** has little of interest, being almost exclusively 19th century in date. The main ground-floor room has 18th-century-style panelling and cornice; six-panel doors throughout. The inserted staircase, which is at the extreme northern end of the centre range, cuts through a most elaborately moulded beam on a north-south axis, a section through which is exposed on the wall to the south of the staircase. The moulding is of roll and fillet type and is probably of late medieval date. The wall on the north side of the staircase has an exposed tie beam aligned east-west. This is roll moulded and, although the evidence for mortices is obscured, the presence of peg holes to the bottom suggests the former existence of a large mullion window beneath the tie beam. Above are three vertical posts which support a collar and in the angle by the window is a corner post, which probably represents the north-east angle of the building before the north projecting range was added.

No.2. The front door opens into a large hall, which has a substantial wall post to the left of the door with two sawn-off mortices for horizontal members. The north and south walls have 18th-century six-panel doors to rooms either side and the scar of a former staircase can be seen against the north wall; Victorian plaster cornice. Another six-panel door in the south corner of the west wall leads through into the two-storey lean-to behind. This has a corridor giving access to the present staircase, which is early 19th century with stick balusters (two to each tread), plain carved open string, moulded handrail and dumpy, turned bottom newel. The first floor has four-panel doors and a corridor to the two-storey lean-to. A scar on the south wall of the north bedroom could mark the continuation of the former staircase referred to above.

There is a large cellar running the full length of this range. It has brick walls and floor and three chamfered cross beams to the north, the ends of which are missing. To the south of these is a reinforced steel joist, at which point the floor steps up to the south, with two plain moulded cross beams to the south, the joists between which are either concealed or removed. It is not possible to ascribe a date to the cellar but it should be noted that it does not run under the two-storey lean-to to the west.

South Priory. The ground-floor room to the south of the large ridge stack at the south end of the long range has exposed close-studded posts above a brick plinth to the front (east) wall. The room to the west in the two-storey lean-to has a chamfered cross beam and exposed 20th-century joists replacing earlier joists, the former position of which are still visible in the cross beam. The close-studded framing is best preserved in the room to the north of the ridge stack, where there is also a chamfered spine beam supported on a carved bracket next to the rebuilt fireplace. 20th-century staircase to first floor. The room on the south side has had the attic floor above removed and is now open to the roof. Apart from the west wall, it is completely timber framed with light vertical studs, most of which are late 20th-century fictive work. Large chimney breast to ridge stack, to the north of which is a room with a boxed-in spine beam which runs southward to die into the chimney breast where it is supported by a corbel.

The two-storey lean-to section to the west has a bedroom to the south and a bathroom to the north. There is a north-south running wall with exposed light timber studding, some of which may be reset. A 20th-century staircase leads to the attic which is lit by the two dormers in the west roof slope. The former roof line is visible to the north of the chimney breast; two roof trusses consisting of principal rafters, collar and clasped purlins. The roof structure is also visible to the south of the stack where the former attic floor has been removed. Collar with position of former arch brace and four peg holes visible on the south side.

The rest of the roof structure of the long range is visible in the roof space of No.2, where a large part of a probably late 16th- or early 17th-century roof structure survives under a 19th-century roof structure. Starting at the south ridge stack above the attic ceiling of South Priory the original roof structure survives to the east plane under the raised 19th-century roof but is completely missing to the west slope, where it has been replaced by the common rafters and ridge piece of the two-storey lean-to.

To the north, at which point there is a drop in level, is a lath and plaster-covered collar and tie beam truss (A), which formerly had nine vertical struts between the horizontal members, only two of which remain; single clasped-purlins and straight windbraces to the north. Immediately to the north of this truss is a stud partition to the apex of the roof. The next truss to the north (B) has raking queen struts, single clasped-purlins and straight windbraces to the north. The next truss (C) repeats exactly the configuration of B and is closely followed by truss D, which was formerly closed with seven vertical studs from tie beam to collar and a king strut above the collar. The wattle and daub infill to this truss has now been partly removed. There is then a slight drop in level and the ridge piece, which has been absent from north of the stud partition immediately to the north of truss A, returns with a lath and plaster ceiling below. The next truss (E) is identical to truss D. Beyond this the roof space is plastered over and of the next truss (F), only the tie beam and a fragment of arch bracing supporting the truncated principal rafter on the east survives.

On a line with this truss access can be gained to the roof space of the two-storey lean-to, from which the wall-plate and very top of the original west wall of the long north-south range can be seen. The wall is of close-studded timber-framed construction like that of the east wall, visible on the ground floor of South Priory. There is a mixture of wattle and daub and red brick infill, the former material predominating. Directly underneath the wall-plate the tops of two two-light mullion windows are visible, one approximately on a line with truss E and the other at the extreme north end, near where the range terminates. Taking the roof trusses visible in South Priory into account, the roof structure of the north-south range appears to have been ten bays in length.

PICTORIAL EVIDENCE

The pictorial evidence for the **church** is extensive and is a useful aid to reconstructing its appearance before the various Victorian restorations. The earliest representation is a crude drawing, dated 23 November 1747, by William Cole to accompany his manuscript history, *Parochial Antiquities of Cambridgeshire*.[14] It shows the north side of the church: long continuous nave and chancel with a flat-pitched lead roof, the east end with stepped buttresses surmounted by pinnacles and a cross to the gable. The east

window has five round-headed lights above a transom and five below with a small doorway beneath the cill of the window. The north aisle with its flat-pitched lead roof stops short of the east end and has an east window of similar style to that in the chancel. The north wall is buttressed in four bays, the east bay having a window with two round-headed lights. The next bay has an infilled archway in which is a large window with two round-headed lights below a transom and more Gothic-looking tracery above. In the remaining bays are mullioned and transomed windows with three round-headed lights above and below the transom. The tower is in four stages with a stepped buttress visible to the north-west corner. There are corner pinnacles and what appears to be chequerwork flint patterning to the parapet. The rectangular shape of the tower is shown by three rectangular openings to the east face of the belfry and two on the north, below which are further windows to the first and second stages. West of the tower is a long, low gabled porch, which has a round-headed window in its north wall.

Oldfield's late 18th-century view, also of the north side of the church,[15] is probably a little more reliable. It shows a four-bay north aisle with stepped buttresses, diagonal to the corners. The square-headed window in the east bay has two trefoil-headed lights and the window in the next bay to the west has two rectangular lights below a transom, above which are four trefoil-headed lights with a quatrefoil above, the whole in a blocked arch-way. The next two bays have three-light mullioned and transomed windows, the upper lights being segmental pointed, the window in the second bay from the west having the pedimented Beldam memorial to its right. In front of both bays is a fenced-in area, probably marking the position of the Beldam vault. Again the tower is shown as rectangular in shape.

Although it shows no windows in the west bays nor the fenced-in area around the vault, the basic authenticity of Oldfield's view is confirmed by J.C. Buckler's pen and ink drawing of 1832 of the church from the north east.[16] This view also shows the east windows to both the north aisle and chancel, the former square headed with five segmental-arched lights under a segmental-pointed relieving arch, the latter of three lights under a pointed hoodmould. There is a slight break between the nave and chancel which is of one bay only and terminates in full-height, stepped diagonal buttresses, which by the later 19th century had been capped by pinnacles.[17] The rectangular tower has an additional rectangular opening directly below the north opening to the belfry's east face. From the south-east corner of the chancel there is a wall running south for a short distance, which then turns at right-angles to the east before disappearing from view.

Probably slightly earlier than Buckler's drawing is a

---

[14] B.L., Add. MS. 5820, fol.19v.

[15] H.R.O., Oldfield Drawings, V, 390.
[16] H.R.O., Buckler Drawings, I, 131.
[17] Hertfordshire Local Studies Library, photographic colln.

watercolour of the town by T. Athow.[18] This shows the church only incidentally and the building is viewed from the east. The drawing does not appear to be particularly accurate as it shows two crudely cusped windows in the side wall of the chancel (not shown in any of the more reliable representations) but it does include the plain corner obelisks to the tower, shown by both Oldfield and Buckler.

The north side of the church is also shown in a photograph taken before the restoration of 1872.[19] The tower is roughcast with plain corner obelisks and boldly projecting string courses, one to the belfry and another directly above the nave roof. Otherwise, apart from the absence of the present chancel, the church looks very much as it does today. An apparently slightly earlier photograph of the south side of the church shows a broad three-light window with blind tracery to its pointed head in the east bay of the medieval aisle.[20]

There are two drawings by Oldfield showing features clearly associated with the church but which are no longer extant.[21] The first is entitled "Ancient Arches adjoining Royston Church" and shows a partly ruined wall pierced by a Romanesque doorway, to the right of which is a four-bay intersecting blind arcade with the remains of a fifth arch to the far right. The height of the ground relative to the capitals of the doorway and arcade shows that the original ground level has risen. The other drawing captioned "Doorway on the other side of the ancient Arches adjoining Royston Church" is clearly of the opposite face of the doorway depicted in the first view. The doorway is of two orders with chevron and lozenge moulding supported by coupled columns with capitals and imposts, only the outer column to the right jamb surviving. Above the arch-way are ashlar voussoirs and the plank door in the doorway has elaborately decorated strap hinges. To the right of the doorway is a splayed, narrow rectangular window, the other side of which is visible in the first view. How the wall, doorway and arcade related to the church is not known but if, as seems likely, they were connected with the former cloister, the wall must have lain somewhere to the south of the monastic nave.

There is good pictorial evidence for the interior of the church before 19th-century restoration. There is a late 18th-century engraving and an early 19th-century drawing by Revd. Thomas Powell of the alabaster effigy of the knight now in the chancel,[22] but the earliest views of the building itself are by J.C. Buckler.[23] One apparently shows the west end of the north aisle with the same effigy lying at the foot of a box pew under a gallery. Fixed to the wall above is the headless statue of the Virgin and child (now in

the chancel) and also shown is an octagonal font (not that presently in the church) with carved font cover. The other view depicts the three eastern bays of the south arcade at this time from the north west. This means that it is the two eastern bays of the original south aisle and the lower 14th-century arch of the eastward extension that are shown. The drawing is useful in that it proves that the present details of all three arches and capitals, although heavily recut in the Victorian restoration, are basically accurate copies of their medieval predecessors. Also visible in the view are the east window of the aisle, which is mullioned and transomed apparently in three lights, those lights above the transom with segmental heads like those in the drawing of the north aisle by Cole. The south window in the eastward extension of the aisle is also visible, although like the east window it is partly obscured by a column. It appears to be in three lights with trefoils and a quatrefoil to the head. The window to the west of this is also shown, recessed with simple Y-tracery under a hoodmould and string course. This shows that the existing pair of windows in the south aisle is purely 19th-century work, probably carried out in the restoration of 1859-61.[24] The drawing also shows parts of the nave and aisle roofs, much as existing, and 18th-century box pews. 18th-century pulpit, reading desk and tester stand at the junction between the east respond of the 13th-century arcade and the 14th-century extension, unfortunately for our purposes obscuring their architectural details. There is no screen or structural division between the nave and old chancel, part of the east wall of which can be seen.

A drawing of 1872 by H.J. Thurnall shows much the same aspect.[25] The tester of the pulpit has now gone and a small font on a slender pedestal stands directly below the reading desk. Also by Thurnall is a slightly later drawing of the same view, almost certainly executed immediately after the 1872 restoration.[26] The present reading desk (the woodwork made up from the medieval screen) is at the south-west corner of the old chancel, the new pews and communion rails of which are already in position. This drawing is also useful for the evidence it provides of the eastern lancet on the south side before the aisle was extended eastwards, showing it to be very similar in appearance to that surviving on the north side. There is another drawing by Thurnall of the box pews on the north side of the nave.[27] These are shown as having re-used early 17th-century panelling with fluted, round-arched and geometrical carving, some of which has now been reset around the walls of the tower. That this view was made before the 1872 restoration is indicated by the presence of the old communion rails and the absence of the reopened lancet in the north wall.

Another important drawing is that by Thomas Milbourn of the elaborately carved Perpendicular timber screen, which

[18] Ashmolean Museum, Oxford, Department of Western Art (Print Room).

[19] H.R.O., D/P 87 29/4.

[20] Hertfordshire Local Studies Library, photographic colln.

[21] H.R.O., Oldfield Drawings, V, 393, 395.

[22] *Gentleman's Mag.*, 67 (1788), 729; B.L. Add. MS. 17,458, fol.186.

[23] H.R.O., Buckler Drawings, I, 32-3.

[24] See note 8.

[25] H.R.O., ROY/15; reproduced in Kingston, op.cit. (note 8), 90.

[26] H.R.O., ROY/9; reproduced in Kingston, op.cit. (note 8), 79.

[27] H.R.O., ROY/16.

is said to have been discovered beneath "old" wainscoting in the chancel before being fitted under the Victorian gallery in the western arch of the south arcade.[28] The screen is in three sections with traceried panels below the mid-rail and tracery divisions in six bays to the top. It has canopied, crocketed niches flanking the central opening and to each end an abundance of quatrefoils and other Gothic motifs. This is the screen used to make up the two prayer desks and pulpit following the 1872 restoration.

A photograph of the east end of the church shows its appearance between the restorations of 1872 and 1891.[29] The east window drawn by Buckler has been replaced by a window with panel tracery in four lights, the eastern lancet on the south is shown before being partially cut away by the Victorian arch below but the existing Victorian pews are already in position.

A late 19th-century photograph shows Priory House from the east before the addition of the projecting north and south ranges.[30] The roof is hipped at both ends but the pitch is the same as now. The existing stacks are shown but the left one is much higher and has elaborate string courses. The pediment is the same as existing but there is no portico. Instead there is a simple latticed porch with a flat roof, flanked by two windows on each floor except to the ground-floor left, which has a wide flat-roofed bay with full-height windows to the front. All the other windows are glazing bar sashes except the two lower right which have been replaced by plate-glass sashes.

CARTOGRAPHIC AND PLAN EVIDENCE

The earliest cartographic evidence is a 1725 map of Therfield which shows the town and church of Royston in the bottom left corner.[31] The representation is a crude one and the orientation of the church is not at all clear. The present nave is shown with a pitched roof and no distinction from the aisles. A porch appears on the south of the building with a row of buildings apparently aligned on a street on the same side, which is known never to have existed on this side of the church. Despite these inaccuracies, the depiction of the tower looks a little more reliable. It is squat and square in plan with three by three windows, corner obelisks and two string courses, one above the nave roof and another to the parapet. The most significant feature of the drawing is that it shows no trace of the former monastic nave.

The tithe map of 1851 is of little use beyond showing the location of the stew-pond to the east of Priory House,[32] while an undated 20th-century plan of the Priory grounds shows glass houses on the south side of the boundary wall

between church and house.[33]

A plan of the church by E. Nash accompanying the citation for a faculty in 1872 shows that the doors at the west end of the aisles were put in and the triple-gabled porch added to the tower at this date.[34] However, plans by William Scott Champion, drawn up for further proposed restoration work in 1876,[35] seem to show the old porch to the west of the tower. They also show that the 13th-century lancets were exposed as part of the 1872 restoration and indicate the paired windows in the south aisle as "new work".

A plan by J.K. Colling accompanying a citation for a faculty in 1890 to build the existing chancel shows the pier to the west of the 14th-century arch in the south arcade as "new work".[36] The north wall of the old chancel is retained and its south-east corner is comprehensively remodelled as a pier to the Victorian extension of the south aisle. The window in the east wall of the old south aisle is shown re-used in the east wall of this extension, which as it had probably only been placed there as part of the 1859 restoration obviously made sound economic sense. A plan of 1911 shows the west gallery occupying the west bay of the nave and aisles, the front of it following the line of the former rood screen.[37]

DOCUMENTARY EVIDENCE

The early post-Dissolution evidence for Royston is particularly rich and relates to both the church and Priory House. An inventory made in March 1537 by the king's commissioners refers to the "churche, lady chappell, halle, buttery and pantry, kechin, bakehouse and brewhouse", the sum total of all the goods and chattels (including the plate) being valued at £46 17s 5d.[38] An undated but slightly later list of items sold to various people refers to the parts of the church and monastery mentioned in the inventory but also lists the following: "Saynt Katrynes alter, cloyster, dorter and a howse adjoynge to the porters lodge", recording the value of the goods (excluding the plate but including the future crops of the sown fields) at £132 13s 6d.[39] The purchasers of church goods included William Chamber (whose memorial brass is at the east end of the present north aisle) and Dorbe Wendy who bought a "payre of organes" for 11s. Thomas More and John Newport bought the cloister and dorter for £24 and Robert Boldewyne the "howse next adjoynge to the porters lodge" for £20. These amounts presumably refer to their values as building materials, suggesting that large parts of the monastery were demolished at this time. No further relevant information is obtained from the ministers' accounts other than that the

[28] H.R.O., ROY/14; reproduced in Kingston, op.cit. (note 8), 85.
[29] H.R.O., D/P 87 29/4.
[30] H.R.O., extra-illustrated edn. of Cussans, xiii, 182.
[31] H.R.O., D/P 107/29/2.
[32] H.R.O., DSA 4/82/2.

[33] H.R.O., D/ERy P13.
[34] H.R.O., DSA 2/1/265.
[35] H.R.O., D/P 87 6/11.
[36] H.R.O., DSA 2/1/282.
[37] H.R.O., 37,423.
[38] P.R.O., E 117/12/30.
[39] P.R.O., E 315/361, fols.67-9.

three bells were valued at £29 and the lead at £28.[40]

Before the Dissolution the town of Royston, which probably originated as a deliberate plantation created at about the same time as the foundation of the priory,[41] lay in five parishes- Barkway and Therfield (Herts.) and Bassingbourn, Kneesworth and Melbourn (Cambs.). It seems that by the Late Middle Ages the townspeople worshipped in the priory church, almost certainly in the nave, and there are a number of recorded benefactions to the fabric of the church.[42]

The advowson of the former priory church, along with the ownership of the priory buildings, was to be granted to Robert Chester but before this change of advowson took place the townspeople were able to buy back the church for their own use. This was accomplished by an act of parliament which established Royston as a parish in its own right: "Forasmuche as the Towne of Royston is a markett Towne situate and bilded to gither and extendeth itself into Fyve severall parishes whereof never a Parrisshe churche of them is within twoo myles of the said towne and somme of them be three myles...forasmuche as the towne of Roiston is a greate and a common thorowefare for the Kinges subjectes and liege people travayling from many and sundry partes of this Realme and in the said Towne is also wekely a great markett whereunto greate and frequent resorte is of all thinhabitauntis of the Countery therunto adjoyning, and yet the said subjectis so travailing nor anny of thinhabitauntis so resorting canne have anny masse or other divine service in the said towne...all which discommodities and inconvenie'es were little p'judiciall to the saide towne at such tyme as the late Priory there stode, the churche of which Priory the poore inhabitauntis of the said towne have bought to their great charge to thintent to have the same their parrish churche and therein to have daily masse and other divine services to be celebrated and done...the said churche late being parcell of the said Pryory of Royston shalbe the parrish churche for all and singulier thinhabitauntis of the said towne of Roiston and that the said churche shalbe named and called from hensfurth the parrish churche of Sainct John the Baptist in the towne of Roiston and that one p'cell of grounde nigh or by the said church shalbe provided and enclosed at the costis and charges of the said inhabitauntis for a cemitory or church yerde...."[43]

It is not by known by what process the money to buy the church was raised or even the cost, although the unsubstantiated reference by Milbourn in the 19th century to its having cost the inhabitants £400 is not incompatible with similar situations elsewhere. The change of dedication of the church is itself representative of the times. Formerly dedicated to St John the Baptist and St Thomas the

Martyr,[44] the latter saint was omitted from the new dedication, as a result of the crown's prohibition of the cult of St Thomas.[45] The act was to take effect as soon as a vicar could be appointed, this being Alexander Stooks, a former canon of the priory, who took up his post in November 1540.[46] This appointment was made by the crown but by the time of the next presentation in 1554 the advowson had passed to Robert Chester.[47]

The conversion of the former priory church into a parish church is also referred to by Leland: "In the toune is but one chirche, the este part wherof servid a late for the Priory of Channons. The weste ende servid for a chapel for the toune. For afore the late Parlament the toune longgid to two or three paroches withoute the toune. Now all the tone is allottid to one paroche and that ys kept in the este ende of the priory and the weste ende ys pullid doune."[48] This clearly indicates that the former nave of the church was demolished at the Dissolution. An inventory of church goods made in 1553 adds little beyond the fact that there were "iii bells in the steple."[49]

It is not known precisely when Chester began the work of converting the former conventual buildings into a house but he entertained Mary of Guise here on her journey from Scotland to France in 1551.[50] That Royston was by then Chester's main residence is suggested by the Court of Exchequer's decision in May 1550 that, as he had been resident more in Royston than in London, he should be exonerated from payment of tax assessed in London.[51]

In 1578 the house was considered by royal surveyors as a potential resting-place on a royal progress but was dismissed as "a very unnecessary hows for the receipt of her Majesty; yt stand adjoyning to the Churche on the sowth syde thereof, not haveing any pleasaunt p'spects any way..."[52] The house is shown in an accompanying sketch-plan prepared at this time, the buildings being grouped around three sides of a courtyard with the principal rooms above cellars. The house is shown to be somewhat irregular in plan measuring about 120ft from north to south and 150ft from east to west. To the east lay an outer court with a gateway and porter's lodge on the south side and a range of lodgings to the north, in which at lower level were three rooms, the one on the east being described as a "bad roome" and the one on the west as a "bad p'lor, 21ft by 15ft." To the west was the inner court with a range of five rooms adjoining the highway on the west, a private entry on the north, followed by a cellar linking to the lodgings on

---

[40] P.R.O., SC6/Hen. VIII/1606, m.1d.
[41] M.W. Beresford & J.K.S. St. Joseph, *Medieval England, An Aerial Survey* (2nd. edn., 1979), 188-9.
[42] *V.C.H.*, iii, 264; Kingston, op. cit. (note 8), 56, 81, 84.
[43] *Statutes of the Realm*, iii (1817), 797.
[44] B.L., Cott. MS. Aug. ii, no.124.
[45] N. Doggett, 'Medieval church dedications in Hertfordshire', *Herts. Past*, 25 (Autumn 1988), 27.
[46] R. Newcourt, *Repertorium Ecclesiasticum Parochiale Londinense* (1708), 876.
[47] Cussans, i, pt.3, 112.
[48] Leland, i, 328.
[49] P.R.O., E 315/497/82.
[50] *Acts of the Privy Council, 1550-52*, 406.
[51] P.R.O., E 115/86/101.
[52] P.R.O., SP 12/125.

the north side of the outer court.

On the south side of the inner court were two pantries, a larder and other offices with a kitchen projecting at right-angles to the south. No buildings are shown on the east side of the court, which was borded by a long passage-way marked "entry." The principal apartments were at upper level, the lodgings on the north side of the outer court again being divided into three rooms, measuring 25ft by 11ft, 25ft by 20ft (parlour), 25ft by 24ft (hall) respectively from east to west. The inner court had a staircase in its north-east corner leading up to a pantry with an "yll" chamber on its west side. A passage-way ran to the north of both pantry and chamber. The west range was also divided into five rooms at upper level, beginning with a small room on the south, followed by a chamber measuring 20ft by 16ft. There was then a roughly centrally-placed staircase, to the north of which was a chamber measuring 21ft by 16ft. This was followed by a small room (the dimensions of which are not given) with a closet on its west side. The northern room, which projected northwards from the north range as on the lower level, measured 22ft by 16ft. The south range had three "yll" chambers with an adjoining "bad" chamber the same length as the centre and west chambers parallel to the south.

It has been pointed out that the lower level of the house was "more than a half-underground cellar, as is demonstrated by the labelling of one of its rooms as a "bad roome" and another as a "bad parlor"...the presence of a "sellar" next to the latter indicat(ing) that the term was being used in the older sense of a storeroom which was as likely to be at ground level as below it."[53] It is tempting to identify the west range of the house shown on the 1578 sketch-plan with the long range of the surviving house, although there is no positive evidence to make this connection. It is also worth noting that the upper floor of the north range to the outer court was wider than the lower floor, suggesting that this range was jettied.

In 1610 the former priory is referred to in a survey, the original of which has now been lost but which is preserved in a mid 18th-century copy by Cole: "The Manor and Mansion House of the said Priory with the Gardens and outhouses contain by Estimacon abt. 12 acres and are situate in Hertfordsh. next the Market Place on the west and a lane leading to the Icknell Street towards the south end of the Town on the backside called the Priory Lane on the south east next the Church and Churchyard in Part and next Icknell Street also in Part on the north and also next the Priory Lane towards the south..."[54]

The next reference to the domestic buildings of the former priory occurs in 1628 when the crown paid £450 to Sir Robert Chester "for houses and land bought of him...and

for rent due by the late king for the use of Sir Robert's house for one year,"[55] this being belated payment for James I's use of the house in 1603/4, while his palace in Kneesworth Street was in preparation.[56]

By c.1600 the duties of the vicar seem to have been neglected and the inhabitants of Royston petitioned the crown for a minister to be appointed. The justices of the peace attested that the church was "utterly ruinated and fallen downe to the ground" as a result of which the privy council granted a licence for collections to be made for its rebuilding.[57] That this was successful is shown by the former presence of a plaster panel under the tower arch with a painted inscription in Latin, which read when translated "In 1601...we having acquired this temple by the gracious influence of Holy God give and consecrate it to thee to Christ and to the spirit sanctifying all things, One Trinity. Oh thou merciful, propitiously hear thy servants, Worshippers of Christ, whenever they call upon thee in this holy place: remember thou thy servants whose power, whose riches and whose faculties of mind and body thou hast deigned to employ in erecting this Noble Temple. Glory to God. The Sun descended, yet Night followed not."[58] This last sentence may be a reference to the death of Elizabeth and the accession of James I. It is possible that the 17th-century work in the church, notably the rebuilt tower and the north arcade, may date to this remodelling.

An inquisition made in 1640 gives a little information on the outbuildings of Priory House: "...capital messuage of late priory of Royston, one little tiled garner opening into the market place used to bestow _____ boards and _____ necessary for fairs, sheep pens standing upon premises, messuage with a fair malt house and other necessary houses newly built and set up upon part of the ground belonging to the capital messuage called the Dove House Yard now opening into the market place."[59]

After this date it is primarily from the accounts of antiquarian visitors that most information about the appearance of the church and Priory House is obtained. The earliest of these accounts is by Weever in 1631, who among other references to the church's monuments, states "In a ruinous wall of this decayed Priory lies the proportion of a man cut in stone, which (say the inhabitants) was made to the memorie of one of the Founders who lieth thereby interred",[60] which is almost certainly a reference to the niche which remains in the boundary wall between the churchyard and Priory House, formerly containing the knight effigy which is now in the present chancel. Chauncy, writing c.1700, gives the following short description: "This

[53] Smith (1992), 54.

[54] B.L., Add. MS. 5820, fols.33-5.

[55] *Cal. State Papers Dom., 1628-29*, 31.
[56] *Cal. State Papers Dom., 1603-10*, 153; *King's Works*, iv, 237-40.
[57] *Acts of the Privy Council, 1599-1600*, 304; Calendar of the Manuscripts of the Marquis of Salisbury Preserved at Hatfield House, pt.x *Hist. MSS. Com. Rep.* (1904), 135.
[58] B.L., Add. MS. 5820, fol.26; Warren, op.cit (note 12), 32.
[59] P.R.O., C 142/602/65.
[60] J. Weever, *Antient Funerall Monuments* (1631), 548.

Church consists of a Nave or Body, with an Ile on either side, and a square Tower somewhat low, in which is a small Ring of five Bells."[61] This description is repeated almost *verbatim* by Defoe,[62] and Salmon is concerned exclusively with the church's monuments, including several late 17th- and early 18th-century tablets "on the Outside the Church wall, next to the Priory."[63] Rather more interest attaches to Stukeley's short description of the site: "The whole precincts of it still remain, and some of the old building; a noble kitchen of brickwork."[64]

A fuller account was compiled shortly afterwards by Cole who visited Royston in 1747: "...There are very few Remains of the old Priory: what do, are on the south east and a little to the west sides: the House to the west called The Priory has some painted small Figures in a Window which look as if they had continued from the old House, which was pulled down of late yeers to make up that wch is now inhabited by Mr Lettice the Tenant to Mr Chester. The Walls of the Priory are still standing: and I was told by Mr Lettice that lately on pulling up the Pavement of an old Hall, they found the Stones wch paved it, were Gravestones turned the wrong way: but he could not say whether there were any Brasses or no: but probably none: they were laid down again in another part of the House.

The Church at present consists of a small Porch at the west side of the Tower wch is very flat but handsome and adorned lately with four Spires, a Nave, two side Isles and a Chancel, if such a bit may be called one, wch is only abt 10 or 12 feet in length the wch however seems to be perfect: by what Leland says afterwards, I should guess that this was only a part of the old Church and that there was more of it at the west end: on the north side there certainly was an adjacent Building: and the N. side pillars are much smaller than those on the S. side: the whole is well leaded and there are 6 Bells in the Tower cast abt 50 years since." He then quotes Leland on the west end of the church having been pulled down, adding "A very large Arch in the Tower, now filled up, confirms my Conjecture. The altar is on an eminence of four steps and is railed in and has new Stalls all around the sides of this little Chancell wch is not above 10 or 12 feet in length; and is wainscoted all round: the Altar Peice is a large Frame wth the Decalogue and Lord's Prayer and Creed. On the south side behind the Wainscote is a Place in the Wall for Holy Water." He then goes on to describe the knight effigy, which is in the present chancel, and other monuments, before continuing "There are three Pillars on each side of the Church; those on the South side are very large and substantial: the handsome new Pulpit stands against the first on the South side: the Font is agst. the N.W. Wall in the corner as you enter the Church under the Gallery wch. is erected against the W. End...Above the Gallery agst. the West Wall on the

Part wch is filled up where was a large Arch are the following verses wrote...(the 1601 Latin inscription)..."[65]

There are unattributed manuscript accounts of the church written in 1737 and 1752 contained in Gough's grangerised copy of Salmon's *History*, but these are concerned chiefly with the monuments and add nothing to Cole's description. Gough himself notes that on a beam over what he terms the chancel arch was an inscription reading "VENITE BENEDICTI ITIMALDICTICTIPHIGHNEM."[66]

Further information is added by early 19th-century visitors like Revd. Thomas Powell, who came to Royston in 1806 and left the following account: "The present Church of the town is said by the inhabitants to be part of the old Priory church and most likely this is so but it is strangely demolished confused and parts built up in Queen Eliz time, the East window is large and fine gothic but mutilated in another window are some ancient heads in painted glass As you enter the building there is part of a fine gothic wood screen with the badge of the four Evangelists small, there is a noble gothic arch which some day or other by its fragments will raise as high an idea of the greatnes of the building of the Priory as the fragments I saw at Newsells in this neighbourhood do of the building of Old Carthage from wence they were brought. At present the church seems to be only part of nave with Isles with a tower thereunto which I conceive was built since the dissolution of the priory."[67]

Brayley and Britton comment that "Only a few remains of the Priory building are now standing, with the exception of the Church", their description of which adds no extra information.[68] Clutterbuck's account of the church shows that the painted plaster inscription of 1601 was still in the eastern arch of the tower at this time, while his reference to brasses "On the North side of the passage, leading from the Porch to the Nave" appears to confirm the unusual length of the west porch shown in Cole's drawing of the church.[69]

NINETEENTH-CENTURY RESTORATIONS OF THE CHURCH

The purpose of this section is not to give a full account of the various 19th-century restorations of the church but to use the evidence from these to cast light on the post-Dissolution appearance of the building and how this was the result of adaptation of the priory church. In 1823 the external walls were replastered, at which time "in the middle of the south wall" of the south aisle, along "with a large quantity of human bones regularly piled up", were found the two headless alabaster figures, which are now in

[61] Chauncy, i, 183.
[62] D. Defoe, *A Tour Through Great Britain*, v (1748 edn.), 202.
[63] N. Salmon, *The History of Hertfordshire* (1728), 358.
[64] W. Stukeley, *Palaeographia Britannia...No.1, Origines Roystonianae* (1743), 51.

[65] B.L., Add. MS. 5820, fols.20-6.
[66] Bodl., Gough Herts 18, Gough's grangerised copy of Salmon's *History of Hertfordshire*, manuscript notes at end of volume.
[67] B.L., Add. MS. 17,452, fol.186v.
[68] Brayley & Britton, vii, 181.
[69] Clutterbuck, iii, 567.

the chancel.[70] The figures were then lost again until 1859 when they were found in the infilled staircase in the south wall of the south aisle. This staircase is said to have been in the position of the large red brick and flint buttress between the first and second bays from the west and could be the explanation for the blocked opening visible in its east face. H.J. Thurnall, writing in 1909 to W.B. Gerish, states that "The burial place of The Priory would be on the south and probably surrounded with cloisters. Some years ago several skulls were turned up near the door that used to open into Priory garden from the Church. That great buttress to the south wall contains the staircase. I saw it opened when a boy but built up again- said to have led to monks' dormitories or somewhere in the priory buildings."[71] The Revd. H. Fowler, however, suggests that the staircase may have been right in the south-west corner of the aisle,[72] which would seem more likely if the staircase led to the monastic dormitory.

Other restoration work was carried out in 1859-61. This seems to have been when the paired windows in the south aisle were discovered and reconstructed. From inscriptions formerly on the bases of columns in the south arcade separating the first and second bays and the second and third bays from the west it appears that these too were reconstructed in this year,[73] a view which is strengthened by the physical evidence. "Restoration" of several other windows seems to have been undertaken between 1859 and 1861, Thurnall later commenting that "anyone who chose to pay for one select(ed) his pattern as he might for a tombstone, exactly according to his individual taste."[74]

A more major restoration took place in 1872. Apart from the discovery of the triple lancets in the north and south walls, evidence for the position of the original chancel arch of the monastic church was found. Following the removal of the 18th-century pews at the bottom of the section of wall separating the original 13th-century arcade from the 14th-century eastward extension, Cussans notes that the "bases of the chancel arch, richly moulded, were brought to light." On the south side below the lancets a piscina with credence was discovered: according to Cussans this was "in keeping with the old windows above it (but it) was filled up with rubbish and plastered over." Cussans also comments that "there was to be seen until recently, a large arch on the western face (of the tower), filled in with masonry, which indicates that the church was formerly of greater extent than at present, while the eastern arch had been opened up in 1838 when the gallery was inserted."[75] Fowler suggests that the chancel arch was probably destroyed by the eastward extension of the arcades in the 14th century, at which time it was replaced by a screen which survived until

the Dissolution.[76]

The present chancel, north-east vestry and organ chamber were erected and the south aisle extended in 1891 but the faculty citations provide no relevant information other than that "it might be found necessary to slightly raise the ancient cills of the old work" of the 13th-century lancets discovered in 1872 when the arcades (it was also originally planned to extend the north aisle) were again lengthened.[77] In the event, of course, the eastern lancet on the south was unceremoniously cut through in much the same way as the centre and western lancets had been cut through in the 14th century. Intriguingly, there is also a reference to the "ancient piscina" on the south side being "preserved as far as possible," despite Cussans's earlier statement that it had been "plastered over." This is probably a reference to the existing 13th-century piscina which was later repositioned in the present chancel.

The restoration of 1891 was observed by the local antiquarian, H.J. Thurnall, who later made several interesting comments to W.B. Gerish on the work undertaken then and at other times. In particular, he refers to the resulting increased level of the adjoining graveyard: "...As to the great rising of the level you should remember that when the Tower was recased an immense lot of builder's stuff was spread, by Edward Nash's orders, among these old headstones of which you speak...Then I take it the quantity of earth thrown out when those Beldam vaults were dug must have been spread behind the cottages (adjoining the north side of the church)." He then goes on to complain about the rubble left after the 1891 work. "Rubble and cement were spread all about, so why wonder at the ground rising? My own siftings are making a terrible rise at the far corner but I began by filling the cellar depressions of the old cottages pulled down there." Thurnall also casts doubt on the accuracy of Kingston's account of the church in his *History of Royston*, stating that his "information was most imperfect with regard to the Church for he had not been here to see the various changes."[78]

A little information on the font now in the church can be obtained from various accounts written in the early 20th century. This font does not appear to be the same as that shown in Buckler's view of the north-west corner of the church and by 1872 there was also a slender pedestal font below the pulpit. According to one account the present font is said to have come from a farmyard at Shingay (Cambs.),[79] while the *R.C.H.M.* claims that it formerly stood in the garden of a house to the north-east of Royston Palace.[80] The *V.C.H.* states that the font had recently been in the churchyard "after being for many years in private

[70] Warren, op. et loc.cit. (note 12).
[71] H.R.O., Gerish colln., Box 64.
[72] Fowler, op. cit. (note 9), 18-19; H.R.O., D/ESa 112.
[73] Kingston, op.cit. (note 8), 186.
[74] H.R.O., Gerish colln., Box 64.
[75] Cussans, i, pt.3, 105; Milbourn, op. cit. (note 9), 224.

[76] Fowler, op. cit. (note 9), 15.
[77] H.R.O., D/P 87 6/13.
[78] H.R.O., Gerish colln., Box 64.
[79] '40th excursion of the East Hertfordshire Archaeological Society', *Trans. East Herts. Arch. Soc.*, 4, pt.3 (1911), 312.
[80] See note 10.

hands."[81] Nothing else is known about any of the three fonts.

An undated, early 20th-century plan by Thurnall shows the church and its surroundings.[82] Apart from the outline of the church before and after the addition of the 1891 chancel, the approximate location of the former vicarage to the north-west of the church is marked. This vicarage, which was demolished before the mid-19th century, when a red brick vicarage was built in London Road, stood next to Church Lane, extending down to Melbourn Street with a passage on its east side at the west entrance gate to the churchyard. No illustrations appear to survive of this building but it is said to have been "a stud and plaster ivy-covered building" at the time of its demolition. It was probably first built immediately after the Dissolution to accommodate the first vicar of Royston, a terrier of 1681 describing the structure by that time as "consisting of three Bayes of Building, in length 54ft, in Breadth at the south end thereof 20ft, at the north end 23ft, Stands siding Eastward upon the Churchyard, Westward upon the Market Lane, butting Northward on Ickleton Street, and Southward on a small Tenement..." The terrier further states that there was a garden measuring 64ft by 30ft and an outhouse on the north side of the churchyard comprising three bays of building measuring 31ft by 12ft.[83]

To the east of the former vicarage and running at right-angles to the north of the church was a range of cottages. These were roughly L-shaped in plan and a small section of the south-east corner of the range is shown in Buckler's north-east view of the church. As far as can be ascertained from this and later photographs, the cottages appear to have been roughcast externally with plain tile roofs. Their date is uncertain, but from the available evidence the suggestion made in an early 20th-century newspaper account that they were of 18th-century origin seems quite plausible.[84] This account states that "it would be a vast improvement in every way if they could be acquired by the parish, taken down and the sites thrown into the churchyard." Evidently, however, the cottages still survived at the time of the preparation of the relevant volume of the *V.C.H.* as a line drawing of the church included in the published volume of 1912 also shows the cottages. By this time, their timber framing, which was of light scantling, had been exposed to view externally.[85]

CONCLUSIONS AND INTERPRETATION

It will be clear from the physical, pictorial and documentary evidence that the post-Dissolution history of the church is complex. Enough information exists to reconstruct with some confidence those parts of the church

which were converted to parochial use at the Dissolution, even if not the precise phasing of the actual works. Leland's description seems to make it clear that the nave was demolished almost immediately after the suppression of the priory in April 1537 and it seems likely that this had already taken place by the time that the church was bought by the townspeople in 1540. Unfortunately, the 1537 survey by the royal commissioners is equivocal in this respect.

Several attempts have been made to reconstruct the appearance of the medieval church, which obviously had some bearing on the form it took after the Dissolution. Perhaps the most convincing of these reconstructions is that put forward by Fowler who postulated a rood screen a bay to the east of the east arch of the tower, and which Milbourn suggests may also have run across the south aisle, being the point where the canons entered the church from the east range of the cloister. Fowler, however, suggests that the screen simply occupied the width of the space between the arcades with the canons' stalls running at right-angles in the next two bays to the east, forming a barrier between the choir and the aisles. The choir was thus about 30ft in length, being terminated to the east by another screen in the chancel arch, which he suggests was destroyed at the time of the eastward extension of the aisles in the 14th century, although the bases of its piers remained to be discovered in the restoration of 1872. The chancel had triple lancets in its north and south walls and there may originally have been a similar arrangement at the east end.[86]

The list (c.1537) of church goods sold to various people refers to "O'r Lady alter" and "Saynt Katrynes alter". These may have been in the north and south choir aisles but one of these, or alternatively one of the other altars which are known to have existed in the Late Middle Ages, may have been situated in the chapel which lay at right-angles to the north aisle.

The reason why the townspeople of Royston chose to utilise the choir and chancel of the church rather than the nave, which presumably in the past had been used for parochial worship, requires some explanation. There is slight evidence to suggest that there was a parochial chapel in Royston. This appears to have been built between 1164 and 1179,[87] which would make its foundation contemporary with that of the priory itself. Nothing further is heard of this chapel and its location is unknown, although there are several references in the 19th century to an extensive "ancient" burial ground in the north part of the town. This burial ground appears to have been centred near the junction of Kneesworth Street and Mill Road, finds including a stone slab or coffin lid, while land in this area

[81] *V.C.H.*, iii, 264.

[82] H.R.O., Gerish colln., Box 64.

[83] H.R.O., D/P 87/1/1.

[84] H.R.O., Gerish colln., Box 64.

[85] *V.C.H.*, iii, 262.

[86] Fowler, op. cit. (note 9), 16; Milbourn, op.cit. (note 9), 278. See also unpublished plan drawn by Fowler, H.R.O., D/ESa 112.

[87] S.A. Moore (ed.), *Cart. Mon. S. Johan de Colcestria*, Trans. Roxburgh Club, ii (1893), 513.

was also formerly known as Chapel Fields.[88] If this burial ground was associated with a chapel-of-ease, it may only have served the parish of Bassingbourn (in which parish it lay), making it likely that the townspeople living in the other parishes would have worshipped in the nave of the priory church. Furthermore, there is no evidence positively to equate the burial ground with a chapel-of-ease, especially as such chapels frequently did not have cemeteries and there were also two hospitals in medieval Royston, the exact location of one of which is not known.[89]

Assuming that there was a parochial chapel in Royston, the absence of later references to it suggests that it may have been abandoned at a relatively early date. Indeed, there is much evidence to indicate that by the Late Middle Ages the townspeople were actively involved in worship at the priory church. Some, such as William Lee of Radwell, were influential enough to secure burial in the church itself, Lee's will of 1527 directing that he was to be buried "in the Church of the Monastery of Royston by the sepultre of Elizabeth my late wife".[90] Others too were probably buried in the monastic cemetery to the south of the priory church.

Wills also provide evidence for building work at the priory church in the early 16th century. The same William Lee left £10 towards the chancel roof, while in 1511 Thomas Chamber had bequeathed 20 marks on condition that the "stepull" be built within two years.[91] Other benefactions to various altars also suggest active use of the monastic church by the townspeople at this time. Although these gifts do not absolutely prove that the townspeople worshipped in the priory church, it seems unlikely that they would have been made with such frequency (especially in the late medieval period) if this had not been the case. Interestingly, none of these benefactions directly refers to the nave of the church, although it should, of course, be remembered that the positions of the altars referred to in the wills are not known.

This raises the possibility that the nave had already been demolished or was ruinous by the time of the Dissolution, although no certainty can be attached to this suggestion. An abandoned and derelict nave would have been reason enough to purchase the monastic choir and chancel for parochial worship, in which case the demolition or plundering of any remains would have quickly followed. Finally, the act of 1540 for the creation of the parish seems to suggest that the townspeople worshipped in the priory church before the suppression as it states in relation to the distance from the town to the neighbouring parish churches that the "discommodities and inconvenie'es were little p'judiciall to the saide towne at such tyme as the late Priory there stode".[92]

Although William Chamber left £7 in 1546 towards the north aisle if the south aisle was "sufficiently made and fynished wt.in three yeres next" of his death,[93] the surviving fabric of the church suggests that relatively little was done in the 60 years following the 1540 act. This is borne out by the reference in 1600 to the church being "utterly ruinated and fallen downe to the ground." There may be considerable exaggeration in this statement or it could conceivably refer to the nave which was no longer required for parochial worship, but the ruinous condition of which could still be used to good effect by the townspeople in their plea for help. As suggested earlier, it is likely that the tower and north arcade were rebuilt at this time and the Jacobean panelling, formerly incorporated in the 18th-century box pews and now lining the walls of the tower, indicates further activity.

Physical evidence for the remodelling of the tower is relatively slight owing to the Victorian refacing, but a break in the surviving wall of the south aisle of the former nave marks a projecting impost which probably carried the arch between aisle and transept. This would be on line with the west face of the old tower, showing that it was originally square in plan rather than rectangular as at present, its current west wall having been built approximately seven feet to the east of the old one. If the accounts of Chauncy and Defoe are to be believed the tower was still square in the early 18th century but Cole's drawing of 1747 shows it as rectangular in shape.

It has been suggested that the west arch of the south arcade was also inserted c.1600. In making this suggestion the *V.C.H.* points out that the western end of the short section of wall separating the two western arches of the arcade has been thinned down to make it fit the east respond and arch of the westernmost opening.[94] As the capital of the respond has the same section as the unaltered capital C in the north arcade, it seems likely that it was originally a detached pier. It is significant that there is just sufficient space for a full arch like those to the east between the respond and the tower. In concluding that the arch was therefore rebuilt of old materials c.1600, the *V.C.H.* also cites the fact that the clerestory window directly above was inserted at about this date.

The argument that the arch was remodelled c.1600 seems more convincing than the alternative view put forward by Fowler that the arch remains in its original form. This conclusion is based on the observation that as the arch, the mouldings of which date to between c.1220 and c.1240, directly abuts the tower, the latter cannot be later than the former.[95] This, however, does not seem to be a safe conclusion when the extent of remodelling to the tower is considered and it appears more probable that both the tower and the west arch of the south arcade were rebuilt

[88] Kingston, op. cit. (note 8), 46-7.
[89] *V.C.H.*, iv, 462-4.
[90] P.R.O., PCC Porch; Kingston, op.cit. (note 8), 46n.
[91] P.R.O., PCC Fetiplace; *V.C.H.*, iii, 264.
[92] See note 43.

[93] P.R.O., PCC 24 Alen; Kingston, op. cit. (note 8), 81.
[94] *V.C.H.*, iii, 262, 264.
[95] Fowler, op. cit. (note 9), 11.

c.1600.

The reason why so much of the church appears to have been rebuilt c.1600 may simply have been neglect over the 60 years following the Dissolution. The acquisition of the church would have placed a considerable strain on the town's resources and it may have been that the cost of the purchase itself meant relatively little money was available to spend on the fabric in succeeding years. An additional factor may have been the demolitions which seem to have taken place at the Dissolution. The removal of the nave and transepts may have substantially weakened the structure of the tower, which combined with a comparative lack of maintenance, necessitated the remodelling programme of c.1600.

If it is difficult to reconstruct the precise sequence of events at the church after the Dissolution, even greater problems surround the domestic buildings of the former priory. Although the documentary evidence is relatively good, it is not easy to relate it to the physical evidence of the surviving building. This suggests that the house was formerly of close-studded timber framed construction, of two storeys under a steeply pitched tiled roof. The phasing of this building is not easy to work out but towards its north end it appears to incorporate a late 16th-century range of three unequal timber framed bays. The truss at the south end of these bays is weathered, suggesting that it was formerly external. An addition to the north with a lateral stack and a staircase to the west was made in the early to mid-17th century, and a timber- framed addition to the south followed shortly afterwards. In the early 18th century the whole of the east elevation was clad in brick with chamfered quoins, at which time the present entrance hall to No.2 was probably created. Later in the century a single-storey wing (subsequently increased in height to two storeys) was added to the south-west, while a corridor and staircase were inserted in the two-storey lean-to section to the west and pilasters and pediment attached to the east front in the early 19th century.[96] The canted bay windows on the east front and the projecting north and south ranges were added after 1887 as none of these features is shown on the 25" Ordnance Survey map of that date.

The late 16th-century range appears to have been open to the roof from the first floor, as indicated by the plastered rebate for floor joists which are visible on the north side of the staircase in No.3, and the two-storey lean-to to the west was originally only of one storey as shown by the 17th-century brickwork in its lower courses. Parts of the surviving building may therefore represent the west range of the larger house shown in the sketch-plan of 1578 and it has been suggested that the remainder may have been demolished by Edward Chester in the second quarter of the 17th century,[97] although on what evidence it is not altogether clear. A late 16th-century date for the origin of

the existing structure seems consistent with the timber mullion windows surviving in the roof space, the earliest parts of the roof structure and the remaining fragments of wall framing. The only feature which can confidently be assigned an earlier date is the ground-floor ceiling beam, a section through which is exposed on the south side of the staircase to No.3. This may be as early as the 14th century, but as it is not at present possible to establish its relationship to the rest of the building, the suggestion that it may simply be re-used cannot be ruled out. It would certainly not be possible from the presence of this beam alone to state that the surviving structure represents any part of the monastic buildings.

On the contrary, the evidence currently available from the surviving fabric tends to support the view that the earliest parts of the building date to the late 16th century and are not a direct conversion of the monastic buildings. The furthest that the evidence can be stretched is to say that the main range of the present house may represent the west range of the larger house shown in the 1578 sketch-plan and that this may in turn be the rebuilt west range of the claustral buildings. In this case the small courtyard shown on the plan to the east of this range would represent a small part of the cloister, which had been partly built over on its north side, and the porter's lodge to the south-east may be the former monastic gatehouse. That the west range of the house shown on the plan is unlikely to represent any other part of the claustral buildings is indicated by the earlier sale of the cloister and dorter to Thomas More and John Newport for £24.[98] As this almost certainly represents their value as building materials, it indicates that they were likely to have been quickly demolished in which case, if the west range shown on the 1578 plan is any part of the claustral buildings, it must be the west range. Clearly, its alignment establishes that it cannot be the south range, while the church itself lay to the north. What counts most, however, against the main range of the existing house representing the rebuilt western claustral range is its considerable distance from the church.

The statement in the accompanying 1578 survey of Priory House that "yt stand(s) adjoyning to the Churche on the sowth syde thereof, not haveing any pleasaunt p'spects any way" suggests, however, that a considerable portion of the probably ruinous nave survived into the last quarter of the 16th century and spoilt the house's northward views. It is therefore particularly unfortunate that the 1578 plan does not indicate the position of the house in relation to the church, as this would help considerably in reconstructing its former plan and possibly in establishing whether or not the present building has evolved from a direct conversion of the western claustral range. Perhaps, though, the church's absence from the plan is simply further indication that the monastic nave had already gone by this date, or that as a ruined structure it was not felt necessary to mark it on the plan. Similarly, if the house had nothing to do with

[96] N.M.R., file 77,788.
[97] Ibid.

[98] See note 39.

the former cloister the reason for the absence of the church is entirely obvious.

The slight possibility that the west range of the house shown on the plan may be a remodelling of the west claustral range is strengthened by the fact that its principal rooms are on the first floor, which would be consistent with the usual presence of an undercroft in a west claustral range. That too much should not be made of this, however, is suggested by the presence of similar rooms in the north range of the house shown in the 1578 plan, which as demonstrated above cannot represent any part of the former monastic buildings.

The difficulty of establishing which, if any, of the monastic buildings were converted to domestic use is paralleled by that of determining the exact date at which this may have occurred. The first post-Dissolution owner of the property was Robert Chester, who having initially rented the house, acquired it from the crown for the sum of £1761 5s in 1540.[99] Chester's career was an interesting one. He was born in 1510 of a Hertfordshire family and found favour at court as a gentleman usher of the king's chamber. In 1544 he was at Calais with 25 archers, who formed the king's bodyguard when he departed for the siege of Boulogne.[100] Chester was knighted in 1551 and was made Sheriff of Essex and Hertfordshire in 1565.[101] He died in 1574.[102]

By this time The Priory had been settled on his son, Edward, who also seems to have had a distinguished career in the employment of the crown, "getting great credytt in respect of his good service in the Low Countries."[103] However, he only outlived his father by three years so it is, perhaps, unlikely that he was responsible for any major building work at the house, a suggestion which is given added weight by the queen's surveyors' unfavourable remarks regarding the property in 1578. A more likely candidate to have commissioned a major remodelling programme would seem to have been Edward's son, Robert, who came into possession on attaining his majority in 1586.[104] He was Sheriff of Hertfordshire in 1599.[105] Although often engaged in litigation concerning the extent of the former priory's possessions,[106] he appears to have carried out work to the house. Certainly, the house was in sufficiently good repair for Chester to entertain James I there in April 1603, a visit which must have been a success to judge by his knighting shortly afterwards,[107] and perhaps even more so by the king's decision to rent the house for a year during the preparation of his own hunting lodge at Royston.

As a result of the lease to the crown, Sir Robert was obliged to live at nearby Cokenach, the other family house of the Chesters, which seems to have been his principal residence until his death in 1640.[108] That the Chesters did not altogether abandon Royston, however, is shown by the reference to Sir Robert's son and heir, Edward, residing there in 1634.[109]

It seems therefore that there are two major phases to the post-Dissolution re-use of the priory buildings at Royston, one occurring between 1540 and the visit of Mary of Guise in 1551, the second after 1578 (or more probably after 1586) but before the visit of James I in 1603, although it is only the second phase which has left any tangible evidence in the surviving structure.

Bibliography

PICTORIAL SOURCES

Hertfordshire Record Office

Buckler Drawings, I, 31-3.

Oldfield Drawings, V, 390, 393, 395.

Extra-illustrated edn. of Cussans, xiii, 182.

Gerish Collection, Box 64.

D/ESa 112.

DSA 2/1/265, 282.

D/P 87 6/11.

37,423.

ROY/9, 14-16.

Public Record Office, London

SP/12/125.

British Library, London

Add. MS. 5820, fol.19v.

Add MS. 17,458, fol.186.

[99] *L.P.*, xvi, g.379 (60).
[100] *L.P.*, xix (2), nos.424, 524 (8).
[101] W.A. Shaw, *The Knights of England*, ii (1906), 65; *P.R.O. List & Indexes No.9, List of Sheriffs for England & Wales* (1898), 45.
[102] *P.R.O. List & Indexes No.26, Index of Inquisitions Post Mortem Preserved in the P.R.O.*, ii (1908), 74.
[103] *V.C.H.*, iii, 260.
[104] Ibid.
[105] *P.R.O., List of Sheriffs*, 64.
[106] *V.C.H.*, iii, 260.
[107] Shaw, op. cit. (note 101), 123.

[108] *V.C.H.*, iii, 261.
[109] W.C. Metcalfe (ed.), *Visitations of Herts. in 1572 & 1634*, Harleian Soc. Publications, 22 (1886), 40.

Ashmolean Museum, Oxford

Department of Western Art (Print Room).

Printed

Gentleman's Magazine, 67 (1788), 729.

PHOTOGRAPHIC EVIDENCE

Hertfordshire Record Office

D/P 87 29/4.

Hertfordshire Local Studies Library, Hertford

Photographic Collection.

CARTOGRAPHIC EVIDENCE

Hertfordshire Record Office

D/P 107/29/2.

DSA 4/82/2.

D/ERy P13.

OTHER PRIMARY SOURCES

Manuscript:-

Public Record Office, London

SC6/Hen. VIII/1606, m.1d; 1607.

E 115/86/101.

E 117/12/30.

E 315/361, fols.67-9.

E 315/497/82.

SP 12/125.

C 142/602/65.

PCC 24 Alen.

PCC 1 Fetiplace.

PCC 24 Porch.

Hertfordshire Record Office

D/ESa 112.

D/P 87/1/1.

D/P 87 6/13; 15.

DSA 2/1/282.

Gerish Collection, Box 64

British Library, London

Add. MS. 5820, fols.20-6; 33-5.

Add. MS. 17,452, fol.186v.

Cott. MS. Aug. ii, no. 124.

Bodleian Library, Oxford

Gough Herts 18.

National Monuments Record, The Royal Commission on Historical Monuments, Swindon

File 77,788.

Printed:-

Acts of the Privy Council, ed. Dasent, J.R., 32 vols. (1890-1970).
Calendar of the Manuscripts of the Marquis of Salisbury Preserved at Hatfield House, pt.x *Historical Manuscripts Commission Report* (1904).
Calendar of State Papers, Domestic Series, of the Reigns of Edward VI, Mary, Elizabeth and James I, 12 vols. (1856-72).
Letters and Papers, Foreign and Domestic, of the Reign of Henry VIII, eds. Brewer, J.S., Gairdner, J. & Brodie, R.H., 21 vols. (1862-1932).
Metcalfe, W.C., (ed.), *Visitations of Herts. in 1572 & 1634*, Harleian Soc. Publications, 22 (1886).
Moore, S.A. (ed.), *Cart. Mon. S. Johan. de Colcestria*, Trans. Roxburgh Club, ii (1893).
P.R.O. List and Indexes No.9, List of Sheriffs for England & Wales (1898).
P.R.O. List and Indexes No.26, Index of Inquisitions Post Mortem Preserved in the P.R.O., ii (1908).
The Statutes of the Realm, from Original Records and Authentic Manuscripts, 11 vols. in 12 (1810-28).
Toulmin Smith, L. (ed.), *The Itinerary of John Leland in or about the Years 1535-43*, i (1906).

SECONDARY SOURCES

Beresford, M.W. & St Joseph, J.K.S., *Medieval England, An Aerial Survey* (2nd. edn., Cambridge 1979).

Brayley, E.W. & Britton, J., *The Beauties of England and Wales, Vol.7, Hertfordshire* (1808).

Bright, P., *The Parish and Priory Church of St John the Baptist, Royston, A History and Guide* (Royston pamphlet, c. 1980).

Chauncy, H., *The Historical Antiquities of Hertfordshire*, i (1700, reprinted Dorking 1975).

Clutterbuck, *The History and Antiquities of Hertfordshire*, iii (1827).

Colvin, H.M. *et al*, *The History of the King's Works*, iv (1982).

Cussans, J.E., *The History of Hertfordshire*, i, pt.3 (1873, reprinted Wakefield 1972).

Defoe, D., *A Tour Through Great Britain*, v (1748 edn.).

Doggett, N.D.B., 'Medieval Church Dedications in Hertfordshire', *Herts. Past*, 25 (Autumn 1988), 22-30, concluded in vol.26 (Spring 1989), 9-16.

'40th excursion of the East Hertfordshire Archaeological Society', *Trans. East Herts. Arch. Soc.*, 4, pt.3 (1911), 312.

Fowler, H., 'Church of St. John the Baptist, Royston', *Trans. St. Albans Archit. & Arch. Soc.*, no vol. no. (1884), 5-19.

Kingston, A., *A History of Royston* (1906).

Knowles, M.D. & Hadcock, R.N., *Medieval Religious Houses* (1953).

Milbourn, T. 'Notes on the history of Royston', *Proceedings of the Evening Meetings of the London and Middx. and Surrey Arch. Socs.* (n.d. but paper read in 1874), 193-278.

Newcourt, R., *Repertorium Ecclesiasticum Parochiale Londinense* (1708).

Royal Commission on Historical Monuments, *An Inventory of the Historical Monuments in Hertfordshire* (1910).

Salmon, N., *The History of Hertfordshire* (1728).

Shaw, W.A., *The Knights of England*, ii (1906).

Smith, J.T., *English Houses 1200-1800: the Hertfordshire Evidence* (1992).

Stukeley, W., *Palaeographia Britannia...No.1, Origines Roystonianae* (1743).

The Victoria History of the Counties of England, *Hertfordshire*, iii (1912), iv (1914).

Warren, J., Appendix to *Origines Roystonianae* (1825).

Weever, J., *Antient Funerall Monuments* (1631).

ST. GILES IN THE WOOD, FLAMSTEAD (BEECHWOOD PARK)

History

Benedictine nunnery founded in the mid-12th century by Roger de Todeni, dissolved March 1537.[1] It was then leased to Sir John Tregonwell,[2] but in the following year the lease was revoked and the manor was granted to Sir Richard Page in exchange for his manor of Molesey (Surrey).[3] Sir Richard died in 1548 and the house passed to his widow, Elizabeth.[4] She married Sir William Skypwith and the property remained with the Skypwith family until c.1575 when it was sold to Richard and Thomas Smith.[5] Thomas Smith sold the manor to Thomas Saunders in 1628.[6] In 1687 Anne, daughter of Thomas's grandson, Thomas and Ellen Saunders, married Sir Edward Sebright. Anne died in 1718 and the property remained with the Sebright family until the 1960s.[7]

THE BUILDINGS

Introduction

Nothing survives above ground of the monastic buildings. Situated in former parkland, some of it landscaped by Capability Brown,[8] about two miles west of Flamstead, the present house dates mainly to the late 17th century with a fine east front added between 1695 and 1702. Several further additions were made in the later 18th and 19th centuries. The nunnery buildings seem to have lain approximately 100 yards to the east, although it is possible that there may be some medieval work in the existing cellars. The house became a preparatory school in 1964 in which use it remains.

Evolution of the house's plan

Although it contains a few earlier fragments (see below), the present house dates mainly to the mid- to late 17th century. Chauncy, writing at the very end of the 17th century, describes it as "a fair brick house of the figure of a Roman H."[9] This seems to be an accurate description of the 17th-century house, which consisted of a main range facing east (the present west range) flanked by north and south cross-wings, projecting further to the east than to the west, the stone quoins of the south wing being discovered during 20th-century alterations to the saloon.[10] Between 1695 and 1702 a taller, U-shaped front range was added to the east, its short wings linking to the east wings of the old house. A shallow staircase hall at the back of the new range was lit from the courtyard (formed between the old and new ranges) and originally had a cupola over, removed c.1800.

Further additions were made in the 18th century, including the Great Room of the 1740s on the north side of the west front and the north and south pavilions of the 1760s. The last major alteration to the main house took place in 1851-4, when the central open courtyard was replaced by a top-lit saloon extending through two floors. The central part of the 17th-century house was also remodelled as a single large room on the ground floor with a central bay window projecting between the external stacks on the west front.[11]

Description

The **east front** is constructed of chequered red and purple brick with vitrified headers in Flemish bond; moulded stone plinth, plain string course and rusticated quoins. Hipped plain tile roof over deep modillioned wooden eaves cornice carried up around pediment. The front is symmetrical in nine bays with a central projecting pedimented section of three bays, the pediment having a painted lead cartouche of the Sebright arms flanked by pointing *putti*. Two storeys and attic; six pedimented dormers in the roof slope, with 16-paned sash windows, alternate with the window bays below. Two tall ridge stacks with moulded capping to either side of the central pediment. Central entrance approached by a wide flight of six stone steps flanked by wrought-iron railings. Tall half-glazed double doors in moulded stone surround with fluted Corinthian pilasters supporting a broken segmental pediment. All the sash windows are 12-paned and horned, being insertions of the 1920s or 1930s, the original sashes having been replaced at an earlier date.[12] The rusticated stone window surrounds, which seem to have replaced stucco surrounds at the same time as the existing sash windows were inserted, are continued down as plain blocks to plinth and string course level on the ground and first floors respectively. The head of each window has a stucco chamfered rusticated applied flat arch with a raised keystone, the upper edges of the voussoirs flanking the keystone having been cut down to give it more prominence. There are decorated iron guards to the lower part of each window.

The left and right returns each have brick ridge stacks with moulded capping directly behind the ridge towards the east end, three dormer windows like those on the east front but less heavily pedimented, and two windows on each floor towards the west end. The window surrounds are the same as on the main front except that the stucco lintels have raised keystones no deeper or higher than the lintels. The

[1] Knowles (1953), 212.
[2] P.R.O., E 315/209, fol.88b; H.R.O., 17,243.
[3] *L.P.*, xiv (2), g.113 (16); Dugdale, iv, 301-2.
[4] B.L., Harl. MS. 1504.
[5] In October 1576 a licence was granted to Richard and Dorothy Skypwith to alienate the manor of Beechwood to Richard and Thomas Smith; P.R.O., C 166/1142.
[6] *V.C.H.*, ii, 196.
[7] D. Warrand, *Hertfordshire Families* (1907), 215; local inf.
[8] Pevsner, 92.
[9] Chauncy, ii, 515.
[10] Smith (1993), 56.

[11] D.O.E. 34th List of Buildings of Special Architectural or Historic Interest, The Borough of Dacorum, 7.
[12] A. Oswald, 'Beechwood Park', *Country Life* (Nov. 12, 1938), 477.

windows themselves are plain casements. On the right return there are smaller windows to the right on each floor. Symmetrically placed on both the main front and the returns are lead downpipes with a decorated garland in relief on each length between eared brackets. They are dated "1702" with the initials "S/E.A." for Edward and Anne Sebright, replacement sections having the lettering "SHS/1962".

At the far west end of each return, where the modillioned eaves cornice terminates at the end of the hipped roof, is a 17th-century integral stack flush with the wall, marking the junction between the 17th- and 18th-century parts of the house. Both stacks are large with moulded capping to the tops of the bases, but that on the south is larger, a straight joint on its south face suggesting that it has been extended from its original proportions. The south stack has five attached diagonal chimneys with moulded capping, the one on the north having only two chimneys. The south stack has two small windows in its face.

West front

This is constructed of 17th-century red brickwork in English bond with remains of 18th-century tuck pointing. Plain Portland stone plinth (probably 18th century), alternating Totternhoe stone angle quoins and continuous string courses, stepped over the first-floor windows to the cross-wings. Two storeys and attic with steeply-pitched roofs, now slated. Long centre section flanked by projecting gabled cross-wings forming H-plan. The main range has four gabled dormers in the roof slope, the centre two more closely spaced, and all directly above four tall cross-windows on the first floor. Between the centre and outer windows are two massive external lateral stacks, truncated at eaves level, across which the string course runs. On the ground floor between and abutting the stacks is a large mid 19th-century seven-light canted bay stone window, which formerly had Jacobean-style strapwork ornamentation to the parapet (now removed); plain casements to either side. The cross-wings also have cross-windows, although the lower right window to the left cross-wing is carried down to form a doorway and the ground-floor windows to the right cross-wing are missing some of their glazing bars. The gables have elaborately decorated bargeboards resting on carved brackets and have pointed pendants directly above the plain casement attic windows. The right cross-wing has an extruded integral lateral stack on its south face with four attached diagonal shafts like those on the returns of the east front: there are the truncated remains of a similar stack on the north side of the left cross-wing. Immediately to the left of this is the so-called Great Room, added by Roger Morris for Sir Thomas Sebright c.1744.[13] This is a tall single-storey range in tuck-pointed red brick with Portland stone plinth, plain projecting dado band and moulded wood architrave to frieze and deep modillioned cornice to parapet, which

conceals a lean-to roof. Four equally-spaced tall cross-windows in moulded stone surrounds with triangular pediments and pulvinated friezes, the left carried down to form a glazed door.

On either side of the east front of the house and deeply set back from it are two-storey red brick north and south pavilions with hipped slate roofs, the former originally housing a kitchen and the latter kitchen and offices. These were added in the 1760s after unexecuted schemes had been prepared by Capability Brown (1754) and Matthew Brettingham (c.1759).[14] The pavilions are of five bays with slightly projecting three-bay centre sections. Each is of English bond brickwork with rusticated stone quoins, moulded plinth, hollow-chamfered stone string course and moulded stucco cornices. The windows are all sashes, six-paned to the first floor and 12-paned on the ground floor. The pavilions were originally linked to the house by three-bay arcades,[15] but these have now been replaced by 19th-century recessed two-storey red brick three-window link blocks with moulded stone plinth, plain string course and stone-coped parapet.

On the north a plum brick screen wall with central iron gates to red brick piers conceals the stable yard. The plum brick stables and coach house (1866) are L-shaped with hipped slate roofs, red brick gauged arches, 16-paned sash windows to the ground floor and eight-paned pivot windows to the first floor, and are now linked to the rear of the north pavilion by a late 20th-century slate-roofed addition. On the south side of the house are extensive mid- to late 19th-century brick service ranges, the most prominent feature of which is a square clock tower, built in the 1850s, with a pyramidal lead roof and weathervane. The clock, which has a moulded stone frame to a circular dial on each face is marked "Northampton 1764" and presumably came from elsewhere. To the south and west of these ranges are a number of late 20th-century school buildings. Further still to the south and west is an extensive complex of 17th- and 18th-century red brick kitchen garden walls, repaired and partially demolished in the late 20th century, forming a polygonal enclosure with cross-walls within.

Interior

The main entrance is on the east front into a large stone-flagged hall which has early 18th-century bolection-moulded wall panelling, moulded skirting and cornice and projecting chimney breast on the south with a marble surround. The three moulded round-headed arches in the west wall were inserted in 1863. Beyond and to the left is the 18th-century main staircase; slender twisted balusters, two to each tread, carved open string, moulded handrail and panelled dado to wall.

[13] J. Lees-Milne, *English Country Houses: Baroque* (1970), 263.

[14] D.O.E. 34th List of Historic Buildings (note 11), 6; P.R.O., C 108/362.
[15] Pevsner, 92.

The large room to the south of the entrance hall was designed as a dining room by William Chambers in the 1760s. It has a deep enriched dentilled cornice with egg and dart moulding. Four moulded doorcases with six-panel doors and a cyma frieze to the cornice. The windows have moulded surrounds with fielded panels to both reveals and shutters. The fine marble chimneypiece with fluted consoles is also by Chambers. The drawing room to the north of the entrance hall probably largely dates to the same scheme of decoration as the dining room. It also has an enriched cornice and three six-panel doors with moulded surrounds and dentilled cornices to enriched cyma friezes. The highly decorated white marble chimneypiece has been attributed to Borri. A decorated papier-mache ceiling, which may have been slightly later, was taken down in the 1960s.[16]

Beyond the entrance hall to the west is a large top-lit rectangular saloon, designed and built by William Burn between 1851 and 1854 for Sir Thomas Gage Saunders Sebright.[17] This has an arcaded gallery of five by three round-headed arches with moulded plaster surrounds and keystones. The arches have glazed doors and balconies. Above is an elaborate plaster ceiling by James Annan with a deep enriched cornice interrupted by consoles with lion masks supporting a coved and beamed ceiling with a large rooflight. Below the gallery the walls are plain but on the ground floor there are elaborate carved doorcases with double doors of the 1860s by Barbetti on the north, east and west. The two doors on the south formerly flanked a Renaissance-style chimneypiece, also by Barbetti, which now forms a reredos in the school chapel, which is situated in the ante-chamber between hall and saloon directly opposite the main staircase.

To the west of the saloon is the present school dining room, in the north wall of which double doors open into a vestibule, which has an early 19th-century built-in bookcase and a plaster cornice of upright leaves and four-panel doors in the east wall with echinus moulding and narrow reeded architraves. Beyond this is a panelled passage, which gives access to the library. This is in the Great Room and was remodelled in its present form by Thomas Cundy in 1804 after earlier schemes by Sir John Soane and Alexandre-Louis de Labriere.[18] The ceiling has a deep cove springing from an egg and dart carved band, which probably dates from the 1740s interior. Built-in oak bookcases with swept corners and reeded frieze with ormolu anthemion line the walls, each bay having a central lozenge with index letter. Above the bookcases painted decoration represents oak panelling and on the east wall is a grey marble chimneypiece, attributed to M. Labrier.[19] Double doors in the north wall lead into the inner library,

also with decoration of 1804. White-painted panelling with winged rod and serpent motifs and bookcases in Empire style with ormolu ornament. White marble fireplace on the north wall and mirrored doors on the east wall opposite the glazed door to the garden. Enriched coved cornice.

On the first floor a continuous gallery runs around the saloon; several of the bedrooms have now been converted into dormitories but one bedroom and associated dressing room were formerly decorated in the 18th-century Chinese style and another in the Adam manner.[20]

Relatively few internal features survive from the pre-18th-century house. The earliest are in the present housemaster's study in the south range. The room is panelled, except on the north wall, with a plain plaster frieze above. The panelling is predominantly square but there is some rectangular panelling, mostly on the east wall, which appears to be an insertion. There is a chamfered beam running north-south. On the south wall is a moulded clunch fireplace with a four-centred arch, foliate carving to the spandrels and stops half-way up the jambs. This is probably early to mid-16th century but the timber overmantel is early Jacobean. It has three decorated round-headed arches with terms (two females and two bearded males) between and deep dentilled and corbelled cresting with four foliate brackets. The moulded panelled strip and shelf over the fireplace are an insertion. There is a sash window and boxed-in wall-post to the right of the fireplace and an inset cupboard to the left with H-hinges. A smaller cupboard in the east wall has butterfly hinges.

Contemporary with the mid- to late 17th-century house are the north and south staircases. The north is more elaborate with closed string, dumpy balusters, heavy moulded handrail and square newels with finials. The bolection-moulded dado on the wall is probably later. The top flight of the south staircase (much altered below) has a simple heavy rail, infilled balustrade and rectangular newel with ogee finial. It is lit by a hollow-chamfered two-light stone mullion window and there is a similar but larger mullioned and transomed window directly below. Both windows are in the original south wall of the 17th-century house. Plank doors in the attic of the south range have recently been replaced by fire doors but the butt-purlin roof structure of the 17th-century house is visible through hatches in the west range.

The cellars of the house are extensive. The fine red brick vaulted wine cellar on the north side of the house, extending partly below the link block and the north pavilion, is 18th century but the cellars at the south end of the house are considerably older. The walls are a mixture of painted brick, flint and clunch block construction, some of the flint and clunch sections forming a chequer-work pattern. It is not possible to date these walls precisely: they

---

[16] D.O.E. 34th List of Historic Buildings (note 11), 9; Oswald, op. et loc. cit.

[17] Pevsner, 92.

[18] D.O.E. 34th List of Historic Buildings (note 11), 6; H. Colvin, *A Biographical Dictionary of British Architects, 1600-1840* (1978), 245.

[19] Pevsner, 92.

[20] A. Oswald, 'Beechwood Park, II', *Country Life* (Nov. 19, 1938), 500-1.

may relate to some of the former nunnery buildings or to the 16th-century domestic conversion; in either case the actual stonework is almost certainly of monastic origin.

PICTORIAL AND PHOTOGRAPHIC EVIDENCE

The earliest known surviving drawing of Beechwood Park is one of the east front of the 17th-century range, apparently made in c.1695. The artist is unknown and it may show some proposed alterations.[21] The centre range is in five bays with two-bay projecting gabled ranges having rusticated quoins to north and south. There is a continuous plinth and first-floor plat band, while the eaves cornice of the centre range continues around the projecting gabled ranges, which have single windows to their attics. No details are shown to these or any of the windows but the attic windows are of reduced proportions and the others are of tall rectangular shape. The centre bay of the main range is occupied by a tall and narrow three-storey gabled porch, which has rusticated quoins to the upper floors and, like the gabled ranges, a continuation of the eaves cornice from the main range. The gable of the porch has its own moulded eaves cornice, cut by a window, and has ball finials to the corners. The coped verges are surmounted by a ball finial and weathervane to the apex of the gable. Round-headed archway with keystone on the ground floor flanked by pilasters supporting a broken segmental pediment. Behind the ridge of the main range there are two rectangular stacks with moulded capping, one to either side of the porch.

An early 19th-century drawing by J.P. Neale, engraved by W. Radclyffe,[22] shows the main front with a closed segmental pediment but, with the exception of the absence of the present decorated window surrounds, otherwise largely as existing today. Pencil sketches and pen and ink drawings of 1838-41 by J.C. Buckler show that by this date the pediment had been closed.[23] They also show the large 17th-century stack on the south side of the house in its original proportions with only four shafts, while both the Neale and the Buckler drawings show four sash windows (again without decorated surrounds but with plain keystones and stone cills) on each floor to the left and right returns and also the round-headed arches to the link blocks.

An early 19th-century coloured view of the rear of the house (attributed to Thomas Fisher) shows a central entrance comprising a half-glazed door with intersecting Gothic tracery to its rectangular fanlight set in a moulded pilastered doorcase with keystone and segmental pediment on console brackets. The doorcase looks late 17th century and is flanked by the prominent lateral stacks, of which

only the bases now survive.[24] In contrast with the chimneys shown in the c.1695 drawing, in this view the stacks are shown to be stepped and to have arched corbelling directly below paired diagonal shafts with moulded capping. These too are probably late 17th century and seem to have survived in this form well into the 20th century.[25] Similar details are shown to the large stack at the junction with the Great Room to the north.

Also shown in the Fisher view are circular windows with cusped quatrefoil glazing bars to the attics of the gables. These also survived into the 20th century but the cusped bargeboards, also shown in this view and which were possibly originally the work of Sir John Sebright in the late 18th century,[26] were recarved in Burn's restoration. All the ground- and first-floor windows are glazing bar sashes and the roof is plain tile rather than the present slate. Also visible are two stacks to the rear of the range, apparently matching the two prominent lateral stacks to the front. The current stone string courses are shown to be of moulded brick, the pattern of those above the first-floor wing windows suggesting that these were originally mullion windows (perhaps of five lights) rather than the sash windows shown.

The plans and drawings relating to Burn's restoration, principally carried out between 1851 and 1854, although dated between 1847 and as late as 1866, are another useful source for the appearance of the house in the 19th century.[27] A plan dated September 1851 shows the canted bay window on the west front and others of 1847 show the arrangement of the central courtyard before the saloon was built. The ground-floor area was occupied by a number of outbuildings, the principal of which was a central single-storey covered passage-way with a slate roof linking the east and west ranges of the house. This feature is shown in a mid 18th-century plan and elevation drawing, which is apparently contemporary with the construction of the passage-way.[28] The passage-way runs westwards from a doorway a little to the north of the staircase in the early 18th-century east range to link with the porch to the 17th-century west range. Once through the porch, one branch of the passage turns at right-angles to the south and the other carries straight on. The room to the north of this is marked as the Old Hall. The elevation of the passage-way shows it to have a recessed lunette window in the centre of each long wall with a continuous impost band running the full length of the wall. In the recess of each long wall is a statue of a male torso placed on a tall pedestal. By the time of Burn's restoration the porch (see above) which the passage-way abutted had three-light windows on the first and second floors.

[21] Smith (1993), 56. There is a copy of this drawing in N.M.R., file 39,611.
[22] B.L., Add. MS. 32,349, fol.86, b; J.P. Neale, *Views of the Seats of Noblemen and Gentlemen in England, Wales, Scotland and Ireland* (1822), no page no's.
[23] B.L., Add. MS. 36,365, fols.3 and 4; H.R.O., Buckler Drawings, IV, 9, 11 and 12.
[24] B.L., Add. MS. 32,349, fol.86, a.; there is a similar pencil drawing by Buckler in H.R.O., Buckler Drawings, IV, 10.
[25] Photograph in Oswald, op. cit. (note 12), 476.
[26] N.M.R., file 39,611.
[27] H.R.O., D/EX 45 B2.
[28] N.M.R., file 39,611.

The clock tower to the south service range is shown pencilled in on a drawing of the service buildings, dated May 1851.[29]

DOCUMENTARY EVIDENCE

A detailed inventory made at the time of the nunnery's suppression in March 1537 survives. It lists the following buildings: "...church (quyre and vestery) [described as in 'good repair'], parlour, kechyn, high chamber, myddle chamber, buttery and backhowsse."[30] The mention of "a table of alabaster for O'r Ladye aulter", sold for 3s 4d, possibly also indicates the existence of a lady chapel.

In August 1537 the site was leased to John Tregonwell, but in the following year the lease was revoked.[31] The reason for this was that the king wished to obtain Sir Richard Page's manor of Molesey. He therefore turned out Tregonwell and granted the former nunnery, along with several lands, to Page in exchange for Molesey. The 1537 lease to Tregonwell contains no useful information on the buildings but the deed of exchange with Page refers to "...the church stepull and churche yarde of the...late nonnery...",[32] while in the letters patent of 1539 the reference to the church steeple is substituted by "campanile" (bell tower), which according to the Ministers' accounts had three bells in it worth £10.[33] All these references show that parts at least of the church survived the suppression, albeit briefly.

At an unknown date between 1539 and 1545, probably in 1544, the former nunnery was visited by Leland, who wrote "...ther I saw in a praty wood side S. Leonardes (Flamstead parish church) on the lifte hand, scant half a mile of toward north weste. Wher of late tyme was a priorie of nunnes. Master Page the knight hath it now in exchaunge for lands of his in Sutherey (Surrey) about the quarters of Hampton Courte. Master Page hath translatid the house, and now much lyith there."[34]

Page died in February 1548 and in March his widow, Elizabeth, leased the house to Sir William Skypwith, whom she was eventually to marry. In this document the house is referred to as the "...mansion house Beechwood late callyd the priory of Saint Gyles in the Wood...",[35] suggesting that some form of domestic conversion or new building had taken place by this date.

In June 1564 Lady Elizabeth and Sir William Skypwith leased part of the house and grounds to John Cheyne of Amersham (Bucks.). Interestingly, the house is referred to

as the "...dwelling house now commonly called Beechwood...",[36] perhaps suggesting that its monastic antecedents were already beginning to be forgotten. The contents of the lease are unusually detailed, probably because the lessors retained part of the premises for their own use. The lease states that Sir William and Lady Elizabeth shall have "...reserved unto them at all tymes the upper end of the house frome the haule porche uppward, the great kytchyn, thre Chambers frome a little entre going to the gardine downe towards the great Orcharde and one stable next unto the Mansion house..." Cheyne and his son "...Henry and their assignes shall have the use of the haule and great kytchin and great buttery in the absens of the said Sir William and the Lady Elizabeth his wiffe..." and the lessors shall be responsible for "reparacions donne upon the said houses walles...".

Later antiquarian accounts of the house are few in number. Chauncy wrote that "There are no Remains of the Old House, Cloysters, Chappel etc but the Mannor-house is a fair Brick House, of the Figure of a Roman H, wherein is yet Part of a curious wrought Bedstead inlaid, and Curtains of green Velvet richly embroidered, said to be the Repository of the said Edw. VI, and in some Windows of the House are the Arms of France and England, quarter'd with a Label of three, said to be taken out of the Glass of the old religious House..."[37] No mention is made of this glass elsewhere, except possibly by the early 20th-century Flamstead historian, I.V. Bullard, who refers to a window with Edward VI's coat-of-arms which "may still be seen there", although he does not give a date or say whereabouts in the house the window was.[38] In the early 19th century the Revd. David Thomas Powell appears to repeat Chauncy's assertion that "there are no remains of the cloyster chappells",[39] although from his description of the site's location it seems that he may have been confusing Beechwood with nearby Markyate.

ARCHAEOLOGICAL INVESTIGATION

No properly recorded archaeological excavation has taken place on the site but the parch marks visible in the grass immediately to the east of the house and early 20th-century accounts of various archaeological discoveries are helpful in pin-pointing the possible location of the former monastic buildings more accurately.

I.V. Bullard, writing at the beginning of this century, states that " until c.1860 the carriage drive through the park went absolutely past the hall door (on the east front). In that year it was put back many yards from it, and the present gravel sweep made. In doing this some stone coffins with bones were discovered. In 1898 Sir Edgar Sebright moved the road still further from the house, and more coffins with

[29] H.R.O., D/EX 45 B2.
[30] P.R.O., E 117/12/30.
[31] See notes 2 and 3.
[32] Dugdale, iv, 302.
[33] H.R.O., 17,244; P.R.O., SC6/Hen. VIII/1606, m.14.
[34] Leland, i, 104; John Chandler, *John Leland's Itinerary, Travels in Tudor England* (1993), xxx-xxxi.
[35] H.R.O., 17,248.

[36] H.R.O., 17,255.
[37] Chauncy, ii, 515.
[38] I.V. Bullard, *Flamstead, Its Church and History* (1902), 19.
[39] B.L. Add. MS. 17,458, fol.158v.

bones were found...".[40] The position of the former drive is borne out by various 19th-century maps.[41] Bullard also writes that "...on the garden (west) side of the present house some of the old house was discovered when work on that portion of the house was in progress, but was covered up when the work was completed."[42]

There is a persistent tradition that the foundations of the former nunnery can be seen as parch marks in the lawn immediately to the east of the house.[43] In dry weather, such as at the time of my inspection in September 1990, clear parch marks are visible directly to the east of the north pavilion. These seem to indicate a rectangular building with thick walls aligned roughly east-west, truncated by the road between the lawn and the ploughed field immediately to the east. This field has a dense scatter of clay peg tile fragments on its western edge.

In 1981 crop-marks were clearly visible in this field at the same time as four walls and other features were discovered during the digging of electrical service trenches. These features were, however, dated by the County Archaeologist, Mike Daniels to the 18th century. In 1990 further pipe laying across the parch marks referred to above located what were assumed to be medieval foundations, but unfortunately the work was not archaeologically monitored.[44] Aerial photographs held in the N.M.R. do not, however, indicate building foundations in this area.[45] It should be noted that the prominent parch marks in the lawn to the west of the house are those of formal gardens laid out in the 19th century.[46]

This archaeological evidence, although far from definitive, is probably sufficient to dismiss alternative suggestions for the site of the former nunnery. The 6" Ordnance Survey map of 1960 locates the site in the village of Flamstead at NGR TL 0794 1478 but there is no corroborative evidence for this. Likewise, a photograph taken in 1906 of "The Old Priory", which was demolished shortly afterwards,[47] shows a building which looks unlikely to have been of monastic origin. The building photographed is a gable-ended two-storey structure with relatively flimsy-looking timber frame and painted brick infill under a plain tile roof. It appears most likely to be of 18th-century date, although it may conceal some earlier fabric as the roof pitch is quite steep. The apparent tracery over the gable end window is simply painted decoration. All this suggests that the name, "The Old Priory", may merely be a romantic conceit of no

substance, although there is a slight possibility that the cottage may have been connected with a former chantry in the parish.[48]

INTERPRETATION AND CONCLUSIONS

Owing to the lack of any substantial fabric earlier than the 17th century in the present house, any interpretation of the immediate post-Dissolution conversion at Beechwood must be based chiefly on documentary evidence. Fortunately, this is quite good and allows some reconstruction of the possible sequence of events after the suppression. The deed of exchange between the king and Sir Richard Page in September 1538 and the letters patent of the succeeding year both suggest that parts at least of the church, which in the suppression inventory had been described as in "good repair", survived the Dissolution. It seems, however, from the absence of a reference to the church in Leland's description of the place that the church did not survive much longer than this and that it did not feature in Page's domestic conversion.

Although it seems likely that the principal conversion was carried out by Page, it is by no means certain that Tregonwell had not already undertaken some work on the buildings before him. Even before he formally obtained the house, Tregonwell seems to have placed some value on the property. On December 31st 1536 he wrote to Thomas Wriotheseley from the former nunnery, seeking his help in securing the house in recompense for eight or nine years' service to the crown.[49] He also wrote to Cromwell at the same time, offering him £100 "to move the king on his behalf."[50] Later, when asked to leave immediately to make way for Page in August 1538, Tregonwell replied to Cromwell, in a letter again sent from the house, that he had already spent £120 in necessaries for husbandry, hedging, making the ground etc, £40 of which had been paid to the king at the time of the suppression.[51] Although this seems to have been money spent on the estate rather than on the conversion of the buildings, this may well have been Tregonwell's intention, even if work had not started when he was ejected from the property.

Tregonwell and Page were both prominent in Henry VIII's court. Tregonwell had been made a privy counsellor by 1532 and took a major part in the Dissolution, supervising many surrenders, chiefly in the south and west.[52] One of his richest prizes was the Benedictine Milton Abbey (Dorset), which he acquired for £1000 in February 1540,[53] and was to convert into a house.[54] This must certainly have proved adequate compensation for the loss of Beechwood, even if he occasionally complained about the lack of reward he

---

[40] Bullard, op. et loc. cit.

[41] E.g. the 1838 tithe map, H.R.O., DSA 4/38/2.

[42] Bullard, op. et loc. cit.

[43] Oswald, op. cit. (note 12), 474; Bullard, op. cit., 6; Bodl., MS. Top. eccl. b.27, fol.53.

[44] S.M.R., PRN 2855; Information from the headmaster of Beechwood Park School, D. Macpherson, Esq.

[45] R.C.H.M., National Library of Air Photographs, Swindon: Accession no. CAP 8195, frame 51-3.

[46] The gardens are clearly shown in various photographs held in the house.

[47] Hertfordshire Local Studies Library, Hertford, photographic colln.

[48] Bullard, op. cit. (note 38), 11.

[49] *L.P.*, xi, no.1391.

[50] *L.P.*, xi, no.1390.

[51] *L.P.*, xiii (2), no.74.

[52] *D.N.B.*, xix, 1099-1100.

[53] *L.P.*, xv, g.282 (90).

[54] Howard (1987), 203.

received for his services.[55]

Page's career seems to have been more chequered. At the time of Anne Boleyn's execution in 1536 he was imprisoned in the Tower but later he was made a privy counsellor and lieutenant of the band of gentlemen pensioners.[56] He was present at the christening of Prince Edward in October 1537 and at the reception for Anne of Cleves at Greenwich in January 1540.[57] Chauncy states "There is a Tradition, that in the Infancy of Edward VI he was removed thither (Beechwood) by the Advice of his Physitians for some time, and did reside in the said Religious House..."[58] It is possible that this event acted as a further incentive for Page to carry out building work at Beechwood. Leland's comment that he "much lyith there" seems to indicate that it was his principal residence and, since embellishing or extending a house for a royal visitor was not confined to Elizabeth's reign, it is quite likely that Page, having exchanged Molesey for Beechwood, would have wished to continue in royal favour by providing accommodation for the young prince.

The lack of surviving physical evidence makes it difficult to establish whether the monastic buildings themselves provided the basis for Page's conversion works or whether the materials were simply re-used to build a new house. The apparently relatively quick disappearance of the church, which may be represented by the parch marks of the rectangular building to the east of the house, may be significant and suggests the latter. The claustral buildings would obviously have directly adjoined the church and as the most likely site for this is some distance from the house, especially from its oldest parts, it seems unlikely that the church or claustral buildings were themselves converted. This hypothesis is further strengthened by the small size of the nunnery (there were only the prioress and seven nuns at the time of the suppression and the foundation charter had stipulated that there should never be more than 13 nuns without the express consent of the founder),[59] which suggests that the buildings are unlikely to have been very large or (if the identification of the church site is correct) to have extended from the area of the parch marks as far as the 17th-century ranges of the present house, which probably directly overlie the 16th-century building.

The presumably small and perhaps rather unimpressive nature of the former monastic buildings makes it probable that a new owner of the site, especially a man as ambitious as Page, would have wished to start afresh and it therefore seems likely that he demolished the existing buildings, if this had not been done already by Tregonwell, and used the materials in the construction of a new house. Positive

evidence even of this is slight. The stone fireplace in the housemaster's study may pre-date the Dissolution but it is equally likely to be marginally later and it may, of course, have been brought in from elsewhere. Similarly, the stonework in the cellar may be monastic in origin, although the loose chequer-work pattern, which bears some resemblance to the more accomplished above-ground post-Dissolution work at Markyate Cell and Berkhamsted Place, suggests that, while the stonework itself may be pre-Dissolution in date, the walls relate directly to the 16th-century house.

This evidence seems to indicate that Page's house stood on the site of its 17th-century successor, especially as the early 18th-century east range of the house appears to occupy virgin ground. The frequent changes of ownership in the second half of the 16th century make it unlikely that major modifications were carried out at that time, although it is probable that the Smith family, who owned the property between c.1575 and 1628, undertook some work to the house.[60]

The core of the present house, however, appears to date to later in the 17th century and Clutterbuck's misquotation of Chauncy that "...the original house was afterwards pulled down by the family of Saunders..." may be a true reflection of the course of events.[61] Chauncy does in fact refer to a remodelling of the house by Thomas Saunders (d. 1693), who "...has made this Mannor an excellent Seat, and the Place of his Residence..."[62] Chauncy was not an antiquary in the same mould as Camden, Stukeley or, at a later period, Gough: he was equally concerned with describing contemporary marvels and it is unfortunate that only the rather mutilated fabric of the 17th-century house remains. Further evidence that Thomas Saunders was responsible for rebuilding the house in the late 17th century comes from the fact that he paid tax on 13 hearths in 1673 in comparison with his father paying for only nine in 1663.[63]

Whatever the qualities of this work and indeed of the 16th-century building which preceded it, they were soon to be overshadowed by Edward and Anne Sebright's fine east wing of 1695-1702. It is this which remains the principal architectural splendour of Beechwood today.

Bibliography

PICTORIAL SOURCES

Hertfordshire Record Office

Buckler Drawings, IV, 9-12.

[55] *D.N.B.*, loc. cit.

[56] *L.P.*, xv, no.14, p.5; D. Starkey (ed.), *Henry VIII, A European Court in England* (1991), 136-8.

[57] *L.P.*, xii (2), no.911; *L.P.*, xv, no.14, p.5.

[58] Chauncy, ii, 514.

[59] *V.C.H.*, iv, 432.

[60] There are certificates of residence for Richard Smith in 1587 and 1591 and for his widow, Margaret, in 1592, P.R.O., E 115/362/82/97, E 115/347/118.

[61] Clutterbuck, i, 361n.

[62] Chauncy, ii, 511.

[63] P.R.O., E 179/375/31; E 179/248/23.

D/EX 45 B2.

British Library, London

Add. MS. 32,349, fol.86, a & b.

Add. MS. 36,365, fols.3-4.

National Monuments Record, The Royal Commission on Historical Monuments, Swindon

File 39,611.

Printed

Neale, J.P., *Views of the Seats of Noblemen and Gentlemen in England, Wales, Scotland and Ireland* (1822), no page nos.

PHOTOGRAPHIC SOURCES

National Library of Air Photographs, The Royal Commission on Historical Monuments, Swindon

Accession no. CAP 8195, frames 51-3.

Hertfordshire Local Studies Library, Hertford

Photographic Collection.

CARTOGRAPHIC EVIDENCE

Hertfordshire Record Office

DSA 4/38/2.

OTHER PRIMARY SOURCES

Manuscript:-

Public Record Office, London

SC6/Hen. VIII/1606, m.14.

E 115/347/118; E 115/362/82/97.

E 117/12/30.

E 179/248/23; E 179/375/31.

E 315/209, fol.88b.

C 108/362; C 166/1142.

Hertfordshire Record Office
17,243-4; 17,248; 17,255.

British Library, London

Add. MS. 17,458, fol.158v.

Harl. MS. 1504.

Bodleian Library, Oxford

MS. Top. eccl. b.27, fol.53.

County Sites and Monuments Record, Hertford

P.R.N. 2855.

Printed:-

Dugdale, W. (ed.), *Monasticon Anglicanum*, (re-ed. Caley, J., Ellis, H. & Bandinel, B., 6 vols. in 8, 1817-30).
Letters and Papers, Foreign and Domestic, of the Reign of Henry VIII, eds. Brewer, J.S., Gairdner, J. & Brodie, R.H., 21 vols. (1862-1932).
Toulmin Smith, L. (ed.), *The Itinerary of John Leland in or about the Years 1535-43*, i (1906).

SECONDARY SOURCES

Bullard, I.V., *Flamstead, Its Church and History* (1902).
Chandler, J., *John Leland's Itinerary, Travels in Tudor England* (Stroud, 1993).
Chauncy, H., *The Historical Antiquities of Hertfordshire*, ii (1700, reprinted Dorking 1975).
Clutterbuck, R., *The History and Antiquities of Hertfordshire*, i (1815).
Colvin, H., *A Biographical Dictionary of British Architects, 1600-1840* (1978).
Department of the Environment 34th List of Buildings of Special Architectural or Historic Interest, The Borough of Dacorum.
Dictionary of National Biography, 22 vols. (revd. edn., Oxford, 1921/2).
Howard, M., *The Early Tudor Country House* (1987).
Knowles, M.D. & Hadcock, R.N., *Medieval Religious Houses* (1953).
Lees-Milne, J., *English Country Houses: Baroque* (1970).
Oswald, A., 'Beechwood Park', *Country Life* (Nov. 12, 1938), 474-8 and 'Beechwood Park, II', ibid (Nov. 19, 1938), 498-502.
Pevsner, N., *Hertfordshire* (2nd edn. revd., Cherry, B., Harmondsworth, 1977).
Smith, J.T., *Hertfordshire Houses: Selective Inventory* (1993).
Starkey, D. (ed.), *Henry VIII, A European Court in England* (1991).
The Victoria History of the Counties of England, *Hertfordshire*, ii (1908); iv (1914).
Warrand, D., *Hertfordshire Families* (1907).

ST MARGARET'S, NETTLEDEN

History

Benedictine nunnery founded c.1130-60 by Henry de Blois, Bishop of Winchester; dissolved 1536.[1] In this year a 21 year lease of the site was made to John Verney,[2] but two years later it was granted to Sir John Daunce, who died in 1545.[3] The property remained with the Daunce family as lessees until 1630 when it was granted by the crown to Francis Keate and John Saunders.[4]

THE SITE

Introduction

The site is situated on high ground in a pasture field centred on NGR TL 0152 1178 at the north-west end of the hamlet of St Margaret's. Until 1895 it was part of a detached portion of the parish of Ivinghoe (Bucks.),[5] but it is now in the Hertfordshire parish of Nettleden with Potten End. Nothing survives of the buildings above ground but the site is clearly marked by a number of well-preserved earthworks, which are not, however, designated as a Scheduled Ancient Monument.

Description

The pasture field containing the site is covered by well-preserved earthworks, ranging from 0.5 to 1.5m in height, which include possible enclosures and building remains. No archaeological survey is known to have been undertaken of these earthworks but the more significant ones are readily observable on the ground. Unfortunately, it has not been possible to trace any aerial photographs of the site.

There is quite a pronounced bank on the west side of the site, which means that the earthwork field is considerably higher than the adjoining arable field. The bank incorporates a considerable quantity of flint. The most obvious feature in the field is the "moat" towards its centre. This takes the form of a roughly rectangular tree-lined depression, at the north-west corner of which the uprooting of two large trees had revealed substantial amounts of flint and tile, along with more modern vitrified brick, at the time of site inspection (November 1990). Another fallen tree at the south-west corner of the "moat" had produced similar results and also a piece of moulded stonework- clunch and probably medieval. Some at least of the tile is peg-holed roof tile and may be medieval in date. The line of a flint wall seems to run along the north side of the "moat" and also to bound its south and west banks. A roughly circular depression lies just to the east of the "moat", containing pieces of brick, tile and medieval pottery: it may mark the location of a well.

THE FORMER BUILDINGS

The evidence for the buildings comes from two main sources, pictorial/cartographic and the written accounts of 18th- and 19th-century antiquaries.

Documentary Evidence

The Commissioners' returns report the house to be in "competent estate" but value the bells, lead and other buildings at only £8 10s 6d and the entire value of the movable goods at £1 13s 4d.[6] The grant to Daunce in April 1538 refers to the "church, campanil(e) and cemetery",[7] but contains no other information on the buildings. This absence of information on the buildings is repeated in later grants of the property and the site is also ignored by early antiquaries such as Leland, Norden and Camden.

The earliest accounts of the site are those by the eccentric Buckinghamshire historian, Browne Willis (1682-1760), who may have visited the site on several occasions.[8] Several of these accounts, which are in manuscript form, contain slightly contradictory information, but taken as a whole they give some impression of the appearance of the site in the early 18th century. Willis originally wrote "Nothing of the antient nunnery as I am informed is standing, it being converted into a dwelling house and the old building intirely demolished",[9] but he was soon to alter this in his "Addenda and Corrigenda" in the same manuscript to "I visited this place; the House seems almost entirely standing, tho it was always small; the parlour and Hall not bad buildings being of Tatenhall (Totternhoe) stone well wrought, behind them stood the church I saw the square of the Tower it was 10 foot high in memory of man; Tradition says three bells were in it and one of them was carried to Nettleden chapell scarce half a mile from it; It was about 12 ft square the church adjoyned to it or rather stood on one side and opened into the Priory House by an arch which is yet visible- The Dragon pierced thro with a sword was I presume the arms of the house it is now broke and scarce discernible there is some pretty painted glass in the parlour window surrounding the outside but no writing- the churchyard is yet so called but I could hear of no corpses or Bones dugg up there- the house seeming to have been built tempore Henricii Septius; the Hall and parlour..."[10] The account breaks off at this point but elsewhere he adds that "the hall and parlor seem to be built

---

[1] Knowles (1953), 218; *V.C.H., Bucks.*, i (1905), 353.
[2] *V.C.H., Bucks.*, iii (1925), 382; *L.P.*, xiii (1), g.887 (20).
[3] *L.P.*, xiii (1), g.887 (20); Dugdale, iv, 271. An account of Daunce's life and career is given in C.T. Martin, 'Sir John Daunce's accounts of money received from the treasurer of the king's chamber temp. Henry VIII', *Archaeologia*, 47 (1883), 295-336.. Elsewhere, however, it is suggested that Daunce died in 1564, Bodl., MS. Willis 101, p.145.
[4] Bodl., MS. Willis 40, p.173.
[5] *V.C.H.*, ii, 317.

[6] Bodl., MS. Willis 34, p.121b.
[7] See note 3.
[8] Bodl., Willis colln.
[9] Bodl., MS. Willis 34, p.40.
[10] Bodl., MS. Willis 34, p.40b.

at Hen.7 days."[11]

Willis then continues "The Fabrick seems to have been but small and mean at the ----, of it there remains very little that is antient: there is a good Hall with antique wainscot but the ---- building is modern, in a word it is a dark uncomfortable dwelling. In a window in is this Coat (illustrated) a Dragon with a crucifix in his mouth and a sword on his back, or, in a Feild gules ----. K. Hen VIII granted this house to John Dauncie, viz. all the lands, mills, tenements etc. ...From Dauncie it descended to Fr. Keate and John Saunders, thence to the Father of Mr Catharall the present Possessor."[12]

A little extra information can be gleaned from elsewhere in the Willis collection; for instance, in answer to a series of queries sent out by Willis to local parsons and other antiquaries, an anonymous correspondent replied that "that part of the Nunnery house which is now called the Hall was formerly used as the Chappell being the most likely part now remaining."[13] In 1711 Willis writes that "One of the bells at Nettleden Church is said to have come from St Margaret's."[14] Elsewhere he refers to four paintings on the reading desk, and "on the pulpit were eight more such paintings the most remarkable of which is a woman with a crucifix in her Hand at her feet a Green dragon [(being the Portrayte of St Margaret) in a different hand];"[15] this too may have come from St Margaret's. Indeed, Willis's very full description of Nettleden shows that it was unusually well furnished for a small parochial chapel; some other features are stated to have come from Ashridge and it is by no means inconceivable that others came from St Margaret's.

Willis's account of St Margaret's is usefully supplemented by the roughly contemporary description written by Edward Steele in c.1714. This states that "(the nunnery) was seated on an even, high and spatious Woody Common, which about A.D.1665 John then Earl of Bridgwater (with the concent of the Tenants) inclosed into Arable land, allowing each inhabitant a large and proportionate share Freehold, now pleasantly Surrounded and plentifuly set with Beech Trees, where is one Lane perfectly Straight and level full 550 paces in length, and about 12 broad, nigh to which, parte of the Building is still Standing [now the Mansion House of Mr John Hooke (alias Catherall)] by which it appears it was built with neatness and great strength, of flints, bricks etc but the Dorecases, Window frames and Quire Stones was of Tatinhal Stone, a Quarry not far off, on one of the Chimnys is a large Tyle, impressed with the Armes of the Principallaty of Wales viz. three Ostridge Feathers within a Ducal Coronet with the Device Ic-dieu (from the Old Saxon Ic-pezn) for I serve, the like whereof is upon the Armes of the Counties Palatine

of Chester and Durham...Besides the above mentioned, their is no Armes remaining, except on the Glass, in a window at the West side of the House, is painted a Small Shield bearing G. a Dragon couchant regardent etc..." Steele then refers to more stained glass "Throughout the same Window, in the midst of each Quarrel, or Pain of Glass, is Small Leopards heads verant Flower-de-Luces O. which on a Field G. is the Armes of the See of Hereford." He concludes with an illustration showing "the exact Form and Proportion of the Armes in the Window."[16]

Steele also wrote an account of Nettleden chapel, where he mentions "three small bells, two of them very ancient, one dedicated to St Lawrence, the other to St Katherine, on which is fixed the impression of one of King Edward the 3d shillings."[17] He does not say that any of the bells came from St Margaret's.

With the exception of a description of the site in c.1740 by the Revd. William Cole,[18] which appears to be based entirely on Willis's account, there do not seem to be any further descriptions until the early 19th century. In 1806 Daniel and Revd. Samuel Lysons wrote that "Part of St Margaret's Nunnery is standing, and occupied as a dwelling-house; it does not appear to be of a much earlier date than the dissolution of the monasteries...The building was, in 1802, almost entire: the parlour and hall, which are of Totternhoe stone, appear to be of the age of Henry VII."[19] Although most of this account obviously derives directly from Willis, the reference to the building being "almost entire" in 1802 suggests that it may have been based partly on personal observation.

The lack of any contemporary description in William Caley's 1823 edition of Dugdale's *Monasticon* makes it likely that all traces of the buildings had disappeared by this date, while in 1858 Kelke wrote "From an old man who lives near the spot I learned that the nunnery was inhabited about forty years ago by a gentleman who died there, a portion of the building looked like a church. There are no visible remains of the convent, chapel or manor house mentioned by Leland, but the site is marked by vestiges of a moat and buried portions of a building surrounded by ancestral trees. The spot is still called Nunnery Close."[20] This absence of visible remains is confirmed by Kelke's contemporary, Sheahan,[21] and Lipscomb simply repeats the account of the Lysons brothers.[22] Not surprisingly there was a local tradition, apparently first recorded by Benjamin Scott in the early 19th century, that "there was once a subterranean passage leading from this old Nunnery to Ashridge..." Equally

[11] Bodl., MS. Willis 101, p.143.
[12] Bodl., MS. Willis 34, p.41b.
[13] Bodl., MS. Willis 1, p.682.
[14] Bodl., MS. Willis 34, p.124b.
[15] Bodl., MS. Willis 102, p.20.

[16] Bodl., MS. Top. gen. e. 79, fols.8-11.
[17] Bodl., MS. Gough Bucks. 5, fol.15.
[18] B.L., Add. MS. 5840.
[19] D. & S. Lysons, *Magna Britannia*, i (1806), 492, 588.
[20] H.R.O., Gerish colln., Box 30.
[21] J.S. Sheahan, *The History and Topography of Buckinghamshire* (1862), 701.
[22] G. Lipscomb, *The History and Antiquities of Buckinghamshire*, iii (1847), 399.

unsurprisingly, excavations in the later 19th century failed to locate it.[23]

The *V.C.H.* merely states that "traces of (the nunnery) site still remain near St Margaret's Farm. The buildings in 1802 were almost entire and the refectory remained until the early 19th century."[24] A contemporary newspaper account is, however, much more informative: "The old Nunnery stood in what is now known as the Nunnery Orchard, of about ten acres in extent, belonging to the adjoining farm. A grove containing some large Spanish and horse chestnut and walnut trees extends from the lane about half-way across the orchard to the space upon which stood the old house, while apple and other fruit trees stand thickly round. There are no remains whatever to be seen of the old buildings, but a few grass-covered mounds denote their position. In the middle of the field is a hole overgrown with bushes, which probably marks the location of one of the old cellars, and at the side of the field is a large pond, mostly dry, nearly surrounded by trees, one of them an enormous beech tree, standing on the bank of the boundary ditch. At the opposite corner of the field is a pond, which was formerly walled round, but there are no signs of any moat ever having existed upon the premises surrounding the buildings. The adjoining farm is known as the Nunnery Farm, and the dwelling-house, with some few signs of antiquity, has been considerably altered and repaired, but still contains several old beams and panelled walls. In the garden are a few pieces of the stonework of the old Nunnery showing mouldings and ornaments...The property upon which the Nunnery stood was acquired by an adjoining owner about seventy years ago, but the purchaser was not an antiquarian, and possessed no ideas of an archaeological nature. The place seems to have been considered by the new owner a blot upon the landscape, and therefore the buildings were totally demolished..."[25]

Pictorial Evidence

There are only two known views of the former nunnery, both made in the early 19th century. Each displays minor differences, which can largely be explained by likely differences in date. More importantly, both appear to be basically consistent with the descriptions given by Willis and Steele approximately a century earlier.

The earlier drawing seems to be that contained in the topographical collections of the Lysons brothers.[26] It is an undated, fairly rough sketch, executed partly in pencil and partly in pen and ink. It was probably made as a preliminary drawing for inclusion in their *Magna Britannia*, although in the event it was not to be included in that publication. The drawing shows the building from the west and depicts a structure in two distinct sections. The

north section is of two storeys and appears to be of flint construction with clunch dressings under a steeply pitched tile roof with exposed rafter ends and double-purlin ends visible to the north gable end. There is a chamfered plinth continuing round to the gable end. The west elevation has a central external lateral stack, apparently built of brick, with quoins up to the point where it tapers above the eaves to a moulded base with triangular offsets and three attached diagonal shafts. To either side of the stack there are windows on both floors, the upper being two-light chamfered mullion windows, the left, drawn in more detail than the right, with leaded latticed lights to the left section. The ground-floor windows are mullioned and transomed with cusped trefoil heads and dripstones. The left window is again depicted in more detail than the right and has leaded latticed lights with iron bars above the transom and is bricked up below. The details of the gable end windows, one on each floor, are not shown except for a bracketed head to the ground-floor window. Attached to the north-east corner of the gable end are the remains of what appears to be the east wall of a former timber-framed structure running off-picture to the north.

The range to the south is longer and lower and seems to project slightly to the front: there are quoins to the north-west angle. The lateral stack is dominant with materials indicated as flint with clunch quoins below the eaves and brick above. It has a chamfered plinth and a chamfered string course roughly on the level of the ground-floor window heads. Another chamfered string course directly above the eaves has a carved band of fleur-de-lys decoration below the moulded base, which supports two attached diagonal shafts with moulded capping, which appear to extend above the ridge of the roof. To the left of the stack is a two-light mullion window on each floor, both with leaded lights, the ground-floor one with a string course above and the upper, of reduced proportions, directly below the eaves. To the right of the stack is another two-light leaded mullion window (this one wider than it is high) with string course above and on the first floor, immediately below the eaves, a three-light mullion window, with leaded latticed lights shown to the left section. To the right of these windows is a pointed recessed doorway, seemingly with a plank door, and to the right of this a small lancet, which appears to have large quoins to each jamb. Above and to the right of the lancet an area of brick patching is indicated. There are exposed rafter ends to the eaves and a possibility that the south end of the roof is hipped. To the right of this is what appears to be a ruined section of building. It stands to the same eaves height, suggesting that it was formerly part of the long range, its truncation perhaps accounting for the possible hipped roof form at this point. The walling is indicated as flint with a chamfered plinth and a diagonal buttress to the south-west corner, but there is not enough detail to the drawing to show openings in this section. Drawn separately from the building is a cusped trefoil-headed window, which seems to be captioned "Chapel on north side".

[23] Quincey Lane, 'St Margaret's Priory', *Herts. Constitutional Mag.*, i (1889), 297.

[24] *V.C.H.*, ii, 317.

[25] H.R.O., Gerish colln., Box 30.

[26] B.L., Add. MS. 9460, fol.124.

The evidence of the Lysons drawing is largely corroborated by the slightly later drawing made by Benjamin Scott in 1819,[27] most differences between the two views being explained by demolitions carried out after the first drawing was made. In the Scott view both stacks are shown truncated at the eaves, although the north one has a small brick section above. The long range is shown cut off immediately to the south of the doorway and there appears to be a weatherboarded barn with thatched roof immediately to the north of the building. Other differences from the Lysons view are less easy to explain. First, the whole building is shown under a continuous roof, although a break is visible between the two sections. The north gable end is timber framed with vertical studs to the apex, below which a number of openings are just visible, including a narrow pointed window with spandrels below a dripstone to the north-west corner on the first floor. The windows to either side of the north stack largely match those in the earlier view. The apparently plain pointed heads of the left ground-floor window, which is partially blocked, are probably the result of inaccurate drawing and, in fact, cusped trefoil heads are shown to the lower right window. The first-floor windows are also blocked. To the south, the tall two-light mullion window to the left of the south stack is shown as a square-headed doorway with moulded jambs, but the details of the windows to the right appear to coincide with those shown in the earlier view. A straight joint, which is not detectable in the other view, is visible to the right and the doorway to the right has a square head similar to that of the doorway to the left of the south stack, but with a dripstone, not the pointed head shown in the other drawing. Above the doorway is a two-light trefoil-headed mullion window. The north gable end has a weathervane to the ridge.

Cartographic Evidence

There is a lack of early map evidence for St Margaret's. A map of 1803 by T. Godman shows four buildings pencilled on in a field,[28] which may be the one where the nunnery earthworks lie but, as the field boundaries shown on this map do not coincide with those on other maps, this cannot safely be used as evidence. More certainty attaches to an undated and unattributed map of the early 19th century which, as it also marks St Margaret's Farm - the farm immediately to the south east of the nunnery earthworks-pinpoints the site exactly.[29] It shows five buildings in the field where the earthworks are situated. The longest building is aligned roughly north-west to south-east and may be the building shown in the two early 19th-century drawings. A smaller L-shaped building is marked to the south east with smaller structures still to both north and south. Significantly, an estate map of 1825 of the same area shows no buildings on the site, although it marks the pond or moat,[30] which still survives in the middle of the field.

This ties in well with the lack of reference to surviving buildings in the 1823 edition of Dugdale's *Monasticon*, referred to above, and it can be stated with some certainty that the buildings were demolished between the time of Scott's drawing in 1819 and 1825.

The 6" Ordnance Survey map of 1883/4 shows quite a number of trees on the site with what appears to be a regularly planted orchard in the north-west corner of the field. Again the surviving moat is clearly marked.

INTERPRETATION AND CONCLUSIONS

The relatively sparse evidence for St Margaret's makes it difficult to come to any positive conclusions about the re-use of the former monastic buildings after the Dissolution. From the Commissioners' returns it is obvious that the house was a poor one. Although in "competent estate", the bells, lead and other buildings were worth only £8 10s 6d and the entire value of the movable goods was put at £1 13s 4d. Never a large community, there were only five nuns (including three novices) and four servants there at the suppression, while the Ministers' accounts valued the house at only £10 4s 1½d.[31]

It is no surprise then that the post-Dissolution use seems to have been low-key. The original grantee of the site, John Verney, was a member of an important landowning family in Buckinghamshire,[32] but the comparatively short period for which he held the site and the absence of any other known connections with the immediate locality perhaps make it unlikely that he carried out any conversion work.

The next owner, Sir John Daunce, who had been Henry VIII's Treasurer of Wars and had been involved with the financing of royal works at Camber, Portsmouth and Portchester,[33] Surveyor-General of crown lands since December 1536,[34] and who had been appointed Commissioner of the Peace for Buckinghamshire in December 1536 and for Oxfordshire in November 1537,[35] was already advanced in years when he acquired the property. It seems unlikely that he too would have embarked on any major programme of remodelling and it seems that the buildings were simply adapted, probably with substantial demolitions, to form a farmhouse and associated farmbuildings. This certainly seems to have been the use of the site during the long ownership by the Catherall family from the second quarter of the 17th century to c.1800.[36]

Both Willis and Steele state that the then surviving

[27] H.R.O., Gerish colln., Box 30.
[28] H.R.O., AH. 2817.
[29] H.R.O., 56,473.
[30] H.R.O., 56,483.

[31] Bodl., MS Willis 34, p.121b; P.R.O., SC6/Hen. VIII/234, m.6.
[32] A prominent member of the family, Sir Ralph Verney, was made Sheriff of Bedfordshire and Buckinghamshire in November 1540; *L.P.*, xvi, g.305 (80).
[33] *King's Works*, iii, 291n; Ibid, iv, 416, 493, 496.
[34] *L.P.*, x, g.1015 (6).
[35] *L.P.*, xi, g.1417 (5); *L.P.*, xii, g.1150 (15).
[36] *V.C.H., Bucks.*, iii (1925), 383.

buildings had been erected during the reign of Henry VII and, although the doorway and lancet window shown in the Lysons view look earlier than this, there is no real evidence to deny the substance of this claim. If the buildings had been so recently erected, their re-use at the Dissolution would have been particularly attractive.

There remains the problem of identifying the original monastic function of the buildings re-used at St Margaret's. In the absence of standing buildings or excavation, we must again rely on Willis and Steele and the two drawings. Despite the reply to the queries sent out by Willis that "That part of the Nunnery house which is now called the Hall (the building then surviving) was formerly used as the Chappell being the most likely part now Remaining", it seems probable that the building shown in the two early 19th-century views was a domestic building of the nunnery. It is, of course, an assumption that the principal building described by Willis and Steele is the same as the one depicted in the two drawings but, on the basis of comparisons, it is probably a valid one. Willis refers to the building which survived in his day as the "parlour and hall" but he also mentions the church tower which stood "ten foot high in the memory of man", suggesting that the church had long been ruinous. The *V.C.H.* is apparently the earliest authority to identify the building which remained in the early 19th century as the refectory. Such a use would, however, be consistent with the appearance of the building shown in the two drawings. It is conceivable therefore that the monastic refectory was converted after the Dissolution to the parlour and hall of a new house, its length and domestic character being particularly suitable for such a function.

As was frequently the case in such situations, some building materials from the former nunnery seem to have found their way elsewhere. Nearby Nunnery Farmhouse is described in the early 20th-century newspaper account referred to earlier: "...the dwelling-house, with some few signs of antiquity, has been considerably altered and repaired, but still contains several old beams and panelled walls. In the garden are a few pieces of the stonework of the old Nunnery showing mouldings and ornaments." Unfortunately, access to the interior of the farmhouse was denied at the time of my site visit but, although some slight irregularities in the roof slope and a large stack at the east end may suggest an earlier core, the purplish brick and machine tiled roof point to a substantial rebuilding of the 1880s. Most of the farmbuildings also appear to be of this date. Again access was refused but the farmer stated that the roof structures are of sawn timber and there seems little reason to doubt this statement.

Both farmhouse and farmbuildings are shown on early 19th-century maps so we know that the farm is at least as early as this, but it is too far away to be connected directly with the former nunnery buildings. Other buildings in the locality may also contain re-used fragments from the nunnery. The early 20th-century newspaper account states that "Over the fireplace in one of the rooms of an old cottage in the hamlet two pieces of the remains have been built into the wall for preservation. These are ornamentally carved stones of the early Decorated period." It has not been possible to identify this cottage or whether it even survives, and nothing is known of the date or circumstances when the supposed fragments found their way to the building.

Finally, mention should be made of the claim by Willis that there were three bells in the tower of the nunnery church and that "...one of them was carried to Nettleden chapell..." In March 1555 two bells from St Margaret's are listed in the "Declaracon of Joise Carleton, wydowe",[37] and as bells were usually highly prized commodities, it is likely that they would have been removed from the nunnery at the time of the Suppression. The number of bells is not, however, specified in the Commissioners' returns and it is possible that one bell was removed to Nettleden before or at the same time as the listing of the other two in 1555. It is worth noting, though, that in his authoritative study of Buckinghamshire church bells, Cocks makes no mention of the "tradition " that one of the Nettleden bells came from St Margaret's.[38]

Bibliography

PICTORIAL SOURCES

Hertfordshire Record Office

Gerish Collection, Box 30.

British Library, London

Add. MS. 9460, fol.124.

CARTOGRAPHIC SOURCES

Hertfordshire Record Office

AH. 2817.

56,473; 56,483.

OTHER PRIMARY SOURCES

Manuscript:-

Hertfordshire Record Office

---

[37] A.H. Cocks, *The Church Bells of Buckinghamshire* (1897), 531.
[38] Ibid, 532.

Gerish Collection, Box 30.

Public Record Office, London

SC6/Hen. VIII/234, m.6.

British Library, London

Add. MS. 5840.

Bodleian Library, Oxford

MS. Willis 1, 34, 40, 101, 102.

MS. Top. gen. e. 79, fols.8-11.

MS. Gough Bucks. 5, fol.15.

Printed:-

Dugdale, W. (ed.), *Monasticon Anglicanum*, (re-ed Caley, J., Ellis, H. & Bandinel, B., 6 vols. in 8, 1817-30).
Letters and Papers, Foreign and Domestic, of the Reign of Henry VIII, eds. Brewer, J.S., Gairdner, J. & Brodie, R.H., 21 vols. (1862-1932).

SECONDARY SOURCES

Cocks, A.H., *The Church Bells of Buckinghamshire* (1897).
Colvin, H.M. *et al*, *The History of the King's Works*, iii (1975); iv (1982).
Knowles, M.D. & Hadcock, R.N., *Medieval Religious Houses* (1953).
Lane, Q., 'St Margaret's Priory', *Herts. Constitutional Mag.*, i (1889), 297.
Lipscomb, G., *The History and Antiquities of Buckinghamshire*, iii (1847).
Lysons, D. & S., *Magna Britannia*, i (1806).
Martin, C.T., 'Sir John Daunce's accounts of money received from the treasurer of the king's chamber temp. Henry VIII', *Archaeologia*, 47 (1883), 295-336.
Sheahan, J.S., *The History and Topography of Buckinghamshire* (1862).
The Victoria History of the Counties of England, *Buckinghamshire*, i (1905); iii (1925).
-*Hertfordshire*, ii (1908).

SOPWELL NUNNERY

History

Benedictine nunnery founded as a dependent cell of St Albans Abbey in c.1140;[1] dissolved in March 1537 and granted to Sir Richard Lee in December 1538.[2] Lee died in 1575,[3] when the property passed to his daughter, Mary and her husband, Humphrey Coningsby.[4] It remained with Mary and her second husband, Ralph Pemberton, until her death in 1610.[5] In 1669 the site was sold to Harbottle Grimston,[6] whose family became the earls of Verulam,[7] with whom it remained until the 20th century.[8]

THE BUILDINGS

Introduction

The ruins of Sopwell Nunnery are situated on open ground on the south-west bank of the River Ver approximately half a mile to the south-east of St Albans Abbey. Most of what is now visible is associated with Lee's remodelling of the nunnery buildings as a house in two distinct phases after the Dissolution. Although partially covered in ivy and other vegetation at the time of site inspection in September 1990, the ruins are in reasonable condition and some consolidation work has been carried out.

DESCRIPTION

Now a roofless ruin, the buildings are of mixed brick and flint construction with clunch dressings.

Plan-form

The principal survival on the site is the west range of Lee's second house. At its northern end the range is double and foundations to the east of the present boundary wall (originally the central wall of the 16th-century hall range, itself on the site of the monastic church) show that the east range was similar in this respect. The wall running at right-angles to the east of the west range is the south wall of a single-storey corridor to the south of the hall. The wall may also be on the site of the south wall of the monastic north cloister walk.

West range

East elevation. The section to the left of the cross-wall has a brick and flint plinth with moulded stone capping. From left to right there is a doorway with moulded surround

(head missing) and a large window, probably originally of four lights, of which the moulded surround and part of the cill and dripstone remain, with the fragments of segmental-headed lights with hollow spandrels to the corners. To the north of this window is a similar window, probably formerly of three lights, the head partly replaced by a concrete lintel. Immediately to the right is another former three-light window, partially infilled by later brickwork, again with fragments of segmental-headed lights to the corners.

Although there is a cross-wall at the present south end of the range , this is likely originally to have been internal and the range probably once extended further to the south. On the first floor, above a moulded stone string course and directly above the ground-floor windows, are the remains of windows of the same dimensions. The brickwork and plinth of the east-west running cross-wall, although not continuous with that of the east elevation of the west range, is apparently bonded into it.

To the right of the cross-wall the first section of walling projects slightly from the section to the left of the cross-wall. It is carried up directly from the cross-wall and has a moulded stone capping which itself is below the moulded string course, continued across from the section to the left of the cross-wall. There is a well-preserved window with the remains of three segmental-headed lights, probably originally with a high transom, the head of the centre light now supported by an inserted brick pier. There are a moulded cill, surround and dripstone as to the other windows. To the right of this is a doorway, which somewhat curiously appears to have its internal face on this side. Brick reveals are visible to the right jamb, the facing material having been robbed from the left jamb. Although there is no distinct sign of a straight joint to either side of the doorway, this suggests that there may have been a porch or some other kind of structure to the east: a stone to the right of the top right corner of the doorway may have had some association with such a feature. Above the doorway are the remains of a roundel with a moulded brick surround.

To the right of the doorway are the vestiges of another window (the left jamb and a small section of cill and dripstone), probably again originally of three lights, the straight joint to the right probably representing the position of its north jamb. To the right again is the base of a projecting red brick chimney stack, which looks like it might have been inserted into a blocked opening. To the right is a further section of brick and flint wall, which turns at right-angles to the west. This probably represents the northern extent of this range and has the remains of the left corner of the dripstone of a window below the first-floor string course, which starts again, with a more elaborate moulding, on this north face. It should be noted that there is no plinth visible to the north of the east-west running cross-wall but it is almost certainly simply buried.

[1] Knowles (1953), 219.
[2] *L.P.*, xii (1), no.571 (1); H.R.O., IV. A. 1.
[3] *D.N.B.*, xi, 811.
[4] *V.C.H.*, ii, 413.
[5] Ibid.
[6] Ibid.
[7] Norah King, *The Grimstons of Gorhambury* (1983), 93.
[8] *V.C.H.*, ii, 413.

The first floor of this section of building only has a string course above the capping over the surviving ground-floor window. Above and slightly to the right of this window is a window of the same dimensions, of which only part of the surround and part of the cill remain. To the right of this window the string course and capping terminate and the wall plane continues at the same projection as around the surviving ground-floor window. In this section of wall a series of straight joints suggests blocked openings but these may be later than either phase of Lee's conversion works. Above and slightly to the right of the remnants of the ground-floor window to the right of the doorway are the remains of the left jamb of a window, with the traces of a brick elliptical relieving arch above. A large section of wall is then missing at first-floor level, beginning again only to the right of the position of the projecting chimney stack. Immediately to the south of the wall's return to the west are the remains of the cill and north jamb of a window, of which not enough survives to determine its original size.

West elevation. The west wall of the west range has now disappeared above ground level to its northern end and is not picked up again until the point where there is a stub projecting to the north at the west end of a cross-wall dividing this range (this internal cross-wall continues the line of the cross-wall to the east of the west range). Then there is a fairly wide gap to an unbroken stretch of brick and flint walling; the opening in this to the ground floor right is probably a later breach and is now supported by a concrete lintel. There is a slightly angled buttress directly to the right of this. The first floor of this latter section of wall has a robbed-out string course (probably originally similar to the other stone string courses on the building). The first-floor window to the north of the buttress is probably not contemporary as its cill cuts the string course and it has a wooden lintel, now supported by a concrete one. To the right of the buttress is another ground-floor opening, again possibly not original, with suggestions of another opening directly above, and then the wall slopes slightly back, dying away into the footings to the south.

North "double" range

The **east elevation** is the external face and is described first. At the south-east corner is the stump of a wall, which ran across eastwards to meet the north-east angle of the west range described above. This wall was the north elevation of the west range and its elaborately moulded string course continues round to the east face of the northern "double" range. To the ground floor left of this is a wide three-centred brick archway with a brick threshold, a plain brick stepped string course directly above and a surviving moulded stone jamb to its left side. There is a moulded stone plinth as on the west range. The wall continues for some distance to the north and then terminates, although the footings and plinth continue, apparently to the point where the wall line meets the northern boundary wall of the northern enclosure, but it should be noted that the ground is very overgrown here.

The first floor of this face of standing wall has the moulded stone surrounds of two narrow two-light windows, the left to the south of the three-centred archway and the right near the north end of the surviving wall.

Interior. The features which have already been described as part of the exterior are not mentioned again unless significant further details can be added. It should be noted that all wall surfaces have remains of lime plaster. Beginning at the south end of the **west range**, this seems to have been divided into four rooms, the largest being to the north and approximately three times the length of the other roughly square-plan rooms. Virtually nothing survives of the south room, save the position of a large first-floor beam end in its north-west corner. The north and south walls of the next room to the north also show the level of the first floor. The south wall has a lean-to scar visible to its west end, suggesting the position of either a staircase or a later lean-to, erected after the building had become ruinous, at this point. The west wall has the remains of a brick fireplace to the south of the surviving first-floor window. The north wall, the position of which is immediately to the north of the southern window in the east wall has a ground-floor doorway in its eastern corner. This is possibly not original and it now has a concrete lintel. Directly above is a first-floor doorway with the remains of a moulded stone surround to its head. The third room to the north has ground- and first-floor doorways to the north wall (the internal continuation of the east-west running wall) in the same position as in the room to the south. The one on the first floor has the same moulding details as the other first-floor doorway and the ground-floor doorway may also be original as it has a segmental brick head on its northern face.

To the north again is a much larger room which has no surviving internal details except the finely moulded stone doorway with roundel above in the east wall, the other side of which has been described above. On its western face the doorway has square lugs to the corners of the head. There are no traces above ground of internal cross-walls in this room.

The west (internal) face of the **north "double" range** has the stub of a cross-wall between the two first-floor windows. This is cut by the large three-centred archway described above, which is thus clearly demonstrated to be an insertion. The positions of three substantial beam ends are also visible. The lower sections of this wall, which is of brick and flint construction, can be seen at right-angles to the west, with its return to north and south, presumably marking the original width of this range.

Other features and boundary walls. To the east of the west range, the east-west running brick and flint and partly lime-plastered wall has a doorway towards its east end. The outer face of this doorway is on the south side and has moulded stone jambs. The wall appears to stand near to its original height towards the west and there is a moulded stone plinth on the south side. The north face of the wall projects slightly at its east end and there is a small projecting range at this point to the south. This has a doorway in its west wall with good-quality ashlar masonry surviving to its north jamb. There seems to have been a staircase or vault over the doorway and there are three segmental-pointed recesses in the north wall with similar but larger recesses in the south and east walls. These recesses may have been for storage.

There are extensive remains of enclosure walls on all sides of the ruins. These appear to have formed inner and outer courtyards, the exact extent of which it is no longer possible to trace. The northern boundary wall is of red brick in English bond, although further to the west behind the modern houses, which lie immediately to the north-west of the ruins, it is of mixed brick and flint construction. The line of this boundary continues westwards until it meets the present road. At its eastern end the northern boundary wall turns at right-angles to the south, where it is again of mixed brick and flint construction. At the point where it meets the staircase projection (referred to above), a moulded stone plinth is visible on the west side, suggesting that here the wall was formerly an outside wall of a building.

To the south of the ruins, the enclosure wall consists only of footings on its east side, while on the south side the brick and flint wall is in fragmentary state. The outer enclosure to the south of this has a very overgrown wall on its southern boundary, which appears to be mainly of red brick, although it contains some flint towards its west end. The western boundary of the site is formed by a fairly substantial bank and ditch of uncertain date, running parallel with the road.

Adjoining the north-west of the north "double" range is an overgrown area of ground forming a square shape, which probably represents another enclosure or courtyard. To the east of the ruins on the same line as the northern boundary referred to above are two brick piers, which may represent part of a gateway. The eastern boundary of this outer enclosure is formed by a red brick wall in Flemish bond and there is another section to the south in mixed bond.

An overgrown area of ground to the west of the ruins conceals the remains of a rectangular building, measuring approximately 288 ft by 23 ft and standing to a maximum of 5 ft high at its east end. It is built of brick in a mixed bond and flint and has a cross-wall in the middle of the long side.

Away from the site of the house very small fragments of the wall which Lee built around the vast park he created can still be seen. In London Road a short section, now consisting only of flint and red brick footings with some moulded clunch, can be seen to the east of the railway bridge. In Old London Road the course of the park wall is marked only by a row of trees on a slight bank, although near the junction with London Road a section of 19th-century brick and flint wall may also indicate its line. More of the wall was, however, visible in this vicinity in the early part of this century.[9]

CARTOGRAPHIC, PICTORIAL AND PHOTOGRAPHIC EVIDENCE

The earliest pictorial representation of the building appears to be on an undated estate map made by Mark Pierce in c.1600.[10] This seems to be quite an accurate perspective drawing and shows a house with its main range aligned roughly east-west with a full-height twin-gabled range projecting at right-angles to the north towards its eastern end and a single-gabled range, also projecting to the north, towards its western end. From the north-east corner of the main range and the north-east corner of the west projecting range a boundary wall encloses a small courtyard, on the south side of which is a small gateway, from which a path leads across to the principal doorway of the main range and northwards to the River Ver. Immediately to the west of the west wall of the courtyard a small rectangular building is tucked into the angle with the north wall, which continues westwards to meet a turret on the western boundary of the site.

On the south side of the main range are two full-height gabled ranges, that to the west continuing the line of the north projecting range and that to the east slightly to the west of the twin-gabled range on the north side. A wall links the inner corners of these ranges, forming a small courtyard which perhaps marks the site of the former cloister. To the centre of the main range two elaborate pinnacles are just visible, possibly on the corner turrets of a porch and in a corresponding position with the doorway on the other side of the range. At right-angles to the range projecting to the south of the main range at its west end is an L-shaped range, the short arm of which appears to be lower than the remainder. To the south-west of this in a large western enclosure is a detached rectangular outbuilding, which may be the same building as that of which the footings remain to the west of the present ruins, although it seems to lie on a different axis in the drawing, running at right-angles to the southern boundary of the western enclosure.

To the east of the courtyard on the north side of the house is another still larger courtyard or precinct, which terminates at its north-east and south-east corners in circular bastions. Immediately to the south-east of the latter of these is what appears to be an octagonal structure on top of a small mound. This might be a dovecote but in view of its apparent location on top of a small mound is perhaps more likely to be some kind of gazebo or pleasure house.

The drawing is of too small a size to indicate the architectural details of the house or associated structures

---

[9] Ibid.
[10] H.R.O., IV. A. 25.

but the main east-west range is shown to have a gable-lit attic storey, the windows are symmetrically placed and several of the gables and the returns of the ranges projecting to the south have tall chimneys.

It is not possible definitely to equate any of the buildings shown on the map with the surviving ruins, but the east-west range is likely to have been the hall range on the site of the medieval church, of which only the east-west running wall to the east of the existing ruins survives today. The principal survival on the site, the north-south range, may be represented by the full-height projection to north and south shown on the map. Significantly, this interpretation seems to tie in fairly well with the archaeological excavation of the site in the 1960s.

The basic accuracy of the c.1600 map is confirmed by an undated mid-17th century estate map, which also shows the house in perspective view.[11] This is more stylised and is probably less reliable but nevertheless matches many of the details of the earlier map and usefully adds a few more. It too shows a main block aligned roughly east-west, although with projecting full-height gables to each end on the north side only. The presence of giant rabbits and stags in the warren to the south shows that this representation of the house was not necessarily intended to be strictly accurate, but significantly it shows a central entrance on the north side of the block and the turrets of a porch in the corresponding position on the south.

The northern boundary of the site is shown in the same location as on the c.1600 map with a rectangular outbuilding along the northern boundary and another to the south-west of the house, both as in the earlier map. An additional outbuilding is, however, shown between the two and a formal gateway in the centre of the west boundary wall. To the south and east of the house an orchard is shown with the north-east corner of the eastern court or precinct occupied by a formal garden. To the south of the house a park pale is shown with a rectangular lodge astride it, the pale dividing the two areas of warren.

Again, the drawing is of too small a size to show much of the details of the house. The entrance on the north side of the main range, however, has four pilasters with carved capitals, the inner two flanking a round-headed doorway. The area between the pilasters is coloured pink, probably representing brickwork, while the rest of the walls are grey to indicate stonework, although in reality this is more likely to have been rendered brick and flintwork. The chimneys and roofs are coloured red, suggesting that they were brick and tiled respectively, while the red colour of the forecourt walls presumably shows that these too were of brick construction.

A map of St Albans, made in 1634 by Benjamin Hare, shows the north front of the main range.[12] It is gable ended of two storeys with five windows on each floor; the tower-like structures visible behind the ridge are part of the porch on the south side. There are full-height ranges at each end, that to the left apparently running at right-angles to the south, while to the right is a detached gable-ended building. In front of all three buildings is a boundary wall and several trees near the house represent its parkland. The map also shows the northern boundary wall of the park which Lee created and the course of the old London Road which was diverted in 1562 as a result of the making of the park.[13]

The next perspective view of the house comes in a map of St Albans drawn by John Oliver in the late 17th century for Chauncy's *History of Hertfordshire*.[14] This depicts the north front of the main range in very similar form to that in the 1634 map. A full-height gable-ended range is shown running parallel and slightly projecting to the right at the rear, while the main range is continued eastwards in a four-bay range with a central gable. Once more a boundary wall is shown in front of the buildings and an orchard to the rear.

A plan of Verulamium made by Stukeley in 1721 also has a perspective view of Sopwell.[15] This too seems to show the north front of the main range, which is indicated to be of 2:2:2:2:2 bays, the central and outer bays having symmetrically placed doorways on the ground floor and the inner bays forming projecting gables with single windows on the ground floor. The central and outer bays each have two ridge stacks.

An estate map of c.1766 shows what was by then a field immediately to the south-east of the house as "The Great Garden."[16] It does not mark the location of the house at all clearly and it seems likely that by then it was already in ruins. Later maps add little further information to that which can be gained from an inspection of the surviving ruins. An 1826 map of St Peter's parish shows the ground-plan of the ruins in much the same form as today.[17] It also usefully confirms the lay-out of the precinct or courtyard walls shown on the c.1600 map, as does the 1840 tithe map of the parish.[18] The 1838 tithe map of St Stephen's parish also shows the situation largely as existing today but, like the 1898 25" Ordnance Survey map, shows more extensive walling surviving to the large enclosures to the east and west of the house.[19]

Turning from representations of Sopwell on maps to those in drawings, we find equally abundant evidence, although

---

[11] H.R.O., XIII. 30.

[12] Reproduced in *V.C.H.*, ii, opp. p.470.

[13] *V.C.H.*, ii, 470.

[14] Chauncy, ii, 428.

[15] Annotated copy of Richard Gough's edn. of Camden's *Britannia*, Bodl., MS. Gough Gen. Top. 61.

[16] H.R.O., D/EV P2.

[17] H.R.O., D/P 93. 29/9.

[18] H.R.O., DSA 4/88/2.

[19] H.R.O., DSA 4/89/2.

none of such early date. The earliest known view is that contained in James Webster's undated mid 18th-century manuscript history of Verulamium and St Albans.[20] It is a small watercolour of 1742 and, although probably not very accurate, seems to be the east view of the ruins. The east boundary wall is in the foreground and part of the main east-west range is visible with a traceried window on the ground floor of its gable end. Also contained in this volume is another watercolour of the nunnery "as it was." In the accompanying text Webster states that he was given a copy by Browne Willis of a drawing which he had found in the library of St Albans Abbey, reputing to show Sopwell as it was in 1420.[21] Presumably then, the watercolour is a copy of Willis's own copy and, perhaps not surprisingly, it does not look very reliable. It shows a substantial church with a tall bell tower, corbelled outwards at the top like a Venetian campanile, with a small square turret covered by a pyramidal roof. Possibly the most significant feature of both drawings is that they were made from the same vantage point, adding further strength to the evidence that Lee converted the nunnery church into the hall range of his house.

A virtually contemporary pen and ink drawing is included in a grangerised copy of Salmon's *History of Hertfordshire*.[22] It is stated to be by Thomas Collinson and to have been presented to Andrew Ducarel on 3 June 1749. It appears to show the north front of the main range of Lee's house and is the only known view to do this. A forecourt wall (presumably the north boundary wall) is shown to the front, apparently of brick construction, although the size of some of the blocks are of a size more usually associated with ashlar masonry. Roughly to the centre of this wall can be seen a pair of rusticated stone gate piers with moulded capping surviving to the left pier and panelled timber double gates. To the left of the gates a wall can be seen running at right-angles to the south to meet the main range behind.

This block survives partly to full height, including the left gable end which can be seen to have an attic window and a corner buttress. A small section of the front wall survives to the right of the gable end and has a doorway to the left on the ground floor and a cross-window, part of the cill of which is missing, high up on the first floor. A cross-wall is visible internally running back from the left jamb of this window and another cross-wall is visible to the right. To the right of this in the rear wall is a tall, narrow, round-headed window. To the right of the second cross-wall a first-floor string course begins and runs along the front wall.

The centre section of the north elevation, aligned on the gateway in the boundary wall to the front, rises up to form a gable with a central square-headed doorway flanked by a cross-window to the left and a narrow round-headed doorway to the right. There are three windows on the first floor and a single window to the attic. All the upper windows are square-headed with segmental-arched lights, the centre and left windows on the first floor mullioned and transomed in three and two lights respectively, the others mullioned in three lights.

The front wall is then missing for a section and then begins again, surviving to eaves height. To the right of the centre gable the back wall can be seen with mutilated openings on both the ground and first floors. A right-angled return from this wall probably represents the stub of a cross-wall.

An undated and unattributed pen and coloured ink drawing, possibly dating to c.1780, in the British Library may show the northern "double" range from the west.[23] It is certainly difficult to reconcile with views of other parts of the ruins and it must be remembered that the west wall of this range has now disappeared completely. It shows a long rectangular two-storey block, apparently surviving to full eaves height at its left end, which slightly projects from the rest of the front wall, which is either at a lower level or survives only to string course height. If the former, the window in its front wall is directly below the eaves. A lancet window with internal hoodmould is visible on the first floor of the left gable end and there is a tall round-headed window to the rear wall on the right. A boundary wall abuts the building at the point where the left section projects from the remainder.

Sparrow's view of the ruins, drawn in 1787 and included in Grose's *The Antiquities of England and Wales*,[24] is much easier to relate to the condition of the site today. It was drawn from the west and shows the surviving north-south range and the north "double" range. It adds important details to our knowledge of the former, such as the presence of a blocked round-headed window over the doorway which has the roundel above, traces of which can still be seen on the east face today. Most interest, however, attaches to the north "double" range, which is shown in a more complete, albeit even then ruinous state. The north end walls survive to eaves height and have tall windows at first-floor level. The dividing spine wall also survives at the north end and the external west wall has the remains of the left jamb of a first-floor window towards its northern end. A boundary wall, presumably enclosing a courtyard, abuts the west wall and has a square-headed doorway in its south face.

An important, undated early 19th-century watercolour of the east side of the remaining ruins depicts a large lump of overgrown masonry in front of the north-south range but behind the east boundary wall and to the right of the wall, which runs at right-angles to the north-south range.[25] This

[20] Library of Society of Antiquaries, MS. 720, J. Webster, *Gleanings of Antiquity from Verolam and St Albans* (n.d.), 134.
[21] Ibid, 138.
[22] Bodl., Gough Herts. 11, opp. p.82.

[23] B.L., K. Top. XV. 83.
[24] Francis Grose, *The Antiquities of England and Wales*, v (1777), no page no.
[25] B.L., Add. MS. 32,351, fol.197 (top).

masonry lump, both external walls of which are visible in this view, does not link with the north-south range and would seem most likely to represent the remains of an outbuilding. Another, more romanticized view confirms the former presence of this masonry lump.[26]

Several views of the ruins from the south east exist. These drawings add a few details to those which can be seen on the ruins today. The most detailed of these views shows the surviving fireplace on the west wall of the north-south range to have been square headed with a semi-circular relieving arch. To the west of the ruins a single-storey gabled building can be seen abutting the inside face of the southern boundary wall.[27] A small romanticized engraving of 1817 by I. Hassell shows a broad lancet on the first floor immediately to the right of the east-west running wall,[28] this being the same window as depicted in a view by Oldfield,[29] as well as being shown from the other side in the drawing by Sparrow referred to earlier.

A large watercolour, dated October 1821,[30] portrays the same broad lancet with its head missing, suggesting that it collapsed or was removed between 1817 and 1821. The head of the lancet is also missing in C.A. Buckler's pencil sketch of the ruins made in June 1832.[31] This sketch also shows a blocked doorway with a four-centred stone head in the southern boundary wall near its south-east corner. The gabled outbuilding on the southern boundary wall had evidently disappeared by this date as a gap can be seen in the wall where it once stood.

This sketch, of which there are also at least two finished pen and ink drawings,[32] shows that the two first-floor windows to the left of the east-west running wall were each divided by both a transom and mullions, the left with three segmental-headed lights above and below the transom, the right with only two. The pen and ink drawing also clearly indicates another blocked doorway in the southern boundary wall to the right of the one with the four-centred stone head. Both doorways are also shown in a photograph of the ruins taken from the same angle in c.1900.[33] This also shows that the north-south range once continued right down to the southern boundary wall, as the lower courses of the east wall of this range are shown extending southwards from its present termination. The southern boundary wall is also shown to incorporate several substantial pieces of clunch.

Various undated early 19th-century drawings by J. Carter

show details of other features associated with the house. One shows a square, carved stone panel with a dripstone depicting a right arm, clothed in a 16th-century embroidered tunic with a puffed shoulder and protected elbow, which has the legend "ET PLAI" to a flowing garland. The hand of the arm, which is bent at the elbow, grips a blazing sword and underneath is the caption "TERRO ET PLAI".[34] The location of the carved panel is not given but it is almost certainly one of the two carved panels referred to by Grose as being "on one of the walls of the garden" (see below). The coat-of-arms was granted to Lee in October 1544.[35]

Other drawings by Carter show the vaulted staircase chamber at the east end of the east-west running wall.[36] One is an accurate, measured ground-plan indicating the niches in the walls, one of the smaller of which is also shown in elevation. Carter also provides a view of a gang of men in the chamber apparently breaking up its stone barrel vaults. The appearance of the chamber in this drawing ties in neatly with the ground-plan and the surviving structure, although the huge ashlar blocks depicted to the vaulting look a little improbable.

DOCUMENTARY EVIDENCE

As with several Hertfordshire former monastic sites, the documentary evidence is most conveniently treated under two headings- official records made in connection with the site and the accounts of antiquarian visitors.

As is frequently the case, little information on the buildings can be gleaned from the Ministers' Accounts beyond the fact that they were in reasonable repair and that the lead on the roofs and the four bells were worth £40 and £18 respectively.[37] More useful is the inventory made of the house by the royal commissioners at its suppression in March 1537.[38] This mentions the following buildings: " the hall, kychen, napery and churche", the total value of the goods being given as only 76s 8d. This, however, did not include the timber and the stone and in the records of the Augmentations Office the sum total of the goods and plate amounted to £11 8s 9d.[39] These also show that the "Tymber worke in the Quyre" was sold for 40s, "the stuffe in the quyre conteyned in the inventory" for 20s, "the stones in the churche wt the vestery Stuff" for 60s, the "Stuff in the parlor conteyned in the Inventory" for 10s and the "Kechyn stuff" for 15s, all to John Shreve and Thomas Maydewell, who were probably local men.

Richard Lee (he was not knighted until 1544) had been bailiff and farmer of the nunnery since 1534,[40] and in

[26] Ibid (centre).

[27] B.L., Add. MS. 32,351, fols.195, 198.

[28] B.L., Add. MS. 32,351, fol.196.

[29] H.R.O., Oldfield Drawings, VIII, 556.

[30] B.L., Add. MS. 32,351, fol.198.

[31] B.L., Add. MS. 36,366, fol.207.

[32] H.R.O., Buckler Drawings, III, 138; Museum of St Albans, Lewis Evans colln., St Albans Scrapbooks, Vol.2.

[33] British Museum, Dept. of Prints and Drawings, Case 21. There are other useful late 19th-century photographs in H.R.O., County Views ST.A (P)/2-9 and the Hertfordshire Local Studies Library, Hertford.

[34] H.R.O., Knowsley Clutterbuck, Vol.1, 104 B.

[35] *D.N.B.*, xi, 811.

[36] H.R.O., Knowsley Clutterbuck, Vol.1, 104 E.

[37] P.R.O., SC6/Hen. VIII/1606, m.8.

[38] P.R.O., E 117/12/30.

[39] P.R.O., E 315/361, fol.64.

[40] *V.C.H.*, ii, 413.

December 1538 he was granted the site,[41] although this was not confirmed until February 1540.[42] The grant refers to the the church, tower and cemetery of the nunnery suggesting that these survived the Dissolution.

The pay-books of James Nedeham, surveyor of the king's works before Lee himself, show that lead from Sopwell was taken to use in building works at the royal manor of The More near Rickmansworth, on which much money was spent between 1534 and 1543.[43] In September 1538, before the grant of Sopwell to Lee, eight fothers, three quarters and 21 pounds of lead were transported to The More and in March/April 1542 a further 13 fothers and seven pounds were removed.[44] It is not clear whether this latter amount of lead had already been removed from Sopwell and kept in storage before it was taken to The More, but this must be a possibility as the grant to Lee had been confirmed in February 1540.

There are no contemporary descriptions of Lee's house: it is not mentioned by either Leland or Norden. The house was, however, stayed in by Elizabeth during a royal progress in 1564 and is referred to briefly in John Shrimpton's manuscript history of St Albans (c.1610),[45] although interestingly the writer asserts that the "stones and chiefe stuffe" of the "fair house" were "taken out of the abbey" and makes no reference to the conversion of the former nunnery buildings.

Chauncy gives no details of the buildings, while Defoe simply says that Sopwell "where they say King Henry was married to Anne of Bolen" is "demolished and secularised,"[46] and Thomas Hearne, writing in 1732, claims that "no vestigia remain."[47] A much fuller account is given by Grose in the 1770s, who states that "From the stile of these ruins, as well as from their being chiefly built with brick, they cannot be of much elder date than the reign of Henry VII or VIII and possibly may be the remains of a mansion built by sir Richard Leigh with some of the materials, and on the site of the nunnery. When Chauncey's History of Hertfordshire was written, this house was entire, or at least is so represented in the plan, and is in some old surveys called Sopewell Hall and Sopewell House. It is said that about fifty or sixty years ago, the buildings here were in such a state as to make lord Grimston doubtful which of the two, this mansion or that of Gorehambury, he should fit up for his residence. On one of the walls of the garden are two square tablets of stone, on each of which is carved a dexter hand and arm completely armed, holding a sword engrailed, with something like a scrawl under it. As these are enclosed, and only to be viewed at a distance, there may possibly be some minute parts or members of this piece of sculpture left out in the description."[48]

In 1793 part of the house had been converted into a smaller dwelling, then in the occupation of a Mr Clark,[49] while in the caption accompanying his view of the ruins, Oldfield writes that "Lord Grimston's kennel of hounds are kept within the site of the building."[50] Brayley and Britton, writing in 1808, say that the "...dilapidations have been so great, that neither the plan of the buildings, nor their appropriation, can now be traced...the ruins of Sopwell are mostly huge fragments of wall, composed of flint and brick: the windows in what appear to have been the chief apartments, are square, and large, with stone frames; some of them have been neatly ornamented. The gardens, which lie contiguous, are now orchards: in the wall, over the door leading into the principal one, is a square tablet of stone, sculptured with the figure of a dexter hand and arm, elevated, and holding a broken sword; above was an inscribed label, now mutilated. In an angle in this garden is a strongly-arched brick building, with various small recesses and niches, constructed within the walls...One of the outbuildings is yet standing at a little distance, and is now used as a barn...An unauthorised tradition represents Henry VIII as having been married to Anne Boleyn in the Chapel here."[51]

This account is repeated almost *verbatim* by S.G. Shaw in 1815,[52] and no further information on the buildings is contained in Caley's and Ellis's edition of Dugdale's *Monasticon*. The buildings are not mentioned by Clutterbuck, while the most useful observation by Cussans is that the house "...appears to have been allowed to fall into decay some 50 or 60 years after its erection."[53]

Both the *V.C.H.* and the *R.C.H.M.* describe the ruins largely as they exist today, although both also mention the moulded doorway, shown in Sparrow's view of the ruins in Grose's *Antiquities*, on the south side of the enclosure abutting the west side of the north "double" range. The *V.C.H.* account also mentions the remains of a small fragment of pilaster to the west of the surviving north-south range, which it suggests marked the position of the main entrance to the site.[54]

[41] H.R.O., IV. A. 1.

[42] *L.P.*, xv, no.282 (123).

[43] Martin Biddle, 'The excavations of the manor of The More, Rickmansworth, Hertfordshire', *Arch. Jnl.*, 116, 136-99; *King's Works*, iv, 164-9.

[44] Bodl., MS. Rawl. D. 809, fols. 2r, 7v. The figures given by Biddle, op. cit., 199 do not take account of the lead transported in 1542.

[45] P.R.O., E 351/3202; H.R.O., 66,296, John Shrimpton, *The Antiquities of Verulam and St Albans* (n.d.), 78.

[46] Chauncy, ii, 257; D. Defoe, *A Tour Through The Whole Island of Great Britain* (1748 edn.), 189.

[47] Bodl., Hearne's Diaries, Vol.137, p.96.

[48] Grose, op. et loc. cit. (note 24).

[49] H.R. Wilton Hall, 'Sopwell' in P.C. Standing (ed.), *Memorials of Old Hertfordshire* (1905), 75.

[50] H.R.O., Oldfield Drawings, VIII, 557.

[51] Brayley & Britton, vii, 109-10.

[52] S.G. Shaw, *The History of Verulam and St Albans* (1815), 218-19.

[53] Cussans, iii, pt.2, 292.

[54] *V.C.H.*, ii, 413.

ARCHAEOLOGICAL INVESTIGATION

Excavations on the site, directed by E.A. Johnson and O.J. Weaver, took place between 1963 and 1966. The results of these have still not been fully published but interim reports were released as the work progressed and these are summarised here.[55]

The priory buildings were found to be on the same site as the later house and were similarly orientated. The church lay on the site of the hall range of Lee's first house with the cloister to the south. This was later demolished and the whole arrangement swept away to be replaced by the double-courtyard plan of Lee's second house.

A considerable deposit of building debris, including painted glass and lead cames, covered the medieval levels when the floors of Lee's first house were laid down. Coin evidence suggested that this cannot have been earlier than the 1550s. The hall range of Lee's first house had a fireplace in its north wall and the south and east ranges of this house followed the plan of their monastic predecessors.

In Lee's second house, the hall range again followed the axis of the former church, although this time it was wider and had a clerestory on its south side, the surviving east-west running wall probably being the south wall of its single-storey aisle or corridor. The excavations also showed that the south ends of the surviving east and west wings were never finished and that the east wing (like the west) was originally "double" at its north end.

One of the most interesting results of the excavations was the evidence they gave for deliberate demolition after the Dissolution. A tile hearth was found against the north wall of the south claustral range and also a lead-melting hearth with much burning around it. On the uppermost floor surface of the church, stripped of its floor tiles, was a round setting of roof tiles edged with bricks, which had been used for lead casting. The excavations also showed that Lee's second house was in turn partially deliberately demolished. A useful plan showing both phases of Lee's house is included in Colin Platt's *Medieval England*.[56]

INTERPRETATION AND CONCLUSIONS

As is frequently the case with former monastic houses, it is not possible to reconstruct precisely the events which occurred at Sopwell directly after the Dissolution. Both the archaeological evidence for the building of the first post-suppression house and the fact that as late as 1542 lead was still being removed for re-use at the king's manor of The More suggest that the conversion did not take place immediately. Similarly, the absence of a reference to the house by Leland, who is thought to have passed through St

Albans in 1539,[57] may also be significant, although the fact that he gives no description of the town itself perhaps indicates that it would be unwise to read too much into this.

While the dating evidence for Lee's first house is not extensive, it seems unlikely to have been constructed before the 1550s. This would tie in well with the fact that Lee withdrew from public life in 1548 and spent almost a decade of retirement in Hertfordshire.[58] This period would indeed have provided ample opportunity for Lee to carry out the work at Sopwell, although it might be thought that he would have wished the major building operations to have been completed before his occupation began. This could have been the case because we do not know at which date he first lived here and, of course, he had other houses as well, including the former priory of Newent in Gloucestershire.[59]

Lee was born in c.1513 of a Hertfordshire family and it is likely that both his father and grandfather were masons. He first came to prominence serving in the king's army at Calais and in 1536 became surveyor and paymaster of the fortifications there, a post he was to hold until 1542. In 1538 he was advising Thomas Wriothesley on the conversion of the former Premonstratensian house of Titchfield. In 1544 he was inspecting and advising on royal fortifications in the north of England and was present at the attack on Edinburgh in the spring of that year. While there he looted the famous brazen font from Holyrood Abbey, which having added a boastful inscription recording the deed, he later presented to St Albans Abbey. As a result of his part in the Scottish campaign he was knighted and in October 1544 was granted a new coat-of-arms. It was at about this time that he became surveyor of the king's works in succession to James Nedeham, who had died the month before.

Lee's entry into the ranks of the gentry was undoubtedly aided by his marriage to Margaret, daughter of Sir Richard Grenville who had been with him at Calais, and his own thrusting and forceful personality. In early 1545 Lee was responsible for the restoration of the defences at Calais and Boulogne but in 1547, after accompanying Protector Somerset in his campaign against the Scots, he resigned the post and withdrew from the public arena. In 1557, however, Lee was again in royal service and for the next few years was heavily involved in the refortification of Berwick and the Scottish border. In 1560 he drew up plans for Upnor Castle (Kent) and was again engaged in works at Berwick. In 1562 Lee was dispatched by Cecil to Dieppe and Le Havre and he remained in demand for his work as a military engineer virtually until the end of his life, the earl of Essex requesting that he should construct a fort near Belfast as late as 1573. Lee died in 1575 and was buried in St Peter's Church in St Albans, where there was formerly a

[55] *Med. Arch.*, 8 (1964), 242; 9 (1965), 179; 10 (1966), 177-80; 11 (1967), 274.
[56] Colin Platt, *Medieval England* (1978), 216.
[57] John Chandler, *John Leland's Itinerary. Travels in Tudor England* (1993), xxx.
[58] *D.N.B.*, xi, 811.
[59] *Cal. Pat. R., Edw. VI, 1547-8*, 108.

brass inscription to his memory in the chancel.[60]

The terms of Lee's will, made in 1570, are particularly interesting.[61] It states that "if any of the persons mentioned in this entail do altar, change, transforme digge cutt dowen or deface the said howses, edifices, buyldynges or walles of the mansion house of the said Syr Rycharde called Lee Hall or Sopwelle Hall...and shall not within the space of three years next folowinge the saide alterynges etc...in like or better form and fashion ereckt buylde upp or make the same againe...from henceforth the sd persons so doing shall forfeit their interest in the premises." This undoubtedly reflects the pride that Lee took in his house and indeed the conversion which he undertook of the former nunnery buildings has all the hall-marks of the most ambitious and daring of such schemes. Re-use of the monastic church as domestic accommodation usually involved considerable practical difficulties and is thus frequently found only as part of the more major conversions. In Hertfordshire this occurred at Wymondley and possibly also at Ashridge and The Priory and The Biggin, Hitchin, although in the latter three cases it was probably the claustral buildings which formed the nucleus of the post-Dissolution conversions. With the exception of Wymondley, none of these Hertfordshire sites forms an especially close parallel to Sopwell, which in its first phase of church transformed into hall range can be more usefully compared with the re-use of the church at high status sites like Netley and Mottisfont in Hampshire and Leez Priory in Essex.

What little is known of the architectural details of Sopwell also tends to confirm that it was a conversion of the first rank. There is a series of stone and plaster medallions at Salisbury Hall in the parish of Shenley near St Albans, which is traditionally believed to have come from Sopwell. A house was built at Salisbury Hall in the early 15th century, but the present building is largely a remodelling carried out for Sir Jeremiah Snow between c.1669 and his death in 1702.[62]

The medallions are located above the panelling in the great hall of Snow's house and are said to have been purchased by Snow from Sir Harbottle Grimston, who bought Sopwell in 1669.[63] It seems likely that Grimston demolished at least some of the buildings at Sopwell and the coincidence between the date of the sale to Grimston and the beginning of Snow's ownership of Salisbury Hall adds credence to the tradition that the medallions were removed from one house to the other. Various other features were probably taken from Sopwell by Grimston for the house at Gorhambury, which also came into his possession at this time.[64]

The *V.C.H.* claims that the medallions are 15th century in date and that their original provenance is not known.[65] If this dating is correct, their style and quality suggest that they are most likely to be Italian but this is ruled out by the fact that five of the six full medallions and the four half-medallions now visible are made of Totternhoe stone. It therefore seems probable that they were commissioned expressly for Lee's house and that they are of English workmanship. The medallions are circular in shape and measure approximately 3 ft in diameter. They show in low relief the heads of Roman emperors and empresses, with their names around the rims, probably copied from Roman coins.

There are thought originally to have been 12 medallions (the numbers vary in different accounts) but, although another medallion and half-medallion have been found buried in a Tudor cellar in the garden,[66] only those referred to above can now be seen at Salisbury Hall. The medallions depict the profile heads of Vespasian, Constantine the Great, Julius Caesar, Marcus Aurelius, Augustus and Trajan, the half-medallions Marcus Antonius, Cleopatra, Zenobia and another unidentified empress. Further evidence that the medallions were formerly at Sopwell comes from the excavation in the grounds of Salisbury Hall of moulded stone door jambs practically identical to those still extant at Sopwell; the possibility that other features were also transferred cannot, of course, be ruled out.[67]

The house at Sopwell appears to have stood for a comparatively short time. An indication that Grimston made little use of the buildings comes from a lease of 1671 to Thomas Ayleward of Hedges, "yeoman", which included the provision that the "great barn now standing at Sopwell...be taken downe and sett up in a Field called Wallnutree."[68] There is a distinct possibility that this barn was the barn of the former nunnery and the fact that it could be taken down and re-erected elsewhere suggests that it was of timber-framed construction.

The great hall of Lee's house appears only to be shown on the various 17th-century maps referred to earlier and in the mid-18th-century views made by James Webster and Thomas Collinson. Thereafter drawings and engravings of the site tend to show the surviving north-south range, suggesting that the hall range had collapsed or been totally demolished during the second half of the 18th century.

Even before Grimston acquired Sopwell in 1669, it seems quite likely that the house had already been abandoned, although the reference to it in John Shrimpton's *History of St Albans* in c.1610 as a "fair house" suggests that it was still maintained in something like its original condition at this date. However, there is quite strong evidence that the

[60] John Harvey, *English Mediaeval Architects* (revd. edn., 1984), 175-7; *King's Works*, iii, 13-14; iv, 410-11.
[61] P.R.O., C 142/189/86.
[62] Smith (1993), 170-1.
[63] *V.C.H.*, ii, 213.
[64] J.S. Rogers, 'The manor and houses at Gorhambury', *Trans. St Albans Archit. & Arch. Soc.*, n.s., 4 (1933-35), 73.

[65] *V.C.H.*, ii, 268.
[66] Pevsner, 337.
[67] Ibid, 322-3n.
[68] H.R.O., IV. H. 7.

house was incomplete at the time of Lee's death in 1575 and that it was in fact never entirely finished. This comes from both the surviving building and the archaeological excavations carried out on the site. The relatively few early antiquarian accounts of the house also suggest that it quickly became ruinous.

Several writers from Shrimpton onwards have stated that Lee used building materials from St Albans Abbey to construct Sopwell. Lee was in fact granted the greater part of the abbey buildings in 1550,[69] and it is quite possible that he used building materials from there at Sopwell, in much the same way that Nicholas Bacon transported materials from St Albans to build his house at Gorhambury in the 1560s.[70]

Nevertheless, it would seem more likely that the former nunnery buildings at Sopwell formed the nucleus of Lee's house. Although it has been suggested that the walls of the church and conventual buildings were entirely rebuilt by Lee,[71] this is by no means certain. In the first phase especially, the ground-plan of the church and claustral buildings was closely followed and it is quite possible that substantial sections of medieval walling were in fact incorporated in the new buildings. This is now difficult to prove from an examination of the surviving ruins, as these largely relate to Lee's second house, but despite the excavator's assertion that the monastic walls were rebuilt during the first phase of the domestic conversion, the idea has certainly not been disproved by the archaeological evidence.

In view of the persistent tradition that materials from St Albans Abbey were re-used by Lee, it is necessary to pay some attention to this claim. It is quite conceivable that stones from the abbey were re-used in the wall with which Lee enclosed the park he created in the 1560s, especially in the northern section which was as close to the abbey as to Sopwell. Furthermore, the date of the formation of the park coincides neatly with the re-use of materials from St Albans at Gorhambury, which would perhaps seem to suggest that this was the period when Lee was most likely to have made use of such materials. However, this cannot have been so as Lee had sold the majority of the former domestic buildings of the abbey to its last abbot, Richard Boreman, in November 1551,[72] unless, of course, he had already removed various building materials and kept them in store.

The re-use of lead from Sopwell by the crown at The More in the 1540s suggests that many of the buildings at Sopwell were ruinous by the time that Lee began work on his first house after 1548. As grantee of the site, Lee presumably would have exercised some control over the demolition which took place there after the Dissolution, but the lead

melting hearths found on the site probably relate to work carried out for the king rather than for Lee.

The date at which Lee decided to abandon his first house and begin work on the new is not known but the fact that it was still unfinished on his death suggests that it was late in his life. This again equates with both the archaeological evidence and the surviving architectural details of the existing ruins. Precisely what the impetus was for Lee's decision to embark on the second phase of building is uncertain but the fashionable double-courtyard plan, which has been compared to that of Sissinghurst (Kent),[73] suggests a house of considerable prestige and ambition.

Lee's interest and perhaps involvement in the property appear to have fluctuated. In 1557 he conveyed the estate to trustees for the use of his younger daughter, Anne, and her heirs,[74] but three years later he leased it to his son-in-law, Humphrey Coningsby, husband to his elder daughter, Mary.[75] This may, however, not be the result of lack of interest in the house but rather the reverse. 1557 was the year in which Lee returned to royal service and it may have been in the event of a premature death or a possible fall from royal favour that he decided to safeguard his home by making it over to trustees. Following the lease to Coningsby the manor was sub-let to various tenants, the first of whom were Edward Greves and John Kettell.[76] If any of these tenants occupied the house, they were almost certainly removed during the second phase of building activity in the 1560s or '70s.

Although Lee was active in royal service virtually until the end of his life, he may have been planning to retire shortly after this remodelling began. He did not live to see the result of his labours and, despite the wording of his will, it appears that his descendants did not share his interest in the place, the house seemingly not surviving the second half of the 17th century.

Bibliography

PICTORIAL SOURCES

Hertfordshire Record Office

Buckler Drawings, III, 138.

Oldfield Drawings, VIII, 556-7.

Knowsley Clutterbuck, Vol.1, 104 B, E.

British Library, London

[69] *Cal. Pat. R., Edw. VI*, iv, 5.
[70] Rogers, op. cit. (note 64), 41.
[71] *Med. Arch.*, 8 (1964), 242; 10 (1966), 178.
[72] *V.C.H.*, ii, 511.

[73] Colin Platt, *Medieval Britain From The Air* (1984), 201-02.
[74] *Cal. Pat. R., Phil. & Mary, 1557-8*, 243.
[75] *V.C.H.*, ii, 413.
[76] *Cal. Pat. R., Eliz., 1560-63*, 70.

Add. MS. 32,351, fols.195-8; 36,366, fol.207.

K. Top. XV. 83.

Bodleian Library, Oxford

Gough Herts. 11, opp. p.82.

Library of Society of Antiquaries

MS. 720, Webster, J., *Gleanings of Antiquity from Verolam and St Albans* (n.d.), 134.

Museum of St Albans

Lewis Evans Collection, St Albans Scrapbooks, Vol.2.

Printed

Grose, F., *The Antiquities of England and Wales*, v (1777), no page no.

PHOTOGRAPHIC SOURCES

Hertfordshire Record Office

ST.A (P)/2-9.

Hertfordshire Local Studies Library, Hertford

Photographic Collection.

British Museum, London

Department of Prints and Drawings, Case 21.

CARTOGRAPHIC EVIDENCE

Hertfordshire Record Office

IV. A. 25.

XIII. 30.

D/EV P2.

D/P 93. 29/9.

DSA 4/88/2; DSA 4/89/2.

Bodleian Library, Oxford

MS. Gough Gen. Top. 61.

OTHER PRIMARY SOURCES

Manuscript:-

Public Record Office, London

SC6/Hen. VIII/1606, m.8.

E 117/12/30.

E 315/361, fol.64.

E 351/3202.

C 142/189/86.

Hertfordshire Record Office

IV. A. 1.

IV. H. 7.

66,296, Shrimpton, J., *The Antiquities of Verulam and St Albans* (n.d.).

Bodleian Library, Oxford

MS. Rawl. D. 809, fols.2r, 7v.

Hearne's Diaries, Vol.137, p.96.

Printed:-

Calendar of Patent Rolls Preserved in the Public Record Office (1903- (in progress).
Letters and Papers, Foreign and Domestic of the Reign of Henry VIII, eds. Brewer, J.S., Gairdner, J. & Brodie, R.H., 21 vols. (1862-1932).

SECONDARY SOURCES

Biddle, M., 'The excavations of the manor of The More, Rickmansworth, Hertfordshire', *Arch. Jnl.*, 116 (1959), 136-99.
Brayley, E.W. & Britton, J., *The Beauties of England and Wales, Vol. 7, Hertfordshire* (1808).
Chandler, J., *John Leland's Itinerary. Travels in Tudor England* (Stroud, 1993).
Chauncy, H., *The Historical Antiquities of Hertfordshire*, ii (1700, reprinted Dorking 1975).
Colvin, H.M. *et al*, *The History of the King's Works*, iii (1975); iv (1982).
Cussans, J.E., *The History of Hertfordshire*, iii, pt.2 (1881, reprinted Wakefield 1972).
Defoe, D., *A Tour Through The Whole Island of Great Britain* (1748 edn.).
Dictionary of National Biography, 22 vols. (revd. edn.,

Oxford 1921/2).

Harvey, J., *English Mediaeval Architects* (revd. edn., Gloucester 1984).

King, N., *The Grimstons of Gorhambury* (Chichester, 1983).

Knowles, M.D. & Hadcock, R.N., *Medieval Religious Houses* (1953).

Med. Arch., 8 (1964), 242; 9 (1965), 179; 10 (1966), 177-80; 11 (1967), 274.

Pevsner, N., *Hertfordshire* (2nd edn., revd. Cherry, B., Harmondsworth, 1977).

Platt, C., *Medieval England* (1978).

-*Medieval Britain From The Air* (1984).

Rogers, J.S., 'The manor and houses at Gorhambury', *Trans. St Albans Archit. & Arch. Soc.*, n.s., 4 (1933-35), 35-112.

Shaw, S.G., *The History of Verulam and St Albans* (1815).

Smith, J.T., *Hertfordshire Houses: Selective Inventory* (1993).

The Victoria History of the Counties of England, *Hertfordshire*, ii (1908).

Wilton Hall, H.R., 'Sopwell' in Standing, P.C. (ed.), *Memorials of Old Hertfordshire* (1905), 74-9.

WARE PRIORY

History

Franciscan friary founded in 1338 by Thomas, second Lord Wake of Liddell.[1] Dissolved in autumn 1538, appearing to have been in the king's hands by Michaelmas that year.[2] In the following year it was held by Robert Byrch at an annual rent of 20s.[3] In 1544 it was granted to his son, Thomas Byrch,[4] who died in 1550.[5] In 1628 the site was sold to Job Bradshaw.[6]

THE BUILDINGS

Introduction

The house is situated at the west end of medieval Ware on the south side of Priory Street near its junction with High Street. The parish church of St. Mary lies a little to the north-east and the River Lea Navigation, a canalisation of the River Lea, is immediately to the south.

The surviving buildings represent the south and part of the west ranges of the cloister with another slightly later range (possibly a guest hall) at right-angles to the west of the latter. Although considerably modified since the Dissolution, partly as the result of an extensive restoration by George Godwin in 1849,[7] the buildings retain a considerable amount of medieval fabric.

In 1919 the house was granted to Ware Urban District Council and since 1974 it has formed the offices of the Town Council. In 1990 parts of the building were used by the County Council Social Services Department and others by a play-group and for storage, the future use of the building then being uncertain. By 1994, however, major restoration work was again in hand, this time under the direction of Donald Insall and Associates, the purpose being to rearrange the Town Council accommodation and to provide a number of new community uses.

The former friary buildings have been collectively known as The Priory since at least the 18th century,[8] and this name is therefore used here when referring to the post-Dissolution house.

DESCRIPTION

Materials

The buildings are of two storeys with attics. The walls are of flint and clunch rubble construction with later red brick to the truncated gable ends. At the time of site inspection in November 1990 all external surfaces were plastered, mostly in 19th- and 20th-century roughcast or cement render, but with recently renewed lime plaster to the north and east walls of the south range and to the east wall of the west range. Further inspection in February 1994 showed that some plaster had been removed from the north wall of the west range, revealing 18th-century red brick, some of it vitrified, apparently replacing an earlier substantial timber frame. The roofs are clay peg tiled, with extensive replacement by machine clay tiles to the rear slopes.

The following description is based on the building's appearance in 1990. Features discovered during 1994 are described later under archaeological evidence.

South Range

North wall.

There are six glazing bar sash windows on the first floor, directly above five segmental arches with a mid-19th-century porch in the angle with the west range to the right. The arches represent the original cloister openings, each with three pointed cinquefoil-headed lights and a moulded plinth running across the base. The centre and left lights of the third arch from the east are infilled, as are all three lights of the next arch from the east and the left light of the west arch. The tracery of each arch is heavily plastered.

The bowed porch in the angle with the west range has a re-used early 17th-century heavy strapwork-panelled door with nail studding and a plainly moulded surround in a segmental-arched recess; broad 19th-century lancets to either side.

There is a moulded eaves cornice and two tall hipped dormers with sashes in the roof slope, the left immediately to the right of the third window from the left and the right directly above the fifth window from the left. There was formerly a tall internal axial stack between these two dormers and another dormer above the westernmost window.[9] There is a buttress with stepped coping terminating at first-floor level to the north-east corner.

East wall (gable end of south range).

This has a red brick stack to the left of the ridge, flush with the gable wall. The attic floor has a 16-paned glazing bar sash window, off centre to the right, and there are two sash windows on the first floor with another at a slightly lower

---

[1] *Cal. Pat. R., 1338-40*, 14.

[2] *L.P.*, xiii (2), no.1021; P.R.O., SC6/Hen. VIII/1617, m.2d.

[3] P.R.O., SC6/Hen. VIII/1618.

[4] *L.P.*, xix, no.610 (68).

[5] *Cal. Pat. R., Ed. VI, 1553*, 342.

[6] H.R.O., 76,899.

[7] R. Walters, 'Ware Priory', *Trans. East Herts. Arch. Soc.*, 1, pt.i (1899), 42; H.R.O.; D/EX 317 P9.

[8] Ms. inventory in private ownership. I am grateful to David Perman for drawing this to my attention and for providing me with a photocopy of the document.

[9] Painting (c.1850) in Town Council Chamber, Ware Priory.

level to the left in a continuous catslide outshut, separated from the others by a wide buttress, which rises to the height of the head of this window.

There is a chamfered string course at first-floor level dying into the top of the buttress at the north-east angle of this range (see above), below which is a square-headed window with two cinquefoil-headed lights and label to the left and an arch-way like those in the north wall to the right.

South wall.

This is separated from the south gable of the west range by a full-height stepped buttress, which has an iron-barred staircase window with glazing bars immediately to the right. To the right on the first floor is a glazing bar sash window, to the right of which is another full-height stepped buttress. Directly to the left of this is a deep round-arched recess, which has a half-glazed door with early 19th-century Gothic-style glazing.[10] To the right of the buttress are the remains of a substantial stepped lateral stack (formerly with a tall internal shaft which rose in the middle of the roof slope),[11] flanked by French windows with glazing bars and substantial moulded transoms and two glazing bar sashes on the first floor. The positions of the French windows were formerly occupied by sash windows.[12] To the far right on the ground floor is an iron-barred square-headed window with a label and two cinquefoil-headed lights.

To the right of this window is a **projecting range** with a steeply pitched hipped roof. This is flint faced and largely late Victorian in appearance, having segmental-arched top-hung leaded casements with internal shutters. There is a plank door under a lean-to hood in the south wall and a projecting corner turret to the first floor at the south-west angle. This turret has the date '1892' and the initials 'RW' (for the then owner, Robert Walters) in its ornamental plasterwork. There is a late 19th-century casement in a bracketed projection to the right of the turret and the ridge has a late 19th-century red brick chimney with elaborate Tudor-style moulded capping.

The range is, however, earlier in origin than any of these features suggest. Various pre-1892 views show glazing bar sashes on both the south and west faces and a tall external stepped stack on the south wall with an arched recess to the bottom; other than this no stacks are shown in pre-1892 views.[13]

Immediately to the east of this range and slightly projecting to the south of it is a Victorian billiard room. This is probably contemporary with the remodelling of the projecting range and the hipped roof is capped by a glazed gable running north-south along its long axis.

West range

East wall.

Projecting at right-angles to the north of the south range, this range has a glazing bar sash window on the first floor above the porch. Immediately to the right of the porch is another claustral arch with a three-light cinquefoil-headed window like those in the north wall of the south range. There is a hip-roofed dormer in the roof slope immediately to the right of the first-floor sash window: this dormer has two side-hung casements to its lower part rather than a full sash window like the other dormers. The plinth to the base of the claustral arch-way continues as a stepped plinth to the right.

North gable wall.

This has symmetrically-spaced glazing bar sash windows on each floor, three to the ground floor, two on the first floor and one of reduced proportions to the attic.

South gable wall.

This is a flush with the south wall of the south range and has three glazing bar sashes on the first floor and two of reduced proportions to the attic. The ground floor has a cross-window, formerly apparently with leaded lights,[14] but now with fixed horizontal sliding sashes, on the left and a smaller glazing bar sash window at a slightly higher level to the right. There is also a window between the two ground-floor windows lighting the cellar.[15] There was formerly a small end stack to this gable.[16]

West wall.

This runs into the south wall of the hall range and formerly had a continuous catslide outshut, its eaves broken to the left by a large hip-roofed dormer.[17] There was a large lateral stack, which may originally have been external or could have served a long-demolished range projecting at right-angles to the west, incorporated in the outshut. One view shows it attached by an iron tie to the roof slope of the west range and another apparently with a coat-of-arms or some other device to its west face.

The truncated remains of both outshut and stack survive, the former with a flat roof, above which in the original external wall of the west range is a 20th-century metal casement. This occupies the approximate position of the

[10] H.R.O., Oldfield Drawings, VI, 373.
[11] H.R.O., Gerish colln., Box 79.
[12] H.R.O., Oldfield Drawings, VI, 373.
[13] For example, painting (c.1850) in Council Chamber; H.R.O., view of 1812 by J. Gosselin (Ware/189); B.L., view by R.M. Batty from an engraving by F. Dukes (Add. MS. 32,352, fol.89).

[14] Painting (c.1850) in Council Chamber; H.R.O., Oldfield Drawings, VI, 373.
[15] Ibid.
[16] H.R.O., Gerish colln., Box 79.
[17] Painting (c.1850) in Council Chamber; early 20th-century photographs in Hertfordshire Local Studies Library, Hertford.

former large hip-roofed dormer and above to the left in the bottom of the main roof slope is a smaller hip-roofed dormer with two-light glazing bar casement. This is party concealed from general view by the east gable wall of the hall range.

Hall range

This range is attached at ground- and first-floor levels to the west wall of the west range, but the lime-plastered and pargetted **east gable** looks directly on to the west roof slope of the west range and has three casement windows at different levels lighting the attic. There was formerly a large external stack, which survived into the early 20th century,[18] against this gable.

North wall.

This is entirely lit by flat-arched two-light cinquefoil-headed windows like those in the south and east walls of the south range, except for one single-light window of the same style but without a traceried head to the far right on the ground floor. All windows except one (see below) have labels. Of the two-light windows, the ground floor has three grouped together to the left of centre and another to the right; there are also two directly below the eaves, one to the centre and the other to the right. To the far left there is one window directly above another, the lower without a label and at a higher level than the other ground-floor windows. It is in fact bisected by the ground-floor ceiling. This window, the single-light window and the right window on the first floor are all iron barred.

Below the higher level ground-floor window there is blocked quatrefoil-shaped opening with iron bars across set in a moulded square recess. This has been interpreted as a dole window.[19] There is a roughly central tall red brick stack directly in front of the ridge and two tall gabled dormers in the roof slope to the right, both with four-paned sashes.

There are a number of differences between the current arrangement of windows in this wall and that shown in 19th-century drawings of the hall range. A watercolour of c.1820 by Thomas Fisher shows the three first-floor windows in the same positions as now but the two central ground-floor openings as single-light windows. The two windows to the left and the two to the right are absent from the Fisher view.[20] A similar situation is depicted in a mid 19th-century painting in the house but this latter view does show the existence of the second and fifth windows from the left on the ground floor, plus the single-light window to the ground floor on the right.[21] Both views show the roof slope without dormers but with a substantial stack to the left gable end (see above, east gable), the stack being

clustered in the Fisher view. The stack directly in front of the ridge is not shown in the Fisher view.

West wall.

This gable wall has stepped angle buttresses to both the north and south corners, rising to a higher level on the north and south faces than on the west. There is a flat-arched three-light cinquefoil-headed window with label to the centre on the first floor (depicted as a door in the Fisher view) and a broad iron-barred window without a traceried head but with a label to the lower right. There was formerly a small end stack directly to the left of the ridge.[22]

South wall.

This is divided into three unequal bays, having three two-light cinquefoil-headed windows with dripstones directly below the eaves, the centre and left windows iron barred and the right with the mullion removed to from a fire escape. To the left of the left window is a small casement window, which is not present in the c.1850 and other earlier views of the building. The ground floor has a brick lean-to on the left and a flat-roofed addition to the right. Between is a pointed single-chamfered archway which has a 20th-century plank door with glazed panels. A chamfered buttress rises above the flat-roofed addition but another similar buttress, visible above the lean-to range in the c.1850 view of the house, has now gone.

There is a small courtyard to the south of this elevation, bounded on the south by a large conservatory/greenhouse, behind which to the north are a number of late 19th- and early 20th-century sheds, storerooms and other outbuildings. The conservatory itself appears to be late 19th century or early 20th century in date and is shown in several photographs taken of the south front at this time.[23] However, it replaces smaller glazed structures in the same position. The c.1850 picture shows a gabled greenhouse and a late 18th-century view by Oldfield depicts a five-bay flat-roofed building which has full-height windows with glazing bars, divided by columns with moulded capitals. This may have served as an orangery or summerhouse/conservatory.

Interior

The building is entered through a stone-flagged **entrance hall**, which has small tiles at the intersections between flags. To the south-west of the door is a pillar, which represents the junction between the south and west ranges of the friary cloister. The mouldings on its east and north faces are the same as on the cloister arches in the south and west ranges. It is flat-faced on its south side and has a figure corbel supporting a respond, from which springs a short three-centred arch dying into a respond supported by

[18] Ibid.
[19] H.R.O., 37,401.
[20] B.L., Add. MS. 32,352, fol.88; Bodl., Gough Maps, 11, fol.57.
[21] Painting (c.1850) in Council Chamber.
[22] Photographs in Hertfordshire Local Studies Library, Hertford.
[23] Ibid.

a figure corbel. The span of this arch probably reflects the width of the medieval cloister. The figure corbel on the north is in the form of a male head wearing a cap and with arms outstretched and bent at the elbow; the south figure corbel is similar but the head is capless. The respond above the north corbel is moulded but the south one is plain. To the north and east of the central pillar are further segmental arches, which represent the south and west cloister arches of the west and south ranges respectively.

Immediately to the east on the same wall as the south figure corbel is an elaborately moulded respond. It serves no apparent purpose and may be reset; alternatively, it may have acted as a light bracket. This, the figure corbels and the arches themselves are likely to be late 14th century in date. Directly to the east of the possible light bracket and in line with the half-glazed door in the south wall of the south range is another arch supported by moulded responds.

To the east of the entrance hall and the passage leading to the door in the south wall is the main part of the **south claustral range**. Before the 1849 restoration this was divided into two rooms, a library to the west and an ante-room to the east. The width of the cloister walk was defined by its original south wall, which formed the north wall of the ante-room. The library to the west incorporated the width of the cloister walk, this section of the south cloister wall having been demolished. This arrangement seems to have been altered radically in the 1849 restoration or shortly afterwards, although apparently not in the way proposed in a drawing of 1849.[24]

A plan of 1867 shows the dividing wall between ante-room and library removed, with a section of wall on the line of the south wall of the cloister walk roughly in the middle of a large drawing room. Only a nib of the original cloister walk wall remained at the junction with the outside wall.[25] Today even these sections of wall have gone and the room is now one large space.

In the fourth claustral arch from the east, which externally is blind, is a narrow elliptical arch springing from carved responds: there are no signs internally of the three blind cinquefoil-headed lights visible to the exterior of this arch. The windows in the south and east walls have internal shutters and several of the windows have Victorian stained glass. Traces of red paint in the window splays are medieval as is the painting in the west splay of the two-light cusped window in the south wall. This is of a crocketed pinnacle surmounted by a lobed trefoil; the colours are red and gold leaf. Higher up the same window splay is a small painted cross. The window has a leaded casement with an elaborately decorated catch.

In the south-east corner of the room, an apparently medieval pointed doorway in a deeply splayed segmental-headed recess leads through to the **projecting range**. This has rough joists running east to west and at the south end there are traces of the fireplace serving the chimney shown in the various 19th-century views of the building. The joists are supported by a central north-south running beam resting on a carved post, which presumably is contemporary with the remodelling of this range in 1892. The joists continue to the west of the central wall beneath the beam, the internal shutters with their elaborate catches in this room also being of 1892.

Returning to the entrance hall, a six-panel door, immediately to the west of the south figure corbel leads into a **store-room**. This door is actually set in the infill of a wider segmental-pointed doorway, above which on the south side is a single chamfered recess, suggesting that the north side has always been the external side of this doorway, which is confirmed by a bracket for a door hinge on the south side. Above the blocked doorway itself on the south side is a hollow chamfered segmental arch.

The blocking of the doorway continues down into the cellar beneath the store-room, showing that the raised floor of the store-room is an insertion. The doorway itself is probably late 14th century in date. In the east wall of the store-room a plank door with H/L hinges leads to another small store-room above the adjacent former wine cellar. This is approached by a doorway in the passage-way leading to the half-glazed door in the south wall and has a brick floor and a timber-framed wall separating it from the store-room to the west. Recesses for wine bottles line its west wall.

At right-angles immediately to the west of the half-glazed door (which has an internal shutter) in the south wall is an arch-way, practically identical to that to the north in line with the half-glazed door. This arch-way is at the foot of the **staircase**. This is probably of the mid-18th century and rises in three flights to the attic. The first two flights have three bobbin balusters to each tread, turned newels, a ramped moulded handrail and a carved open string. The top flight has a plain closed string.

Returning again to the entrance hall, a six-panel door directly opposite the one to the store-room leads into the ground-floor room of the west range. This is now the **Council Chamber** and has fine early to mid-18th-century fittings. It is fully panelled except for a moulded cornice and the area occupied by the cloister arch on the east wall. The 18th-century fireplace on the west wall has a garlanded eared surround with tiny dentils to the mantel shelf and reeded pilasters flanking a centre panel with dentilled cornice above. The rather heavy coffered plaster ceiling is Victorian. A six-panel door to the left of the fireplace leads to the adjoining **Members' Room**, which is also fully panelled, and forms the eastern room of the **hall range**. Here, though, the panelling is probably 19th century in date. The restored quatrefoil-shaped 'dole hole' in the north wall is deeply splayed.

---

[24] H.R.O., D/EX 317 P9.
[25] B.L. Map Room, Maps 137 a.3 (11).

To the south of this room a narrow passage runs the whole length of the hall range. On its south side is a two-light cinquefoil-headed window (concealed externally by the flat-roofed addition), the west light now blocked, and to the west of this window is the pointed doorway referred to above. The passage is spanned by two steeply-pointed corbelled arches, one immediately to the west of the two-light window and the other at the point where the passage turns at right-angles to the north at the west end of the range.

The rooms to the north of the passage are largely featureless except for a blocked, pointed 14th-century arch-way in the west cross-wall of the room with the paired windows. The arch-way is hollow chamfered on its east (internal) face.

At the east end of the hall range the passage turns at right-angles to the south to continue eastwards across the west range. To the south outside the medieval building are the former butler's pantry and scullery,[26] now converted into lavatories and with no features earlier than the 20th century visible. To the east of these is the **kitchen**, which has a large inglenook fireplace, to the north of which was formerly an infilled two-light cinquefoil-headed window,[27] recently brought to light again during the recent renovation work (see below under Archaeological evidence) To the north of the passage there were previously a closet and secondary staircase.[28]

The **first floor** has been much altered. The town clerk's room and the adjoining room (formerly one room - the morning room) has dado panelling and a late 18th-century cornice. There are plain plaster cornices and six-panel doors in the other first-floor rooms, which have an essentially late 18th- to early 19th-century character.

The **attic** of both south and west ranges is occupied by a large caretaker's flat, which is devoid of any architectural features. The roof structure of both these ranges is only visible in the roof space. The projecting range has a central king-post truss, which probably dates to the remodelling of 1892. Both the south and west ranges have a continuous scissor-braced roof with coupled rafters and no ridge piece. The tops of the collars are visible but it is not possible to establish whether there was originally a collar purlin and crown-post beneath. A downward-sloping brace visible in a cupboard in the attic towards the west end of the south range may be a brace from a crown-post, as in the hall range, but this is not conclusive. The east gable end of the south range is constructed of 17th-century brick and there are remains of a wattle and daub partition towards the west end of this range, suggesting that there was originally a clear break between the south and west ranges, similar to that which still exists between the latter and the hall range.

Now, however, the roof structure runs through to meet that of the west range. There has been removal of some of the scissor bracing and other remodelling of the roof structure towards the south end of this range and, along with the post-medieval brickwork of the south gable end, this suggests that, just as the south range may originally have extended further to the east, the west range may formerly have extended southwards towards the river.[29]

The original form of the roof structure is clearer in the hall range where the physical evidence is usefully supplemented by a mid-19th-century print, showing the roof structure open from first-floor level, and an accompanying commentary published in *The Builder*.[30] Unfortunately, it is not certain, either from the print or from the text, that the drawing shows the roof structure as it actually existed in 1849, or whether it is simply a reconstruction of how it may originally have appeared, or how it could look again after restoration. The reference in the commentary to "a required increase in the number of rooms having led to its conversion into an additional storey" is almost certain to refer to the hall range shown in the print, but this is not specifically stated and it is possible that this may refer to the south and west ranges which, as suggested above, may originally have had the same type of roof construction as the hall range.

This, however, is probably being too cautious and, while it is possible to interpret the print as a true representation of the roof structure in 1849, with the present attic storey being an insertion of that or a later date, this on balance also seems unlikely. Added weight is given to this assumption by the commentary's statement that the building was "about to be restored" and the restoration which did in fact take place under George Godwin in 1849/50. The plans relating to this work have already been referred to above and, although they show only the ground floor of the building, it seems that the principal intention was to uncover rather than to conceal monastic fabric. This does not mean that the work was intended to be strict archaeological reconstruction. This is indicated by the addition of the porch in the angle between the south and west ranges, the removal of the rear wall of the south claustral walk and other short sections of medieval walling and the proposed demolition and rebuilding on a larger scale of the south projecting range, which in the event never took place.

Nevertheless, the proposals also included the unblocking of the windows in the claustral arches (again never fully implemented), as is shown by a detailed drawing of a window with cusped cinquefoil-headed lights, suggesting that the tracery,[31] while probably based on surviving

[26] Ibid.
[27] *R.C.H.M.*, 228; H.R.O., D/EX 317 P10.
[28] B.L. Map Room, Maps 137 a.3 (11).

[29] P.E. Locke, 'The Priory: an historic building in need of repair' in *Saving Ware's Historic Priory* (The Rockingham Press, 1992), 16. I am grateful to Mr Locke for providing me with a copy of his unpublished 1990 report for Donald Insall and Associates on the building.
[30] G. Godwin, 'Note on Ware Priory', *The Builder*, 7 (1849), 342.
[31] H.R.O., D/EX 317 P11.

medieval work,[32] dates principally to this time.

Furthermore, writing in 1887 the then owner, R. Walters, stated that the owner in 1849, Martin Hadsley Gosselin, "contemplated a reconstruction (of the roof) on extensive lines".[33] This clear statement and the nature of the other restoration work carried out at that time make it most unlikely that if such an impressive feature as the open roof of the hall range had survived intact in 1849 that it would have been effectively destroyed by the insertion of a full attic storey.

This concentration on establishing the authenticity of the print in *The Builder* may seem unnecessarily pedantic but it is important in deciding how much weight can be placed on it as evidence. The conclusion is that it is almost certainly a reconstruction drawing but in many ways a remarkably accurate one. It shows the correct number and form of windows in the north, south and west walls and the range is divided into four bays. Three slightly cambered tie beams sit on the wall-plate, above which ashlar pieces link to the common rafters. In the centre of each tie beam is a tall crown-post with moulded base and cap. Below the cap the crown-post is octagonal in section but above it is square with chamfered edges. From the cap rise four chamfered curving braces, those to east and west supporting the collar purlin and those to north and south attaching to the common rafters. Above the collar purlin the roof structure is exactly as surviving in the south and west ranges. The arrangement of the roof structure shown in the print is borne out by the completely remaining crown-post in the attic of the hall range and is striking testimony to the accuracy of the drawing. This crown-post is the one to the truss dividing the two eastern bays of the range and is the one closest to the eye in *The Builder* drawing.

With the next truss to the west, however, the physical evidence does not completely agree with the drawing. Here the crown-post, unlike that shown in the drawing which is octagonal below the cap, is square in section. The post is partly concealed by a partition but there are no traces of a moulded cap or base. There is only one brace, sloping upwards to the north and, while other mortices may be hidden by the partition, only one more is actually visible, directly below the existing brace on the northern face of the crown-post. This suggests either the existence of a former downward-sloping brace or that the whole post is re-used.

Neither crown-post or what is visible of the tie beam below the eastern post shows any sign of smoke blackening but what can be seen of the upper roof structure (i.e. the common rafters and scissor bracing) through small hatches to the west of the western crown-post indicates possible traces of smoke blackening.

DOCUMENTARY EVIDENCE

The early post-Dissolution documentary history of the site is relatively slight and not particularly helpful. For instance, the Ministers' Accounts and the grant of the site to Thomas Byrch in 1544 provide no details of the buildings.[34]

The site is, however, referred to in 1590 in the verse "The Tale of Two Swannes" by William Vallans as "Byrches house, that whilom (once) was the Brothers Friers place..."[35] and in 1631 John Weever gives the following description: "A Frierie, whose ruins, not altogether beaten downe, are to be seene at this day."[36] This and his mention of two funerary monuments appear to suggest that parts of the church still remained at this date.

The building is also mentioned in the memoirs of Lady Anne Fanshawe, who with her husband, Sir Richard, rented the house in 1658,[37] but no details are given. A more comprehensive account of the property is, however, given in a survey of 1715, which incidentally refers to the house as "The Priery".[38] This survey, which takes the form of a household inventory, gives a full description of the building and shows it to be very different from the surviving structure. It was made when Robert Hadsley the younger took possession and indicates that the building was very much larger than it is now. It mentions the following rooms and structures- "brewe house, kitchin, counting house, litle parler and closet, litle rome out of the parler, darey, porch, great seler, litle seler, roome over the seler, pasage in to the great parlor, great parler, closet in the great parler, litle roome beyond the great parler, further roome beyond the great parler, cole house, one borded shop at the ende of the house over against the Chapell, nessarey, litle chamber next to the malten, malt house, best chamber, further chamber, litle garat, great garat, porch going out of the garden, a sumer house, great gates, litle gate, barne next the stable, house beyond the barne, barne next to the kill house, dust hous, kill house, malt loft, three malt shops, leden sestarn and barly chamber."

Although it is difficult positively to equate these rooms and structures with the surviving building, the "great parler" would seem to refer to the south range and the "litle roome beyond the great parler" would seem to be in the projecting range to the south. It is also worth noting the existence of the chapel and the large number of outbuildings, several of which were associated with malting, Ware's principal industry from the 16th to the

---

[32] Although there are no pre-1850 drawings showing the cloister arches, the cinquefoil-headed lights of the arches appear to be based on genuine medieval work.

[33] R. Walters, *Ware Priory* (1926 pamphlet), 47.

[34] P.R.O., SC6/Hen. VIII/1617-20, 1632-3; *L.P.*, xix, no.610 (68).

[35] 'A Tale of Two Swannes' is contained in William Vallans's 'Account of Several Parts of Hartfordshire', which appears as a prefix to Thomas Hearne's 1769 edition of volume 5 of John Leland's *Itinerary* (Bodl., Douce HH 169).

[36] J. Weever, *Ancient Funerall Monuments* (1631), 544.

[37] C. Fanshawe (ed.),*Memoirs of Lady Fanshawe...Written by Herself* (1829), 126.

[38] See note 8.

20th century.[39]

Apart from long lists of window shutters, locks, latches and catches in each room, relatively little further detail is given of the building or its fittings and furnishings. Several of the rooms including the closet in the "litle parler", the "great parler" and several chambers are "wenscoted" and another chamber is "halfe wencoted". There are "wenscote" (ie panelled) doors and shutters in many of the rooms; the porch has "three setles with six bordes fited to the endes" and the "porch going out of the garden" has "two setles". In the "further roome beyond the great parler there is a deale Closet and four shelfes in it" and the "chapell" has "one great ___ store three dores to it with three lockes and keyes". "One dormer window (is) taken downe and left in the great garat with two sheetes of glass".

It is not possible to identify any features connected with the former friary, although as mentioned above, the "great parler" and the rooms beyond would seem to be associated with the south range. The reference to a chapel may be to one created after the Dissolution: the friary church is almost certain to have disappeared by this date but the possibility that the chapel mentioned in the survey may originally have been the private chapel of the prior cannot be entirely discounted.

The Priory is again referred to in the late 18th century in a manuscript note in Richard Gough's copy of Salmon's *History of Hertfordshire* where it is described thus: "The priory has some considerable remains; being converted into a house inhabited by Mr Hadsley; several arches as of cloisters and a whole wing of buildings with antient square windows are intire".[40] This description is useful, not so much for the limited information it contains, but for the suggestion that the building was by then not much larger than the surviving structure. This inference is confirmed by the description and accompanying view of The Priory in *The Beauties of England and Wales* (1808).[41]

PICTORIAL EVIDENCE

Compared with many former monastic houses in Hertfordshire, the pictorial and early photographic record for Ware Priory is particularly good. There are no especially early views of the building but the late 18th- and early 19th-century drawings made of the house are generally compatible with each other.

Reference has already been made to Oldfield's view of the south front, which usefully confirms the authenticity (in position at least) of the surviving Gothic-traceried windows on this side of the building. Similarly, Thomas Fisher's

view of The Priory from the north-west (c.1820) is helpful in distinguishing the genuine medieval windows in the hall range from those inserted in the 19th century.[42] It shows all the existing windows on the first floor of the north front but on the ground floor it shows only two single-light windows to the centre. It also shows a boarded hatch to the centre of the first floor on the west gable end and a large clustered stack to the east gable end.

However, the drawings of c.1850 kept in the house and which depict the building in its immediate post-1849 restoration state, show the same fenestration pattern as today, except that the lower left window on the north front of the hall range is absent and the paired two-light windows in the centre are shown as single-light windows, as in the Fisher watercolour. The west gable end has two traceried windows as existing. If these drawings are compared with the 1849 plan showing the proposed alterations, we see that the lower left window was unblocked or inserted only at this time, along with the window immediately to the right of the paired single-light windows. The two-light window directly to the left of the paired single-light windows and the single-light window to the right are, however, marked on the 1849 plan, showing that they were either unblocked or inserted after c. 1820. The 1867 plan shows the same situation as in 1849: interestingly, the paired single-light windows are still indicated in this form, showing that their enlargement to two lights must post-date 1867.

Other noteworthy late 18th- and early 19th-century drawings of The Priory include those by J. Storer for *The Beauties of England and Wales*, a print by R.M. Batty from an engraving by F. Jukes,[43] and a view by Joshua Gosselin (1812),[44] while there are several useful late 19th- and early 20th-century photographs in the Hertfordshire Record Office and the Local Studies Library.[45] Another late 19th-century photograph in the Bodleian Library, Oxford shows the south projecting range before its remodelling in 1892, with a sash window to the first floor of each face where the projecting corner tower is now situated.[46]

Surviving maps provide little further information on the former plan of the building, all post-dating the house's apparent reduction in size during the 18th century.[47]

SALES PARTICULARS

These are another useful source of information on the building in the 19th and early 20th centuries. Those of 1867 provide a detailed ground-floor plan of the building,

[39] L. Munby, *The Hertfordshire Landscape* (1977), 198-9; *V.C.H.*, iv, 208-9.

[40] Bodl., MS. Gough Herts. 18; Ms. note between pp.246-7 of annotated copy of Nathaniel Salmon's *History of Hertfordshire* (1728).

[41] Brayley & Britton, vii, 251-2.

[42] See note 20.

[43] B.L., Add. MS. 32,352, fol.89; Map Room, K. 15. 59. c.

[44] H.R.O., Ware/189.

[45] H.R.O., Ware/16, Ware/194; Gerish colln., Boxes 78 & 79; Hertfordshire Local Studies Library, Hertford.

[46] Bodl., MS. top. eccl. b 28, fol.13.

[47] H.R.O., map of 1841 (63,620); 1844 Tithe map (PC 35); mid-19th-century plans of The Priory (D/EX 317 P8 & D/ECh P13).

reference to which has already been made. Also especially informative are those of 1906 and 1913.[48] The 1906 particulars report that the drawing room (the ground-floor room of the south range) "is divided by stone arches so as to form three rooms if so desired". All evidence for this arrangement has now been obliterated but can be seen in the plan of 1867 and in late 19th-century photographs of the room. The sub-dividing walls are not marked on the 1849 plan where the room is shown divided into a different arrangement, and the photographs of elliptical-shaped arches with traceried decoration, along with painted Gothic-style tracery decoration on the south and west walls, suggest that this arrangement was little earlier than 1867. The 1906 particulars also state that what is now the Members' room is "panelled in oak brought from an old church in Somerset".

ARCHAEOLOGICAL EVIDENCE

Until 1994 there had been only limited archaeological investigation of The Priory and its grounds. There is a somewhat enigmatic reference to the "further extent of the house eastwards (being) ascertained by the discovery of foundations in 1892,"[49] the date suggesting that this discovery may have been connected with the remodelling of the south projecting range in that year.

A souvenir programme for a fete held at The Priory in 1919 states that "further evidence for the original extent of the priory was the discovery of massive red brick foundations on the north side of the house when a large chestnut tree came down in May 1918".[50]

In 1954 massive wall footings were exposed in a sewer trench to the north of the building. The foundations were of chalk, both rammed and of rubble and lay approximately 3ft below the surface, averaging 3ft 6" in height above the natural gravel. These walls were considered to be those of the friary church.[51]

The laying of another parallel sewer trench in 1977 produced very similar results. Again two substantial sections of walling were located with a rammed chalk floor between. The northern wall was over 3ft thick, while close examination of the south wall revealed the beginning of a cross-wall with a buttress to the south. All appeared to be contemporary, the main south wall being of the same thickness as the north. The sewer trench also cut through two inhumation burials, which post-dated the destruction of the building to which the walls belonged. As in 1954, the walls were interpreted as those of the friary church,

enabling a reconstruction plan of the friary buildings to be made.[52]

In 1990, following the fall of a large cedar tree, further limited investigations were made to the west of the line of the 1954 sewer trench. The corner of a masonry building was exposed with demolition deposits within and a possible cellar beneath. The demolition deposits included a distinct layer of clay peg tile, which presumably came from the destruction of the building's roof. The building fragment uncovered lay on the same alignment as the surviving friary buildings and the walls uncovered in the sewer trenches.

From this archaeological evidence two alternative interpretations have been put forward; first, that the structure was associated with the public nave of the friary church, for example as an almshouse or watching closet, in an open-court plan. On the other hand, if the friary had followed the closed-court arrangement, the structure may have formed part of a range extending northwards from the claustral buildings to adjoin the nave of the church.[53] This interpretation is largely based on the possible opening observed on the east side of the exposed structure but, in view of the very limited area investigated, it is really only safe to say that the walls uncovered in 1990, along with those in 1954 and 1977, may be associated with the friary church and possibly with some form of range linking with the cloister to the south.

Until the recent repair project, archaeological work on the surviving building was even more limited than that carried out below ground. In 1951 removal of plaster to the west range exposed the jamb of a third claustral arch, which had the same mouldings as the other claustral openings.[54] A number of undated black and white photographs in the County Sites and Monuments Record of the north-east angle buttress to the south range show it to be chiefly of brick construction, indicating that the buttress is of post-medieval date.[55] The recent repairs have, however, provided the opportunity for more detailed recording to take place,[56] and my own observations, albeit limited by difficulties in arranging access, have also led to the recognition of hitherto unknown features.

Externally, the selective removal of render from the north wall of the **west range** has shown it to be basically of 18th-century red brick construction, some of it vitrified, although there is a faint suggestion that the brick under the ground-floor windows may be earlier than that under those

[48] H.R.O., 37,401; D/ELe B16.
[49] Walters op. cit. (note 7), 42; H.P. Pollard 'Franciscan and Benedictine monuments of Ware' in P.C. Standing (ed.), *Memorials of Old Hertfordshire* (1905), 54.
[50] H.R.O., 79,899.
[51] *East Herts. Arch. Soc. Newsletter*, 5 (1954); H.R.O., D/EGm 298 & Ware/167-78.
[52] Clive Partridge, 'Rescue excavations at Ware Priory', *Herts. Arch.*, 7 (1979), 143-5.
[53] M. Morris, *Ware Priory, A Note on Some New Evidence* (Hertfordshire Archaeological Trust, 1990), 3.
[54] *Trans. East Herts. Arch. Soc.*, 13 (1950-54), 65; H.R.O., D/EGm 298.
[55] S.M.R., PRN 4014.
[56] Recording work, both above and below ground, was being undertaken by the Hertfordshire Archaeological Trust. I am grateful to Tom McDonald of the Trust for discussing his preliminary findings with me and to Donald Insall and Associates for giving me access to the site at this time.

on the first floor. The top of the wall-post to the north-east corner (underbuilt in brick) and a short angle brace supporting the original tie beam, which is truncated to the left of the left first-floor window, were also exposed by the render removal. Stripping of roughcast render from the first floor of the **projecting range** to the south of the south range revealed Victorian yellow brick, but also several pieces of re-used medieval stonework. On the west gable of the **hall range** rapid drying of the damp render had clearly exposed the outline of a crown-post truss with diagonal downward braces between the collar and the tie beam.

Internally, the repair work has been much more extensive, the principal features revealed at the time of inspection in February 1994 being as follows:
Ground floor. The inner leaf of the north wall of the **south range** is of studwork, running parallel with which the footings of the south wall of the south claustral walk were visible on the ground, directly below a massive east-west running beam strengthened by a steel strap. Most of the ceiling joists in this room are modern, although some wider timbers have been re-used. An old beam rests above the wall separating the staircase and the cellar to the west, which has modern joists. In the former **kitchen** a fictive two-light Gothic blind "window" recess in an infilled clunchstone doorway with cambered head could be seen to the north of the large external lateral stack, immediately to the south of which is another later blocked doorway. The stack had two flues visible externally (revealed by the demolition of the formerly adjoining 20th-century flat-roofed addition), one on the ground floor and one on the first floor. What appear to be medieval floor layers were also visible in a trench immediately to the west, further suggesting the former presence of a range running to the west in this position.

In the **hall range** removal of plaster showed the south wall to be of mixed flint and brick construction and its doorway to be of modern date. The corridor running parallel with the south wall was seen to be a recent insertion as the joists above it run through to abut the south wall. At the time of inspection joists were exposed to several other parts of the ceiling, most notably in the two rooms to the west of the Council Chamber, where their considerable width shows them to be of medieval date. The room at the west end of the range has modern joists.

First Floor. The most significant discoveries in terms of the 16th-century conversion of the building to domestic use are in the south range, where the second and third sash windows from the east in the north wall and the western sash in the south wall were seen to be inserted into the brick infill of late 16th-century windows, the cambered and chamfered clunchstone heads of which survive, that to the second window from the east in the north wall being of greater width than the others. Above the cambered head of the window on the south side the medieval wall-plate and ashlar pieces were also exposed at the time of inspection.

Immediately to the east of this window the lath and plaster of the north-south running partition wall had been partially removed, showing it to be of stud construction with a crudely inserted round-headed doorway towards its southern end. Immediately to the north of the doorway the character of the partition wall changes, an exposed wattle and daub infill panel suggesting that from this point at least, where the wall apparently supports a north-south running beam, it is of much earlier construction. The eastern face of this wall and the wall running at right-angles to the east from its south-western corner form a square-shaped room, which the removal of later wall surfaces has revealed to have square oak panelling of c.1600 to its south, east and west sides.

Similar panelling could also be seen to the east wall of the similarly-shaped room to the east, the removal of lath and plaster from this wall revealing a carved timber mullion re-used as a stud to which the panelling is fixed. To the east again a chamfered cross-beam ceiling runs across the partitions of several later rooms, with several heavy medieval joists also exposed in the south-eastern corner, while in the corridor running east-west along the south side of the range the southern end of a north-south aligned tie beam could be seen above the ashlar pieces. The wall-plate beneath had been supported by a reinforced steel joist, following the removal of the chimney breast at this point. A number of very wide floorboards were visible in the **south projecting range**, confirming that it is considerably older than suggested by its external appearance.

Plaster stripping had been far less extensive in the **west range** at the time of inspection and no early features were visible. Three substantial north-south beams supporting the roof structure above were, however, exposed in the **hall range**. That to the west is chamfered and is clearly contemporary with a similar chamfered east-west running beam, forming a cross-beam ceiling to what once must have been a single large room at the west end of this range. The presence of this cross-beam ceiling suggests that at this end the attic floor it supports was inserted no later than the 17th century. In the eastern half of the range, however, the relatively insubstantial ceiling joists suggest that the second floor was put in much later and possibly only after 1849, the view usually expressed in other accounts of the building.[57] Further evidence that the hall range was originally a separate, albeit physically attached structure from the west range is shown by the small infilled gap visible between a fourth tie beam at the eastern end of the range and the wall-plate of the west range. Rafter feet could be seen overlapping the wall-plate, indicating that the west range was built before the hall range. Further wide floorboards were visible at several points in the hall range.

In the **attic** limited lath and plaster removal has added little to the previously available information on the roof structure. However, removal of an east-west partition

---

[57] Locke, 1992, op. cit. (note 29), 18 ; Ms. report (1982) by Richard Hewlings in N.M.R., file 81,117.

immediately to the west of the western crown-post in the hall range uncovered an upward brace to the west, corresponding with the already exposed brace to the north. Removal of the partition also revealed that the crown-post is limewashed on its eastern face. Again it was not possible to gain access to the upper parts of the roof structure in the hall range, but the stripping of lath and plaster from the lower parts of the rafters to the eastern half of this range on the south side confirms that they are not smoke blackened in this part of the roof: in fact, they also are limewashed. In the south range empty mortices indicate the former presence of ashlar pieces on the north side, to match those still surviving on the south.

INTERPRETATION AND CONCLUSIONS

There can be little doubt that the south and west ranges and the hall range projecting to the west are substantially medieval in their fabric. There is some uncertainty about their precise date but there seems no reason to follow the assertion by Walters that the arches in the present entrance hall are earlier than the 14th century. As he says himself, this "would presuppose some earlier building than Wake's foundation",[58] and there is no direct evidence to suggest that there was a previous building on the site.

Although both contain minor inaccuracies, the most complete descriptions of the building are still those by the *V.C.H.* and the *R.C.H.M.*[59] Both consider that "nothing earlier than late 15th-century work survives". However, while the original windows in the hall range are clearly of this date, this view would not seem to be supported either by the basic form or by the tracery details of the claustral arches in the south and west ranges. As we have seen, the existing tracery to the claustral arches was reworked (if not inserted) during the restoration of 1849/50, just as in the hall range new windows were inserted and alterations made to the existing ones between c.1820 and 1849/50. The situation is further complicated by the mouldings of all the windows and claustral arches being covered in painted cement render, so that it is impossible to distinguish between restoration and what may be genuine medieval work.

However, the basic authenticity of the present form of the claustral arches themselves was confirmed by the uncovering of the moulded jamb of the blocked arch in the west range in 1951, which would seem to suggest a late 14th-century date for these features. We also have the statement by Walters that "several old windows have been disclosed and opened out, and where repair was necessary reverentially treated".[60] This appears to relate to work he carried out himself, although the possibility that it is a reference to modifications earlier in the century or, indeed, to alterations to earlier 19th-century work cannot be ruled out. Similarly, while there was doubtless much restoration, the statement also suggests that the tracery of the windows in the hall range and the claustral arches was essentially repaired as existing.

The recent survey of the building by Peter Locke of Donald Insall Associates, as part of a feasibility study for future uses of The Priory, follows Walters in suggesting that there may be some fabric in the present building which pre-dates the foundation of the friary in 1338. Locke suggests that the pointed blocked doorway to one of the cross walls on the ground floor of the hall range and the similar doorway in its south wall are both of 13th-century date. He also points out that "various features and inconsistencies in the plan form and structure suggest the possibility of remnants of a pre-existing building in the (hall) wing" and that "...the disposition of the main lower walls of the wing is not incompatible with a classic 'hall house' plan."[61]

The use of the site before the friary's foundation is not known. The patent roll of Edward III for Thomas Wake to found the friary mentions "...one messuage and seven acres of land with appurtenances in Ware for **newly** erecting an oratory, houses and other buildings then necessary."[62] It is perhaps dangerous to read too much into this, especially as the grant does not specifically state that there were no existing buildings on the site, but the implication seems to be that it was essentially an empty site.

In 1372 Blanche, Lady Wake, gave the friars a further four acres of land with the buildings thereon valued at 2s *per annum* for the enlargement of their house,[63] but as the original seven acres seem to correspond with the later extent of The Priory grounds,[64] this would appear to be a distinct area of land, not directly connected with the site of the friary buildings.

The grants do not therefore give any positive information about the buildings on the friary site, although it should be remembered that by 1338 the days when friars lived in simple wooden huts had long gone,[65] and that any substantial buildings on the site would almost certainly have been re-used by the new community.

Nevertheless, the pointed arches of the two doorways in the hall range do not necessarily confirm a 13th- or even a 14th-century date, and in fact that on the south side has now been shown to be of modern construction. Pointed archways continued to be built in the 15th century and the rendered wall in which the internal doorway is situated makes it impossible to tell whether the arch-way, even if it is of the 13th century, could in fact simply be re-used from elsewhere. The hard cement-rendered walls of The Priory

[58] Walters, op. cit. (note 7), 42.
[59] *V.C.H.*, iii, 392; *R.C.H.M.*, 228-9.
[60] Walters, op. cit. (note 7), 42.

[61] Locke, 1990, op. cit. (note 29), 14.
[62] *Cal. Pat. R., 1338-40*, 14.
[63] *Cal. Pat. R., 1370-74*, 185.
[64] *Hertfordshire Mercury* (19 May 1906).
[65] B. Hamilton, *Medieval Religion in the West* (1986), 32-3.

are, indeed, a considerable hindrance to its archaeological interpretation, a fact which the recent renovation work has done little to alter.

Locke also observes that the 17th-century brickwork visible in the roof space to the east gable of the south range suggests that this range has been truncated, which would be consistent with the reference to the discovery in 1892 of foundations to the east of the surviving building. He also points out that the "makeshift carpentry" towards the southern end of the west range and "the comparatively modern brickwork" of its flush south gable end are indications "that this wing might originally have extended further southwards towards the river", having later been rebuilt in truncated form. Although it is not certain that this range has not been rebuilt on exactly the same lines as previously, this seems a distinct possibility and a long projecting range in this position could have served as an infirmary.

The original lay-out of the south and west ranges is unclear but the presence of the integral cloister arcades means that only the first floor can have been open to the roof and the absence of crown-posts makes even this uncertain. The ground floor of the south range may originally have been divided into two rooms by a north-south cross-wall behind the cloister walk, an arrangement which is shown in the plan of 1849 (see above). The ground-floor plan of the west range is even less certain but the former kitchen in the south-west corner of the building may occupy the site of the original kitchen.[66]

Leaving aside Locke's suggestion that the hall range may pre-date the foundation of the friary, the most noticeable feature of its ground floor is the small number of original windows in its north wall. Remembering that only two single-light windows are shown in the Fisher watercolour of c.1820, it seems possible that the ground floor was used primarily for storage and may have served as some kind of undercroft. Against this idea, however, it should be noted that the 1849 plan shows another ground-floor window, which has since been destroyed, in the south wall. The ground floor of this range appears to have been divided into three rooms by north-south cross-walls, that to the west containing the infilled doorway, the one to the east being rather less thick. The 1849 plan shows that the corridor on the south side did not exist before this date.

The first-floor plan of both the south and west ranges is difficult to reconstruct, although on the strength of parallels from elsewhere (see below) it is likely that the frater occupied the south range. Less weight should be given to the assertion by both the *R.C.H.M.* and A.R. Martin that the south projecting range may have been associated with the frater pulpit.[67]

In the hall range the elaborate carpentry of the eastern crown-post shows that it was intended to be visible from below and the attic floor is clearly an insertion, albeit that it now seems the floor in the two western bays was put in some two centuries before that to the eastern end. The plain crown-post to the centre of the range is embedded in a rebuilt north-south partition. Neither crown-post shows any sign of smoke blackening but what little can be seen through small hatches of the scissor bracing and common rafters to the west of the partition appears to show traces of smoke blackening. Owing to the impossibility of close inspection this is not conclusive and the rafters may in any case be re-used. This may, however, indicate that the area to the west of the partition was originally open to the roof from the ground floor, while the two bays to the east were fully screened off, unheated and only open to the roof from first-floor level, a suggestion strengthened by the recent discovery of flat medieval-looking joists to the corresponding part of the ground floor. In short, the original appearance of the roof structure of this range probably took a form similar to that seen in the 1849 print from *The Builder*, even if there was never a single open space on the first floor as shown in this drawing. The length of both crown-posts and the carpentry details of the eastern post suggest a 15th-century date for the roof structure.

The surviving fragments of the medieval friary are therefore the south and part of the west claustral ranges with a hall range at right-angles to the west. This may have served as a guest house, the two western bays of which seem originally to have been fully open to the roof, or were possibly heated by a portable brazier at first-floor level. The south range seems to have extended further to the east, although it is unlikely that the cloister itself extended further than the easternmost arch, probably returning to the north at the point where the building now ends. The west range may also have extended further to the south, while the buttresses to the hall range indicate that it is likely to retain its medieval proportions.

The church lay to the north and the monastic cemetery probably to the west. In 1802 four stone coffins were found near the western extremity of The Priory grounds but the description and illustration of these, along with the associated finds, seem to indicate a Roman rather than medieval date.[68] Owing to the fragmentary nature of the archaeological evidence, the plan of the church remains conjectural but, as at the Franciscan friaries of Newgate, London and Walsingham,[69] there seems to have been a small court between the north side of the cloister and the church, which were linked by a covered walk-way. The likely arrangement of this is shown in a reconstruction plan of the friary by A.G. Davies.[70] Details of the internal appearance of the church are not known but the recently

[66] *R.C.H.M.*, 228.
[67] Ibid; A.R. Martin, *Franciscan Architecture in England* (1937), 141.

[68] Partridge, op. et loc. cit. (note 52); Pollard, op. cit. (note 49), 55; *Gents. Mag.*, 72 (1802), 393; Bodl., Gough Maps, 11, fols.54v-56v.
[69] Martin, op. cit., 29.
[70] Partridge, op. cit. (note 52), 145.

published excavation results from Greyfriars, Oxford provide a useful parallel, albeit from a site of rather higher status.[71]

Indeed, comparisons with other Franciscan houses are helpful in reconstructing the possible lay-out of the claustral buildings. It was standard practice to incorporate the cloister walks into the claustral ranges themselves, there being surviving examples at Walsingham and Dunwich,[72] and evidence for this arrangement at Bedford, London and Yarmouth.[73] This practice was followed too by the Dominicans, as at Bristol, Hereford, Newcastle and Norwich,[74] while it was also used by the Carmelites and the Gilbertines, with examples in Hertfordshire at The Priory and The Biggin, Hitchin respectively.[75]

Plans of other Franciscan houses also point to the likelihood of the frater occupying the range opposite the church. Parallels can be found at Denny, Dunwich and Walsingham,[76] and probably also at Oxford.[77] The west range was sometimes occupied by the guest house, as at Canterbury and Walsingham,[78] but at Ware it seems more likely to have been situated in the hall range projecting to the west.

It is impossible to be certain as to how many of the friary buildings were utilised in the post-Dissolution conversion, but the fact that at least the south range was in domestic use by c.1600 has been established by the recent discovery of the square oak panelling and cambered stone window heads on its first floor, and it is quite clear that the house was much larger in the second half of 16th century than it is today. The reference by Weever, however, to "A Frierie, whose ruines, not altogether beaten downe, are to be seene at this day" suggests that much of the complex was unused by the Byrch family, while his mention of two surviving memorials is similarly far from conclusive proof that the church survived into the early 17th century. The friary church at Oxford had been almost entirely demolished by 1544,[79] and, while the archaeological evidence for the church at Ware is currently not sufficient to allow accurate dating of its demolition, the proximity of the parish church perhaps makes it unlikely that the friary church survived for any significant time after the Dissolution. The reference to a chapel in the inventory of 1715 is probably to a small domestic chapel in the house and should not be confused with the former friary church.

Little is known of the Byrch family, who acquired the site after the Dissolution. Thomas Byrch, who succeeded Robert Byrch in 1544 is described in the grant as a "yeoman of the crown" and as a scrivener and accountant.[80] Walters suggests that he may have been an agent of Cromwell,[81] but as Cromwell had been disgraced and dead since 1540, the reference to Byrch receiving Ware Priory in fee "for his services" is more likely to be for services to the crown.[82]

Finally, the reference in "The Tale of Two Swannes" by William Vallans to the site as "Byrches house" is perhaps more useful than this simple statement at first appears. As at Cheshunt, the reference in itself gives no indication as to the precise use of the buildings but it possibly indicates that the Byrch family, who were to hold the property until 1628, had made a substantial house out of the former friary, a suggestion strengthened by the late 16th-century cambered stone window heads and the slightly later oak panelling on the first floor of the south range. Which member of the Byrch family was principally responsible for this it is not possible to tell, but we can be more certain that the comparatively recent date of the claustral buildings, linked to their closeness to both town and river, made the friary an attractive proposition for residential conversion.

Bibliography

PICTORIAL SOURCES

Hertfordshire Record Office

Oldfield Drawings, VI, 373.

D/EX 317 P9-11.

Ware/189.

Gerish Collection, Box 79.

37,401.

British Library, London

Add. MS. 32,352, fol.88-9.

Map Room, Maps 137 a.3 (11); K. 15. 59. c.

Bodleian Library, Oxford

Gough Maps 11, fols.54v-56v, 57.

[71] T.G. Hassall, C.E. Halpin, M. Mellor et al, 'Excavations in St. Ebbe's, Oxford, 1967-1976: Part I: late Saxon and medieval domestic occupation and tenements, and the medieval Greyfriars', *Oxoniensia*, 54 (1989), 140-94.

[72] Martin, op. cit., 30.

[73] Ibid.

[74] Ibid.

[75] See reports on The Priory and The Biggin, Hitchin.

[76] Martin, op. cit., 32.

[77] Hassall et al, op. cit., 193.

[78] Martin, op. cit., 34.

[79] T.G. Hassall, C.E. Halpin, M. Mellor, 'Excavations in St. Ebbe's, Oxford, 1967-76: Part II: post-medieval domestic tenements and the post-Dissolution site of the Greyfriars', *Oxoniensia*, 49 (1984), 173, 271.

[80] *L.P.*, xix, no.610 (68).

[81] Walters, op. cit. (note 7), 41.

[82] *L.P.*, xix, no.610 (68).

Miscellaneous

Paintings (c.1850) hung in Council Chamber, Ware Priory.

PHOTOGRAPHIC SOURCES

Hertfordshire Record Office

Ware/16; 194.

Gerish Collection, Boxes 78-9.

Hertfordshire Local Studies Library, Hertford

Photographic Collection.

Bodleian Library, Oxford

MS. top. eccl. b 28, fol.13.

CARTOGRAPHIC SOURCES

Hertfordshire Record Office

D/ECh P13.

D/EX 317 P8.

PC 35.

63,620.

OTHER PRIMARY SOURCES

Manuscript:-

Public Record Office, London

SC6/Hen. VIII/1617-20, 1632-3.

Hertfordshire Record Office

37,401.

76,899.

79,899.

D/EGm 298.

D/ELe B16.

Ware/167-78.

Bodleian Library, Oxford

Douce HH 169.

MS. Gough Herts. 18.

National Monuments Record, The Royal Commission on Historical Monuments, Swindon

File 81,117.

County Sites and Monuments Record, Hertford

P.R.N. 4014.

Printed:-

Calendar of Patent Rolls Preserved in the Public Record Office (1903- (in progress).
Letters and Papers, Foreign and Domestic, of the Reign of Henry VIII, eds. Brewer, J.S., Gairdner, J. & Brodie, R.H., 21 vols. (1862-1932).

SECONDARY SOURCES

Brayley, E.W. & Britton, J., *The Beauties of England and Wales, Vol. 7, Hertfordshire* (1808).
East Herts. Arch. Soc. Newsletter, 5 (1954).
Fanshawe, C. (ed.), *Memoirs of Lady Fanshawe...Written by Herself* (1829).
Gentleman's. Magazine, 72 (1802), 393.
Godwin, G., 'Note on Ware Priory', *The Builder*, 7 (1849), 342.
Hamilton, B., *Medieval Religion in the West* (1986).
Hassall, T.G., Halpin, C.E., Mellor, M., 'Excavations in St. Ebbe's, Oxford, 1967-76: Part II: post-medieval domestic tenements and the post-Dissolution site of the Greyfriars', *Oxoniensia*, 49 (1984), 153-275.
-'Excavations in St. Ebbe's, Oxford, 1967-1976: Part I: late Saxon and medieval domestic occupation and tenements, and the medieval Greyfriars', *Oxoniensia*, 54 (1989), 140-94.
Hertfordshire Mercury (19 May 1906).
Locke, P.E. 'The Priory: an historic building in need of repair' in *Saving Ware's Historic Priory* (Ware, 1992), 15-23.
-Unpublished 1990 report on the building for Donald Insall and Associates.
Martin, A.R., *Franciscan Architecture in England* (Manchester, 1937).
Morris, M. *Ware Priory, A Note on Some New Evidence* (Hertfordshire Archaeological Trust, Hertford 1990).
Munby, L., *The Hertfordshire Landscape* (1977).
Partridge, C., 'Rescue excavations at Ware Priory', *Herts. Arch.*, 7 (1979), 143-5.
Pollard, H.P., 'Franciscan and Benedictine monuments of Ware' in Standing, P.C. (ed.), *Memorials of Old*

Hertfordshire (1905), 53-7.

Royal Commission on Historical Monuments, *Hertfordshire* (1910).

Trans. East Herts. Arch. Soc., 13 (1950-54), 65.

The Victoria History of the Counties of England, *Hertfordshire*, iii (1912); iv (1914).

Walters, R., 'Ware Priory', *Trans. East Herts. Arch. Soc.*, 1, pt.i (1899), 39-43.

    - *Ware Priory* (1926 pamphlet).

Weever, J., *Antient Funerall Monuments* (1631).

WYMONDLEY PRIORY

History

Initially established as a hospital between 1203 and 1207, the Augustinian priory here was founded by Richard de Argentin before 1218.[1] Dissolved in April 1537 and first leased and then granted to James Nedeham, surveyor of the king's works,[2] the property remained in the Nedeham family until 1733.[3]

THE BUILDINGS

Introduction

The principal surviving structure is almost certainly the western part of the nave of the priory church, converted into a house by James Nedeham after 1537 with additions carried out for his son John, and grandson, George, in the later 16th century. To the south is the 15th-century monastic barn. A moat, of which the drawbridge remained until the mid-19th century,[4] originally enclosed the church, conventual buildings and barn, but now only survives in parts, principally on the south and east. A boundary wall to the east of the house contains several fragments of moulded medieval stonework. Approximately 500 yards to the north-east of the house is a conduit head, which is probably of monastic origin, and to the north-west of the house a dovecote (now converted into a cottage) may also be of pre-Dissolution date.

There is some evidence to suggest that the first conversion on the site was of relatively high status and may have included the majority of the claustral buildings as well as the western part of the nave of the monastic church. Later in the 16th century the house appears to have been reduced in size, although the three gables on the north side are probably additions of this period. Chauncy, writing in c.1700, mentions the cloisters (which almost certainly lay to the north) and a "chappel consecrated since the Dissolution".[5] An estate map of 1731 shows the outline of a larger building than the present house and it is possible that this represents the whole of the nave with crossing, transepts and transeptal chapels.[6] The three latter structures and the eastern part of the nave have now been demolished, possibly as the result of a fire in the second half of the 18th century.

Various minor additions were made to the house in the 18th and 19th centuries, the chief of which was a single-storey wrap-around lean-to on the north and west elevations. In 1973-74 major renovations were carried out but at the time of inspection in November 1989 the house was unoccupied and there were plans to convert the barn to residential or office use.

The house ('The Priory')

This appears to have been formed from the western part of the aisleless nave of the 13th-century church, with a parallel and lower 16th-century addition on the south and three late 16th-century gables projecting beneath the ridge of the original building on the north. The whole structure, which is of two storeys with attics, is now cement rendered under a plain tile roof but the surviving medieval building is known to have been constructed mainly of flint rubble with uncoursed knapped flint facing, except for the east end of the south wall, the top of the west gable end and the buttress at the west end which are faced with regularly coursed limestone blocks. There are limestone dressings throughout. There has, however, been much rebuilding of the medieval fabric in 16th-century and later brick. The original north wall is now almost completely of brick, as is the upper part of the east gable end, the centre section of the south wall on both floors and virtually all the west gable end, much of the latter belonging to the renovations of 1973-74. The 16th-century south-western block is also of red brick (English bond) with some diaper patterning in vitrified brick to its west gable end. There is similar red brickwork to the three northern gables, which are timber framed to their apices.[7] As with the surviving medieval building all of this is concealed externally by cement render of 1973-74.

All the external joinery, apart from a single two-light wooden mullion window directly above the lean-to in the angle with the south-western addition on the south elevation, was replaced in 1973-74. Several 16th-century mullioned and transomed windows (most notably to the first floor of the three northern gables) had survived until then but others had been renewed in the 18th and 19th centuries: the pre-1973 fenestration pattern, however, survives largely intact. There are two ridge stacks roughly to the centre of the main range, both with red brick diagonal shafts, the eastern one on a substantial rendered base with dripstones. There were also formerly several other stacks, the most prominent of which, shown on a drawing of c.1790 by H.G. Oldfield,[8] was a large external lateral stack on the west face of the western gable on the north elevation. The south-west range retains a plain brick stack to its east gable end, which was reduced in height in 1973-74.[9]

North elevation:- This is dominated by the triple gables referred to above, with large eight-light mullioned and transomed windows on each floor except for the ground-floor centre, which has a large 20th-century door flanked by contemporary tall narrow windows. The left and centre

[1] Knowles (1953), 160, 321.
[2] *L.P.*, xiii, p.589; H.R.O., 21,339-21,344.
[3] *V.C.H.*, iii, 190.
[4] Noel Farris, *The Wymondleys* (1989), 148.
[5] Chauncy, ii, 110.
[6] H.R.O., 44,215.
[7] D.O.E. 54th List of Historic Buildings, District of North Hertfordshire, 28 May 1987, 87; N.M.R., photographs in parish boxes.
[8] H.R.O., Oldfield Drawings, VII, 418, 451.
[9] N.M.R. photographs (note 7).

gables have pronounced bulges in the render at tie beam level which suggest that they were originally jettied at this point. There was formerly a single-storey lean-to, shown on the c.1790 drawing, which ran from approximately the middle of the centre gable to the west wall of the west gable and incorporated the large stack mentioned above. This lean-to was later extended to fill in the angle between the west wall of the west gable and the north wall of the main range, at which time the external stack was probably demolished. The extended lean-to had a Victorian canted bay window projecting from its west wall.[10] The access from the extension of the lean-to into the main range appears to have destroyed the 13th-century walling at this point.[11]

West elevation:- The main range has two windows on the first floor directly above French windows to the ground floor and a single three-light window to the attic. The lower south-west range is flush with the main range and has a window on both floors. There is a stepped buttress at the junction between the two ranges which may be original 13th-century work. Before 1973 there was a hip-roofed porch to the left of the main range and a canted bay window to the lower range: both were Victorian. The c.1790 drawing shows a wooden cupola housing a bell to the gable of the south-west range with a circular clock face directly below. Both are absent on George Buckler's pen and ink drawing of 1840,[12] but the clock mechanism still survives internally.

South elevation:- The south-west range has a window on each floor with a later single-storey lean-to in the angle with the main range against its east end. A blocked doorway survives under the plaster to the left of the ground-floor window.[13] The main range has a two-light wooden mullion window (referred to above) directly over the lean-to and a window on each floor to the centre; two-light gabled dormer in roof slope.

East elevation:- The main range has a window on each floor, including to the attic. There is a small window at the junction with the flush north gabled projection, which has another small window to the right.

Interior.

General description.

This was much altered in 1973-74 with new staircases, doors and other joinery. The plan before this was largely the result of the 16th-century domestic conversion with modifications from the 17th century to the early 20th century. The western part of what appears to be the south wall of the monastic nave survives between the main range and the south-west addition and its line is continued by the

external wall to the east of the south-west projection. More of the nave north wall survives and forms the division between the main range and the triple-gabled north range. Both walls are approximately 3ft thick, where of original construction, and survive to eaves level.

The other principal survivals from the early 13th-century church are the roof structure (described below), two tall lancet windows in the original south wall and a fine processional doorway in the west part of the north wall. The lancet windows, fully uncovered in the alterations of 1973-74,[14] are at present first-floor level, the eastern one giving access to the south-west range, the western one currently blocked. Both have rebated outer arches, deep internal splays and nook-shafts with moulded capitals supporting finely moulded two-centred arches. There are traces of red paint (probably medieval) on the east capital of the west arch. The processional doorway is of the same date as the lancets and has a fine moulded arch of multiple rolls and hollows (recently restored) on its external face.

The internal arrangement of the house was extensively altered in 1973-74 and it is therefore more useful to describe it in terms of the plan drawn by the *V.C.H.* in 1912, which is the earliest reliable plan known to exist.[15] This obviously incorporates the additions and alterations made in the 18th and 19th centuries, but also clearly indicates the extent of the 16th-century and early 17th-century modifications. These converted the western part of the nave into living quarters by inserting a first floor and attic and two massive back-to-back fireplaces, separated by a narrow passage-way which is present on all three floors. A parallel addition was made to the south-west and the three gables were added to the north wall.

Ground floor:- To take the room to the west first, which at the time of the *V.C.H.* account served as the dining room, this has a large fireplace with a reset wooden lintel which has ogee stops and is probably of late 16th-century date. The north and south walls have full-height square and rectangular panelling, much restored in 1973-74 but probably belonging to the late 16th or early 17th century. There are contemporary ceiling beams and joists.

There was formerly a wall running west from the north-west corner of the fireplace to the west wall, apparently built in the late 16th or early 17th century, creating a passage-way, which later incorporated a straight-flight staircase of uncertain but probably 18th- or 19th-century date. This passage-way, parallel with the north wall of the nave, ran almost the full length of the building with another passage-way (now blocked) running at right-angles between the two chimney breasts.

The room to the east of the eastern chimney breast, divided at the time of the *V.C.H.* account into the kitchen and

---

[10] H.R.O., County Views WYM. LT/3; Farris, op. cit. (note 4), 165.
[11] *V.C.H.*, iii, 189.
[12] H.R.O., Buckler Drawings, III, 106.
[13] N.M.R. photographs (note 7).

[14] *Med. Arch.*, 18 (1974), 191.
[15] *V.C.H.*, iii, 189.

several smaller service rooms, has 16th-century beams and joists and a reset massive plain wooden lintel to the fireplace. The south-west range (the present kitchen) has flat 16th-century joists and a large, originally integral end stack to the east wall. On the north side of the house the infilled processional doorway from the nave to the former cloister is situated in the angle with the west wall of the west gable. In the north-east corner of the east gable is a late medieval traceried recess (probably a piscina or aumbry and possibly reset) with part of a wall painting, probably of c.1600 and depicting a powerfully built warrior in classical armour holding a sword, above. There was formerly a "small plain old stair" in this area,[16] but this is now gone. This would appear to have been the staircase rising up by a square-panelled wall with a moulded handrail, turned balusters and a circular newel-post with moulded plinth and capitals, of which there is a photograph in the N.M.R.[17] The staircase looks to have been of early 18th-century date.

According to the *V.C.H.* there was a doorway, infilled by the time that the *V.C.H.* account was written, in the eastern (external) wall with a splayed four-centred arch. It has been suggested that this wall, which is partly of brick construction, is of late 16th-century date,[18] in which case the doorway was probably also of this period. That this wall may not, however, have been external in the original conversion is suggested by the 1731 map, which appears to show that the converted building formerly extended much further to the east.

First Floor:- The beams of the inserted attic floor are visible jutting out into the centre gable on the north side in the void above the modern staircase and similarly in the first-floor room of the east gable, suggesting that the flooring in of the nave pre-dates the addition of the gables. The western chimney breast is of red brick construction and has a moulded stone fireplace with four-centred arch under a depressed three-centred brick relieving arch. The fireplace is now mostly infilled and has a smaller brick fireplace inserted in its right corner. Although J.T. Smith has dated the relieving arch to the mid-17th century,[19] the moulding and shape of the stone fireplace would seem to indicate a mid-16th-century date and suggest that it served an important room to the west: the rooms currently to the west are the result of modern sub-divisions. The larger rooms to the east no longer have any features of interest, but several were formerly panelled, including a room to the east front and the long east-west passage-way with square and oak rectangular panelling like that found on the ground floor.[20]

The two 13th-century lancet windows in the south wall of the former nave are cut by the inserted 16th-century floor but at such a level for them to serve as doorways into the south-west range: the west lancet is, however, currently infilled by a modern partition wall.

The south-west range has a collar and tie beam roof in three bays with clasped purlins and curved windbraces. The west bay has an attic floor but this is absent to the centre and east bays, which may have formed a single large room open to the roof at first-floor level, the eastern tie beam appearing to be a later insertion. This idea is strengthened by the fact that the west tie beam has mortices to its underside suggesting a close-studded partition. The mortices stop some distance short of the nave wall which at this point contains the west lancet, implying that there was a doorway at this point. This would have led into a small closet in the north-west corner of this range, the former existence of which is shown by the presence of mortices to the underside of the beam running west at right-angles from the western tie beam. A doorway to the closet at this point means that the lancet window could have been open as a doorway contemporaneously with the existence of the west room and closet, although obviously this is not proven. The attic chamber contains the clock mechanism, access being obtained through a door directly above the tie beam.

Attic (of main range):- This contains the roof structure of the 13th-century church, although this is fully exposed only in the west room. It is of single-framed construction without purlins consisting of individual rafter couples, each with a collar, straight braces below the collar and ashlar pieces (most clearly visible to the first floor on the south side) near the feet of the rafters descending vertically to sole-pieces over twin wall-plates. Photographs taken of the western section of the roof structure during the refurbishment works of 1973-74 show what look like traces of smoke blackening to many of the rafters, but it would be unwise to read too much into this as similar deposits can be seen in photographs taken of the roof structure of the south-west range at the same time.[21] This range is known to have had a first floor and chimney stack from the start and while some of its roof timbers may have been re-used from elsewhere, there is no sign that this was the case. This apparent smoke blackening is therefore very slender evidence on which to suggest that the main body of the house is not in fact the remains of the monastic church, but another building originally open to the roof and heated by a ground-floor hearth.[22] Whether the deposits seen in the photographs were caused by smoke blackening or were the result of the major fire which is known to have taken place in the 18th century,[23] is no longer possible to establish as the roof timbers in the main roof structure are now all black painted.

The attic of the west gable on the north side has its timber

[16] Ibid, 188.
[17] N.M.R. photographs (note 7).
[18] Unpublished report by Adrian Gibson (1973), Hertfordshire Local Studies Library, Hertford, H 726.7.
[19] Smith (1992), 188.
[20] N.M.R. photographs (note 7).

[21] Ibid.
[22] Smith (1993), 218; N.M.R., file 77,959.
[23] Farris, op. cit. (note 4), 173-4.

frame exposed internally, comprising a queen-strut truss with curved windbraces to clasped purlins and narrow red brick infill panels. The centre gable has a similar roof structure but the windbraces are straighter. The attic of the west gable shows that the top of the nave north wall is of red brick: presumably it was rebuilt when the gables were added in the late 16th century.

Other buildings

Also within the moated platform, the largely water-filled ditch of which survives on the south and east and partially on the north and west sides, is the former monastic **barn**. This magnificent timber-framed building is of aisled construction measuring 109 x 39 ft externally and is of nine bays. It is clad in weatherboarding under a vast plain tile roof, which extends almost to the ground with hipped ends and gablets. There are later, probably 18th-century, hip-roofed lean-tos at each end, that to the west open fronted. There is a central gabled porch set within the line of the aisle on both north and south sides and a later porch on the north near the west end. There were formerly gabled hatched dormers to either side of the porch on the south side.[24]

The **interior** remains almost completely unaltered. The jowled arcade posts of heavy square section are supported on peninsular oak plates resting on stone sills dividing the aisles into compartments. There are arched braces to the arcade-plates and long curved braces to the heavy cambered tie beams. The roof has butt-purlins in two tiers with curved windbraces, the upper purlins carried on collars and the lower on raking queen-posts. The aisle ties each have inclined queen-posts directly supporting a clasped purlin. The aisle walls are constructed of alternating heavy studs and quartered poles: these are not designed for wattle and daub infill so the barn is likely to have been weatherboarded from the beginning.[25] There are slightly curved braces above the mid-height rail in the end walls, the curve more pronounced at the east end. The heavy flat rafters are original and have a mortice on the faces directly above the arcade-plates. Several of the principal rafters have mortices directly below the collar, some on one roof slope only but others corresponding to both north and south sides.

There is some controversy over the date of the barn. Some authorities have claimed that it is of 13th-century origin,[26] but most are agreed that it dates to the late 15th century.[27] Radiocarbon dating has, however, obtained a date of c.1260 from an apparently re-used timber so, despite the current lack of a more accurate dendrochronological assessment, it is possible that the present barn is a rebuilding of an earlier structure.[28] Nevertheless, the constructional details all suggest a late rather than early medieval date for the surviving building.

Adjoining the barn on the west are 19th-century pigsties and other outbuildings, which incorporate some 16th-century red brick and medieval moulded stonework within their fabric. To the west again are a 17th-century barn and 18th-century stable. The three-bay barn, the west end of which lies over an infilled part of the moat, is on the south and has the stable attached to its east end projecting to the north. Both are weatherboarded, the barn with a corrugated iron roof over thatch and the stables with a plain tile roof. There is another weatherboarded barn with a plain tile roof closing the yard to the north of the stable. All three structures are much altered and do not contain any re-used medieval work.

To all sides of the house are boundary walls. Although these contain re-used medieval stonework, they are unlikely to be earlier than the 17th century and do not appear to represent any medieval boundaries, or to be associated with the 16th-century conversion work. The walls are best preserved to the east of the house, where they stand approximately 6ft high and incorporate much medieval flintwork and dressed clunch. The walls here form a rectangular shape (now a garden area) and it has been suggested that the southern section is on the line of the monastic cemetery enclosure although there is no positive evidence to substantiate this.[29] The north face of this stretch of wall contains a post-medieval bee bole with segmental head. The walls to the north and north-west of the house are largely brick built and were probably constructed when this section of the moat was infilled.

Approximately 140 yards to the north-west of the house and immediately to the north of the priory stew-pond is a former **dovecote**, which was converted into a cottage in the late 19th century. The building is square in plan and of narrow red brick construction in English bond with blue brick diaper patterns. It has a steeply pitched hipped plain tile roof with large gablets on the east and west. These are now pargetted but originally had entrances for doves. Access is now on the west through a half-glazed door under a segmental head with square label; there is a 19th-century three-light casement under a similar head to the left and a three-light casement directly below the eaves to the centre. The south elevation has a narrow window under a similar head to the right. The central stack is a 19th-century insertion and there are prominent single-storey modern additions to the north and east. A drawing of 1840 by George Buckler shows the building in its pre-conversion state.[30] An entrance, probably the only one, is on the north and there is pronounced diaper patterning to the west

[24] Bodl., MS. top. eccl. b.27, fol.53.

[25] D.O.E. List (note 7), 88.

[26] W. Horn, 'The great tithe barn of Cholsey, Berkshire', *Jnl. Soc. Archit. Hist.*, 22 (1963), 18-19.

[27] Pevsner, 243.

[28] R. Berger, 'The potential and limitations of radiocarbon dating in the Middle Ages: the radiochronologist's view' in R. Berger (ed.), *Scientific Methods in Medieval Archaeology* (1970), 133.

[29] D.O.E. List (note 7), 88.

[30] H.R.O., Buckler Drawings, III, 106.

elevation. There is a chamfered plinth (still surviving) and a moulded eaves cornice, now gone.

The date of the dovecote is problematic. It is certainly of 16th-century date but if monastic in origin must date to the 1530s or possibly the 1520s at the earliest. However, it could equally well have been built in the 1540s or 1550s. No dovecote is mentioned in a survey of 1537 but this, of course, is not conclusive. It may be worth noting that the building's brickwork is very similar to that of the surviving fragment of the house built by Robert Gostwick at the former Augustinian abbey of Warden (Beds.) after 1545,[31] and even more particularly to that of the 16th-century barns with blue brick diaper patterns at the same site. There is also a dovecote of similar construction but with a timber-framed upper storey at nearby Wymondley Bury.[32]

Approximately 500 yards to the north-east of the house is the former **conduit head**. This is now in almost totally ruinous condition and even that part still surviving is mostly the result of reconstruction by Colonel Unwin Heathcote and F. Johnstone Page in c.1905.[33] It is a small roofless rectangular building standing in a copse of trees, with only the gabled south wall remaining to full height. This is of narrow red brick in English bond to the bottom part, rebuilt in early 20th-century plum red brick to the gable. The other walls survive as footings only and are constructed of uncoursed flint rubble. The south wall has a central clunch doorway with a three-centred arch in two orders, imposts and stone jambs with a corbelled brick course above. On the internal face the doorway has a segmental rere-arch and splayed jambs with a round-headed niche to each side. There are remains of a central north window flanked by niches and triple recesses to the side walls. At the time of inspection in November 1989 the ruined building was completely dry inside but when visited by the East Hertfordshire Archaeological Society in August 1906, shortly after its reconstruction, the conduit head was described as "shaped like an oblong bath,... full of water, communicating with springs close by and conveying water to the Priory".[34]

A watercolour of c.1790 by Oldfield depicting the interior of the building in an unruined and apparently unrestored state shows that there were then two tiers of niches, the lower forming seats, although interestingly only two wide recesses are shown to the bottom tier on the east and west sides.[35] The top tier on these sides also has a small splayed segmental-headed window in place of the central niche. The watercolour shows a roof structure of collar and tie beam trusses with curved windbraces to single purlins. Also depicted in the painting is a central basin. This

appears too in the *V.C.H.* plan of 1912 with a rounded end towards the door,[36] although it is shown square-ended by Oldfield.

Another contemporary Oldfield watercolour of the exterior of the building represents it with a possibly thatched roof, the entrance doorway set in a slight projection and what may have been brick diapering to the gable above.[37] This all suggests that the c.1905 rebuilding may not have been strictly accurate, a view also taken by the *V.C.H.* which states that "as no record of the old building could be found, the new work was copied from another old building elsewhere."[38]

Chauncy refers to the conduit which provided "sufficient water to turn the spit in the kitchen (of the house) upon all occasions",[39] a use which it continued to serve until the mid-19th century.[40] The provision of a piped water supply from natural springs indeed seems to have been the original function of the conduit, with elm water pipes recorded as having been ploughed up along its length in c.1920,[41] but the conduit house itself may also have served a more recreational purpose. Oldfield in the caption to his watercolours of the building writes that "it appears... by the benches in the niches to have been a sort of pleasant retreat in the heat of summer for the Religious Inhabitants of the Priory who might here enjoy their wine diluted with the cool chrystal spring, rising in the middle of the building".

Whether or not this was the case is impossible to establish but it is perhaps more likely that such a practice was enjoyed by James Nedeham and his successors than by the Augustinian canons. Indeed, like the dovecote, the date of the conduit house is difficult to pinpoint with any accuracy. It may be of monastic origin but the surviving doorway and the former roof structure, which was similar to that in the 16th-century parts of the house, tend to suggest a late 16th-century date. The difficulty of determining a more accurate date is further complicated by the remodelling of c.1905.

Other features. The church bells are not included in the inventory of March 1537 but a month later they are recorded as weighing 24 hundredweight.[42] The four bells were subsequently sold to the parish of Graveley, where they are referred to in a document of 1557 as the "iiij belles of Graveley sum tyme belongyng to the Priore of Wymondelay Parva."[43] The other goods mentioned in the 1537 survey were bought by James Nedeham but it is likely that some building materials were sold to local people. It has been claimed, however, that the choir stalls were taken

[31] Howard (1987), 201.

[32] *V.C.H.*, iii, 189; *R.C.H.M.*, 149.

[33] 'Twenty fourth excursion of the East Hertfordshire Archaeological Society, 30 August 1906', *Trans. East Herts. Arch. Soc.*, 3 (1906), 230-1; *Herts. Express* (8 September 1906).

[34] Ibid.

[35] H.R.O., Oldfield Drawings, VII, 411.

[36] *V.C.H.*, iii, 189.

[37] H.R.O., Oldfield Drawings, VII, 411.

[38] *V.C.H.*, iii, 189.

[39] Chauncy, ii, 110.

[40] *V.C.H.*, iii, 189.

[41] Farris, op. cit. (note 4), 144.

[42] P.R.O., SC6/Hen. VIII/1606, m.11.

[43] T. North and J. Stahlscmidt, *The Church Bells of Hertfordshire* (1886), 32.

to the parish church of Stevenage.[44] It has not been possible to trace the original reference for this and, if it did occur, precisely when and why this happened is not clear: there is no known connection between Wymondley and Stevenage either before or after the Dissolution. It is enough to state here that the Stevenage choir stalls with their misericords are of sufficiently high quality to have come from a monastic church, while there are many parallels elsewhere for the transfer of fittings from monastic to parish churches at the Dissolution.[45]

DOCUMENTARY AND MAP EVIDENCE

From the physical evidence of the 13th-century doorway in the north wall of the former nave and the height of the south windows which do not allow for a cloister walk beneath them, it appears that the cloister lay to the north, a feature not uncommon in Augustinian houses.[46] It may be, however, as Stuart Rigold has suggested that in a small house like Wymondley there was never a complete claustral plan,[47] a suggestion perhaps made more credible by its origins as a hospital.

A visitation of 1530 by John Rayne, chancellor to the diocese of Lincoln, helps a little in identifying the position of the claustral and other buildings.[48] The repair of the frater is mentioned and its position may have been the usual one, directly opposite the church. In this case, the dorter would have occupied the first floor of the east claustral range with the chapter house, referred to in 1442 and on the priory seal,[49] below to the north of the north transept. An inventory of 1537, made just before the suppression, lists a hall, servants' chamber, kitchen, bakehouse, brewhouse, buttery and pantry but it is not possible from this alone to identify their precise locations.[50] In addition, the visitation of 1530 mentions a bell tower at the west end of the church.[51]

Chauncy's statement of c.1700 that "This Priory has been a

fair old building with cloysters" rather implies that the cloister had disappeared by this date, but this is by no means certain and it is no longer possible to establish whether or not it formed an integral part of the post-Dissolution conversion. It is, however, quite likely that it did as the 1530 visitation suggests that much was done at about this time to put the conventual buildings in order.

Although 100 marks had been spent on repairs since Prior Weston had taken office in 1520, the chancel and nave of the church were still in need of repair at the time of the 1530 visitation. Two windows in the east part of the church had been renewed, however, and the refectory repaired. The bell tower was being rebuilt after it had collapsed owing to an apparent lack of maintenance and Rayne was assured that the stonework would be finished by midsummer. The four bells from the old tower remained.[52] This may have been a detached structure as there is no reference to its collapse having caused damage to other buildings.

Although the precise condition of the priory is not easy to ascertain from this information (the word *ruinosus* which appears frequently in the records of the visitation can mean anything from total collapse to simply requiring maintenance), it seems that not only had most of the buildings received some attention between 1520 and 1530 but that further repairs were carried out after 1530. If this was the case, the church and refectory are likely to have been in relatively sound condition in 1537 and the prior would have been unlikely to have neglected his own lodgings, probably the 'hall' referred to in the inventory of that year.

It seems quite likely therefore that the church (or at least the nave) and possibly the refectory and prior's lodging/hall formed the nucleus of the first conversion on the site. The house at this stage may thus have been of courtyard plan around the former cloister and it is possibly this to which Chauncy refers. He also mentions a "chappel...consecrated since the Dissolution". This may have been in the former refectory, with the western part of the nave serving as the hall of Nedeham's new house, although the possibility that the chapel was a separate post-Dissolution structure cannot be discounted.

It is difficult to date the 16th-century conversion and the additions to the north and south of the nave with any degree of exactness. The work may have been carried out by Nedeham but it may equally well have been undertaken by his son or grandson. The phasing of this operation is discussed in detail below but all that can be said with absolute certainty from the documentary evidence is that the domestic conversion took place between c.1540 and c.1600. Certainly, there seems no reason categorically to

[44] F. Bottomly, *Abbeys, Churches and Monasteries of Great Britain* (1981), 218.

[45] For instance, the choir stalls in the parish churches at Lancaster and Richmond were originally at Cockersand and Easby respectively; L. Butler and C. Given-Wilson, *Medieval Monasteries of Great Britain* (1979), 120, 222. In Wales, the choir stalls and screen were transferred from Chirbury Priory (Shropshire) to Montgomery at the Dissolution and the north nave arcade and roof at Llanidloes (Montgomeryshire) are said to have come from Cwmhir Abbey (Radnorshire); Richard Haslam, *The Buildings of Wales; Powys* (1979), 140-1, 166.

[46] As at Dorchester-on-Thames (Oxon.), Hinchingbrooke (Hunts.), Lacock (Wilts.) and Leez and St Osyth (Essex). It has, however, been suggested that the cloister may have lain to the south; G. Burleigh, K. Matthews & D. Went, *Wymondley Priory, Hertfordshire: An Archaeological Evaluation* (North Hertfordshire District Council Museums, 1989), 3-4.

[47] Letter from Stuart Rigold to Noel Farris, 1974, Hertfordshire Local Studies Library, Hertford H 726.7.

[48] Farris, op. cit. (note 4), 157.

[49] A. Hamilton Thompson (ed.), *Visitations of Religious Houses, 1436-49*, iii, Lincs. Rec. Soc., 21 (1929), 396-7 ; the seal is reproduced in *V.C.H.*, iv, opp. p.434.

[50] P.R.O., E 117/12/30.

[51] Farris, op. cit. (note 4), 157.

[52] H.E. Salter (ed.), *A Subsidy Collected in the Diocese of Lincoln in 1526* (1909), 192.

state, as some writers have done,[53] that it belongs entirely to the latter part of the period.

Further documentary evidence for the relatively good condition of the church in 1537 comes from a bill of £15 4s 8d paid by Nedeham to the former prior, John Atow, "for repairs this year made on the house and church buildings of the former Priory where they were greatly ruined and defective".[54] In fact, £5 more than this was set aside for maintenance in this year, which suggests that repairs were still ongoing after the Dissolution.[55]

On Nedeham's death in 1544 the property passed to his son, John, who held it until his death in 1591, the house then falling to his son, George, who died in 1626.[56] Little is known from documentary sources of the house in the 17th and 18th centuries. Chauncy records that George Nedeham, who succeeded to the property in 1658, "much improved the Priory" and in 1662 the property was assessed for 16 hearths.[57] Exactly what he did, however, is not clear and in 1733 the house left the Nedeham family when it was sold to Samuel Vanderplank.[58] At some time after 1731, the date of the estate map referred to earlier, the eastern part of the nave and all parts of the church to the east were destroyed. A local tradition records that this was the result of a disastrous fire but,[59] as suggested below, the parts of the church to the east of the present east wall of the house may have been ruinous long before the 18th century.

It is tempting to equate the formerly greater extent of the house with a survival of the eastern part of the church long after the Dissolution and it is possible to interpret the roughly cruciform shape of this larger building as following the plan of the church. Certain irregularities, however, suggest that these now long-demolished ranges represent structures added after the suppression, albeit on the site of the eastern end of the church. Likewise, if the once greater extent of the building does represent the crossing, transepts and quire of the monastic church, they may not have survived as habitable structures but may have been shown on the map simply because their walls remained above ground. It is also worth noting that the map appears to show the main range of the house extending further to the west than is the case today. Whether the reduction in size during the second half of the 18th century represents simply the clearance of wall footings or more extensive demolition, the reduction had clearly taken place by 1776 when another estate map was drawn.[60] This, and enclosure and estate maps of 1811,[61] show the main house to be no larger than now.

ARCHAEOLOGICAL EVIDENCE

Only limited archaeological work has been carried out on the site. In November 1989 as part of a proposal to convert the house into a training centre, the North Hertfordshire District Council Museums Field Archaeology Section was commissioned to carry out a field evaluation. Four trial trenches were dug in the position of the proposed new buildings, one immediately to the south of the house and three to the north-east of the barn outside the courtyard to the south and east of the house. The former produced inconclusive traces of a pre-Dissolution building, which the excavator tentatively suggests may show that the cloister in fact lay to the south of the church. Alternatively, it is possible that the structure located relates to the pre-priory hospital phase of the site. In the other three trenches the most significant discovery was a large linear "negative feature", which while it could be regarded as the cellar or undercroft of a building, has been interpreted as part of the moated system, apparently sub-dividing the island into two roughly equal-sized parts. This ditch may have separated the church and conventual buildings from the barn, although it seems to have stopped short of the trench excavated immediately to the south of the house. The ditch appears to have been backfilled by 1731 as it is not shown on the estate map of that year.[62] An eastern extension remains, however, and runs eastwards towards a spring which formed a secondary water supply for the moat. Neither the date of this feature or whether it formed part of the original moated system is known but it appears to be shown on the 1731 map.

Outside the moated platform in the surrounding pasture fields is an extensive series of earthworks, clearly visible both on the ground and from the air.[63] To the south is a hollow-way aligned on the possibly original causeway across the moat, while to the east is a well-defined area of ridge and furrow field system. To the north are house platforms and enclosures, bounded on the west by ponds and to the east by a hollow-way. The line of the water course linking the conduit head to the moated enclosure surrounding the house is also readily discernible, although at its north-eastern end it is now largely piped and ploughed over. At its south-western end, immediately to the north of the moat, the water course runs into a long linear feature, possibly a monastic fishpond, which is shown as two separate ponds on the 1731 map.

These earthworks have not been investigated or fully recorded, but it has been suggested that they represent a deserted medieval settlement, which was either associated with the agricultural work of the priory or was depopulated when it was founded.[64] The former is the more likely and it is possible that the settlement was not in fact depopulated

---

[53] *V.C.H.*, iii, 188-9; Pevsner, 243.

[54] P.R.O., SC6/Hen. VIII/1606, m.11.

[55] Ibid.

[56] P.R.O., PCC 21 Pynnyng; *V.C.H.*, iii, 190.

[57] Chauncy, ii, 110; P.R.O., E 179/375/30.

[58] *V.C.H.*, iii, 190.

[59] Farris, op. cit. (note 4), 173-4.

[60] H.R.O., 44,212.

[61] H.R.O., QS/E 81; D/EX 234 P13.

[62] H.R.O, 44,215; Burleigh et al (note 46), 16.

[63] S.M.R., PRN 1037, 0159; R.C.H.M., National Library of Air Photographs, Swindon: Accession nos. CAP 8211, frame 61 & 62, CAP 8194, frame 31.

[64] Burleigh et al, op. cit., 1.

until after the Dissolution. In this connection, the designation of the field immediately to the north of the house as "The Park" on the 1731 map may be significant. There is apparently no other documentary evidence relating to a park at Wymondley, but one may well have been created by the Nedehams in the second half of the 16th century, which would explain the abandonment of the medieval settlement. Some but not all of the earthworks are now designated as a scheduled ancient monument.[65]

INTERPRETATION AND CONCLUSIONS

Reference has been made already to the difficulty of dating exactly the 16th-century work on the house. It would seem unlikely that James Nedeham, with his knowledge and experience of building, would have done little or nothing to the property he acquired in April 1538, especially as he already seems to have been responsible for the priory's finances since its closure a year earlier.[66] It is possible that the fact he originally held the house on a lease (from December 1537) and did not purchase it until some months later may have acted as some disincentive to immediate and expensive conversion work,[67] but there is no direct evidence to support this and in any case the gap between the two events was extremely slight. Furthermore, it seems that the majority of the buildings were in a comparatively good state of repair at the suppression. Much work had recently been done on the church itself and as some of this seems to have taken place after the Dissolution, this rather suggests that Nedeham intended to convert the church from the beginning.

That the church itself was chosen for conversion and the speed with which the site was acquired both suggest that Nedeham had ambitious plans for the former priory. Church conversions, such as at the Hampshire houses of Netley, Titchfield, Mottisfont and rather later at Buckland (Devon), were often among the most daring transformations of ex-monastic property. Most were carried out by men of high status who were able to afford the high costs such work entailed, were not afraid of the possible accusations or consequences of sacrilege and were anxious to have an unusual and prestigious house. The latter was perhaps the most compelling driving force and is exactly the motive one would expect of a man like Nedeham. Indeed, as surveyor of the king's works, Nedeham was already gaining direct experience of converting former monastic buildings into royal residences at Dartford, Rochester and St Augustine's Abbey, Canterbury.[68]

Another reason that the church itself was selected for conversion may have been simply that it was in good condition. The repair works of c.1520 to 1530 were carried out before the first talk of suppression and, although it

seems likely that the immediate post-Dissolution repairs were undertaken because conversion was intended, the relatively good state of the church before the Dissolution may have been a contributory factor in its selection for conversion in the first place. This said, it should be recalled that the church was not the only building repaired in the period c.1520 to 1530. The refectory was also then newly rebuilt. However, although it is not positively known that the refectory did not form part of the conversion, it certainly seems that the church formed the nucleus of the new house and it appears likely that reasons other than simply sound walls and a watertight roof provided the stimulus for this.

Although it seems reasonably clear that at least the western part of the nave formed the core of Nedeham's new house, it is much more difficult to establish what became of the eastern part, the crossing and the quire and whether they too initially formed part of the conversion. The estate map of 1731 shows that they still survived in plan at least by this date, although this does not necessarily prove that they also remained as standing buildings: they may well have been ruinous. The east wall of the present house is thought to be late 16th century in date and, although not as thick as the walls of the former nave, it is certainly substantial enough to have been built as an external wall, an idea further strengthened, albeit not proven, by the former presence within it of a doorway.

Certainly, to have converted the entire church to domestic use would have been a major undertaking but perhaps this was the original intention. Possibly this was embarked upon or even accomplished, but proved to be too ambitious, a cross-wall then being built to separate the nave from the rest of the church, which was thus allowed to fall into disrepair. Alternatively, of course, it may never have been intended to convert more than the western part of the church. Indeed, there are several other examples of church conversions, like Woodspring (Somerset) and Buckland (Devon),[69] where only part of the church was converted, the remainder being demolished. Yet another possibility is that the east wall simply formed an internal wall of a larger conversion. These are perhaps all ideas which could be clarified by further archaeological excavation.

At the time Nedeham was granted the priory, he had a house at Chislehurst (Kent), where he was probably resident, and also a house in London,[70] but it nevertheless seems that he intended to make Wymondley his main residence, an idea strengthened by the retrospective memorial erected by his grandson in Little Wymondley parish church.[71] This makes it all the more likely that he

[65] D.O.E. List of Scheduled Ancient Monuments, National Monument Number 11,518.
[66] P.R.O., SC6/Hen. VIII/1606, m.11.
[67] *L.P.*, xiii, p.589; H.R.O., 21,339- 21,344.
[68] *King's Works*, iv, 68-74, 234-7 and 59-63.

[69] Bettey (1989), 128; Howard (1987), 144.
[70] John Harvey, *English Mediaeval Architects* (revd. edn., 1984), 212.
[71] *V.C.H.*, iii, 191. Only the brass plate of the monument now survives, the remainder having been destroyed c.1875, a faculty for this work having been obtained in 1874; H.R.O., DSA 2/1/267. In 1878 J.E. Cussans described it as having been an "excessively ugly monument of

would have instigated the first conversion scheme.

Precisely what had been achieved by the time of Nedeham's death in 1544 is impossible to say but it is probable that he intended to transform the former priory into a substantial country house. Although it is almost certain that it was never completed, this house appears to have been much larger in its first post-monastic phase than the remaining structure would indicate. Quite apart from Chauncy's reference to "cloysters" and the 1731 map evidence, which both suggest a considerably larger building than now survives, it would seem unlikely that if Nedeham was prompted to convert the church to domestic use partly on account of its good condition, he would have ignored the equally recently rebuilt refectory. This is particularly so as its most likely position, directly opposite the church in the north claustral range, would have led to the creation of a convenient and fashionable courtyard plan. If there was also a prior's lodging, assuming for the moment that the reference to a hall in the 1537 inventory is not to the refectory, this may have been in the west claustral range. If so, it is likely that, along with the dormitory in the east range, this would have been transformed into lodgings as the church appears to have served as the hall and parlour of Nedeham's new house.

It is not possible to say whether it was Nedeham or one of his successors who added the south-west range, but several authorities have dated the gables on the north front to c.1600,[72] which would make them the work of Nedeham's grandson, George, although there is no direct documentary evidence for this. The addition of the gables suggests that, if it was not already the case, the north front had become the main entrance front to the house by this date. Inside the house, the presence of late 16th-century panelling across the internal face of the west processional doorway in the north wall of the former monastic nave raises the possibility that, although the house may have originated with a courtyard plan based on the monastic cloister, it had been reduced in size by the end of the century through the removal of the claustral ranges, albeit that the three gabled projections were then added to the north wall of the former church.

The suggestion that the house had declined in importance as early as 1600 is not entirely consistent with some of the features of this period which still remain or formerly existed in the building. For example, the panelling seems to have been considerably more extensive before the refurbishment works of the 1970s when much of it was destroyed or replaced by "replica" panelling. It is therefore not possible to date the panelling exactly or even to be certain that it was not imported from elsewhere at a later date, but the panelling does at least suggest a house of some status.

More revealing of the relative importance of the house at the end of the 16th century was the discovery in 1973-74 of a wall painting in a late medieval traceried recess in the north-east corner of the building. The purpose of this recess is unclear but the late 16th-century painting of running soldiers in classical armour is work of the highest quality.[73] It has been suggested that the recess is where the south walk of the cloister would have been,[74] but as it is located in what is clearly a late 16th-century addition (the eastern of the three gabled projections), it is much more probable that it has been reset. In this case, it may have served as the piscina of the chapel which Chauncy says was "consecrated since the Dissolution" and the position of which is not known.[75] As only part of the painting is now exposed, it is not possible to say whether the subject depicted was of a secular or religious nature and this suggestion must remain tentative. All that can really be concluded is that although the house appears to have been reduced in scale by the end of the 16th century, it remained an important building, a status that it was to retain throughout the following century during which further alterations were carried out.[76]

It is difficult to visualise now the type of house created by James Nedeham and his successors. It should be remembered that they would probably have wished to disguise the most obvious ecclesiastical features of the building. Thus, although the lancet windows in the south wall of the former nave are at the right level to serve as doorways connecting with the south-west range, it must be questioned whether they functioned as such in the 16th-century house. If they did, it is likely that the 13th-century nook-shafts would have been concealed from view. Similarly, as referred to above, the west processional doorway in the north wall of the nave is still concealed on its south side by late 16th-century panelling. It is in fact the work of later antiquaries and restorers which has "unpicked" these features and it is only in the roof structure that the fabric of the monastic church would have remained visible in the 16th-century house and this, of course, would only have been seen in the attic.

Bibliography

PICTORIAL SOURCES

Hertfordshire Record Office

Buckler Drawings, III, 106.

---

plaster, resembling a four-post bedstead", *History of Hertfordshire*, 2, pt.iii (1878), 60: in fact, it appears to have been quite a handsome Jacobean wall monument, illustrated by Oldfield a century earlier, H.R.O, Oldfield Drawings, VII, 440-1.
[72] Pevsner, 243; *R.C.H.M.*, 149.

[73] N.M.R., file 77,959.
[74] D.O.E. List (note 7), 87.
[75] Chauncy, ii, 110.
[76] Smith (1993), 218.

Oldfield Drawings, VII, 411, 418, 440-1, 451.

CARTOGRAPHIC SOURCES

Hertfordshire Record Office

44,212.

44,215.

QS/E 81.

D/EX 234 P13.

PHOTOGRAPHIC SOURCES

Hertfordshire Record Office

County Views WYM. LT/3.

National Library of Air Photographs, the Royal Commission on Historical Monuments, Swindon

Accession nos. CAP 8211, frames 61 & 62; CAP 8194, frame 31.

National Monuments Record, The Royal Commission on Historical Monuments, Swindon

Red Boxes.

File 77,959.

Bodleian Library, Oxford

MS. top. eccl. b.27, fol.53.

County Sites and Monuments Record, Hertford

P.R.N. 1037, 0159.

OTHER PRIMARY SOURCES

Manuscript:-

Public Record Office, London

SC6/Hen. VIII/1606, m.11.

E 117/12/30.

E 179/375/30.

PCC 21 Pynnyng.

Hertfordshire Record Office

DSA 2/1/267.

21,339-21,344.

Hertfordshire Local Studies Library, Hertford

H 726.7.

Printed:-

Hamilton Thompson, A. (ed.), *Visitations of Religious Houses, 1436-49*, iii, Lincs. Rec. Soc., 21 (1929).

Letters and Papers, Foreign and Domestic, of the Reign of Henry VIII, eds. Brewer, J.S., Gairdner, J. & Brodie, R.H., 21 vols. (1862-1932).

Salter, H.E. (ed.), *A Subsidy Collected in the Diocese of Lincoln in 1526* (Oxford, 1909).

SECONDARY SOURCES

Berger, R., 'The potential and limitations of radiocarbon dating in the Middle Ages: the radiochronologist's view' in Berger, R. (ed.), *Scientific Methods in Medieval Archaeology* (Berkeley, 1970), 89-139.

Bettey, J., *The Suppression of the Monasteries in the West Country* (Gloucester, 1989).

Bottomly, F., *Abbeys, Churches and Monasteries of Great Britain* (1981).

Burleigh, G., Matthews, K. & Went, D., *Wymondley Priory, Hertfordshire: An Archaeological Evaluation* (North Hertfordshire District Council Museums, Hitchin 1989).

Butler, L. & Given-Wilson, C., *Medieval Monasteries of Great Britain* (1979).

Chauncy, H., *The Historical Antiquities of Hertfordshire*, ii (1700, reprinted Dorking 1975).

Colvin, H.M. *et al*, *The History of the King's Works*, iv (1982).

Cussans, J.E., *The History of Hertfordshire*, ii, pt.3 (1878, reprinted Wakefield 1972).

Department of the Environment 54th List of Historic Buildings, District of North Hertfordshire, 28 May 1987.

Department of the Environment List of Scheduled Ancient Monuments, National Monument Number 11,518.

Farris, N., *The Wymondleys* (Hertford, 1989).

Harvey, J., *English Mediaeval Architects* (revd. edn., Gloucester 1984).

Haslam, R., *The Buildings of Wales; Powys* (Harmondsworth, 1979).

Hertfordshire Express (8 September 1906).

Horn, W., 'The great tithe barn of Cholsey, Berkshire', *Jnl. Soc. Archit. Hist.*, 22 (1963), 13-23.

Howard, M., *The Early Tudor Country House* (1987).

Knowles, M.D. & Hadcock, R.N., *Medieval Religious Houses* (1953).

Med. Arch., 18 (1974), 191.

North, T. & Stahlscmidt, J., *The Church Bells of Hertfordshire* (1886).

Pevsner, N., *Hertfordshire* (2nd edn., revd. Cherry, B., Harmondsworth 1977).

Royal Commission on Historical Monuments, *An Inventory of the Historical Monuments in Hertfordshire* (1910).

Smith, J.T., *English Houses 1200-1800: the Hertfordshire Evidence* (1992).

-*Hertfordshire Houses: Selective Inventory* (1993).

'Twenty fourth excursion of the East Hertfordshire Archaeological Society, 30 August 1906', *Trans. East Herts. Arch. Soc.*, 3 (1906), 230-1.

The Victoria History of the Counties of England, *Hertfordshire*, iii (1912); iv (1914).